Tibetan-English Dictionary of Buddhist Terminology

(Revised and Enlarged Edition)

ནང་དོན་རིག་པའི་མིང་ཚིག

བོད་དབྱིན་ཤན་སྦྱར།

Tibetan-English Dictionary of Buddhist Terminology

(Revised and Enlarged Edition)

Tsepak Rigzin

LIBRARY OF TIBETAN WORKS AND ARCHIVES

Second Revised Edition 1993
Reprint 2003

ISBN: 81-85102-88-0

Published by the Library of Tibetan Works and Archives, Dharamsala, and printed at Indraprastha Press (CBT), 4 Bahadur Shah Zafar Marg, New Delhi-110 002

FOREWORD

It gives us pleasure to bring out this second edition of the *Tibetan-English Dictionary of Buddhist Terminology*. The present edition has been revised and upgraded since it's first, and has been expanded with hundreds of new entries from various sources. For example, many new words have been added to the selected lists of terms from the Mahavyutpatti (bye-brag tu rtogs-par byed-pa chen-mo) and from many other collected writings and lexicons. Attempts have been made to provide Sanskrit equivalents wherever possible in Romanised transliterated form with care. The English translations and definitions have been selected to provide a general meaning aimed at leading to a deeper understanding of Buddhist concepts.

Of course, a project of such encyclopedic scope would be exceedingly difficult to complete single-handedly, if not impossible. Nonetheless, Mr. Tsepak Rigzin of the Library's Translation Bureau is to be recognized and congratulated for his vision in undertaking such a timely project, as well as for his painstaking labour.

It is hoped that this Dictionary will not only serve as a reference tool but also as a handy book for providing overview of Tibetan Buddhism. Both students and scholars of Tibetan Buddhist culture will find it useful.

Gyatsho Tshering
DIRECTOR

INTRODUCTION

When I was informed that a revised edition of my previous *Tibetan-English Dictionary of Buddhist Terminology* was due, I was immediately reminded of both the features (and the flaws) of the first edition. Having never seen myself as a Tibetan Buddhist studies scholar or as a qualified translator, I must confess that the compliments and criticisms that I have received have been extremely rewarding. The entire process of compiling this dictionary, from beginning to end, has been an extremely rewarding learning experience. Over two thousand new entries have been incorporated in this edition—all within the short period of time derived from maximum usage of my office hours as well as of my weekend holidays. With the exception of some minor editing and changes, the majority of these new entries have been directly translated from the glossary found in the three volumes of the *Grand Tibetan-Chinese Dictionary*.

Many of the first edition's redundant entries have been reduced to a minimum by giving cross references wherever possible in Tibetan transliterated form following the Turrell Wylie system of transliteration. Attempts have been made to occasionally provide sanskrit equivalents in romanised transliterated form based on the standard dictionaries (primarily splitting the words for better comprehension). The purpose of incorporating sanskrit in romanised form is to enable more advanced students to go into a deeper study and research. Every care has been taken in revising and editing the sanskrit words provided herein; although I do not claim these to be absolutely free of flaws. Readers are therefore advised to take care and caution while using these words. In all, I hope that the modifications and changes I have made will prove helpful to all readers. The unfortunate presence of any overlooked mistakes in this dictionary reflects the sheer gift of my own ignorance and carelessness.

Finally, I would like to add that the production of this edition has been a gross experience of the interdependent nature of my own life and the lives of my associates. The biggest change has been the Library's purchase of a computer (an advantage not known during its first edition); but also the assistance of many well wishers and scholars. It is to these people that I give my inexpressible thanks: to the many teachers in my life who taught me everything from the alphabet to philosophy; Ku-Ngo Gyatsho Tshering, Director of this institute, for his unflagging interest and encouragement; Jeremy Russell, for his many years of association at the Translation Bureau; Ms. Marguerite Mullins for her moral support; Robert Moyer for his editorial assistance in revising the english part and Mr. Sangye Tandar, LTWA's Tibetan Language Officer for revising the Tibetan spellings; Dr. Christoph Cüppers, a learned Tibetologist friend, for his generous time and erudition in revising and editing the sanskrit equivalents and for providing extremely valuable suggestions; Mr. Tsering Dhendup, our Computer Geshe for his guidance through the computer world; and finally to Scott Heftler, for finalization—design, layout, formatting, proof-reading, and incorporating corrections. Mr. Heftler's work was done on a Macintosh Classic that was kindly made available by the Tibetan Medical Institute's Dr. Namgyal Qusar.

As always, I thank all those whose moral support has actually caused me to move along with this project.

Tsepak Rigzin
Research and Translation Officer
Library of Tibetan Works & Archives
Dharamsala

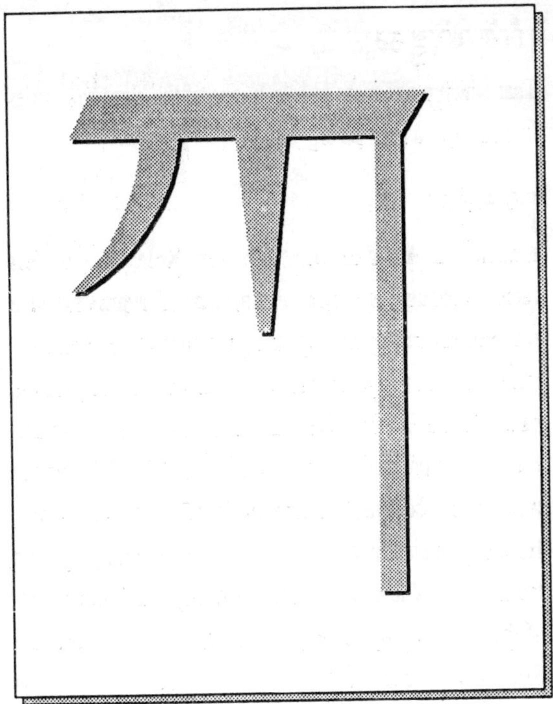

ཀ་དག་ལྷན་སྐྱེས།

Innately pure from the beginning; the primordial principle

ཀ་དག་གདོད་མའི་གཞི་ལུགས།

The nature of primordial purity; the primordial reality.

ཀ་དག་ཁྲེགས་ཆོད།

The primordial breakthrough-path. A core transmission of the secret rDzog Chen practice, the quintessential instruction for liberating lazy disciples effortlessly. Through the mastering of this instruction one is able to maintain the meaning of primordial reality in its instinctive and natural mode by way of gaining awareness within oneself, reaching a conclusion upon hearing the words and introducing inner confidence upon liberation, through understanding the intrinsically abiding self-arisen primordial mind otherwise stabilized but to be released only by means of four modes of liberating it (see grol-lugs-chen-po bżhi).

ཀ་ཁོལ་མ།

This is a text of religious history, a will left by King Songtsen Gampo and concealed in a pillar marked with tree leaves in the Lhasa Cathedral, which was later discovered by the great teacher, Atiśa. This text is also known by the name *Guide to Lhasa* (lha-sa'i dkar-chag).

ཀ་ཏྱཱའི་བུ།

Kātyāyana/ A direct disciple of Buddha Śākyamuni known especially for his knowledge of Vinaya, and who was also the founder of the Theravādin tradition, one of the four main schools of the Theravāda tradition.

ཀ་དག

1. Primordially pure or pure from the beginning; the original mode of abidance of that which is basically unarisen; a term used in Nyingma teachings. 2. Emptiness.

ཀ་གདམས་པ་བདེ་གཤེགས།

Kadampa Desheg. His real name is Sherab Senge, but is also known by the name Pobpa Thaye. Born in the Water-Tiger year (1122) of the second sexagenerary at Dokham, eastern Tibet, he built Kathog monastery in the Palyul district of the Kham region. He was a great master belonging to the Nyingma tradition. He died in the Water-Mouse year (1192).

ཀ་ཋ་ཡ།

Spear-noose; harpoon; a spear with a noose at its end used as a tantric implement.

ཀ་ནིཥྐ།

Kaniṣka/ An early Indian King. With his military power he conquered small kingdoms and built the Gandhola kingdom during the first century, but at the end of his life became a Buddhist and erected many temples and stupas. He accepted Ācārya Āryaśūra (rta-dbyangs) as his teacher and patronized Buddhist activities. He also invited many Arhats to Kashmir and composed the treatise known as *Mahāvibhanga* (bye-brag chen-po).

ཀ་མ་ལ་ཤཱི་ལ།

Kamalaśila/ An Indian Ācarya professing the philosophy of the Yogācārya Madhyamaka school which developed in the eastern part of India during the eighth century A.D. During the reign of King Tri-Song Deu-Tsan he was invited to Tibet and defeated the Chinese monk Hashang Mahāyāna holding 'ton-mun', the instantaneous path of enlightenment, as opposed to the Bodhisattva doctrine of 'chen-min', the gradual path of enlightenment, in a philosophical contest. As a consequence, he wrote *Triple Stages to Enlightenment* (sgom-rim rnam gsum) and established the latter tradition of doctrine.

ཀརྩེ་སྒོ་བཞིའི་མཆོད་རྟེན།

A stupa with four gates built on the highway north of the Lhasa cathedral. It is believed to be a holy place where the great meditator, Thangtong Gyalpo spent many years practising meditation before 1368 A.D.

ཀརྨ་བཀའ་བརྒྱུད།

The Karma Kagyud Tradition of Tibetan Buddhism; one of the many lineages of Kagyud traditions founded by the first Karmapa Dusum Khyenpa (1110-1193), who was a distinguished disciple of Gampopa (see sgam-po-pa). He established Tsurphu Monastery, the main seat of his tradition, in the north-west of Lhasa. In India, the main centre of Karma Kagyud has been re-established in Rumtek, Sikkim.

ཀི་ལི་ཀི་ལིའི་སྒྲ་ཅན།

That which pronounces ki-li ki-li, one of the eight cemeteries (see dur-khrod chen-po brgyad).

ཀུ་མཱ་ར་ཛཱི་བ།

Kumārajīva. A a great translator from Kotan (li-yul). His father, although of Indian origin, married a princess of a northern Kotan (li-yul) king, and gave birth to this translator there. At a young age he entered monkhood, and received the name Zhonu Tsering. He studied Sanskrit language and Hīnayāna Buddhist doctrines, but later entered into Mahāyāna tradition and became erudite in the Middle View philosophy. He was proficient in both Tibetan and Chinese language. He translated the *Diamond Cut Sūtra* and major and minor texts of the *Wisdom Perfection* texts, the *White Lotus Sūtra*, the *Stainless Wisdom Sūtra*, the *Root Middle Way* text of Nāgārjuna, Āryadeva's *Four Hundred Stanzas* and many other treatises. He had many disciples and passed away at the age of seventy.

ཀུ་རུ་ཀུ་ལླེ།

A goddess of power called Rigje-ma (rig-byed-ma) common to Sakya's golden transmission lineage (gser-chos).

ཀུ་ཤ

The Kuśa grass, literally meaning that which dispels evil or the supreme grass. It has a fine and rich, crispy tassel of leaves, it is sweet flavoured, moderate to digest, and has the power to prolong one's life and increase the essential energy of the human body.

ཀུ་ཤའི་གྲོང་ཁྱེར།

Kuśinagarī/ The city of Kusha, Kushinagara where Buddha

Śākyamuni passed away into parinirvāṇa. Located close to the border of India and Nepal near Gorakhpur.

ཀུ་ས་ར།

An Indian pandit who was invited to Tibet during the reign of King Songtsen Gampo. He translated many tantric texts of different levels from Sanskrit into Tibetan.

ཀུ་སུ་ལུ།

A Yogi mendicant; a yogi who practices the art of tantric exorcism and penance.

ཀུ་སུ་ལུའི་ཚོགས་གསོག

A cut-ritual (gcod) practice in which one offers one's body as a feast (tshog) to accumulate merit.

ཀུན་དཀྲིས།

The ever-binding factors; fetters. Those categories of delusions that are responsible for making repeated obstacles for one's mind during meditation on calm-abiding (śamatha) and equanimity (upekṣā/ btang-snyoms). There are four (see kun-dkris bzhi) and three levels of wrong activities which can be categorized as follows. If a wrong activity is committed fulfilling all the four factors, such a wrong activity becomes great; if only the first, i.e. not regarding a breach as a fault, is present and the others are absent, such a wrong activity becomes middling; and if all other three are present, except not regarding a breach as fault, it becomes weak.

ཀུན་དཀྲིས་བརྒྱད།

Aṣṭa paryavasthāna/ The eight ever-binding factors; eight fetters. The delusions that disturbs the mind repeatedly during meditation on calm-abiding (śamatha) and equanimity (btang-snyoms). These are: 1. རྨུགས་པ། styāna/ mental sloth 2. གཉིད། middha/ sleep 3. རྒོད་པ། auddhatya/ agitation 4. འགྱོད་པ། kaukartyam/ regret 5. ཕྲག་དོག īrṣyā/ jealousy 6. སེར་སྣ། mātsarya/ miserliness 7. ངོ་ཚ་མེད་པ། ahrīkya/ lack of shame 8. ཁྲེལ་མེད་པ། anapatrāpyam/ lack of concern for others.

ཀུན་དཀྲིས་བཅུ།

Daśa paryavasthāna/ The ten ever-binding factors; the ten fetters: 1-8. (see above, kun-dkris brgyad) 9. ཁྲོ་བ། krodha/ anger 10. འཆབ་པ། mrakṣa/ concealment.

ཀུན་དཀྲིས་བཞི།

Catvāri paryavasthāna/ The four ever-binding factors; the four fetters. A breach of the Bodhisattva or tantric vows is complete if these four factors are present: 1. ཉེས་དམིགས་མི་ལྟ་བ། not regarding the breach as wrong 2. སྤྱོད་འདོད་མ་ལོག་པ། not wishing to avoid it in the future 3. དགའ་མགུ་བྱེད་པ། rejoicing in misdeeds 4. ངོ་ཚ་དང་ཁྲེལ་མེད་པ། not being ashamed or embarrassed.

ཀུན་མཁྱེན་ཀློང་ཆེན།

The Omniscient Lama Longchen Rabjam (1308-1363). A Nyingma Lama regarded as a great visionary by all the four schools of Tibetan Buddhism; who was influenced greatly by a vision of Ācārya Padmasambhava. Out of more than two hundred treatises some of his major works include the *Seven Treasures* (see klong-chen mdzod-bdun), *Triple Relaxation* (ngal-gso skor gsum) and *Triple Self Liberation* (rang-grol skor gsum).

ཀུན་གྱིས་བཀུར་བའི་སྡེ།

Saṃmatīya/ A school of Buddhist philosophy (see mang-pos bkur-ba'i sde).

ཀུན་དགའ་རྒྱལ་མཚན།

The real name of Sakya Paṇḍita (see sa-skya pandi-ta).

ཀུན་དགའ་སྙིང་པོ།

Kunga Nyingpo (1092-1158). One of the five foremost masters of the Sakya tradition. He was the abbot of the Sakya monastic university at Sakya for forty-six years.

ཀུན་དགའ་བོ།

Ānanda; one of the twelve close disciples of Buddha Śākyamuni known for his knowledge of scriptures. He was second of the seven hierarchs (see ston-pa'i gtad rabs-bdun) after the passing away of Buddha and recited by heart the Sūtrapitaka during the first council held at Rājagṛha. He was also one of the main disciples who attended Buddha's teachings on the four tantras of medicine.

ཀུན་འགྲོ།

A. Space B. Snake C. Mental factor or factors (see below) that accompanies every instance of mind or mental activity.

ཀུན་འགྲོ་ལྔ།

Pañca sarvagaḥ/ Five ever-functioning mental factors. Mental factors that accompany every instance of mind and mental activity. These are: 1. ཚོར་བ། vedanā/ feeling 2. འདུ་ཤེས། samjñā/ recognition 3. སེམས་པ། centanā/ perception 4. རེག་པ། sparśa/ contact 5. ཡིད་ལ་བྱེད་པ། manasikāra/ attention.

ཀུན་འགྲོའི་རྒྱུ།

Ever-functioning cause. One of the six types of causes (see rgyu-drug). Those delusions (phra-rgyas) that occur in or travel through all the three realms of existence and act as an obstacle for attaining the state of liberation (nirvāṇa).

ཀུན་ཉོན་གྱི་དབང་པོ་ལྔ།

The five feelings (see tsor-ba lnga) within the mental continuum of ordinary persons.

ཀུན་དུ་རྒྱུ་ཆེན་པོ་ལྔ།

The five great disciples; the five ascetics (see 'khor lnga-sde bzang-po).

ཀུན་དུ་རྒྱུ་གནག་ལྷས་ཀྱི་བུ།

Maskarin Gośaliputra. One of the six non-Buddhist teachers; a self-professed teacher of Hindu philosphy during the time of Buddha Śakyamuni. He taught that the sufferings of all sentient beings were spontaneous without any reliance upon causes and conditions.

ཀུན་དུ་བརྗོད་པའི་ཆོ་འཕྲུལ།

Ādeśanā prātihārya/ Miracle of speech. The power of Buddha enables him to read others minds (meritorious or non-meritorious) and teach accordingly.

ཀུན་དུ་བརྟགས་པའི་མཚན་ཉིད།

Parikalpita lakṣaṇa/ Imputed phenomena. One of the three phenomena (see mtsan-nyid gsum). The existence of a thing by mere conceptual labelling, i.e. the confused mind labels persons and phenomena by misconception and identifies existents as I, self, mine or name, upon imputation.

ཀུན་དུ་བཟང་པོ།

Samantabhadra/ A. Those existents that are pure or virtuous throughout all of its parts. B. The sphere of reality (dharmadhātu) or the nature truth body (dharmakāya). C. Tathāgata Samantabhadra. D. Bodhisattva Samantabhadra, one of the eight close spiritual sons of Buddha Śākyamuni (see nye-ba'i sras-brgyad). E. According to the Bon tradition, the complete enjoyment body (sambhogakāya).

ཀུན་རྟོག

Saṁkalpa/ A. Thorough investigation; the process of

conceptual analysis. B. Thoughts, concepts, conceptualization and imagination.

ཀུན་བརྟགས།

Parikalpita/ Conceptual imputation; intellectual imputation; artificial labelling or imputation. Misconception of the true nature of phenomena developed through reasoning rooted in philosophical and intellectual study or training.

ཀུན་བརྟགས་གཉིས།

The two types of imputed phenomena. 1. རྣམ་གྲངས་པའི་ཀུན་བརྟགས། pariyāya parikalpita/ nominally imputed phenomena 2. མཚན་ཉིད་ཡོངས་སུ་ཆད་པའི་ཀུན་བརྟགས། alakṣaṇa parikalpita/ imputed phenomena lacking identity.

ཀུན་བརྟགས་པའི་གཟུགས།

Parikalpita rūpa/ Imputed form. Forms seen in imagination, e.g. horse, elephant, house, etc., seen in a dream, and seeing all surroundings filled with skeletons in concentration meditation (samādhi).

ཀུན་བརྟགས་ཀྱི་ཉོན་མོངས་པ།

Parikalpita kleśa/ Imputed delusions. Deluded views and such that disturb the peace of mind as a result of wrong conceptual labelling of the meaning of reality imposed by a mind tainted with a wrong philosophy.

ཀུན་བརྟགས་ཀྱི་མ་རིག་པ།

Parikalpita avidyā/ Imputed ignorance. Lack of understanding of the mode of reality of phenomena conjoined with deluded views of a wrong philosophy.

ཀུན་བརྟགས་པའི་སྟོབས།

Parikalpita bala/ Power of imputation. Lack of attachment towards all outer and inner phenomena; having seen all phenomena as being empty and lacking self nature through wisdom combined with concentration (samādhi).

ཀུན་བདེ་གླིང་།

A monastery established in the Wood-Tiger year (1794) located to the south-west of the Potala palace in Lhasa. Tagtra Rinpoche was the chief Lama of this monastery. Two masters of this lineage have been regents of Tibet.

ཀུན་བདེན་གྱི་སྤང་བྱ་བདུན།

Seven abandonments of the truth of origin. The seven things abandoned by a person having seen the truth of origin of all sufferings within this desire realm. These are: 1. མ་རིག་པ། avidyā/ ignorance 2. འདོད་ཆགས། rāga/ desire-attachment 3. ཁོང་ཁྲོ། pratigha/ hatred-anger 4. ང་རྒྱལ། māna/ pride 5. ཐེ་ཚོམ། vicikitsā/ doubt 6. ལོག་ལྟ། mithyādṛṣṭi/ wrong views 7. ལྟ་བ་མཆོག་འཛིན། dṛṣṭiparāmarśa/ views holding wrong moral disciplines as superior.

ཀུན་འདར་མ།

Literally 'all-shaking'. This refers to the central energy channel. It is called this because the central energy channel is responsible for generating the essential drop, bliss within energy, and bliss from wind-energy.

ཀུན་ནས་ཉོན་མོངས་པ།

Saṁkleśa/ Thoroughly afflicted phenomena. The six primary delusions (see rtza-nyon drug) and twenty near-delusions (see nye-nyon nyi-shu) motivated by cause or intent that motivates.

ཀུན་ནས་ཉོན་མོངས་པ་དང་རྣམ་པར་བྱང་བ།

Saṁkleśa vaiyadānika/ Thoroughly afflicted and purified phenomena. The ever-afflictive and the ever-wholesome side of phenomena. The truth of suffering and origin are the ever-afflictive and the truth of cessation and path are the ever-wholesome side.

ཀུན་ནས་ཉོན་མོངས་པའི་བདེན་པ།

Samkleśa satya/ The thoroughly afflicted phenomena. This refers to the truth of origin of suffering.

ཀུན་ནས་ཉོན་མོངས་ཕྱོགས་ཀྱི་དབང་པོ་བཅུ་བཞི།

The fourteen faculties of the ever-afflicted phenomena. 1-6. མིག་གི་དབང་པོ་ནས་ཡིད་ཀྱི་དབང་པོ་བར་དྲུག eye faculty to mental faculty. 7. ཕོའི་དབང་པོ། puruṣendriya/ faculty of maleness 8. མོའི་དབང་པོ། strīndriya/ faculty of femaleness 9. སྲོག་གི་དབང་པོ། jīviendriya/ faculty of life-force 10. བདེ་བའི་དབང་པོ། sukhendriya/ faculty of joy 11. སྡུག་བསྔལ་གྱི་དབང་པོ། duḥkhendriya/ faculty of suffering 12. ཡིད་བདེའི་དབང་པོ། sauamasyendriya/ faculty of mental pleasure 13. ཡིད་མི་བདེའི་དབང་པོ། daurmanasyendriya/ faculty of mental displeasure 14. བཏང་སྙོམས་ཀྱི་དབང་པོ། upekṣendriya/ faculty of neutrality.

ཀུན་ནས་ཉོན་མོངས་ཕྱོགས་ཀྱི་འགྲེལ་ཆང་ང་གསུམ།

The fifty three divisions of ever-afflicted phenomena: 1-5. ཕུང་པོ་ལྔ pañca skandha/ five aggregates (see phung-po lnga) 6-11. དབང་པོ་དྲུག ṣaḍ indriya/ six sense faculties (see dbang-po drug) 12-17. རྣམ་ཤེས་དྲུག ṣaḍ vijñāna/ six consciousnesses (see rnam-shes tsogs-brgyad, 1-6) 18-23. ཡུལ་དྲུག སྐྱེ་མཆེད་དྲུག ṣaḍ saṃvṛta/ six sources of perception (see bskyed-mched drug) 24-29. རེག་པ་དྲུག ṣaḍ sparśa/ six contacts (see reg-pa drug) 30-35. ཚོར་བ་དྲུག ṣaḍ vedanā/ six feelings (see tsor-ba drug) 36-41. འབྱུང་བ་དྲུག ṣaḍ bhūta/ six elements ('byung-ba drug) 42-53. རྟེན་འབྲེལ་བཅུ་གཉིས། dvadaśanga pratītyasamutpāda/ twelve links of interdependent origination (see rten-'brel yan-lag bcu-gnyis).

ཀུན་སྤངས།

A. Complete abandonment or thorough release. B. The primary vein (rtza) of the heart. C. A mendicant, a recluse. D. The state of liberation (nirvāṇa).

ཀུན་བྱེད་རྒྱལ་པོ།

The universal principle. A. Mind or consciousness. B. Emptiness. C. The god, Brahma. D. In rDzogs-chen doctrine it refers to the basic mind, the Tathāgata essence or Buddha nature which is the origin of all phenomena within saṁsāra and beyond, or the basis or source of all misconceptions and liberation. E. A tantric text in Nyingma secret mantrayāna. Its full name is: *byang-chub-kyi sems kun-byed rgyal-po lta-ba nam-mkh'a ltar mth'a-bdus med-pa'i rgyud le'u brgyad-cu rtza-bzhi pa.* (Sarva dharma mahaśanti bodhicittakulayarāja) Translated by Śrī Sengha and Vairocana.

ཀུན་འབྱུང་བདེན་པ།

The truth of origin of suffering. All those karma and delusions that become causes for the origination of the impure world and its inhabitants including the human body.

ཀུན་འབྱུང་བདེན་པའི་ཁྱད་ཆོས་བཞི།

Catvāri saṁvṛttisatya guṇa/ The four features of the truth of the origin of suffering. 1. རྒྱུ། hetu/ cause 2. ཀུན་འབྱུང་། samudaya/ origin of all 3. རབ་སྐྱེས། prabhava/ production 4. རྐྱེན། pratyayaḥ/ condition.

ཀུན་འབྱུང་བདེན་པའི་རྣམ་པ་བརྒྱད།

Aṣṭa samudaya satyaguṇa/ The eight features of the truth of origin. 1. འདོད་ཆགས་དང་བྲལ་བའི་རྣམ་པ། turning away from desire-attachment 2. མི་གནས་པའི་རྣམ་པ། non-abidance 3. ཞི་བའི་རྣམ་པ། peacefulness 4. འདོད་ཆགས་མེད་པའི་རྣམ་པ། lack of desire-attachment 5. ཞེ་སྡང་མེད་པའི་རྣམ་པ། lack of hatred-anger 6. གཏི་མུག་མེད་པའི་རྣམ་པ། lack of closed-mindedness 7. ཉོན་མོངས་མེད་པའི་རྣམ་པ། lack of delusion 8. སེམས་ཅན་མེད་པའི་རྣམ་པ། lack of sentient beings.

ཀུན་སྦྱོར་གསུམ།

Tri saṁyojana/ The three constant fetters; three ever-binding factors. These refer to the three types of delusions that are abandoned upon reaching the Path of Seeing (third of the five paths). 1. འཇིག་ལྟ་ཀུན་བཏགས། satkāyadṛṣṭi/ the intellectually acquired view of the transitory collection (of I or mine) that obstructs a person from achieving liberation 2. ཚུལ་ཁྲིམས་དང་བརྟུལ་ཞུགས་མཆོག་འཛིན། śilavrata parāmarśa/ the view that holds wrong moral disciplines and practices as superior and that obstructs a person by way of taking a wrong path as the right path 3. ཐེ་ཚོམས་ཉོན་མོངས་ཅན། kliṣṭa vicikitsā/ doubt that obstructs a person by generating a wavering attitude towards the (right) path.

ཀུན་སྦྱོར་དགུ

Nava saṁyojana/ The nine constant fetters; nine ever-binding factors. These are the ever-binding: 1. རྗེས་སུ་ཆགས་པ། rāga/ attachment 2. ཁོང་ཁྲོ་བ། krodha/ anger 3. ང་རྒྱལ། māna/ egotistic pride 4. མ་རིག་པ། avidya/ ignorance 5. ལྟ་བ། dṛṣṭi/ wrong view 6. མཆོག་འཛིན། parāmarśa dṛṣṭi/ view of superiority 7. ཐེ་ཚོམ། vicikitsā/ doubt 8. ཕྲག་དོག īrṣyā/ jealousy 9. སེར་སྣ། mātsarya/ miserliness.

ཀུན་རྫོབ་ཀྱི་ཀུན་རྫོབ།

The obscuring conventional phenomena. One of the three conventional truths. For instance, an illusion, a mirage, a cataract (mi-yor), etc., that cannot perform their respective functions properly.

ཀུན་རྫོབ་ཀྱི་སྐྱབས།

Saṁvṛti śaraṇa/ The conventional refuge; the conventional object of worship, e.g. an image of Buddha Śākyamuni.

ཀུན་རྫོབ་གཉིས།

The two conventional existences; the two types of relative existence. 1. ཡང་དག་ཀུན་རྫོབ། saṁyag saṁvṛti/ correct conventional truth, e.g. a pillar 2. ལོག་པའི་ཀུན་རྫོབ། mithya saṁvṛti/ incorrect conventional truth, e.g. a mirror image.

ཀུན་རྫོབ་རྟོགས་པའི་ཤེས་རབ།

Saṁvṛti pratijñāna/ A. Wisdom that has gained mastery over the five sciences of learning (see rig-pa'i gnas lnga). B. Wisdom understanding conventional phenomena; the discriminative awareness that understands things on the conventional level of truth, e.g. a wisdom understanding the illusory nature of phenomena.

ཀུན་རྫོབ་བདེན་པ།

Saṁvṛti satya/ The conventional truth; the relative truth; generally referring to phenomena other than emptiness.

ཀུན་རྫོབ་བྱང་ཆུབ་ཀྱི་སེམས།

Saṁvṛti bodhicitta/ The conventional bodhicitta; the conventional mind of enlightenment. This includes the wishing bodhicitta (see smon-pa sems bskyed) and the committed bodhicitta (see 'jug-pa sems-bskyed).

ཀུན་རྫོབ་གསུམ།

The three types of conventional truths. These are: 1. ཀུན་རྫོབ་ཀྱི་ཀུན་རྫོབ། conventional nature of the conventional truth. 2. ཡང་དག་པ་མ་ཡིན་པའི་ཀུན་རྫོབ། incorrect conventional truth and 3. ཡང་དག་པའི་ཀུན་རྫོབ། correct conventional truth. Or: 1. བཏགས་པའི་ཀུན་རྫོབ། upacāra saṁvṛti/ the imputed conventional existence 2. ཤེས་པའི་ཀུན་རྫོབ། the known conventional existence 3. བརྗོད་པའི་ཀུན་རྫོབ། the expressed conventional existence.

ཀུན་གཞི་རྣམ་ཤེས།

Ālayavijñāna/ The foundational consciousness; mind basis of all; one of the eight types of consciousnesses (see rnam-shes tsogs-brgyad) asserted by the Mind Only school of Buddhist philosophy; believed to be primary and the store-house of all mental imprints.

ཀུན་གཞི་གནས་ཀྱི་འཁོར་ལོ།

The point at the heart level where all energy channels are collected.

ཀུན་བཟང་མཆོད་སྤྲིན།

Samantabhadra pūjāmegha/ A cloud of Samantabhadra's offerings; in the sūtra tradition this refers to the panoply of offerings filling all of space and formed by Bodhisattva's holding one material of offering from which emanates many duplicates, each emanating further duplicates; in the tantra tradition this refers to an offering of non-duality of bliss and emptiness.

ཀུན་བཟང་ཐུགས་ཀྱི་བསྟན་པ།

In the Nyingma tradition this refers to the doctrine of Dzog-pa chen-po.

ཀུན་སློང་།

Samutthāna/ Motivation; a primary consciousness directed towards a goal. There are two types of motivation. 1. རྒྱུའི་ཀུན་སློང་། causal motivation 2. དུས་ཀྱི་ཀུན་སློང་། actual motivation at the time of action.

ཀོང་སྤྲུལ་ཡོན་ཏན་རྒྱ་མཚོ།

Kongtrul Yonten Gyatso (1813-1899). Also knows as Garwang Lodoe Thaye, was born in the Water-Bird year of the fourteenth sexagenerary at Dokham. He compiled *The Jewel Treasure* (rin-chen gter mdzod), *The Instruction Treasure* (gdams-ngag mdzod) and *The Secret Transmission Treasure* (bka'-brgyud sngags-mdzod), and discovered *The Treasure of Knowledge* (shes-bya mdzod) and *The Uncommon Secret Treasure* (thun-min gsang-ba'i mdzod). These are known as the Five Treasures. He composed texts on medicine, poetry and others, comprising almost a hundred volumes in all.

ཀླུ།

Nāga/ A kind of being regarded as belonging to the animal class; believed to abide in subterranean realms, having control over rain, ponds, rivers and soil productivity. Some are helpers while others can bring retribution if disturbed. Often in Buddhist art and in written accounts, they are portrayed as being half man and half snake. Generally serpents and snakes are recognised as nāgas.

ཀླུ་སྒྲུབ།

Nāgārjuna/ The great Nāgārjuna, founder of the Madhyamaka school of philosophy and of the lineage of the profound teachings of emptiness (see zab-mo lta brgyud). His works include *The Six Treatises* (see rigs-tshogs drug), *Letter to a King* (bshes-spring), and *Jewel Garland* (rin-chen phreng-ba).

ཀླུ་སྒྲུབ་ཀྱི་ཐུགས་སྲས་བདུན།

The seven spiritual sons of Nāgārjuna. 1. ཤཱཀྱ་མི་ཏྲ། Śākyamitra 2. ཀླུའི་བྱང་ཆུབ། Nāgabodhi 3. འཕགས་པ་ལྷ། Āryadeva 4. མ་ཏང་ཀི Mataṅga 5. སངས་རྒྱས་བསྐྱངས། Buddhapalita 6. ལེགས་ལྡན་འབྱེད། Bhāvaviveka 7. སློབ་དཔོན་དཔའ་བོ། Aśvaghośa.

ཀླུ་ཆེན་བརྒྱད།

Aṣṭa mahā nāgarāja/ The eight nāga kings. There are two ways of listing these. A. 1. ཀླུའི་རྒྱལ་པོ་མཐའ་ཡས། Nāgarāja Ananta

2. ཀླུའི་རྒྱལ་པོ་འཇོག་པོ། Nāgarāja Takṣaka 3. ཀླུའི་རྒྱལ་པོ་སྟོབས་རྒྱུ། Nāgarāja Karkoṭaka 4. ཀླུའི་རྒྱལ་པོ་རིགས་ལྡན། Nāgarāja Kulika 5. ཀླུའི་རྒྱལ་པ་ནོར་རྒྱས། Nāgarāja Vāsuki 6. ཀླུའི་རྒྱལ་པོ་དུང་སྐྱོང་། Nāgarāja Saṅkhapāla 7. ཀླུའི་རྒྱལ་པོ་པདྨ། Nāgarāja Padma 8. ཀླུའི་རྒྱལ་པོ་ཝ་རུ་ཎ། Nāgarāja Varuṇa B. 1-7. as listed in A and 8. ཀླུའི་རྒྱལ་པོ་པདྨ་ཆེན་པོ། Nāgarāja Mahāpadma.

ཀླུ་གཉན།

A. Malignant or harmful nāgas. B. Lord of the earth. There are two types of these, known as nāgas or gnyan. These are spirits belonging to the category of animals or hungry ghost.

ཀློང་ཆེན་སྙིང་ཐིག

A treasure doctrine of the Nyingma tradition, mind-revelation of Rigzin Jigme Lingpa (1729-1798).

ཀློང་ཆེན་མཛོད་བདུན།

The seven treasure texts. The treatises composed by Longchen Rabjampa (see kun-mkhyen klong-chen rab-'byams), a fourteenth century master of the Nyingma tradition. These are: 1. གྲུབ་མཐའ་མཛོད། *The Treasure of Philosophy* 2. ཐེག་ཆེན་མཛོད། *The Greater Vehicle Treasure* 3. ཡིད་བཞིན་མཛོད། *The Wish Granting Treasure* 4. མན་ངག་མཛོད། *The Treasure of Transmission* 5. ཆོས་དབྱིངས་མཛོད། *The Treasure of Reality* 6. གནས་ལུགས་མཛོད། *The Treasure of Nature* 7. ཚིག་དོན་མཛོད། *The Treasure of Words and Meanings*.

ཀློང་ཆེན་རབ་འབྱམས།

The great master Longchen Rabjampa (see kun-mhyen klong-chen rab-'byams).

ཀློང་སྡེ།

The Centrists. A transmission of Atiyoga practice within rDzogs-chen doctrine, the lineage of which comes from Longde Dorje Zampa, Ācārya Śrī Simha the great translator, Vairocana and others. This doctrine professes that within the self-arisen primordial wisdom, i.e. the subjective ever wholesome wisdom, all appearances of objective phenomena dissolve into their own mode of appearance. Since both subjective wisdom and the objective phenomena do not exist as being subject and object, therefore, without applying analysis as to whether they are existent or not, all phenomena are by nature established in their primordial state of liberation and unlimited sphere of reality.

དཀའ་ཐུབ།

Tapas/ Asceticism; austere practices.

དཀར་པོ་རྣམ་གསུམ།

The three lay masters of Sakya tradition. 1. Sachen Kunga Nyingpo (1092-1158) 2. Sonam Tzemo (1142-1182) 3. Jetsun Dakpa Gyaltsen (1147-1158).

དཀར་པོ་ས་བོན་གྱི་སྟོབས།

The power of the white seed. The strong determination to collect merit and eliminate obstacles in order to develop an enlightened attitude; one of the five powers (see stobs-lnga); the wish to be able to develop the enlightened attitude in one's future lifetimes, generated at the time of death.

དཀར་པོའི་ལས།

White karma; wholesome karma. The process of activity whereby happiness and fortunate consequences follow as the result of previously committed virtuous actions. Synonymous with all virtuous actions.

དཀར་པོའི་ཆོས་བཞི།

Catvāri śukladharma/ The four white actions; the four wholesome actions. The four virtuous actions producing white karmic results which prevent the degeneration of bodhicitta, the enlightened motive of a Bodhisattva, namely: 1. སྲོག་གམ་ཐ་ན་བཞད་གད་ཀྱི་ཕྱིར་ཡང་ཤེས་བཞིན་དུ་རྫུན་མི་སྨྲ་བ། abandoning consciously telling lies at the cost of one's life or even for a joke 2. སེམས་ཅན་ལ་གཡོ་སྒྱུ་མེད་པར་བསམ་པ་དྲང་པོར་གནས་པ། being unbiased in helping all sentient beings without having ulteriour thoughts 3. སེམས་ཅན་ཀུན་ལ་སྟོན་པའི་འདུ་ཤེས་སྐྱེད་ཅིང་དོན་གནས་ཀྱི་བསྔགས་པ་བརྗོད་པ། recognizing all Bodhisattvas as teachers and praising them as they deserve throughout the four directions 4. གདུལ་བྱ་རྣམས་ཉི་ཚེ་བའི་ཐེག་པར་མི་འདོར་བར་རྫོགས་པའི་བྱང་ཆུབ་འཛིན་དུ་འཇུག་པ། inspiring all sentient beings to strive for the attainment of supreme enlightenment.

དཀར་ཕྱོགས་ཀྱི་ལྷ།

The gods and goddesses of the white side. This includes all divinities that align with the virtuous and righteous factions.

དཀོར།

Dhana/ Spiritual material. Offerings made to the objects of refuge, in a temple, to a monastic community or to an individual lama. It can also means offerings misused by a monk or nun or else monks and nuns spoiled by too many offerings.

དཀྱིལ་འཁོར།

Maṇḍala/ A. Round shaped, e.g. the full moon. B. A complete feature of something, e.g. of face. C. In tantra, this constitutes the complete celestial mansion or abode of a principal deity surrounded by his or her retinue, representing the paths and fruits of that particular cycle of practices. Often maṇḍalas may be either painted on a scroll, carved on wood or drawn with coloured sand.

དཀྱིལ་འཁོར་རྒྱལ་མཆོག

The supramundane victorious maṇḍala . Also called dkyil-'khor rgyal mchog-gi ting-nge-'dzin. Roughly translated as meditation on the supramandane deity, one of the three stages of meditation on the generation stage practice of tantra, in which one visualizes and places all deities of a particular cycle of practice in their respective place of the maṇḍala by imagining them as having emanated from the essential drop of the principal deity in union with his or her partner.

བཀའ།

Buddha vacana/ Teachings or words of Buddha. Either originally spoken by Buddha himself, recorded in any of the three collections (lung-gi sde-snod gsum) or the insight and realizations (rtogs-pa'i chos) within Buddha's mental continuum.

བཀའ་བརྒྱུད།

Kagyud Tradition. One of the four Tibetan Buddhist traditions holding the commissioned lineage of Buddha Vajradhara. In Tibet, this transmission was divided into two schools, the Shangpa Kagyud started by Mahasiddha Kyungpo Nyaljor (978-1079) and the Dakpo Kagyud by Lhodrak Marpa (1012-1099). The Dakpo Kagyud tradition was further divided into four sub-schools known as the four major schools of the Kagyud tradition (see bKa'-brgyud che-bzhi) and its sub-school. Phagdu Kagyud developed into eight sub-schools known as Digung, Taglung, Drugpa, Yasang, Trophu, Shugseb, Yelpa and Martsang.

བཀའ་བརྒྱུད་ཆེ་བཞི།

The four major schools of the Kagyud tradition. 1. འབའ་རོམ། Barong Kagyud established by Barompa Darma Wangchuk 2. ཕག་གྲུ Phagdru Kagyud established by Phagdru Dorjee Gyalpo (1110-1170) 3. ཀརྨ་ཚང་། Karma Kagyud established by Karma Duesum Khyenpa (1110-1193) 4. ཚལ་པ། Tsalpa Kagyud established by Tsalpa Tsondru Dakpa, a disciple of Ongom Tsultrim Nyingpo.

བཀའ་འགྱུར།

Kangyur; the collection of Buddha's teachings translated from Sanskrit into Tibetan, generally consisting of 108 volumes, but the number varies according to different editions.

བཀའ་ཆེན།

Kachen; the title or academic degree awarded at Tashi Lhunpo monastery, probably equivalent to the Geshe Degree of other monastic institutions.

བཀའ་ཉན།

Ājñākara/ Attendant; member of a retinue; minister.

བཀའ་བསྟན།

A. The collection of Buddhist canons, the teachings of Buddha and their commentaries by Indian master-scholars; the former consists of 108 volumes and the latter 225, varying slightly according to the edition. B. The collection of sacred scriptures.

བཀའ་ཐང་སྡེ་ལྔ་།

The Annals; the five prophetic texts. The five texts left as wills by Guru Padmasambhava as discovered by Ogyan Lingpa from Samye and Yeldag in the Wood-Bird year (1285) of the fifth sexagenerary. These are texts concerning: 1. རྒྱལ་པོ་བཀའ་ཐང་། the king (rgyal-po bka'-thang) 2. བཙུན་མོ་བཀའ་ཐང་། the queen (btsun-mo bka'-thang) 3. བློན་པོ་བཀའ་ཐང་། the ministers (blong-po bka'-thang) 4. ལོ་པཎ་བཀའ་ཐང་། the scholars and translators (lo-pan-bka'-thang) 5. ལྷ་འདྲེ་བཀའ་ཐང་། the gods and spirits (lha-'dre bka'-thang).

བཀའ་དྲིན་གསུམ་ལྡན།

Tri parigrahaka gurū/ He possessing the three kindnesses. According to the sūtra tradition, this refers to a spiritual master from whom one has received vows, teachings and oral tansmission, and according to tantra, this refers to a spiritual master from whom one has received initiation, tantric teachings and oral transmissions.

བཀའ་གདམས།

Kadampa tradition. A tradition of Tibetan Buddhism founded by Atiśa. Dromtonpa, Potowa and Chekawa are some of the great masters belonging to this tradition.

བཀའ་གདམས་སྐུ་མཆེད་གསུམ།

The three spiritual brothers of the Kadampa tradition. 1. ཕུ་ཆུང་བ་གཞོན་ནུ་རྒྱལ་མཚན། Puchungwa Zhonu Gyaltsen 2. པོ་ཏོ་བ་རིན་ཆེན་གསལ། Potowa Rinchen Sel 3. སྤྱན་སྔ་བ་ཚུལ་ཁྲིམས་འབར། Chengwa Tsultrim Bar.

བཀའ་གདམས་རྙིང་མ།

The Kadampa tradition accepting the three doctrine and four deities (see bka'-gdams lha-chos bdun) passed down from Dromtonpa to Je Tsong Khapa.

བཀའ་གདམས་གདམས་ངག

The Kadampa's teachings. These constitute the basic view or philosophy as transmitted by the founder of the Kadampa tradition, Atiśa, to Chen-ngawa on the Four Noble Truths, the transmission of teachings on dependent arising as transmitted by Phuchungba, and the teachings on the two truths (conventional and ultimate) as transmitted by Naljorpa.

བཀའ་གདམས་པ་ཆོས་བུ་ཆོས།

The father and son transmission of Kadampa doctrine. The secret transmission of the Kadampa tradition, rooted in Atisha as received by Dromtonpa Gyalwe Jungne, is known as the father-transmission (pha-chos); that received by Ngog Loden

Sherab and Khuton Tsondru is known as the son-transmission (bu-chos).

བཀའ་གདམས་ཕུགས་ནོར་བཅུ།

The ten innermost jewels of the Kadampa tradition. A. གཏད་པ་བཞི། The four entrustments: 1. བློ་ཕུགས་ཆོས་ལ་གཏད། entrusting yourself to the dharma as the simplest way of thought 2. ཆོས་ཕུགས་སྤྲང་ལ་གཏད། entrusting yourself to poverty as the simplest way of practising dharma 3. སྤྲང་ཕུགས་ཤི་ལ་གཏད། entrusting yourself to death as the extreme consequence of poverty 4. ཤི་ཕུགས་གྲོག་པོ་སྐམ་པོ་ལ་གཏད། entrusting yourself to an empty cave as the simplest place to die. B. རྡོ་རྗེ་གསུམ། The three diamond hard resolutions: 1. ཐེབས་མེད་རྡོ་རྗེ། the resolution to reject objections from parents, etc. to one's practising in seclusion 2. ཁྲེལ་མེད་རྡོ་རྗེ། the resolution to face embarrassment 3. ཡེ་ཤེས་རྡོ་རྗེ་དང་འགྲོགས་པ། the resolution to abide by promised practices. C. བུད་སྙེགས་ཐོབ་གསུམ། The three—expulsion, finding and attaining: 1. མི་གྲལ་ནས་བུད། self expulsion from human society 2. ཁྱི་གྲལ་སྙེགས། finding the company of dogs 3. ལྷ་གྲལ་ཐོབ། attaining heavenly status.

བཀའ་གདམས་ཕོ་བྲང་།

The Kadampa palace, name of two chambers at Radreng and Tashi Lhunpo.

བཀའ་གདམས་མན་ངག་པ།

Kadampas of the instruction lineage. The lineage of Kadampa teachings coming from the Kadampa master Chen-ngawa to Jayulwa, primarily based on study and practice of the *Graded Path* teachings combined with the *Heart Sūtra of Dependent Origination* and oral transmission of the masters.

བཀའ་གདམས་རྩ་གཞུང་།

The fundamental texts of Kadampa tradition. *Entering the Two Truths* བདེན་གཉིས་ལ་འཇུག་པ། and *Instruction on Middle View* དབུ་མའི་མན་ངག, composed by Atiśa, primarily concerning the middle way teaching; *Lamp of Essential Moral Conduct* སྤྱོད་བསྡུས་སྒྲོན་མི། and *Essential Conduct* སྤྱོད་བསྡུས། primarily concerning activity or behavior; and *Lamp on the Path to Enlightenment* བྱང་ཆུབ་ལམ་སྒྲོན། concerning both.

བཀའ་གདམས་གཞུང་དྲུག

The six texts of Kadampa tradition. Treatises which formed the fundamental basis of practice of the past Kadampa masters. These are: *Life Stories of Buddha* སྐྱེས་རབས། and *Specific Teachings* ཆེད་དུ་བརྗོད་པའི་ཚོམས། for inspiring faith and devotion; *Bodhisattva Grounds* བྱང་ས། and *Ornament of Collection of Sūtras* མདོ་སྡེ་རྒྱན for producing meditative concentration; and *Guide to Bodhisattva's Way of Life* སྤྱོད་འཇུག and *Compendium of Precepts* བསླབ་བཏུས། for developing wholesome behavior.

བཀའ་གདམས་གཞུང་པ་བ།

Kadampas of the textual lineage. The lineage of Kadampa teachings coming from the Kadampa master Geshe Potowa to Sharawa, primarily based on study and practice of the Graded Path teachings combined with the major texts of the Kadampa tradition (see bka'-gdams gzhung-drug).

བཀའ་གདམས་ལམ་རིམ་པ།

Kadampas of the path lineage. The lineage of Kadampa teachings coming from the Kadampa master Gonpowa to Neuzur, primarily based on study and practice of the Graded Path teachings combined with miscellaneous texts of the Kadampa tradition.

བཀའ་གདམས་ལྷ་བཞི།

The four deities of the Kadampa tradition; the four divinities of the Kadampas. 1. ཐུབ་པ། Buddha Śākyamuni 2. སྤྱན་རས་གཟིགས། Avalokiteśvara 3. སྒྲོལ་མ། Tārā 4. མི་གཡོ་བ། Acalā.

བཀའ་གདམས་ལྷ་ཆོས་བདུན།

The four deities and three texts of the Kadampa tradition. 1-4. (see bka'-gdams lha-bzhi). 5-7. (see sde-snod gsum).

བཀའ་གདམས་གསར་མ།

The New Kadampa. The lineage of teachings directly originating from Tsong Khapa, based on the examples of the life and deeds of past Kadampa masters inclusive of the middle way view and secret mantrayāna paths. This refers to the Gelug tradition.

བཀའ་བསྡུ་གསུམ།

The Three Buddhist Councils. The first council was held during the same summer of the Buddha's passing into parinirvāṇa at Rājagṛha sponsored by King Ajātaśatru, in which Ānanda recited the collection of Sūtra teachings and Upāli recited the collection of Abhidharma teachings. The second council was held 110 years after Buddha's parinirvāṇa at Vaishālī sponsored by King Ashoka. At that time, monks, especially from Magadha, who had transgressed their vows were expelled and thus the code of monastic discipline was revised. The third council was held at Pataliputra 137 years after Buddha's passing into parinirvāṇa during the reign of King Kaniṣka. The purpose of this council was to create harmony amongst the different schools of philosophy.

བཀའ་པོད་ལྔ།

The five major texts. The five subjects of Buddhist philosophy studied in the Geshe Degree curriculum in the great monastic universities of Tibet and India. 1. ཕར་ཕྱིན། prajñāpāramitā/ Perfection of Wisdom 2. དབུ་མ། madhyamaka/ Middle Way 3. ཚད་མ། Pramāṇa/ Valid Cognition 4. མཛོད། Abhidharma/ Treasure of Knowledge 5. འདུལ་བ། Vinaya/ Monastic Discipline.

བཀའ་བབ་བཞི།

A. The four great disciples of Marpa: 1. རྔོག་ཆོས་སྐུ་རྡོ་རྗེ། Ngog Choku Dorje 2. མཚུར་སྟོན་དབང་གི་རྡོ་རྗེ། Tsurton Wangi Dorje 3. མེས་སྟོན་ཆེན་པོ། Meton Chenpo 4. མི་ལ་རས་པ། Milarepa. B. The four commissioned lineages: 1. སྒྱུ་ལུས་དང་འཕོ་བའི་བཀའ་བབ། the yoga of illusory body and consciousness transference 2. རྨི་ལམ་གྱི་བཀའ་བབ། thè yoga of dreams 3. འོད་གསལ་གྱི་བཀའ་བབ། the yoga of clear light mind 4. གཏུམ་མོའི་བཀའ་བབ། the yoga of psychic heat.

བཀའ་བཞི་པ།

Kazhipa. A Geshe Degree conferred on someone who has merely studied and fulfilled the requirements of an examination after completing his study on the Perfection of Wisdom (phar-phyin), the Middle Way View (dbu-ma), the Monastic Discipline ('dul-ba) and the Treasure of Knowledge (mdzod).

བཀའ་ལུང་།

Oral transmission; prophesy; prediction.

བཀོད་མའི་ཆུ་ལྟ་བུའི་སེམས་བསྐྱེད།

Pravasravaṇodaka cittotpāda/ Fountain-water-like Bodhimind. The bodhicitta or motive of enlightenment associated with the power of retention (see gzungs/ dhāraṇī) and confidence possessed by the Bodhisattva on the three pure grounds, i.e. the 8th, 9th and 10th grounds.

བཀྲ་ཤིས་རྟགས་བརྒྱད།

Aṣṭa maṅgalacihna/ The auspicious signs; the eight auspicious emblems. 1. གདུགས། chattra/ an umbrella 2. གསེར་ཉ།

suvarṇamatsya/ a pair of golden fish 3. བུམ་པ། kalaśa/ a treasure vase 4. པད་མ། padma/ a lotus 5. དུང་དཀར། śaṅkha/ a white conchshell with whorls turning to the right 6. དཔལ་བེའུ། śrīvatsa/ an endless knot 7. རྒྱལ་མཚན། dhvaja/ a banner of victory 8. འཁོར་ལོ། dharmacakra/ a wheel of doctrine.

བཀྲ་ཤིས་རྫས་བརྒྱད།

Aṣṭa maṅgala dravya/ The eight lucky articles; the eight auspicious substances. 1. མེ་ལོང་། ādarśa/ a looking-glass/ mirror 2. གི་ཝང་། gorocanā/ medicinal concretion from the brains of elephants 3. ཞོ། dadhi/ curd 4. རྩྭ་དུར་བ། dūrvā/ fine green grass 5. ཤིང་ཏོག་བིལ་བ། bilva/ śrīphala/ a wood-apple 6. དུང་དཀར་གཡས་འཁྱིལ། dakṣiṇāvartaśaṅkha/ a right-whorled conchshell 7. ལི་ཁྲི། sindhūra/ vermillion 8. ཡུངས་དཀར། sarṣapa/ white mustard seed.

ཀང་གླིང་།

Human thighbone trumpet; femur trumpet. This is used as a ritual implement in certain tantric practices of exorcism to remind one of death and impermanence.

ཀང་མིག་པ།

Ṛṣi Akṣapāda/ Rishi Akshapada. Founder of the non-Buddhist school of philosophy called Nyāya (see rig-pa can-pa).

ཀུ་ཐབས་སུ་གནས་པ།

Steyasaṁvāsika/ Living a lie. The lifestyle of living like a monk without having received monk vows; or without changing one's heart, even though one has externally taken the vows.

རྐྱང་མ།

Lalanā/ The left energy channel. The left channel in our body which is white in colour and stands adjacent to the central channel. It runs from the level of the eyebrows to the point between the navel. The specific details vary according to the lineage of the practice concerned.

རྐྱེན།

Pratyaya/ Conditions. Conditions or circumstances which are a necessary prerequisite for a cause to produce an effect.

རྐྱེན་གསུམ།

Tri pratyayāḥ/ The three types of conditions. 1. གཡོ་བ་མེད་པའི་རྐྱེན། nrīha pratyaya/ unchanging condition 2. མི་རྟག་པའི་རྐྱེན། anitya pratiyaya/ impermanent condition 3. ནུས་པའི་རྐྱེན། samartha pratyaya/ effective condition.

རྐྱེན་བཞི།

Catvāri pratyayāḥ/ The four conditions; the four conditions for a cognition. 1. རྒྱུ་རྐྱེན། hetu pratyaya/ causal condition 2. དམིགས་རྐྱེན། ālambana pratyaya/ objective condition 3. བདག་རྐྱེན། adhipati pratyaya/ fundamental condition 4. དེ་མ་ཐག་རྐྱེན། samanantara pratyaya/ immediate condition.

སྐོག་གྱུར།

Parokṣa/ Hidden phenomenon; obscure phenomenon. A phenomenon that cannot initially be cognized by a direct perception but can only be understood by an inference generated in dependence upon a correct reason, e.g. impermanence of a vase.

སྐོག་ཆོས།

Parokṣa dharma/ The secret transmission. Oral transmission of certain doctrines handed down by Lamas only to ripe and deserving disciples.

སྐད་ཅིག་མ།

Ekakṣaṇa/ Momentary. An impermanent thing—the definition of impermanence.

སྐད་ཅིག་མའི་སྦྱོར་བ།

Kṣaṇikaprayoga/ The momentary training; the training of a single-instant; the yoga of the last moment before enlightenment. The seventh of the eight topics (see dngos-po brgyad), exclusive to the path of Ārya Bodhisattva.

སྐད་ཅིག་མའི་སྦྱོར་བ་མཚན་ཉིད་ཀྱི་ཆོས་བཞི།

Catvāri kṣaṇika prayoga dharmāḥ/ The four topics that characterize the momentary training. 1. རྣམ་པར་སྨིན་པའི་སྐད་ཅིག་སྦྱོར་བ། vipāka kṣaṇika prayoga/ the fruitional or matured momentary training 2. རྣམ་པར་མ་སྨིན་པའི་སྐད་ཅིག་སྦྱོར་བ། avipāka kṣaṇika prayoga/ non-fruitional or immature momentary training 3. མཚན་ཉིད་མེད་པའི་སྐད་ཅིག་སྦྱོར་བ། alakṣaṇa kṣaṇika prayoga/ momentary training lacking characteristics 4. གཉིས་སུ་མེད་པའི་སྐད་ཅིག་སྦྱོར་བ། advaya kṣaṇika prayoga/ non-dual momentary training.

སྐབས་གསུམ་པ།

He who sees the three times; the gods. Metaphorically used for the gods who see the three times (past, present and future) through clairvoyance.

སྐལ་མཉམ་གྱི་རྒྱུ།

Sabhāga hetu/ Congruent cause; equal-state cause. A cause that subsequently produces something of similar type to itself; one of the six types of causes (see rgyu-drug).

སྐལ་བ་དྲུག ཕུན་སུམ་ཚོགས་པ་དྲུག

Ṣaḍ sampanna bhāga/ The six fortunate possessions; six excellent riches. Excellent: 1. དབང་ཕྱུག īśvara saṃpanna bhāga/ power and wealth 2. གཟུགས། rūpa saṃpanna bhāga/ physical form 3. དཔལ། dhānya saṃpanna bhāga/ glory 4. གྲགས་པ། kīrtī saṃpanna bhāga/ fame or reputation 5. ཡེ་ཤེས། jñāna saṃpanna bhāga/ wisdom 6. བརྩོན་འགྲུས། vīrya saṃpanna bhāga/ enthusiastic perseverance.

སྐུ་ངེས་པ།

Kāya niyata/ Certainty of body; certainty of physical form. The feature of a Buddha's Complete Enjoyment Body (sambhogakāya), who is adorned with the 32 major marks (see mtsan bzang-po sum-cu rtsa-gnyis) and 80 minor marks (see dpe-byed bzang-po brgyad-bcu).

སྐུ་ལྔ།

Pañca kāya/ The five bodies of a Buddha. A. The five bodies of a Buddha. 1-3. (see sku-gsum) 4. ངོ་བོ་ཉིད་སྐུ svabhāvakāya/ Nature Truth Body 5. མི་འགྱུར་རྡོ་རྗེའི་སྐུ avikāra vajrakāya/ Immutable Varja Body. B. In some Nyingma tantra these are listed as: 1-3. (see sku-gsum) 4. མི་འགྱུར་རྡོ་རྗེའི་སྐུ avikāra vajrakāya/ Immutable Vajra Body 5. མངོན་པར་བྱང་ཆུབ་པའི་སྐུ abhisaṃbodhikāya/ Fully Enlightened Body.

སྐུ་གཉིས།

Dvi kāya/ The two bodies of a Buddha. 1. གཟུགས་སྐུ rūpakāya/ Form Body 2. ཆོས་སྐུ dharmakāya/ Truth Body.

སྐུ་ཐང་།

Thangka painting; scroll painting. Traditional Tibetan Buddhist art of painting Buddhas, Bodhisattvas, deities and various mystical representations upon a canvas.

སྐུ་ཐུགས་ཟུང་འཇུག

The union of body and mind. The unity of the illusory body and the clear light mind of a yogi.

སྐུ་གདུང་།

A. Dead body. B. Relics. C. A stūpa containing relics or remains of a holy being.

སྐུ་ཕྲེང་།

Incarnate lineage. The lineage of successive incarnate lamas or a single incarnation who is such a succession.

སྐུ་རྫུ་འཕྲུལ་གྱི་ཆོ་འཕྲུལ།

Kāya ṛddhi pratiharya/ Physical miraculous activity. One of the three miraculous activities of a Buddha (see cho-'phrul rnam-gsum) by which sentient beings are tamed and lead to the righteous path.

སྐུ་བཞི།

Catvāri kāya/ The four bodies of a Buddha. 1. ངོ་བོ་ཉིད་སྐུ svabhāvakāya/ Nature Truth Body 2. ཡེ་ཤེས་ཆོས་སྐུ jñānakāya/ Wisdom Truth Body 3. ལོངས་སྐུ saṃbhogakāya/ Complete Enjoyment Body 4. སྤྲུལ་སྐུ nirmānakāya/ Emanation Body.

སྐུ་གསུམ།

The three bodies of a Buddha. 1. ཆོས་སྐུ། dharmakāya/ Truth Body 2. ལོངས་སྐུ། saṃbhogakāya/ Complete Enjoyment Body 3. སྤྲུལ་སྐུ། nirmāṇakāya/ Emanation Body.

སྐུ་གསུམ་ལམ་འཁྱེར།

Taking the three bodies of a Buddha as paths. The tantric practice of taking death as the dharmakāya, the intermediate state of rebirth as the sambhogakāya and the rebirth as the nirmāṇakāya of a Buddha in one's meditation practice.

སྐུར་འདེབས།

Abhyākhyāna/ Depreciation; underestimation. The assertion of the existence of something that does not exist conventionally, or to under rate somebody's qualities below deserving limits. For instance, asserting the non-existence of the law of causality.

སྐྱ་བསེང་གི་བུ་ལྔ།

Pāṇḍava/ The Pandavas. 1. གཡུལ་ངོར་བརྟན་པ། Yudhiṣṭhira 2. འཇིགས་སྡེ། Bhīmasena 3. རིགས་མེད། Nakula 4. སྲིད་སྒྲུབ། Arjuna 5. ལྷ་བཙས། Sahadeva.

སྐྱབས་གསུམ།

Tri śaraṇa/ The three objects of refuge; the three protectors—Buddha, Dharma and Sangha.

སྐྱབས་ཀྱི་སྦྱིན་པ།

Śaraṇa dāna/ The generosity of giving protection; the way of giving protection to somebody afraid of or in a crucial situation. One of the three types of giving (see sbyin-pa rnam-gsum).

སྐྱབས་གསུམ་འཛིན་པའི་དགེ་བསྙེན།

Tri śaraṇagrāhaka upāsaka/ a lay person ordained by refuge precepts. A Buddhist layman who has taken formal refuge or vow of precepts to accept the Three Jewels as the ultimate object of refuge for one's life-time. One of the four nominally ordained lay persons (see dge-bsnyen btags-pa-ba bzhi).

སྐྱིད་གྲོང་འཕགས་པ།

The Avalokiteśvara of Kyidrong. According to a common belief among Tibetans, the Tibetan King Songtsen Gampo once emanated himself in the form of a Gelong and came to Nepal, where he fell a sandal tree in which he is said to have found four self-born images of Avalokiteshvara. The Kyidrong Phagpa is one of them.

སྐྱིལ་ཀྲུང་བཞི།

Catvāri paryaṅka/ The four cross-legged positions. 1-3. three vajra cross-legged positions (see next) 4. བདེ་སྟོང་གི་སྐྱིལ་ཀྲུང་། cross-legged position of non-dual bliss and void.

སྐྱིལ་ཀྲུང་གསུམ།

Tri paryanka/ The three vajra cross-legged positions of the energy channels, wind and drops རྩ་རླུང་ཐིག་ལེའི་རྡོ་རྗེ་སྐྱིལ་ཀྲུང་གསུམ། Synonymous with rdo-rje skyil-krung gsum.

སྐྱེ་དགུ སྒུ།

Prajā/ Sentient being; living being. Lit: nine-fold births refering to all beings for they take rebirth from the desire realm within the three realms; the form realm within the three realms; and from the formless realm within the three realms.

སྐྱེ་མཆེད།

Āyatana/ Sources of perception; the senses and their respective objects.

སྐྱེ་མཆེད་བཅུ་གཉིས།

Dvādaśa āyatanāni/ Twelve sources of perception. A. 1-6. Six outer sources of perception (see yul-drug) B. 7-12. Six inner sources of perception (see dbang-po drug).

སྐྱེ་མཆེད་དྲུག་གི་རྟེན་འབྲེལ།

Ṣaḍ āyatana pratītyasamutpāda/ The interdependent link of six sources of perception; the link of six cognitive faculties. The fifth link in the twelve linked chain of interdependent origination; the period of time when the six sense powers of a foetus first emerge although they are still unable to distinguish objects of sense.

སྐྱེ་གནས་བཞི།

Catvāro yonayaḥ/ The four types of birth. The four types of sentient beings differentiated according to the way they are born. 1. མངལ་སྐྱེས། jārāyu jāḥ/ those born from a womb 2. སྒོང་སྐྱེས། aṇḍa jāḥ/ those born from an egg 3. དྲོད་གཤེར་ལས་སྐྱེ་བ། saṁsveda jāḥ/ those born from heat and moisture 4. རྫུས་སྐྱེས། upapādukā jāḥ/ those born miraculously.

སྐྱེ་བ།

Jāti/ The birth-state; birth. One of the four states of existences of a being (see srid-pa bzhi) in genral; for human beings, the very moment of conception in the mother's womb.

སྐྱེ་བ་ངོ་བོ་ཉིད་མེད་པ།

Utpattiniḥ svabhāvatā/ One of the three lackings of identity. Because all phenomena are generated, or come into being in reliance upon causes and conditions, not only does a multi-coloured rope lack a snake's existence, but also, it's inherent existence as a rope, as it is the product of many threads wound together. Therefore, it lacks inherent existence.

སྐྱེ་བ་སྤྲུལ་སྐུ།

Janma nirmāṇakāya/ The Emanation Body of a Buddha by birth. The way a Buddha takes an emanated form of a god, animal, bridge and living beings in order to tame sentient beings.

སྐྱེ་མེད་དོན་གྱི་གསུང་།

The ultimate teachings lacking birth. One of the five teachings (see gsung lnga) of a Buddha according to Nyingma tradition. This refers to the inexpressible reality itself which forms the basis or root of all meanings. Consequently, it is also called the ultimate teaching of the unborn truth body (chos-sku skye-med don-gyi gsung).

སྐྱེ་མེད་བདེ་ཆེན།

Ajāta mahāsukha/ The unborn great bliss. This refers to the state of liberation or state beyond suffering.

སྐྱེ་སྲིད།

Upapattibhava/ The state of birth or existence. One of the four states of existence, e.g. the consciousness that has just connected to the conception taken place in the womb.

སྐྱེས་ཐོབ་ཀྱི་མུ་སྟེགས་པ།

A non-Buddhist by birth. Those who hold the wrong view that phenomena exist truly by way of their own accord.

སྐྱེས་བུ་གསུམ།

The three types of persons (see skys-bu chung-ngu, spyes-bu'-bring and skyes-bu chen-po).

སྐྱེས་བུ་ཆུང་ངུ།

Adhama puruṣa/ Person of small scope. A practitioner who merely seeks a higher state of rebirth impelled by fear of the lower rebirths.

སྐྱེས་བུ་ཆུང་བ་ཁྱད་པར་ཅན།

Viśeṣakādhama puruṣa/ The superior person of small scope. A practitioner who has generated disgust of the experience of this life and has produced an uncontrived or natural interest in a better future life through contemplating the difficulty and significance of finding a human rebirth endowed with leisure (see dal-ba brgyad) and endowments (see 'byor-ba bcu), and impermanence.

སྐྱེས་བུ་ཆུང་ངུའི་ལམ།

Adhama puruṣa mārga/ The paths of a person of small scope. The intent or wish for, primarily, seeking a higher rebirth within cyclic existence (saṁsāra) for the sake of oneself alone.

སྐྱེས་བུ་ཆེན་པོ།

Uttama puruṣa/ Person of great scope. A practitioner with great spirit who voluntarily seeks to place all sentient beings throughout the expanse of space in the state of complete enlightenment (Buddhahood), and who therefore is able to work extensively for the sake of others.

སྐྱེས་བུ་ཆེན་པོའི་ལམ།

Uttama puruṣa mārga/ The paths of a person of great scope. All paths of the greater vehicle (Mahāyāna) that are conjoined by resolute intent (lhag-bsam), the sixth of the seven-fold causes and result (see rgyu-'bras man-ngag bdun) transmission.

སྐྱེས་བུ་ཐ་མ།

Anta puruṣa/ The person of small scope (same as skyes-bu chung-ngu).

སྐྱེས་བུ་འབྲིང་།

Madhyama puruṣa/ Person of middling scope. A practitioner who wishes himself or herself to be free of the sufferings of cyclic existence and seeks to achieve the state of liberation.

སྐྱེས་བུ་འབྲིང་གི་ལམ།

Madhyama puruṣa mārga/ The paths of a person of middling scope. All those paths that are conjoined with a wish primarily to achieve the state of liberation for one's own sake by being disgusted with the marvels of cyclic existence (saṁsāra).

སྐྱེས་བུ་ཟུང་བཞི།

Catvāri yampuruṣa/ Four categories of a person (on the paths). 1. རྒྱུན་ཞུགས། śrotāpanna/ Stream-winner 2. ཕྱིར་འོང་། sakṛdāgāmin/ Once-returner 3. ཕྱིར་མི་འོང་། anāgāmin/ Never-returner 4. དགྲ་བཅོམ། arhat/ Foe-destroyer.

སྐྱེས་བུ་གསུམ་གྱི་ལམ་རིམ།

The stages of paths of the three types of persons and the texts that explain these paths.

སྐྱེས་བུས་བྱེད་པའི་འབྲས་བུ།

Pauruṣeya phala/ Fruit produced by a person. The commonly shared environment and the general conditions of life in this universe as experienced by an individual being, who is dependent upon them.

སྐྱེས་རབས།

Jātaka/ Life stories (jātakas); rebirth stories. Accounts of Bodhisattva practices that Buddha encountered in his previous lives; a geniune examplary teaching.

སྐྱོ་ཤས།

Kheda/ Attitude of disgust. A subdued state of mind which is disgusted with the uncontrolled cycle of birth, sickness and death that ultimately desires liberation, thus transforming into renunciation.

སྐྱོན་ཡོན།

Doṣa and guṇa/ Faults and good qualities; merits and demerits.

སྐྱོབ་པ་འཇིག་རྟེན་མགོན་པོ།

Kyopa Jigten Gonpo (1143-1217). The founder and one of the foremost masters of the Drikung Kagyu tradition of Tibetan Buddhism.

སྐྱོར་དཔོན།

Class monitor in a monastic university.

སྐྱོར་གྲྭ

A regular class in a monastery where students recite the texts by heart at an assembly after they have memorized them.

སྐྲ་ཤད་འཛག་སྣང་།

Keśoṇḍuka/ A false appearance of falling hair. An example of what a person with a cataract seems to see with distorted non-conceptual sensory perception.

བརྐྱངས་ཕྱག

Full-length prostration.

བསྐལ་ཆུང་།

The small aeon. According to the Abhidharma tradition, a small aeon refers to the extent of time it takes for the human life-span to increase from ten years of age up to a maximum of eighty-thousand at a rate of only one year every century, as well as to decrease down to a minimum of ten years of human life span at the same rate, i.e. one year every century. This comes to billions of human years.

བསྐལ་ཆེན།

Mahākalpa/ The great aeon. According to Abhidharma tradition, every cycle of eighty small aeons comprises one great aeon. This comes to trillions of human years. A great aeon consists of eighty intermediate aeons divided into twenty aeons of formation, persistence, dissolution and vacuity.

བསྐལ་ཆེན་གྲངས་མེད།

Asaṃkyeya kalpa/ An incalculable aeon. One sixtieth of a great aeon, i.e. the sixty digit number of years in calculation. Thrice this limit of calculation becomes the three great countless aeons (skal-chen grangs-med gsum).

བསྐལ་དོན།

Obstructions. Obstructions caused either by an object, time or nature that do not allow the visual perception of something.

བསྐལ་དོན་གསུམ།

The three-fold obstructions. 1. དུས་ཀྱི་བསྐལ་དོན། obstruction by time, e.g. not enabling one to perceive something due to a duration of time 2. ཡུལ་གྱི་བསྐལ་དོན། obstruction by object, e.g. not enabling one to perceive something due to distant location of the object of perception 3. རང་བཞིན་ནམ་ངོ་བོའི་བསྐལ་དོན། obstruction by nature or identity, e.g. not enabling one to perceive something due to the inherent subtlety.

བསྐལ་པ།

Kalpa/ An aeon; world age.

བསྐལ་པ་གཉིས།

The two aeons. 1. སྒྲོན་བསྐལ། The aeon of light (sgron-bskal), referring to that period when the doctrine of Buddha flourishes. 2. མུན་བསྐལ། The aeon of darkness (mun-bskal), referring to that period when the doctrine of Buddha does not flourish.

བསྐལ་པ་གཉིས་ལྡན།

The two-fold aeon. Following the further degeneration of the three-fold aeon, it is believed that people will observe only two of the ten virtuous activities; this period is known as the two-fold aeon and is equivalent to eight hundred and sixty-four thousand human years.

བསྐལ་པ་བར་མ།

Antara kalpa/ The intermediate aeon. According to the Abidharma tradition, two small aeons make an intermediate aeon. This comes to billions of human years.

བསྐལ་པ་བར་མ་གསུམ།

The aeons that falls within eighteen intermediate periods. This comprises the three aeons known as the aeon of starvation, the aeon of sickness and the aeon of weapons.

བསྐལ་པ་རྫོགས་ལྡན།

Kṛtayuga/ The perfect aeon; the excellent aeon. According to the Abhidharma tradition, it is explained that after the origination of human beings in this universe for a long period the system of private ownership did not exist and the people were perfectly pure in their moral conduct committing no non-virtues, i.e. they upheld all of the ten virtuous activities. This period is known as the perfected aeon and is said to be equivalent to one million seven hundred and twenty-eight thousand human years.

བསྐལ་པ་ཡ་ཐོག

The earliest aeon. This refers to the fortunate aeon (bskal-pa rdzogs-ldan) during which human beings lived to the age of ten thousand years, and were nourished by natural oil from the ground and unharvested crops such as rice seedlings.

བསྐལ་པ་གསུམ་ལྡན།

Tretā yuga/ The three-fold aeon. Following the degeneration of the perfected aeon, it is said that people will observe only three of the ten virtuous activities; this period is known as the three-fold aeon. This period is equivalent to one million two hundred and ninety-six thousand human years.

བསྐལ་པའི་དུས་བཞི།

The four periods of an aeon: 1. the fortunate (see bskal-pa rdzogs-ldan) 2. the three-fold (see bskal-pa gsum-ldan) 3. the two-fold (see bskal-pa gnyis-ldan) 4. The corrupt age (see rtsod-idam-gyi dus).

བསྐྱེད་རིམ།

Utpattikrama/ The generation stage practice. The tantric practice of transforming appearance, sound and wisdom respectively into a deity, mantra and wisdom of that particular meditational deity in order to purify the four types of birth along with their latencies.

བསྐྱེད་རིམ་ཕྲ་མོ།

The subtle generation stage practice. Meditation on the implements of a deity, i.e. the subtle vajra meditative concentration.

བསྐྱེད་རིམ་རགས་པ།

The gross generation stage practice. Tantric meditation on the face and arms of a deity.

བསྐྱོད་ལས།

A limit of calculation. The fifty-fifth fraction of the sixtieth limit of counting according to the Abhidharma tradition.

ཁ་སྐོང་སྦྱིན་སྲེག

Complementary fire-pūja. A commitment of performing the rite of fire-pūja at the conclusion of a retreat on a particular deity in order to purify the omissions and commissions one may have made in the course of meditation on that deity.

ཁ་ཅིག

Opponent; another view point. Proponents of a philosophical position other than one's own or other than those held by the author of a philosophical treatise, who introduces his opponent's views by the phrase 'kha-chig', then proceeds to refute them.

ཁ་ཆེམས།

An oral will. An oral testament given, especially at the time of death, describing how one's affairs are to be handled.

ཁ་དོག་གི་ཟིལ་གནོན་བཞི།

The four surpassing concentrations on colors. One of the eight surpassing concentrations, in which a yogi visualizes the four colors blue, yellow, white and red as radiant and luminous through the power of meditation and thus gains control of magical hallucinations.

ཁ་བདེའི་རྟེན་འབྲེལ་སྒོ་འབྱེད།

Welcoming the day through reciting words of auspiciousness. This refers to the custom of greeting everybody with the words, "Good luck and happy New Year. May you be prosperous forever," thereby offering and accepting bits of chang, and phye-mar, i.e. sweet ground roasted barley.

ཁ་ན་མ་ཐོ་བ།

Avadya/ Misdeeds. All wrong doings, non-virtues and negative activities prone to produce pain and suffering as their consequences.

ཁ་ན་མ་ཐོ་བ་གཉིས།

The two types of misdeeds; two kinds of non-virtues. 1. བཅས་པའི་ཁ་ན་མ་ཐོ་བ། pratikṣepaṇa sāvadya/ proscribed misdeed 2. རང་བཞིན་གྱི་ཁ་ན་མ་ཐོ་བ། natural misdeed.

ཁ་ན་མ་ཐོ་བའི་སྒྲིབ་པ།

Avadyāvaraṇa/ The obscuration from misdeeds. The ten non-virtues and other wrong doings. These are also called karmic obscurations (las-kyi sgrib-pa).

ཁ་བབ་ཆུ་བཞི།

The four great rivers coming from the four directions of Mt. Kailash. 1. གངྒཱ། The Ganges from the opening of a rock like an elephant to the east; 2. སིནྡྷུ། the Sindhu from the opening of a rock like a peacock to the south; 3. པཀྵུ། the Pakshu from the opening of a rock like a horse to the west, which is also known as the Yarlung river; and 4. སི་ཏཱ། Sita from the opening of a rock like a lion to the north.

ཁ་སྦྱོར་ཡན་ལག་བདུན་ལྡན།

Saptāṅga saṁbhukta/ The seven features of divine embrace; the seven features of Buddhas in sambhogakāya form. 1. ལོངས་སྤྱོད་རྫོགས་པའི་ཡན་ལག saṁbhogāṅga/ complete enjoyment 2. ཁ་སྦྱོར་གྱི་ཡན་ལག saṁbhuktāṅga/ kissing 3. བདེ་བ་ཆེན་པོའི་ཡན་ལག mahāsukhāṅga/ great bliss 4. རང་བཞིན་མེད་པའི་ཡན་ལག abhāvaṅga/ non-inherent existence 5. སྙིང་རྗེས་ཡོངས་སུ་གང་བའི་ཡན་ལག saṁpūrṇakaruṇāṅga/ completely overwhelmed by compassion 6. རྒྱུན་མི་ཆད་པའི་ཡན་ལག anācchedāṅga/ uninterrupted contuinity 7. འགོག་པ་མེད་པའི་ཡན་ལག anirodhāṅga/ non-cessation.

ཁ་གསག

Lapanā/ Flattery. One of the five means of wrong livelihood (see log-'tso lnga), getting someone to give you something by flattering him or her.

ཁང་ཚན།

Monastic house. A smaller community within a monastic univeristy in which monks from one geographical area live.

ཁམས།

Dhātu/ A. A locality, region, domain or realm. B. A family or caste. C. Elements or nature. D. Cause or seed. E. Spheres, faculty or senses.

ཁམས་དཀར་དམར།

The white and red constituents; semen and blood.

ཁམས་ལྔ།

Pañca dhātu/ The five elements. A. Generally the: 1. ས། bhū/ earth 2. ཆུ། jala/ water 3. མེ། tejas/ fire 4. རླུང་། anila/ wind 5. ནམ་མཁའ། ākāśa/ space. B. In medical tantras and astrology these are identified as: 1. ཤིང་། vṛkṣa/ wood 2. མེ། tejas/ fire 3. ས། bhū/ earth 4. ལྕགས loha/ iron 5. ཆུ། jala/ water.

ཁམས་ལྔའི་ཡོན་ཏན།

The natural qualities of the five elements. The earth element has five qualities—sound, touch, taste, form and smell; the water element has four—sound, touch, taste and form; the fire element has three qualities—sound, touch and taste; the wind element has two qualities—sound and touch; and the space element has only one quality—being capable of producing sound.

ཁམས་བཅོ་བརྒྱད།

Aṣṭadaśa dhātu/ The eighteen spheres of perception. 1-6. དམིགས་པ་ཡུལ་གྱི་ཁམས་དྲུག the six objects as the bases—1. གཟུགས rūpa/ form 2. སྒྲ། śabda/ sound 3. དྲི། gandha/ smell 4. རོ། rasa/ taste 5. རེག་བྱ། spraṣṭavya/ tangible object 6. ཆོས། dharma/ phenomena 7-12. རྟེན་དབང་པོའི་ཁམས་དྲུག the six sense powers as the reliance (see dbang-po drug) 13-18. བརྟེན་པ་རྣམ་ཤེས་ཀྱི་ཁམས་དྲུག the six consciousnesses that rely upon senses (see rnam-shes tsogs-brgyad, 1-6).

ཁམས་དྲུག

The six elements. 1-5. (see khams-lnga) 6. རྣམ་ཤེས། vijñāna/ consciousness.

ཁམས་དྲུག་ལྡན།

Human beings possessing six elements. According to Vajrayāna teachings the rebirth of human beings is superior for tantric practices due to the fact that human being possesses the six elements (see khams-drug).

ཁམས་བཞི།

Catvāri dhātu/ The four elements (see khams-lnga, 1-4).

ཁམས་གསུམ།

Traidhātu/ The three realms. 1. འདོད་ཁམས། kāma dhātu/ the desire realm 2. གཟུགས་ཁམས། rūpa dhātu/ the form realm 3. གཟུགས་མེད་ཁམས། arūpa dhātu/ the formless realm.

ཁམས་གསུམ་ས་དགུ

Traidhātu nava bhūmi/ The three realms and nine levels. 1. འདོད་ཁམས། kāma dhātu/ desire realm 2. བསམ་གཏན་དང་པོ། prathama dhyāna/ first concentration 3. བསམ་གཏན་གཉིས་པ། dvitīyadhyāna/ second concentration 4. བསམ་གཏན་གསུམ་པ། tritīyadhyāna/ third concentration 5. བསམ་གཏན་བཞི་པ། caturthadhyāna/ fourth concentration 6. ནམ་མཁའ་མཐའ་ཡས། ākāśāntya/ infinite space 7. རྣམ་ཤེས་མཐའ་ཡས། vijñānāntya/ infinite consciousness 8. ཅི་ཡང་མེད། ākiṁcanya/ nothingness 9. སྲིད་རྩེ། bhavāgra/ peak of cyclic existence.

ཁས་འཆེས་པའི་དགེ་སློང་།

Pratijñābhikṣu/ A nominal bhikṣu; an insincere monk. A person who claims to be a monk without having received monastic vows or by having lost the vows through transgressing any of the root vows.

ཁུ་ཁྲག

Semen and menstrual blood; semen and egg. Male and female substances.

ཁུ་རྔོག་འབྲོམ་གསུམ།

The three principal disciples of Atiśa the Great. They are ཁུ་སྟོན་བརྩོན་འགྲུས་གཡུང་དྲུང་། Khuton Tsondru Yung Drung, རྔོག་ལེགས་པའི་ཤེས་རབ། Ngog Legpe Sherab, and འབྲོམ་སྟོན་རྒྱལ་བའི་འབྱུང་གནས། Dromton Gyalwe Jungne.

ཁུར་བཞི།

Catvāri bhāra/ The four burdens. 1. ཕུང་པོའི་ཁུར། skandha bhāra/ burden of aggregate 2. བརྩོན་འགྲུས་ཀྱི་ཁུར། vīrya bhāra/ burden of effort 3. ཉོན་མོངས་པའི་ཁུར། kleśa bhāra/ burden of delusions 4. དམ་བཅའི་ཁུར། pratijñā bhāra/ burden of pledges.

ཁེངས་པ། ཁེངས་དྲེགས།

Stambha/ Conceit; pride; arrogance; haughtiness.

ཁོང་དུ་ཆུད་པའི་ལེའུ་གསུམ།

The three chapters of total comprehension. This refers to the first three durations of the ten sets of five hundred years being the life-span of Buddha Śākyamuni's doctrine. These three are known as དགྲ་བཅོམ་པའི་ལེའུ། the chapter of Arhats, ཕྱིར་མི་འོང་བའི་ལེའུ། the chapter of Never-returners and རྒྱུན་དུ་ཞུགས་པའི་ལེའུ། the chapter of Stream-winners.

ཁོང་རྩུབ།

Cruel-minded; nasty; conniving.

ཁོན་འཛིན།

Vaira/ Grudge. Stubbornly holding a grudge and seeking to take revenge.

ཁོར་ཡུག་གི་རི།

The surrounding mountains. According to Abhidharma this refers to the iron mountains surrounding the outskirts of the four cardinal directions. The outer circumference of this is said to be three crores six lakhs twenty-six thousand and twenty five (3,602,625) yojanas.

ཁྱབ་འཇུག་པ།

Vaiṣṇava/ Viṣṇu worshippers. A propounder of non-Buddhist tenets who follow Viṣṇu, asserting a permanent and partless self. The practice of vase-like meditation and meditation on the syllable OM is asserted as their path of liberation.

ཁྱབ་འཇུག་གི་འཇུག་པ་བཅུ།

The ten emanations of Viṣṇu. 1. ཉ། matsya/ a fish 2. རུས་སྦལ། kacchapa/ a tortoise 3. ཕག་རྒོད། vārāha/ a wild pig 4. མིའི་སེང་གེ། narasiṁha/ human-lion 5. ར་མ་ཙ། rāmā candra/ the God Rama 6. མིའུ་ཐུང་། vāmana/ a dwarf 7. ནག་པོ། kṛṣṇa/ the God Krishna 8. པར་ཤུ་ར་མ། ṛṣī parkurama/ the Saint Parku 9. ཤཱཀྱ་ཐུབ་པ། Śākyamuni/ Buddha Śākyamuni 10. ཀལྐི། Kṛkici/ the son of a Brahmin.

ཁྱབ་པ།

Vyāpti/ Pervasion. A logical relationship e.g., if "X" is pervasive with "Y," then all instances of "X" are necessarily "Y," but all "Y" are not necessarily "X."

ཁྱབ་པ་སྒོ་བརྒྱད།

Aṣṭa vyāptidvāra/ Eight types of pervasion. A logical relationship, in which the eight requirements of congruency for two things are mutually inclusive. ཡིན་ཁྱབ་གཉིས། 1. if it is "X" it is "Y" 2. if it is "Y" it is "X" མིན་ཁྱབ་གཉིས། 3. if it is not "X" it is not "Y" 4. if it is not "Y" it is not "X" ཡོད་ཁྱབ་གཉིས། 5. if there is "X" there is "Y" 6. if there is "Y" there is "X" མེད་ཁྱབ་གཉིས། 7. if there is no "X" then there is no "Y" 8. if there is no "Y" then there is no "X".

ཁྱབ་པ་འདུ་བྱེད་ཀྱི་སྡུག་བསྔལ།

Saṁskāra dhuḥkhatā/ Pervasive suffering. The most subtle suffering inherent in the very nature of the five contaminated aggregates which, like a magnet, attract suffering directly or indirectly.

ཁྱབ་པ་རྣལ་མ་བཞི།

Mūla vyāpti/ Four positive pervasions. 1. རྗེས་ཁྱབ། subsequent pervasion (see rjes-khyab) 2. ལྡོག་ཁྱབ། counter pervasion (see ldog-khyab) 3. འགལ་ཁྱབ། contrary pervasion ('gal-khyab) 4. ཐུར་ཁྱབ། downward pervasion (see thur-khyab).

ཁྱབ་པའི་དམིགས་པ།

Spharaṇālaṃbana/ Pervasive object. One of the four meditative objects (see rnal-'byor-gyi dmigs-pa bzhi) of a yogi practising mental quiescence meditation (zhi-gnas) in which the suchness that pervades all existents is taken as the object of developing samatha.

ཁྱབ་པའི་དམིགས་པ་བཞི།

Catvāri spharaṇālaṃbana/ Four objects of pervasion. The pervasive objects of mental quiescence are: 1. རྣམ་པར་རྟོག་པ་དང་བཅས་པའི་གཟུགས་བརྙན། savikalpa/ conceptual pervasive object 2. རྣམ་པར་རྟོག་པ་མེད་པའི་གཟུགས་བརྙན། nirvikalpa/ nonceptual pervasive object 3. དངོས་པོའི་མཐའ། vastvanta/ extreme of existence 4. དགོས་པ་ཡོངས་སུ་འགྲུབ་པའི་དམིགས་པ། kṛtyānuṣṭhāna/ perfectly established purpose.

ཁྱབ་བྱེད་ཀྱི་རླུང་།

The pervasive wind energy. One of the five principal winds (see rtza-ba'i rlung lnga) located at the heart, it spreads liquids such as blood throughout the body, and is responsible for the movements of the body and limbs.

ཁྲིམ་པ་སུན་འབྱིན།

Disturbing the householder's faith; an act of placing bad impressions about the Sangha community in the eyes of householders.

ཁྲི་དྲུག་འགྲོགས།

Six ornaments of a throne; six adornments of a throne. A. 1. བྱ་ཁྱུང་། an eagle 2. ཀླུ་གདེངས་ཀ་ཅན། a water-spirit (nāga) with multiple hoods behind the head 3. ཆུ་སྲིན། a crocodile-like sea monster (makara) with a criss-cross ornmental pattern on its body 4. མཛེས་པའི་བུ་ཆུང་། a fine looking youth wearing tree leaves as garments 5. རི་དྭགས་ཤ་རལ་ཅན། a large unicorn-like animal having a mane of flesh and a single horn 6. གླང་པོ་ཆེ་རྒྱན་ལྡན། an elephant adorned with ornaments and holding a vase in its trunk B. 1. སེང་གེ simha/ a lion 2. གླང་ཆེན། hastin/ an elephant 3. རྟ་མཆོག aśva/ a supreme horse 4. མ་བྱ། mayūra/ a peacock 5. ཤང་ཤང་། garuḍa/ a garuḍa bird 6. ཕུད་ཀྱི་མི། vīra puruṣa/ a strong man.

ཁྲིད།

Discourse; teaching; explanation; transmission.

ཁྲིད་བརྒྱུད།

Lineage of a teaching. A transmission of the lineage of a teaching in which a scriptural text is explained word by word from written commentaries and oral tradition.

ཁྲིད་ལུང་།

Oral transmission. A discourse in which a textual transmission is given by the recitation of a text, often with a brief explanation.

ཁྲིད་ཆེན་བརྒྱད།

The eight great transmissions; the eight great teachings. A. ཕྱག་ཆེན་ཁྲིད་ཆེན་བརྒྱད། The eight great transmissions on the Great Seal (mahāmudrā): 1. བླ་མ་སྐུ་གསུམ་གྱི་ཁྲིད། teaching on guru devotion and the three bodies of a Buddha 2. བྱམས་སྙིང་རྗེའི་ཁྲིད། teaching on love and compassion 3. རྒྱུ་འབྲས་རྟེན་འབྲེལ་གྱི་ཁྲིད། teaching on causality and dependent origination 4. ལྔ་ལྡན་བདུད་རྩི་ཐིགས་པའི་ཁྲིད། the drop of nectar-like five-fold instructions on the Great Seal 5. ལྷན་ཅིག་སྐྱེས་སྦྱོར་གྱི་ཁྲིད། teaching on simultaneous brith and unification 6. ནཱ་རོ་ཆོས་དྲུག་གི་ཁྲིད། teaching on the six yogas of Naropa (see na-ro chos-drug) 7. ཆོས་བརྒྱད་མགོ་སྙོམས་ཀྱི་ཁྲིད། teaching on subduing the eight worldly concerns (see 'jig-rten chos-brgyad) 8. གསང་སྤྱོད་ལོག་སྒོམ་གྱི་ཁྲིད། teaching on the reversed method of meditation on secret mantra doctrine. B. ལམ་རིམ་ཁྲིད་ཆེན་བརྒྱད། The eight great texts on the Graded Path (lam-rim): 1. ལམ་རིམ་ཆེན་མོ། the extensive text 2. ལམ་རིམ་འབྲིང་། the midddling text and 3. ལམ་རིམ་ཆུང་ངུ་། the short texts by Tsong Khapa 4. ལམ་རིམ་གསེར་ཞུན་མ། *Refined Gold* by the Third Dalai Lama, Sonam Gyatso (1543-1588) 5. ལམ་རིམ་འཇམ་དཔལ་ཞལ་ལུང་། *Instruction from Manjuśri* by the Fifth Dalai Lama, Ngawang Lobsang Gyatso (1617-1682) 6. ལམ་རིམ་བདེ་ལམ། *Convenient Path* by the first Panchen Lama, Lobsang Choegyan (1570-1662) 7. ལམ་རིམ་མྱུར་ལམ། *Quick Path* by the Second Panchen Lama, Lobsang Yeshi (1663-1737) 8. ལམ་རིམ་ལེགས་གསུང་ཉིང་ཁུ། *Essence of Elegent Sayings* by Dakpo Ngawang Dakpa.

ཁྲུ།

Hasta/ Cubit. 1. The length measuring from the elbow to the main joints of the little finger with the hand in a fist or the length of measurement from the elbow to the tip of middle finger. The former is called the short cubit and the latter the full-length cubit. 2. According to Vinaya, dividing one's body into seven equal proportions, a cubit equals the length covered within two parts of the whole.

ཁྲུས་བྱ་བ།

Taking a bath. One of the three requirements before a disciple is prepared to enter the maṇḍala during an initiation. A disciple visualizes taking a bath from the water of the ritual vase. This is symbolically done by sipping, rinsing and spitting water just before entering the hall of initiation. The other two requirements are making prostration and offering a maṇḍala to the master.

ཁྲུས་གསུམ་བྱེད་པ།

Taking a three-fold bath. A practice of Kriyā tantra. ཕྱིའི་ཁྲུས་ཡན་ལག་ལྔ་ཁྲུས། Taking the outer bath by washing the five limbs of the body, ནང་གི་ཁྲུས་རྩ་ལྟུང་དག་པར་བྱེད་པ། taking the inner bath by purifying the root downfalls and གསང་བའི་ཁྲུས་མཚན་རྟོག་དག་པར་བྱེད་པ། taking the secret bath by casting away all negative conceptual thoughts and imaginations.

ཁྲེལ་མེད།

Anapatrāpya/ Inconsideration; indifference to blame. Lack of concern for the consequences of actions done to others or the lack of any sense of embarassment.

ཁྲེལ་ཡོད་པའི་ནོར།

Apatrāpyaadhana/ The wealth of sense of concern. One of the seven wealths of the Āryas (see 'phags-nor bdun). Avoiding committing wrong doings because of sense of embarrassment in regard to others. In other words, one tries to protect the wholesome deeds and avoid committing wrong-doings. This is analogous to the precious minister.

ཁྲོ་གཉེར།

Bhṛkuti/ Wrinkles of wrathfulness. A sign of wrath on the nose or brow of a tantric meditational deity.

ཁྲོ་ཕུ་བཀའ་བརྒྱུད།

Khrophu Kagyud Tradition. A lineage of the Kagyu tradition of Tibetan Buddhism coming from Phagmo Drupa's disciple Rinpoche Gyaltsab and his younger brother Kunden Repa, through Khrophu Lotsawa, Jampa Pel and others.

ཁྲོ་བ།

Krodha/ Wrath; aggressiveness.

ཁྲོ་བོ་བཅུ།

Ten wrathful deities; the ten protectors. 1. གཤིན་རྗེ་གཤེད། Yamāntaka 2. གཞན་གྱིས་མི་ཐུབ་པ། Aparājita 3. རྟ་མགྲིན། Hayagrīva 4. བདུད་རྩི་འཁྱིལ་བ། Amṛtakuṇḍalin 5. མི་གཡོ་བ། Acala 6. འདོད་རྒྱལ Takkirāja/ Kāmarāja 7. དབྱུག་སྔོན་ཅན། Nīladaṇḍa 8. སྟོབས་པོ་ཆེ། Mahābala 9. གཙུག་ཏོར་འཁོར་བསྒྱུར། Uṣṇīṣacakravartin 10. གནོད་མཛེས་རྒྱལ་པོ། Śumbharāja. According to Guhyasamāja these are the ten wrathful deities of the four directions, four intermediate directions, zenith and nadir.

ཁྲོ་བོ་བཅུ་གཅིག

Eleven wrathful deities. 1-10. (see above, khro-bo-bcu) 11. རྡོ་རྗེ་ས་འོག Vajrapātāla.

ཁྲོ་བོའི་བཞད་པ་བརྒྱད།

The eight terrifying laughs of a wrathful deity. སྡིགས་པའི་གད་མོ་ཧ་ཧ། Ha Ha as the threatening; དགྱེས་པའི་གད་མོ་ཧེ་ཧེ། He He as the pleasing; སྒེག་པའི་གད་མོ་ཧི་ཧི། Hi Hi as the elegant; and ཟིལ་གྱིས་གནོན་པའི་གད་མོ་ཧོ་ཧོ། Ho Ho as the outshining laugh.

ཁྲོམས་ཚོགས་ཀྱི་ཚུལ།

The manner of being in a crowded assembly. One of the manners of visualizing the merit field (tshogs-zhing) in which one visualizes the principal deity in the center surrounded by other masters and disciples forming a circle of a crowded assembly.

མཁན་པོ།

Upādhyāya/ An abbot or abbess. The head of a monastery or the principal master from whom monastic vows are received.

མཁན་བརྒྱུད།

Upādhyāya paramparā/ The abbot lineage. A. The ordination

lineage of monastic vows. B. The lineage of abbots of a monastery, also called 'abbot lineage' (mkhan-rabs).

མཁན་སློབ།

A. The master and his disciple. B. The Abbot and Assistant Abbot. According to the Vinaya tradition a spiritual master who fulfills the three qualities of being: 1. pure in the observance of moral discipline as the foundation of all qualities 2. learned in the ritual and rites explained in the Vinayapitaka scriptures 3. extremely compassionate towards the sick and friendless.

མཁན་སློབ་སྤྱིའི་མཚན་ཉིད་དྲུག

Six characteristics of the abbot and assistant abbots in general. 1. ཚུལ་ཁྲིམས་དང་ལྡན་པ། purity of moral discipline 2. འདུལ་བའི་ཆོ་ག་ཤེས་པ། knowledge of monastic code 3. ནད་པར་སྙིང་བརྩེ་བ། kindness towards sick people 4. ནང་འཁོར་དག་པ། purity of close disciples 5. ཆོས་དང་ཟང་ཟིང་གིས་ཕན་འདོགས་པ། benefiting others with dharma teachings and giving material aid 6. དུས་སུ་འདོམས་པ། knowledge of the proper time to give teachings.

མཁའ་ཁྱབ་ཀྱི་ཏིང་ངེ་འཛིན།

A universal meditative concentration free of being biased or sectarian in nature.

མཁའ་འགྲོ

Ḍākinī/ sky-goer; sky-walker. Female celestial beings capable of flying through space, residing in a pure land or within cyclic existence. In tantras ḍākinis are the class of female deities embodying the wisdom aspect of a practitioner who has attained the uncommon siddhi. A goddess born in the pure land of a Buddha is also known as Ḍākinī.

མཁའ་འགྲོ་སྡེ་ལྔ།

Pañca ḍākinī/ The five families of ḍākinīs. 1. ཤར་རྡོ་རྗེ་མཁའ་འགྲ Vajra ḍākinī to the east 2. ལྷོ་རིན་ཆེན་མཁའ་འགྲོ Ratna ḍākinī to the south 3. ནུབ་པད་མ་མཁའ་འགྲོ Padma ḍākinī to the west 4. བྱང་ལས་ཀྱི་མཁའ་འགྲོ Karma ḍākinī to the north 5. དབུས་སངས་རྒྱས་མཁའ་འགྲོ Buddha ḍākinī in the centre.

མཁའ་འགྲོ་སྙིང་ཐིག

The Heart Drop Doctrine of Ḍākinī. A secret Nyingma transmission of Guru Padmasambhava given to Khado Yeshe Tsogyal that was later discovered by Padma Ledrel Tsal from a treasure (i.e. Terma).

མཁའ་སྤྱོད།

Khasarpaṇa/ A. A practitioner who utilizes the sky as the realm of existence. B. A ḍākinī.

མཁའ་སྤྱོད་ཀྱི་དངོས་གྲུབ།

Khasarpaṇa siddhi/ The Siddhi of Khechari field. One who has either attained the eight worldly siddhis (see 'jig-rten pa'i dbang-phyug brgyad), one of the eight common siddhis (see thun-mong gi dngos-grub brgyad), or has the capability to travel into the celestial Khechari fields such as the land of six gods of the desire realm (see 'dod-lha rigs-drug).

མཁའ་སྤྱོད་སྐོར་གསུམ།

The three cycles of Khasarpaṇa ḍākinī teachings of the Sakya tradition of Tibetan Buddhism. 1. ན་རོ་མཁའ་སྤྱོད། Naro Khacho 2. ཨིནྡྲ་མཁའ་སྤྱོད། Indra Khacho 3. མཻ་ཏྲི་མཁའ་སྤྱོད། Metri Khacho.

མཁའ་སྤྱོད་ཆུང་ངུ།

The Lesser Khasarpaṇa. Those practitioners who utilize space or fly in the sky of the form realm, six gods of the desire realm (see 'dod-lha rigs-drug), human world or otherwise being uncertain in terms of their destination.

མཁའ་སྤྱོད་ཆེན་པོ།

The Greater Khasarpaṇa. Those practitioners who possess the following eight qualities: 1. རྡུལ་ཕྲ་རབ་ཀྱི་ངོ་བོ་ཉིད་དང་། who can transform their body into a size as tiny as dust particles 2. ལུས་ཡང་བ་ཉིད་དང་། who has a light body 3. འཇིག་རྟེན་གསུམ་པོ་མཐའ་དག་ཁྱབ་པར་བྱེད་པ་ཉིད་དང་། who can fly throughout the three realms of existence (see khams-gsum) 4. སངས་རྒྱས་ཀྱི་ཡོན་ཏན་འཐོབ་པ་དང་། who are capable of attaining the qualities of a Buddha 5. ཡེ་ཤེས་ཀྱི་སྣང་བ་གསལ་བ་དང་། whose primordial wisdom is penetrative 6. བརྟན་པ་དང་། whose primordial body is stable 7. སྐྱེ་བོ་ཐམས་ཅད་བདག་ཉིད་ཀྱི་དབང་དུ་གྱུར་པ་དང་། who has the power of control over all creatures 8. འདོད་དགུར་སྒྱུར་བ་བཅས་ཡོན་ཏན་བརྒྱད་དང་ལྡན་པའི་མཁའ་སྤྱོད། who fulfills all wishes.

མཁའ་སྤྱོད་ཀྱི་གནས།

Khasarpaṇa kṣetra/ The Ḍākinī Land.

མཁའ་སྤྱོད་དབང་པོ།

The lord of the sky, garuḍa bird.

མཁའ་སྤྱོད་མ།

Khasarpaṇa goddess.

མཁའ་ལ་རྒྱུ་བའི་ཡི་དྭགས།

The hungry ghosts travelling in the sky, e.g. the malignant spirits and dwarves ('u-rang) of the human world.

མཁས་པའི་དམིགས་པ།

Paṇḍitālaṁbana/ The object of the wise ones. One of the four objects of calm-abiding (śamatha) meditation (see rnal-'byor gyi dmigs-pa bzhi). One who has the wisdom to judge his or her objects of meditation with respect to the aggregates, the spheres, the sources of perception, the links of dependent arising, and those that are and are not suitable to be taken as the object for developing calm abiding meditation.

མཁས་པའི་ཡོན་ཏན་ལྔ།

Pañca paṇḍitālaṁbana/ The five qualities of a master-scholar. 1. མང་དུ་ཐོས་པ། extensive hearing & study 2. དོན་ལ་མཁས་པ། mastery over meaning 3. ཡི་གེ་ལ་མཁས་པ། mastery over diction 4. ངེས་པའི་ཚིག་ལ་མཁས་པ། mastery over definite words 5. སྔོན་དང་ཕྱི་མའི་མཐའ་དགོངས་པ་ལ་མཁས་པ། mastery over interpretation of the previous and latter contexts.

མཁས་པའི་བྱ་བ་གསུམ།

The three activities of a master-scholar. 1. འཆད་པ། preaching 2. རྩོད་པ། debating 3. རྩོམ་པ། writing.

མཁས་བཙུན་བཟང་གསུམ།

Learned, pure, wise. A person who is knowledgeable in the sciences of learning, is morally pure with respect to the three gates of activity and unsullied by negativities, and has the pure spirit to benefit others.

མཁྱེན་པ།

Jñāna/ Knowledge; wisdom; understanding; insight.

མཁྱེན་པ་གཉིས།

Two kinds of knowledge. 1. ཇི་ལྟ་བ་མཁྱེན་པ། yathāvajjñāna/ knowledge of all conventional phenomena 2. ཇི་སྙེད་པ་མཁྱེན་པ། yāvajjñāna/ knowledge of all ultimate phenomen.

མཁྱེན་པ་གསུམ།

Three kinds of knowledge. 1. གཞི་ཤེས། vastujñāna/ the omniscient mind 2. ལམ་ཤེས། mārgajñāna/ the knowledge of paths 3. རྣམ་མཁྱེན། sarvajñāna/ the knowledge of bases.

མཁྱེན་པ་ལྔ།

The five knowledges. Same as the five wisdoms (see ye-shes lnga).

མཁྱེན་གསུམ་གྱི་ཆོས་སུམ་ཅུ།

The thirty topics that characterize the three knowledges explained in the *Ornament of Clear Realization* (Abhisamayālaṅkāra). These constitute the ten topics that characterize the omniscient mind (see rnam-mkhyen mtshon-byed-kyi chos bcu), the eleven topics that characterize the knowledge of the paths (see lam-shes mtshon-byed-kyi chos bcu-bcig) and the nine topics that characterize the knowledge of the bases (see gzhi-shes mtshon-byed-kyi chos-dgu).

མཁྱེན་གསུམ་བསྡུས་སྒོམ།

Meditation on the union of the three knowledges/wisdoms. Condensed, abbreviated meditation on the three wisdoms i.e. basic wisdom, path wisdom and omniscient wisdom.

འཁོན།

The Khon lineage. The patriarchal lineage of the hierarchies of the Sakya tradition. It is said that a celestial being known by the name Yapang Kye (g.ya'-spang-skyes) tamed Kyareng Tragme (skya-rengs khrag-med), a demon, and accepted his wife Yadrug Silema (g.ya'-'brug si-le-ma) to his court as his bride who gave birth to a son. This being the result of combat between a demon and a celestial being the descendants of this lineage came to be known as Khon, the 'combat lineage'. The present lineage holder is His Holiness Sakya Trizin, who is based at Rajpur, India.

འཁོན་པ་བཟླུམས་པའི་གསོ་སྦྱོང་།

The confession ceremony for pacifying disputes. One of the ceremonies of the monastic community held at irregular intervals whenever there is a need to hold such an assembly to pacify a major dispute between Sangha communities.

འཁོར་སྒྱུར་གྱི་འཁོར་ལོའི་ཁྱད་ཆོས་དྲུག

The six qualities of the wheel of a universal monarch. These are: 1. མྱུར་དུ་འགྲོ་བ། speedy 2. གཞན་དུ་འགྲོ་བ། migrant 3. མ་རྒྱལ་བ་ལས་རྒྱལ་བར་བྱེད་པ། victorious over those uncaptured 4. རྒྱལ་བ་རྣལ་དུ་འགོད་པ། controls those already captured 5. མཐོ་བ་ལ་འཕར་བ། eliminates those above 6. དམའ་བ་ལ་འབབ་པ། debases those beneath.

འཁོར་སྒྱུར་གྱི་ཉེ་བའི་རིན་ཆེན་བདུན།

The seven near precious articles of a universal monarch. These are: 1. རལ་གྲི་རིན་པོ་ཆེ། precious sword 2. པགས་པ་རིན་པོ་ཆེ། precious skin 3. ཁྱིམ་རིན་པོ་ཆེ། precious householder 4. ཚལ་རིན་པོ་ཆེ། precious garden 5. གོས་རིན་པོ་ཆེ། precious garment 6. ལྷམ་རིན་པོ་ཆེ། precious shoes 7. མལ་ཆ་རིན་པོ་ཆེ། precious bedding.

འཁོར་སྒྱུར་ལྔ།

Pañca cakravartin/ The five universal monarchs. These are: 1. ང་ལས་ནུ། Māndhātṛ 2. མཛེས་པ། Cāru 3. ཉེ་མཛེས་པ། Upacāru 4. མཛེས་ལྡན། Cārumanta 5. ཉེ་མཛེས་ལྡན། Upacārumanta.

འཁོར་ངེས་པ།

Certainty of disciples. A feature of a sambhogakāya Buddha who only teaches to a circle of Ārya Bodhisattva disciples.

འཁོར་ལྔ་སྡེ་བཟང་པོ།

Pañca bhadrapariṣadyā/ The five ascetics. The group of five disciples who were the direct recipients of Buddha's First Turning of the Wheel of Doctrine at Varanasi. 1. ཀུན་ཤེས་ཀཽཎྜི་ནྱ། Ajñānata Kauṇḍinya 2. རྟ་ཐུལ། Aśvajit 3. རླངས་པ། Vāṣpa 4. མིང་ཆེན། Mahānāma 5. བཟང་ལྡན། Bhadrika.

འཁོར་རྣམ་བཞི།

Catvāri pariṣadyāḥ/ The four types of followers of Buddha Śākyamuni. 1. ཁྱིམ་པ་ཕོ་མོ་གཉིས། male and female householders 2. རབ་བྱུང་ཕོ་མོ་གཉིས། novice monks and nuns 3. དགེ་སློང་ཕ་མ་གཉིས། fully ordained monks and nuns 4. དགེ་བསྙེན་ཕ་མ་གཉིས་ ordained layman and laywomen.

འཁོར་ཕུན་སུམ་ཚོགས་པ།

Sampanna pariṣadḺa/ The perfect retinue. One of the five excellences (see phun-sum tshogs-pa lnga); the fact that a Buddha is being encircled by Bodhisattvas who have attained the spiritual grounds and the knowledge bearers (tantrikas).

འཁོར་བ།

Saṁsāra/ Cyclic existence (saṁsāra). The vicious beginningless cycle of rebirth, fraught with sufferings of birth, sic ness, aging and death, arising from ignorance as contrast to the state of peace, liberation.

འཁོར་བ་ཉམས་ལེན།

The practice of saṁsāra. The practice of forbearance and willingly accepting the pains and sufferings within cyclic existence.

འཁོར་བའི་ཁྱིམ།

A. The household of saṁsāra, family life. B. the queen's palace.

འཁོར་བའི་འཁོར་ལོ་ཆ་ལུ་པ།

The painting of the wheel of life traditionally depicted on the wall of the portico of a monastery.

འཁོར་བའི་དགྲ།

The enemy of saṁsāra. A. The wisdom realizing selflessness. B. The state of liberation.

འཁོར་བའི་རྒྱ་མཚོ།

The ocean of saṁsāra. The immeasurable and unlimited suffering that seems to have no beginning and no end of its own.

འཁོར་བའི་རྒྱུན།

The continuity of saṁsāra. The continuity of this aggregate propelled by karma and delusion that knows no beginning.

འཁོར་བའི་སྒོ།

Saṁsāra dvāra/ The door of saṁsāra. Karma and delusion.

འཁོར་བའི་འཆིང་བ།

Saṁsāra bandhana/ The bindings of saṁsāra. The karma and delusion that binds us within samsaric life.

འཁོར་བའི་སྡུག་བསྔལ།

Saṁsāra duḥkhatā/ The sufferings within saṁsāra. The sufferings of birth, old age, sickness, death and of hunger, thirst and the like.

འཁོར་བའི་སྣ་འདྲེན།

The leader of saṁsāra. The truth of origin of suffering; the karma and delusion that spearheads every experience within saṁsaric life.

འཁོར་བའི་རྩ་བ།

Saṁsāra mūla/ The root of saṁsāra. The six root delusions that bind us to saṁsāra; desire-attachment, hatred-anger, pride, ignorance, deluded views or philosophy, and doubt.

འཁོར་བའི་ལམ།

Saṁsāra mārga/ The paths of saṁsāra. A. The twelve links of interdependent origination (see rten'brel yan-lag bcu-gnyis). B. The non-virtuous activities.

འཁོར་བའི་ལམ་གསུམ།

The three paths within cyclic existence; the circle of three paths. 1. ཉོན་མོངས་པའི་ལམ། kleśa mārga/ the path of delusions that give rise to accumulation of karmas 2. ལས་ཀྱི་ལམ། karma mārga/ the path of karma that give rise to sufferings 3. སྡུག་བསྔལ་གྱི་ལམ། duḥkhatā mārga/ he path of suffering that give rise to continuous generation of karmas and delusions.

འཁོར་ལོ་ལྔ།

Pañca cakra/ The five channel wheel. 1-4. (see 'khor-lo bzhi') 5. གསང་གནས་སུ་བདེ་སྐྱོང་འཁོར་ལོ། the wheel of sustaining bliss at the secret organ.

འཁོར་ལོ་ཆེན་པོ་བཞི།

Catvāri mahācakra/ The four great wheels. 1. མཐུན་པར་གྱུར་པའི་ཡུལ་ན་གནས་པ། living in a harmonious environment 2. སྐྱེས་བུ་དམ་པ་ལ་བརྟེན་པ། relying upon a holy or spiritual person 3. སྨོན་ལམ་བཏབ་པ། making prayers 4. བསོད་ནམས་བསགས་པ། having accumulated merits. This is also called the four wheels of the god and men (lha-dang mi-rnams-kyi 'khor-lo bzhi).

འཁོར་ལོ་ཆེན་པོ་རྫོགས་རིམ་བྱིན་རླབས་བཞི།

The great wheel of four-fold blessings according to the completion stage practice of tantra. 1. ལུས་བྱིན་རླབས། blessings of body 2. ངག་བྱིན་རླབས། blessings of speech 3. ཡིད་བྱིན་རླབས། blessings of mind 4. དེ་ཁོ་ན་ཉིད་ཀྱི་བྱིན་རླབས། blessings of the suchness.

འཁོར་ལོ་རྣམ་གསུམ།

The three-fold wheels. 1. ཀློག་པ་ཐོས་བསམ་གྱི་འཁོར་ལོ། the wheel of study through reading, listening and contemplation 2. སྤོང་བ་བསམ་གཏན་གྱི་འཁོར་ལོ། the wheel of abandonment through concentration 3. བྱ་བ་ལས་ཀྱི་འཁོར་ལོ། the wheel of service through activities.

འཁོར་ལོ་བཞི།

Catvāri cakra/ The four channel wheels. 1. སྙིང་ཁར་ཆོས་ཀྱི་འཁོར་ལོ། the wheel of great bliss at the crown 2. མགྲིན་པར་ལོངས་སྤྱོད་ཀྱི་འཁོར་ལོ། the wheel of enjoyment at the throat 3. ལྟེ་བར་སྤྲུལ་པའི་འཁོར་ལོ། the wheel of phenomena the heart 4. གཙུག་ཏོར་དུ་བདེ་ཆེན་གྱི་འཁོར་ལོ། the wheel of emanation at the navel.

འཁོར་ལོ་རིམ་པ་གསུམ།

The three turnings of the wheel of doctrine (see below).

འཁོར་ལོ་གསུམ།

Tri cakra/ A. The three-fold wheels (see above 'khor-lo rnam-gsum). B. The three turnings of the wheel of doctrine. (see below).

འཁོར་ལོ་དང་པོ།

Prathama dharmacakra/ The first turning of the wheel of doctrine. The first teaching at Dear Park, Sarnath, in which Buddha Śākyamuni expounded the Four Noble Truths and set forth the basis of the Hīnayāna philosophy that phenomena have a truly eixstent nature.

འཁོར་ལོ་བར་པ།

Madhya dharmacakra/ The second turning of the wheel of doctrine. The teaching at Vulture Peak (Gṛdhrakūṭa) in which Buddha Śākyamuni taught the Perfection of Wisdom Sūtras, the teaching which is the basis of the Middle View philosophy, introducing the doctrine that all phenomena lack a truly eixstent nature.

འཁོར་ལོ་ཐ་མ།

Antya dharmacakra/ The third turning of the wheel of doctrine. The teaching at Vaishālī in which Buddha Śākyamuni taught the Sūtra of Clear Discrimination, the teaching laying the basis of the Mind-Only School and introducing the doctrine that imputed phenomena lack a truly existent nature, but dependent and thoroughly established phenomena are truly existent.

འཁོར་ལོས་སྒྱུར་བའི་རྒྱལ་པོ།

Cakravartin/ The universal monarch. The monarchs wielding wheels in their hands. These monarchs appear only during the time when the human life span stretches between infinite to eighty thousand years.

འཁོར་གསུམ།

The three wheels. A. མཚོན་ཆ་མདའ་གྲི་མདུང་གསུམ། The arrow, sword and spear B. The three turnings of the wheel of doctrine (see 'khor-lo gsum) C. བྱེད་པ་པོ་དང་། བྱ་བའི་ལས། བྱ་བའི་ཡུལ་གསུམ། The three circles of an activity, e.g. the agent, the activity and the goal D. ལུས་ངག་ཡིད་གསུམ། The body, speech and mind.

འཁོར་གསུམ་རྣམ་དག

The purity of the three circles. The Bodhisattva's practice at the seventh Bodhisattva ground of sealing all the three—agent, activity and goal—as lacking inherent existence in nature.

འཁོར་གསུམ་རྣམ་པར་མི་རྟོག་པ།

The lack of conceptual imagination of the three circles. The wisdom that is free of any conceptual recognition of the three—agent, activity and goal—as having any inherent identity of their own, and knows these as being empty or free of inherent existence.

འཁྱེར་སོ་གསུམ་གྱི་རྣལ་འབྱོར།

The three modes of yoga; the yogic practice of the triple ways. 1. སྣང་བ་སྐུའི་འཁྱེར་སོ། the yoga of taking all appearances as the body of a Buddha 2. སྒྲ་གྲགས་གསུང་གི་འཁྱེར་སོ། the yoga of taking all sounds as the speech of a Buddha 3. དྲན་རྟོག་ཐུགས་ཀྱི་འཁྱེར་སོ། the yoga of taking all thoughts as the mind of a Buddha.

འཁྲུགས་པ་སྡེབ་པའི་བསྟན་བཅོས།

A compiled treatise. A treatise that is a compilation of fragments on a particular topic from all sūtras, e.g., the *Ornament of Discourses* (mahāyānasūtrālaṃkāra/ mdo-sde-rgyan) or the *Compendium of Precepts* (śikṣasamucchaya/ bslab-btus).

འཁྲུལ་རྒྱུ།

The cause or condition of deceptive cognition. A. The ultimate cause of deceptive knowledge, e.g. mistaking all that is selfless or non-inherently existent as having self or inherently existence. B. The temporary cause of deceptive perception, e.g. misjudging things through defective vision.

འཁྲུལ་རྒྱུ་བཞི།

The four causes of deceptive perception or knowledge. 1. འཁྲུལ་རྒྱུ་གནས་ལ་ཡོད་པ། deception caused by the venue, e.g. seeing trees as running while one is journeying in a boat 2. འཁྲུལ་རྒྱུ་རྟེན་ལ་ཡོད་པ། deception caused by sense faculty, e.g. seeing falling hairs by a person with cataract 3. འཁྲུལ་རྒྱུ་ཡུལ་ལ་ཡོད་པ། deception cause by the object, e.g. seeing a wheel of sparks from swinging a flaming fire-brand or torch in a circle 4. འཁྲུལ་རྒྱུ་དེ་མ་ཐག་རྐྱེན་ལ་ཡོད་པ། deception caused by immediate conditions, e.g. seeing the surroundings like a ball of fire when a person is in outrageous anger or wrath.

འཁྲུལ་སྣང་།

False appearance; deceptive appearance. The mode of appearance of seeing things as different from their actual mode of abidance.

འཁྲུལ་ཞིག་པ།

One who has released all deceptions. A person who has realized emptiness through releasing all misconceptions.

འཁྲུལ་ཤེས།

Bhrānta jñāna/ A. Misconception; misunderstanding. Wrong ideas and ways of judging things because of one's misunderstanding or recognition. B. Deceptive cognition. An awareness that is deceived with respect to the object that appears to it (snang-yul), synonymous with apparent direct perception (see mngon-sum ltar-snang).

གང་མང་གི་ཞི་བ།

Resolution by the majority. One of the seven ways of pacifying quarrels and arguments (see rtsod-pa zhi-byed-kyi chos-bdun) within the Saṅgha community according to the Vinaya rules. If any dispute could not be resolved through the eight appellate procedures (see mngon-sum brgyad kyis zhi-ba), it is then decided by throwing tooth sticks, and whichever of the sides gets the majority of the sticks is considered the winner.

གང་ཟག

Pudgala/ A person. Any person, man or creature imputed upon any of the five aggregates. Lit: ups and downs, meaning such beings have both merits and demerits occasionally growing (gang-ba) or waning (zag-pa/ 'jig-pa).

གང་ཟག་གི་བདག་འཛིན་གཉིས།

Dvi pudgalātmagrāha/ Two kinds of grasping at the self of a person. 1. གང་ཟག་གི་བདག་འཛིན་ལྷན་སྐྱེས། sahaja pudgalātmagrāha/ innate grasping at the self of a person 2. གང་ཟག་གི་བདག་འཛིན་ཀུན་བཏགས། parikalpita pudgalātmagrāha/ intellectual grasping at the self of a person.

གང་ཟག་གི་གདགས་གཞི།

The basis of imputation of a person. The five aggregates comprising form, feeling, recognition, perception and consciousness.

གང་ཟག་གི་བསམ་པ་ལ་དགོངས་པ།

Pudgalāśayābhiprāya/ Determining the interest of a person. A type of interpretative teaching of Buddha, e.g. the teaching, highlighting the importance of the practice of generosity as the best, in which Buddha's basic intention is to teach the equal importance of the practice of six perfections.

གང་ཟག་སྔ་གོན།

Individual preparation. A ritual and rite for the Saṅgha community preparing for their three months rainy season retreat.

གང་ཟག་སྙན་བརྒྱུད།

The human whispered lineage. The lineage of the three inner yogas according to the Nyingma tradition—Mahāyoga, Anuyoga and Atiyoga transmissions passed to successive disciples stemming from Ācārya Padmasambhava and the great scholar, Vimalamitra.

གང་ཟག་བདག་མེད།

Pudgala nairātmya/ Selflessness of person. In its highest sense it is the lack of inherent existence of person. According to the Vaibhāṣika, Sautrāntikas, Cittamātrins and Svātrantikas selflessness of person is either the non-existence of a permanent, single, independent person or the non-existence of a self-sufficient substantially existent person. According to Prāsaṅgika the selflessness of person is either non-existence of a self-sufficient substantially existent person or non-existence of an inherently existent person.

གང་ཟག་བདག་མེད་ཕྲ་མོ།

Sūkṣama pudgalanairātmya/ Subtle selflessness of person. According to Vaibhāṣikas, Sautrāntikas, Cittamātrins and Svātantrikas it is the non-existence of a self-sufficient substantially existent person, and according to Prāsaṅgika it is the non-inherently existent person.

གང་ཟག་བདག་མེད་རགས་པ།

Sthūla pudgalanairātmya/ Coarse selflessness of person. According to the Vaibhasika, Sautrantikas, Cittamatrins and Svatantrikas the coarse selflessness of person is the non-existence of a permanent, single, independent person, and according to Prāsaṅgika it is the non-existence of self-sufficient substantially existent person.

གང་ཟག་བདག་འཛིན།

Pudgalātmagrāha/ Grasping at the self of person. The misconception of the self of person as being truly existent. The perverted conception of a person being inherently existent.

གང་ཟག་མ་ཡིན་པའི་ལྡན་མིན་འདུ་བྱེད་ཉེར་གསུམ།

Twenty-three impersonal, non-associated compositional factors; phenomena that are neither form or consciousness nor a person. 1. ཐོབ་པ། prāpta/ attainment 2. འདུ་ཤེས་མེད་པའི་སྙོམས་འཇུག asaṃjñāsamāpatti/ meditative absorption without discrimiantion 3. འགོག་པའི་སྙོམས་འཇུག nirodhasamāpatti/ meditative absorption of cessation 4. འདུ་ཤེས་མེད་པ་པ། asaṃjñatā/ one without discrinative awareness 5. སྲོག prāṇa/ life-force 6. རིགས་མཐུན་པ། nikāyasabhāga/ similar category 7. སྐྱེ་བ། jāti/ birth 8. རྒ་བ། jarā/ aging 9. གནས་པ། sthiti/ sustenance 10. མི་རྟག་པ། anitya/ impermanence 11. མིང་གི་ཚོགས། nāmakāya/ collection of names 12. ཚིག་གི་ཚོགས། padakāya/ collection of words 13. ཡི་གེའི་ཚོགས། vyañjanakāya/ collection of letters 14. སོ་སོ་སྐྱེ་བོ་ཉིད། pṛthagjanatā/ state of being an ordinary person 15. འཇུག་པ། pravṛtti/ engagement 16. སོ་སོར་ངེས་པ། pratiniyama/ distinct existence 17. རྣལ་འབྱོར། yoga 18. jāva/ rapidity 19. གོ་རིམ། anukrama/ order/ system 20. དུས། kāla/ time 21. ཡུལ། deśa/ place 22. གྲངས། saṁkhyā/ number 23. ཚོགས་པ། bheda/ group.

གང་ཟག་བཞི།

Catvāri pudgala/ Four types of persons; four categories of persons. 1. མུན་པ་ནས་མུན་པར་འགྲོ་བ། person moving from darkness to darkness 2. མུན་པ་ནས་སྣང་བར་འགྲོ་བ། person moving from darkness to light 3. སྣང་བ་ནས་སྣང་བར་འགྲོ་བ། person moving from light to light 4. སྣང་བ་ནས་མུན་པར་འགྲོ་བ། person moving from light to darkness.

གངས་ཏི་སེ།

Mt. Kailash. Also called the holy mountain (gangs rin-po-che) located in the district of Purang in Ngari region of western Tibet, and is venerated by Bonpos, Hindus and Buddhists alike. It is located at a height of 6656 meters above sea level, and is the source of the river Ganges. After every cycle of twelve years in the Horse year, a grand ceremony of special pilgrimage takes place.

གཎ་གཡོག

The wooden stick used for beating the wooden gong used in a monastery to call the community for a congregation. Also called gandi-the'u.

གཎྜི།

Gaṇḍī/ Wooden gong. A long gong of wood, beaten as a bell to call the congregation of monks and nuns to bi-monthly ceremony, work, mourn at the demise of a fellow monk, and for other emergency matters.

གར་གྱི་ཉམས་དགུ

Nava nātakabalā/The nine features of dance. 1. སྒེག་པ། lāsya/ charming 2. དཔའ་བ། vīra/ heroic 3. མི་སྡུག་པ། aśubha/ ugly 4. དྲག་ཤུལ། ūgra/ aggressive 5. བཞད་གད། hasita/ smiling 6. krodha/ wrathful 7. སྙིང་རྗེ། kāruṇika/ compassionate 8. རྔམས་པ། adbhūta/ frightening 9. ཞི་བ། śānti/ peaceful.

གར་ཐིག་དབྱངས་གསུམ།

Dancing, drawing and chanting. The three-fold trainings of the monks—performing monastic dance, learning how to draw or build a maṇḍala and chanting of prayers.

གལ་ཆེན་སྦྱོང་བའི་ས།

The path of significant purification. According to Nyingma tradition, this is the third ground of a Yogi referring to the third level of the Path of Preparation (second of the five paths), where all manifest delusions obstructing the actualization of the clear light mind on the Path of Seeing (third of the five paths) are dispelled.

གུ་རུ་མཚན་བརྒྱད།

The eight manifestations of Guru Rinpoche. 1. གུ་རུ་ཤཱཀྱ་སེང་གེ། Guru Śākya Senge 2. གུ་རུ་པདྨ་སཾབྷ། Guru Padmasambhava 3. གུ་རུ་ཉི་མ་འོད་ཟེར། Guru Nyima Odzer 4. གུ་རུ་སེང་གེ་སྒྲ་སྒྲོག Guru Senge Dradog 5. གུ་རུ་རྡོ་རྗེ་གྲོ་ལོད། Guru Dorje Drolo 6. གུ་རུ་མཚོ་སྐྱེས་རྡོ་རྗེ། Guru Tsokye Dorje 7. གུ་རུ་པདྨ་རྒྱལ་པོ། Guru Padma Gyalpo 8. གུ་རུ་བློ་ལྡན་མཆོག་སྲེད། Guru Loden Chokse.

གུ་རུ་རིན་པོ་ཆེ།

Guru Padmasambhava. An Indian pandit of the eighth century, and an incarnation of Buddha, who introduced the tantric form of Buddhism into Tibet and is revered by all traditions of Tibetan Buddhism, especially the Nyingma tradition.

གོ་སྒྲུབ།

Saṁnāhapratipatti/ Achievement through armour. A Bodhisattva's practice of carrying out all the six perfections within the practice of each perfection. Synonymous with 'Bodhisattva wisdom' (byang-sems kyi mkhyen-pa).

གོ་ཆའི་བརྩོན་འགྲུས།

Saṁnāha vīrya/ Armour-like effort. One of the three types of efforts or enthusiastic perseverence (see brtzon-'grus rnam-gsum) with which a practitioner would happily endure suffering in order to help liberate others from suffering.

གོ་ཆའི་ལྷ་ཡུམ་དྲུག

The six goddesses of putting on the armour. These are 1. རྡོ་རྗེ་ཕག་མོ། Vajravārāhī 2. གཤིན་རྗེ་མ། Yāminī 3. རྨོངས་བྱེད་མ། Mohinī 4. སྐྱོང་བྱེད་མ། Saṃcālinī 5. སྐྲག་བྱེད་མ། Saṃtrāsinī 6. ཙཎྜི་ཀཱ། Caṇḍikā.

གོ་མི་དགེ་བསྙེན།

Gomi Upāsaka. A layman who in addition to observing the eight precepts of the one day vows (see bsnyen-gnas yan-lag brgyad) receives permission to shave his head and wear robes if he so chooses.

གོང་མའི་ཆ་མཐུན་ལྔ།

Pañcordhoa-bhāgīya-kleśā/ Five fetters with respect to the higher realm. 1. གཟུགས་ཀྱི་འདོད་ཆགས། rūpa rāga/ longing desire of the form realm 2. གཟུགས་མེད་པའི་འདོད་ཆགས། arūpa rāga/ longing desire of the formless realm 3. རྒོད་པ། āuddhatya/ mental agitation 4. ང་རྒྱལ། manas/ egotistic pride 5. རྨོངས་པ། avidyā/ deluded ignorance.

གོང་མའི་ཆ་མཐུན་གྱི་ཀུན་སྦྱོར་ལྔ།

The five constant fetters of the higher realms (see above, gong-ma'i cha-mthun lnga).

གོང་སའི་སྙོམས་འཇུག་དག་པ་བ་བཞི།

The four pure meditative absorptions of the higher (form and formless) realm. 1. གནས་པ་ཆ་མཐུན། aid to existence 2. ཉམས་པ་ཆ་མཐུན། aid to degeneration 3. ཁྱད་པར་ཆ་མཐུན། aid to regeneration 4. ངེས་འབྱེད་ཆ་མཐུན། aid to definitive discrimination.

གོང་མའི་གནས་གཙང་ལྔ།

The five pure states of gods in the higher realm (the form and formless realms). Synonymous with the five pure states (see gnas-gtsang lnga).

གོང་སའི་སྙོམས་འཇུག

The meditative absorption of the higher realm, i.e. the meditative absorptions of the form and formless realms.

གོང་སའི་དབང་པོ།

The lord of the higher realm. This may mean: A. Brahma, the lord of the form realm B. The sensory faculties within the higher realms.

གོར་གོར་པོ།

The hard-fleshy foetus. The fourth of the five stages of foetus development of a human being in the womb of a mother during its fourth week when the foetus is just able to resist pressure.

གོས་སྔོན་ཅན།

Nilāmbaradhara/ The one with blue robes. This may mean: A. Sky B. Vajrapāni C. Saturday (Saturn) D. Mahābala (stobs-bzang) the brother of Viṣṇu (khyab-'jug).

གྱ་ནོམ་སྣང་།

Sudarśana/ The excellent experience. The sixth state of the fourth level of concentration. The gods in this state enjoy ecstatic bliss of body and mind and see the supreme dharma (chos-kyi mchog). One of the five pure states of gods.

གྱེན་རྒྱུའི་རླུང་།

Upward-moving wind energy. One of the five energy winds (see rtza-ba'i rlung-lnga) that controls swallowing, speaking and breathing, and seated in the centre of the chest.

གྱི་ན་བ།

A. Ordinary person B. Inferior one C. Lethargic.

གྲགས་ཆེན་བཅོ་བརྒྱད།

The eighteen major texts. Eighteen major texts of Buddhist studies in the Sakya monastic universities. 1. སོ་སོར་ཐར་པའི་མདོ། *Individual Liberation Sūtra* (pratimoksa sūtra) 2. འདུལ་བ་མདོ་རྩ་བ། *Root Discipline Sūtra* (vinaya sūtra) 3. མངོན་རྟོགས་རྒྱན། *Ornament of Clear Realisation* (abhisamayālaṃkāra) 4. མདོ་སྡེ་རྒྱན། *Ornament of Discourses* (mahāyānasūtrālaṃkāra) 5. རྒྱུད་བླ་མ། *Sublime Continuum* (uttaratantra) 6. དབུས་མཐའ་རྣམ་འབྱེད། *Clear Distinction Between the Middle and Extremes* (madhyāntavibhāga) 7. ཆོས་དང་ཆོས་ཉིད་རྣམ་འབྱེད། *Clear Distinction Between Phenomena and their Reality* (dharmādharmatāvibhāga) 8. སྤྱོད་འཇུག *Guide to Boddhisattva's Way of Life* (bodhicāryāvatāra) 9. དབུ་མ་རྩ་བ་ཤེས་རབ། *Root Wisdom* (mūla madhyamaka kārikā) 10. བཞི་བརྒྱ་པ། *Four Hundred Stanzas* (catuḥśataka) 11. དབུ་མ་འཇུག་པ། *Entering the*

Middle Way (madhyamakāvatāra) 12. མངོན་པ་ཀུན་བཏུས། *Compendium of Knowledge* (abhidharmasamuccaya) 13. མངོན་པ་མཛོད། *Treasure of Knowledge* (abhidharmakośa 14. ཚད་མ་ཀུན་བཏུས། *Compendium of Valid Cognition* (pramāṇasamuccaya) 15. ཚད་མ་རྣམ་འགྲེལ། *Commentary on Valid Cogntion* (pramāṇavarttika) 16. ཚད་མ་རྣམ་ངེས། *Discernment of Valid Cognition* (pramāṇaviniścaya) 17. ཚད་མ་རིགས་གཏེར། *Treasure of Valid Cognition* (pramāṇayuktinidhi) 18. སྡོམ་གསུམ་རབ་དབྱེ། *Distinction Between the Three Vows* (trisaṃvarapravedha).

གྲགས་པ་རྒྱལ་མཚན།

Sakya Lama Dakpa Gyaltsen (1147-1216). A great master of the Sakya tradition of Tibetan Buddhism, said to have taken many previous births as Indian and Tibetan Mahāsiddhas. He composed many works including commentaries to the *Cakrasaṃvara* tantra, *Hevajra* and so forth.

གྲགས་པ་ཉམས་པའི་རྒྱུ་དྲུག

The six causes of defamation. 1. རྒྱན་པོ་འགྱེད་པ། gambling 2. འདུས་པ་ལ་བལྟ་བ། witnessing public fair 3. ལེ་ལོ། laziness 4. ཆང་འཐུང་བ། taking intoxicants 5. སྡིག་གྲོགས་བསྟེན་པ། associating with non-virtuous friends 6. མཚན་མོ་གྲོང་དུ་འགྲོ་བ། wandering about at night.

གྲགས་པའི་རྗེས་དཔག

Inference by notion. An inferential cognition based on popular convention. For instance, the idea infering that 'that with rabbit' can be called 'moon'. One of the three inferential cognitions (see rjes-dpag gsum).

གྲགས་པའི་མཚན་མ།

Valid notion. Something that needs no explanation for it is obvious to all.

གྲགས་པའི་བསལ་བ།

The exclusion by notion. A term used in Buddhist logic studies. Any expression or assertion that is absolutely contradictory to common notion, e.g. to call a vase a moon or to state that a human skull is a clean substance.

གྲང་དམྱལ་བརྒྱད།

Aṣṭa śītanaraka/ Eight cold hells. 1. ཆུ་བུར་ཅན། arbudaḥ/ blistering 2. ཆུ་བུར་རྡོལ། nirarbudaḥ/ broken blister 3. སོ་ཐམ། aṭaṭaḥ/ chattering teeth 4. ཨ་ཆུ་ཟེར་བ། huhuvaḥ/ 'a-chu' sneezing 5. ཀྱི་ཧུད་ཟེར་བ། hahavaḥ/ 'kye-hud' crying 6. ཨུད་པལ་ལྟར་གས་པ། utpalaḥ/ utpala-like splits (on petals) 7. པད་མ་ལྟར་གས་པ། padmaḥ/ lotus-like splits (on petals) 8. པད་མ་ལྟར་ཆེན་པོ་གས་པ། mahāpadmaḥ/ big lotus-like splits (on petals).

གྲངས་ཅན་པ།

Saṁkhyā/ The Enumerators. Propounders of non-buddhist tenets also called Kapilas, who assert that all objects of knowledge can be enumerated into twenty-five categories of phenomena (see she-bya nyer-lnga). They also assert that the Fundamental Principle which is partless, permanent and the agent of all actions, pervades all phenomena. There are two main schools of Saṃkhyās—the theistic and the non-theistic.

གྲི་གུག

A curved knife. A curved knife with a vajra handle on the lateral face. A ritual implement held by a tantric deity.

གྲུབ་མཐའ།

Siddhānta/ Tenets; pholosophical theory. The study of philosophical positions and principles of the classical Buddhist and non-Buddhist schools of thought.

གྲུབ་མཐའ་སྨྲ་བ་གཉིས།

The two schools of philosophy. 1. ནང་པའི་གྲུབ་མཐའ་སྨྲ་བ། school of Buddhist philosophy and 2. ཕྱི་རོལ་པའི་གྲུབ་མཐའ་སྨྲ་བ། school of non-Buddhist philosophy.

གྲུབ་མཐའ་སྨྲ་བ་བཞི།

The four schools of philosophy; the four classical schools of Buddhist philosophy. 1. བྱེ་བྲག་སྨྲ་བ། Vaibhāṣika 2. མདོ་སྡེ་པ། Sautrāntika 2. སེམས་ཙམ་པ། Cittamātra 4. དབུ་མ་པ། Mādhyamika.

གྲུབ་པའི་འབྲས་བུའི་ཡན་ལག

The set of actualized results. Birth, aging and death are the set of actualized results in the twelve links of interdependent origination.

གྲུབ་བདེ་དབྱེར་མེད་ཀྱི་རྫས་གཅིག

Indivisible substances of simultaneous existence. Two separate substances that exist and are produced simultaneously; therefore their origination, sustenance and disintegration takes place at the same time. These two are both substances, and the appearance of one necessitates the appearance of the other, e.g. vase and its colour.

གྲུབ་བདེ་རྫས་གཅིག

Substances of simultaneous existence. The simultaneity of different, reversed entities—the production, sustenance and disintegration of which takes place at the same time, and are necessarily substances.

གྲུབ་པའི་སྤྱོད་པ།

The conduct of a Mahāsiddha. One of the four ways of utilizing tantric realizations. An adept having actualized the feat of utilizing the sky through tantric practices, complements this with practices of the six perfections according to tantra, and finally gains a state of three-fold vajra conduct of body, speech and mind of a deity.

གྲུབ་པའི་དབང་ཕྱུག

A lord of actualization; Mahāsiddha. One who has attained supreme realizations of either or both the sūtra and tantra traditions.

གྲུལ་བུམ།

Kumbhāṇḍa/ A monstorous demigod somewhat like a vampire in western mythology; a kind of spirit.

གྲོང་འཇུག

Entering a corpse. The practice of entering a corpse. An exalted tantric practice through which a yogi having gained control of his energy winds and mind purposely abandons his body and transfers his consciousness into another serviceable corpse. This enables him to maintain his life even after the break up of his original body in order to fulfil the purpose of other sentient beings. The great yogi Dharma Dhode, the son of Lama Marpa, is said to have demonstrated this practice.

གྲོལ་ལུགས་ཆེན་པོ་བཞི།

The four great releases or liberations. A transmission of rDzogs-chen practice in which four ways of releasing Rigpa (intutive mind) into dharmakāya are explained. These are: 1. ཡེ་གྲོལ། Primordial release 2. རང་གྲོལ། self-release 3. གཅེར་གྲོལ། bare release 4. མཐའ་གྲོལ། limitless release.

གླིང་དྲུག

The six continents. According to *Kālacakra* tantra these are: 1. ཟླ་བའི་གླིང་། moon continent 2. འོད་དཀར་གྱི་གླིང་། white light continent 3. ཀུ་ཤའི་གླིང་། kusha grass continent 4. མིའམ་ཅིའི་གླིང་། probable human continent 5. ཁྲུང་ཁྲུང་གི་གླིང་། crane continent 6. དྲག་པོའི་གླིང་། agitated continent. These are also called the six domains of riches because although the mountains, oceans and continents within the cool ranges do not get light from the sun and the moon, human beings survive by rays of light emanated from their bodies and enjoy as much wealth as the gods do.

གླིང་བདུན།

The seven continents. 1-6. (see above, gling-drug) 7. འཛམ་གླིང་ཆེན་པོ། jambu dvīpa/ the world we live in.

གླིང་ཕྲན་བརྒྱད།

Aṣṭa kṣudradvīpāh/ The eight sub-continents. 1-2. ལུས་དང་ལུས་འཕགས། Deha and Videha around the east. 3-4. རྔ་ཡབ་དང་རྔ་ཡབ་གཞན། Cāmara and Apara Cāmara around the south 5-6. གཡོ་ལྡན་དང་ལམ་མཆོག་འགྲོ Śāthā and Uttaramantriṇa/ around the west 7-8. སྒྲ་མི་སྙན་དང་སྒྲ་མི་སྙན་གྱི་ཟླ། Kurava and Kaurava around the north.

གླིང་བཞི།

The four continents. 1. ཤར་ལུས་འཕགས་པོ། Pūrvavideha to the east 2. ལྷོ་འཛམ་བུ་གླིང་། Jambudvīpa to the south 3. ནུབ་བ་ལང་སྤྱོད། Avaragodāniya to the west 4. བྱང་སྒྲ་མི་སྙན། Uttarakuru to the north.

གླུ་དབྱངས་ཀྱི་ངེས་པ་བདུན།

The seven principles of sounds and chanting 1. དྲུག་སྐྱེས་རྨ་བྱའི་སྐད་ལྟར་སྒྲོག drug-skyes like the sound of a peacock 2. དྲང་སྲོང་གླང་སྐད་ཀྱིས་ཅོམ། drang-srong like the sound of a mendicant 3. ས་འཛིན་སྐྱེས་ནི་ར་ཡི་སྐད། sa-'dzin-skyes like the sound of a goat 4. བར་མ་ཁྲུང་ཁྲུང་སྒྲ་སྒྲོག་བཞིན། bar-ma like the sound of a crane 5. ལྔ་ལྡན་མེ་ཏོག་ལྡན་དུས་སུ། ཁུ་བྱུག་སྐད་སྙན་སྒྲོག་ལྟ་བུ། lnga-ldan like the sound of a kucoo during the spring 6. བློ་གསལ་རྟ་སྐད་ལྟ་བུར་འཆེར། blo-gsal like the sound of a horse 7. འཁོར་ཉན་གླང་པོའི་སྒྲ་ལྟ་བུ། 'khor-nyan like the sound of an elephent.

གླུ་དབྱངས་ལྟ་བུའི་སེམས་བསྐྱེད།

Gītopamā cittotpāda/ The song-like bodhicitta. The Bodhisattva motive of enlightenment associated with primordial cognition possessed by the Bodhisattva on the tenth stage, surpassing the practice of primordial wisdom.

གླུད།

Scapegoat. A clay or dough effigy of a person consecrated and sent away as ransom to appease harmful spirits which causes sickness or interference.

གླེང་གཞིའི་སྡེ།

The introductory teachings. One of the twelve scriptual categories (see gsung-rab yan-lag bcu-gnyis); teachings given by Buddha to specific people. For instance, the sūtra that prescribes the act of stealing as a proscribed misdeed because of the behaviour of Nor-can, the son of a potter.

གློ་བུར་གྱི་དྲི་མ།

Adventitious defilement; incidental stains. Usually refers to all obscurations that temporarily obscure the pristine mind.

གློ་བུར་རྣམ་དག་གི་ཆར་གྱུར་པའི་ངོ་བོ་ཉིད་སྐུ།

Nature truth body that is pure from adventitious stains. For instance, the noble truth of cessation within Buddha's mental continuum.

དགག་པ།

Pratisedha/ A negative phenomenon. An object which is realized through the explicit elimination of an object of negation. For instance, a non-vase thing.

དགག་བྱ།

Pratiṣedhya/ An object of negation. An object of refutation, or that which is to be disproved in a logical argument.

དགག་བྱ་གཉིས།

The two objects of refutation. 1. ལམ་གྱི་དགག་བྱ། mārga pratiṣedhya/ refutation on the path of practice 2. རིགས་པའི་དགག་བྱ། yukti pratiṣedhya/ refutation through logical analysis.

དགག་བྱའི་ཆོས།

Pratiṣedhya dharma/ The object of refutation; antithesis. That which is to be refuted in a logical argument, the opposite of the subject and the predicate taken together in a logical syllogism.

དགག་བྱའི་མཐའ་བཞི།

Catvāri pratiṣedhyāntā/ The four extremes to be refuted. 1. ཡོད་པའི་མཐའ། astyanta/ extreme of existence 2. མེད་པའི་མཐའ། nāstyanta/ extreme of non-existence 3. གཉིས་ཀའི་མཐའ། ubhyānta/ extreme of being both 4. གཉིས་ཀ་མ་ཡིན་པའི་མཐའ། advyānta/ extreme of being neither.

དགག་བྱའི་བདག

Pratiṣedhyātman/ The self to be refuted. The self to be refuted, the direct opposite of the selflessness to be explicitly negated when one realizes the true selflessness.

དགག་བྱའི་བདག་གཉིས།

The two kinds of self to be refuted. 1. གང་ཟག་གི་བདག pudgalātman/ self of a person 2. ཆོས་ཀྱི་བདག dharmātman/ self of a phenomenon.

དགག་བྱའི་དོན་སྤྱི།

Pratiṣedhyārthasāmānya/ Meaning generality or generic image of an object to be refuted.

དགག་དབྱེ།

Pravāraṇā/ The ceremony of lifting the restrictions. Lifting restrictions particularly laid down for individual monks during the three month rainy season retreat; the last day of the rainy season retreat.

དགག་གཞི།

The basis of negation. For instance, the vase being the basis of negation upon which the conception of that vase being a permanent phenomena is refuted or expelled.

དགག་བཞག་སྤོང་གསུམ།

Refutation, establishment and responding to an assertion. A traditional scholarly means of refuting the stand of others, through establishing one's own position and responding to the criticism of one's own position. A systematic debate in the study of Buddhist logic should fulfill these three essential factors.

དགའ་ལྡན།

Tuṣita/ A. The Heaven of Joy. The Tuṣita Buddha field; the pure land where the future Buddha, Maitreya would give teachings, also called the joyous field of virtue and mental happiness (dga'-ldan yid-dga' chos-'dzin); one of the six heavens of the gods of desire realm. It is also known to be the heaven for Bodhisattvas obstructed by a single birth from attaining Buddhahood. B. The Ganden monastery founded by Je Tsong Khapa in 1408.

དགའ་ལྡན་ཕྱག་རྒྱ་ཆེན་པོ།

The Mahāmudrā of the Gelug tradition. A transmission of developing calm abiding and penetrative insight meditation by taking one's mind as the object of meditation in the Gelug tradition as a means to finding the right view through meditation.

དགའ་ལྡན་ཁྲི་པ།

The holder of Ganden throne; the successor to the throne of Je Tsong Khapa.

དགའ་བ་ཚད་མེད།

Immeasurable joy. One of the four immeasurables (see tsad-med bzhi). A meditation on joy in which one takes immeasurable sentient beings as one's object of meditation and wishes them never to be separated from a genuine happiness free of suffering.

དགའ་བ་བཞི།

The four joys. The joys experienced through the flow of melting regenerative fluid in stages from crown to secret organ in the highest tantric practices. 1. དགའ་བ། muditā/ joy 2. མཆོག་དགའ། pramuditā/ great joy 3. ཁྱད་དགའ། viśeṣa muditā/ exalted joy 4. ལྷན་སྐྱེས་ཀྱི་དགའ་བ། sahaja muditā/ innate joy.

དགའ་བ་ཡང་དག་བྱང་ཆུབ་ཀྱི་ཡན་ལག

Prītisaṁbodhyaṅga/ The perfect joy as a limb to enlightenment. One of the seven limbs of enlightenment (see byang-chub yan-lag bdun), the contentment and benefit that is physically and mentally received by the joy of reaching the first Bodhisattva ground.

དགའ་བཞི་འཕྲུལ་གྱི་ལྷ་ཁང་།

The miraculous cathedral of four-fold joy. Another name of the Lhasa cathedral. The name was given due to jubiliance shown by man, gods, nāgas and spirits at the beginning of the building of the Lhasa cathedral.

དགེ་སྐོས།

A monk disciplinarian. The monk in charge of enforcing the monastic rules and regulations.

དགེ་བསྙེན།

Upāsaka/ Ordained lay person. A layman or laywoman who has taken any or all of the five precepts—not killing, not lying, not indulging in sexual misconduct, not stealing and not taking intoxicants.

དགེ་བསྙེན་དངོས་གནས་པ་གསུམ།

The three fully fledged lay persons. 1. ཡོངས་རྫོགས་དགེ་བསྙེན། a full fledged ordained lay person observing all the five vows until death while remaining as a householder e.g. Marpa, the great translator. 2. ཚངས་སྤྱོད་དགེ་བསྙེན། a full fledged ordained lay person observing all the five vows until death and leading a life of celibacy e.g. Candragomin. 3. གོ་མི་དགེ་བསྙེན། a full fledged ordained lay person observing all the eight vows of a one day vow holder (see bsnyen-gnas yan-lag brgyad) until death and who wears robes.

དགེ་བསྙེན་བཏགས་པ་བ་བཞི།

The four nominal ordained lay persons. 1. སྐྱབས་འགྲོ་ཙམ་གྱི་དགེ་བསྙེན། a lay person ordained merely through seeking refuge in the three jewels 2. སྣ་གཅིག་དགེ་བསྙེན། an ordained lay person observing only one of the four root vows 3. སྣ་གཉིས་ཙམ་བསྲུང་བའི་དགེ་བསྙེན། an ordained lay person observing only two of the four root vows 4. སྣ་གསུམ་ཙམ་བསྲུང་བའི་དགེ་བསྙེན། an ordained lay person observing three of the four root vows.

དགེ་བསྙེན་དྲུག

The six kinds of ordained lay persons (upāsaka). 1. སྐྱབས་འགྲོའི་དགེ་བསྙེན། an ordained lay person (merely) by having taken refuge in the three jewel 2. སྣ་གཅིག་དགེ་བསྙེན། an ordained lay person observing only one of the five vows 3. སྣ་དགའི་དགེ་བསྙེན། an ordained lay person observing only two of the five vows 4. ཕལ་ཆེར་དགེ་བསྙེན། an ordained lay person observing three of the five vows 5. ཡོངས་རྫོགས་དགེ་བསྙེན། a full-fledged ordained lay person observing all the five vows 5. ཚངས་སྤྱོད་དགེ་བསྙེན། an ordained lay person observing all the five vows until death, and leading a life of celibacy.

དགེ་སྟོང་སྡིག་སྟོང་།

Emptiness of virtue and non-virtue. The lack of inherent existence of both virtue and non-virtue in their ultimate sense.

དགེ་འདུན།

Saṅgha/ The holy community; the supreme assembly; the Saṅgha. One of the three objects of refuge conventionally represented by the community of monks and nuns (above three or four) devoted to study and practice of the teachings of Buddha, and ultimately, the Saṅgha comprises those on and above the path of seeing (Āryas).

དགེ་འདུན་ཀུན་ར།

The debate courtyard or the main assembly hall of a monastic community.

དགེ་འདུན་དབྱེན་འབྱེད་པ།

Creating a schism in the Saṅgha community. Causing disunity in the monastic community with at least four people on each side. Such an act constitutes one of the five heinous crimes (see mtsams-med lnga).

དགེ་འདུན་གྱི་དབྱེན་གསུམ།

The three schisms within a monastic community. 1. འཁོར་ལོའི་དབྱེན། schism by a defection, i.e., by way of diverting devotion to a non-Buddhist teacher and precepts during the presence of Buddha Śākyamuni himself or his hierarchies 2. ལས་ཀྱི་དབྱེན། schism by behavior 3. འཁྲུགས་ལོང་གི་དབྱེན། schism by dispute .

དགེ་འདུན་ཉི་ཤུ།

Viṁśatiḥ saṅgha/ The twenty Saṅgha members. The twenty exemplary Saṅgha members comprising 1-5. རྒྱུན་ཞུགས་ལྔ། the five stream-winners 6-8. ཕྱིར་འོང་གསུམ། the three once-returners 9-18. ཕྱིར་མི་འོང་བཅུ། the ten never-returners 19. དགྲ་བཅོམ་ཞུགས་པ། the enterers into Arhatship 20. བསེ་རུ་ལྟ་བུའི་རང་སངས་རྒྱས། the rhinoceros-like solitary realizer (see bse-ru lta-bu'i rang sangs-rgyas).

དགེ་འདུན་ཐ་དད་པ།

A Saṅgha of different orders. The Saṅgha members belonging to different schools within the same tradition.

དགེ་འདུན་ཕལ་པོ་ཆེའི་སྡེ་པ་ལྔ།

The five Mahāsānghika schools. 1. ཤར་གྱི་རི་བོའི་སྡེ་པ། Purvaśaila 2. ནུབ་ཀྱི་རི་བོའི་སྡེ། Aparaśaila 3. གངས་ཀྱི་རི་བོའི་སྡེ། Himavata 4. འཇིག་རྟེན་ལས་འདས་པར་སྨྲ་བའི་སྡེ། Lokottaravādin 5. རྟག་པར་སྨྲ་བའི་སྡེ། Prajñāpativādin.

དགེ་འདུན་དབུ་སྡེ་གཉིས།

The two honourable classes of Saṅgha. 1. རབ་བྱུང་དགེ་འདུན་གྱི་སྡེ། the ordained monks 2. གོས་དཀར་ལྕང་ལོ་ཅན་གྱི་སྡེ། the tantrikas bearing matted hair knots on their head, as were honoured by King Tri Ralpa Chen, who spread two silken scarves bound to his head and let a member of each class of Saṅgha be seated on these scarve cushions as a mark of his respect and devotion to them.

དགེ་འདུན་བཙུན་པ།

The honoured Saṅgha, referring to the community of monks and nuns who hold moral disciplines as laid down in the Vinaya teachings.

དགེ་འདུན་བཞི་སྡེ།

The four-fold Saṅgha members. A group of four fully ordained monks already on the paths of attainments or a gathering of four fully ordained monks in their ordinary state having received their Bikṣu ordination by means of four-fold requests.

དགེ་འདུན་གསུམ།

The three Saṅgha members. 1. སོ་སོ་སྐྱེ་བོའི་དགེ་འདུན། the ordinary fully ordained Saṅgha member—a group of four or more ordinary saṅgha members who have all received their full ordination of a Bikṣu by means of four-fold requests 2. སློབ་པའི་དགེ་འདུན། Saṅgha member on the path of a trainee—any Saṅgha member who is on or above the stream-winner's path, up to the path leading to Arhatship 3. མི་སློབ་པའི་དགེ་འདུན། Saṅgha member on the path of no-more learning—a person who has already attained the state of an Arhat.

དགེ་ལྡན་པའི་སྨོན་ལམ་ལྔ་།

The five prayers of Gelug tradition. 1. བཟང་སྤྱོད་སྨོན་ལམ། Prayer of Good Deeds 2. བྱམས་སྨོན། Prayer of Buddha Maitreya 3. ཐོག་མཐའ་མ། Prayer of Beginning and the End 4. བདེ་སྨོན། Prayer of the Blissful Fields 5. སྤྱོད་འཇུག་སྨོན་ལམ། Prayer of the Deeds of a Bodhisattva.

དགེ་བ་བཅུ།

Daśakuśalāni/ The ten virtues. 1. སྲོག་གཅོད་སྤོང་བ། prāṇātighātād virati/ abandoning the act of killing 2. མ་བྱིན་པར་ལེན་པ་སྤོང་བ། adattādānād virati/ abandoning the act of stealing 3. ལོག་གཡེམ་སྤོང་བ། kāmamithyācārād virati/ abandoning the act of indulging in sexual misconduct 4. རྫུན་སྤོང་བ། mṛṣāvādāt prativirati/ abandoning the act of telling a lie 5. ཕྲ་མ་སྤོང་བ། pāiśunyāt prativirati/ abandoning the act of slandering 6. ཚིག་རྩུབ་སྤོང་བ། pāruṣyāt prativirati/ abandoning the act of using harsh words 7. ངག་འཁྱལ་སྤོང་བ། Saṁbhinna pralāpat prativirati/ abandoning the act of indulging in idle gossip 8. བརྣབ་སེམས་སྤོང་བ། abhidhyāyāḥ prativirati/ abandoning the act of being coveteous 9. གནོད་སེམས་སྤོང་བ། vyāpādāt prativirati/ abandoning the act of harming others 10. ལོག་ལྟ་སྤོང་བ། mithyādṛṣṭeḥ prativirati/ abandoning upholding wrong views or philosophies.

དགེ་བ་བཅུ་གཅིག

Eka daśa kuśaláni/ Eleven virtuous mental factors. 1. དད་པ། śraddhā/ faith 2. ངོ་ཚ་ཤེས་པ། hrī/ sense of shame 3. ཁྲེལ་ཡོད་པ། apaltavyam/ sense of dread of blame 4. འདོད་ཆགས་མེད་པ། alobha/ lack of desire 5. ཞེ་སྡང་མེད་པ། adveṣa/ lack of hatred 6. གཏི་མུག་མེད་པ། amoha/ lack of stupidity 7. བརྩོན་འགྲུས། vīrya/ virtuous effort 8. བག་ཡོད། apramāda/ conscientiousness 9. ཤིན་སྦྱངས། praśrabdhi/ suppleness 10. བཏང་སྙོམས། upekṣā/ equanimity 11. རྣམ་པར་མི་འཚེ་བ། ahiṁsā/ not harming others.

དགེ་བ་བཅུ་གཉིས།

Dvadaśa kuśalāvi/ The twelve virtues. 1. ངོ་བོ་ཉིད་ཀྱི་དགེ་བ། svabhāvakuśala/ natural virtue 2. འབྲེལ་བའི་དགེ་བ། saṁbandhakuśala/ associate virtue 3. རྗེས་སུ་འབྲེལ་བའི་དགེ་བ། anubandhakuśala/ concordant virtue 4. ཀུན་སློང་གི་དགེ་བ། samutthānakuśala/ motivated virtue 5. དོན་དམ་གྱི་དགེ་བ། paramārthakuśala/ ultimate virtue 6. སྐྱེ་བས་ཐོབ་པའི་དགེ་བ། upapattipratilambhikakuśala/ virtue acquired by birth 7. སྦྱོར་བའི་དགེ་བ། prayogakuśala/ virtue acquired through learning 8. ཕན་འདོགས་པའི་དགེ་བ། upakārikuśala/ beneficial virtue 9. ཡོངས་སུ་འཛིན་པའི་དགེ་བ། parigrāhakakuśala/ fully acquired virtue 10. གཉེན་པོའི་དགེ་བ། pratipakṣakuśala/ antidotal virtue 11. ཉེ་བར་ཞི་བའི་དགེ་བ། upaśamakuśala/ fully pacified virtue 12. རྒྱུ་མཐུན་གྱི་དགེ་བ། niṣyandakuśala/ virtue congruent to its cause.

དགེ་བའི་དེ་བཞིན་ཉིད་གཉིས།

The two virtuous suchnesses; the two wholesome realities. 1. གང་ཟག་གི་བདག་མེད། pudgalanairātmya/ selflessness of a person 2. ཆོས་ཀྱི་བདག་མེད། dharmanairātmya/ selflessness of a phenomenon.

དགེ་བའི་རྩ་བ་གསུམ།

The three root virtues. 1. འདོད་ཆགས་མེད་པའི་དགེ་བའི་རྩ་བ། alobha/ root virtue devoid of desire 2. ཞེ་སྡང་མེད་པའི་དགེ་བའི་རྩ་བ། adveṣa/ root virtue devoid of hatred 3. གཏི་མུག་མེད་པའི་དགེ་བའི་རྩ་བ། amoha/ root virtue devoid of mental stupidity.

དགེ་བའི་ཡིད་གཉིས།

The two mental virtues; the two virtuous minds. 1. སྐྱེས་ཐོབ་ཀྱི་དགེ་བ། virtuous mind by birth 2. སྦྱོར་བྱུང་གི་དགེ་བ། virtuous mind by training.

དགེ་བའི་བཤེས་གཉེན།

Kalyāṇamitra/ Spiritual master; spiritual friend; religious teacher; a Guru.

དགེ་བའི་བཤེས་གཉེན་གྱི་མཚན་ཉིད་བཅུ།

Daśa kalyāṇamitra guṇā/ The ten qualities of a spiritual master; the ten requisites of a Mahāyānist teacher. 1. ལྷག་པ་ཚུལ་ཁྲིམས་ཀྱི་བསླབ་པས་དུལ་བ། being humble due to his higher training of morality 2. ལྷག་པ་ཏིང་ངེ་འཛིན་གྱི་བསླབ་པས་ཞི་བ། being calm due to his higher training of concentration 3. ལྷག་པ་ཤེས་རབ་ཀྱི་བསླབ་པས་ཉེ་བར་ཞི་བ། being pacified due to his higher training of wisdom 4. ལུང་གི་ཡོན་ཏན་གྱིས་ཕྱུག་པ། being rich in oral transmission 5. སྟོང་པ་ཉིད་རྟོགས་པ། having realized emptiness 6. སློབ་མ་ལས་ཡོན་ཏན་ལྷག་པ། being more learned than his students 7. སྨྲ་མཁས་པ། being skillful in preaching 8. བརྩེ་བ་དང་ལྡན་པ། being compassionate 9. བརྩོན་འགྲུས་དང་ལྡན་པ། being hard working 10. སྐྱོ་ངལ་སྤོང་པ། having no regrets or lamentation.

དགེ་བའི་བཤེས་གཉེན་བསྟེན་པའི་སྐབས་ཀྱི་སེམས་དགུ།

Nine attitudes of relying on a Guru/ spiritual master. 1. བུ་མཛངས་པ་ལྟ་བུའི་སེམས། attitude like that of a wise son 2. རྡོ་རྗེ་ལྟ་བུའི་སེམས། vajra-like attitude 3. ས་གཞི་ལྟ་བུའི་སེམས། attitude like the foundational ground 4. ཁོར་ཡུག་གི་རི་ལྟ་བུའི་སེམས། attitude like the surrounding mountain 5. བྲན་གཡོག་ལྟ་བུའི་སེམས། attitude like that of a servant 6. ཐེམ་པ་ལྟ་བུའི་སེམས། attitude like that of a staircase 7. སྒོ་ཁྱི་ལྟ་བུའི་སེམས། attitude like that of a watch-dog 8. ཕྱག་དར་ལྟ་བུའི་སེམས། attitude like that of a broom 9. གྲོགས་བཟང་པོ་ལྟ་བུའི་སེམས། attitude like that of a good friend.

དགེ་བའི་ས་མང་བཅུ་གཅིག

The eleven virtuous levels of thought (see dge-ba bcu-gcig). These eleven levels of thought accompany a perfect virtuous state of mind.

དགེ་སྦྱོང་།

Śramaṇa/ A practitioner of virtue. A general name for any person ordained as a novice monk or nun, or a fully ordained monk or nun or the whole Saṅgha, who have vowed to attain the state of liberation by means of observing the precepts of the individual liberation vows (pratimokṣa) in his or her endeavour to eliminate delusions and pacify sufferings within saṁsāra.

དགེ་སྦྱོང་གི་ཆོས་བཞི།

The four precepts of a monk; the four principles of a monk. 1. གཤེ་ཡང་སླར་མི་གཤེ་བ། ākruṣṭena na pratyākroṣṭitavyam/ not to scold another although being scolded 2. ཁྲོས་ཀྱང་སླར་མི་ཁྲོ་བ། roṣitena na pratiroṣitavyam/ not to become angry when incited to anger 3. བརྡེགས་ཀྱང་སླར་མི་རྡེག་པ། tādite na prativāḍitavyam/ not to hit another in return when being hit 4. མཚང་བྲུས་ཀྱང་སླར་མཚང་མི་འབྲུ་བ། bhaṇḍitena na pratibhaṇḍitavyam/ not to reveal another's faults when he does so.

དགེ་སྦྱོང་གི་འབྲས་བུ་བཞི།

The four fruits of a trainee. 1. རྒྱུན་དུ་ཞུགས་པའི་འབྲས་བུ། the fruit of a Stream-winner 2. ཕྱིར་འོང་བའི་འབྲས་བུ། the fruit of a Once-returner 3. ཕྱིར་མི་འོང་བའི་འབྲས་བུ། the fruit of a Never-returner 4. དགྲ་བཅོམ་པའི་འབྲས་བུ། the fruit of an Arhat.

དགེ་སྦྱོང་ཚུལ་གྱི་འབྲས་བུ།

The fruit of a trainee. The path of thorough liberation which is compositional and the truth of cessation that is a non-compositional attainment.

དགེ་རྩ།

Mūla kuśala/ The root of virtue. Any wholesome act or practice such as of giving and honouring that results in happiness and benefit.

དགེ་ཚུལ།

Śramaṇera/ A novice monk. A monk observing thirty-six precepts according to the pratimokṣa vows (dge-tsul-gyi blang-'das so-drug).

དགེ་ཚུལ་གྱི་སྤང་བྱ་ཡན་ལག་བཅུ།

Daśa śramaṇera prahātavya dharmā/ The ten precepts of a novice monk; the ten limbs of abandonment for a novice. 1. སྲོག་གཅོད་སྤོང་བ། prāṇātighātād virati/ to avoid taking life 2. མ་བྱིན་པར་ལེན་པ་སྤོང་བ། adattādānād virati/ to avoid stealing 3. མི་གཙང་སྤྱོད་སྤོང་བ། kāmamithyācārād virati/ to avoid engaging in sexual misconduct 4. རྫུན་སྤོང་བ། mṛṣāvādāt virati/ to avoid telling lies 5. མྱོས་འགྱུར་སྤོང་བ། madyapāna virati/ to avoid taking intoxicants 6. གར་སོགས་སྤོང་བ། nāṭaka virati/ to avoid dancing, etc. 7. འཕྲེང་སོགས་སྤོང་བ། mālāya virati/ to avoid wearing garlands, etc. 8. མལ་སྟན་ཆེ་མཐོ་སྤོང་བ། ucchaśayana mahāśayana virati/ to avoid using high and luxurious beds and seats 9. དུས་མིན་ཁ་ཟས་སྤོང་བ། vikāta bhojana virati/ to avoid taking untimely food 10. གསེར་དངུལ་ལེན་པ་སྤོང་བ། jātarūparajata virati/ to avoid accepting gold and silver.

དགེ་ཚུལ་གྱི་བླང་འདས་སོ་དྲུག

The thirty-six precepts of a novice monk. 1. མི་གསོད་པ་སྤོང་བ། to avoid killing a human being 2. དུད་འགྲོ་དང་བཅས་པ་བརྡེག་པ་སྤོང་བ། to avoid harming living beings 3. དུད་འགྲོ་དང་བཅས་པ་སྤྱོད་པ་སྤོང་བ། to avoid using water containing living creatures 4. དུད་འགྲོ་གསོད་པ་སྤོང་བ། to avoid killing animals 5. མ་བྱིན་པ་ལེན་པ་སྤོང་བ། to avoid stealing 6. མི་གཙང་སྤྱོད་སྤོང་བ། to avoid indulging in sexual misconduct 7. རྫུན་སྨྲ་བ་སྤོང་བ། to avoid telling lies (about super-human attainment) 8. གཞི་མེད་སྐུར་འདེབས་སྤོང་བ། to avoid accusing a bhikṣu or novice groundlessly of a defeat (pham-pa) 9. བག་ཙམ་གྱི་སྐུར་འདེབས་སྤོང་བ། to avoid deprecating a bhikṣu or novice by insinuation 10. དགེ་འདུན་དབྱེན་འབྱེད་པ་སྤོང་བ། to avoid creating schism in the Saṅgha community 11. དེ་རྗེས་ཕྱོགས་པ་སྤོང་བ། to avoid following such a faction 12. ཁྱིམ་པ་བསུན་འབྱིན་པ་སྤོང་བ། to avoid disturbing the householders' faith 13. ཤེས་བཞིན་གྱི་རྫུན་སྤོང་བ། to avoid knowingly telling a lie 14. ཤེས་ངོར་བྱེད་པ་སྤོང་བ། to avoid making false accusations as a favour to a friend 15. འཕྱ་བ་སྤོང་བ། to avoid despising a Saṅgha steward 16. ཟས་ཙུང་གི་ཕྱིར་སྐུར་བ་འདེབས་པ་སྤོང་བ། to avoid accusing a monk of teaching Dharma for material gain 17. ལྷག་མའི་སྐུར་བ་འདེབས་པ་སྤོང་བ། to avoid accusing a bhikṣu groundlessly of commiting a remainder-transgression 18. བསླབ་པ་མི་སྤོང་བ། to avoid not listening to the advice of an elder 19. འབྲས་ཆེན་འགེབས་པ་སྤོང་བ། to avoid accepting food that is more than one's share 20. ཆང་འཐུང་བ་སྤོང་བ། to avoid taking liquor 21. གླུ་སོགས་སྤོང་བ། to avoid singing 22. གར་སོགས་སྤོང་བ། to avoid dancing etc. 23. རོལ་མོ་བྱེད་པ་སྤོང་བ། to avoid playing musical instruments 24. རྒྱན་སོགས་སྤོང་བ། to avoid wearing ornaments 25. དྲི་དང་ཁ་དོག་འཆང་བ་སྤོང་བ། to avoid using colourful costumes 26. སྤོས་ཉུག་བྱེད་པ་སྤོང་བ། to avoid using aromatic scents 27. ཕྲེང་བ་སོགས་སྤོང་བ། to avoid wearing garlands, etc. 28. ཁྲི་སྟན་ཆེ་མཐོ་སྤོང་བ། to avoid using luxurious seats and beds 29. དེར་འདུག་པའམ་ཉལ་བ་སྤོང་བ། to avoid sleeping or sitting upon luxurious seats and beds 30. ཁྲུ་གང་ལྷག་གི་ཁྲི་སྟན་སྤྱོད་པ་སྤོང་བ། to avoid using high thrones or beds more than a cubit in height

31. རིན་འདུག་པའམ་ཉལ་བ་སྤོང་བ། to avoid sleeping or sitting upon high thrones or beds more than a cubit in height 32. ཕྱི་དྲོའི་ཁ་ཟས་སྤོང་བ། to avoid eating food after noon 33. གསེར་དངུལ་ལེན་པ་སྤོང་བ། to avoid accepting and keeping gold and the like 34. ཁྱིམ་པའི་རྟགས་འཆང་བ་སྤོང་བ། to avoid maintaining a layman's way of life 35. རབ་བྱུང་གི་རྟགས་སྤངས་པ་མི་སྤོང་བ། to avoid abandoning a monk's way of life 36. མཁན་པོར་གསོལ་བ་བཏབ་པ་ལས་མ་ཉམས་པ། to avoid refusing service to one's abbot and teachers.

དགེ་ཚོགས།

The collection of virtues. The collection of merits (bsod-nams kyi tshogs) and the collection of insights (ye-shes kyi tshogs).

དགེ་སློང་།

Bhikṣu/ A fully ordained monk. A monk observing two hundred and fifty-three vows according to the Mūlasarvāstivādin tradition according to Tibetan monastic discipline.

དགེ་སློང་ལྔ།

Pañca bhikṣu/ The five types of fully ordained monks (gelong/ bhikṣu). 1. སློང་བའི་དགེ་སློང་། bhiksuta iti bhikṣu/ an alm seeking bhikṣu 2. མིང་གི་དགེ་སློང་། saṁjñābhikṣu/ a bhikṣu in name 3. ཁས་འཆེ་བའི་དགེ་སློང་། pratijñā bhikṣu/ a nominal bhikṣu 4. གསོལ་བཞིའི་ལས་ཀྱི་དགེ་སློང་། jñāpati caturtha karmano pasampanno bhikṣu/ a bhikṣu by four-fold request 5. ཉོན་མོངས་དང་བྲལ་བའི་དགེ་སློང་། bhinnakleśatvad bhikṣu/ a bhikṣu who is free of delusions.

དགེ་སློང་གི་བསླབ་བྱ།

The precepts of a fully ordained monk. The five classes of vows to be observed—the class of defeats, remainders, abandoning downfalls, propelling downfalls and faults, comprising all the two hundred and fifty-three precepts.

དགེ་སློང་མའི་བསླབ་བྱ།

The precepts of a fully ordained nun. The three hundred and sixty-four vows classed as eight defeats, twenty remainders, thirty-three abandoning downfalls, one hundred and eighty propelling downfalls, eleven individual confessions and one hundred and twelve faults.

དགེ་སློབ་མ།

Śikṣamānā/ A probationary novice nun. One of the seven types of individual liberation vow holders, who is a novice nun on two years probation before being ordained as a Bhikṣuṇī, observing the six root dharmas (see rtsa-ba'i chos drug) and the six auxiliary dharmas (see rjes-mthun gyi chos drug) in addition to her novice vows.

དགོངས་གཏེར།

The mind treasure teachings. Those cycle of teachings revealed spontaneously from within by a highly realized master and recorded in writing. This kind of teaching is particularly renowned in the Nyignma tradition of teaching Buddhism.

དགོངས་པ།

Abhiprāya/ A. Thought, idea or view point. B. Honorific for mind. C. The essential point. D. Permission.

དགོངས་པ་ཅན་བཞི།

Catvāro bhiprāyā/ The four interpretative sūtras primarily stressing the basic intention of Buddha. 1. མཉམ་པ་ཉིད་ལ་དགོངས་པ། samatābhiprāya/ determining the samenesses 2. དོན་གཞན་ལ་དགོངས་པ།། arthāntarābhiprāya/ determining some other meaning 3. དུས་གཞན་ལ་དགོངས་པ། kālāntarābhiprāya/ determining some other time 4. གང་ཟག་གི་བསམ་པ་ལ་དགོངས་པ།

pudgalāntarābhiprāya/ determining the interest of a particular person.

དགོངས་པ་བརྡའི་གསུང་།

The teaching through symbolic gestures. One of the five ways of imparting teaching (see gsung lnga) by a sambhogakāya Buddha who transmits teachings to his circle of disciples through physical gestures and the meaning is understood by the disciples. A special lineage of transmission as asserted by the Nyingma tradition of Tibetan Buddhism.

དགོངས་པ་ཡོངས་སུ་འགྲུབ་པ།

Complete fulfillment of the thought. One of the four objects of pervasion (see khyab-pa'i dmigs-pa bzhi). The experience of self-transformation from this impure body to a pure body as a result of repeated training of complete attention and familiarity with the chosen object of calm-abiding (zhi-gnas) and penetrative insight (lhag-mthong) meditation.

དགོན་པ།

Monastery; monstic univerity; a hermitage.

དགོན་པ་བ།

A. A recluse. B. A hermit. C. Gonpawa, a master of the Kadampa tradition.

དགྲ་བཅོམ་པ་མཐོང་ཐོབ་པ།

Arhat dṛṣṭiprāpti/ Foe-destroyer by correct view; the intelligent Foe-destroyer.

དགྲ་བཅོམ་པ་དད་མོས་པ།

Arhat śraddhādhimukta/ Foe-destroyer by devotion; faith; the less-intelligent Foe-destroyer.

དགྲ་བཅོམ་བདུན།

The seven Arhats. The seven early Indian masters who were responsible for the compilation of the seven treatises on knowledge (see mngon-pa sde bdun). They were: 1. ཀཏྱའི་བུ། Kātyāyana 2. དབྱིག་བཤེས། Vasumitra 3. བྲམ་ཟེ་ལྷ་སྐྱིད། Brahmiṇ Devotsava 4. ཤཱ་རིའི་བུ། Śāriputra 5. མོའུ་གལ་གྱི་བུ། Maudgalyāyana 6. གསུས་པོ་ཆེ། Mahākauṣṭhila 7. གང་པོ། Pūrṇa.

དགྲ་བཅོམ་པ་གཉིས།

The two types of Arhats. A. In regard to their degree of abandonments: 1. ཤེས་རབ་ཀྱིས་རྣམ་པར་གྲོལ་བ། one who is liberated by means of the wisdom path 2. གཉིས་ཀའི་ཆ་ལས་རྣམ་པར་གྲོལ་བ། one who is liberated by means of both the wisdom and method paths. B. In regard to their status: 1. ཉན་ཐོས་དགྲ་བཅོམ་པ། śravaka arhat/ the hearer Arhat 2. རང་རྒྱལ་དགྲ་བཅོམ་པ། pratyekbuddha arhat/ the solitary-realizer Arhat.

དགྲ་བཅོམ་པ་དྲུག

Six types of Foe-destroyers. 1. ཡོངས་སུ་ཉམས་པའི་ཆོས་ཅན། Foe-destroyer liable to degeneration 2. འཆི་བར་སེམས་པའི་ཆོས་ཅན། Foe-destroyer wishing to die 3. རྗེས་སུ་སྲུང་བའི་ཆོས་ཅན། Foe-destroyer protecting his state of realization 4. གནས་པ་ལ་མི་བསྐྱོད་པའི་ཆོས་ཅན། Foe-destroyer immutably abiding in his state of realization 5. རྟོགས་པའི་འོས་སུ་གྱུར་བའི་ཆོས་ཅན། Foe-destroyer destined to generation of realization 6. མི་འཁྲུགས་པའི་ཆོས་ཅན། Foe-destroyer never liable to transformation.

དགྲ་བཅོམ་པ་གསུམ།

The three types of Arhats. 1. ཉན་ཐོས་དགྲ་བཅོམ། śravaka arhat/ the hearer Arhat 2. རང་རྒྱལ་དགྲ་བཅོམ། pratyekabuddha arhat/ the solitary-realizer Arhat 3. སངས་རྒྱས་དགྲ་བཅོམ། buddha arhat/ the Buddha Arhat.

དགྲ་བཅོམ་པའི་གོ་འཕང་།

The state of a Foe-destroyer; Arhatship. The state of liberation or the 5th path of no-more learning, attained by Arhats after perfecting training of the 4th path. According to Lower Vehicle it is the culmination of four stages of perfection—the Stream-winner, Once-returner, Never-returner and Arhatship, and according to the Higher Vehicle, it is either the state of liberation or the state of omniscience.

དགྲ་བཅོམ་པའི་ཕུང་པོ་མཐའ་མ།

The last aggregate of an Arhat. The aggregate of an Arhat who has attained nirvāṇa with remainder (see lhag-bcas myang-'das) as asserted by the schools of Buddhist philosophy of and below Svātantrika Mādhyamika.

དགྲ་བཅོམ་པའི་འབྲས་བུ།

Arhatphala/ The fruit of an Arhat. One of the four fruits of a trainee (see dge-sbyong-gi 'bras-bu bzhi). One who has released himself or herself of all the abandonments of the three realms to be eliminated on the path of meditation, and thereby has overcome all the foes of the four devils (māras) (see bdud-bzhi).

དགྲ་བཅོམ་འབྲས་གནས།

Arhatphalaniṣraya/ Abider in the fruit of an Arhat. One of the eight persons of enterer and abider amongst the Twenty Saṅgha members. A person belonging to the lower vehicle who has eliminated all the nine delusions to be abandoned on the peak level (srid-rtse) of existence.

དགྲ་བཅོམ་ཞུགས་པ།

Enterer in the path of an Arhat. One of the eight persons of enterer and abider amongst the Twenty Saṅgha members. One who is engaged in the act or process of eliminating all the delusions covering the first concentration stage up to the peak level of existence.

བགེགས་བསྐྲད།

Vighna/ Expelling the interfering forces. A rite performed at the beginning of a maṇḍala ritual and initiation, when all those forces interfering with the performance of a maṇḍala ritual and initiation are given sacrificial cakes (gtor-ma) and sent away from the place by way of emanating wrathful deities through generating divine pride.

མགལ་མེའི་འཁོར་ལོ།

Alātacakra/ A fire-wheel. A circle of fire formed by swinging a flaming fire-brand or torch in a circle thereby creating the illusion of a flaming wheel.

མགུ་བ་སྤྱོད་པ།

Pleasing services. The offering of services such as washing dishes, shoe-shining and the like by an individual monk to the Saṅgha community of which he is a member, for having committed a breach of any of the thirteen remainders (lhag-ma).

མགོན་སྐྱ།

The monk who does the invocation rite of a dharma protector in a monastery.

མགྲོན་ཆེན་བཞི།

The four classes of guests; the four classes of guests of offering. 1. དཀོན་མཆོག་སྤྱིའི་མགྲོན། the Three Jewels as the guest of honor 2. མགོན་པོ་ཡོན་དན་གྱི་མགྲོན། the lords of protectors as the guest of qualities 3. འགྲོ་དྲུག་སྙིང་རྗེའི་མགྲོན། the six classes of beings as guests for compassion 4. གདོན་བགེགས་ལན་ཆགས་ཀྱི་མགྲོན། the spirits and malignant forces as guests of karmic retribution.

འགལ་ཁྱབ།

Virūddhavyāpti/ Contrary pervasions. The pervasion in a logical syllogism that whatever is the reason is not the predicate in the given logical syllogism. One of the four positive pervasions (see khyab-pa rnal-ma bzhi). This pervasion is also called correct contrary pervasion ('gal-khyab rnal-ma).

འགལ་ཁྱབ་ཕྱིན་ཅི་ལོག

Viparyaya virūddhavyāpti/ Wrong contrary pervasion. The pervasion in a logical syllogism that whatever is the reason is not that which is not the predicate. Synonymous with subsequent pervasion (see rjes-khyab).

འགལ་བ་གཉིས།

Two types of contradictions. A. By means of their reverse identity there are two: 1. ལྷན་ཅིག་མི་གནས་འགལ། ekatrāsthita virūddha/ contradiction not abiding simultaneously, e.g. hot and cold 2. ཕན་ཚུན་སྤང་འགལ། anyānyaparihāra virūddha/ contradictions canceling each other, e.g. is and isn't. B. By means of their manner of contradiction there are two: 1. དངོས་འགལ། bhāva virūddha/ direct contradiction, e.g. permanent and impermanent 2. བརྒྱུད་འགལ། avedhavirūddha/ indirect contradiction, e.g. pillar and vase.

འགལ་བ་མི་མཐུན་ཕྱོགས།

Virūddha vipakṣa/ Contradictory dissimilar factor. An opposite factor of the predicate in a logical syllogism.

འགལ་བ་བཞི།

Four types of contradictions. (see above, 'gal-ba gnyis A, 1-2 and B, 1-2).

འགལ་བ་གསུམ།

Three types of contradictions. 1-2 (see A. 1-2 above) 3. ཚད་མའི་གནོད་འགལ། contradiction by valid cognition.

འགོ་བའི་ལྷ།

A personal god or inhuman force. A god or inhuman force believed to be the personal protector of an individual inseparable from oneself like the shadow of one's body.

འགོ་བའི་ལྷ་ལྔ།

Pañca devā/ Five personal gods or inhuman forces. 1. ཡུལ་ལྷ། deśa deva/ the local god 2. ཕོ་ལྷ། puruṣa deva/ the male god of a man 3. མོ་ལྷ། strī deva/ the female god of a woman 4. དགྲ་ལྷ། śatru deva/ the enemy combating god 5. སྲོག་ལྷ། prāṇa deva/ the life-force god.

འགོག་བདེན།

Nirodha satya/ The noble truth of cessation. The total pacification of all karmas and delusions through application of the path within oneself.

འགོག་བདེན་བཅུ་གཉིས།

Dvadaśa nirodha satya/ The twelve types of truth of cessation. 1. མཚན་ཉིད་ཀྱི་འགོག་པ། lakṣaṇa nirodha/ characterised cessation 2. ཟབ་པའི་འགོག་པ། gambhīra nirodha/ profound cessation 3. བརྡའི་འགོག་པ། sāṁketa nirodha/ symbolic cessation 4. དོན་དམ་པའི་འགོག་པ། parārtha nirodha/ ultimate cessation 5. ཡོངས་སུ་མ་རྫོགས་པའི་འགོག་པ། aparipūrṇa nirodha/ unperfected cessation 6. ཡོངས་སུ་རྫོགས་པའི་འགོག་པ། paripūrṇa nirodha/ perfected cessation 7. རྒྱན་བཅས་འགོག་པ། sālaṅkāra nirodha/ adorned cessation 8. རྒྱན་མེད་འགོག་པ། anālaṅkāra nirodha/ unadorned cessation 9. ལྷག་བཅས་འགོག་པ། avaśeṣa nirodha/ residual cessation 10. ལྷག་མེད་འགོག་པ། nirvaśeṣa nirodha/ non-residual cessation 11. ཁྱད་པར་དུ་འཕགས་

པའི་འགོག་པ། viśesta nirodha/ exalted cessation 12. རྣམ་གྲངས་པའི་འགོག་པ། prayāya nirodha/ nominal cessation.

འགོག་བདེན་གྱི་ཁྱད་ཆོས་བཞི།

Catvāri nirodhaḥ satya guṇā/ Four attributes of the noble truth of cessation. 1. འགོག་པ། nirodha/ cessation 2. ཞི་བ། śānta/ peace 3. གྱ་ནོམ་པ། praṇīta/ excellence 4. ངེས་འབྱུང་། niḥsaraṇam/ renunciation.

འགོག་བདེན་གྱི་རྣམ་པ་བཅུ་དྲུག

Sadaśa nirodha satyākāra/ The sixteen aspects of the noble truth of cessation. These are the aspects of internal emptiness and so on of the sixteen emptinesses (see stong-pa nyid bcu-drug).

འགོག་བདེན་གྱི་སྤང་བྱ་བདུན།

Sapta nirodha satya prahātavya/ Seven abandonments of the path of cessation. These concern the objects of elimination having actualized the truth of cessation within this desire realm, which are: 1. མ་རིག་པ། avidyā/ ignorance 2. འདོད་ཆགས། rāga/ desire-attachment 3. ཁོང་ཁྲོ། pratigha/ hatred-anger 4. ང་རྒྱལ། māna/ ego/ pride 5. ཐེ་ཚོམ། vicikitsā/ doubt 6. ལོག་ལྟ། mithyā drsti/ wrong views holding wrong philosophy as right.

འགོག་པའི་སྙོམས་འཇུག

Nirodhasamāpatti/ The meditative absorption in cessation. A state of meditation achieved in reliance upon the meditative absorption at the peak level of cyclic existence (srid-rtse), in which a yogi can remain for many aeons through stopping all gross feelings and perceptions. Synonymous with the emancipation of cessation ('gog-pa'i rnam-par thar-ba).

འགྱུར་བ་མ་ངེས་པའི་ས།

The unchangeable path. According to Nyingma teachings it refers to the first ground attained on the level of the first yogic stage.

འགྱུར་བའི་སྡུག་བསྔལ།

Vipariṇāmaduḥkhatā/ The suffering of change. The fact that all happiness in cyclic existence changes to dissatisfaction and suffering. One of the three types of suffering (see sdug-bsngal gsum).

འགྱེད་ཆེན་བཞི།

The four great feasts. The feast offered in Cut-ritual (gcod) practices. 1. དཀར་འགྱེད། the white feast 2. དམར་འགྱེད། the red feast 3. ཁྲ་འགྱེད། the multi-colored feast 4. ནག་འགྱེད། the black feast.

འགྱོད་པ།

Kaukṛtya/ Regret; contrition. A secondary mind necessary for confession of negativities. One of the four changeable mental factors (see gzhan-'gyur bzhi).

འགྲུབ་བྱེད་ཀྱི་ཡན་ལག

Actualizing causes. Craving, grasping and becoming are the actualizing causes in the twelve links of interdependent origination, for these are responsible for activating, at death, the seeds of karmic instinct implanted in one's mind which determine one's next rebirth.

འགྲོ་བ།

Gati/ Migrators; sentient beings. Generally classified into two categories: 1. the unfortunate beings (ngan-'gro) 2. the fortunate beings (bde-'gro).

འགྲོ་བ་རིགས་དྲུག

The six types of beings; the six types of migrators. 1. ལྷ། deva/ gods 2. མི། manuṣya/ human beings 3. ལྷ་མ་ཡིན། asura/

demigods 4. དམྱལ་བ། naraka/ hell beings 5. ཡི་དྭགས། preta/ hungry ghosts 6. དུད་འགྲོ། tiryak/ animals.

རྒོད་པ་རགས་པ།

Coarse mental agitation. In the practice of single-pointed concentration, losing one's focal object after having held it for any period of time is recognized as coarse mental agitation.

རྒོད་པ་ཕྲ་མོ།

Subtle mental agitation. In the meditation to develop single-pointed concentration, when one part of the mind wanders to an object of attraction, and away from the focal object of meditation (even if not completely lost).

རྒྱ་རིམ་པ་བདུན།

The seven codes of translation. The convention of translation followed by the Tibetan translators. 1. ཚིག་འདྲ་མི་འགྲུག་པ་ཚིག་གི་རྒྱ། there must be a corresponding number of words per sentence 2. ཚིག་རྐང་མི་འགྲུག་པ་ཤད་ཀྱི་རྒྱ། the number of full stops must correspond to the number of sentences 3. ཚིག་དོན་མི་འགྲུག་པ་ལེའུ་རྒྱ། the number of chapters must correspond to the number of subjects 4. ཤོ་ལོ་ཀ་མི་འགྲུག་པ་བམ་པོའི་རྒྱ། each volume must contain a set of verses 5. བམ་པོ་མི་འགྲུག་པ་བམ་པོའི་གྲངས་ཀྱི་རྒྱ། there must be a constitent number of volumes within a set 6. མཐའ་མི་འཚོལ་བ་སྡེ་ཐིག་གི་རྒྱ། there must be clear, consistent margins 7. གླེག་བམ་མི་འགྲུག་པ་གདོང་ཡིག་གི་རྒྱ། there must be an identifying title on each volume.

རྒྱ་ཆེན་སྤྱོད་རྒྱུད།

Vaipulyatantra/ The lineage of extensive deeds. The lineage of teachings and practice coming from Maitreya, Asaṅga and Vasubandhu mainly emphasizing the method aspect of Buddha's teachings.

རྒྱགས་པ་བརྒྱད།

Aṣṭa mada/ Eight types of Haughtinesses. Eight types of conceited delight. 1. རིགས་བཟང་བས་རྒྱགས་པ། conceited delight by family or lineage 2. གཟུགས་ཀྱིས་རྒྱགས་པ། conceited delight by physical qualities 3. ལང་ཚོས་རྒྱགས་པ། conceited delight by youthful feature 4. ནད་མེད་པས་རྒྱགས་པ། conceited delight by being free of sickness 5. ནོར་གྱིས་རྒྱགས་པ། conceited delight by being wealthy 6. དབང་ཡོད་པས་རྒྱགས་པ། conceited delight by being powerful 7. བཟོ་རིག་ཤེས་པས་རྒྱགས་པ། conceited delight by being knowledgeable in arts and sciences 8. མང་དུ་ཐོས་པས་རྒྱགས་པ། conccitcd delight by being a scholar.

རྒྱང་གྲགས།

Krośa/ Five hundred armspans. A measurement of length equal to 500 fathoms or armspans; the distance of about 1 kilometer, the reach of hearing or five hundred bows' length.

རྒྱང་འཕེན་པ།

Cārvāka/ The Hedonists. A proponent of non-Buddhist tenets who assert the non-existence of past and future lives and that the mind arises adventitiously from the body as light is kindled from the lamp.

རྒྱན་བཅས་དགྲ་བཅོམ་པ།

The ornamented Foe-destroyer. A Hearer of lower intellectual capacity who is mainly concerned with the practice of mental quiescence meditation, who, when he attains the state of Arhatship is free both from the obscurtions to liberation and obscurations to meditative absorption, and also attains the six extra-sensory perceptions or clairvoyances.

རྒྱན་དྲུག་མཆོག་གཉིས།

The six ornaments and two excellences. The eight great Indian masters. 1. ཀླུ་སྒྲུབ། Nāgārjuna 2. འཕགས་པ་ལྷ། Āryadeva 3.

ཐོགས་མེད། Asaṅga 4. དབྱིག་གཉེན། Vasubandhu 5. ཕྱོགས་གླང་། Dignāga 6. ཆོས་གྲགས། Dharmakīrti 7. ཡོན་ཏན་འོད། Guṇaprabha 8. ཤཱཀྱ་འོད། Śākyaprabha.

རྒྱན་དྲུག་ཕྱག་མཚན།

The six adornments and implements. 1. རུས་པའི་དབུ་རྒྱན། human skull crown 2. མགུལ་རྒྱན། necklace 3. སྙན་རྒྱན། ear-ring 4. གདུ་བུ། bracelets and anklets 5. སེ་རལ་ཁ། jewel sash worn across shoulder (se-ral-kha) 6. འོག་པག jewel net sash worn as a girdle or lower garment.

རྒྱན་མེད་དགྲ་བཅོམ།

Anālaṅkārārhat/ The unornamented Foe-destroyer. A hearer of higher level intellectual capacity who is mainly concerned with the practice of special insight meditation and, who, on attaining the state of Arhatship does not attain extra-sensory perceptions or clairvoyances.

རྒྱན་བཞི།

The four ornaments; the four adorments. 1. ཚུལ་ཁྲིམས་ཀྱི་རྒྱན། ornament of moral discipline 2. ཏིང་ངེ་འཛིན་གྱི་རྒྱན། ornament of meditative concentration 3. ཤེས་རབ་ཀྱི་རྒྱན། ornament of wisdom 4. གཟུངས་ཀྱི་རྒྱན། ornament of retentive power.

རྒྱལ་ཆེན་བཞི།

The four great kings. The gods or evil spirits included in the category of the first level of gods in the desire realm 1. གནོད་སྦྱིན་ལག་ན་གཞོང་ཐོགས། Karoṭapāṇayodeva གནོད་སྦྱིན་ལག་ན་ཕྲེང་ཐོགས། Mālādhāra 3. རྟག་མྱོས། Sadāmāda 4. སྡེ་དཔོན་ཆེན་པོ། Pratihāra. Or the four directional protectors 1. ཡུལ་འཁོར་སྲུང་། Dhṛtarāṣṭra in the east 2. འཕགས་སྐྱེས་པོ། Virūḍhaka in the south 3. སྤྱན་མི་བཟང་། Virūpākṣa in the west 4. . རྣམ་ཐོས་སྲས། Vaiśravaṇa in the north.

རྒྱལ་པོ་ཀྲི་ཀྲིའི་རྨི་ལམ་བཅུ།

The ten prophetic dreams of Kṛkirājā; the ten apocalyptic dreams of King Kṛki. The dreams that correspond to various negative occurences in Buddha's teachings after his passing away. 1. གླང་པོ་ཆེ་ལུས་སྐར་ཁུང་ནས་ཐོན་ཀྱང་མཇུག་མ་དེ་ལ་ཐོགས་པ། an elephant's body is outside but his tail is caught in the window 2. གླང་པོ་ཆེ་ཕལ་པས་ཕྱོས་ཀྱི་གླང་པོ་ཆེ་སྐྲོད་པ། 'an ordinary elephant is driving away a superior elephant 3. མི་གཙང་བའི་གོས་པའི་སྤྲེའུ་ཞིག་གིས་སྤྲེའུ་གཞན་ལ་མི་གཙང་བ་བསྐུད་པ། a monkey covered with excrement is spreading it on other monkeys 4. སྤྲེའུ་གཅིག་གིས་སྤྲེའུ་ཚོགས་ལ་དབང་བསྐུར་བ། a monkey is giving initiation to a group of monkeys 5. ཙན་དན་སྦྲུལ་གྱི་སྙིང་པོ་དང་ཤིང་ཕལ་པ་མགོ་སྙོམས་པ། the sandal-wood tree is counted equal with other trees 6. མུ་ཏྲི་གང་དང་སྲུ་ཏིག་ཏྲི་གང་བརྗེ་བ། a bowl of pearl is exchanged for a bowl of barley flour 7. གཙུག་ལག་ཁང་གི་ཉེ་འཁོར་ན་ཡོད་པའི་མེ་ཏོག་དང་འབྲས་བུ་རྐུན་པོས་འཁྱེར་བ། thieves steal the flowers and fruits from around the temple 8. གཙང་ཞིང་ཡིད་དུ་འོང་བའི་ཁྲོན་པས་སྐོམ་པའི་མིས་ཇེས་སུ་སྙེགས་ཀྱང་ཆུ་འཐུང་མི་ནུས་པ། a man dying of thirst finds clear water in a well but is unable to drink it 9. སྐྱེ་བོ་མང་པོ་སྡེ་རིས་སུ་བཅད་ནས་རྩོད་པ། people gathered in many groups are quarreling with each other 10. རས་ཡུག་གཅིག་མི་བཅོ་བརྒྱད་ཀྱིས་བགོས་པས་ཐམས་ཅད་ལ་ཆ་ཚང་བ་རེ་ཐོབ་ཅིང་རྩ་བའི་རས་ཡུག་མ་ཉམས་པ། a piece of cloth is shared among eighteen people yet each receives the whole cloth and the original remains intact.

རྒྱལ་པོ་ལྟ་བུའི་སེམས་བསྐྱེད།

The king-like Bodhimind. The bodhicitta associated with the five extra-sensory perceptions possessed by a Bodhisattva on the three pure levels of the path—the eighth, ninth and t[illegible]h grounds.

རྒྱལ་པོའི་ཁབ།

Rājagṛha/ A holy Buddhist place to the east of Bodhgaya. It is believed to be the place where Rāja Bimbisāra's palace stood during Buddha's time. Buddha taught many sūtras here, and the first Buddhist Council was also held here.

རྒྱལ་བ་རིགས་ལྔ།

Pañcā jinā/ The five families of Buddha. 1. རྣམ་པར་སྣང་མཛད། Vairocana, white 2. མི་བསྐྱོད་པ། Akśobhya, blue 3. རིན་ཆེན་འབྱུང་གནས། Ratnasaṃbhava, yellow 4. འོད་དཔག་མེད། Amitābha, red 5. དོན་ཡོད་གྲུབ་པ། Amoghasiddhi, green. When Buddha རྒྱལ་བ་རྡོ་རྗེ་འཆང་། Vajradhāra, deep blue in colour, is added on top of this list, it becomes the six Buddha families.

རྒྱལ་བའི་མཛད་ཆེན་བརྒྱད།

Eight great festivals connected with Buddha Śākyamuni. 1. ལྷ་ལས་བབས་པ། His descent from Tuṣita heaven 2. ལྷུམས་སུ་ཞུགས་པ། His entering of mother's womb 3. སྐུ་བལྟམས་པ། His birth 4. རབ་ཏུ་བྱུང་བ། His renunciation of worldly life and becoming a monk 5. སངས་རྒྱས་པ། His attainment of complete enlightenment 6. ཆོས་འཁོར་བསྐོར་བ། His turning the wheel of doctrine 7. ཆོ་འཕྲུལ་བསྟན་པ། His performance of miracles 8. མྱ་ངན་ལས་འདས་པ། His passing into parinirvāṇa.

རྒྱལ་སྲིད་སྣ་བདུན།

The seven precious royal emblems. 1. འཁོར་ལོ་རིན་པོ་ཆེ། cakra ratna/ precious wheel for power and authority 2. ནོར་བུ་རིན་པོ་ཆེ། maṇi ratna/ precious jewel for marvelous property 3. བཙུན་མོ་རིན་པོ་ཆེ། strī ratna/ precious queen, as the queen 4. བློན་པོ་རིན་པོ་ཆེ། mantrī ratna/ precious minister as the minister of state 5. གླང་པོ་རིན་པོ་ཆེ། hastin ratna/ precious elephant for power and courage 6. རྟ་མཆོག་རིན་པོ་ཆེ། aśva ratna/ precious horse for strength and discipline 7. དམག་དཔོན་རིན་པོ་ཆེ། senāpati ratna/ precious military commander as the military force of a Universal Monarch.

རྒྱས་འགྱུར་གྱི་རིགས།

The maturing Buddha nature; the transformational Buddha nature. The Buddha nature enlightened and developed through sincere practice, that ultimately transforms into the form body of a Buddha.

རྒྱུ་རྐྱེན།

Hetupratyaya/ Causes and conditions; causal condition.

རྒྱུ་སྐྱབས།

Hetu śaraṇa/ Causal refuge. The Buddha, Dharma and Saṅgha in those who have already developed them. Buddhists accept them as their examplary objects of refuge.

རྒྱུ་གཉིས།

The two types of causes. A. By nature: 1. ཉེར་ལེན་གྱི་རྒྱུ། upādāna hetu/ the fundamental cause 2. ལྷན་ཅིག་བྱེད་རྐྱེན། saha bhū hetu/ imultaneously arisen cause. B. By way of giving rise to results: 1. དངོས་རྒྱུ། bhāva hetu/ direct cause 2. བརྒྱུད་རྒྱུ། saṁbandha hetu/ indirect cause.

རྒྱུ་མཐུན་གྱི་འབྲས་བུ།

Niṣyandaphala/ The results corresponding to its cause. The fruits of a karmic action experienced or ripened with its nature corresponding to its cause. This has two: 1. བྱས་པ་རྒྱུ་མཐུན་གྱི་འབྲས་བུ། the fruits corresponding to its actions, e.g. the fact that a person who may have been a sinner in the past life has the natural urge to do similar actions in this life. 2. མྱོང་བ་རྒྱུ་མཐུན་གྱི་འབྲས་བུ། the fruits corresponding to its experience, e.g. the fact that a person who practices generosity in this life would become rich in his future life.

རྒྱུ་དྲུག

Ṣaḍ hetavaḥ/ The six types of causes; the six causes. 1. བྱེད་རྒྱུ། kāraṇa hetu/ acting cause 2. ལྷན་ཅིག་འབྱུང་བའི་རྒྱུ། sahabhū hetu/ simultaneously arising cause; innately born cause 3. སྐལ་མཉམ་གྱི་རྒྱུ། sabhāga hetu/ equal-state cause 4. མཚུངས་ལྡན་གྱི་རྒྱུ། saṁprayukta hetu/ concomitant cause 5. ཀུན་འགྲོའི་རྒྱུ། sarvatraga hetu/ omnipresent cause 6. རྣམ་སྨིན་གྱི་རྒྱུ། vipāka hetu/ ripening cause.

རྒྱུ་རྡོ་རྗེ་འཛིན་པ།

The adamantine cause. The primordial reality abiding within the mental continuum of sentient beings which is qualified by three basic features: 1. unchangeable 2. self-awarness 3. the great and supreme bliss.

རྒྱུ་འབྲས་མན་ངག་བདུན།

The seven-fold cause and effect precepts. A lineage of meditation for cultivating the mind of enlightenment. 1. མར་ཤེས། recognizing all sentient beings as one's mother 2. དྲིན་དྲན། being mindful of their kindness 3. དྲིན་གཟོ། repaying their kindness 4. ཡིད་འོང་གི་བྱམས་པ། heart-warming love 5. སྙིང་རྗེ། compassion 6. ལྷག་བསམ། resolute intention 7. བྱང་ཆུབ་ཀྱི་སེམས། mind of enlightenment.

རྒྱུ་མཚན་ལྡན་པའི་ཡིད་དཔྱོད།

Presumption or correct belief that is based on reason. One of the five types of presumptions resulting from some reason that is either incorrect or, if correct, not understood.

རྒྱུ་གཟུགས།

The causal form. Forms that retain the entity of elements. These comprise earth or soil, water or liquid, fire or warmth, and wind.

རྒྱུད།

Tantra/ A. Tantra; classification of Buddha's teachings concerning the speedier method of attaining Buddhahood. B. Mental continuum; mind stream.

རྒྱུད་ཀྱི་འཆད་ཐབས་བཞི།

The four ways of explaining a tantric text. 1. དོན་ཁོག་ཕུབ་གིས་ནམ་མཁའི་དབྱིངས་འཇལ་ལྟར་ཕུབ། presenting the summary of the text in the manner of a garuda bird floating in the sky 2. དཀྱུས་ཀྱི་ས་སྐྱག་མོ་ནགས་ལ་མཆོང་བ་ལྟར་བཅད། explaining the body of text in the manner of a lion leaping in the forest 3. ཚིག་གི་དོན་རུས་སྦལ་དལ་གྱིས་འགྲོ་བ་ལྟར་བཤད། explaining the meaning of the words literally in the manner of a tortoise's gait 4. མན་ངག་གི་དོན་མུ་ཏིག་བསྒྲར་ལ་བརྒྱུས་པ་བཞིན་བསྒྱུ་བ། passing the transmission in the manner of pearls woven on the string.

རྒྱུད་གཉིས།

Two classes of tantra. 1. ཕ་རྒྱུད། father tantra 2. མ་རྒྱུད། mother tantra.

རྒྱུད་སྟོད་སྨད།

The upper and lower tantric college of Gelug tradition. Tsong Khapa's disciple Jetsun Sherab Senge established the lower tantric college in 1433, and the upper tantric college instituted by his disciple Neying Jetsun Kunga Dhondup in 1474 in Lhasa.

རྒྱུད་སྡེ་དྲུག

Saḍ tantrapiṭakā/ The six classes of tantra. 1. བྱ་རྒྱུད། kriyā tantra/ action tantra 2. སྤྱོད་རྒྱུད། cārya tantra/ performance tantra 3. རྣལ་འབྱོར་རྒྱུད། yoga tantra 4. ཕ་རྒྱུད། pitā tantra/ father tantra 5. མ་རྒྱུད། mātā tantra/ mother tantra 6. གཉིས་མེད་རྒྱུད། advaya tantra/ non-dual tantra. The first are known as the three outer classes of tantra and the latter three as the three inner classes of tantra.

རྒྱུད་སྡེ་བདུན།

Sapta tantra piṭakā/ The seven classes of tantra. According to Atiśa's *Lamp on the Path to Enlightenment* these are: 1. བྱ་བའི་རྒྱུད། kriyā tantra/ action tantra 2. སྤྱོད་པའི་རྒྱུད། cārya tantra/ performance tantra 3. རྟོག་པའི་རྒྱུད། savitarka tantra/ conceptual tantra 4. གཉིས་ཀའི་རྒྱུད། ūbhya tantra/ dual tantra 5. རྣལ་འབྱོར་གྱི་རྒྱུད།

yoga tantra 6. རྣལ་འབྱོར་ཆེན་པོའི་རྒྱུད། mahāyoga tantra/ great yoga tantra 7. རྣལ་འབྱོར་བླ་ན་མེད་པའི་རྒྱུད། anuttarayoga tantra/ highest yoga tantra.

རྒྱུད་སྡེ་བཞི།

Catvāri tantra piṭakā/ The four classes of tantra. 1. བྱ་བའི་རྒྱུད། kriyā tantra/ action tantra 2. སྤྱོད་པའི་རྒྱུད། cārya tantra/ performance tantra 3. རྣལ་འབྱོར་རྒྱུད། yoga tantra 4. རྣལ་འབྱོར་བླ་ན་མེད་པའི་རྒྱུད། anuttarayoga tantra/ highest yoga tantra.

རྒྱུད་པ་གསུམ།

The three types of lineages. 1. གདུང་རྒྱུད། family lineage 2. སྐུ་རྒྱུད། reincarnation lineage 3. སློབ་རྒྱུད། disciple lineage.

རྒྱུད་གསུམ།

The three integerations; the three principles. A. རྒྱུན་ཆགས་གསུམ། The three regular principles of practice at a teaching session: 1. ཕྱག་འཚལ་བ། making prostration 2. མདོ་འདོན་པ། reciting a sūtra 3. བསྔོ་བ་བྱེད་པ། making dedication. B. ས་སྐྱ་པའི་ལམ་འབྲས་ལྟར་རྒྱུད་གསུམ་སྐོར་ཚུལ། The integration of the actual path and fruit practice according to Sakya tradition, being the secret mantra vajrayāna practice drawn into three principles: 1. ཀུན་གཞི་རྒྱུ་རྒྱུད་ལ་འཁོར་འདས་དབྱེར་མེད་ཀྱི་ལྟ་བ་སྐྱོང་བ། maintaining the view of the inseparability of saṁsāra and nirvāṇa within the fundamental mental continuum (kun-gzhi rgyu-rgyud) as the causal principle. 2. ལུས་ཐབས་རྒྱུད་ལ་དབང་བཞི་དང་འབྲེལ་བའི་ལམ་བསྒོམ་པ། meditating on the paths connected to the fourfold initiations upon one's body as the method principle. 3. མཐར་ཐུག་འབྲས་བུའི་རྒྱུད་ལ་སྐུ་ལྔ་ཡེ་ཤེས་ལྔའི་ཡོན་ཏན་འཆར་བ། attaining the qualities of the five bodies and five primordial wisdoms at the end as the resultant principle.

རྒྱུན་དུ་འཇོག་པ།

Continual fixation. The second of the nine stages of mental fixation or placement (see sems-gnas dgu) in the practice of mental quiescence meditation; the stage at which one increases one's attention on the object of meditation.

རྒྱུན་བཤགས་ཀྱི་ཡན་ལག་བདུན་པ།

The seven regular confession practices. 1. སྡིག་པ་བཤགས་པ། pāpadeśanā/ confession of non-virtues 2. རྗེས་སུ་ཡི་རང་བ། anumoda/ rejoicing in virtues 3. དོན་དམ་བྱང་ཆུབ་ཀྱི་སེམས་བསྐྱེད་པ། paramārthacittopāda/ generating the ultimate mind of enlightenment 4. སྐྱབས་སུ་འགྲོ་བ། śaraṇa/ taking refuge 5. སྨོན་སེམས་བསྐྱེད་པ། praṇidhicittopāda/ generating the aspiring mind of enlightenment 6. འཇུག་སེམས་བསྐྱེད་པ། prasthānacittopāda/ generating the engaging mind of enlightenment 7. བསྔོ་བ། pariṇāma/ dedicating the virtues.

རྒྱུའི་རྒྱུད།

The causal principle. The reality of mind that abides unchangeable like space within the minds of sentient beings and Buddhas. According to sūtras this refers to the Tathāgata essence—the naturally abiding buddha nature. In the lower tantras this is known by various names like the suchness of self (bdag-gi de kho-na nyid), the mind of enlightenment and the mind of Samantabhadra (kun-tu bzang-po'i sems). According to the highest yoga tantra this principle is known as the union of E-VAṂ (e-vam zung-'jug).

རྒྱུའི་ཐེག་པ།

Hetuyāna/ Causal vehicle. The common vehicle known as the perfection vehicle, the slower path of practice for the attainment of Buddhahood.

རྒྱུའི་རྟེན་འབྲེལ་དྲུག

Ṣaḍ pratītyasamutpāda/ The six causal interdependent principles. The elements of the outer natural phenomena—earth, water, fire, wind, space and time.

རྒྱུའི་དབང་།

The causal initiations. Those stages of initiations that are given to prepare a disciple to become a ripe receptacle, otherwise known as the initiation to ripen a disciple who is not yet ripe.

སྒོ་མ་བཞི།

The four guardian goddesses. In the secret mantra maṇḍalas the four gates or entrances of the maṇḍala: 1. ལྕགས་ཀྱུ་མ། Aṅkuśī 2. ཞགས་པ་མ། Pāśī 3. ལྕགས་སྒྲོག་མ། Śṛṅkhalā 4. དྲིལ་བུ་མ། Gaṇṭā.

སྒོ་གསུམ།

The three gates of activity. ལུས་ངག་ཡིད་གསུམ། Body, speech and mind.

སྒོམ་སྤང་སྐོར་དགུ

The nine levels of delusions to be abandoned on the path of meditation. སྒོམ་སྤང་ཆེ་འབྲིང་ཆུང་གསུམ་རེ་རེར་ཆེ་འབྲིང་ཆུང་སྐོར་གསུམ་རེ་རྩིས་པའི་སྐོར་དགུ The great, middling and small levels of delusions of each of the great, middle and small delusions to be abandoned on the path of meditation.

སྒོམ་སྤང་བཅུ།

The ten delusions to be abandoned on the path of meditation. According to *Abhidharmakosa* there are four of the desire realm, three of the form realm, and three of the formless realm.

སྒོམ་སྤང་བཅུ་དྲུག

The sixteen delusions to be abandoned on the path of meditation. This follows the tradition of *Abhidharma-samuccaya* (see sgom-spang nyon-mongs bcu-drug).

སྒོམ་སྤང་འཇུག་པ་གཟུང་རྟོག

Bhāvanāheyavṛttigrāhyakalpa/ Conceptual apprehension of objects of cultivation to be eliminated on the path of meditation.

སྒོམ་སྤང་ཉོན་མོངས་བཅུ་དྲུག

Ṣoḍaśa bhāvanāheyakleśā/ The sixteen delusions (which are obscurations to liberation) to be abandoned on the path of meditation. འདོད་པའི་ཁམས་བསྡུས་ཀྱི་དྲུག ṣaḍ kāmadhātu kleśā/ Six of the desire realm: 1. འདོད་ཆགས། rāga/ desire-attachment 2. ཁོང་ཁྲོ། krodha/ anger 3. ང་རྒྱལ། māna/ pride 4. མ་རིག་པ། avidyā/ ignorance 5. འཇིག་ལྟ། satkāyadṛṣṭi/ view of the transitory collection 6. མཐར་ལྟ། antagrāhadṛṣṭi/ extreme view. གཟུགས་ཀྱི་ཁམས་བསྡུས་ཀྱི་ལྔ། pañca rūpadhātu kleśā/ Five of the form realm: 1. འདོད་ཆག rāga/ desire-attachment 2. ང་རྒྱལ། māna/ pride 3. མ་རིག་པ། avidyā/ ignorance 4. འཇིག་ལྟ། satkāyadṛṣṭi/ view of the transitory collection 5. མཐར་ལྟ། antagrāha dṛṣṭi/ extreme view. གཟུགས་མེད་ཁམས་བསྡུས་ཀྱི་ལྔ། pañca arūpadhātu kleśā/ Five of the formless realm: 1. འདོད་ཆགས། rāga/ desire-attachment 2. ང་རྒྱལ། māna/ pride 3. མ་རིག་པ། avidyā/ ignorance 4. འཇིག་ལྟ། satkāyadṛṣṭi/ view of the transitory collection 5. མཐར་ལྟ། antagrāhadṛṣṭi/ extreme view.

སྒོམ་སྤང་བཏགས་འཛིན་རྟོག་པ།

Bhāvanāheyaprajñāptigrāhakalpa/ Conceptual apprehension of imputed existence to be abandoned on the path of meditation.

སྒོམ་སྤང་ལྡོག་པ་གཟུང་རྟོག

Bhāvanāheyanirvṛttigrāhyakalpa/ Conceptual apprehension of objects of elimination to be abandoned on the path of meditation.

སྒོམ་སྤང་རྫས་འཛིན་རྟོག་པ།

Bhāvanāheyadravyagrāhakakalpa/ Conceptual apprehension of substantial existence to be abandoned on the path of meditation.

སྒོམ་སྤང་བཞི་བརྒྱ་བཅུ་བཞི།

The four hundred and fourteen delusions to be abandoned on the path of meditation. This list includes all delusions to be abandoned on the path of meditation within the three realms and nine levels (see khams-gsum sa-dgu). These are འདོད་པའི་སྒོམ་སྤང་ལྔ་བཅུ་རྩ་བཞི། the fifty-four of the desire realm, གཟུགས་ཁམས་ཀྱི་སྒོམ་སྤང་བརྒྱ་དང་བརྒྱད་ཅུ། one hundred and eighty of the form realm, གཟུགས་མེད་ཁམས་ཀྱི་སྒོམ་སྤང་བརྒྱ་དང་བརྒྱད་ཅུ། one hundred and eighty of the formless realm.

སྒོམ་ལམ་གྱི་བྱེད་པ་དྲུག

Six functions of the path of meditation; six benefits of the path of meditation. 1. སེམས་ཀུན་ཏུ་ཞི་བ། peaceful mind 2. ཐམས་ཅད་ལ་འདུད་པ། self-disciplined and humble 3. ཉོན་མོངས་པའི་ཕྱོགས་ལས་རྒྱལ་བ། victory over defilements 4. ཕྱི་ནང་གི་གནོད་པས་བརྫི་བ་མེད་པ། no occasion for attack from internal and external evils 5. བྱང་ཆུབ་མྱུར་དུ་སྒྲུབ་པ། ability to achieve enlightenment 6. རང་གང་དུ་གནས་པའི་ས་ཕྱོགས་དེ་ཉིད་ཀྱང་མཆོད་པའི་རྟེན་ཉིད་དུ་འགྱུར་བ། the worthiness of being worshipped wherever one abides.

སྒོམ་ལམ་ཕྱིར་མི་ལྡོག་པའི་རྟགས་བརྒྱད།

The eight marks of irreversibility on the path of meditation. 1. སྐྱེ་བ་ལ་ཟབ་པ། profundity of production 2. འགག་པ་ལ་ཟབ་པ། profundity of stopping 3. དེ་བཞིན་ཉིད་ལ་ཟབ་པ། profundity of reality 4. ཤེས་པ་ལ་ཟབ་པ། profundity of objects of knowledge 5. སྤྱོད་པ་ལ་ཟབ་པ། profundity of knowledge 6. profundity of practice 7. གཉིས་མེད་ལ་ཟབ་པ། profundity of non-duality 8. ཐབས་མཁས་ལ་ཟབ་པ། profundity of skillful means.

སྒོམ་ལམ་རྩེ་སྦྱོར།

Bhāvanāmārga mūrdhaprayoga/ The peak training on the path of meditation. A path of practice within the continuum of a Bodhisattva on the path of meditation which is a direct antidote to the seed of eliminations to be abandoned on the path of meditaiton

སྒྱུ་མའི་དཔེ་བཅུ་གཉིས།

Dvadaśa māyopamā/ The twelve examples of illusory nature; the twelve similes to prove lack of true existence of a conjurer's display. 1. སྒྱུ་མ། māyā/ an illusion 2. ཆུ་ཟླ། udakacandra/ a reflection of the moon in the water 3. མིག་ཡོར། pratibhāsa/ hallucination 4. སྨིག་རྒྱུ། marīci/ a mirage 5. རྨི་ལམ། svapna/ a dream 6. བྲག་ཆ། pratiśabda/ an echo 7. དྲི་ཟའི་གྲོང་ཁྱེར། gandharvanagara/ the city of smell-eaters 8. མིག་འཕྲུལ། indrajāla/ a magic play 9. འཇའ་ཚོན། indracāpa/ a rainbow 10. གློག vidyut/ a bolt of lightening 11. ཆུ་བུར། budbud/ a water bubble 12. མེ་ལོང་ནང་གི་གཟུགས་བརྙན། pratibimba/ a reflection in a mirror.

སྒྱུ་རྩལ་དྲུག་ཅུ་རེ་བཞི།

The sixty-four arts. The thirty skills of arts and crafts (see bzo-rig-gi sgyu-rtsal sum-cu), the eighteen arts of music (see rol-mo'i sgyu-rtsal bco-brgyad), the seven principles of songs and chanting (see glu-dbyans-kyi nges-pa bdun), and the nine features of dance (see gar-gyi nyams-dgu), all rooted in the ancient Indian culture.

སྒྱུ་ལུས་ཀྱི་སྐུ་གཉིས།

Two types of illusory body. 1. ཀུན་རྫོབ་ཀྱི་སྒྱུ་ལུས་ཀྱི་སྐུ། saṁvṛti māyākāya/ the conventional illusory body 2. དོན་དམ་པའི་སྒྱུ་ལུས་ཀྱི་སྐུ། paramārtha māyākāya/ the ultimate illusory body.

སྒྱུ་ལུས་བདུན།

The seven types of illusory body. The seven different illusory bodies: 1. དཔེའི་སྒྱུ་མ། exemplary illusory body 2. སྣང་བ་སྒྱུ་མ། appearance illusory body 3. རྨི་ལམ་སྒྱུ་མ། dream illusory body 4. བར་དོ་སྒྱུ་མ། illusory body of the intermediate state of rebirth 5. འོད་གསལ་སྒྱུ་མ། clear light illusory body 6. སྤྲུལ་པ་སྒྱུ་མ། emanation illusory body 7. ཡེ་ཤེས་སྒྱུ་མ། wisdom illusory body.

སྒྲ་བཅུ་གཅིག

The eleven types of sound. 1. ཡིད་དུ་འོང་བའི་སྒྲ། pleasant 2. ཡིད་དུ་མི་འོང་བའི་སྒྲ། unpleasant 3. གཉིས་ཀ་མིན་པ། neither pleasant nor unpleasant 4. ཟིན་པའི་སྒྲ། conjoined sound 5. མ་ཟིན་པའི་སྒྲ། unconjoined sound 6. མ་ཟིན་པའི་སྒྲ། neither conjoined nor unconjoined 7. འཇིག་རྟེན་གྱི་གྲགས་པ། popular sound 8. གྲུབ་པས་བསྟན་པ། philosophical expression 9. ཀུན་བརྟགས་པ། imputed sound 10. འཕགས་པའི་ཐ་སྙད་བཏགས་པ། utterances pronounced by Āryas 11. འཕགས་པ་མ་ཡིན་པའི་ཐ་སྙད་བཏགས་པ། utterances pronounced by non-Āryas.

སྒྲ་སྙན་ལྟ་བུའི་སེམས་བསྐྱེད།

The delightful sound-like Bodhimind. The mind of enlightenment associated with the gaiety of dharma possessed by the Bodhisattva on the tenth level.

སྒྲ་མཐའི་དེ་ཉིད།

The suchness of sound. An action tantra meditation practice. A practitioner concentrates and analyses the sound of a mantra into its subtler and subtler forms and finally places his or her mind within the non-conceptual level of experiencing the suchness of sound at its final stage. This helps a meditator to produce the wisdom of penetrative insight meditation (vipaśyanā).

སྒྲ་དོན་མཐུན།

Logical sound. An expression or statement that fits the popular convention, e.g. the statement, 'sound is permanent'.

སྒྲ་དོན་མི་མཐུན།

Illogical sound. An expression or statement that does not fit the popular convention, e.g. the statement, 'sound is impermanent'.

སྒྲ་དོན་གཉིས་ཀ་སྣང་བའི་རྟོག་པ།

The conceptual cognition of sound generality (see sgra-spyi) and meaning generality (see don-spyi). For instance, the idea of conceptual cognition of a vase in the mind of a person learned in conventions.

སྒྲ་སྤྱི།

Sound generality. Generic image based only on hearsay about an object, e.g. the image of a sound in one's mind having heared the expression, 'vase'.

སྒྲ་བྱུང་ཚད་མ།

Sabda pramāna/ Valid cognition based on verbal indication. It is the sound generality based entirely on hearsay and not on previous direct apprehension of the object such as through sense consciousness, etc. It is permanent and is the appearing object to a conceptual mind that apprehends the object.

སྒྲ་ལ་གཞོལ་བའི་ཡན་ལག

Concentration on sound. One of the four types of recitation of mantra in meditation (see bzlas-brjod yan-lag bzhi). The practice of reciting the mantra according to performance tantra. This involves concentrating on the mantric syllables visualized upon a moon disk as self-resounding.

སྒྲའི་ལྷ།

Śabda deva/ The sound deity. One of the six types of deities in action tantra. This involves meditation on the mantric syllables visualized in the maṇḍala as self-resounding and emitting and drawing rays of light.

སྒྲར་གནས་ཀྱི་དེ་ཉིད།

Suchness abiding upon sound. A practice of meditation on the suchness of concentration according to action tantra. This involves meditation on all the mantric syllables visualized as encircling the moon disk at one's heart along with the moon disk itself as producing sound similar to one's ritual bell, and thus maintaining concentration upon it. A basis for developing calm abiding meditation.

སྒྲིབ་པ་ལྔ་།

The five types of obscurations. According to some traditions these are: 1. འདོད་ཆགས། kāmacchanda/ desire-attachment 2. རྨུགས་པ། styāna/ mental sloth 3. གཉིད་དང་འགྱོད་པ། nindrā kāukṛtya/ sleep and regret 4. གཡེང་བ། vikṣepa/ mental distraction 5. due་ཚོམ། vicikitsā/ doubt.

སྒྲིབ་པ་གཉིས།

The two obstructions; two obscurations. 1. ཉོན་མོངས་པའི་སྒྲིབ་པ། kleśāvaraṇa/ delusive obscuration to liberation 2. ཤེས་བྱའི་སྒྲིབ་པ། jñānāvaraṇa/ obstructions to omniscience.

སྒྲིབ་པ་སྤང་པའི་སེམས་བསྐྱེད་གཉིས།

The two types of Bodhicitta completely free from obscurations. 1. Bodhicitta like a flowing river (see chu-bo'i rgyun lta-bu'i sems-bskyed) 2. Cloud-like Bodhicitta (see sprin lta-bu'i sems-bskyed).

སྒྲིབ་པ་བཞི།

The four types of obscurations. A. ལམ་གྱི་དགག་བྱ་སྒྲིབ་པ་བཞི། The four obscurations of the paths: 1. འདོད་ཆེན་གྱི་སྒྲིབ་པ། obscurations of the desirous ones 2. མུ་སྟེགས་པའི་སྒྲིབ་པ། obscurations of the hedonists (tīrthikas) 3. ཉན་ཐོས་ཀྱི་དམན་སྒྲིབ། obscurations of the hearers (śrāvakas) 4. རང་རྒྱལ་གྱི་དམན་སྒྲིབ། obscurations of the solitary realizers (pratekyabuddhas). B. 1. ཉོན་སྒྲིབ། kleśāvaraṇa/ delusive obscurations 2. ཤེས་སྒྲིབ། jñānāvaraṇa/ obscurations to omniscience 3. ཆགས་སྒྲིབ། sarāgāvaraṇa/ obscurations of attachment 4. ཐོགས་སྒྲིབ། sapratigāvaraṇa/ impeding obscurations. C. 1. ལས་ཀྱི་སྒྲིབ་པ། karmakāvaraṇa/ karmic obscurations 2. ཉོན་མོངས་པའི་སྒྲིབ་པ། kleśāvaraṇa/ delusive obscurations 3. ཤེས་བྱའི་སྒྲིབ་པ། jñānāvaraṇa/ obscurations to omniscience 4. སྙོམས་འཇུག་གི་སྒྲིབ་པ། samāpattyāvaraṇa/ obscurations to meditative absorption.

སྒྲིབ་པ་གསུམ།

The three obscurations. A. 1-2. (see sgrib-pa gnyis, above) 3. ལས་ཀྱི་སྒྲིབ་པ། karmakāvaraṇa/ karmic obscuration. B. 1. ཆགས་པའི་སྒྲིབ་པ། sarāgāvaraṇa/ obscuration to attachment 2. ཐོགས་པའི་སྒྲིབ་པ། sapratigāvaraṇa/ impeding obscuration 3. དམན་པའི་སྒྲིབ་པ། hīnāvaraṇa/ obscuration to the lower.

སྒྲིབ་བྱེད་ཀྱི་དྲི་མ་དགུ

The nine obstructing stains. 1-3. དུག་གསུམ་གྱི་བག་ལ་ཉལ་བ་གསུམ། the three poisonous delusions in their latent state 4. དེ་དག་གི་ཀུན་ནས་ལྡང་བ་དྲུག the six secondary delusions (see rtsa-nyon-drug) arising from the three root delusions 5. མ་རིག་བག་ཆགས་ཀྱི་ས། the instinctive level of ignorance 6. ཐེག་དམན་གྱི་མཐོང་སྤང་། the abandonments on the path of seeing of the lesser vehicle 7. ཐེག་དམན་གྱི་སྒོམ་སྤང་། the abandonments on the path of meditation of the lesser vehicle 8. མ་དག་ས་བདུན་གྱི་སྤང་བྱ། the abandonments on the seven impure levels of Bodhisattvas 9. དག་པ་ས་གསུམ་གྱི

སྤང་བྱ། the abandonments on the three pure levels of Bodhisattvas.

སྒྲུབ་བརྒྱུད།

The practice lineage. The lineage of reclusive lamas and their disciples who mainly do intensive meditation in isolated places and seldom give public teachings or compose texts.

སྒྲུབ་འཇུག

Affirming perception; assertive perception. All direct perceptions affirming their objects of knowledge as they are as a whole without being specific with respect to different aspects of their object, e.g. the direct perception with regard to a vase.

སྒྲུབ་ཐབས།

Sādhana/ The method of accomplishment (sādhana). The text of practice aimed at the actualization of reality through meditation. It involves an entire system of visualization, recitation, rituals and meditation concerning a deity or the cycle of deities.

སྒྲུབ་ལྡོག་རིགས་གཅིག་པ།

Things of the same production and reverse identity. For instance, the idea or thought that the sound of a bell and flute are same with respect to their being produced from solid things.

སྒྲུབ་པ།

A. Positive phenomenon. A phenomenon that can be understood without having to understand what is opposite to it or, in general, without recourse to conception, e.g. a vase. B. Practice; accomplishment; achievement; attainment; realization.

སྒྲུབ་པ་བཀའ་བརྒྱད།

The eight Kagyad deities. The eight deities of the Nyingma tradition primarily of the generation stage practice of tantra. These are: 1. འཇམ་དཔལ་སྐུ། 'jam-dpal sku 2. པདྨ་གསུང་། pad-ma gsung 3. ཡང་དག་ཐུགས། yang-dag thugs 4. བདུད་རྩི་ཡོན་ཏན། bdud-rtsi yon-tan 5. ཕུར་པ་ཕྲིན་ལས། phur-pa phrin-las 6. མ་མོ་བོད་གཏོང་། ma-mo bod-gtong 7. དམོད་པ་དྲག་སྔགས། dmod-po drag-sngags 8. འཇིག་རྟེན་མཆོད་བསྟོད། 'jig-rten mchod-bstod. The first five are transworldly deities and the latter three worldly deities.

སྒྲུབ་པ་སྒོམ་ལམ་ལྔ།

The five paths of meditation of achievement, with respect to its: 1. སྒོམ་ལམ་གྱི་ངོ་བོ། nature 2. འབྲས་བུའི་ཁྱད་པར། fruits 3. བྱེད་ལས་ཀྱི་ཁྱད་པར། function 4. གནས་སྐབས་ཀྱི་ཁྱད་པར། temporary features 5. མཐར་ཐུག་གི་ཁྱད་པར། ultimate features.

སྒྲུབ་པའི་ཆེད་དུ་བྱ་བ་གསུམ།

The three great accomplishments; the three great objectives of a Bodhisattva. 1. སེམས་དཔའ་ཆེན་པོ། mahāsattva/ great being 2. སྤོང་བ་ཆེན་པོ། mahāprahāṇa/ great abandonment 3. རྟོགས་པ་ཆེན་པོ། mahādhigama/ great insight.

སྒྲུབ་པའི་མཆོད་པ།

The offering of practice. The practice of offering one's own Dharma practices and collection of virtues as an object of offering. The best offering one can make to those worthy of making offerings.

སྒྲུབ་པའི་སྤྱོད་པ།

The activity of practice. One of the four ways of utilizing realizations (see spyod-pa'i sgo-bzhi) according to action tantra in which one transforms articles of offering, body and resources into gods of desire realms and Vidyādhāras or ḍākinīs of the same rank.

སྒྲུབ་པའི་མཎྜལ།

The symbolic maṇḍala. A maṇḍala arranged on an altar made of gold or metal bases or otherwise upon which the fivefold heaps of precious stones or grains are created and visualized as the five Buddha families. Such a maṇḍala primarily symbolizes the deities as objects of worship.

སྒྲུབ་པའི་དམིགས་པ་བཅུ་གཅིག

The eleven objects of accomplishment; the eleven objects of the Bodhisattva paths. 1. བླང་བྱ་དགེ་བ། virtuous objects to be cultivated 2. དོར་བྱ་མི་དགེ་བ། non-virtuous objects to be abandoned 3. ལུང་མ་བསྟན། unspecified objects which are neither 4. འཇིག་རྟེན་པ། worldly objects 5. འཇིག་རྟེན་ལས་འདས་པ། transworldly objects 6. ཟག་བཅས། contaminated objects 7. ཟག་མེད། uncontaminated objects 8. འདུས་བྱས། composite objects 9. འདུས་མ་བྱས། non-composite 10. ཐུན་མོང་བའི་ཡོན་ཏན། common qualities 11. ཐུན་མོང་མ་ཡིན་པའི་ཡོན་ཏན། uncommon qualities.

སྒྲོ་བཏགས།

Samāropa/ Overestimation; exaggeration; superimposition; hypostatization. Exaggerating the meaning or significance of the mode of abidance of a phenomenon without any basis; taking something as existing in a certain way when it does not actually exist in that way.

སྒྲོན་མ་བཞི།

The four types of lamps. The paths that allow direct perception of the enlightened body of the inseparable reality and awareness at the actual stage of rDzogs-chen meditation following the leap-over system (thod-rgal). These are: 1. རྒྱང་ཞགས་ཆུ་ཡི་སྒྲོན་མ། the distant water lamp 2. རིག་པ་དབྱིངས་ཀྱི་སྒྲོན་མ། the lamp of reality of awareness 3. ཐིག་ལེ་སྟོང་པའི་སྒྲོན་མ། the lamp of emptiness of drop 4. ཤེས་རབ་རང་བྱུང་གི་སྒྲོན་མ། the lamp of self-born wisdom.

བརྒྱད་གཏོར།

The Torma ritual of the eigth. A religious ceremony of the four-faced Mahākāla held on the 8th of the 3rd Tibetan month. The ceremony involves offering of sacrificial cakes through invocation rites and rituals to Mahākāla and all other dharma protectors.

བརྒྱུད་པ་དྲུག

The six lineages or transmissions. The six lineages of transmissions according to the Oral (bka'-ma) and Treasure (gter-ma) lineages in Nyingma tradition. Thcsc arc: 1. རྒྱལ་བ་དགོངས་པའི་བརྒྱུད་པ། Buddha's intention lineage 2. རིག་འཛིན་བརྡའི་བརྒྱུད་པ། Vidyādhāra's symbolic lineage 3. གང་ཟག་སྙན་ཁུང་གི་བརྒྱུད་པ། disciple's whispered lineage 4. བཀའ་བབ་ལུང་བསྟན་གྱི་བརྒྱུད་པ། the commissioned prophetic lineage 5. སྨོན་ལམ་དབང་བསྐུར་གྱི་བརྒྱུད་པ། the lineage of prayers and empowerment 6. མཁའ་འགྲོ་གཏད་རྒྱའི་བརྒྱུད་པ། the lineage protected by ḍākinīs. The first three lineages are common to both the Oral and Treasure transmissions whereas the latter three are unique to the revealers of treasure teachings.

བརྒྱུད་པ་རྣམ་པ་ལྔ།

The five types of lineages. The five lineages of Buddhism according to the way it spread in India. 1. འདུལ་བའི་བརྒྱུད་པ། the vinaya lineage 2. གསང་སྔགས་ཀྱི་བརྒྱུད་པ། the secret mantra lineage 3. རྒྱ་ཆེན་སྤྱོད་བརྒྱུད། the extensive practice lineage 4. ཟབ་མོ་ལྟ་བརྒྱུད། the profound view lineage 5. སྙིང་པོ་དོན་བརྒྱུད། the essential meaning lineage.

བརྒྱུད་པ་གསུམ།

The three types of lineages. A. According to the graded path teaching tradition of Sūtrayāna, these are: 1. ཟབ་མོ་ལྟ་བརྒྱུད། the profound view lineage 2. རྒྱ་ཆེན་སྤྱོད་བརྒྱུད། the extensive practice lineage 3. ཉམས་ལེན་བྱིན་རླབས་ཀྱི་བརྒྱུད། the blessed practice lineage.

B. According to the secret mantra teaching tradition of the Nyingma school, these are: 1. རིང་བརྒྱུད་བཀའ་མ། the distant oral lineage 2. ཉེ་བརྒྱུད་གཏེར་མ། the close treasure lineage 3. ཟབ་མོ་དག་སྣང་གི་བརྒྱུད་པ། the profound pure vision lineage.

བསྐུར་བ་ཞིམ་པོར་དགོངས་པ།

Interpretive sūtras for the purpose of encouragement. For instance, the sūtras in which Buddha taught those of weak aptitude that, 'enlightenment can be achieved through striving hard in the accumulation of two types of merits'.

བསྒྲལ་བའི་ཞིང་བཅུ།

The ten heinous crimes. An enemy of the Buddha Dharma who has committed ten serious non-virtues and is therefore an object to be captured and killed. 1. སངས་རྒྱས་བསྟན་པ་བཤིག་པ། destroying the Buddha's teaching 2. དཀོན་མཆོག་དབྱུ་འཕང་སྨོད་པ། disparaging the three jewels of refuge 3. དགེ་འདུན་གྱི་འདུན་སྐོར་འཕྲོག་པ། appropriating the wealth of the Sangha community 4. ཐེག་ཆེན་ལ་སྨོད་པ། disparaging the Mahāyāna 5. བླ་མའི་སྐུ་ལ་བསྒོ་བ། threatening the body of a guru 6. རྡོ་རྗེ་སྤུན་གྲོགས་སྒྱུན་འབྱེད་པ། causing disunity amongst vajra friends 7. སྒྲུབ་པ་ལ་བར་དུ་གཅོད་པ། hindering the practice of Dharma 8. དམ་ཚིག་ཉམས་པ་དང་བྲལ་བ། dropping the spiritual pledges 9. བརྩེ་བ་སྙིང་རྗེ་གཏན་ནས་མེད་པ། lacking compassion 10. ལས་འབྲས་ལ་ལོག་པར་ལྟ་བ། holding wrong views or philosophy.

བསྒྲིབས་ལུང་མ་བསྟན།

The obscured unspecified phenomena. The delusive unspecified phenomena. The delusions within the form and formless realms that are obstructions to attaining Ārya paths, and hence hinder actualization of uncontaminated paths, and are not non-virtues because these do not give rise to suffering or misery, therefore these become unspecified phenomena. For example, the innately born self or ego.

བསྒྲུབ་མཆོད།

Accomplishment ceremony. A grand tantric ceremony involving the creation of a maṇḍala, offering of services, and performance of the ritual and rites of generating oneself into a deity, generating the deity in front and into the vase, etc.

བསྒྲུབ་བྱ།

Sādhya/ The thesis; that which is to be established. The subject and the predicate in a correct logical syllogism taken together as that which is to be proved.

བསྒྲུབ་བྱའི་ཆོས།

Sādhyadharma/ Predicate. That which is to be proved in relation to the subject in a given logical syllogism, e.g. 'impermanence' as the predicate when the given syllogism is, 'Take sound, it is impermanent because it is a functional thing'.

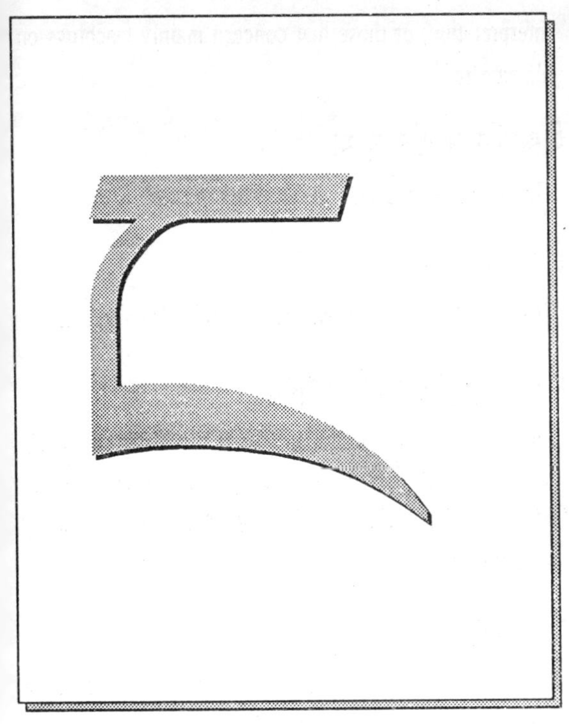

ང།

I; self; me. Mahāyāna philosophical systems do not assert the existence of an independent, self-existent, unchanging self, because if such a self were to exist, a person would be unchanging and would be unable to purify himself of fettering passions etc., and attain Buddhahood. What is accepted is a relative, impermanent, changeable, conscious-entity self, which is the continuation of one's former life, to this and future lives and is also the basis for the ripening of karma.

ང་རྒྱལ་བདུན།

Sapta māna/ The seven kinds of pride; the seven prides. 1. ང་རྒྱལ། māna/ pride, a feeling of arrogance or superiority; one of the six root delusions (see rtsa-nyon drug). 2. ཆེ་བའི་ང་རྒྱལ། mahāmāna/ exalted pride, the feeling of superiority amongst the equals. 3. ང་རྒྱལ་ལས་ཀྱང་ང་རྒྱལ། mānātimāna/ exaggerated pride, a puffed-up feeling that you are higher than the extremely high 4. ངའོ་སྙམ་པའི་ང་རྒྱལ། asmimāna/ egotistic pride, a feeling that you are the only one who can do some specific thing correctly; more philosophically, the pride that mistakenly appropriates any of the five aggregates as the 'I'. 5. མངོན་པའི་ང་རྒྱལ། abhimāna/ presumptuous pride, a feeling that you have realized something, or that you know something, when actually you do not. 6. ཅུང་ཟད་སྙམ་པའི་ང་རྒྱལ། ūnamāna/ modest pride, a feeling that though you may be equal with your friends you are a little better than them. 7. ལོག་པའི་ང་རྒྱལ། mithyāmāna/ perverted pride, a feeling of pride in your unwholesome habits and qualities.

ང་རྒྱལ་དང་གསལ་སྣང་།

The divine pride and vision. A basic requirement of tantric practices in which one tries to counteract one's ordinariness by generating divine pride of being the deity of the respective practice, and visualizing both oneself and the surroundings as the celestial mansion or abode.

ང་ཙམ།

The mere 'I'; the conventionally existent 'I' representing the person at a relative level.

ངག་གི་གནས་བརྒྱད།

The eight sound sources. 1. ཁོག་པ། uvular 2. མགྲིན་པ། guttural 3. རྐན། palatal 4. ལྕེ། tongue 5. སྣ། nasal 6. སོ། dental 7 སྡྲི་སོ། alveolar 8. མཆུ། labial.

ངན་འགྲོའི་སྡུག་བསྔལ།

Durgati dukha/ The sufferings of the unfortunate beings. The miseries and suffering encountered by the three types of beings in the lower realms. The suffering from heat and cold for hell beings, the suffering of hunger and thirst for hungry ghosts, and the suffering of becoming a beast of burden and exploitation for animals.

ངན་སྔགས།

Black magic. The art of casting spells and curses on others.

ངན་སོང་གི་གནས་བཅུ།

The ten states of bad rebirth. 1-8. states of the eight hot and cold hells (see tsha-dmyal brgyad and grang-dmyal brgad) 9. ཡི་དྭགས། hungry ghost state 10. དུད་འགྲོ animal state.

ངར་འཛིན།

Ahaṁkāra/ Ego-grasping; self-grasping; self-preoccupation. The concept of taking the mere 'I' upon oneself as the truly existent 'I' or 'self'.

ངལ་ཞིང་དུབ་པའི་མཐའ།

The extreme of ascetic practice; the extreme practice of self-mortification by depriving the body of the means of living. One of the extremes of living to be avoided by monks.

ངལ་གསོ་སྐོར་གསུམ།

The three cycles of relaxation. The three famous texts of practice composed by Longchen Rabjampa, a Nyingma master of the fourteenth century. 1. སེམས་ཉིད་ངལ་གསོ། *Relaxation of the Suchness of Mind*, relaxation through meditation on the suchness of mind 2. སྒྱུ་མ་ངལ་གསོ། *Relaxation of the Illusions*, relaxation through pacifying illusory appearances 3. བསམ་གཏན་ངལ་གསོ། *Relaxation of Samādhi*, relaxation through meditation on concentrations.

ངེས་དོན་གྱི་མདོ།

Nītārtha sūtra/ Definitive teachings. Those teachings of Buddha acceptable as they are which do not require interpretation, or those that concern mainly teachings on ultimate truth.

ངེས་དོན་གྱི་རྡོར་དྲིལ།

The definitive vajra and bell. The bliss and void.

ངེས་དོན་གྱི་ཨ་ཐུང་།

The subtle life-sustaining energy wind (srog-'dzin phra-ba).

ངེས་དོན་གྱི་དབང་པོ་གསུམ།

The three indispensable faculties; the three necessary faculties. 1. སྲོག་གི་དབང་པོ། faculty of life-force 2. ཡིད་ཀྱི་དབང་པོ། faculty of mind 3. བཏང་སྙོམས་ཀྱི་དབང་པོ། faculty of indifferent feeling.

ངེས་པ་ལྔ།

The five certainties; the five definite features of a Sambhogakāya Buddha. 1. གནས་ངེས་པ། certainty of place; that they always reside in the richly adorned Buddha-field called 'Heaven-below-non' 2. སྐུ་ངེས་པ། certainty of body; they are always adorned with thirty-two major and eighty minor marks (see mtshan bzang-po sum-bcu rta-gnyis & dpe-byed bzang-po brgyad-bcu) 3. དུས་ངེས་པ། certainty of time; that they will live for as long as saṁsāra is not emptied of sentient beings 4. ཆོས་ངེས་པ། certainty of teachings; that they always teach the greater vehicle doctrine 5. འཁོར་ངེས་པ། certainty of disciples; that they always teach to a circle of Ārya Bodhisattva disciples.

ངེས་པར་རྒྱུ་བ།

Niścāravāyu/ The definitely running wind energy. The wind energy for the cognitive faculty of touch. One of the five secondary energy winds (see yan-lag-gi rlung lnga).

ངེས་འབྱུང་།

Niryāṇa/ Renunciation; wish to be liberated. A thought of definite release from cyclic existence wishing freedom from the cycle of unending sufferings within saṁsāra. A prime necessity for carrying out a pure Dharma practice.

ངེས་འབྱུང་སྒྲུབ་པ།

The definitely occuring achievement. The path existing at the last three pure levels of the Bodhisattva grounds.

ངེས་འབྱུང་སྒྲུབ་པ་བརྒྱད།

The eight definitely occuring achievements; definitely occuring achievement to: 1. ཆེད་དུ་བྱ་བ་གསུམ་དུ་ངེས་པར་འབྱུང་བ། the three great objectives 2. མཉམ་པ་ཉིད་དུ་ངེས་པར་འབྱུང་བ། the samenesses 3. སེམས་ཅན་ཐམས་ཅད་ཀྱི་དོན་དུ་ངེས་པར་འབྱུང་བ། attain the purpose of all sentient beings 4. འབད་མེད་ལྷུན་གྲུབ་ཏུ་ངེས་པར་འབྱུང་བ། effortless achievement 5. མཐའ་ལས་འདས་པར་ངེས་པར་འབྱུང་བ། the state beyond extremes 6. ཐོབ་པའི་མཚན་ཉིད་དུ་ངེས་པར་འབྱུང་བ། the actuality of achievement 7. རྣམ་མཁྱེན་དུ་ངེས་པར་འབྱུང་བ། omniscient knowledge 8. ལམ་གྱི་ཡུལ་ཅན་གྱི་ངེས་པར་འབྱུང་བ། objects of the path.

ངེས་འབྱུང་སྒྱུ་སྤྲད།

Fictitious renunciation. Temporarily produced sense of renouncing worldly life that does not last.

ངེས་འབྱེད་ཆ་མཐུན་བཞི།

Catvāri nirvedhabhāgīya/ The four levels of the path of preparation. 1. དྲོད། uṣman/ heat level 2. རྩེ་མོ། mūrdha/ peak level 3. བཟོད་པ། kṣānti/ patience 4. ཆོས་མཆོག lankikāgradharma/ supreme Dharma.

ངེས་འབྱེད་ཡན་ལག

Nirvedhāṅgā/ Level of the path of preparation. One of the seventy topics of the perfection of wisdom training; the path of preparation at the level of aspirational Bodhicitta.

ངེས་ལེགས་ཀྱི་རྒྱུ།

Niḥśreyasa hetu/ The cause of definite goodness. The wisdom paths: primarily the wisdom understanding selflessness as cause for attainment of either liberation or full enlightenment.

ངོ་བོ་ཉིད།

Svabhāva/ A. The natural feature; natural identity. B. The mode of abidance of phenomena.

ངོ་བོ་ཉིད་ཀྱི་དགེ་བ།

The natural virtue. The eleven virtuous secondary mental factors (see dge-ba bcu-gcig).

ངོ་བོ་ཉིད་ཀྱི་མི་དགེ་བ།

The natural non-virtue. The six root delusions (see rtsa-nyon drug) and the near delusions (see nye-nyon nyi-shu) that are mental factors responsible for producing all negative behaviours.

ངོ་བོ་ཉིད་ཀྱི་ལུང་མ་བསྟན།

Svabhāvatāvyākṛta/ The natural unspecified phenomena. Those classes of phenomena that are neither virtuous nor non-virtuous by their nature. For instance, the elements, aggregates and sources of perception.

ངོ་བོ་ཉིད་སྐུ་གཉིས།

Svabhāvakāya/ The two types of nature truth body. The two bodies of a Buddha being totally pure of two stains: 1. རང་བཞིན་རྣམ་དག་གི་ངོ་བོ་ཉིད་སྐུ the natural truth body 2. གློ་བུར་

རྣམ་དག་གི་ངོ་བོ་ཉིད་སྐུ the truth body free of adventitious defilements. In other words, these are the emptiness of a Buddha's mind and the truth of cessation within the continuum of a Buddha.

ངོ་བོ་ཉིད་སྐུའི་མཚན་ཉིད་ལྔ།

The five features of a nature truth body. These are: 1. འདུས་མ་བྱས་པ། non-compositional 2. དབྱེར་མེད་པ། inseparable 3. མཐའ་གཉིས་སྤངས་པ། free of two extremes 4. སྒྲིབ་པ་གསུམ་ལས་གྲོལ་བ། free of three obscurations 5. རང་བཞིན་གྱིས་འོད་གསལ་བ། luminous by nature.

ངོ་བོ་ཉིད་སྐུའི་ཡོན་ཏན་ལྔ།

The five qualities of nature truth body. These are: 1. གཞལ་དུ་མེད་པ། incognizable 2. གྲངས་མེད་པ། infinite 3. བསམ་དུ་མེད་པ། inconceivable 4. མཉམ་པ་མེད་པ། incomparable 5. དྲི་མས་དག་པ། pure of stains.

ངོ་བོ་ཉིད་སྟོང་པ་ཉིད།

Svabhāva śūnyatā/ The emptiness of own nature. The lack of inherent identity of the reality of form and sound etc.

ངོ་བོ་ཉིད་མེད་པ་གསུམ།

The three identityless phenomena; the three identitylessnesses. 1. མཚན་ཉིད་ངོ་བོ་ཉིད་མེད་པ། laksana niḥsvabhāvatā/ identitylessness of characteristics 2. སྐྱེ་བ་ངོ་བོ་ཉིད་མེད་པ། utpatti niḥsvabhāvatā/ identitylessness of production 3. དོན་དམ་པ་ངོ་བོ་ཉིད་མེད་པ། paramārtha niḥsvabhāvatā/ identitylessness of ultimate phenomena.

ངོ་བོ་ཉིད་གསུམ།

The three natural existents. 1. ཀུན་དུ་བརྟགས་པའི་ངོ་བོ་ཉིད། parikalpita svabhāva/ imputed phenomena 2. གཞན་གྱི་དབང་གི་ངོ་བོ་ཉིད། paratantra svabhāva/ dependent phenomena 3. ཡོངས་སུ་གྲུབ་པའི་ངོ་བོ་ཉིད། parinispanna svabhāva/ thoroughly established phenomena; ultimate phenomena.

ངོ་མཚར་ལྔ་ལྡན་འཛམ་གླིང་གི་ནོར་འཛིན།

The five-fold marvels of this world's treasure holders. These are the five supreme worlds of this continent: 1. དབུས་སུ་རྒྱ་གར་རྡོ་རྗེ་གདན་ཤཱཀྱ་ཐུབ་པའི་ཞིང་། Bodhgaya of India in the centre, the land of Buddha Śākyamuni 2. ཤར་དུ་རྒྱ་ནག་རི་བོ་རྩེ་ལྔ་འཇམ་དཔལ་དབྱངས་ཀྱི་ཞིང་། Mt. Waute of China in the east, the land of Mañjuśrī 3. ལྷོ་ན་རི་བོ་པོ་ཏ་ལ་སྤྱན་རས་གཟིགས་ཀྱི་ཞིང་། Mt. Potala in the south, the land of Ārya Avalokiteśvara 4. ནུབ་ན་ཨོ་རྒྱན་མཁའ་འགྲོའི་གླིང་པད་མ་འབྱུང་གནས་ཀྱི་ཞིང་། Ogyan Dākinī land in the west, the land of Padmasambhava 5. བྱང་ན་ཤམ་བྷ་ལ་ཆོས་རྒྱལ་རིགས་ལྡན་གྱི་ཞིང་། Shambhala in the north, the land of Dharmarāja Kulikas.

དངོས་ཀྱི་ཉེར་ལེན།

The real fundamental cause. That cause which is responsible for producing its own substantial continuity as its result. For instance, a log of wood becomes the fundamental cause for producing coals from its burning.

དངོས་གྲུབ་བརྒྱད།

The eight spiritual feats; the eight types of higher attainments. 1. རལ་གྲི། invisibily from a sword 2. རིལ་བུ། pills 3. མིག་སྨན། eye-lotion 4. རྐང་མགྱོགས། swift footedness 5. བཅུད་ལེན། elixir/extracting the essence 6. མཁའ་སྤྱོད། walking in space 7. མི་སྣང་བ། invisibility 8. ས་འོག walking underground. When the list concerns nine feats the feat of subduing and benefitting other is added.

དངོས་གྲུབ་གཉིས།

Two types of attainments; two actual attainments. 1. མཆོག་གི་

དངོས་གྲུབ། supreme higher attainments 2. ཐུན་མོང་གི་དངོས་གྲུབ། common higher attainments.

དངོས་འགལ་གཉིས།

Two types of direct contradictions. 1. ཕན་ཚུན་སྤངས་འགལ། direct contradiction cancelling each other, e.g. is and is not 2. ལྷན་ཅིག་མི་གནས་འགལ། contradiction not abiding simultaneously, e.g. hot and cold.

དངོས་རྒྱུ།

Sājñātkāraṇa/ Direct cause; actual cause. A cause which generates its result directly, i.e. in the immediate next moment, e.g. fire as the cause of smoke.

དངོས་སྟོབས་རྗེས་དཔག

Vastubalānumāna/ Inferential cognition based on evidence.

དངོས་པོ།

Vastu/ Thing; impermanence; functional phenomenon.

དངོས་པོ་བརྒྱད།

Aṣṭa padārtha/ The eight topics of the *Ornament of Clear Realization* (abhisamayālaṃkāra). 1. རྣམ་མཁྱེན། sarvajñāna/ the omniscient mind 2. ལམ་ཤེས། mārgajñāna/ the knowledge of the paths 3. གཞི་ཤེས། vastujñāna/ the knowledge of the basis 4. རྣམ་རྫོགས་སྦྱོར་བ། sarvākārābhisaṁbodha/ the complete training of all aspects 5. རྩེ་མོའི་སྦྱོར་བ། mūrdhaprayoga/ the peak training 6. མཐར་གྱིས་སྦྱོར་བ། anupūrvaprayoga/ the serial training 7. སྐད་ཅིག་མའི་སྦྱོར་བ། kṣaṇikaprayoga/ the momentary training 8. འབྲས་བུ་ཆོས་སྐུ phalam dharmakāya/ the resultant truth body.

དངོས་པོ་སྟོང་པ་ཉིད།

Bhāva śūnyatā/ The emptiness of things; the emptiness of the five aggregates. One of the four summarising types of emptiness added to the sixteen to make up twenty types of emptiness (see stong-pa nyid nyi-shu).

དངོས་པོ་མེད་པ་སྟོང་པ་ཉིད།

Abhāva śūnyatā/ The emptiness of non-things; the emptiness of impermanent phenomena, e.g. emptiness of nirvāṇa. One of the eighteen emptinesses.

དངོས་པོ་མེད་པའི་ངོ་བོ་ཉིད་སྟོང་པ་ཉིད།

Abhāva svabhāva śūnyatā/ The emptiness of reality of that which lacks true existence. One of the sixteen emptinesses.

དངོས་མིང་།

Mūla nāma/ A real name. Any term or name initially given by an arbitrary designator to denominate a thing unmistakenly, e.g. the term 'vase'.

དངོས་པོ་ཡོད་པར་སྨྲ་བ།

Proponents of true existence. School of Buddhist and non-Buddhist philosophy asserting the truly existent nature of phenomena.

དངོས་པོའི་མཐའ་ལ་དམིགས་པ།

The object of the extreme of existence. One of the four objects of pervasion (see khyab-pa'i dmigs-pa bzhi). The assertion or acceptance of a limit of existence either of conventional reality or ultimate reality. For instance, the statement that all phenomena are included in the four noble truths and not otherwise. Or to say that all phenomena lack inherent existence and if not there is no other way of their existence.

དངོས་མེད་ངོ་བོ་ཉིད་ཀྱི་མཐར་གྱིས་སྦྱོར་བ།

Abhāva svabhāva pūrva prayoga/ The serial training in the entitylessness of phenomena. The Bodhisattva path from the

Mahāyāna path of accumulation upto the moment preceding the last instant of the path of meditation.

མངལ་སྐྱེས་ཁམས་དྲུག

The six constituents of a womb-born human of this world. 1. རུས་པ། asthi/ bone 2 རྐང་། majjā/ marrow and 3. ཁུ་བ། śukra/ regenerative fluid obtained from father 4. ཤ māṁsa/ flesh 5. ལྤགས་པ། tvak/ skin 6. ཁྲག rudhira/ blood obtained from mother. According to some other systems these are 1. ས། pṛthivī/ earth 2. ཆུ། aba/ water 3. མེ། teja/ fire 4. རླུང་། vāyu/ wind 5. རྩ། nāḍī/ energy-channels 6. ཐིག་ལེ། śukra/ essential drops.

མངལ་གྱི་གནས་སྐབས་ལྔ།

The five stages of growth in the womb; the five stages of foetal development in the womb. 1. མེར་མེར་པོ། the oral-shaped foetus 2. ནུར་ནུར་པོ། the viscous foetus 3. གོར་གོར་པོ། the soft fleshy foetus 4. འཁྲང་འགྱུར། the hard fleshy foetus 5. འབུར་པོ་ལྔ། the five protuberances—the two legs, two arms and head.

མངོན་འགྱུར།

Pratyakṣa/ Manifest phenomena. Obvious phenomena that can be cognized directly by sensory perception.

མངོན་འགྱུར་བཅུ།

The ten factors. The ten directly present factors for conducting a ceremony of full ordination. 1. སྟོན་པ་མངོན་འགྱུར། accepting the teacher 2. སངས་རྒྱས་མངོན་འགྱུར། accepting the Buddha 3. ཆོས་མངོན་འགྱུར། accepting the Dharma 4. མཁན་པོ་མངོན་འགྱུར། accepting the abbot 5. སློབ་དཔོན་མངོན་འགྱུར། accepting the assistant abbot 6. བསྙེན་པར་རྫོགས་པ་འདོད་པ་མངོན་འགྱུར། wishing to receive ordination 7. ཡོ་བྱད་མངོན་འགྱུར། the presence of monk's articles 8. ཡོངས་སུ་དག་པ་མངོན་འགྱུར། the performance of the ordination ceremony 9. གསོལ་བ་མངོན་འགྱུར། requesting the ceremony 10. ལས་མངོན་འགྱུར། activity (of monks).

མངོན་མཐོ།

Higher status; superior rebirth. The attainment of a more fortunate rebirth such as a fully endowed human being's or a god's. One of the two basic human aims for making progress on the spiritual paths to Buddhahood.

མངོན་འདོད་ཀྱི་དད་པ།

Longing faith. Aspirational faith longing to attain one's desired spiritual goal.

མངོན་པ་གཉིས།

A. The two abhidharmas: 1. དོན་དམ་པའི་ཆོས་མངོན་པ། paramārtha abhidharma/ the ultimate abhidharma, e.g. the uncontaminated wisdom understanding emptiness 2. བརྡར་བཏགས་པའི་ཆོས་མངོན་པ། saṁketikābhidharma/ the nominal abhidharma, e.g. the contaminated wisdom understanding emptiness and the *Abhidharma* texts. B. The two *Abhidharma* texts: 1. མངོན་པ་ཀུན་བཏུས། *Compendium of Knowledge* (abhidharmasamuccaya) by Ārya Asanga 2. མངོན་པ་མཛོད། *Treasure of Knowledge* (abhidharmakośa) by Ācārya Vasubandhu.

མངོན་པ་སྡེ་བདུན།

The seven treatises on phenomenology. The seven principal treatises of the Mūlasarvāsti-vādin school of philosophy. These are: 1. ཀཏྱའི་བུས་མཛད་པའི་ཡེ་ཤེས་ལ་འཇུག་པ། *Entering the Wisdom* by Katyayana 2. དབྱིག་གཉེན་གྱིས་མཛད་པའི་རབ་ཏུ་བྱེད་པ། *Thorough Discernment* by Vasumitra 3. བྲམ་ཟེ་ལྷ་སྐྱིད་ཀྱིས་མཛད་པའི་རྣམ་ཤེས་ཀྱི་ཚོགས། *Collection of Consciousnesses* by Brahmin Devotsava 4. ཤཱ་རིའི་བུས་མཛད་པའི་ཆོས་ཀྱི་ཚོགས། *Dharma Aggregates* by Śariputra 5.

མོའུ་འགལ་གྱི་བུས་མཛད་པའི་གདགས་པའི་བསྟན་བཅོས། *Treatise on Imputation* by Maudgalyāyana 6. གསུས་པོ་ཆེས་མཛད་པའི་འགྲོ་བའི་རྣམ་གྲངས། *Enumeration of Migrators* by Mahākausṭhila 7. གང་པོས་མཛད་པའི་ཁམས་ཀྱི་ཚོགས། *Collection of Spheres* by Pūrṇa.

མངོན་པའི་སྡེ་སྣོད།

Abhidharma piṭaka/ The basket of teaching on knowledge (abhidharmapiṭaka). That category of Buddha's teachings which reveals mainly the instruction on higher training of wisdom.

མངོན་པར་འགྲུབ་པའི་སྲིད་པ།

Formative existence. An epithet of the intermediate state of rebirth.

མངོན་པར་ཤེས་པ་དྲུག

Ṣaḍ abhijñā/ The six extra-sensory perceptions; the six clairvoyances; the six extraordinary knowledges. 1. རྫུ་འཕྲུལ་གྱི་མངོན་ཤེས། ṛddhi vidhi jñāna/ knowledge of miracles 2. ལྷའི་མིག་གི་མངོན་ཤེས། divyaṁ cakṣu/ knowledge of the divine eye 3. ལྷའི་རྣ་བའི་མངོན་ཤེས། divyaṃ śrotra jñānam/ knowlege of the divine ear 4. གཞན་སེམས་ཤེས་པའི་མངོན་ཤེས། paracitta jñānam/ knowledge of other's thoughts 5. སྔོན་གནས་རྗེས་དྲན་གྱི་མངོན་ཤེས། pūrva nivāsānusmṛti jñānam/ knowledge of recollecting past lives 6. ཟག་པ་ཟད་པའི་མངོན་ཤེས། āśrava kṣaya jñānam/ knowledge of the extinction of contamination.

མངོན་བྱང་གི་གསུང་།

The teachings through enlightened energy or blessings. One of the five teachings (see gsung-lnga) of a Buddha. According to the Nyingma tradition this refers to the simultaneous and natural establishment of all sounds within their source of reality that knows no cessation, also called the blessed teachings from intuitive awareness.

མངོན་བྱང་ལྔ།

A. The five modes of enlightenment; a generation stage practice of visualizing a deity. 1. ཟླ་བ་ལས་བྱང་ཆུབ་པ། enlightenment from moon 2. ཉི་མ་ལས་བྱང་ཆུབ་པ། enlightenment from sun 3. ས་བོན་ལས་བྱང་ཆུབ་པ། enlightenment from the seed syllable 4. ཕྱག་མཚན་ལས་བྱང་ཆུབ་པ། enlightenment from the deity's implements 5. སྐུ་རྫོགས་པ་ལས་བྱང་ཆུབ་པ། enlightenment from the entire entity of the body. B. The process of generating oneself into a fully enlightened deity: 1. ཟླ་བ་མེ་ལོང་ཡེ་ཤེས་ལས་བྱང་ཆུབ་པ། visualizing the moon as the mirror-like wisdom of a Buddha 2. ཉི་མ་མཉམ་ཉིད་ཡེ་ཤེས་ལས་བྱང་ཆུབ་པ། visualizing the sun as the wisdom of sameness of a Buddha 3. ས་བོན་དང་ཕྱག་མཚན་སོར་རྟོགས་ཡེ་ཤེས་ལས་བྱང་ཆུབ་པ། visualizing the seed syllable and implements of a deity as the wisdom of individual discrimination 4. ཐམས་ཅད་འདྲེས་པ་བྱ་གྲུབ་ཡེ་ཤེས་ལས་བྱང་ཆུབ་པ། visualizing the combination of all (moon, sun, seed syllable and implements) as the wisdom of accomplishments 5. སྐུ་རྫོགས་པ་ཆོས་དབྱིངས་ཡེ་ཤེས་ལས་བྱང་ཆུབ་པ། visualizing the full-fledged body of a Buddha as the wisdom of reality.

མངོན་སུམ་བཞི།

The four direct perceptions. 1. indriya pratyakṣa/ sensory direct perception 2. citta pratyakṣa/ mental direct perception 3. svasaṁveda pratyakṣa/ direct perception of self-awareness 4. yogi pratyakṣa/ yogic direct perception.

མངོན་སུམ་འཁྲུལ་རྒྱུ་ཅན།

Pratyakṣa bhrānta hetu/ Deceptive direct perception. A direct perception that is affected by a deceptive cause.

མངོན་སུམ་བཅད་ཤེས།

Paricchinna pratyakṣa/ Subsequent direct perception. A direct perception following the original or the first instance of direct cognition.

མངོན་སུམ་ལྟར་སྣང་།

Pratyakṣābhāsa/ Apparent direct perceptions. A direct perception that is mistaken with respect to its appearing object (snang-yul), e.g. the inferential understanding cognizing sound as impermanent.

མངོན་སུམ་ལྟར་སྣང་བདུན།

Seven apparent direct perceptions. 1. འཁྲུལ་བའི་རྟོག་པ། the distorted thought 2. ཀུན་རྫོབ་པའི་རྟོག་པ། the conventional thought 3. རྗེས་དཔག་གི་རྟོག་པ། the inferential thought 4. རྗེས་དཔག་ལས་བྱུང་བའི་རྟོག་པ། the thought resulting from inferential cognition 5. དྲན་པའི་རྟོག་པ། the recollecting thought 6. མངོན་འདོད་ཀྱི་རྟོག་པ། the speculative thought 7. རྟོག་མེད་ལོག་པ། non-conceptual wrong perception.

མངོན་སུམ་ལྟར་སྣང་རབ་རིབ་ཅན།

Taimira pratyakṣābhāsa/Blurred apparent direct perception.

མངོན་སུམ་ཡིད་མ་གཏད།

Absent-minded direct perception; inattentive direct perception.

ལྔ་བརྒྱ་ཕྲག་བཅུ།

The ten phases of five hundred years each. This refers to five thousand years being the life span of Buddha Śākyamuni's teachings divided into ten phases of five hundred years each. These are: 1. དགྲ་བཅོམ་པ་དང་། the Arhat period 2. ཕྱིར་མི་འོང་བ། the period of the Never-returner 3. རྒྱུན་ཞུགས་ཀྱི་འབྲས་བུ་ཐོབ་པ་སྟེ་ཡེ་ཤེས་ཁོང་དུ་ཆུད་པའི་ལེའུ་གསུམ། the period the Stream-winners—all known as the three phases of realization. 4. ལྷག་མཐོང་དང་། the wisdom period 5. ཏིང་ངེ་འཛིན། the period of meditative concentration 6. ཚུལ་ཁྲིམས་ཏེ་བསླབ་པའི་ལེའུ་གསུམ། the period of moral discipline known as the three phases of three trainings. 7. མངོན་པ་དང་། the period of the knowledge 8. མདོ་སྡེ། the period of discourses 9. འདུལ་བ་སྟེ་ལུང་གི་ལེའུ་གསུམ། the period of monastic discipline known as the three periods of oral transmission 10. ལྟ་སྤྱོད་རྣལ་མ་མེད་པར་རབ་བྱུང་གི་རྟགས་ཙམ་འཛིན་པའི་ལེའུ། the period of corrupt moral discipline in which only a corrupt view, corrupt philosophy and corrupt monastic discipline shall survive.

ལྔ་ལྡན་གྱི་ཁྲིད།

The five-fold transmission on Mahāmudrā. A lineage of transmission of the Mahāmudrā practice for beginners, as formulated by the great Kagyud master Drigung Kyopa Jigten Gonpo (1143-1217). 1. བྱང་ཆུབ་ཀྱི་སེམས་སྒོམ་པ། meditation on bodhicitta 2. རང་ལུས་ལྷར་སྒོམ་པ། meditation on one's body as that of a deity 3. བླ་མ་ལྷར་སྒོམ་པ། meditation on guru devotion 4. མི་རྟོག་པའི་ལྟ་བ་སྒོམ་པ། meditation on the non-conceptual view 5. བསྔོ་སྨོན་གྱིས་རྒྱས་འདེབས་པ། dedication at the end.

སྔ་དར།

The Early Spread; the Early Propagation. The early spread of Buddhism in Tibet beginning from 7th century and its propagation during the reign of the three religious kings of Tibet until the eclipse of Buddha's teaching during the reign of King Lang Darma.

སྔགས།

Mantra; words of power; incantation; mind-protector. Formulae of words chanted as powers; very often this word 'sngags' is used as a synonym for tantra.

སྔགས་ཀྱི་ཆེ་བ་བཞི།

The four distinguishing features of Tantra. 1. མ་རྨོངས་པའི་ཁྱད་པར། clear and unconfusing 2. ཐབས་མང་བའི་ཁྱད་པར། manifold methods 3. དཀའ་བ་མེད་པའི་ཁྱད་པར། easier to practice 4. དབང་པོ་རྣོ་བའི་ཁྱད་པར། requires sharp intellect.

སྔགས་ཀྱི་ཐེག་པ།

Mantrayāna/ The Mantrayāna. The secret mantra vehicle meant for persons of highly sharp faculty who aspire to taking the results as a path and simultaneous actualization of both the causes and results of one's practice.

སྔགས་ཀྱི་གནས་སྐབས་བཞི།

The four states of tantric experience. 1. གཉིད་སད་པའི་གནས་སྐབས། awaking state 2. རྨི་ལམ་གྱི་གནས་སྐབས། dream state 3. གཉིད་མཐུག་གི་གནས་སྐབས། state of deep sleep 4. བཞི་པའི་གནས་སྐབས། the fourth state (old-aged stage).

སྔགས་སྡེ་གསུམ།

The three classes of mantra; three types of mantra incantation: 1. གསང་སྔགས། secret mantra symbolizing the union of both method and wisdom paths 2. རིག་སྔགས། wisdom mantra symbolizing the method aspect of the paths 3. གཟུངས་སྔགས། retention (dhāraṇi) mantra symbolizing the wisdom aspect of the paths.

སྔགས་སྡོམ།

Mantra saṁvara/ The tantric vows (see rta-ltung bco-bryag and nyes-byed zhi-cu zhe-drug).

སྔགས་ཕྱོགས་ཀྱི་ཡན་ལག་བདུན།

The seven limb practices of the tantric tradition. 1. ཕྱག་འཚལ་བ། prostration 2. མཆོད་པ། offering 3. བཤགས་པ། confession 4. རྗེས་སུ་ཡི་རང་། rejoicing 5. སྐྱབས་སུ་འགྲོ་བ། taking refuge 6. བྱང་ཆུབ་མཆོག་ཏུ་སེམས་བསྐྱེད་པ། generation of the mind of enlightenment 7. བསྔོ་བའི་ཡན་ལག dedication.

སྔགས་རམས་པ།

Tantric graduate. A geshe who has also earned a tantric degree from any of the two tantric colleges in the Gelug system of monastic education.

སྔོན་དུས་ཀྱི་སྲིད་པ།

Pūrvanivāsa/ The prior existence. The period of existence between the second moment of connecting to one's new life in the womb and death.

བསྔོ་བ་སྒོམ་ལམ།

Pariṇāma bhāvanā mārga/ The path of meditation on dedication. The Mahāyāna path of meditation which transforms 'root of virtues' of self and others for the attainment of complete enlightenment.

བསྔོ་བ་སྒོམ་ལམ་བཅུ་གཉིས།

The twelve paths of meditation on dedication. 1. དགེ་བའི་རྩ་བ་ཡོངས་སུ་བསྔོ་བའི་བསྔོ་བ། thorough dedication of the roots of virtue 2. དམིགས་མེད་རྣམ་པ་ཅན་གྱི་བསྔོ་བ། dedication free from the apprehension of a truly existent nature 3. ཕྱིན་ཅི་མ་ལོག་པའི་མཚན་ཉིད་ཅན་གྱི་བསྔོ་བ། dedication marked by the absence of wrong views 4. དོན་དམ་པར་ངོ་བོ་ཉིད་ཀྱིས་དབེན་པའི་བསྔོ་བ། dedication devoid of an ultimate truly existent nature 5. སངས་རྒྱས་དང་བསོད་ནམས་རང་བཞིན་དྲན་པའི་བསྔོ་བ། dedication recollecting the Buddha, merits and the ultimate nature 6. ཐབས་ལ་མཁས་པའི་བསྔོ་བ། dedication that is skillful in means 7. མཚན་མ་མེད་པའི་བསྔོ་བ། dedication without signs 8. སངས་རྒྱས་ཀྱི་སྣང་ཞིང་དགྱེས་པ་ཞེས་བྱ་བའི་བསྔོ་བ། dedication enjoined or permitted by the Buddhas 9. ཁམས་གསུམ་དུ་མ་གཏོགས་པའི་བསྔོ་བ། dedication beyond the three realms 10. བསོད་ནམས་ཆེན་པོ་འབྱུང་བའི་བསྔོ་བ་ཆུང་ངུ། lesser dedication giving rise to great merits 11. བསོད་ནམས་ཆེན་པོ་འབྱུང་བའི་བསྔོ་བ་འབྲིང་། middling dedication giving rise to great merits 12. བསོད་ནམས་ཆེན་པོ་འབྱུང་བའི་བསྔོ་བ་ཆེན་པོ། great dedication giving rise to great merits.

ཅང་ཏེའུ།

Hand drum. A small drum usually identified with the ones held in the hands of a god or goddess as their implement.

ཅི་ཡང་མེད་པའི་སྐྱེ་མཆེད།

Ākiṁcanyāyatana/ The domain of nothingness. One of the four means of emanation within the formless realm; the domain of concentration within the formless realm where a person remains fixed to the idea that there exists nothing other than consciousness because of not seeing anything, and thus remains fully absorbed in it as one's object of meditation.

ཅུང་ཟད་ལྐོག་གྱུར།

Slightly hidden phenomena; slightly obscure phenomena, e.g. impermanence.

ཅོ་འདྲི་བ།

Viḍambanā/ To blame; reproach; scoff at. Also refers to a sense of competetiveness.

གཅིག་དུ་བྲལ།

Neither being one nor many. A logical way of analyzing the mode of existence of phenomena that cannot be beyond being one or many.

གཅེར་བུ་པ།

Digambara/ Jain; Lit: the Naked Ones. Proponents of non-Buddhist tenets who assert that all objects of knowledge are included in nine categories: 1. སྲོག prāṇa/ life-force 2. ཟག་པ། āstrava/ contamination 3. སྡོམ་པ། saṁvara/ vows 4. ངེས་པར་རྒ་བ། avaśyajarā/ old-agedness 5. འཆིང་བ། bandhana/ bindings (delusions) 6. ལས། karma 7. སྡིག་པ། akalyāṇa/ non-virtue 8. བསོད་ནམས། puṇya/ merits 9. ཐར་པ། mokṣa/ liberation. They believe that liberation can be attained through resorting to practices of asceticism such as going naked, not speaking and so forth.

གཅོད།

Cutting-off ritual. The practice primarily common to the Zhi-byed tradition of Tibetan Buddhism formed by Phadampa Sangye. The term is derived from the nature of the instructions on which this practice is based; that love, compassion and bodhicitta sever selfishness; the view of emptiness severs the root of cyclic existence (saṁsāra); and the common practices sever the four demonic forces (see below).

གཅོད་ལུགས་ཀྱི་བདུད་བཞི།

The four demonic forces of the cutting-off ritual. 1. ཐོགས་བཅས། obstructive forces 2. ཐོགས་མེད། non-obstructive forces 3. དགའ་སྤྱོད། joyous forces 4. སྙེམས་བྱེད། haughty forces.

བཅད་ཤེས།

Subsequent cognition; re-cognition. An awareness which is not a new correct perception or conception, but apprehends what has already been apprehended in its stream of cognition, e.g. the second moment of visual perception of a vase.

བཅས་པའི་ཁ་ན་མ་ཐོ་བ།

Pratikṣepana sāvadya/ Proscribed non-virtue; declared misdeed; misdeed by decree. For instance, actions such as eating after noon, drinking intoxicants, etc., that are declared to be non-virtuous for monks and nuns by Buddha, although these do not constitute non-virtue by nature.

བཅས་རང་གི་ཉེས་པ།

The misdeed by nature and proscription (see bcas-pa'i kha-na ma tho-ba and rang-bzhin gyi kha-na ma-tho-ba).

བཅུད་ལེན།

Rasāyana/ The art of elixir; extracting the essence. An austure practice by which a practitioner temporarily avoids eating gross food and sustains himself by regularly consuming consecrated pills and engaging in meditation.

བཅོ་ལྔ་མཆོད་པ།

The prayer festival on the 15th. The celebration of Buddha's defeat of the six non-Buddhist teachers (see mu-stegs-kyi ston-pa drug) on the 15th of the first Tibetan month. Tsong Khapa marked this event as the Great Prayer Festival.

བཅོམ་ལྡན་འདས།

Bhagavat/ The Victorious Conqueror; Supramundane Victor; Buddhas.

བཅོས་མ།

Kṛtrima/ Artificial; contrived. A temporary artificial state of mind generated or created within an enthusiastic virtuous state of mind.

བཅོས་མིན་སྙིང་རྗེ།

Akṛtrima karuṇā/ Natural compassion; uncontrived compassion; spontaneous compassion.

ལྕགས་མཁར།

A. Iron house or fort. B. A wrathful tantric propitiation ritual of throwing sacrificial cake with nine or sixteen edges invoking Yamarāja Chagkhar.

ཆ་ཅན་ཆ་མེད།

Part and partless; divisible and indivisible.

ཆ་མཉམ་པའི་ཐེ་ཚོམ།

Sambhāgiya vicikitsā/ Evenly balanced doubt. An indecisive wavering evenly balanced between correct and incorrect conclusions; one of the three types of doubt (see the-tsom gsum).

ཆ་དང་ཆ་ཅན།

Parts and that consisting of parts; pair and one of the pairs.

ཆགས་པའི་བསྐལ་པ།

Aeon of formation. The twenty intermediate aeons covering the period of time since the formation of the outer world until the birth of one inhabitant in the realm of the hell-without-respite.

ཆགས་བྲལ་ལྔ།

The five types of freedom from attachment. The five different aspects of being free of attachment. 1. ཕྱོགས་གཅིག་ལ་ཆགས་བྲལ་བ། freedom from being attached to one aspect 2. མཐའ་དག་ལ་ཆགས་བྲལ་བ། freedom from being attached to all 3. རྟོགས་པའི་ཆགས་བྲལ་བ། freedom from being attached to realizations 4. གནོན་པའི་ཆགས་བྲལ་བ། freedom from attachment of having subdued 5. ལེགས་པར་སྟོན་པའི་ཆགས་བྲལ་བ། freedom from being attached to elegant teachings.

ཆང་བུ།

A leftover portion of food, squeezed between the fingers and offered to hungry ghosts; an after-meal rule of giving the remainders to spirits that Buddha has prescribed for monks and nuns.

ཆད་ལྟ།

Uccheda dṛṣṭi/ View of nihilism; nihilism. For instance, asserting the non-existence of the cause and effect, former and future lives, severence or exhaustion of existence at death, etc.

ཆད་སྟོང་།

Uccheda śūnyatā/ Nihilistic emptiness. The emptiness upon realization of which rejects the existence of its base.

ཆད་མཐའ།

Ucchedānta/ The extreme of nihilism. A kind of belief that something validly exitent is non-existent.

ཆུ་བོ་བཞི།

A. The four torrents. 1. སྲིད་པའི་ཆུ་བོ། saṁsāra/ torrent of cyclic existence 2. སྲིད་པའི་ཆུ་བོ། tṛṣ/ torrent of craving 3. མ་རིག་པའི་ཆུ་བོ། avidyā/ torrent of ignorance 4. ལྟ་བའི་ཆུ་བོ།

dṛṣṭi/ torrent of wrong view. B. The four big rivers. 1. གང྄་ཱ། Ganges 2. པཀྵུ། Indus/ Sindhu 3. སི་ཏཱ། Brahmaputra/ Pakshu 4. སིནྡྷུ། Yamuna.

ཆུ་བོའི་རྒྱུན་ལྟ་བུའི་སེམས་བསྐྱེད།

Bodhimind like a flowing river. The mind of enlightenment primarily in accord with the path within the mental continuum of a Buddha in his physical form.

ཆུ་དབང་ལྔ།

The five types of water initiations. 1. དཀྱིལ་འཁོར་གྱི་ཕྱིའི་འཇུག་སྒོའི་བུམ་པ། vase initiation concerning the rites outside the mandala 2. དཀྱིལ་འཁོར་གཉིས་པར་ལྷ་ཐམས་ཅད་ཀྱི་བུམ་པ། vase initiation of all the concerned deities within the mandala 3. གསུམ་པར་ཉན་རང་གི་བུམ་པ། vase initiation of the hearers and solitary realizers 4. བཞི་པར་བྱང་སེམས་ཀྱི་བུམ་པ། vase initiation of the Bodhisattvas 5. ལྔ་པར་སངས་རྒྱས་ཀྱི་བུམ་པ། victorious vase initiation of the Buddha.

ཆུ་ཡན་ལག་བརྒྱད་ལྡན།

Eight qualities of good water; a water possessing the eight sublime qualities. 1. བསིལ་བ། śīta/ cool 2. ཡང་བ། lagu/ light/ refreshing 3. ཞིམ་པ། svāduka/ sweet/ tasty 4. འཇམ་པ། komala/ smooth 5. དྭངས་བ། prasanna/ clear 6. དྲི་ང་བ་མེད་པ། nirāmagandha/ free of bad odour 7. འཐུང་ན་མགྲིན་པ་ལ་བདེ་བ། kanṭhasukha/ soothing to throat to drink 8. འཐུང་ན་ལྟོ་བ་ལ་བདེ་བ། udarasukha/ harmless to stomach to drink.

ཆུ་རིགས་བདུན།

Seven types of water resources. 1. ཆར་ཆུ། rain water 2. གངས་ཆུ། snow water 3. ཆུ་ཀླུང་གི་ཆུ། river water 4. ཆུ་མིག་གི་ཆུ། pond water 5. ཁྲོན་པའི་ཆུ། well water 6. བ་ཚྭ་ཅན་གྱི་ཆུ། salty water 7. ཤིང་གི་རྩ་ཆུ། water from the roots of trees.

ཆེ་བའི་ང་རྒྱལ།

Mahāmāna/ Pride of superiority. The feeling that one, in general, is equal to all, in general, yet, is superior in one particular respect.

ཆེ་བའི་ཡོན་ཏན་བདུན།

The seven qualities of greatness; the seven superior features. 1. རིགས་བཟང་བ། good family 2. གཟུགས་བཟང་བ། good physical features 3. གཉེན་འཁོར་གཡོག་འཛོམས་པ། big circle of kith and kin or attendants 4. འབྱོར་པ་ཆེ་བ། wealthy 5. དབང་ཐང་ཆེ་བ། powerful 6. ཤེས་རབ་ཆེ་བ། great wisdom 7. ལུས་སྟོབས་དང་ལྡན་པ། strong body.

ཆེད་དུ་བརྗོད་པའི་སྡེ།

Udānavarga/ Impersonal utterances of Buddha's teachings; the class of impersonal teachings. Those categories of Buddha's teachings uttered not for specific disciples but in general without being requested for the purpose of flourishing of the Buddha Dharma.

ཆེན་པོ་ལྔ།

The five greatnesses; the five great qualities of space. 1. གཟུགས་མེད་པ། formless 2. ཐོགས་པ་མེད་པ། unobstructive 3. རྟག་པ། permanent 4. མི་འགྱུར་བ། unchangeable 5. མི་འཕོ་བ། untransforming.

ཆེན་པོ་སྟོང་པ་ཉིད།

Mahā śūnyatā/ The great emptiness; the emptiness of that which is great. Lack of true and independent existence of the ten directions. One of the sixteen emptinesses.

ཆེན་པོ་བདུན།

The seven greatnesses; the seven features of a true Mahāyānist. 1. དམིགས་པ་ཆེན་པོ། great objective 2. སྒྲུབ་པ་

ཆེན་པོ། great practice 3. ཡེ་ཤེས་ཆེན་པོ། great wisdom 4. བརྩོན་འགྲུས་ཆེན་པོ། great effort 5. ཐབས་ལ་མཁས་པ་ཆེན་པོ། great skill in means 6. ཡང་དག་སྒྲུབ་པ་ཆེན་པོ། great perfect accomplishment 7. ཕྲིན་ལས་ཆེན་པོ། great enlightened activity.

ཆོ་ག་གསུམ་བསྐྱེད།

The three stages of generating a deity. The practice of meditation by means of visualizing a deity's seed syllable on a lotus, sun or other cushions, from which there arises the implements and the mantric syllable; the complete transformation of which then enables a person to generate the concerned deity complete with all features.

ཆོ་འཕྲུལ་དུས་ཆེན།

The day of great miracles. The celebration of Buddha's taming of devils and spirits from the first to fifteenth of the first Tibetan month. Je Tsong Khapa instituted the Great Prayer Festival during this period.

ཆོ་འཕྲུལ་བཞི།

Catvāri prātihārya/ The four miraculous ways; the four meditative concentrations according to yoga tantra. 1. ཏིང་ངེ་འཛིན་གྱི་ཆོ་འཕྲུལ། miracles of concentration 2. བྱིན་གྱིས་རློབས་པའི་ཆོ་འཕྲུལ། miracles of blessings 3. དབང་བསྐུར་བའི་ཆོ་འཕྲུལ། miracles of empowerment 4. མཆོད་པའི་ཆོ་འཕྲུལ། miracles of offering rites.

ཆོ་འཕྲུལ་གསུམ།

The three miraculous ways of a Buddha. 1. སྐུ་རྫུ་འཕྲུལ་གྱི་ཆོ་འཕྲུལ། miracles of body 2. གསུང་ཀུན་དུ་བརྗོད་པའི་ཆོ་འཕྲུལ། miracles of speech 3. ཐུགས་རྗེས་སུ་བསྟན་པའི་ཆོ་འཕྲུལ། miracles of mind.

ཆོས།

Dharma. A. Teachings of Buddha. B. A phenomenon.

ཆོས་ཀྱི་རྐང་པ་བཞི།

The four legs of Dharma. The division of periods in view of the life span of Buddha's teachings, which are: 1. རྫོགས་ལྡན། the perfected aeon (see bskal-pa rdzogs-ldan) 2. གསུམ་ལྡན། the threefold aeon (see bskal-pa gsum ldan) 3. གཉིས་ལྡན། the twofold aeon (see bskal-pa gnyis ldan) 4. རྩོད་ལྡན། the quarrelsome aeon (see rtsod-ldan gyi dus).

ཆོས་ཀྱི་སྐྱེ་མཆེད་ཀྱི་གཟུགས།

Dharmāyatana rūpa/ The form of the source of mental faculty. The objects for generating the perception of mental faculty, e.g. fine particles and the physical body of a dream state.

ཆོས་ཀྱི་སྐྱེ་མཆེད་ཀྱི་གཟུགས་ལྔ།

The five types of forms of the spheres of phenomena. 1. བསྡུས་པ་ལས་གྱུར་བའི་གཟུགས། compounded form 2. མངོན་པར་སྐབས་ཡོད་པའི་གཟུགས། occasionally manifesting form 3. ཡང་དག་པར་བླངས་པ་ལས་བྱུང་བའི་གཟུགས། form arising from vows and precepts 4. ཀུན་བརྟགས་པའི་གཟུགས། imputed form 5. དབང་འབྱོར་བའི་གཟུགས། conjured form.

ཆོས་ཀྱི་ཁམས།

Dharma dhātu/ The faculty of dharma. One of the eighteen spheres (see khams bco-brgyad), feeling, recognition, perception, non-revelatory form and all non-compositional factors, i.e. non-functional phenomena.

ཆོས་ཀྱི་ཁམས་ཀྱི་འདུས་མ་བྱས་བརྒྱད།

Aṣṭa dharma dhātu asaṁskṛta/ The eight non-compositional factors of the dharma constituents. 1. དགེ་བའི་དེ་བཞིན་ཉིད། kuśala tattva/ the virtuous reality 2. མི་དགེ་བའི་དེ་བཞིན་ཉིད།

akuśala tattva/ the non-virtuous reality 3. ལུང་མ་བསྟན་གྱི་དེ་བཞིན་ཉིད། avyākṛtya tattva/ the unspecified reality 4. ནམ་མཁའ། akāśa/ space 5. སོ་སོར་བརྟགས་འགོག pratisamkhyā nirodha/ the analytical cessation 6. སོ་སོར་བརྟགས་མིན་གྱི་འགོག་པ། apratisamkhyā nirodha/ the non-analytical cessation 7. མི་གཡོ་བའི་འགོག་པ། acala nirodha/ the immutable cessation 8. འདུ་ཤེས་དང་ཚོར་བ་འགོག་པ། saṁjñā vedanā nirodha/ the cessation of perception and feeling.

ཆོས་ཀྱི་བདག་མེད།

Dharma nairātmya/ Selflessness of phenomena. In its highest sense it is the lack of inherent existence of phenomena other than persons. There are two types—the gross and subtle selflessness of phenomena.

ཆོས་ཀྱི་བདག་འཛིན།

Grasping at the self of phenomena. The misconception of phenomena as having true existence. It has two kinds: 1. innate grasping at the self of phenomena 2. intellectual grasping at the self of phenomena.

ཆོས་ཀྱི་སྡོམ་བཞི།

The four seals of Dharma (see lta-ba bkar-btags-kyi phyag-rgya bzhi).

ཆོས་ཀྱི་དབྱིངས་ཀྱི་ཡེ་ཤེས།

Dharmadhātu jñāna/ The primordial wisdom cognizing the reality of phenomena. The lack of inherent nature or the emptiness of the five aggregates.

ཆོས་དཀོན་མཆོག

Dharma ratna/ The Dharma Jewel; the doctrine. The true cessation and path within the mental continuum of an Ārya; conventionally it is represented by the scriptures and books on the teachings of Buddha.

ཆོས་སྐུ།

Dharmakāya/ The Truth Body; dharmakāya. The foundation of all qualities, the source of the four kāyas; the impersonal Buddha. It has two kinds—the natural truth body and the wisdom truth body of a Buddha.

ཆོས་སྐུའི་ཆོས་བཞི།

Catvāri dharmakāya dharmāḥ/ The four topics or features of the Truth Body. One of the seventy topics of the perfection of wisdom teachings which are the four aspects of dharmakāya or a Buddha's being: 1. ངོ་བོ་ཉིད་སྐུ svabhāvakāya/ nature truth body 2. ཡེ་ཤེས་ཆོས་སྐུ jñānakāya/ wisdom truth body 3. ལོངས་སྐུ། saṁbhogakāya/ complete enjoyment body 4. སྤྲུལ་སྐུ nirmāṇakāya/ emanation body.

ཆོས་ཁམས་བཅུ་དྲུག

The sixteen faculties of dharma spheres. According to the *Compendium of Knowledge* (abhidharmasamuccaya) these are: 1-5. ཆོས་ཀྱི་སྐྱེ་མཆེད་པའི་གཟུགས་ལྔ། the five types of forms of the spheres of phenomena (see chos-kyo skye-mched-pa'i gzugs-lnga) 6. ཚོར་བ། the aggregate of feeling 7. འདུ་ཤེས། the aggregate of recognition 8. འདུ་བྱེད། the aggregate of perception 9-16. འདུས་མ་བྱས་བརྒྱད། the eight types of non-compositional factors (see 'dus-ma byas brgyad).

ཆོས་ཁམས་བདུན།

The seven faculties of dharma spheres. According to the *Treasure of Knowledge* (abhidharmakośa) these are: 1. ཚོར་བའི་ཕུང་པོ། the aggregate of feeling 2. འདུ་ཤེས་ཀྱི་ཕུང་པོ། the aggregate of recognition 3. འདུ་བྱེད་ཀྱི་ཕུང་པོ། the aggregate of perception 4. རྣམ་པར་རིག་བྱེད་མིན་པའི་གཟུགས། non revelatory form 5-7. འདུས་མ་བྱས་གསུམ། the three non compositional factors (see 'dus-ma byas gsum).

ཆོས་གོས་རྣམ་གསུམ།

The three kinds of Dharma robes. 1. ཆོས་གོས། བླ་གོས། 'chogo'—the yellow upper robe which can be worn by all monks and nuns 2. སྣམ་སྦྱར། 'namja'—yellow upper robe worn only by fully ordained monks 3. མཐང་གོས། 'thango'—monks' and nuns' lower robe.

ཆོས་རྒྱལ་མྱ་ངན་མེད།

Dharmarāja Aśoka/ The Indian king Aśoka, 3rd century B.C., who came into contact with Buddhist teachings after repenting the widespread slaughter and misery he had caused in numerous wars. In the later part of his life, he became a devout Buddhist and propagated Buddha's teaching far and wide.

ཆོས་བརྒྱད་རོ་སྙོམས།

The equal taste of eight worldly concerns (see 'jig-rten chos-brgyad). The fact that one has freed oneself of these concerns and thus makes and does not effect one's way of life.

ཆོས་ལྔ།

Pañca dharmāḥ/ Five phenomena; five features. 1. མིང་། nāma/ name 2. མཚན་མ། nimitta/ marks 3. རྣམ་རྟོག vikalpa/ conceptualization 4. དེ་བཞིན་ཉིད། tathatā/ reality 5. མི་རྟོག་ཡེ་ཤེས། akalpanā jñāna/ non-conceptual wisdom.

ཆོས་མངོན་པ།

Abhidharma/ The knowledge. The set of teachings and treatises concerning the training of higher wisdom and the study of metaphysics and cosmology.

ཆོས་ཅན།

Dharmin/ Subject. Subject of the proposition in a dialectical syllogism standing for a subject on which the thesis is established, e.g. 'sound' is the subject when the thesis 'sound is impermanent' is to be proved in a correct logical syllogism.

ཆོས་ཅན་བརྗོད་པའི་སྒྲ།

The statement expressing the subject. A statement in which the subject of concern for both the speaker and listener is presented as the basis of discussion, e.g. the statement, 'sound is a thing'. Here 'sound' is shown as the basis of a (functional) thing but does not exclude other qualities of sound such as its being impermanent and an object of knowledge.

ཆོས་བརྗོད་ཀྱི་སྒྲ།

A statement expressing quality. A statement in which the subject of concern for both the speaker and listener is presented as the quality of discussion, e.g. the statement, 'impermanence of sound'. This statement not only distinguishes impermanence of sound from the impermanence of others, such as a vase or pillar, but also excludes discussing the qualities of other phenomena within the topic of discussion.

ཆོས་ཉིད།

Dharmatā/ Intrinsic nature; suchness; empty nature.

ཆོས་ཉིད་ཀྱི་རིག་པ།

The reasoning of common sense. One of the four types of reasoning (see rigs-pa bzhi). Well-known common notions that are naturally accepted as true, e.g. rivers always flow downward and fire blazes upward.

ཆོས་ཐམས་ཅད་སྟོང་པ་ཉིད།

Sarvadharma śūnyatā/ The emptiness of all phenomena. The lack of true existence of outer and inner phenomena, i.e. the fact that these being impermanent, miserable, empty and lack self-identity are non-inherent in nature.

ཆོས་བདུན་ལྡན་གྱི་མི།

Humans possessing seven features. The qualities of human beings living in this world during the first aeon. 1. བརྫུས་ཏེ་སྐྱེ་བ། they were born miraculously 2. ཚེ་ལོ་དཔག་མེད་ཐུབ་པ། enjoyed an immeasurable life-span 3. དབང་པོ་ཀུན་ཚང་བ། possessed perfect sense faculties 4. རང་ལུས་འོད་ཀྱིས་ཁྱབ་པ། had self-illuminated body 5. མཚན་བཟང་རྗེས་མཐུན་གྱིས་བརྒྱན་པ། possessed similitudes of the major and minor marks of a Buddha 6. ཟས་རགས་པ་ལ་མ་བརྟེན་པར་དགའ་བའི་ཟས་ཀྱིས་འཚོ་བ། lived on the food of joy without eating gross food 7. རྫུ་འཕྲུལ་གྱིས་ནམ་མཁའ་ལ་འཕུར་བ། miraculously flew in the sky.

ཆོས་དྲན་པ་ཉེར་བཞག

Dharma smṛtyūpasthāna/ Close contemplation of phenomena. The meditation on the emptiness and selflessness of the thoroughly purified and negative aspects of phenomena.

ཆོས་སྤྱོད་བཅུ།

Daśa dharmacaryaḥ/ The ten spiritual trainings; the ten monastic trainings. 1. ཡི་གེ་འབྲི་བ། lekhanā/ writing 2. མཆོད་པ་འབུལ་བ། pūjanā/ worshipping 3. སྦྱིན་པ་གཏོང་བ། dānam/ generosity 4. ཆོས་ཉན་པ། śravaṇam/ hearing Dharma 5. འཛིན་པ། udgrahaṇam/ memorizing 6. ཀློག་པ། vācanam/ reading 7. འཆད་པ། prakāśanā/ preaching 8. ཁ་ཏོན་དུ་བྱ་བ། svādhyāyanam/ recitation 9. ཆོས་ཀྱི་དོན་སེམས་པ། dharmārtha cintanā/ contemplation on Dharma 10. ཆོས་ཀྱི་དོན་སྒོམ་པ། dharmārtha bhāvanā/ meditation on Dharma.

ཆོས་ཕུང་།

Dharma skandha/ A heap of doctrine. One heap of Buddha's doctrine constitute a set of teachings which contains the complete instructions to counteract one of the eighty-four thousand delusions.

ཆོས་ཕུང་བརྒྱད་ཁྲི་བཞི་སྟོང་།

Caturasīti sahastraṇi dharma skandhāḥ/ The eighty-four thousand heaps of doctrine. The entire teachings of Buddha incorporated into four groups of antidotes against four thousand delusions. 1. འདོད་ཆགས་ཀྱི་གཉེན་པོར་ཉིས་ཁྲི་ཆིག་སྟོང་། twenty-one thousand heaps of doctrine as antidotes to desire-attachment 2. ཞེ་སྡང་གི་གཉེན་པོར་ཉིས་ཁྲི་ཆིག་སྟོང་། twenty-one thousand heaps of doctrine as antidotes to hatred-anger 3. གཏི་མུག་གི་གཉེན་པོར་ཉིས་ཁྲི་ཆིག་སྟོང་། twenty-one thousand heaps of doctrine as antidotes to closed-mindedness 4. དུག་གསུམ་ཐུན་མོང་བའི་གཉེན་པོར་ཉིས་ཁྲི་ཆིག་སྟོང་།twenty-one thousand heaps of doctrine as antidotes to all the three root delusions in equal proportions.

ཆོས་དབྱིངས།

Dharmadhātu. The sphere of reality.

ཆོས་གཟུངས།

Retention of Dharma. The power of memorization and retention of an unlimited number of words, phrases and mystic formulae (mantra) for an infinite period of time having only heard them once.

མཆོག་དབང་གོང་མ་གསུམ།

The three higher supreme initiations. The latter three initiations of the highest anuttarayogatantra that ripen a disciple's mental continuum having entered into the maṇḍala. 1. གསང་དབང་། secret initiation 2. ཤེས་རབ་ཡེ་ཤེས་ཀྱི་དབང་། wisdom initiation 3. ཚིག་དབང་། word initiation.

མཆོག་བཞི།

Catvāri uttama dharmāḥ/ The four supreme qualities. 1. རྒྱུན་

ཀྱི་མཆོག་ཐོས་པ། study as the supreme ornament 2. བདེ་བའི་མཆོག་སེམས་བསྐྱེད། generating the mind of enlightenment as the supreme happiness 3. ནོར་གྱི་མཆོག་སྦྱིན་པ། generosity as the supreme wealth 4. གྲོགས་ཀྱི་མཆོག་མི་བསླུ་བ། sincerity as the supreme friend.

མཆོད་རྟེན་ཆ་བརྒྱད།

Aṣṭa stūpāḥ/ The eight types of stūpas. 1. བདེ་གཤེགས་མཆོད་རྟེན། Tathāgata stūpa 2. བྱང་ཆུབ་མཆོད་རྟེན། Bodhi stūpa 3. ཆོས་འཁོར་མཆོད་རྟེན། Dharmacakra stūpa 4. ཆོ་འཕྲུལ་མཆོད་རྟེན། Prātihārya stūpa/ miracle stūpa 5. ལྷ་བབ་མཆོད་རྟེན། stūpa of descent from Tuṣita field 6. དབྱེན་བསྡུམ་མཆོད་རྟེན། stūpa for pacifying a schism among the sangha community 7. རྣམ་རྒྱལ་མཆོད་རྟེན། Vijayāni stūpa/ victory stūpa 8. མྱང་འདས་མཆོད་རྟེན། Parinirvāṇa stūpa.

མཆོད་པ།

Pūjā/ A. Worship service. B. Offerings to the gods and divinities. C. The material and immaterial medium of offerings.

མཆོད་པ་ཆ་བརྒྱད།

The eight-fold offerings. 1. མཆོད་ཡོན། water for the mouth 2. ཞབས་བསིལ། water for the feet 3. མེ་ཏོག flower 4. བདུག་སྤོས། incense 5. མར་མེ། lamp 6. དྲི་ཆབ། scented water 7. ཞལ་ཟས། food 8. རོལ་མོ། music.

མཆོད་པ་གཉིས།

Two types of offerings. Offerings made to the object of refuge has two: 1. ཟང་ཟིང་གི་མཆོད་པ། offering of material goods 2. སྒྲུབ་པའི་མཆོད་པ། offering of practice; or 1. དངོས་འབྱོར་གྱི་མཆོད་པ། offerings actually arranged 2. ཡིད་ཀྱིས་སྤྲུལ་པའི་མཆོད་པ། offerings made in the imagination.

མཆོད་པ་བཞི།

Catvāri pūjāḥ/ Four types of offerings. A. 1. ཕྱིའི་མཆོད་པ། outer offering 2. ནང་གི་མཆོད་པ། inner offering 3. གསང་བའི་མཆོད་པ། secret offering 4. དེ་ཁོ་ན་ཉིད་ཀྱི་མཆོད་པ། offering of suchness. B. The four religious festivals of offerings instituted during the reign of King Mune Tsanpo: 1. ལྷ་སར་འདུལ་བའི་མཆོད་པ། offering of Vinayapiṭaka at Lhasa 2. ཁྲ་འབྲུག་ལ་མངོན་པའི་མཆོད་པ། offering ceremony of Abhidharmapiṭaka at Tradrug 3-4. བསམ་ཡས་ལ་མདོ་སྡེ་དང་བྱང་ཆུབ་ཀྱི་མཆོད་པ། offering ceremony of Sūtrapiṭaka and enlightenment at Samye.

མཆོད་པའི་ཡོ་བྱད།

The offering articles; the objects of offering to be made to the three objects of refuge.

མཆོད་རྫས་བཅུ།

Daśa pūjā dravyāḥ/ The ten objects of offering; ten kinds of offering. The set of ten different offerings made to deities. 1. མེ་ཏོག puṣpa/ flowers 2. ཕྲེང་བ། mālā/ garlands 3. བདུག་སྤོས། dhūpa/ incense 4. བྱུག་པ། vilepanam/ scent 5. ཕྱེ་མ། cūrṇa/ food 6. ན་བཟའ། vastra/ cloth 7. རྒྱན། alam/ ornament 8. གདུགས། chattram/ umbrella 9. རྒྱལ་མཚན། maṅgala dhvaja/ victory banner 10. བ་དན། patākā/ flags.

འཆབ་བཅས།

A concealed non-virtue; concealment of non-virtues deliberately in an attempt to show one's purity.

འཆི་ཆུང་།

Alpa mṛtyu/ The small death. The death that occurs within the life of an intermediate state being (bar-do) at the completion of each week.

འཆི་བདག་གི་བདུད་རགས་པ།

Coarse interferences from the lord of death. This refers to the death incurred through force of karma and delusion.

འཆི་བདག་གི་བདུད་ཕྲ་མོ།

Subtle interferences from the lord of death. This is the severence of the life-force (srog) within the continuum of an Ārya.

འཆི་འཕོ་བའི་རྒྱུ་གསུམ།

Tri cyutihetu/ The three causes of transmigration; the three causes of death. 1. ཚེ་ཟད་པ། āyukṣaya/ exhaustion of life-span 2. བསོད་ནམས་ཟད་པ། puṇyakṣaya/ exhaustion of merits 3. ལས་ཟད་པ། karmakṣaya/ exhaustion of karma.

འཆི་འཕོ་བའི་སྔ་ལྟས་ལྔ།

The five signs of imminent death for a god. 1. ལུས་ཀྱི་འོད་དང་བཀྲག་གདངས་ཉམས་པ། they lose lustre and brightness of their body 2. སྟན་ལ་སྡོད་པར་མི་འདོད་པ། they dislike to sit on their cushions 3. མེ་ཏོག་གི་ཕྲེང་བ་རྙིང་པ། their garlands fade away 4. གོས་རྙིང་ཞིང་དྲི་མ་ཆགས་པ། their robes are worn out and smell bad 5. ལུས་ལ་རྡུལ་ཆུ་འབྱུང་བ། their body is covered with sweat.

འཆི་བ་འོད་གསལ།

The clear light of death; the subtle mind that manifests at death following the experience of the stages of dissolution of the elements and the gross minds of a person.

འཆི་སེམས་གསུམ།

The three types of death-experience; the three levels of thought at death. 1. དགེ་བའི་འཆི་སེམས། virtuous state of mind 2. མི་དགེ་བའི་འཆི་སེམས། non-virtuous state of mind 3. ལུང་མ་བསྟན་པའི་འཆི་སེམས། indifferent state of mind.

འཆི་སྲིད།

The death state. The state existing during the last moment of death or during the period of experiencing the clear light of death.

འཆིང་གྲོལ་གྱི་བདག

Bandhana muktātman/ The self that binds and from which we must be free. The truly existent self, misconceived to be the real self; the cause of uncontrolled rebirth in cyclic existence, freedom from which is the attainment of liberation.

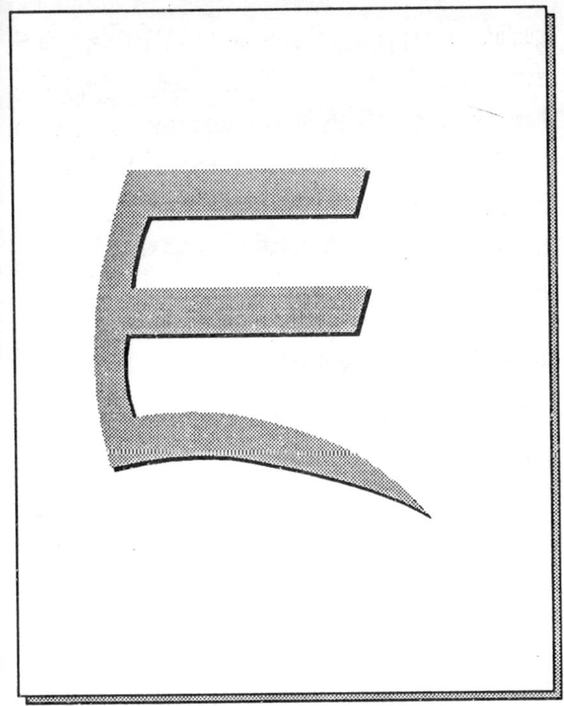

ཇི་སྙེད་པ།

Yāvat/ All that exists; all conventional things; refering to all phenomena other than emptiness.

ཇི་ལྟ་བ།

Yathā/ A thing as it is; thatness; refering to the ultimate truth—emptiness which is other than the conventional aspect of all phenomena.

ཇི་ལྟ་ཇི་སྙེད།

Yathā yāvat/ All that exists; innumerable; infinite; without exception.

ཇོ་ནང་པ།

The Jonang school. A school of Tibetan Buddhism akin to the Kagyud tradition instituted by Tāranātha and his followers. During the 11th century the view of Other Emptiness (gzhan-stong) was asserted by Yomo Mikyod Dorjee, and a monastic institution for the study and preservation of this philosophy was established at Jonang by Kunpang Thugje Tsondru, and later Dolpo Sherab Gyaltsen became a propounder of this philosophy.

ཇོ་བོ་རྗེ་དཔལ་ལྡན་ཨ་ཏི་ཤ།

Atiśa Dīpaṇkara Śrī Jñāna (982-1054). The celebrated Buddhist Paṇḍit from Bengal, who came to Tibet in 1042 and lived there for a number of years. He was one of the principal figures during the revival of Buddhism in Tibet in the 11th century. He passed away in Nyethang near Lhasa. His *Lamp on the Path to Enlightenment* (bodhipathapradīpa) was the source of the 'lamrim' tradition in Tibet.

ཇོ་བོ་མི་བསྐྱོད་རྡོ་རྗེ།

The venerable Mikyo Dorje image. An image of Buddha Śākyamuni believed to be similar to him in his eighth year of age that was brought to Tibet during the reign of King Songtsen Gampo by his Nepalis wife, Bhrikuti. In the past it was housed at Ramoche temple.

ཇོ་བོ་ཤཱཀྱ་མུ་ནེ།

The venerable Śākyamuni image. An image of Buddha Śākyamuni believed to be similar to himself in his twelfth year of age that was brought to Tibet during the reign of King Songtsen Gampo by his Chinese wife, Kongjo, as her dowry. Presently it is housed at Lhasa Tsuglag Khang.

འཇའ་ལུས།

Rainbow body. A yogic way of dying whereby one's body transforms into rays of light without leaving any trace of his physical body.

འཇང་དགུན་ཆོས།

The winter debate session at Jangphu monastery courtyard situated to the south-west of Lhasa in which monks of each of the three largest Gelug universities of Central Tibet gather.

འཇིག་རྟེན་ཆོས་བརྒྱད།

Astau lokikadharmāḥ/ The eight worldly concerns; the eight concerns for an ordinary person to be happy and unhappy about. 1. རྙེད་པ་དང་། lābha/ gain 2. མ་རྙེད་པ། alābha/ loss 3. སྙན་པ་དང་། yaśa/ reputation 4. མི་སྙན་པ། ayaśa/ infamy 5. བསྟོད་པ་དང་། praśaṁsā/ praise 6. སྨད་པ། nindā/ degradation 7. བདེ་བ་དང་། sukham/ pleasure 8. མི་བདེ་བ། duḥkham/ misery.

འཇིག་རྟེན་དང་འཇིག་རྟེན་ལས་འདས་པའི་སྲུང་མ།

The worldly and transworldly protectors of Dharma. The Dharma protectors who have and have not attained the level of an Ārya possessing direct insight into emptiness.

འཇིག་རྟེན་བདུན།

Sapta loka/ The seven worlds; the seven realms of existence. A. 1-6. འགྲོ་བ་རིགས་དྲུག་གི་འཇིག་རྟེན། ṣad jagati/ the realm of six migrators (see 'gro-ba rigs-drug) 7. བར་དོའི་འཇིག་རྟེན། antarabhāva loka/ the realm of the intermediate state of rebirth. B. 1-3. ངན་སོང་གི་གནས་གསུམ། tri durgati avasthā/ the realm of three lower beings (hell, animal and hungry ghosts) 4-5. འདོད་པའི་ལྷ་མི་གཉིས་ཀྱི་འཇིག་རྟེན། manusya deva loka/ the realm of gods and human beings of the desire realm 6-7. གཟུགས་གཟུགས་མེད་ཀྱི་ལྷའི་འཇིག་རྟེན། rūpa arūpa dhātu loka/ the realm of gods of the form and formless realms.

འཇིག་རྟེན་པའི་དབང་ཕྱུག་བརྒྱད།

The eight mundane powers. These are similar to the eight qualities of the great Vajrayoginī. 1. གཟུགས་ཤིན་ཏུ་ཕྲ་བ། extremely subtle body 2. ཡང་བ། light body 3. ཤིན་ཏུ་ཆེ་བ། huge body 4. གར་ཡང་ཕྱིན་པ། enjoying freedom of movement 5. གསལ་བར་འོས་པ། luminous body 6. དབང་པོ་ཉིད། completely luminous 7. དབང་བསྒྱུར་བ་ཉིད། conquering others or magnetic 8. གང་དུ་འདོད་པར་གནས་པ། enjoying freedom of residence.

འཇིག་རྟེན་པའི་ལམ་བརྒྱད།

Aṣṭa laukika mārgāḥ/ The eight worldly paths; the eight mundane paths. 1-4. བསམ་གཏན་བཞི། catvāri dhyānāḥ/ the four types of meditative concentrtion (see bsam-gtan gyi snyoms-'jug bzhi). 5-8. གཟུགས་མེད་བཞི། catvāri arūpa samāpattayaḥ/ the four types of formless meditative absorptions (see gzugs-med snyoms-'jug bzhi).

འཇིག་རྟེན་ལས་འདས་པའི་ལམ་དགུ

Nava lokottara mārgāḥ/ The nine types of transworldly paths. ལམ་བདེན་གྱི་ངོ་བོར་གྱུར་པའི་འཕགས་རྒྱུད་ཀྱི་ལམ། 1-4. བསམ་གཏན་གྱི་སྙོམས་འཇུག་བཞི། the four states of absorption of the form realm (see bsam-gtan gyi snyoms-'jug bzhi) 5-8. གཟུགས་མེད་ཀྱི་སྙོམས་འཇུག་བཞི། the four states of absorption of the formless realm (see gzhugs-med kyi snyoms-'jug bzhi) 9. འགོག་པའི་སྙོམས་འཇུག the absorption of cessation ('gog-pa'i snyoms-'jug) that retains the nature of the truth of the paths within the mental continuum of an Ārya.

འཇིག་ལྟ།

Satkāyadṛṣṭi/ The view of the transitory collection; the wrong view of apprehending the collection of the five aggregates (see phung-po lnga) as the 'I' or 'mine', and hence the basis of all misconceptions or ego graspings.

འཇིག་ལྟ་ཉི་ཤུ།

Viṁśat satkāyadṛṣṭi/ The twenty views of the transitory

collection. 1. གཟུགས་བདག་ཏུ་ལྟ་བ། view of grasping at form as being the self 2. གཟུགས་བདག་གིར་ལྟ་བ། view of grasping at form as being mine 3. གཟུགས་ལ་བདག་རང་བཞིན་གྱིས་ཡོད་པར་ལྟ་བ། view of grasping at form as possessing the self 4. བདག་ལ་གཟུགས་རང་བཞིན་གྱིས་ཡོད་པར་ལྟ་བ། view of grasping at form as abiding within the self. དེ་བཞིན་ཚོར་བ། འདུ་ཤེས། འདུ་བྱེད། རྣམ་པར་ཤེས་པའི་ཕུང་པོ་ལའང་དེ་བཞིན་ལྟ་བ་བཞི་བཞི་སྟེ་ཉི་ཤུའོ། Similarly for sound, smell, taste and touch—grasping them as the self, as being mine, as possessing the self and as abiding within the self, makes twenty.

འཇིག་ལྟ་ལྷན་སྐྱེས་གཉིས།

Dvi sahaja satkāyadrṣṭi/ The two innate graspings of the view of transitory collection; the ignorance of grasping at 'I' and 'I possessor' within the minds of all sentient beings. 1. ངར་འཛིན་གྱི་བདག་འཛིན་དང་། ahaṁkāra/ grasping at self 2. ང་ཡིར་འཛིན་པའི་བདག་འཛིན། mamakāra/ grasping at mine.

འཇིག་པ་རྣམ་གསུམ།

Tri nāśa/ The three types of destruction. 1. མཚོན་ཆའི་འཇིག་པ། destruction by weapons 2. ནད་རིམས་ཀྱི་འཇིག་པ། destruction by sickness 3. མུ་གེའི་འཇིག་པ། destruction by famine. Or 1. མེའི་འཇིག་པ། destruction by fire 2. ཆུའི་འཇིག་པ། destruction by water 3. རླུང་གི་འཇིག་པ། destruction by wind.

འཇིག་པའི་རྩེ་མོ་གསུམ།

The three peak immune states of existence. The second, third and fourth concentration states that are immune to the cosmic destruction caused by fire, water and wind elements.

འཇིགས་པ་བརྒྱད།

The eight fears. 1. ང་རྒྱལ་སེང་གེའི་འཇིགས་པ། fear which is like a lion, analogous to pride 2. གཏི་མུག་གླང་པོའི་འཇིགས་པ། fear which is like an elephant, analogous to ignorance 3. ཞེ་སྡང་མེའི་འཇིགས་པ། fear which is like a fire, analogous to hatred 4. ཕྲག་དོག་སྦྲུལ་གྱི་འཇིགས་པ། fear which is like a snake, analogous to jealousy 5. ལྟ་ངན་རྐུན་པོའི་འཇིགས་པ། fear which is like a thief, analogous to wrong view 6. སེར་སྣ་ལྕགས་སྒྲོགས་ཀྱི་འཇིགས་པ། fear which is like one chained with irons, analogous to miserliness 7. འདོད་ཆགས་ཆུ་བོའི་འཇིགས་པ། fear which is like a raging river, analogous to desire 8. ཐེ་ཚོམ་ཤ་ཟའི་འཇིགས་པ། fear which is like a cannibal, analogous to doubt.

འཇིགས་པ་ལྔ།

The five fears; the five types of fears encountered by Bodhisattvas on the path of accumulation and the path of preparation. 1. འཚོ་བ་མེད་པའི་འཇིགས་པ། fear of not finding livelihood 2. མི་བསྔགས་པའི་འཇིགས་པ། fear of not being praised 3. འཁོར་གྱི་འཇིགས་པ། fear of not finding followers 4. འཆི་བའི་འཇིགས་པ། fear of death 5. ངན་འགྲོའི་འཇིགས་པ། fear of falling into lower rebirth.

འཇིགས་སྲིད།

Craving for freedom from fear; yearning for freedom from fear and disgust, e.g. the fear of parting from this body at death.

འཇུ་མི་ཕམ།

Mipham Jamyang Nyamgyal Gyatso (1846-1912). A great scholar of the Nyingma tradition. He is well known for his learnedness and mastery of all the ten sciences of learning (see rig-gnas bcu). His treatises on Buddhist philosophy have been adapted as the syllabus of study in many Nyingma colleges.

འཇུག་སྒོ་རྣམ་གསུམ།

The three entrances; the threefold commitments. 1. བསྟན་པ་ལ་འཇུག་པའི་སྒོ་སྐྱབས་འགྲོ། taking refuge in the three jewels is the entrance into Buddhism 2. ཐར་པ་ལ་འཇུག་པའི་སྒོ་ངེས་འབྱུང་། renunciation is the entrance to the state of liberation (nirvāṇa) 3. ཐེག་ཆེན་དུ་འཇུག་པའི་སྒོ་སེམས་བསྐྱེད། generation of the mind of enlightenment is the entrance to the greater vehicle path (mahāyāna).

འཇུག་སྒོམ།

Prasthāna bhāvanā/ Formal meditation; stabilized meditation. A practice of meditation in which a meditator single-pointedly fixes his or her mind on an object without examining the aspects of the object analytically.

འཇུག་སྒྲུབ།

Prasthāna pratipatti/ Achievement through engagement; achievement through training. A Bodhisattva path which is mainly concerned with the training of enthusiastic perseverance applied either in the causal or resultant practices of the greater vehicle within the Peak Training (see rtse-mo'i sbyor-ba).

འཇུག་སྒྲུབ་དགུ

Nine achievements through engagement; nine achievements through training. Achievement through engagement in: 1. བསམ་གཏན་གཟུགས་མེད་ལ་འཇུག་པའི་འཇུག་སྒྲུབ། the meditative concentration and absorption within the formless realm 2. ཕར་ཕྱིན་དྲུག་ལ་འཇུག་པའི་འཇུག་སྒྲུབ། the six perfections 3. མཐོང་ལམ་དང་སྒོམ་ལམ་ལ་འཇུག་པའི་འཇུག་སྒྲུབ། the path of seeing and meditation 4. ཚད་མེད་བཞི་ལ་འཇུག་པའི་འཇུག་སྒྲུབ། the four immeasurables 5. བདེན་གྲུབ་ཀྱི་དམིགས་པ་མེད་པ་ལ་འཇུག་པའི་འཇུག་སྒྲུབ། the absence of the apprehension of true existence 6. འཁོར་གསུམ་རྣམ་པར་དག་པ་ལ་འཇུག་པའི་འཇུག་སྒྲུབ། the threefold purity 7. ཆེད་དུ་བྱ་བ་གསུམ་ལ་འཇུག་པའི་འཇུག་སྒྲུབ། the threefold goals 8. མངོན་ཤེས་དྲུག་ལ་འཇུག་པའི་འཇུག་སྒྲུབ། the six extra sensory perceptions 9. རྣམ་མཁྱེན་ལ་འཇུག་པའི་འཇུག་སྒྲུབ། the omniscient mind.

འཇུག་གནས་ལྡང་གསུམ།

The threefold practices of entering, abidance and awakening. A special feature of meditation without signs according to action tantra. 1. ཕུང་སོགས་ཀྱི་ཆོས་ཐམས་ཅད་ལ་རྣམ་པར་དཔྱད་དེ་སྐྱེ་མེད་དུ་རྟོགས་པ་ནི་འཇུག་པ། entering into realizing all phenomena as lacking inherent production by way of applying analysis 2. མི་རྟོག་པའི་ངོ་བོ་མཉམ་དུ་གྱུར་པ་ནི་གནས་པ། abiding within non-conceptual realization of reality 3. དེ་ལས་མ་རྟོགས་པའི་འགྲོ་བ་རྣམས་ལ་སྙིང་རྗེ་ཆེན་པོ་ལྷག་པར་འཇུག་པ་ནི་ལྡང་བ། awakening with the special meditation on great compassion for those without such a realization.

འཇུག་པ་སེམས་བསྐྱེད།

Prasthāna cittotpāda/ The committed Bodhicitta; the venturing mind of enlightenment. The mind of enlightenment that is committed in the Bodhisattvas' practices as opposed to being commited only in spirit.

འཇུག་པའི་སྤྱོད་པ།

The activity of entering into practice. One of the four ways of utilizing realizations (see spyod-pa'i sgo-bzhi) according to action tantra, in which one attempts to transform oneself into a proper receptacle of initiations by means of observing the precepts connected to the respective deity after having received the initiation of that deity.

འཇོག་བྱེད།

Definition; nature; meaning. An explanation of a point which gives a partial explanation of the object defined.

རྗེ་ཙོང་ཁ་པ།

Tsong Khapa (1357-1419). The founder of the Gelug order of Tibetan Buddhism known for his revival of the Kadampa tradition. He also elucidated the most subtle meanings of sūtra and tantra in innumerable discourses and his collected works comprise 18 volumes. His teachings and those of his two main disciples Gyaltsab-Je and Khedrub-Je remain in the heart of the Gelug tradition.

རྗེ་བཙུན་གོང་མ་ལྔ།

The five foremost masters of the Sakya tradition. 1. ས་ཆེན་ཀུན་དགའ་སྙིང་པོ། Sachen Kunga Nyingpo (1092-1158) 2. རྗེ་བཙུན་བསོད་ནམས་རྩེ་མོ། Sonam Tzemo (1142-1182) 3. རྗེ་བཙུན་གྲགས་པ་རྒྱལ་མཚན། Dakpa Gyaltsen (1147-1216) 4. ས་སྐྱ་པཎྜི་ཏ་ཀུན་དགའ་རྒྱལ་མཚན། Sakya Paṇḍita Kunga Gyaltsen (1182-1251) 5. འགྲོ་མགོན་ཆོས་རྒྱལ་འཕགས་པ། Drogon Choegyal Phagpa (1235-1280).

རྗེ་གཟིགས་པ་ལྔ་ལྡན།

Khedrub Je's five visions of his master Je Tsong Khapa. 1. གླང་པོ་ཆེ་དཀར་པོ་ཞིག་ལ་ཆིབས་པ། riding on a white elephant 2. ནོར་བུ་མུ་ཏིག་སོགས་ཀྱིས་སྤྲས་པའི་ཁྲི་གཅིག་གི་སྟེང་དུ་བཞུགས་པ། seated on a throne adorned with jewels and so forth 3. སེང་གེ་དཀར་པོ་ཞིག་ལ་ཆིབས་པ། riding on a white snow lion 4. སྟག་འཇིགས་སུ་རུང་བ་ཞིག་ལ་ཆིབས་པ། riding on a terrifying tiger 5. སྤྲིན་དཀར་པོའི་ཕུང་པོ་གཅིག་གི་དབུས་སུ་བྱོན་པ། resting amidst a huge mass of white clouds.

རྗེ་རིན་པོ་ཆེའི་མཛད་ཆེན་བཞི།

The four great deeds of Je Tsong Khapa. 1. དགའ་ལྡན་གྱི་དཀྱིལ་འཁོར་བསྒྲུབ་མཆོད། the construction of a maṇḍala and making grand offerings at Ganden monastery 2. རྫིང་ཕྱིའི་བྱམས་པ་ཞིག་གསོས། renovation of Maitreya's statue in Zingchi 3. ལྷ་སར་ཆོ་འཕྲུལ་སྨོན་ལམ། the great prayer festival at Lhasa 4. གཉལ་གྱི་ལུང་རྣ་ཆེན་མོ། the great religious ceremony of Nyal.

རྗེས་ཁྱབ།

Subsequent pervasion; second logical mark. The pervasion in a correct logical syllogism that whatever is the reason is necessarily that predicate. There are two types of this pervasion called the རྗེས་ཁྱབ་རྣལ་མ། positive and རྗེས་ཁྱབ་ཕྱིན་ཅི་ལོག reversed subsequent pervasions.

རྗེས་མཐུན་གྱི་ཆོས།

Anurūpa dharma/ Similitudes; approximate features. A quality or feature to be included in a particular category while not being exactly synonymous with that category, e.g. the qualities of an Ārya Bodhisattva on the last moment of the tenth level which are similar to those of a Buddha.

རྗེས་གྲུབ་ཀྱི་མིང་།

Subsequent given name. A way of giving a name to anything or any person after its existence for reasons of similarity or relationship or otherwise, e.g., to call a puppy a tiger or sunrays the sun.

རྗེས་ཆོག

The concluding rite or ceremony. The concluding rite following a ceremony of accomplishment of a rite of a maṇḍala. This can be of various forms such as: performing a fire ritual of peace; increasing activity to please the deity and to redress any omission or duplication of a ritual; worshiping and making offering to the maṇḍala and giving sacrificial cakes to the directional protectors of the maṇḍala; making prostration and apology to the maṇḍala; bidding the wisdom being (see ye-shes-pa) to their abode and dissolving the pledge being (see dam-tsig pa) into oneself and dismantling the sand powdered maṇḍala; and simply dedicating the virtues and chanting verses of auspiciousness.

རྗེས་ཐོབ་སྒྱུ་མ་ལྟ་བུའི་སྟོང་པ་ཉིད།

The experience of emptiness like an illusion at the post-meditation stage. The experience of all that is seen, heard about or recollected like that of an illusory feat after arising from meditative equipoise on emptiness at an actual session.

རྗེས་དྲན་ལྔ།

Pañca anusmṛtayaḥ/ The five recollections. A set of five Kadampa precepts. 1. སྐྱབས་གནས་བླ་མ་དྲན་པ། recollecting one's spiritual master as the object of refuge 2. ལུས་ལྷའི་རང་བཞིན་དྲན་པ། recollecting one's body as being a divine body 3. ངག་བཟླས་བརྗོད་ཀྱི་རང་བཞིན་དྲན་པ། recollecting one's speech as being mantra 4. འགྲོ་བ་ཐམས་ཅད་ཕ་མར་ཤེས་པ། recollecting all sentient beings as one's mother 5. སེམས་ཀྱི་གནས་ལུགས་སྟོང་པར་ཤེས་པ། recollecting the reality of mind as being empty.

རྗེས་དཔག

Anumāna/ Inferential cognition; inferential understanding. A direct conceptual understanding of an obscure phenomenon, generated in reliance upon a correct reason, e.g. the cognition of the impermanence of a vase. There are two types of inferential cognition: 1. རང་དོན་རྗེས་དཔག svārthānumāna/ inference for self 2. གཞན་དོན་རྗེས་དཔག parārthānumāna/ inference for others; or 1. རྗེས་དཔག་ཡང་དག the correct inference 2. རྗེས་དཔག་ལྟར་སྣང་། the imperfect inference.

རྗེས་དཔག་བཅད་ཤེས།

Anumāna paricchinna jñāna/ Subsequent inferential cognition. A non-new understanding of an obscure phenomenon that is the continuity of understanding, or the continuing subsequent understanding originally generated by a previous inferential cognition, e.g. the second instant of inference understanding impermanence.

རྗེས་དཔག་ཚད་མ།

Anumāna pramāṇa/ Valid inferential cognition. The fresh, new inferential understanding of an obscure phenomenon, e.g. the first moment of inferential cognition of the impermanence of a vase generated by reason of its being a product.

རྗེས་དཔག་གསུམ།

Three types of inferential cognition. 1. དངོས་སྟོབས་རྗེས་དཔག inference through cogent evidence 2. གྲགས་པའི་རྗེས་དཔག inference through popular convention 3. ཡིད་ཆེས་རྗེས་དཔག inference through conviction in valid scriptures.

རྗེས་གཞིག

Gradual dissolution. A generation stage practice of tantra in which a practitioner meditates on the gradual dissolution of the maṇḍala into clear light and finally into oneself.

རྗེས་སུ་གནང་བའི་བཀའ།

Anujñā vacana/ The approved teachings; authorized teachings. The introductory words that occur at the beginning of a sūtra such as, 'Thus I have heard, once the Blessed One was dwelling . . .' which were spoken by Ānanda and others. These words were spoken because of an injunction by lord Śākyamuni Buddha to introduce the actual body of the sūtra in this way after or subsequent to his passing into parinirvāṇa.

རྗེས་སུ་དྲན་པ་ལྔ།

Pañca anusmṛtayaḥ/ The five recollections; the five points of constant recollection according to the Kadampa tradition (see rjes-dran lnga).

རྗེས་སུ་དྲན་པ་བཅུ།

Daśānusmṛtayaḥ/ The ten recollections. 1-6. (see rjes-su dran-pa drug, below) 7. དབུགས་ཕྱི་ནང་རྒྱུ་བ་རྗེས་སུ་དྲན་པ། the moment of breath 8. སྐྱེ་བ་རྗེས་སུ་དྲན་པ། birth 9. འཆི་བ་རྗེས་སུ་དྲན་པ། death 10. ལུས་ཀྱི་རྣམ་པ་རྗེས་སུ་དྲན་པ། forms of the body.

རྗེས་སུ་དྲན་པ་དྲུག

Ṣaḍ anusmṛtayaḥ/ The six types of recollection. The six things to be constantly remembered by all Buddhists. Recollection of: 1. བླ་མ་རྗེས་སུ་དྲན་པ། guru-anusmṛti/ the spiritual master 2. སངས་རྒྱས་རྗེས་སུ་དྲན་པ། buddhānusmṛti/ the Buddha 3. ཆོས་རྗེས་སུ་དྲན་པ། dharmānusmṛti/ the Dharma 4. དགེ་འདུན་རྗེས་སུ་དྲན་པ། saṅghānusmṛti/ the Saṅgha 5. ཚུལ་ཁྲིམས་རྗེས་སུ་དྲན་པ། śīlānusmṛti/ moral-discipline 6. གཏོང་བ་རྗེས་སུ་དྲན་པ། tyāgānusmṛti/ giving.

རྗེས་སུ་ཡི་རང་སྒོམ་ལམ་གཉིས།

The two types of paths of meditation on admiration. A. 1. ཐབས་ལ་མཁས་པས་དགེ་བའི་རྩ་བ་ལ་རྗེས་སུ་ཡི་རང་བ། admiring the roots of virtue by skillful means 2. དམིགས་པས་དགེ་བའི་རྩ་བ་ལ་རྗེས་སུ་ཡི་རང་བ། admiring the roots of virtue by the non-apprehended view. B. 1. ཀུན་རྫོབ་པའི་རྗེས་སུ་ཡི་རང་བ་སྒོམ་ལམ། the conventional path of meditation on admiration 2. དོན་དམ་པའི་རྗེས་སུ་ཡི་རང་བ་སྒོམ་ལམ། the ultimate path of meditation on admiration.

བརྗེ་བ་རྣམ་གསུམ།

Tri parivartana/ The three transformations; the three alterations. The three tranformations a new monk or nun is supposed to undertake at their ordination. 1. རྟགས་དང་ཆ་ལུགས་བརྗེ་བ། veṣa parivartana/ changing their way of life 2. བསམ་པ་བརྗེ་བ། āśāya parivartana/ changing their thought 3. མིང་བརྗེ་བ། nāma parivartana/ changing their name.

བརྗེད་ངས།

Muṣitasmṛtitā/ Forgetfulness. Technically it is a secondary mental factor responsible for the slackening of attention to virtuous objects and causing distraction; one of the five hindrances to mental quiescence meditation (see ngyes-pa lnga).

བརྗོད་བྱེད་ཀྱི་སྒྲ།

Abhidhāna śabda/ Expressive sound. Synonymous with sound that reveals meaning to sentient beings, e.g. the expression 'impermanence'.

བརྗོད་དུ་མེད་པ།

Anabhilāpya/Inexpressible; incommunicable; e.g. emptiness.

བརྗོད་དུ་མེད་པའི་བདག

Anabhilāpyātman/ An inexpressible self; a self that is neither substantially one with nor different from the five aggregates, neither permanent nor imprmanent as propounded by the Vaiputrīya, a sub-school of Vaibhāṣika and many other non-buddhist philosophers.

བརྗོད་པ་ཚིག་གི་གསུང་།

The literal teachings of expression. One of the five teachings (see gsung-lnga) of a Buddha according to the Nyingma tradition. The way a Nirmaṇakāya Buddha teaches various disciples, the meaning simultaneously being understood by each according to their own language.

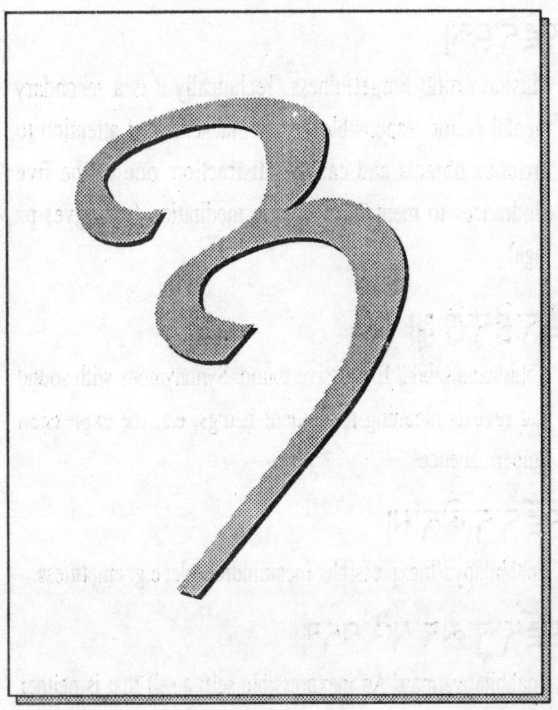

ཉན་ཐོས།

Śrāvaka/ A Hearer. Originally, those disciples of Buddha who actually listen to Buddha's teachings and also propagate these to others. Their goal is to achieve nirvāṇa for themselves. The four noble truths and the twelve links of independent origination are their primary fields of study and practice.

ཉན་ཐོས་ཀྱི་རྣལ་འབྱོར་མངོན་སུམ།

Śrāvaka yogi pratyakṣā/ The yogic direct perception of a Hearer. The knowledge and wisdom of a Śrāvaka trainee on the Hearers' path of seeing and meditation cognizing the sixteen aspects of the four noble truths (see mi-rtag sogs bcu-drug).

ཉན་ཐོས་ཀྱི་ལམ་ཤེས་པའི་ལམ་ཤེས།

The path-wisdom which understands the Hearer path. The Bodhisattva wisdom that understands the impermanence or emptiness of any or all of the four noble truths.

ཉན་ཐོས་ཀྱི་ས་བདུན།

Sapta śrāvakabhūmayaḥ/ The seven Hearer levels; the seven stages of a Hearer. 1. རིགས་ཀྱི་ས། gotra bhūmi/ the level of family 2. བརྒྱད་པའི་ས། aṣṭamaka bhūmi/ the level of the eighth 3. མཐོང་བའི་ས། darśana bhūmi/ the level of seeing 4. སྲབ་པའི་ས། tanū bhūmi/ the level of narrow 5. འདོད་ཆགས་དང་བྲལ་བའི་ས། vigata rāga bhūmi/ the level free of desire 6. བྱས་པ་རྟོགས་པའི་ས། kṛtāvi samaya bhūmiḥ/ the level of actualizing deeds 7. དཀར་པོ་རྣམ་པར་མཐོང་བའི་ས། śukla vidarśanā bhūmi/ the level of seeing white dharma.

ཉན་ཐོས་ཉེ་འཁོར་བཅུ།

The ten close Śrāvaka disciples of Buddha Śākyamuni. 1. ཤཱ་རིའི་བུ། Śariputra 2. མོའུ་འགལ་གྱི་བུ། Maudgalyāyana 3. འོད་སྲུང་ཆེན་པོ། Mahākaśyapa 4. ཀུན་དགའ་བོ། Ānanda 5. སྒྲ་གཅན་འཛིན། Rāhula 6. ཀཱ་ཏྱའི་བུ། Kātyāyana 7. མ་འགགས་པ། Aniruddha 8. གང་པོ། Pūrna 9. རབ་འབྱོར། Subhūti 10. ཉེ་བར་འཁོར། Upāli.

ཉན་ཐོས་སྡེ་པ་བཅོ་བརྒྱད།

Aṣṭadaśa śrāvaka nikāyāḥ/ The eighteen schools of Hearers. The eighteen schools branched from the four main schools of Hearers (see nyan-thos rtsa-ba'i sde-pa bzhi). 1-7. ཐམས་ཅད་ཡོད་སྨྲའི་སྡེ་པ་བདུན། seven schools of Mūlasarvāstivādin tradition (see gzhi thams-cad yod-par smra-ba'i sde-bdun) 8-12. ཕལ་ཆེན་སྡེ་པ་ལྔ། five schools of Mahāsāṃghika tradition (see dge-'dun phal-chen gyi sde-pa lnga) 13-15. གནས་བརྟན་པའི་སྡེ་པ་གསུམ། three schools of Sthavira tradition (see gnas-brtan-sde-pa) 16-18. མང་པོས་བཀུར་བའི་སྡེ་པ་གསུམ། three schools of Sammitīya tradition (see mang bkur sde-pa gsum).

ཉན་ཐོས་རྩ་བའི་སྡེ་པ་བཞི།

Catvāri mūla śrāvaka nikāyāḥ/ The four main schools of Hearers. 1. ཐམས་ཅད་ཡོད་པར་སྨྲ་བའི་སྡེ། Mūlasarvāstivādin tradition 2. ཕལ་ཆེན་པའི་སྡེ། Mahāsāṁghika tradition 3. གནས་བརྟན་པའི་སྡེ། Sthavira tradition 4. མང་པོས་བཀུར་བའི་སྡེ། Sammitīya tradition.

ཉན་ཐོས་ལ་ཡོད་པ་དང་རྗེས་སུ་མཐུན་པའི་རྣམ་མཁྱེན་གྱི་རྣམ་པ་སུམ་ཅུ་སོ་བདུན། ཉན་ཐོས་དང་ཐུན་མོང་བའི་རྣམ་པ་སོ་བདུན།

The thirty-seven features of the omniscient mind common to Hearers and Solitary Realizers. 1-4. དྲན་པ་ཉེ་བར་བཞག་པ་བཞི། catvāri smṛtyūpasthānāḥ/ the four close contemplations (see dran-pa nye-bar bzhag-pa bzhi). 5-8. ཡང་དག་པར་སྤོང་བ་བཞི། catvāri samyak prahāṇāḥ/ the four perfect abandonments (see yang-dag spong-ba bzhi). 9-12. རྫུ་འཕྲུལ་གྱི་རྐང་པ་བཞི། catvāri ṛddhipādāḥ/ the four limbs of miracles (see rdzu-'phrul-gyi rkang-pa bzhi). 13-17. དབང་པོ་ལྔ། pañcendriyāṇi/ the five faculties (see dbang-po lnga). 18-22. སྟོབས་ལྔ། pañca balāni/ the five powers (see stobs-lnga). 23-29. བྱང་ཆུབ་ཀྱི་ཡན་ལག་བདུན། sapta bodhyaṅgāni/ the seven limbs of enlightenment (see byang-chub yan-lag bdun). 30-37. འཕགས་ལམ་ཡན་ལག་བརྒྱད། aṣṭāryāṅga mārga/ the eight noble paths (see 'phags-lam yan-lag brgyad).

ཉམས་མགུར།

Spiritual songs. Songs of spiritual transformation revealing a meditator's experience and insight.

ཉམས་བརྒྱད།

The eight features of dance. 1. སྒེག་པ། charming 2. དྲག་ཤུལ། aggressive 3. དཔའ་བ། heroic 4. སྙིང་རྗེ། compassionate 5. མི་སྡུག་པ། ugly 6. བཞད་པ། smiling 7. རྨད་པ། magnificent 8. འཇིགས་རུང་། frightening.

ཉམས་སྣང་བན་བུན།

Blurred experience. Unclear yet multi-faceted appearances.

ཉམས་རྟོགས།

Experiences and insights; spiritual realization gained through proper meditation practices.

ཉམས་པ་རྣམ་གསུམ།

The three degenerations. A. That of: 1. ཚུལ་ཁྲིམས་ཉམས་པ། śīla vipanna/ moral discipline 2. ལྟ་བ་ཉམས་པ། dṛṣṭi vipanna/ view 3. ཆོ་ག་ཉམས་པ། ācāra vipanna/ rites. B. The three degenerations of monks' and nuns' precepts, i.e. from: 1. ཁྱིམ་པའི་རྟགས་སྤོང་བ་ལས་ཉམས་པ། giving up the householder's way of life 2. རབ་བྱུང་གི་རྟགས་འཆང་བ་ལས་ཉམས་པ། accepting the tradition of a monk or nun 3. མཁན་པོར་གསོལ་བ་བཏབ་པ་ལས་ཉམས་པ། having requested the abbot for ordination.

ཉམས་ལེན་བྱིན་རླབས་ཀྱི་བརྒྱུད་པ།

The lineage of blessed practices. According to the Lam-rim tradition of Je Tsong Khapa this lineage originates from Buddha Śākyamuni to Mañjuśrī to Śāntideva and so on. In tantric tradition, particularly of the Kagyud tradition this lineage begins from Buddha Vajradhāra to Tilopa, Naropa, Dombhipa, Atiśa and so on.

ཉལ་བའི་རྣལ་འབྱོར།

The yoga of sleep. A practice of yoga in sleep state usually carried out during the middle phase of dawn by laying down in the manner of a lion's resting position. In the secret mantrayāna practice it means going to bed and sleeping within the recognition of the clear light of emptiness.

ཉི་མ་ལྟ་བུའི་སེམས་བསྐྱེད།

Ādityopamacittotpāda/ The sun-like bodhicitta. The mind of enlightenment associated with the perfection of power possessed by Bodhisattvas on the ninth level.

ཉི་མའི་གཉེན།

The kinsman of the sun. An epithet of Buddha Śākyamuni derived from a legend concerning his ancestry.

ཉི་མའི་ཆ་བཅུ་བཞི།

The fourteen divisions of daylight. 1. སྐྱ་རེངས་ཤར་བ། first light 2. ཉི་མ་མ་ཤར་ཙམ། just before sun rise 3. ཉི་མ་ཤར་བ། the first glimpse of the sun 4. ཉི་མའི་བརྒྱད་ཆ་ཙམ་ཤར་བ། one eighth of the sun risen 5. ཉི་མའི་བཞི་ཆ་ཙམ་ཤར་བ། one fourth of the sun risen 6. སྔ་དྲོའི་དུས། morning 7. གུང་ཚིག་གོང་ཙམ། late morning 8. གུང་ཚིག noon 9. ཕྱི་དྲོའི་དུས། late afternoon 10. ཉི་མའི་བཞི་ཆ་ཙམ་ལུས་པ། one fourth of the sun remaining 11. ཉི་མའི་བརྒྱད་ཆ་ཙམ་ལུས་པ། one eighth of the sun remaining 12. ཉི་མ་མ་ནུབ་ཙམ། last glimpse of the sun 13. ཉི་མ་ནུབ་པ། sunset 14. ཉི་མ་ནུབ་ནས་སྐར་མ་མ་ཤར་ཙམ་གྱི་དུས། sunset to first starlight.

ཉི་ཚེ་བའི་དམྱལ་བ།

Pratyekanaraka/ The occasional hells. The hells surrounding the hot and cold hell realms that experience happiness and suffering during day and night alternatively.

ཉིན་མཚན་དུས་དྲུག

Six sessions throughout the day and night. 1. སྔ་དྲོ། morning 2. ཉིན་གུང་། afternoon 3. ཕྱི་དྲོ། twilight 4. སྲོད། late evening 5. ནམ་གུང་། midnight 6. ཐོ་རངས། pre-dawn.

ཉིང་མཚམས་སྦྱོར་བ།

Connecting to rebirth. The instant that consciousness collapses into the parent's mixture of sperm and blood in the womb of a mother during rebirth. The instant of conception in the womb.

ཉི་འཁོར་ལྷག་པ་བཅུ་དྲུག

The sixteen neighbouring hells. The four hell states on each of the four directions of the hell without respite are known as the sixteen neighbouring hell states. These are namely: 1. མེ་མ་མུར། kukūlam/ the fiery embers 2. རོ་མྱགས་ཀྱི་འདམ། kuṇapam/ the swamp of filth 3. སྤུ་གྲིའི་ཐང་། kṣuradhāra/ the razor-filled path 4. རལ་གྲིའི་ཚལ། asidhāra/ the forest of sword-leaves .·

ཉི་བརྒྱུད་གཏེར་མ།

The close lineage of treasure teachings. The great Ācārya Padmasambhava and other accomplished masters have left many holy religious texts hidden under rocks and mountains with their prophesied instructions of the time, and the persons who would collect them and spread those teachings far and wide in future. This lineage exclusive to the Nyingma tradition of Tibetan Buddhism is known as the close lineage treasure teaching.

ཉི་ཉོན་ཉི་ཤུ།

Dvadaśa upakleśāḥ/ The twenty secondary afflictions; the twenty approximate delusions. The twenty delusions tha arises in dependence upon the six root delusions (see rtsa nyon drug). 1. ཁྲོ་བ། krodha/ anger 2. འཁོན་འཛིན། upanāha malice 3. འཆབ་པ། mrakṣa/ concealment 4. འཚིག་པ pradāsa/ outrage 5. ཕྲག་དོག īrṣyā/ jealousy 6. སེར་སྣ mātsaryam/ miserliness 7. སྒྱུ། māyā/ ceceit 8. གཡོ། śāṭhyam dishonesty 9. རྒྱགས་པ། mada/ haughtiness 10. རྣམ་པར་འཚེ་བ། vihiṃsā/ harmful intent 11. ངོ་ཚ་མེད་པ། āhrikyam/ non embarrassment 12. ཁྲེལ་མེད་པ། anapatrāpyam/ non consideration 13. མ་དད་པ། āśraddhyam/ lack of faith 14. འ

ལོ། kausīdyam/ laziness 15. བག་མེད། pramāda/ non-conscientiousness 16. བརྗེད་ངས། muṣitasmṛtitā/ forgetfulness 17. ཤེས་བཞིན་མ་ཡིན་པ། asamprajanyam/ non-introspection 18. བྱིང་བ། nimagṇa/ dullness 19 རྒོད་པ། auddhatyam/ agitation 20. རྣམ་གཡེང་། vikṣepa/ mental wandering.

ཉེ་བར་ལེན་པ་བཞི།

Upādānam/ The four compulsive acquisitions; the four negative acquirements by the force of delusions in a person. The hundred and eight delusions are included in these four. 1. འདོད་པ་ཉེ་བར་ལེན་པ། that of desire 2. ལྟ་བ་ཉེ་བར་ལེན་པ། that of view 3. བདག་ཏུ་ལྟ་བ་ཉེ་བར་ལེན་པ། that of the view of self 4. ཚུལ་ཁྲིམས་དང་བརྟུལ་ཞུགས་མཆོག་འཛིན། that of holding wrong moral conduct as superior.

ཉེ་བའི་མཚམས་མེད་ལྔ།

The five secondary heinous non-virtues; the five approximate heinous crimes; the five secondary crimes of immediate retribution. 1. མ་དགྲ་བཅོམ་པ་སུན་ཕྱུང་བ། disrobing an ordained female Foe-destroyer 2. བྱང་སེམས་དུ་ངེས་ནས་གསོད་པ། killing a Bodhisattva knowlingly 3. སློབ་པ་གསོད་པ། killing a trainee 4. དགེ་འདུན་གྱི་འདུ་སྒོ་འཕྲོག་པ། misappropriation of SaḤngha property 5. མཆོད་རྟེན་བཤིགས་པ། destroying a stūpa.

ཉེ་བའི་རིན་ཆེན་སྣ་བདུན།

The seven semi-precious possessions. 1. ཁང་བཟང་རིན་པོ་ཆེ། harmya/ precious mansion 2. མལ་ཆ་རིན་པོ་ཆེ། śayana/ precious bedding 3. ལྷམ་རིན་པོ་ཆེ། pulā/ precious shoes 4. རལ་གྲི་རིན་པོ་ཆེ། khadga/ precious sword 5. གོས་རིན་པོ་ཆེ། cīvara/ precious clothing 6. པགས་པ་རིན་པོ་ཆེ། carman/ precious skin 7. ཚལ་རིན་པོ་ཆེ། vana/ precious forest.

ཉེ་བའི་སྲས་ཆེན་བརྒྱད།

Aṣṭopaputrāḥ/ The eight close disciples of Buddha Śākyamuni. 1. འཇམ་དཔལ་དབྱངས། Mañjuśrī 2. ཕྱག་ན་རྡོ་རྗེ། Vajrapāṇi 3. སྤྱན་རས་གཟིགས། Avalokiteśvara 4. ས་ཡི་སྙིང་པོ། Kṣitigarbha 5. སྒྲིབ་པ་རྣམ་སེལ། Sarvanirvaraṇa Viskambhin 6. ནམ་མཁའི་སྙིང་པོ། Ākāśagarbha 7. བྱམས་པ། Maitreya 8. ཀུན་ཏུ་བཟང་པོ། Samantabhadra.

ཉེར་བསྡོགས།

Sāmantaka/ The preparatory stage. A preparatory virtuous state of concentration within the sphere of the form and formless realm that directly generates an actual state of meditative concentration of either the form or formless absorption. There are eight types of preparatory meditative concentrations.

ཉེར་ལེན་གྱི་རྒྱུ།

The substantial cause. That cause which gives rise to the result that abides in its own substantial continuity or subsequent similar type, e.g. the clay from which a pot is made is the main substantial constituent of it.

ཉེས་པ་ལྔ།

Pañca doṣāḥ/ Five faults; five hinderances to mental quiescence meditation. 1. ལེ་ལོ། kausīdyam/ laziness 2. གདམས་ངག་བརྗེད་པ། upadeśa saṁpramoṣa/ forgetting instructions 3. བྱིང་རྒོད། dullness and agitation 4. མངོན་པར་འདུ་མི་བྱེད་པ། abhisaṁskāra pratipakṣa/ non-application of antidotes 5. མངོན་པར་འདུ་བྱེད་པ། anābhisaṁskāra pratipakṣa/ over-application of antidotes.

ཉེས་བྱས་བཞི་བཅུ་ཞེ་དྲུག

The forty-six faults; the fourty-six secondary transgressions of Bodhisattva vows. སྦྱིན་པ་དང་འགལ་བ་བདུན་ནི། Seven associated with the perfection of giving 1. དཀོན་མཆོག་གསུམ་ལ་སྒོ་གསུམ་གྱིས་མི་མཆོད་པ། not making offerings to the Three Jewels every day by means of body, speech and mind 2.

འདོད་པའི་སེམས་ཀྱིས་གཏམ་བརྗོད་པ་སོགས་དེའི་རྗེས་སུ་འཇུག་པ། indulging in worldly pleasures such as in talking by means of attachment 3. བསླབ་པ་རྒན་པ་རྣམས་དང་ཡོན་ཏན་ཅན་ལ་གུས་པར་མི་བྱེད་པ། being disrespectful to the senior trainees and those who are knowledgeables 4. ཆོས་སོགས་ཀྱི་ཚིག་དོན་དྲིས་པ་ལ་ནི་དེའི་ལན་མི་འདེབས་པ། not giving answers to those who ask questions relating to Dharma 5. དད་པས་མགྲོན་དུ་བོས་པ་ན་མི་རུང་བ་མེད་བཞིན་བདག་གིར་མི་བྱེད་པ། declining an invitation without good reason extended in good faith 6. གསེར་ལ་སོགས་པ་ཕུལ་ཡང་ཞེན་པ་མེད་པ་ལེན་པར་གསུངས་པ་ལས་ལེན་པར་མི་བྱེད་པ། refusing to accept offerings of gold and the like when it is said to be permissible to accept them with a mind free of attachment 7. ཆོས་འདོད་པ་ལ་སྦྱིན་པར་མི་བྱེད་པ། not giving Dharma to those who desire it. ཚུལ་ཁྲིམས་དང་འགལ་བ་དགུ་ནི། Nine associated with the perfection of morality 1. ཚུལ་ཁྲིམས་འཆལ་བ་ཡལ་བར་འདོར་བ། neglecting those who have broken their moral commitments 2. ཕ་རོལ་དད་པའི་ཕྱིར་སྒོ་གསུམ་བཙུན་པར་སློབ་པར་མི་བྱེད་པ། not using one's three gates of activities to effect trainings that cause others to generate faith 3. ཁུར་ཁུར་བ་སོགས་སེམས་ཅན་གྱི་གནས་སྐབས་ཀྱི་དོན་ལ་བྱ་བ་ཆུང་ངུར་ཡང་མ་བརྩོན་པ། not making efforts to benefit others in order to help others even to the extent of carrying their luggage and the like 4. སྙིང་བརྩེར་བཅས་ན་མི་དགེ་མེད་པས་བྱ་བ་ངན་པ་ཀློག་ཕྱིར་ཆིག་རྩུབ་སོགས་ཤེས་བཞིན་མི་བྱེད་པ། refusing to do negative actions even though it is taught that these are free of negativities when motivated by compassion 5. འཚོ་བ་ལོག་པ་དང་དུ་ལེན་པ། practicing wrong livelihood 6. སྒོ་གསུམ་འཆལ་ཞིང་རབ་ཏུ་ཁོད་པ། indulging in frivolous activites by body, speech and mind 7. དགོས་པ་མེད་པར་འཁོར་བ་ཁྱིམ་པའི་རྟེན་གཅིག་པུས་བགྲོད་པར་སེམས་པ། thinking without good reason that a Bodhisattva can attain enlightenment solely by being in the midst of samsaric household life 8. གྲགས་པ་མ་ཡིན་པ་མི་སྤོང་བ། not avoiding a bad reputation 9. ཉོན་མོངས་དང་བཅས་ཀུང་ཤེས་བཞིན་དུ་འཆོས་པར་མི་བྱེད་པ། not helping someone to avoid a situation when you know others do it forced by their negativities. བཟོད་པ་དང་འགལ་བ་བཞི་ནི། Four associated with the perfection of patience 1. གཤེ་བ་ལ་ལན་དུ་གཤེ་བ་ལ་སོགས་པ་བཞི། the four such as retaliating a harm with harm and so on (see dge-sbyong gi chos-bzhi) 2. ཁྲོས་པ་རྣམས་ནི་ཡལ་བར་དོར་བ། neglecting to apologize those who were incited into anger by oneself 3. ཕ་རོལ་གྱི་ཤད་ཀྱིས་ཆགས་པ་སྤོང་བ། not accepting others' sincere apologies 4. གཞན་ཁྲོས་པའི་སེམས་ཀྱིས་རྗེས་སུ་འཇུག་པ། letting oneself be carried out by anger against others. བརྩོན་འགྲུས་དང་འགལ་བ་གསུམ་ནི། Three associated with the perfection of effort 1. རྙེད་བཀུར་འདོད་པའི་ཕྱིར་འཁོར་རྣམས་སྡུད་པ། gathering a circle of followers out of desire for profit or reputation 2. ལེ་ལོ་ལ་སོགས་པའི་ཆོས་ལ་མི་སྦྱོར་བ་སེལ་བར་མི་བྱེད་པ། not trying to eliminate habits such as laziness that are obstacles to the practicing Dharma 3. གཞན་དྲངས་པ་སོགས་ཀྱི་ཕྱིར་མ་ཡིན་པར་ཆགས་པས་བྱི་མོའི་གཏམ་ལ་བརྟེན་པ། indulging in gossips out of attachment other than in conversation to help others བསམ་གཏན་དང་འགལ་བ་གསུམ་ནི། Three associated with the perfection of concentration 1. ཏིང་ངེ་འཛིན་གྱི་དོན་མི་འཚོལ་བ། not making efforts to find the meaning of concentration 2. བསམ་གཏན་གྱི་སྒྲིབ་པ་ལྔ་སྤོང་བར་མི་བྱེད་པ། not overcoming the five obstacles to concentration (see nyes-pa lnga) 3. བསམ་གཏན་གྱི་རོ་ཤིན་སྦྱངས་ཀྱི་བདེ་བ་ལ་ཡོན་ཏན་དུ་བལྟ་བ། being attached to the taste or ecstatic suppleness of the meditative concentration ཤེས་རབ་དང་འགལ་བ་བརྒྱད་ནི། Eight associated with the perfection of wisdom 1. ཉན་ཐོས་ཀྱི་ཐེག་པ་སྤོང་བར་བྱེད་པ། abandoning the Lower Vehicle 2. རང་ཚུལ་ཐེག་ཆེན་ཡོད་བཞིན་དེ་ལ་བརྩོན་པ་དགོས་པ་མེད་པར་བརྩོན་བྱ་མིན་པའི་ཕ་རོལ་གྱི་བསྟན་བཅོས་ལ་བརྩོན་པ། putting a great effort in studying the doctrine of the Lower Vehicle and other subjects even though they serve no significant purpose for one has already embarked on to the study and practice of the Greater Vehicle 3. དགོས་པའི་དབང་གིས་བརྩོན་པར་བྱེད་ཀྱང་དེ་ལ་ཡོན་ཏན་དུ་བལྟ་བར་དགའ་བ། although it is necessary to study other subjects for good reasons, but being engrossed in them with pleasure 4. ཐེག་པ་ཆེན་པོ་སྤོང་བར་བྱེད་པ་སྙེ་དེ་ལ་མི་བརྩོན་པ། not making effort in the study and practice of the Greater Vehicle teachings and abandoning them 5. བག་མེད་ཙམ་གྱིས་བདག་ལ་བསྟོད་ཅིང་གཞན་ལ་སྨོད་པ། praising oneself and criticising others with negligence 6. ཆོས་ཀྱི་དོན་དུ་འགྲོ་བར་མི་བྱེད་པ། making no effort to study or practice Dharma 7. དེ་ལ་སྨོད་ཅིང་ཡི་གེར་མཆོག་ཏུ་བཟུང་ནས་དེ་ཙམ་ལ་ཡིད་རྟོན་པ། neglecting the study and practice of Dharma and prefering to read other non-Dharma materials 8. སེམས་ཅན་དོན་བྱེད་དང་འགལ་བ་ལ་བཅུ་གཉིས། Twelve associated with not giving assistance and care to others. གཞན་དོན་ལས་ཉམས་ཉེས་པ་བཞི། Of these there are four for not giving assistance to others, which are: 1. གཞན་གྱི་དགོས་པའི་དོན་ཅི་ཡང་རུང་བའི་གྲོགས་སུ་འགྲོ་བར་མི་བྱེད་པ། not going to the assistance of those seeking help for their purpose 2. ནད་པའི་རིམ་གྲོ་བྱ་བ་སྤོང་བ། neglecting to offer service to the sick 3. གཞན་གྱི་ལུས་སྡུག་བསྔལ་སེལ་བར་ནུས་བཞིན་མི་བྱེད་པ། not acting to dispel sufferings of others although one is capable of giving help 4. ཤེས་བཞིན་དུ་བག་མེད་པ་ལ་རིགས་པ་མི་སྟོན་པ། not helping others to overcome their bad habits knowingly. གཞན་ལ་ཕན་མི་འདོགས་པའི་ཉེས་པ་དྲུག Six faults for not benefiting others: 1. ཕན་པ་བྱེད་པ་ལ་ལན་དུ་ཕན་མི་འདོགས་པ། not returning help of those who benefit oneself 2. གཞན་གྱི་སེམས་མྱ་ངན་གྱིས་གདུང་བ་སེལ་བར་མི་བྱེད་པ། not relieving the distress of others 3. ནོར་འདོད་པ་ལ་སེར་སྣ་མེད་ཀྱང་ལེ་ལོས་སྦྱིན་པར་མི་བྱེད་པ། not giving material help to those who seek charity out of laziness even though one lack miserliness 4. རང་གི་འཁོར་རྣམས་ཀྱི་གནས་སྐབས་ཀྱི་དོན་མི་བྱེད་པ། not giving assistance to one's disciples to fulfill their temporary benefits 5. ཆོས་དང་མི་བསྟུན་པ་མེད་པའི་གཞན་གྱི་བློ་དང་མཐུན་པར་མི་འཇུག་པ། not acting in accordance with the inclinations of others when these do not contradict Dharma 6. ཆོས་ལ་འཇུག་པའི་དགོས་པ་མེད་པས་ཡོན་ཏན་དང་བསྔགས་པ་སྒྲ་བར་མི་བྱེད་པ། not praising the good qualities of others unless there is a special purpose of turning their mind to Dharma ངན་པ་ཚར་མི་གཅོད་པའི་ཉེས་པ་གཉིས། Two faults for not subduing an evil person. 1. ཕ་རོལ་པོའི་རྐྱེན་དང་འཚམས་པར་བྱ་བ་རྩུབ་མོས་ཚར་མི་གཅོད་པ། not subduing others with wrathful actions when it is harmonious to their evil conduct 2. རྫུ་འཕྲུལ་དང་བསྡིགས་པ་ལ་སོགས་པ་མི་བྱེད་པ། not performing miracles and threatening actions, or so on.

ཉོན་མོངས་ཀྱི་རྒྱུ་དྲུག

The six causes of generating delusions. 1. རྟེན། basis 2. དམིགས་པ། object 3. འདུ་འཛི། public gatherings 4. བཤད་པ། speaking 5. གོམས་པ། familiarity 6. ཡིད་ལ་བྱེད་པ། mental reflection.

ཉོན་སྒྲིབ།

Kleśāvaraṇa/ Delusive obscurations. Obstacles to liberation primarily preventing liberation from cyclic existence. There are two types : 1. ཉོན་སྒྲིབ་ཀུན་བཏགས། prajñāpti kleśāvaraṇa/ the intellectually acquired obscuration to liberation 2. ཉོན་སྒྲིབ་ལྷན་སྐྱེས། sahaja kleśāvaraṇa/ innately acquired obscuration to liberation.

ཉོན་མོངས།

Kleśa/ Defilement; delusion; affliction. A mental state that produces turmoil and confusion thus disturbing mental peace and happiness.

ཉོན་མོངས་སྐྱེ་བའི་རྒྱུ་དྲུག

The three causes of generating delusions. 1. ཉོན་མོངས་པའི་བག་ལ་ཉལ་བ་མ་སྤངས་པ། non-elimination of latent delusions 2. ཉོན་མོངས་སྐྱེ་བའི་ཡུལ་ཉེ་བར་གནས་པ། close association with the object prone to generate delusions 3. རྩལ་བཞིན་མ་ཡིན་པར་ཡིད་ལ་བྱེད་པ། entertaining wrong thoughts.

ཉོན་མོངས་ལྔ།

Pañca kleśāḥ/ The five types of delusions. 1. ཀུན་སྦྱོར། constant fetters (see kun-sbyor gsum or dgu) 2. ཕྲ་རྒྱས། subtle increase (phra-rgyas) 3. འཆིང་བ། bindings 4. ཉེ་ཉོན། near delusions 5. ཀུན་དཀྲིས། ever-binding factors (see kun-dkris bzhi).

ཉོན་མོངས་ཅན་གྱི་རེག་པ་གསུམ།

The three contacts of a delusive mind. 1. མ་རིག་པའི་རེག་པ། contact with ignorance 2. གནོད་སེམས་ཀྱི་རེག་པ། contact with harmful intention 3. རྗེས་སུ་ཆགས་པའི་རེག་པ། contact with attachment.

ཉོན་མོངས་ཆུང་ངུའི་ས་མང་བཅུ།

Daśālpakleśabhūmikāḥ/ Ten mental attitudes of the minor delusions (see 1-10 nye-nyon nyi-shu). These are called minor because of being weaker by nature of their accompanying mental factors, weaker by nature of abandonment and weaker by nature of the primary mind which is their basis.

ཉོན་མོངས་ཆེན་པོའི་ས་མང་དྲུག

Ṣaḍ mahākleśa bhūmikāḥ/ Six mental attitudes of the major delusions. 1. མ་དད་པ། aśraddya/ lack of faith 2. ལེ་ལོ། kausīdya/ laziness 3. གཏི་མུག moha/ ignorance 4. བྱིང་བ། nimagna/ mental cloudiness 5. རྒོད་པ། auddhātya/ mental agitation 6. བག་མེད་པ། pramāda/ unconscientiousness.

ཉོན་མོངས་གཉིས།

The two delusions. 1. ཉོན་མོངས་ཀུན་བཏགས། intellectually acquired delusions 2. ཉོན་མོངས་ལྷན་སྐྱེས། innately born delusions.

ཉོན་མོངས་དུག་ལྔ།

The five delusive poisons; the five poisonous delusions. 1. འདོད་ཆགས། desire-attachment 2. ཁོང་ཁྲོ hatred-anger 3. མ་རིག་པ། ignorance 4. ང་རྒྱལ། pride 5. ཕྲག་དོག jealousy.

ཉོན་མོངས་རྣམ་སྦྱོང་གི་དམིགས་པ།

Object for eliminating delusions. One of the four objects of a Yogi (see rnal-'byor gyi dmigs-pa bzhi) meditating on the development of mental quiescence meditation in which a meditator either sees the lower concentration levels as grosser and the higher as subtler or takes either of the sixteen features of the four noble truths (see mi-rtag sogs bcu-drug) as his or her object of meditation for developing śamatha.

ཉོན་མོངས་པའི་དྲི་མ་དྲུག

The six stains of delusions. The six stains or gross thoughts that arise in reliance upon delusions. 1. སྒྱུ། deception 2. གཡོ། dishonesty 3. རྒྱགས་པ། conceit 4. འཚིག་པ། outrage 5. ཁོན་འཛིན། grudge 6. རྣམ་འཚེ། harmfulness.

ཉོན་མོངས་པའི་བྱེད་ལས་བཅུ།

The ten functions of delusions. 1. རྩ་བ་བརྟན་པར་བྱེད་པ། it stabilizes the root of delusion 2. རྒྱུན་གནས་པར་བྱེད་པ། it keeps the continuity of delusion 3. ཞིང་དུ་སྒྲུབ་པར་བྱེད་པ། it establishes its own goal 4. རྒྱུ་མཐུན་པར་སྒྲུབ་པར་བྱེད་པ། it establishes results similar to itself 5. ལས་ཀྱི་སྲིད་པ་མངོན་པར་སྒྲུབ་པར་བྱེད་པ། it establishes karmically linked existence 6. རང་གི་ཚོགས་ཡོངས་སུ་འཛིན་པར་བྱེད་པ། it treasures its own collection of delusions 7. དམིགས་པ་ལ་ཀུན་དུ་རྨོངས་པར་བྱེད་པ། it makes its objectives unclear 8. རྣམ་པར་ཤེས་པའི་རྒྱུན་འཁྲིད་པར་བྱེད་པ། it leads to the continuity of consciousness 9. དགེ་བའི་ཕྱོགས་ལས་གཡོ་བར་བྱེད་པ། it misdirects oneself from wholesome activities 10. ཁམས་ལས་མི་འདའ་བའི་རྩལ་

གྱིས་འཆིང་བའི་དོན་དུ་ཁྱབ་པར་བྱེད་པ། it multiplies as a binding force without transcending the delusive realms.

ཉོན་མོངས་པའི་ལམ་གསུམ།

The three paths of delusions. 1. ཉོན་མོངས་པའི་ལམ། path of delusions 2. ལས་ཀྱི་ལམ། karmic path 3. སྐྱེ་བའི་ཀུན་ནས་ཉོན་མོངས་པའི་ལམ། path of rebirth.

ཉོན་མོངས་གསུམ།

The three delusions. 1. ཉོན་མོངས་པ་ཀུན་ནས་བསླང་པའི་ཉོན་མོངས། kleśasaṁkleśa/ delusions arising from other delusions 2. ལས་ཀྱི་ཀུན་ནས་བསླང་པའི་ཉོན་མོངས། karmasaṁkleśa/ delusions arising from karma 3. སྐྱེ་བའི་ཀུན་ནས་བསླང་པའི་ཉོན་མོངས། utpattisaṁkleśa/ delusions arising from birth.

ཉོན་ཡིད།

Kleśa manas/ The deluded mind. One of the eight groups of consciousnesses (see rnam-shes tshogs-brgyad). It is recognized as an obstructive unspecified primary consciousness (sgrib lung-ma bstan) that takes the foundation or fundamental consciousness (see kun-gzhi rnam-shes) as its object and maintains ego-grasping with respect to it until the person has attained the Ārya path.

ཉོན་ཡིད་རྣམ་ཤེས།

Kleśa vijñāna/ The deluded consciousness; the afflicted mind. It is one of the eight types of consciousnesses (see rnam-shes tshogs-brgyad) asserted by the Cittamātrin school of thought. The deluded mind is an obstructed and unspecified conceptual consciousness that takes the foundational consciousness as its focal object and grasps at it as being a substantially existent self, etc.

གཉན་པོ་གསང་བ།

The extremely secret teachings. This name is given to the collection of mdo-sde za-ma tog, snying-po yi-ge drgug-ma, spang-skong phyag-rgya, and a golden stūpa found from a casket that fell from the sky during the reign of King Lha Thothori Nyan Tsan (5th century A.D.), the 27th officially recognized king of Tibet. This is considered the beginning of Buddhism in Tibet.

གཉིད་དུས་ཀྱི་འོད་གསལ།

Nidrā prabhāsvara/ The clear light of sleep; the clear light mind of sleep state. The practice of activating the subtle mind during sleep; a part of completion stage yoga of tantra.

གཉིས་སྟོང།

Ubhaya śūnyatā/ Non-duality or separate simultaneous sources between the consciousness and its object. It can also mean the non-duality of bliss and void.

གཉིས་སྟོང་གི་དེ་ཁོ་ན་ཉིད།

Ubhaya tathātā/ The reality of non-duality; the thatness of non-duality.

གཉིས་སྣང།

Ubhayābhāsa/ Dualistic appearance; mundane appearance. The duality of the object of apprehension and the consciousness that apprehends it.

གཉིས་མེད་ཀྱི་རྒྱུད།

Advaya tantra/ The non-dual tantra. That of anuttarayoga tantra in which equal emphasis is placed on the development of the mind of clear light and the illusory body.

གཉིས་སུ་མེད་པའི་སྐད་ཅིག་སྦྱོར་བ།

Advayaka kṣanikaprayoga/ The momentary training in non-duality. The final instant of the path of meditation of a Bodhisattva's training during which he or she realizes the non-duality of the object and object-perceiver directly within a single instant of time.

གཉུག་མའི་དགེ་འདུན།

Nivāsita saṅgha/ The permanent resident monk. A monk who has been staying at the same monastery ever since his admission in that monastery.

གཉུག་མའི་ཡེ་ཤེས།

The primordial wisdom; the naturally abiding intutive mind or awareness, also called the basic wisdom.

གཉེན་པོ་སྟོབས་བཞི།

Catvāri pratipakṣabalāni/ The four opponent forces; the four strong antidotes. 1. རྟེན་གྱི་སྟོབས། force of reliance 2. གཉེན་པོའི་སྟོབས། force of overcoming misdeeds through antidotes 3. རྣམ་པར་སུན་འབྱིན་པའི་སྟོབས། force of repentence 4. ཉེས་པ་ལས་སླར་ལྡོག་པའི་སྟོབས། force of not repeating the misdeeds.

གཉེན་པོ་འདུ་བྱེད་བརྒྱད།

Aṣṭa pratipakṣasaṁskārāḥ/ The application of eight antidotes. Eight antidotes applied to eliminate the five faults to mental quiescence meditation (śamatha). 1-4. ལེ་ལོའི་གཉེན་པོར་དད་པ། འདུན་པ། རྩོལ་བ། ཤིན་སྦྱངས། faith, aspiration, enthusiastic perseverance and ecstasy as antidotes to laziness. 5. གདམས་ངག་བརྗེད་པའི་གཉེན་པོར་དྲན་པ། mindfulness as an antidote to forgetting the instructions (losing object of meditation) 6. བྱིང་རྒོད་ཀྱི་གཉེན་པོར་ཤེས་བཞིན། alertness as an antidote to mental dullness and agitation 7. མངོན་པར་འདུ་མི་བྱེད་པའི་གཉེན་པོར་འདུ་བྱེད་པ། application of antidotes to counter their non-application 8. མངོན་པར་འདུ་བྱེད་པའི་གཉེན་པོར་འདུ་མི་བྱེད་པ། non-application of antidotes to counter their application.

གཉེན་པོ་ལྡེམ་པོར་དགོངས་པ།

Pratipakṣābhisandhi/ Interpretive sūtras concerning antidotes. For instance, the sūtra which says, 'father and mother are to be killed', taught to king Ajātaśatru in order to calm his regrets temporarily and to teach him to eliminate ignorance and karma ultimately.

གཉེན་པོ་ཕྱོགས་ཀྱི་གཞི་ཤེས།

Pratipaksa vastujñāna/ The knowledge of basis categorized as an antidote. The sixth of the nine topics that characterize the knowledge of the basis; a Mahāyāna path that is a superior path of wisdom and method identical with the basic wisdom within the continuum of a Mahāyānist Ārya. This wisdom exists from the path of seeing to the path of no more learning.

གཉེན་པོ་དགེ་བ་བརྒྱད།

Aṣṭa pratipakṣa kuśalāni/ The eight antidotal virtues. Antidotal virtue through: 1. རྣམ་པར་སུན་འབྱིན་པའི་གཉེན་པོ། overcoming negative forces 2. གཞིའི་གཉེན་པོ། counteracting one's virtuous forces 3. ཐག་སྲིང་བའི་གཉེན་པོ། prolonging one's virtuous forces 4. རྣམ་པར་གནོན་པའི་གཉེན་པོ། subduing the negative forces 5. བྲལ་བའི་གཉེན་པོ། separating from negative forces 6. ཉོན་སྒྲིབ་ཀྱི་གཉེན་པོ། counteracting the obstructions to liberation 7. ཤེས་སྒྲིབ་ཀྱི་གཉེན་པོ། counteracting the obstructions to omniscience 8. སྤོང་བའི་གཉེན་པོ། elimination of negative forces.

མཉན་ཡོད།

Śrāvastī/ The capital of the kingdom of Kosala, where Buddha Śākyamuni passed 25 rainy seasons. It is called the place where Buddha defeated the Heterodox teachers through miracles.

མཉམ་གནས་ཀྱི་རླུང་།

The equalizing wind; the equally abiding energy wind. One of the five energy winds in the body (see rtsa-ba'i rlung lnga) that controls the digestive process of assimilation of nutrition and separation of waste materials located at the third stage of the stomach. This wind is also called the fire-dwelling wind (me-gnas-kyi rlung).

མཉམ་པ་ཉིད་ལྔ།

The five samenesses; the five universal qualities of all Bodhisattvas. 1. བདག་གཞན་མཉམ་ཉིད། both self and other are equal 2. ཕན་གནོད་མཉམ་ཉིད། both self and others are equal in wishing to be benefitted and not wishing to be harmed 3. འཇིག་རྟེན་ཆོས་བརྒྱད་མཉམ་ཉིད། both self and others are equal in having the eight worldly concerns (see 'jig-rten chos-brgyad) 4. སྲིད་ཞི་མཉམ་ཉིད། both the cyclic existence and the state of liberation are the same.

མཉམ་པ་ཉིད་བཅུ།

The ten samenesses; the ten samenesses of all phenomena as: 1. མཚན་ཉིད་མེད་པ་མཉམ་པ་ཉིད། asvabhāva samatā/ lacking truly existent features 2. མཚན་མ་མེད་པ་མཉམ་པ་ཉིད། alakṣaṇa samatā/ lacking truly existent signs and marks 3. མཐའ་བཞི་ལས་སྐྱེ་བ་མེད་པ་མཉམ་པ་ཉིད། ajāti samatā/ lacking production from the four extremes—self, others, both and neither both. 4. མ་སྐྱེས་པ་མཉམ་པ་ཉིད། ajātaka samatā/ being unproduced 5. དབེན་པ་མཉམ་པ་ཉིད། śūnyā samatā/ being empty 6. གདོད་མ་ནས་རྣམ་པར་དག་པ་མཉམ་པ་ཉིད། adhiśuddha samatā/ being primordially pure 7. སྤྲོས་པ་མེད་པ་མཉམ་པ་ཉིད། niṣprapañca samatā/ lacking conceptual elaboration 8. བླང་བ་དང་དོར་བར་བྱ་བ་མིན་པ་མཉམ་པ་ཉིད། anupadeyāheya samatā/ not being objects of cultivation and elimination 9. ཆོས་ཐམས་ཅད་མི་ལམ་དང་། མིག་གཡོར་དང་། གཟུགས་བརྙན་དང་། སྤྲུལ་པ་ལྟ་བུར་མཉམ་པ་ཉིད། svapna māyā udakacandra pratibimba nirmaṇopama samatā/ being like a dream, hallucination, moon in the water, reflection and emanation 10. དངོས་པོ་དང་དངོས་པོ་མེད་པ་མཉམ་པ་ཉིད། bhāva-abliāva samatā/ being a thing or non-thing. The first seven indicate the subtle selflessness of phenomena and the eighth, subtle selflessness of person, whereas the last two show emptiness pertaining to both.

མཉམ་པ་ཉིད་ལ་དགོངས་པ།

Samatābhiprāya/ Interpretative sūtra determining the samenesses; e.g., the sūtra. 'I shall be Buddha Maitreya at that time', in which the basic intention of Buddha was to reveal that all the Buddhas are equal in having attained the three equal states (see mnyam pa nyid gsum).

མཉམ་པ་ཉིད་གསུམ།

The three samenesses; the three equal states of all Buddhas. 1. ཚོགས་བསགས་པ་མཉམ་པ་ཉིད། equal in terms of having accumulated merits 2. ཆོས་སྐུ་ཐོབ་པ་མཉམ་པ་ཉིད། equal in terms of having attained the Truth Body 3. གཞན་དོན་བྱེད་པ་མཉམ་པ་ཉིད། equal in terms of working for the welfare of others.

མཉམ་བཞག་ཡེ་ཤེས།

The wisdom of meditative equipoise. A wisdom of single pointed concentration in the process of directly eliminating or having eliminated its respective object of abandonemt. In general there are two: 1. བར་ཆད་མེད་ལམ། the uninterrupted path 2. རྣམ་གྲོལ་ལམ། the path of thorough liberation.

རྙིང་མ།

The Ancient School; the Nyingma Tradition. A first major school of Tibetan Buddhism introduced in Tibet by Guru Padmasambhava, the great Indian mahāyogi who came to Tibet in the 8th century.

ཉིང་མའི་ཐེག་པ་རིམ་པ་དགུ

The nine vehicles of the Nyingma tradition. 1. ཉན་ཐོས་ཀྱི་ཐེག་པ། the Hearers' vehicle 2. རང་རྒྱལ་གྱི་ཐེག་པ། the Solitary Realizers' vehicle 3. བྱང་སེམས་ཀྱི་ཐེག་པ། the Bodhisattvas' vehicle 4. བྱ་རྒྱུད་ཀྱི་ཐེག་པ། the action tantra vehicle 5. སྤྱོད་རྒྱུད་ཀྱི་ཐེག་པ། the performance tantra vehicle 6. ཡོ་གའི་ཐེག་པ། the yoga tantra vehicle 7. མ་ཧཱ་ཡོ་གའི་ཐེག་པ། the mahāyoga tantra vehicle 8. ཨ་ནུ་ཡོ་གའི་ཐེག་པ། the anuttarayoga tantra vehicle 9. ཨ་ཏི་ཡོ་གའི་ཐེག་པ། the atiyoga tantra vehicle.

སྙན་བརྒྱུད།

The whispered lineage. A lineage of secret teachings transmitted only to the closest disciples through direct communication with their root teacher or meditational deity.

སྙན་བརྒྱུད་བཞི།

The four types of whispered lineages. 1. ཆོས་གང་ལུང་དང་བཅས་པ། having received oral transmissions of every teaching one has received 2. ལུང་མན་ངག་དང་བཅས་པ། having all oral transmissions with instructions from the teacher 3. མན་ངག་བརྒྱུད་དང་ལྡན་པ། having all instructions coming through the proper lineage 4. བརྒྱུད་པ་བྱིན་རླབས་དང་ལྡན་པ། having all lineages blessed.

སྙིགས་དུས།

Kaliyuga/ The degenerate age; the decadent period. The period when the tradition of Buddha's teachings are no longer pure and the world situation makes it difficult to practice properly. This also refers to the period of the universe when the lifespan of human beings is declining from one hundred to ten years.

སྙིགས་མ་ལྔ

Pañca kaṣāyāḥ/ The five dregs; the five degenerations. 1. ཚེ་སྙིགས་མ། āyuḥ kaṣāya/ degenerated life-span 2. ཉོན་མོངས་སྙིགས་མ། kleśa kaṣāya/ degenerated delusions 3. སེམས་ཅན་སྙིགས་མ། sattva kaṣāya/ degenerated persons 4. དུས་སྙིགས་མ། kalpa kaṣāya/ degenerated time 5. ལྟ་བ་སྙིགས་མ། dṛṣṭi kaṣāya/ degenerated view.

སྙིང་གར་ཐོག་མར་ཆགས་པའི་རྩ་བརྒྱད།

The eight channels initially formed at the heart. 1. དབུ་མ། the central channel 2. རོ་མ། the right channel 3. རྐྱང་མ། the left channel 4. ཤར་གྱི་གསུམ་སྐོར་མ། the triple circle of the east 5. ལྷོའི་འདོད་མ། the desirous one of the south 6. ནུབ་ཀྱི་བདུད་བྲལ་མ། the one free of hindrance of the west 7. བྱང་གི་ཁྱིམ་མ། the householder of the north 8. གཏུམ་མོ། the fiery one.

སྙིང་རྗེ་རྣམ་གསུམ།

The three types of compassion. 1. སེམས་ཅན་ཙམ་ལ་དམིགས་པའི་སྙིང་རྗེ། compassion merely observing sentient beings 2. ཆོས་ལ་དམིགས་པའི་སྙིང་རྗེ། compassion observing the doctrine 3. དམིགས་མེད་ལ་དམིགས་པའི་སྙིང་རྗེ། compassion observing the lack of true existence.

སྙིང་རྗེས་ཞི་ལ་མི་གནས་པའི་ལམ་ཤེས།

Karuṇā na śamesthiti mārga jñāna/ The knowledge of the path which through compassion does not abide in the extreme of peace. The path of Mahāyāna Āryas categorized as negating the extreme of peace for the sake of sentient beings. It exists from the first level of a Bodhisattva up to the state of Buddhahood.

སྙིང་པོ་ལྔ

The five essentials. 1. བུ་རམ། molasses 2. ཞུན་མར། molten

butter 3. སྦྲང་རྩི། honey 4. ཏིལ་མར། sesame oil 5. ལན་ཚྭ། salt.

སྙིང་པོ་དོན་གསུམ།

The three essential practices. 1. ཚེ་འདི་ར་ཡི་དམ་སྒོམ་པ། meditation on one's deity in this life 2. འཆི་ཁར་འཕོ་བ་སྒོམ་པ། meditation on consciousness transference at death 3. བར་དོར་བསྲེ་བ་སྒོམ་པ། practising merging with the three bodies of a Buddha in the intermediate state.

སྙོམས་འཇུག

Samāpatti/ Meditative absorption. The state of single-pointed concentration within the form and formless realm in which a person's primary mind and secondary minds are fully absorbed in its object of meditation.

སྙོམས་འཇུག་གཉིས།

The two types of meditative absorptions of serial advancement: 1. འགོག་པའི་སྙོམས་འཇུག nirodha samāpatti/ the meditative absorption of cessation 2. འདུ་ཤེས་མེད་པའི་སྙོམས་འཇུག naivasamjñā na samjñāyatana/ the meditative absorption without-perception.

སྙོམས་འཇུག་བཞི།

The four types of meditative absorptions. The single-pointed meditative absorptions within the four states of the formless realm. 1. ནམ་མཁའ་མཐའ་ཡས་སྐྱེ་མཆེད། ākāśāntya samāpatti/ meditative absorption of infinite space 2. རྣམ་ཤེས་མཐའ་ཡས་སྐྱེ་མཆེད། vijñānāntya samāpatti/ meditative absorption of infinite consciousness 3. ཅི་ཡང་མེད་པའི་སྐྱེ་མཆེད། ākincanyāyatana samāpatti/ meditative absorbtion of nothingness 4. སྲིད་རྩེའི་སྙོམས་འཇུག ཡོད་མིན་མེད་མིན་སྐྱེ་མཆེད། bhavāgra samāpatti/ meditative absorption of the peak of existence, neither with perception nor without non-perception.

སྙོམས་འཇུག་དགུ

The nine types of meditative absorptions. 1-4. གཟུགས་ཁམས་ཀྱི་བསམ་གཏན་བཞི། བསམ་གཏན་བཞི། meditative absorptions of the four states of concentration within the form realm 5-8. གཟུགས་མེད་སྙོམས་འཇུག་བཞི། catvāri arūpadhātu samāpatti/ meditative absorptions of the four states of concentration within the formless realm 9. འགོག་པའི་སྙོམས་འཇུག nirodha samāpatti/ meditative absorption of the cessation.

བསྙེན་སྒྲུབ་ཡན་ལག་བཞི།

The four limbs of the approaching retreat. The ways of being in retreat. 1 བསྙེན་པ། approaching through visualizing a symbolic being 2. ཉེ་བར་བསྙེན་པ། the near achievement of a wisdom being 3. སྒྲུབ་པ། actual achievement 4. སྒྲུབ་པ་ཆེན་པོ། the great achievement.

བསྙེན་གནས་ཡན་ལག་བརྒྱད།

The eight precepts of an upāsaka. Vows to be observed by a one day vow holder. 1 སྲོག་གཅོད་སྤོང་བ། prāṇātighātād virati/ not killing 2. མ་བྱིན་པར་ལེན་པ་སྤོང་བ། ādattādānād virati/ not stealing 3. མི་ཚངས་སྤྱོད་སྤོང་བ། kāmamithyācārād virati/ not indulging in sexual activity 4. བརྫུན་སྤོང་བ། mṛṣāvādāt virati/ not telling a lie 5. ཆང་སྤོང་བ། madya pānam/ not taking intoxicants 6. གར་སོགས་སྤོང་བ། gānā nāṭaka virati/ not singing and dancing 7. ཕྱི་དྲོའི་ཁ་ཟས་སྤོང་བ། not taking a meal after noon 8. མལ་སྟན་ཆེ་མཐོ་སྤོང་བ། not using high and luxurious seat or bed.

བསྙེན་པ་བཞི།

The types of retreat practices; the four types of close practices. 1. ལུས་ཀྱི་བསྙེན་པ། kāya-āsevita/ close practice of body, by being in retreat for a definite time 2. གྲངས་ཀྱི་བསྙེན་པ། saṁkhya-āsevita/ close practice of numbers, through chanting a specified number of mantras 3. མཚན་མའི་བསྙེན་པ། lakṣaṇa-āsevita/ close practice of signs, through visualizing and dissolving oneself into the wisdom being 4. སེམས་བརྟན་གྱི་བསྙེན་པ། cittadṛḍha-āsevita/ close practice of conviction, by accomplishing the gross level of the generation stage practices.

ཏིང་ངེ་འཛིན་གྱི་དཀྱིལ་འཁོར།

Samādhi maṇḍala/ The concentration maṇḍala. The single-pointed concentration of visualizing the entire maṇḍala.

ཏིང་ངེ་འཛིན་གྱི་གེགས་ཉེས་པ་ལྔ།

The five faults in the development of concentration (see nyes-pa lnga).

ཏིང་ངེ་འཛིན་གྱི་ཆོ་འཕྲུལ།

The miracles of meditative concentration. One of the four miracles according to yoga tantra meditation (see cho-'phrul bzhi). This involves meditation through visualizing Vairocana in the centre, Akṣobhya to the east, Ratnasambhava to the south, Amitābha to the west, and Amoghasiddhi to the north encircled by four Bodhisattva each of their own family.

ཏིང་ངེ་འཛིན་གྱི་ཚོགས།

The requirements for developing meditative concentration. The virtuous forces indispensible for achieving calm abiding meditation.

ཏིང་ངེ་འཛིན་གསུམ།

The three meditative concentrations. A. According to the generation stage practice of mahāyoga tantra in the Nyingma tradition these are: 1. དེ་བཞིན་ཉིད་ཀྱི་ཏིང་ངེ་འཛིན། tathatāsamādhi/ meditative concentration of suchness 2. རབ་ཏུ་སྣང་བའི་ཏིང་ངེ་འཛིན། prabhāsasamādhi/ the all-apparent meditative concentration 3. རྒྱུའི་ཏིང་ངེ་འཛིན། hetusamādhi/ the causal concentration. B. According to the generation stage practice of yoga tantra and above, the three yogas of the generation stage in general are: 1. དང་པོ་སྦྱོར་བའི་ཏིང་ངེ་འཛིན། the initial preparatory meditative concentration 2. ལས་རྒྱལ་མཆོག་གི་ཏིང་ངེ་འཛིན། the supramundane activity meditative concentration 3. དཀྱིལ་འཁོར་རྒྱལ་མཆོག་གི་ཏིང་ངེ་འཛིན། the supramundane maṇḍala meditative concentration.

ཏིང་ངེ་འཛིན་སེམས་དཔའ།

Samādhi sattva/ The concentration being. The visualization of a seed syllable or implement at the heart of the wisdom being in the deity one has visualized.

ཏིང་ལོ།

The miniature fire balls. Flaming small dough balls thrown into one's mouth during the course of a Vajrayoginī initiation.

གཏད་པ་བཞི།

The four entrustments. The first four of the ten innermost jewels of the Kadampa tradition (see bka'-gdams phugs-nor bcu). The four are entrusting yourself to: 1. བློ་ཕུགས་ཆོས་ལ་གཏད། the Dharma as the simplest way of thought 2. ཆོས་

ཕུགས་སྤྲང་ལ་གཏད། poverty as the simplest way of practising Dharma 3. སྤྲང་ཕུགས་ཤི་ལ་གཏད། death as the extreme consequence of poverty 4. ཤི་ཕུགས་གྲོག་པོ་སྐམ་པོ་ལ་གཏད། an empty cave as the simplest place to die.

གཏད་རབས་བདུན།

The seven successors of the Buddha (see ston-pa'i gtad rabs-bdun).

གཏན་པ་མེད་པའི་སྦྱིན་པ།

Lavish generosity. The practice of selfless and continuous giving to the needy with total openness.

གཏན་ཚིགས་ཆེན་པོ་ལྔ།

The five great logical reasons. The five types of logical reasons to establish the middle way view. 1. གཅིག་དུ་བྲལ་གྱི་གཏན་ཚིགས། the reasoning of either being one or many 2. རྡོ་རྗེ་གཟེགས་མའི་གཏན་ཚིགས། the reasoning called vajra prongs 3. ཡོད་མེད་སྐྱེ་འགོག་གི་གཏན་ཚིགས། the reasoning of existence and non-existence, and production and cessation 4. མུ་བཞི་སྐྱེ་འགོག་གི་གཏན་ཚིགས། the reasoning negating birth from four alternatives.

གཏན་ཚིགས་རིག་པ།

Hetuvidyā/ The science of logic. One of the five major fields of study (see rig-gnas che-ba lnga), i.e. the study of Buddhist logic.

གཏན་ལ་ཕབ་པའི་སྡེ།

The set of finalized discourse. One of the twelve scriptural categories (see gsung-rab yan-lag bcu-gnyis) which explains the distinction of the individual and general category of phenomena, e.g. the set of discourse on knowledge.

གཏི་མུག

Moha/ Closed-mindedness; ignorance. An active misconception or a negative mental state obstructing the knowledge of reality.

གཏུམ་མོ།

Caṇḍālī/ Psychic fire; inner heat. The fine radiant blood cells or drops in the nature of the fire element, obtained from one's mother, which abide within the navel channel-wheel; realized practitioners ignite this element and generate sublime bliss thus using it as a means to experience enlightenment.

གཏུམ་མོའི་འབར་འཛག

The ignition and emission of psychic heat. The practice of meditation of igniting psychic heat or fire at the navel level and the emission of a drop or drops of bodhicitta from the short 'A' syllable visualized at the crown chakra.

གཏུར་བུ།

Vṛṣikā/ The square cloth for wrapping the yellow robes of monks and nuns.

གཏེར་ཆོས།

The treasure teachings. The extremely sublime secret texts of teachings hidden under rocks, trees, water etc., by Ācārya Padmasambhava and others because of the lack of appropriate disciples at that time. These texts were concealed for the benefit of future disciples and contained instructions for the ḍākinīs to guard and the appropriate discoverer to reveal these.

གཏེར་ལྟ་བུའི་སེམས་བསྐྱེད།

The treasure-like Bodhicitta. The mind of enlightenment

associated with the perfection of giving possessed by Bodhisattvas on the path of seeing.

གཏེར་སྟོན།

Discoverer of treasure. Realized master-scholars who discover texts, images and mystic articles connected to a highly sophisticated cycle of teachings. This tradition is very familiar to the Nyingma order of Tibetan Buddhism.

གཏོང་བ་རྗེས་སུ་དྲན་པ།

Tyāgānusmṛti/ Recollection of giving. The reflection on giving and the qualities of giving.

གཏོར་མ།

Bali/ Ritual cakes; sacramental cakes. A component of an offering usually made of barley flour (tsam-pa) and moulded butter, symbolizing deities and their retinues or the spirits, etc. Tormas can be of different sizes ranging from the size of one finger to one or two feet or more.

བཏགས་མིང་།

A nominal name; alias. A name which is not the actual term originally formulated to designate a specific meaning or a thing, but a later (perhaps vulgar or common) secondary term designating the same thing, e.g. 'the rabbit bearer' (ri-bong-can) refering to the moon. There are two types of nominal names: 1. འདྲ་བ་རྒྱུ་མཚན་དུ་བྱས་ནས་བཏགས་པའི་མིང་། nominal name because of similar features, e.g. calling a man a monkey 2. འབྲེལ་བ་རྒྱུ་མཚན་དུ་བྱས་ནས་བཏགས་པའི་མིང་། nominal name because of relationship, e.g. calling sunrays the sun.

བཏགས་ཙམ་གྱི་ང་།

The mere label of an 'I'; the conventionally existent 'I' or point of view of an 'I' that exists by mental labelling alone.

བཏགས་ཡོད།

Designated phenomena; imputed phenomena. Phenomena that exists only in dependence upon the sound and concept that imputes them. For instance, time and person.

བཏགས་ཡོད་ཆོས་གསུམ།

The three features of an imputed phenomena. 1. རང་ཉིད་མཚོན་བྱ་ཡིན་པ། being subject to definition 2. རང་གི་མཚན་གཞིའི་སྟེང་དུ་གྲུབ་པ། that which exists upon its own examples 3. རང་གི་མཚན་ཉིད་ལས་གཞན་པའི་ཆོས་གཞན་གྱི་མཚོན་བྱ་མི་བྱེད་པ། that which does not become a subject to be defined other than by its own definition.

རྟག་ཆད།

The views of eternalism and nihilism. According to Prāsaṅgika Mādhyamika this would be views asserting the true existence and total non-existence of phenomenon respectively.

རྟག་པ།

Nitya/ Permanence; unconditioned phenomena which are not dependent on causes and conditions.

རྟག་མཐའ།

The extreme of eternalism. Belief that something which is not validly existent is existent, e.g. the inherent-existence of a thing.

རྟགས།

Hetu/ A. Signs; marks. B. Reasons in the study of Buddhist logic.

རྟགས་ཚུལ་དང་པོ།

The first mode of reasoning; the first mark of logical reasoning. The presence of the posited reason in the subject or the pervasion of the subject by the reason in a given correct logical syllogism.

རྟགས་ཚུལ་གཉིས་པ།

The second mode of reasoning; the second mark of logical reasoning. The pervasion of the predicate by the reason in a syllogism.

རྟགས་ཚུལ་གསུམ་པ།

The third mode of reasoning; the third mark of logical reasoning. The non-pervasion of the negative of the predicate by the reason in a syllogism.

རྟགས་ལྟར་སྣང་གསུམ།

Tri hetvābhāsa/ The three wrong reasons. 1. མ་གྲུབ་པའི་རྟགས། asiddhahetu/ unestablished reason 2. འགལ་བའི་རྟགས། viruddhahetu/ contradictory reason 3. མ་ངེས་པའི་རྟགས། Anaikāntika-hetu/ uncertain reason.

རྟགས་ཡང་དག་གསུམ།

Tri saṁyag hetavaḥ/ The three correct reasons. 1. འབྲས་རྟགས་ཡང་དག kārya hetu/ correct reason of effect 2. རང་བཞིན་གྱི་རྟགས་ཡང་དག svabhāva hetu/ correct reason of nature 3. མ་དམིགས་པའི་རྟགས་ཡང་དག anupalabdhi hetu/ correct reason of non-cognition.

རྟགས་ཡང་དག་ལ་རྒོལ་བའི་སྒོ་ནས་དབྱེ་ན་གཉིས།

The two types of correct reasons according to the disputants. 1. རང་དོན་གྱི་རྟགས་ཡང་དག correct for one's own purpose 2. གཞན་དོན་གྱི་རྟགས་ཡང་དག correct reason for the other's purpose.

རྟགས་ཡང་དག་ལ་བསྒྲུབ་བྱའི་ཆོས་ཀྱི་སྒོ་ནས་དབྱེ་ན་གཉིས།

The two types of correct reasons according to the way they are applied to the predicate. 1. སྒྲུབ་རྟགས། positive reason 2. དགག་རྟགས། negative reason.

རྟགས་ཡང་དག་ལ་བསྒྲུབ་ཚུལ་གྱི་སྒོ་ནས་དབྱེ་ན་གསུམ།

The three types of correct reasons according to the way they are established. 1. དོན་སྒྲུབ་ཀྱི་རྟགས་ཡང་དག that which establishes meaning 2. ཐ་སྙད་སྒྲུབ་ཀྱི་རྟགས་ཡང་དག that which establishes name 3. ཐ་སྙད་འབའ་ཞིག་སྒྲུབ་ཀྱི་རྟགས་ཡང་དག that which establishes only names.

རྟགས་ཡང་དག་ལ་བསྒྲུབ་བྱའི་སྒོ་ནས་དབྱེ་ན་གསུམ།

The three types of correct reasons according to the thesis. 1. དངོས་སྟོབས་ཀྱི་རྟགས། reason based on cogent evidence 2. གྲགས་པའི་རྟགས། reasons based on renown 3. ཡིད་ཆེས་ཀྱི་རྟགས། reasons based on conviction.

རྟགས་ཡང་དག་ལ་མཐུན་ཕྱོགས་ལ་འཇུག་ཚུལ་གྱི་སྒོ་ནས་དབྱེ་ན་གཉིས།

The two types of correct reasons according to the way they are applied to the similar cases of the predicate. 1. མཐུན་ཕྱོགས་ལ་ཁྱབ་བྱེད་དུ་འཇུག་པའི་རྟགས། pervasive application to similar cases 2. དེ་ལ་ཆ་གཉིས་སུ་འཇུག་པའི་རྟགས། dual application to similar cases.

རྟགས་རིགས།

Signs and reasonings. Science of reasoning, one of the basic texts for logical studies in monastic universities.

རྟེན།

Āśraya/ A. Basis; support; that upon which something relies. B. A dependent basis such as our rebirth. C. Ritual objects, icons, images, offerings, deities and representations of Buddhas and Bodhisattvas.

ེན་གྱི་དབང་པོ་བདུན།

The seven faculties of reliance; the seven powers that the mind depends upon in order to produce a mental perception. 1-5. དབང་པོ་གཟུགས་ཅན་པ་ལྔ། the five physical faculties (see khams bco-brgyad, B 1-5) 6. ཡིད་ཀྱི་དབང་པོ། the faculty of consciousness 7. སྲོག་གི་དབང་པོ། the faculty of life.

ན་ཅན་གྱི་དབང་པོ་གཉིས།

The two faculties of basis of sex. 1. ཕོའི་དབང་པོ། the male organ 2. མོའི་དབང་པོ། the female organ.

ན་ཅིང་འབྲེལ་བར་འབྱུང་བ།

ratītyasamutpāda/ Interdependent origination; dependent co-origination. The meeting or coincidence of causes and onditions for creating a thing or a situation. In general, the welve links of interdependent origination dealing with the ycle of rebirth, and in its highest sense it is the proof of all henomena being dependent on each other and hence lacking nherent existence.

ན་དང་བརྟེན་པ།

he basis and the dependent; the reliance and the reliant; the esidence and the resident.

ན་འབྲེལ་གྱི་དཔེ་ཆོས་བཅུ་གཉིས།

he twelve analogies for the twelve links of dependent rigination. 1. མ་རིག་པ་ནི་རྒན་མོ་ལོང་བ་དང་འདྲ། ignorace is nalogous to a blind old woman 2. འདུ་བྱེད་རྫ་མཁན་ཞིག་དང་འདྲ། connecting karma is analogous to a potter moulding pot 3. རྣམ་ཤེས་སྤྲེའུ་དང་འདྲ། consciousness is like a onkey looking out of a window 4. མིང་གཟུགས་གྲུར་གཞུག་པ་དང་འདྲ། name and form are analogous to a man rowing a oat 5. སྐྱེ་མཆེད་ཁང་གསར་རྫོགས་པར་གྲུབ་པ་དང་འདྲ། sources f perception is analogous to a prosperous-looking house 6. རེག་པ་ཕོ་མོ་འཁྱུད་པ་དང་འདྲ། contact is analogous to a man and woman embracing each other 7. ཚོར་བ་མིག་ལ་མདའ་བསྣུན་པ་དང་འདྲ། feeling is analogous to an arrow piercing an eye 8. སྲེད་པ་ཆང་གིས་གཟི་བ་དང་འདྲ། craving is analogous to a drunken man 9. ལེན་པ་སྤྲེའུས་ཤིང་ཏོག་འཐོག་པ་དང་འདྲ། grasping is analogous to a monkey picking fruits 10. སྲིད་པ་བུད་མེད་སྦྲུམ་མ་དང་འདྲ། existence is analogous to a pregnant woman 11. སྐྱེ་བ་ཕྲུ་གུ་བཙས་པ་དང་འདྲ། birth is analogous to the birth of a child 12. རྒ་ཤི་མི་རོ་འཁུར་བ་དང་འདྲ། aging and death is analogous to a corpse being carried to cremation.

རྟེན་འབྲེལ་ཡན་ལག་བཅུ་གཉིས།

Dvādaśāṅga pratītyasamutpāda/ The twelve links of dependent origination. 1. མ་རིག་པ། avidyā/ ignorance 2. འདུ་བྱེད་ཀྱི་ལས། saṁskāra/ connecting karma 3. རྣམ་ཤེས། vijñānam/ consciousness 4. མིང་གཟུགས། nāma rūpam/ name and form 5. སྐྱེ་མཆེད། āyatanam/ sources of perception 6. རེག་པ། sparśa/ contact 7. ཚོར་བ། vedanā/ feeling 8. སྲེད་པ། tṛṣṇā/ craving 9. ལེན་པ། upādānam/ grasping 10. སྲིད་པ། bhava/ existence 11. སྐྱེ་བ། jāti/ birth 12. རྒ་ཤི jarā maraṇam/ aging and death.

རྟེན་འབྲེལ་ཡན་ལག་བཞི།

The four links of dependent origination. 1. འཕེན་བྱེད་ཀྱི་ཡན་ལག projecting causes being ignorance, connecting karma and consciousness. 2. འཕངས་པའི་ཡན་ལག projected results being name and form, sources of perception, contact and feeling. 3. མངོན་པར་འགྲུབ་པར་བྱེད་པའི་ཡན་ལག the materializing causes being craving, grasping and existence. 4. མངོན་པར་འགྲུབ་པའི་ཡན་ལག materialized results being birth, aging and death.

རྟོག་གེ་པ།

Tarkika/ Dialectician; logician. Those who explain the hidden nature of phenomena through reasonings.

རྟོག་གེ་སྨྲ་ལྔ།

Pañca tarkavāda/ The five schools of logic; the five schools of Hindu philosophy. 1. གྲངས་ཅན་པ། Sāṁkhya 2. རྒྱང་འཕེན་པ། Lokāyata 3. བྱེ་བྲག་པ། Vaiśeṣika 4. རིག་པ་ཅན་པ། Vedāntika 5. གཅེར་བུ་པ། Nirgrantha.

རྟོག་གེའི་ཚིག་དོན་བརྒྱད།

Aṣṭa tarkapadārtha/ The eight topics of logicians; the eight topics of discussion in the *Valid Cognition* (pramāṇavartika) text. 1. མངོན་སུམ་ཡང་དག། saṁyak pratyakṣa/ correct direct perception 2. མངོན་སུམ་ལྟར་སྣང་། abhāsa pratyakṣa/ wrong direct perception 3. རྗེས་དཔག་ཡང་དག saṁyag anumāna/ correct inferential perception 4. རྗེས་དཔག་ལྟར་སྣང་། abhāsa anumāna/ wrong inferential perception 5. སྒྲུབ་ངག་ཡང་དག saṁyag vāca/ correct argument 6. སྒྲུབ་ངག་ལྟར་སྣང་། abhāsa vāca/ wrong argument 7. སུན་འབྱིན་ཡང་དག saṁyag dūṣana/ correct refutation 8. སུན་འབྱིན་ལྟར་སྣང་། abhāsa dūṣana/ wrong refutation.

རྟོག་པ།

Vitarka/ A. Rough investigation. B. Conceptualization or imagination. C. Chapter. D. Conceptual awareness.

རྟོག་པ་དོན་མཐུན།

Conceptual awareness that conforms to reality, e.g. the correct inferential cognition apprehending the impermanence of sound.

རྟོག་པ་དོན་མི་མཐུན།

Conceptual awareness that does not conform to reality, e.g. a wrong conceptual thought apprehending a rabbit with horns.

རྟོག་མེད་ལོག་ཤེས།

Distorted non-conceptual awareness, e.g. the mistaken eye consciousness to which a mountain appears blue.

རྟོག་པ་བརྗོད་པའི་སྡེ།

Utterences of realizations (Avadānam); parables. One of the twelve scriptural categories that explains a topic with illustrations and examples for easy comprehension.

རྟོགས་པའི་བསྟན་པ།

The transmission of insights. One of the two kinds of Buddha's teachings that comprises insights and realizations gained through practice of the trainings.

རྟོགས་པས་བསྡུས་པ་དྲུག

The six qualities of Buddha's insight or realization from amongst the eighteen unshared qualities of a Buddha. 1. འདུན་པ་ཉམས་པ་མི་མངའ་བ། non-degenerating aspiration 2. བརྩོན་འགྲུས་ཉམས་པ་མི་མངའ་བ། non-degenerating effort 3. དྲན་པ་ཉམས་པ་མི་མངའ་བ། non-degenerating mindfulness 4. ཤེས་རབ་ཉམས་པ་མི་མངའ་བ། non-degenerating wisdom 5. ཏིང་ངེ་འཛིན་ཉམས་པ་མི་མངའ་བ། non-degenerating meditative concentration 5. རྣམ་པར་གྲོལ་བ་ཉམས་པ་མི་མངའ་བ། non-degenerating of thorough liberation.

རྟོན་པ་བཞི།

The four reliances; the four correct reliances. The four principles to be followed when one embarks on a Buddhist path or teaching. 1. གང་ཟག་ལ་མི་རྟོན་ཆོས་ལ་རྟོན། relying on teachings and not on the person 2. ཚིག་ལ་མི་རྟོན་དོན་ལ་རྟོ

relying on meaning and not on the words 3. རྣམ་ཤེས་མི་རྟོན་ཡེ་ཤེས་ལ་རྟོན། relying on wisdom and not on an ordinary mind 4. དྲང་དོན་ལ་མི་རྟོན་ཡེ་ཤེས་ལ་རྟོན། relying on definitive teachings and not on interpretive teachings.

ལྟ་ངན་བཅུ་དྲུག

Ṣoḍaśa kudṛṣṭayaḥ/ The sixteen wrong views; the view that: 1. བདག་འདས་པའི་དུས་ན་བྱུང་བར་ལྟ་བ། the self has existed in the past 2. བདག་འདས་པའི་དུས་ན་མ་བྱུང་བར་ལྟ་བ། the self did not exist in the past 3. བདག་འདས་པའི་དུས་ན་བྱུང་བ་དང་མ་བྱུང་བ་གཉིས་ཀ་ཡིན་པར་ལྟ་བ། the self has both existed and not existed in the past 4. བདག་འདས་པའི་དུས་ན་བྱུང་བ་དང་མ་བྱུང་བ་གཉིས་ཀ་མ་ཡིན་པར་ལྟ་བ། the self has neither existed nor not existed in the past 5. འཇིག་རྟེན་རྟག་པར་ལྟ་བ། the world is permanent 6. འཇིག་རྟེན་མི་རྟག་པར་ལྟ་བ། the world is impermanent 7. འཇིག་རྟེན་རྟག་པ་དང་མི་རྟག་པ་གཉིས་ཀ་ཡིན་པར་ལྟ་བ། the world is both permanent and impermanent 8. འཇིག་རྟེན་རྟག་པ་དང་མི་རྟག་པ་གཉིས་ཀ་མིན་པར་ལྟ་བ། the world is neither permanent nor not impermanent 9. བདག་མ་འོངས་པའི་དུས་ན་འབྱུང་བར་ལྟ་བ། the self will exist in the future 10. བདག་མ་འོངས་པའི་དུས་ན་མི་འབྱུང་བར་ལྟ་བ། the self will not exist in the future 11. བདག་མ་འོངས་པའི་དུས་ན་འབྱུང་བ་དང་མི་འབྱུང་བ་གཉིས་ཀ་ཡིན་པར་ལྟ་བ། the self will both exist and not exist in the future 12. བདག་མ་འོངས་པའི་དུས་ན་འབྱུང་བ་དང་མི་འབྱུང་བ་གཉིས་ཀ་མིན་པར་ལྟ་བ། the self will neither exist nor not exist in the future 13. འཇིག་རྟེན་མཐའ་དང་ལྡན་པར་ལྟ་བ། the world has an end 14. འཇིག་རྟེན་མཐའ་དང་མི་ལྡན་པར་ལྟ་བ། the world has no end 15. འཇིག་རྟེན་མཐའ་དང་ལྡན་པ་དང་མི་ལྡན་པ་གཉིས་ཀ་ཡིན་པར་ལྟ་བ། the world has both an end and no end 16. འཇིག་རྟེན་མཐའ་དང་ལྡན་པ་དང་མི་ལྡན་པ་གཉིས་ཀ་མིན་པར་ལྟ་བ། the world has neither an end nor no end.

ལྟ་བ་ཉི་ཤུ་རྩ་བརྒྱད།

Aṣṭaviṁśati kudṛṣṭayaḥ/ The twenty-eight wrong views. 1. མཚན་མར་ལྟ་བ། wrong view of truly existent marks 2. བཏགས་པ་ལ་སྐུར་འདེབས་ཀྱི་ལྟ་བ། wrong view deprecating imputed phenomena 3. ཀུན་རྟོག་ལ་སྐུར་འདེབས་ཀྱི་ལྟ་བ། wrong view deprecating conceptualization 4. དེ་ཁོ་ན་ཉིད་ལ་སྐུར་འདེབས་ཀྱི་ལྟ་བ། wrong view deprecating suchness 5. ཡོངས་སུ་འཛིན་པའི་ལྟ་བ། wrong view of thorough apprehension 6. སྒྱུར་བའི་ལྟ་བ། the inconsistent wrong view 7. ཁ་ན་མ་ཐོ་བ་མེད་པའི་ལྟ་བ། wrong view without moral faults 8. ངེས་པར་འབྱུང་བའི་ལྟ་བ། wrong view of definite release 9. དབང་ཟ་བའི་ལྟ་བ། wrong view of power 10. རབ་ཏུ་འཁྲུགས་པའི་ལྟ་བ། completely confused view 11. ཕྱིན་ཅི་ལོག་ཏུ་ལྟ་བ། perverted wrong view 12. འཕེལ་བའི་ལྟ་བ། multiplying wrong view 13. ཁས་མི་ལེན་པའི་ལྟ་བ། unaccepted wrong view 14. ངན་གཡོའི་ལྟ་བ། deceitful wrong view 15. བཀུར་བསྟིའི་ལྟ་བ། wrong view of devotion 16. རྨོངས་པ་བསྟན་པའི་ལྟ་བ། wrong view revealing ignorance 17. རྩ་བའི་ལྟ་བ། the fundamental wrong view 18. ལྟ་བ་ལ་ལྟ་བ་མ་ཡིན་པར་བལྟ་བ། wrong view refuting the right view 19. སྦྱོར་བ་སེལ་བའི་ལྟ་བ། wrong view rejecting the cause 20. ངེས་འབྱིན་མ་ཡིན་པའི་ལྟ་བ། wrong view that is not an aid to liberation 21. སྒྲིབ་པ་ལ་སོགས་པར་ལྟ་བ། wrong view of the obstructions, etc. 22. སྡིག་པ་འཕེལ་བའི་ལྟ་བ། wrong view multiplying the non-virtues 23. འབྲས་བུ་མེད་པའི་ལྟ་བ། wrong view lacking fruits 24. ཆད་པས་བཅད་པའི་ལྟ་བ། the nihilistic wrong view 25. སྐུར་བ་འདེབས་པའི་ལྟ་བ། the deprecating wrong view 26. བསྙད་པ་མ་ཡིན་པའི་ལྟ་བ། the inoffensive wrong view 27. ལྟ་བ་ཆེན་པོ། the great wrong view 28. མངོན་པའི་ང་རྒྱལ་གྱི་ལྟ་བ། wrong view of presumptuous pride.

ལྟ་སྟངས་ཀྱི་དངོས་གྲུབ་བརྒྱད།

The eight powerful glances; the eight yogic glances. The feats gained as signs of perfecting the first stage of anuttarayoga tantra practices. 1. ཤིང་ཏོག་འབྲས་བུ་མ་སྨིན་པ་ལྟ་སྟངས་བྱས་པ་ཙམ་གྱིས་ས་ལ་ལྟུང་བར་བྱེད་པ། the power to cast down unripened fruits by a mere glance 2. མཁྲིགས་ཤིང་གྱེན་དུ་སྐྱེས་པ་ལྟ་སྟངས་བྱས་པ་ཙམ་གྱིས་ཐུར་དུ་འགུག་པར་བྱེད་པ། the power to bend a straight tree by a mere glance 3. རྒྱང་རིང་གི་མེ་ཏོག་དྲི་ལྡན་རྣམས་ལྟ་སྟངས་བྱས་པ་ཙམ་གྱིས་དྲུང་དུ་འདུ་བར་བྱེད་པ། the power to collect fruits and flowers of a distant place 4. དྲིགས་རྩུབ་ལྡན་པའི་དུད་འགྲོ་སོགས་ལྟ་སྟངས་བྱས་པ་ཙམ་གྱིས་དབང་དུ་འདུ་བར་བྱེད་པ། the power to control wild and fierce animals by a mere glance 5. ཤིང་ཏོག་འབྲས་བུ་ས་ལ་ལྟུང་བ་དག་ལྟ་སྟངས་བྱས་པ་ཙམ་གྱིས་སླར་གྱེན་དུ་འདྲེན་པར་བྱེད་པ། the power to restore fruits that have previously been cast down by oneself, by a mere glance 6. མཁྲིགས་ཤིང་ཐུར་དུ་བཀུག་པ་དག་ལྟ་སྟངས་བྱས་པ་ཙམ་གྱིས་སླར་གྱེན་དུ་སྒྲོར་བར་བྱེད་པ། the power to restore trees that have previously been bent down by oneself, by a mere glance 7. རྒྱང་རིང་གི་མེ་ཏོག་དྲི་ལྡན་མདུན་དུ་བཀུག་པ་རྣམས་ལྟ་སྟངས་བྱས་པ་ཙམ་གྱིས་སླར་རྒྱང་རིང་དུ་འཕངས་པར་བྱེད་པ། the power to send back fruits and flowers that have previously been collected infront of onself, by a mere glance 8. དྲིགས་རྩུབ་ལྡན་པའི་དུད་འགྲོ་བཀུམ་པ་དག་ལྟ་སྟངས་བྱས་པ་ཙམ་གྱིས་སླར་དབུགས་འབྱིན་པར་བྱེད་པ། the power to revive wild and fierce animals that have previously been killed by oneself, by a mere glance.

ལྟ་ན་སྡུག

Sudarśana/ Beautiful; good-looking; beautiful to behold.

ལྟ་བ་བཀའ་བཏགས་ཀྱི་ཕྱག་རྒྱ་བཞི།

The four seals of Buddhist doctrine. 1. འདུས་བྱས་ཐམས་ཅད་མི་རྟག་པ། all products are impermanent 2. ཟག་བཅས་ཐམས་ཅད་སྡུག་བསྔལ་བ། all contaminated things are miserable 3. ཆོས་ཐམས་ཅད་སྟོང་ཞིང་བདག་མེད་པ། all phenomena are empty and selfless 4. མྱ་ངན་ལས་འདས་པ་ཞི་བ། nirvāṇa is peace.

ལྟ་བ་ལྔ།

Pañca dṛṣṭayaḥ/ The five views. The five views of deluded wisdom. 1. འཇིག་ཚོགས་ལ་ལྟ་བ། satkāya dṛṣṭi/ view of the transitory collection 2. མཐར་འཛིན། antagrāha dṛṣṭi/ extreme view 3. ལྟ་བ་མཆོག་འཛིན། dṛṣṭi parāmarśa/ holding wrong views as superior 4. ཚུལ་ཁྲིམས་དང་བརྟུལ་ཞུགས་མཆོག་འཛིན། śīlavrataparāmarśa dṛṣṭi/ holding bad ethics and discipline to be superior 5. ལོག་ལྟ། mithyā dṛṣṭi/ perverted view.

ལྟ་བ་གཉིས།

A. 1. སྒྲོ་འདོགས་ཀྱི་ལྟ་བ། view of over estimation 2. སྐུར་འདེབས་ཀྱི་ལྟ་བ། view of underestimation. B. 1. རྟག་ལྟ། view of eternalism 2. ཆད་ལྟ། view of nihilism.

ལྟ་མིན་ལྔ།

The five non-views. The five mental factors that are not views but are deluded minds. 1. འདོད་ཆགས། rāga/ desire-attachment 2. ཁོང་ཁྲོ། krodha/ hatred 3. ང་རྒྱལ། māna/ pride 4. མ་རིག་པ། avidyā/ ignorance 4. ཐེ་ཚོམ། vicikitsā/ doubt.

ལྟུང་བ།

Āpatti/ Downfalls; A category of monk's precepts the transgression of which becomes a downfall.

ལྟུང་བ་སྡེ་ལྔ།

Pañcāpatti dharma/ The five classes of downfalls. 1. ཕམ་པ། pārājika/ defeats 2. ལྷག་མ། saṁghāvaśeṣaḥ/ remainders 3. ལྟུང་བྱེད། pāyattikā/ propelling downfalls 4. སོར་བཤགས། pratideśanīya/ individual confessions 5. ཉེས་བྱས། duṣkṛtam/ faults.

ལྟུང་བ་ན་སྨད།

The minor partial downfalls. The breach of one of the four factors constituting a transgression of a monk's vows.

ལྟུང་བ་ཆེས་ན་སྨད།

The major partial downfalls. The breach of two or more factors constituting a transgression of a monk's vows.

ལྟུང་བ་འབྱུང་བའི་སྒོ་བཞི།

The four doors of downfalls. 1. མི་ཤེས་པ། ignorance 2. བག་མེད་པ། unconscientiousness 3. ཉེན་མོངས་མང་བ། disrespect 4. མ་གུས་པ། excess of delusions.

ལྟུང་བཤགས།

The confession of moral faults; the sūtra of confession in reliance upon the thirty-five Buddhas.

ལྟེ་བ་སྤྲུལ་པའི་འཁོར་ལོ།

The wheel of emanation at the navel. The sixty-four petals of energy-channels located at the level of the navel like the upturned ribs of an umbrella branched out of the central energy-channel at the heart.

སྟ་གོན་གྱི་ཆོ་ག

The preparatory rites. A part of the initiation ritual for empowerment preparing the ground for the actual initiation ceremony. This entails preparatory rites for appeasing goddesses of the site chosen for initiation venue, preparatory rite concerning the deities of the practice, preparatory rites for the vase and preparatory rite for the disciples.

སྟག་ལུང་བཀའ་བརྒྱུད།

Taglung Kagyud tradition. One of the lineages of the Kagyud tradition of Tibetan Buddhism stemming from the master Taglung Thangpa Chenpo.

སྟོང་མཆོད།

The thousand offerings. The set of one thousand of each of the five-fold offerings—flower, incense, butter lamp, scented water and food traditionally represented by torma.

སྟོང་པ་ཉིད།

Śūnyatā/ Emptiness. The lack of inherent existence of phenomena; the highest view of reality in Buddhist philosophy.

སྟོང་པ་ཉིད་བཅུ་དྲུག

Ṣoḍaśa śūnyatā/ The sixteen emptinesses. 1. ནང་སྟོང་པ་ཉིད། adhyātma śūnyatā/ the internal emptiness 2. ཕྱི་སྟོང་པ་ཉིད། bahirdhā śūnyatā/ the external emptiness 3. ཕྱི་ནང་སྟོང་པ་ཉིད། adhyātma bahirdhā śūnyatā/ the emptiness of both external and internal 4. སྟོང་པ་ཉིད་སྟོང་པ་ཉིད། śūnyatā śūnyatā/ he emptiness of emptiness 5. ཆེན་པོ་སྟོང་པ་ཉིད། mahā śūnyatā/ the emptiness of the great 6. དོན་དམ་པ་སྟོང་པ་ཉིད། paramārtha śūnyatā/ the emptiness of the ultimate 7. འདུས་བྱས་སྟོང་པ་ཉིད། saṁskṛta śūnyatā/ the emptiness of the collected phenomena 8. འདུས་མ་བྱས་སྟོང་པ་ཉིད། asaṁskṛta śūnyatā/ the emptiness of the uncollected phenomena 9. མཐའ་ལས་འདས་པ་སྟོང་པ་ཉིད། atyanta śūnyatā/ the emptiness of that beyond extremes 10. ཐོག་མ་དང་ཐ་མ་མེད་པ་སྟོང་པ་ཉིད། anavarāgta śūnyatā/ the emptiness of that without beginning or end 11. དོར་བ་མེད་པ་སྟོང་པ་ཉིད། anavakāra śūnyatā/ the emptiness of that which is not to be abandoned 12. རང་བཞིན་སྟོང་པ་ཉིད། prakṛti śūnyatā/ the emptines of nature 13. ཆོས་ཐམས་ཅད་སྟོང་པ་ཉིད། sarva dharma śūnyatā/ the emptiness of all phenomena 14. རང་གི་མཚན་ཉིད་སྟོང་པ་ཉིད། svalakṣaṇa śūnyatā/ the emptiness of self-marks 15. མི་དམིགས་པ་སྟོང་པ་ཉིད། anupalambha śūnyatā/ the emptiness of non-apprehension 16. དངོས་པོ་མེད་པའི་ངོ་བོ་ཉིད་སྟོང་པ་ཉིད། abhāva svabhāva śūnyatā/ the emptiness of the lack of truly existent identity.

སྟོང་པ་ཉིད་བཅོ་བརྒྱད།

Aṣṭadaśa śūnyatā/ The eighteen emptinesses. On the list of the sixteen emptinesses add: 17. དངོས་པོ་མེད་པ་སྟོང་པ་ཉིད། abhāva śūnyatā/ the emptiness of the lack of a thing 18. ངོ་བོ་ཉིད་སྟོང་པ་ཉིད། svabhāva śūnyatā/ the emptiness of naturalness.

སྟོང་པ་ཉིད་ཉི་ཤུ།

Viṁśati śūnyatā/ The twenty emptinesses. One top of the list of the sixteen emptinesses add: 17. དངོས་པོ་སྟོང་པ་ཉིད། bhāva śūnyatā/ the emptiness of a thing 18. དངོས་པོ་མེད་པ་སྟོང་པ་ཉིད། abhāva śūnyatā/ the emptiness of the lack of a thing 19. རང་གི་ངོ་བོ་སྟོང་པ་ཉིད། svabhāva śūnyatā/ the emptiness of self-nature 20. གཞན་གྱི་ངོ་བོ་སྟོང་པ་ཉིད། parabhāva śūnyatā/ the emptiness of other-nature. These four are also separately called as the four emptinesses (stong-pa nyid bzhi).

སྟོང་པ་ཉིད་སྟོང་པ་ཉིད།

Śūnyatā śūnyatā/ The emptiness of emptiness. The lack of inherent existence of emptiness itself.

སྟོང་པ་བཞི།

The four empties; the four voids. The four empties or the sense of vacuity that arises in conjuction with the four states of subtle consciousnesses, viz. the mind of radiant white appearance, the mind of radiant red increase, the mind of black near-attainment and the clear light mind, respectively while experiencing the stages of dissolution at death. These are: 1. སྟོང་པ། the empty 2. ཤིན་ཏུ་སྟོང་པ། the extremely empty 3. ཆེན་པོ་སྟོང་པ། the great empty 4. ཐམས་ཅད་སྟོང་པ། the all empty.

སྟོང་པའི་བསྐལ་པ།

Śūnyā kalpa/ The empty aeons. The twenty intermediate aeons after the destruction of this universe and the formation of the next during which sentient beings are born either in the formless or form realm.

སྟོང་སང་།

A state of vacuity. A state of expereincing an overwhelming sense of emptiness that a yogi experiences in his meditative concentration on emptiness.

སྟོང་གསུམ་གྱི་འཇིག་རྟེན་ཁམས།

The Three Thousand World Realms. According to the Abhidharma tradition, the first thousand world system refers to one thousand world realms each containing the four continents, the sub-continents, the sun, the moon and the planets. A thousand times the first thousand world realms makes the second thousand world realm, known as the Intermediate World Realm (stong-bar ma'i 'jig-rten-gyi khams). A thousand times the second thousand world realms makes the third thousand world realms known as the Great Thousand World of the Three Thousand (stong-sgum-gyi stong-chen-po'i 'jig-rten-gyi khams).

སྟོད་འདུལ།

The Upper Vinaya lineage. The lineage of ordination that comes from the Ngari region of western Tibet. Lha Lama Yeshi Od, the Ngari King invited the Indian Paṇḍita Dharmapāla, his disciple Sādhupāla, Guṇapāla and Prajñāpāla from whom Gyalwa Sherab of Zhang Zhung received ordination, who then passed the lineage to his disciples Paljor and Jangchub Senge. Thus this lineage came to be known as the Upper Vinaya lineage.

སྟོན་པའི་གཏད་རབས་བདུན།

The Seven Successors of the Buddha. 1. འོད་སྲུང་། Kāśyapa 2. ཀུན་དགའ་བོ། Ānanda 3. ཤ་ནའི་གོས་ཅན། Śāṇavāsin 4. ཉེར་སྦས། Upagupta 5. དྷི་ཏི་ཀ Dhitika 6. ནག་པོ། Kṛṣṇa 7. ལེགས་མཐོང་ཆེན་མོ། Mahāsudarśana.

སྟོན་པའི་མཛད་ཆེན་བཞི།

The four great festivals of Buddha Śākyamuni. 1. ལྷ་ཡུལ་ནས་བབ་པའི་དུས་ཆེན། His descent from the Tuṣita god realm 2. ཆོས་འཁོར་དུས་ཆེན། His turning of the wheel of doctrine 3. ཆོ་འཕྲུལ་དུས་ཆེན། His day of victory through miracles 4. སངས་རྒྱས་པའི་དུས་ཆེན། His attainment of complete enlightenment.

སྟོབས་ཀྱི་ཕ་རོལ་ཏུ་ཕྱིན་པ་བཅུ།

Daśa balapāramitā/ The ten perfections of powers. 1. བསམ་པའི་སྟོབས། āśaya bala/ the power of intention 2. ལྷག་པའི་བསམ་པའི་སྟོབས། adhyāśaya bala/ the power of resolute intention 3. གཟུངས་ཀྱི་སྟོབས། dhāraṇī bala/ the power of retention 4. ཏིང་ངེ་འཛིན་གྱི་སྟོབས། samādhi bala/ the power of concentration 5. ཡང་དག་པར་འགྱུར་བའི་སྟོབས། saṁyak prayoga bala/ the power of perfect application 6. དབང་གི་སྟོབས། the power of authority 7. སྤོབས་པའི་སྟོབས། pratibhāna bala/ the power of confidence 8. སྨོན་ལམ་གྱི་སྟོབས། praṇidhāna bala/ the power of prayers 9. བྱམས་པ་ཆེན་པོ་དང་སྙིང་རྗེ་ཆེན་པོའི་སྟོབས། mahāmaitrī mahākaruṇā bala/ the power of great love and compassion 10. དེ་བཞིན་གཤེགས་པ་ཐམས་ཅད་ཀྱི་བྱིན་གྱིས་རླབས་པའི་སྟོབས། sarva tathāgata adhiṣṭhāna bala/ the power of the blessings of all the Buddhas.

སྟོབས་ལྔ།

The five powers; the five forces. A. The five powers within the thirty-seven limbs of enlightenment. 1. དད་པའི་སྟོབས། śraddha bala/ the power of faith 2. བརྩོན་འགྲུས་ཀྱི་སྟོབས། vīrya bala/ the power of enthusiastic perseverance 3. དྲན་པའི་སྟོབས། smṛti bala/ the power of mindfulness 4. ཏིང་ངེ་འཛིན་གྱི་སྟོབས། samādhi bala/ the power of concentration 5. ཤེས་རབ་ཀྱི་སྟོབས། prajñā bala/ the power of wisdom. B. The five forces according to the seven-point mind training 1. དཀར་པོ་ས་བོན་གྱི་སྟོབས། śuklabīja bala/ the power of the white seed 2. འཕེན་པའི་སྟོབས། āśaya bala/ the power of intention 3. སུན་འབྱིན་པའི་སྟོབས། dūsaṇa bala/ the power of repulsion 4. གོམས་པའི་སྟོབས། abhyāsa bala/ the power of familiarity 5. སྨོན་ལམ་གྱི་སྟོབས། praṇidhāna bala/ the power of prayers.

སྟོབས་བཅུ།

The ten powers (see de-bzhin gshegs-pa'i stobs-bcu or byang-chub sems-pa'i stobs-bcu).

སྟོབས་དྲུག

The six powers; the six forces. The six powers that are aids to the attainment of the nine stages of mental fixation (see sems-gnas dgu) in the training of mental quiescence meditation. 1. ཐོས་པའི་སྟོབས། śrūta bala/ the power of hearing 2. བསམ་པའི་སྟོབས། āśaya bala/ the power of contemplation 3. དྲན་པའི་སྟོབས། smṛti bala/ the power of mindfulness 4. ཤེས་བཞིན་གྱི་སྟོབས། saṁprajānya bala/ the power of alertness 5. བརྩོན་འགྲུས་ཀྱི་སྟོབས། vīrya bala/ the power of enthusiastic perseverance 6. གོམས་པའི་སྟོབས། abhyasa bala/ the power of familiarity.

བརྟག་པ་རྣམ་པ་བརྒྱད།

The eight sciences of examination. 1. ས་གཞི་བརྟག་པ། the examination of earth 2. རིན་པོ་ཆེ་བརྟག་པ། the examination of jewels 3. ལྗོན་ཤིང་བརྟག་པ། the examination of trees 4. གོས་བརྟག་པ། the examination of cloth 5. བུད་མེད་བརྟག་པ། the examination of women 6. རྟ་བརྟག་པ། the examination of horses 7. གླང་པོ་ཆེ་བརྟག་པ། the the examination of elephants 8. སྐྱེས་བུ་བརྟག་པ། the examination of men.

བརྟན་མ་བཅུ་གཉིས།

The Twelve Dharma Protectors; the twelve sister-protectors of Tibet who have promised to protect the Buddha Dharma, belonging to the class of mother tantra. 1. རྡོ་རྗེ་ཀུན་གྲགས་མ། Dorje Kundakma 2. རྡོ་རྗེ་གཡའ་མ་སྐྱོང་། Dorje Yamakyong 3. རྡོ་རྗེ་ཀུན་བཟང་མ། Dorje Kunzangma 4. རྡོ་རྗེ་གེགས་ཀྱི་གཙོ། Dorje Gegkyi-Tzo 5. རྡོ་རྗེ་སྤྱན་གཅིག་མ། Dorje Chen Chigma 6. རྡོ་རྗེ་དཔལ་གྱི་ཡུམ། Dorje Pelgyi Yum 7. རྡོ་རྗེ་དྲག་མོ་རྒྱལ། Dorje Dragmo Gyal 8. རྡོ་རྗེ་ཀླུ་མོ་དཀར་མོ། Dorje Lumo Karmo 9. རྡོ་རྗེ་བོད་ཁམས་སྐྱོང་། Dorje Bodkham Kyong 10. རྡོ་རྗེ་སྨན་གཅིག་མ། Dorje Men Chigma 11. རྡོ་རྗེ་གཡར་མོ་སིལ། Dorje Yarmo Sil 12. རྡོ་རྗེ་གཡུ་སྒྲོན་མ། Dorje Yudron Ma.

བརྟུལ་ཞུགས།

Vrata/ Ascetic practices. A term used to denote acts of penance involving religious practices; often associated with torturing one's body and exposing it to physical hardship for the attainment of spiritual goals. For a true Buddhist, these extreme practices are forbidden, however in tantric practice they are sometimes deemed necessary.

བརྟེན་པ་རྣམ་ཤེས་ཀྱི་ཁམས་དྲུག

The six consciousnesses that rely upon sensory powers (see khams bco-brgyad).

བརྟེན་པ་གཞིའི་ས།

The ground of basic reliance. According to the Nyingma teachings this is the second spiritual ground attained during the first yogic stage. Since all realizations at this stage becomes the basis or foundation for achieving the path of preparation and others, it is knows as the ground of basic reliance.

བརྟེན་པའི་ཁྱད་པར་འགྲོ་བའི་ས།

The ground of reliance for exalted progression. According to the Nyingma teachings this refers to the sixth ground attained at the level of the path of seeing, whereupon a Bodhisattva, in reliance upon directly seeing the meaning clear light, progresses higher and higher in achieving the twelve thousand spiritual qualities. Therefore, the sixth ground is known as the ground of reliance for exalted progression.

བསྟན་འགྱུར།

The Tangyur; the commentarial canon. The collection of Tibetan translations of early Indian commentaries to Buddha's teachings which runs into 225 volumes with slight variations between different editions.

བསྟན་བཅོས།

Śāstra/ Treatises; commentarial works; commentarial texts.

བསྟན་བཅོས་ལྷར་སྣང་དྲུག

The six types of imperfect commentarial works; the six classes of imperfect commentarial works. 1. དོན་མེད་པའི་བསྟན་བཅོས། the meaningless commentary 2. དོན་ལོག་པའི་བསྟན་བཅོས། the misleading commentary 3. ངན་གཡོའི་བསྟན་བཅོས། the deceptive commentary 4. བརྩེ་བྲལ་གྱི་བསྟན་བཅོས། the uncompassionate commentary 5. ཐོས་པ་ལྷུར་ལེན་གྱི་བསྟན་བཅོས། that which stresses study 6. རྩོད་པ་ལྷུར་ལེན་གྱི་བསྟན་བཅོས། that which stresses debate.

བསྟན་བཅོས་ཡང་དག་གསུམ།

The three types of perfect commentarial works; the three classes of perfect commentaries. 1. དོན་དང་ལྡན་པའི་བསྟན་བཅོས། the meaningful commentary 2. སྡུག་བསྔལ་སྤོང་བའི་

བསྟན་བཅོས། that which dispells sufferings 3. སྒྲུབ་པ་ལྷུར་ལེན་གྱི་བསྟན་བཅོས། that which stresses practice.

བསྟན་པ།

Śāsana/ Teaching; doctrine. Teachings spoken by Buddha himself, or recorded into writing by later disciples in the form of commentaries. Technically, Buddha's teachings can be subsumed under two categories: the transmission of oral and recorded teachings (see lung-gi bstan-pa) and the transmission of insights (see rtogs-pa'i bstan-pa).

བསྟན་པ་སྔ་དར།

The Early Spread; the early period of Buddhism. The introduction of Buddhism during the Tibetan King Lha Tho-Tho-Ri Nyan-Tsen, and its steady spread until the irreligious King Lang Darma who destroyed it in the 10th century. This period of propagation of Buddhism in Tibet is known as the period of the early spread.

བསྟན་པ་ཕྱི་དར།

The Later Spread; the later period of Buddhism. The revival of Buddhism in the 12th century starting from the eastern and western part of Tibet after a setback during the reign of King Lang Darma is known as the period of the later spread in the history of Tibetan Budhism.

བསྟན་བསྲུང་།

The protectors of the doctrine; the Buddhist protectors.

བསྟོད་ཆེན་བཞི།

The four great praises; the four eulogies authorized by Je Tsong Khapa. 1. སྟོན་པ་ལ་བསྟོད་པ་རྟེན་འབྲེལ་བསྟོད་པ། Praise of Dependent Origination, in praise of Buddha Śākyamuni 2. བྱམས་བསྟོད་གཉེན་གཤིན་མ། The Rapproachment, in praise of Maitreya 3. འཇམ་དབྱངས་ལ་བསྟོད་པ་བསྟོད་སྤྲིན་རྒྱ་མཚོ། The praise of Ocean of Clouds, in praise of Mañjuśrī 4. རྣམ་རྒྱལ་མ་ལ་བསྟོད་པ་ས་གསུམ་འགྲོ་བའི་རེ་བསྐོང་། Fulfilling the Wishes of Beings in the Three Realms, in praise of Vijayanī.

བསྟོད་ཚོགས།

The eulogies. The collection of writings of the Buddha, Bodhisattvas, masters and scholars in praise of any being or object of veneration.

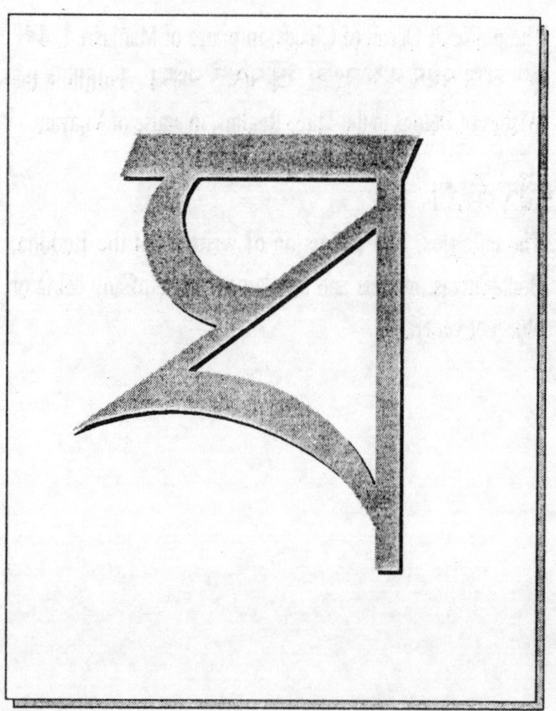

ཐ་སྙད།

Vyavahāra/ Name; terms; jargon; convention.

ཐ་སྙད་མཁན་པོ།

A. A glib person, only interested in words or literal conventions. B. One who was the first to give names to things, a name abbot.

ཐ་སྙད་བདེན་པ།

Vyavahārasatya/ The conventional truth. A phenomenon that is real only to an ordinary consciousness, i.e. to a consciousness other than the meditative equipoise of an exalted being (Arya).

ཐ་སྙད་ལྔ་ལྡན་གྱི་མི།

A person possessing five features. According to the Vinaya tradition these are: 1. མི་ཡིན་པ། being a person 2. སྨྲ་ཤེས་པ། being able to speak 3. དོན་གོ་བ། being able to understand the meaning of a language 4. ཤེས་པ་རང་བཞིན་དུ་གནས་པ། being in possession of a sound mind 5. མ་ནིང་སོགས་མིན་པ། being neither an eunuch nor a hermaphrodite.

ཐ་སྙད་གསུམ།

The three features of a person. 1. མི་ཡིན་པ། being a person 2. ཤེས་པ་རང་བཞིན་དུ་གནས་པ། having sound mind 3. འདོད་ཁམས་པའི་ས་པ་ཡིན་པ། living in the desire realm.

ཐ་དད་བཞི།

Catvāri bhedāḥ/ The four types of differences; the four separate existences. 1. རང་ལྡོག་ཐ་དད་པ། separate self-reversed identity 2. ངོ་བོ་ཐ་དད་པ། separate nature 3. རིགས་ཐ་དད་པ། separate family or class 4. རྫས་ཐ་དད་པ། separate substantial entity.

ཐ་མའི་ཆ་མཐུན་ལྔ།

The five fetters with respect to the last realm (also called, tha-ma'i cha-mthun-gyi kun-sbyor lnga); the five fetters that bind one in the desire realm. 1-3. མཐོང་སྤང་ཀུན་སྦྱོར་གསུམ། the three constant fetters to be abandoned on the path of seeing (see mthong-spang kun-sbyor gsum). 4. འདོད་པ་ལ་འདུན་པ། kāmacchanda/ admiration for sensual objects 5. གནོད་སེམས། vyāpāda/ malicious thought.

ཐ་མལ་གྱི་འཆི་བ།

The ordinary death; natural death.

ཐ་མལ་སྣང་ཞེན།

Compulsive attraction to ordinary appearances. The idea of oneself as an ordinary person which must be abandoned through generating divine pride in the practice of deity yoga in order to produce divine vision and pride.

ཐབས་ཀྱི་དཀྱིལ་འཁོར།

Upāya maṇḍala/ The method maṇḍala. The maṇḍalas representing paths: 1. རྡུལ་མཚོན་གྱི་དཀྱིལ་འཁོར། sand powdered maṇḍala 2. རས་བྲིས་ཀྱི་དཀྱིལ་འཁོར། maṇḍala painted on cloths 3. ཚོམ་བུའི་དཀྱིལ་འཁོར། heaped up maṇḍala (this could be just a heap of sand, grains, stones or metal erected for the purpose of representing a maṇḍala).

ཐབས་ཀྱི་ཐེག་པ།

Upāya yāna/ The method vehicle. The tantric path is known as the method vehicle due its four special features (see gsang-sngags-kyi khyad-chos bzhi) that makes it superior in comparison to the perfection vehicle.

ཐབས་མཁས་བཅུ་གཉིས།

The twelve skillful means of a Bodhisattva. 1. སེམས་ཅན་ཐམས་ཅད་ལ་སྙིང་རྗེ་དང་ལྡན་པ། he is compassionate towards all beings 2. རང་བཞིན་ཇི་ལྟ་བ་བཞིན་མཁྱེན་པ། he knows their nature as it is 3. བླ་མེད་བྱང་ཆུབ་མངོན་དུ་བྱེད་འདོད་པ། he aspires to attain supreme enlightenment 4. འཁོར་བ་མི་གཏོང་བ། he does not release himself from cyclic existence 5. ཉོན་མོངས་ཅན་མ་ཡིན་པས་འཁོར་བར་འཁོར་བ། he is able to take repeated rebirths in cyclic existence because he is not under the sway of delusions 6. འཚང་རྒྱ་འདོད་པས་བརྩོན་འགྲུས་འབར་བ། he strives hard for the attainment of Buddhahood 7. དགེ་བའི་རྩ་བ་ཆུང་ངུ་རྣམས་ཚད་མེད་པར་སྒྱུར་བར་བྱེད་པ། he transforms minor roots of virtue into immeasurable virtue 8. དཀའ་ཚེགས་ཆུང་ངུས་དགེ་རྩ་ཆེན་པོ་འགྲུབ་པར་བྱེད་པ། he accumulates enormous virtue with little effort 9. བསྟན་པ་ལ་འགྲན་པ་རྣམས་ཀྱི་ཁོང་ཁྲོ་འཇོམས་པར་བྱེད་པ། he pacifies anger in those wishing to harm Buddha's doctrine 10. བར་མར་གནས་པ་རྣམས་བསྟན་པ་ལ་འཇུད་པར་བྱེད་པ། he turns the minds of those indifferent to the doctrine 11. ཞུགས་པ་རྣམས་སྨིན་པར་བྱེད་པ། he matures the minds of those engaged in the teachings 12. སྨིན་པ་རྣམས་གྲོལ་བར་བྱེད་པ། he liberates those who are matured.

ཐབས་མཁས་པའི་ཉེ་བའི་གཞི་ཤེས།

The knowledge of the basis near to the resultant mother due to skill in means.

ཐབས་མཁས་སྦྱོར་བ་བཅུ།

The ten trainings in skillful means. The special qualities of a Bodhisattva on the three pure grounds—the eighth, ninth and tenth. 1. བདུད་བཞི་ལས་རྒྱལ་བའི་སྦྱོར་བ། victorious from the four demons (see bdud-bzhi) 2. དོན་དམ་པར་མི་གནས་ཤིང་ཐ་སྙད་དུ་གནས་པའི་སྦྱོར་བ། abides in relative state and not in ultimate 3. གཞན་དོན་སྔོན་གྱི་སྨོན་ལམ་གྱིས་འཕེན་པར་བྱེད་པའི་སྦྱོར་བ། projects the fulfilment of others' goals through the power of past prayers 4. ཐུན་མོང་མ་ཡིན་པའི་སྦྱོར་བ། uncommon trainings 5. ཆོས་ཐམས་ཅད་ལ་བདེན་པར་རང་བཞིན་མེད་པའི་སྦྱོར་བ། apprehension of the lack of truly existent or the inherent nature of all phenomena 6. བདེན་པར་མི་དམིགས་པའི་སྦྱོར་བ། lack of grasping at true existence 7. མཚན་མ་མེད་པའི་སྦྱོར་བ། lack of grasping at signs of true existence 8. སྨོན་པ་མེད་པའི་སྦྱོར་བ། lack of truly existent aspiration 9. ཕྱིན་ཅི་ལོག་བཞི་ལས་གྲོལ་བའི་རྟགས་ཀྱི་སྦྱོར་བ། has four irreversible signs 10. རྟོགས་པ་ཚད་མེད་པའི་སྦྱོར་བ། has immeasurable insight into realizations.

ཐབས་མ་ཡིན་པའི་རིང་བའི་གཞི་ཤེས།

The knowledge of the basis distant from the resultant mother due to lack of skill in means.

ཐབས་ཤེས་ཟུང་འབྲེལ།

The union of method and wisdom. The union of the mind of enlightenment and emptiness as method and wisdom respectively.

ཐམས་ཅད་ཡོད་པར་སྨྲ་བའི་སྡེ།

Mūlasarvāstivāda School. One of the eighteen Hinayāna schools. They assert all phenomena as included in the five categories (see gzhi-lnga), recite sūtras in Sanskrit, their abbots are necessarily those belonging to the king's lineage, their multi-patched yellow upper shawl bears a wheel or lotus symbol, their Bikṣus bear surnames with bhadra or Hridhya, they assert the three times as substantially existent, and they propound that through meditation on the selflessness of person and the accumulation of merits for three countless aeons an individual gains full enlightenment. There are seven sub-schools of this tradition (see gzhi thams-cad yod-par smra-ba'i sde-pa bdun).

ཐར་པ།

Mokṣa/ Nirvāṇa; state of liberation. Freedom from the sufferings of cyclic existence through overcoming the obscurations to liberation (nyon-sgrib). A state of peace, and the primary goals of the Śrāvakas and Pratyeka buddhas.

ཐལ་འགྱུར་ཁྱབ་པ་སྒོ་བརྒྱད།

The eight types of logical pervasion. 1. རྗེས་ཁྱབ་རྣལ་མ། correct subsequent pervasion (see rjes-khyab rnal-ma) 2. རྗེས་ཁྱབ་ཕྱིན་ཅི་ལོག wrong subsequent pervasion (see rjes-khyab phyin-ci-log) 3. ཐུར་ཁྱབ་རྣལ་མ། correct downwards pervasion (see thur-khyab rnal-ma) 4. ཐུར་ཁྱབ་ཕྱིན་ཅི་ལོག wrong downward pervasion (see thur-khyab phyin-ci-log) 5. ལྡོག་ཁྱབ་རྣལ་མ། correct counter pervasion (see ldog-khyab rnal-ma) 6. ལྡོག་ཁྱབ་ཕྱིན་ཅི་ལོག wrong counter pervasion (see ldog-khyab phyin-ci-log) 7. འགལ་ཁྱབ་རྣལ་མ། correct contrary pervasion (see khyab rnal-ma) 8. འགལ་ཁྱབ་ཕྱིན་ཅི་ལོག wrong contrary pervasion (see khyab phyin-ci-log).

ཐལ་འགྱུར་བ།

Prāsaṅgika School; the consequentialists. A school of Mādhyamika philosophy regarded as the highest of all Buddhist schools of philosophy representing Buddha Śākyamuni's ultimate view of reality. This school asserts not only the lack of true existence of all phenomena but also their lack of inherent or natural existence and establishes dependent origination and emptiness as mutually inclusive. Nāgārjuna followed by Buddhapālita and Candrakīrti are considered the proponents of this school.

ཐིག་ལེ།

Bindu/ Śukra/ Drop; essential drop, the seed for generating great bliss in the tantric practice of the male and female regerative fluid.

ཐིག་ལེ་དཀར་དམར།

The white and red drops; the white seminal drops and red seminal drops of the father and mother respectively.

ཐུགས་ཀྱིས་བྱིན་གྱིས་བརླབས་པའི་བཀའ་གསུམ།

The three kinds of Buddha's teachings resulting from his mental blessing. Teachings through: 1. བསམ་གཏན་གྱི་བྱིན་གྱིས་བརླབས་པའི་བཀའ། the blessings of concentration 2. སྙིང་རྗེའི་བྱིན་གྱིས་བརླབས་པའི་བཀའ། the blessings of compassion 3. ཆོས་ཉིད་ཀྱིས་བྱིན་གྱིས་བརླབས་པའི་བཀའ། the blessings of reality.

ཐུགས་དཀྱིལ།

Citta-maṇḍala/ The Mind Maṇḍala. The divine maṇḍala visualized and retained in concentration meditation.

ཐུགས་ལྔ།

The five types of minds of a Buddha. According to the

Nyingma tradition these are: 1. མི་རྟོག་ཆེན་པོའི་ཐུགས། the great non-conceptual mind 2. མཉམ་པ་ཆེན་པོའི་ཐུགས། the great balanced mind 3. འགྲོ་བ་གྲོལ་བའི་ཐུགས། the mind for liberating sentient beings 4. མི་ཕྱེད་རྡོ་རྗེའི་ཐུགས། the indestructible adamantine mind 5. མངོན་བྱང་གི་ཐུགས། the totally enlightened mind.

ཐུགས་ལྗགས་སྤྱན་གསུམ།

The three—heart, tongue and eye balls. Some of the highly realized masters leave their heart, tongue and eye balls untouched by fire at their cremation as a source of inspiration and devotion, symbolizing their blessings of body, speech and mind as relics for their followers.

ཐུགས་བདེན་པའི་བྱིན་གྱིས་བརླབས་པའི་བཀའ།

The words of truth blessed by Buddha's mind. A type of teaching blessed by Buddha which can be heard from trees, sky, rays of lights, music, etc.

ཐུན་དྲུག་བླ་མའི་རྣལ་འབྱོར།

The six-session guru yoga. The practice of the generation and completion stage yogas, technically to be done in six sessions of a day—dawn, morning, afternoon, evening, early night and late night. In the Gelug tradition, it is often recognized as a text of daily commitment after having received initiation into the highest class of tantra.

ཐུན་མིན་ལོངས་སྐུའི་མཎྜལ།

The uncommon sambhogakāya maṇḍala. A practice of maṇḍala offering made to one's spiritual master visualizing him or her as being a Sambhogakāya Buddha residing within a fully adorned Buddha field surrounded by an infinite number of goddesses.

ཐུན་མོང་གི་བཀའ་བབས་བཞི།

The four common transmissions. 1. ཕྱག་ཆེན་གྱི་བཀའ་བབས། the transmission of Mahāmudrā 2. ཕ་རྒྱུད་ཀྱི་བཀའ་བབས། the transmission of father tantra 3. མ་རྒྱུད་ཀྱི་བཀའ་བབས། the transmission of mother tantra 4. འོད་གསལ་གྱི་བཀའ་བབས། the transmission of clear light.

ཐུན་མོང་གི་དངོས་གྲུབ་བརྒྱད།

Aṣṭa sādhāraṇa siddhayaḥ/ The eight common powerful attainments; the eight common feats; the eight siddhis common to both Buddhist and Hindu traditions. According to Buddhist tantra, these are believed to be the external signs of maturing the completion stage practices. 1. རིལ་བུའི་དངོས་གྲུབ། siddhi of pills 2. མིག་སྨན་གྱི་དངོས་གྲུབ། siddhi of eye lotion 3. ས་འོག་གི་དངོས་གྲུབ། siddhi of travelling underground 4. རལ་གྲིའི་དངོས་གྲུབ། siddhi of the sword 5. ནམ་མཁར་འཕུར་བའི་དངོས་གྲུབ། siddhi of flying-in-the-sky 6. མི་སྣང་བའི་དངོས་གྲུབ། siddhi of invisibility 7. འཆི་བ་མེད་པའི་དངོས་གྲུབ། siddhi of immortality 8. ནད་འཇོམས་པར་བྱེད་པའི་དངོས་གྲུབ། siddhi of healing sickness.

ཐུན་མོང་གི་ཐེག་པ་གསུམ།

The three common vehicles. According to the Nyingma tradition these are: 1. ཉན་ཐོས་ཀྱི་ཐེག་པ། the Hearer's vehicle 2. རང་རྒྱལ་གྱི་ཐེག་པ། the Solitary Realizer's vehicle 3. བྱང་སེམས་ཀྱི་ཐེག་པ། the Bodhisattva's vehicle.

ཐུན་མོང་སྤྲུལ་སྐུའི་མཎྜལ།

The common nirmāṇakāya maṇḍala. A practice of maṇḍala offering in which one visualizes all the excellent riches of gods and human beings, roots of virtues and resources in the form of the maṇḍala articles and are offered to one's own spiritual master visualizing him or her as being a Nirmāṇakāya Buddha.

ཐུན་མོང་བའི་དབང་ཕྱུག་གི་ཡོན་ཏན་བརྒྱད། དབང་ཕྱུག་བརྒྱད།

The eight common features of glory; the eight qualities or siddhis common to worldly feats. 1. གཟུགས་ཕྲ་བའི་ཡོན་ཏན། subtle physical form 2. གཟུགས་རགས་པའི་ཡོན་ཏན། gross physical form 3. ཡང་བའི་ཡོན་ཏན། weighing little 4. ཁྱབ་པའི་ཡོན་ཏན། all pervasive 5. ཡང་དག་པར་ཐོབ་པའི་ཡོན་ཏན། perfect attainments 6. རབ་ཏུ་གསལ་བའི་ཡོན་ཏན། perfect luminosity 7. བརྟན་པའི་ཡོན་ཏན། ever-firm 8. འདོད་རྒུ་འབྱུང་བའི་ཡོན་ཏན། fulfillment of all wishes.

ཐུན་མོང་བའི་སྲུང་འཁོར།

The common protection wheel. The meditation and visualization of a protection wheel common to all the four classes of tantra.

ཐུན་མོང་མ་ཡིན་པའི་བཀའ་བབས་བཞི།

The four exclusive transmissions. 1. གཏུམ་མོའི་བཀའ་བབས། the transmission of psychic heat 2. སྒྱུ་ལུས་ཀྱི་བཀའ་བབས། the transmission of the illusory body 3. འོད་གསལ་གྱི་བཀའ་བབས། the transmission of clear light 4. ཕོ་བ་དང་བར་དོའི་བཀའ་བབས། the transmission of consciousness transference and the intermediate state yoga.

ཐུན་མོང་མ་ཡིན་པའི་དབང་ཕྱུག་གི་ཡོན་ཏན་བརྒྱད།

The eight uncommon features of glory; the eight qualities or siddhis uncommon to Tathāgatas. 1. སྐུའི་ཡོན་ཏན། quality of body 2. གསུང་གི་ཡོན་ཏན། quality of speech 3. ཐུགས་ཀྱི་ཡོན་ཏན། quality of mind 4. འཕྲིན་ལས་ཀྱི་ཡོན་ཏན། quality of virtuous energy. 5. རྫུ་འཕྲུལ་གྱི་ཡོན་ཏན། quality of miracles 6. ཀུན་ཏུ་འགྲོ་བའི་ཡོན་ཏན། quality of universal appearance 7. གནས་ཀྱི་ཡོན་ཏན། quality of abode 8. ཅི་འདོད་ཀྱི་ཡོན་ཏན། quality of wish-fulfillment.

ཐུན་མོང་མ་ཡིན་པའི་རྣམ་མཁྱེན་གྱི་རྣམ་པ་སུམ་ཅུ་རྩ་དགུ། རྣམ་མཁྱེན་གྱི་ཐུན་མོང་མ་ཡིན་པའི་རྣམ་པ་སུམ་ཅུ་རྩ་དགུ

The thirty-nine qualities exclusive to the Omniscient Mind. 1-10. སྟོབས་བཅུ། dasa balāni/ the ten powers (see de-bzhin gshegs-pa'i stobs-bcu) 11-14. མི་འཇིགས་པ་བཞི། catvāri vaiśāradyāḥ/ the four fearlessnesses (see mi-'jigs-pa bzhi) 15-18. སོ་སོར་ཡང་དག་པར་རིག་པ་བཞི། catvāri pratideśaniyāḥ/ the four specific perfect understandings (see so-sor yang-dag rig-pa bzhi) 19-36. ཆོས་མ་འདྲེས་པ་བཅོ་བརྒྱད། astādaśāvenika dharmāḥ/ the eighteen unshared qualities of a Buddha (see ma-'dres-pa bco-brgyad) 37-39. རྣམ་མཁྱེན་ཉིད་ཀྱི་རྣམ་པ་གསུམ། the three exclusive qualities of the Omniscient Mind itself: 1. དེ་བཞིན་ཉིད་ཀྱི་རྣམ་པ། the aspect of suchness 2. རང་བྱུང་གི་རྣམ་པ། the aspect of spontaneity 3. སངས་རྒྱས་ཉིད་ཀྱི་རྣམ་པ། the aspect of the fully enlightened being himself.

ཐུན་མཚམས།

Intervals between meditation sessions; post-meditational periods.

ཐུན་བཞིའི་རྣལ་འབྱོར།

The four session yoga. The meditation practiced in the four sessions of a day: 1. ཐོ་རངས། early dawn 2. སྔ་དྲོ། morning 3. ཉིན་གུང་། day time (afternoon) 4. སྲོད། dusk.

ཐུར་ཁྱབ།

Downward pervasion. The pervasion that whatever is that predicate is the reason in a logical syllogism.

ཐུར་ཁྱབ་རྣལ་མ།

Correct downward pervasion. The pervasion that whatever is the predicate is the reason in a logical syllogism. Synonymous with downward pervasion (see thur-khyab, above).

ར་ཁྱབ་ཕྱིན་ཅི་ལོག

Wrong downward pervasion. The pervasion in a logical syllogism that whatever is the predicate is not the reason.

ར་སེལ་གྱི་རླུང་།

The downward moving wind; One of the five principal energy-winds (see rtsa-ba'i rlung lnga) that control the lower sphincter muscles, holding and discharging faeces, urine, semen and menstrual blood.

་ཚོམ་གསུམ།

Tri viciktsā/ The three types of doubt. 1. དོན་འགྱུར་གྱི་ཐེ་ཚོམ། doubt inclining towards fact/ factual doubt 2. དོན་མི་འགྱུར་གྱི་ཐེ་ཚོམ། doubt inclining away from fact/ non-factual doubt 3. ཆ་མཉམ་པའི་ཐེ་ཚོམ། evenly balanced doubt.

ག་ཆེན།

Mahāyāna/ The Greater Vehicle. The Bodhisattva vehicle leading to full enlightenment and is superior in seven ways (see chen-po bdun) from the lower vehicles of the Hearers and Solitary Realizers. It has two types: 1. ཕར་ཕྱིན་ཐེག་པ། the perfection vehicle 2. སྔགས་ཀྱི་ཐེག་པ། the secret mantrayāna vehicle.

ག་ཆེན་གྱི་སྒྲུབ་པ་སྒོམ་ལམ།

Mahāyāna pratipatti bhāvanā mārga/ The Mahāyāna path of meditation of achievement. The uncontaminated Mahāyāna path of meditation which is a cause for the attainment of the realizations of the first to the tenth level of the Bodhisattva's path.

ག་ཆེན་སྒོམ་ལམ་གྱི་བྱེད་པ།

Mahāyāna bhāvanā mārga karaṇa/ The function of the Mahāyāna path of meditation; the benefits derived through meditation on the Mahāyāna path of meditation.

ཐེག་ཆེན་སྒྲུབ་པ་བཅུ་གསུམ།

The thirteen achievements of Mahāyāna; the thirteen trainings of the Mahāyāna path: 1-4. ངེས་འབྱེད་ཆ་མཐུན་བཞི། the four levels of the path of preparation (see nges-'byed cha-mthun bzhi) 5. མཐོང་ལམ། path of seeing 6. སྒོམ་ལམ། path of meditation 7. གཉེན་པོའི་སྒྲུབ་པ། achievement through antidotes 8. སྤོང་བའི་སྒྲུབ་པ། achievement through elimination 9. དེ་དག་ཡོངས་སུ་གཏུགས་པའི་སྒྲུབ་པ། achievement through forsaking discrimination between antidotes and abandonments 10. ཤེས་རབ་སྙིང་བརྩེའི་སྒྲུབ་པ། achievement through the unity of wisdom and compassion 11. སློབ་མ་ཐུན་མོང་མ་ཡིན་པའི་སྒྲུབ་པ། achievement for uncommon practitioners 12. གཞན་དོན་གོ་རིམ་དུ་བྱེད་པའི་སྒྲུབ་པ། achievement through persistently working for the welfare of others 13. ཡེ་ཤེས་རྩོལ་བ་མི་མངའ་བའི་སྒྲུབ་པ། achievement through effortless wisdom.

ཐེག་ཆེན་སྒྲུབ་པ་རང་དབང་དུ་འཇུག་པའི་རྒྱུ་སྤྱན་ལྔ།

The five eyes (see span-lnga) that are the cause for engaging independently in the Mahāyāna path of achievements.

ཐེག་ཆེན་སྒྲུབ་པའི་ཆེད་དུ་བྱ་བ་གསུམ།

The three aims of Mahāyāna achievements. 1. སེམས་དཔའ་ཆེན་པོ། mahāsattva/ greatness of thought 2. སྤོང་བ་ཆེན་པོ། mahāprahāṇa/ greatness of elimination 3. རྟོགས་པ་ཆེན་པོ། adlṅgamamahattva/ greatness of insights.

ཐེག་ཆེན་སྒྲུབ་པའི་དམིགས་པ་བཅུ་གཅིག

The eleven objects of observation of the Mahāyāna achievements. 1. དགེ་བ། kuśala/ wholesome phenomena 2. མི་དགེ་བ། akuśala/ unwholesome phenomena 3. ལུང་མ་བསྟན། avyākṛta/ unspecified phenomena 4. འཇིག་རྟེན་པ། lokika/

worldly phenomena 5. འཇིག་རྟེན་ལས་འདས་པ། lokottara/ transworldly phenomena 6. ཟག་བཅས། sāsrava/ contaminated phenomena 7. ཟག་མེད། anāsrava/ uncontaminated phenomena 8. འདུས་བྱས། saṁskṛta/ conditioned phenomena 9. འདུས་མ་བྱས། asaṁskṛta/ unconditioned phenomena 10. ཐུན་མོང་བ། sādhāraṇa/ common qualitites 11. ཐུན་མོང་མ་ཡིན་པ། asādhāraṇa/ uncommon qualities.

ཐེག་ཆེན་འཕགས་པ།

Mahāyāna Ārya/ A Mahāyānist Noble Being; a Mahāyāna Ārya. A practitioner of the greater vehicle on or above the path of seeing who has gained direct insight into emptiness.

ཐེག་ཆེན་མོས་པ་སྒོམ་ལམ།

Mahāyānādhimukti bhāvanā mārga/ Mahāyāna path of meditation of belief. The Mahāyāna path of meditation that is believed to be the source of fulfilling the purpose of self, others and both.

ཐེག་ཆེན་གསོ་སྦྱོང་།

The Mahāyāna precepts or vows. An ordination of the Mahāyāna tradition normally accepted for twenty hours during special occasions in the presence of a master or an image of the Buddha, taken by both lay and ordained Buddhists. This entails generating the mind of enlightenment and pledging to follow the footsteps of Buddhas and Bodhisattvas of the past in accordance with the ritual text of this ordination. On top of not eating meat, there are eight precepts to be observed (see bsnyen-gnas yan lag bzhi) conjoined with the motive of enlightenment.

ཐེག་མཆོག་འཁོར་ལོ་བཞི།

The four wheels of the supreme vehicle; the four essential factors for a Mahāyānist practitioner. 1. མཐུན་པར་གྱུར་པའི་ཡུལ་ན་གནས་པ། living in a conducive place 2. སྐྱེ་བོ་དམ་པ་ལ་བརྟེན་པ། relying upon a holy person 3. སྨོན་ལམ་བཏབ་པ། making prayers 4. བསོད་ནམས་བསགས་པ། accumulating merits.

ཐེག་པ་ཆེན་པོའི་དགེ་བའི་བཤེས་གཉེན་གྱི་མཚན་ཉིད་བཅུ།

Daśa mahāyāna kalyāṇamitra guṇāḥ/ The ten qualities of a Mahāyāna spiritual master. 1. ལྷག་པ་ཚུལ་ཁྲིམས་ཀྱི་བསླབ་པས་དུལ་བ། in his higher training of discipline he is humble 2. ལྷག་པ་ཏིང་ངེ་འཛིན་གྱི་བསླབ་པས་ཞི་བ། in his higher training of concentration he is peaceful 3. ལྷག་པ་ཤེས་རབ་ཀྱི་བསླབ་པས་ཉེ་བར་ཞི་བ། in his higher training of wisdom he has pacified his ego 4. ལུང་གི་ཡོན་ཏན་གྱིས་ཕྱུག་པ། he is rich in lineages and oral teachings 5. སྟོང་པ་ཉིད་རྟོགས་པ། he has realized emptiness 6. སློབ་མ་ལས་ཡོན་ཏན་ལྷག་པ། he has higher qualities than his disciples 7. སྨྲ་མཁས་པ། he is skillful in teaching 8. བརྩེ་བ་དང་ལྡན་པ། he is compassionate 9. བརྩོན་འགྲུས་དང་ལྡན་པ། he is hard working 10. འཁོར་བ་ལ་སྐྱོ་ངལ་བསྐྱེད་དུ་བཟུག་པ། he inspires aversion of cyclic existence.

ཐེག་པ་གཉིས།

The two vehicles. A. 1. ཐེག་ཆེན། Mahāyāna/ the greater vehicle 2. ཐེག་དམན། Hīnayāna/ the smaller vehicle. B. 1. རྒྱུ་ཕ་རོལ་ཏུ་ཕྱིན་པའི་ཐེག་པ། the causal perfection vehicle 2. འབྲས་བུ་གསང་སྔགས་ཀྱི་ཐེག་པ། the resultant mantra vehicle.

ཐེག་པ་རིམ་པ་དགུ

The nine vehicles; the nine paths (see rnying-ma'i theg-pa rim-pa dgu).

ཐེག་པ་གསུམ།

Triyāna/ The three vehicles; the three causal vehicles. 1. ཉན་ཐོས་ཀྱི་ཐེག་པ། śrāvaka yāna/ Hearer's vehicle 2. རང་རྒྱལ་གྱི་

ཐེག་པ། pratyekabuddha yāna/ Solitary Realizer's vehicle 3. ཐེག་ཆེན་གྱི་ཐེག་པ། mahāyāna/ Greater vehicle.

ག་དམན།

Hīnayāna/ Lower vehicle; the lesser vehicle. Path followed by Śrāvakas and Pratekya Buddhas which leads to the attainment of liberation from cyclic existence.

ག་དམན་དགྲ་བཅོམ་པ་གཉིས།

Dvi hīnayāna arhat/ The two Arhats of the lower vehicle. 1. the ཉན་ཐོས་ཀྱི་མི་སློབ་པ། Arhat of the Hearer vehicle 2. རང་སངས་རྒྱས་ཀྱི་མི་སློབ་པ། Arhat of the Solitary realizer's vehicle.

ག་དམན་ས་བརྒྱད།

Aṣṭa hīnayāna bhūmayaḥ/ The eight spiritual grounds of the lower vehicle. 1. དཀར་པོ་རྣམ་པར་མཐོང་བའི་ས། śukla vidarśanā bhūmi/ the ground of seeing virtuous dharma 2. རིགས་ཀྱི་ས། gotra bhūmi/ the ground the family 3. བརྒྱད་པའི་ས། aṣṭamaka bhūmi/ the eighth ground 4. མཐོང་བའི་ས། darśana·bhūmi/ the ground of seeing 5. བསྲབས་པའི་ས། tanū bhūmi/ the ground of subtleness 6. འདོད་ཆགས་དང་བྲལ་བའི་ས། vigata rāga bhūmi/ the ground free of attachment 7. བྱས་པ་སྲུང་བའི་ས། kṛtāvi bhūmi/ the ground of protecting deeds 8. བྱས་པ་རྟོགས་པའི་ས། kṛtāvi samaya bhūmi/ the ground of realizing deeds.

ར་ཟུག་གི་དངོས་པོ།

The unchangeable phenomenon; the permanent existents.

ག་མ་དང་ཐ་མ་མེད་པའི་སྟོང་པ་ཉིད།

Anavarāgraśūnyatā/ The emptiness of that which is without beginning or end. One of the sixteen types of emptinesses (see stong-nyid bcu-drug), the emptiness of the beginninglessness and endlessness of cyclic existence.

ཐོགས་མེད།

Ārya Asaṅga. The brother of Vasubandhu and the founder of the Cittamātrin school of thought. He was the pioneer of the lineage of extensive deeds (rgya-chen spyod-rgyud) and is famous for bringing the *Five Works of Maitreya* (see byams-chos sde-lnga) from Tuṣita heaven. His works include the *Five Treatises of Asanga* (see sa sde-lnga) and the *Two Compendiums* (see sdom rnam-gnyis).

ཐོགས་རེག་ཅན་གྱི་དངོས་པོ།

Tangible objects; obstructive things.

ཐོས་བསམ་སྒོམ་གསུམ།

Śruta cintā bhāvanā/ The threefold practice of study, contemplation and meditation.

མཐའ་ཁོབ་ཀྱི་མི།

A human from a remote place. To be born as a barbarian or among men dwelling in a country far from the place of the eight conducive factors (see dal-ba brgyad) preventing the practice of religion.

མཐའ་གཉིས།

The two extremes. A. 1. རྟག་མཐའ། nityānta/ extreme of eternalism 2. ཆད་མཐའ། ucchedānta/ extreme of nihilism. B. 1. སྲིད་པ་འཁོར་བའི་མཐའ། extreme of cyclic existence—saṁsāra 2. ཞི་བ་མྱང་འདས་ཀྱི་མཐའ། extreme of peace—nirvāṇa. C. 1. ཡོད་མཐའ། astyanta/ extreme of existence 2. མེད་མཐའ། ananta/ extreme of non-existence. D. 1. བཟང་མཐའ། extreme of good 2. ངན་མཐའ། extreme of evil.

མཐའ་བཞི།

A. The four extreme beliefs in the inherent existence: 1. བདག་ལས་སྐྱེ་བ། ātmaja/ production from self 2. གཞན་ལས་

སྐྱེ་བ། paraja/ production from others 3. གཉིས་ཀ་ལས་སྐྱེ་བ། ubhayaja/ production from both 4. རྒྱུ་མེད་ལས་སྐྱེ་བ། akāraṇaja/ production without causes. B. The four ends: 1. སྐྱེས་མཐའ་འཆི་བ། death as the end of birth 2. འདུས་མཐའ་བྲལ་བ། separation as the end of meeting 3. བསགས་མཐའ་འཛད་པ། exhaustion as the end of accumulation 4. མཐོ་མཐའ་ལྟུང་བ། downfall as the end of an elevated position. C. The four extremes: 1. ཡོད་མཐའ། extreme of existence 2. མེད་མཐའ། extreme of non-existence 3. གཉིས་ཀའི་མཐའ། extreme of being both 4. གཉིས་མིན་གྱི་མཐའ། extreme of being neither.

མཐའ་ལས་འདས་པ་སྟོང་པ་ཉིད།

Atyanta śūnyatā/ That emptiness of that which is beyond extremes. One of the sixteen types of emptinesses (see stong-pa nyid bcu-drug), the emptiness of reality free of the two extremes—the extreme of existence and non-existence.

མཐར་གྱིས་གནས་པའི་སྙོམས་འཇུག་དགུ

The nine meditative absorptions existing in series. 1-4. བསམ་གཏན་གྱི་སྙོམས་འཇུག་བཞི། catvāri dhyāna samāpattayaḥ/ the four types of meditative absorptions of the form realm (see bsam-gtan-gyi snyoms-'jug-bzhi) 5-8. གཟུགས་མེད་ཀྱི་སྙོམས་འཇུག་བཞི། catvāri arūpa samāpattayaḥ/ the four types of meditative absorptions within the formless realms (see gzugs-med snyoms-'jug-bzhi) 9. འགོག་པའི་སྙོམས་འཇུག nirodha samāpatti/ the meditative absorption of cessation.

མཐར་གྱིས་སྦྱོར་བ།

Anupūrva prayoga/ The Serial Training. A Bodhisattva's wisdom which through serial meditation upon the 173 aspects of the three wisdoms (the basis, path and resultant wisdom) gains firm understanding of these aspects.

མཐར་གྱིས་སྦྱོར་བ་མཚོན་བྱེད་ཀྱི་ཆོས་བཅུ་གསུམ།

Tridaśa anupūrva prayoga lakṣaṇāni/ The thirteen topics charactesed by serial training. 1-6. ཕ་རོལ་ཏུ་ཕྱིན་པ་དྲུག་གི་མཐར་གྱིས་སྦྱོར་བ། The serial training of the six perfections (see phar-phyin drug) 7-12. རྗེས་སུ་དྲན་པ་དྲུག་གི་མཐར་གྱིས་སྦྱོར་བ། the serial training of the six recollections (see rjes-su dran-pa drug) 13. ངོ་བོ་ཉིད་མེད་རྟོགས་པའི་སྦྱོར་བ། the serial training understanding the lack of true entity.

མཐར་མངོན་པར་རྫོགས་པ་སངས་རྒྱས་ཚུལ།

The way in which Buddha finally attained Perfect Enlightenment. After accumulating merits for three countless aeons, he attained complete enlightenment in the celestial abode known as Akaniṣṭa, the Heaven Beneath None, in the name of Buddha Indraketudhvaja (dbang-po-tog) and displayed his attainment of enlightenment at Bodhgaya. This is the view of the *Descent into Lanka Sūtra* (lankāvatāra).

མཐར་ལྟ།

The extreme view. An extreme view of nihilism that takes the self from the view of the transitory collection (see 'jigs-lta) as its object and apprehends it as being permanent or non-capable of connecting to subsequent rebirth. The function of such a view hinders the realization of the middle way path.

མཐར་ཐུག་གི་སྒྱུ་ལུས།

The ultimate illusory body. The attainment of the state of union of a no-more learner, i.e. the sambhogakāya being of a Buddha by means of severing the karma and delusion through the force of the spontaneously born wisdom of the clear light mind ('od-gsal lhan-cig skyes-pa'i ye-shes).

མཐར་ཐུག་གི་འབྲས་བུའི་ཁྱད་ཆོས་གསུམ།

The three qualities of the ultimate result or fruit. 1. ངོ་བོ་ག

ནས་དག་པ་རིག་སྟོང་དབྱེར་མེད། the inseparability of intuitive awareness and emptiness as the primordial nature 2. རང་བཞིན་ལྷུན་གྱིས་གྲུབ་པ་གསལ་སྟོང་དབྱེར་མེད། the inseparability of clarity and emptiness as the spontaneous reality 3. ཐུགས་རྗེ་ཀུན་ལ་ཁྱབ་པ་སྣང་སྟོང་དབྱེར་མེད། the inseparability of appearance and emptiness as the all pervading compassion.

མཐུན་རྐྱེན་ལྔ།

The five favourable conditions. The five-fold conditions required of someone wishing to accept ordination as a monk or nun. 1. ཡུལ་མཆོག་གསུམ་དང་མཁན་སློབ་བཞུགས་པ་དང་། རྒྱུད་ཚོགས་སུ་མ་ཚང་ཞིང་སྡོམ་རོ་མེད་པ། the presence of the Three Jewels, abbot and masters as the object of receiving ordination and not forsaking vows already received 2. ཆོག་སྔ་མ་སྔོན་དུ་སོང་བ། having already made a personal request 3. རྟགས་སྐྲ་དང་ཁ་སྤུ་བྲེགས་ཤིང་ཡོ་བྱད་ཚང་བ། possession of all the necessary articles required of an ordained person, and having a shaved head and beard as the signs 4. བསམ་པ་རྒྱུད་ཀྱི་ཀུན་སློང་དང་ལྡན་ཞིང་ངེས་འབྱུང་གི་བསམ་པས་ཟིན་པ། one's mind being conjoined with the thought of renunciation, as the motivation. 5. ཆོ་ག་སྦྱོར་དངོས་མཇུག་གསུམ་ཚང་བ། conducting the rituals in its entirety from the preliminary to the conclusion.

མཐོ་རིས་ཀྱི་ཡོན་ཏན་བདུན།

Sapta svargaguṇāḥ/ The seven qualities of higher rebirth. 1. རིགས་བཟང་བ། kulaguṇa/ better family-lineage 2. གཟུགས་མཛེས་པ། rūpaguṇa/ attractive physical features 3. ཚེ་རིང་བ། cirāyuroguṇa/ long life 4. ནད་མེད་པ། arogaguṇa/ good health 5. སྐལ་བ་བཟང་བ། saubhāgyaguṇa/ good fortune 6. ནོར་ཕྱུག་པ། wealthy 7. ཤེས་རབ་ཆེ་བ། prajñāguṇa/ good wisdom.

མཐོང་ཆོས་བདེར་གནས་ཀྱི་ལམ་ལྔ།

The five paths bestowing peace in this life. 1. ནམ་མཁའ་མཐའ་ཡས་ཀྱི་དངོས་གཞིའི་སྙོམས་འཇུག the actual meditative absorption of infinite space 2. རྣམ་ཤེས་མཐའ་ཡས་ཀྱི་དངོས་གཞིའི་སྙོམས་འཇུག the meditative absorption of infinite consciousness 3. ཅི་ཡང་མེད་ཀྱི་དངོས་གཞིའི་སྙོམས་འཇུག the actual meditative absorption of nothingness 4. སྲིད་རྩེའི་དངོས་གཞིའི་སྙོམས་འཇུག the actual meditative absorption of the peak of existence 5. འགོག་པའི་རྣམ་ཐར། the actual meditative absorption of emancipation in cessation.

མཐོང་ཐོབ་པ།

Dṛṣṭi prāpta/ One who has attained the correct view; a devotee by reason.

མཐོང་སྤང་ཀུན་སྦྱོར་གསུམ།

The three constant fetters to be abandoned on the path of seeing. 1. འཇིག་ལྟ་ཀུན་བཏགས། satkāya dṛṣṭi/ intellectual view of the transitory collection 2. ཚུལ་ཁྲིམས་དང་བརྟུལ་ཞུགས་མཆོག་འཛིན། śīlavrataparamārśa/ holding bad ethics and discipline to be superior 3. ཐེ་ཚོམ་ཉོན་མོངས་ཅན། kliṣṭavicikitsā/ deluded doubt.

མཐོང་སྤང་འཇུག་པ་གཟུང་རྟོག་དགུ

The nine conceptions of grasping at the objects of engagement to be abandoned on the path of seeing. Grasping at: 1. ཐེག་ཆེན་གྱི་ལམ་འབྲས་སྤྱི་ལ་དམིགས་པ། the general Mahāyāna paths and fruits 2. ཐེག་ཆེན་ལམ་གྱི་ངོ་བོ་ལ་དམིགས་པ། the nature of the Mahāyāna paths 3. ཐེག་ཆེན་ལམ་གྱི་མི་མཐུན་ཕྱོགས་སེལ་བའི་ནུས་པ་ལ་དམིགས་པ། the power to eliminate negative forces from the Mahāyāna paths 4. གཞན་དོན་བྱེད་པ་པོའི་ནུས་པ་ལ་དམིགས་པ། the power of the persons who work for the welfare of others 5. གཞན་དོན་བྱ་བའི་འབྲས་བུ་ལ་དམིགས་པ། the results of benefiting others 6.

ཐེག་ཆེན་གྱི་རིགས་ལ་དམིགས་པ། the Mahāyāna lineage 7. ཐེག་ཆེན་ལམ་གྱི་ཡུལ་ལ་དམིགས་པ། the objects of the Mahayana paths 8. ལམ་གྱི་འབྲས་བུ་རང་དོན་ལ་དམིགས་པ། the personal benefit which is the result of the paths 9. གཞན་དོན་བྱ་བའི་ལས་ལ་དམིགས་ནས་བདེན་གྲུབ་ཏུ་ཞེན་པ། the activities for benefiting others. The mode of grasping is conceiving those practices as being truly existent objects to be cultivated.

མཐོང་སྤང་བཏགས་འཛིན་རྟོག་པ་དགུ

The nine conceptions of grasping at the imputed objects to be eliminated on the path of seeing. The grasping at: 1. འབྲས་བུ་དོན་དུ་གཉེར་བྱ་མི་ཐོབ་པ་ལ་དམིགས་པ། fruits which are impossible to attain 2. ལམ་ལ་ཕྱིན་ཅི་ལོག་ཏུ་ཞེན་པ་ལ་དམིགས་པ། wrong apprehension of the paths 3. དགག་སྒྲུབ་བདེན་པར་འཛིན་པ་ལ་དམིགས་པ། truly existent negative and positive phenomena 4. ཆོས་ལྡན་མི་ལྡན་བདེན་པར་འཛིན་པ་ལ་དམིགས་པ། truly existent phenomena with or without qualities 5. གནས་ལུགས་ཀྱི་དོན་བདེན་པར་འཛིན་པ་ལ་དམིགས་པ། truly existent conceptions of the mode of reality 6. ཐེག་ཆེན་གྱི་ལམ་དང་འགལ་བ་དམན་པའི་རིགས་ཉམས་པ་ལ་དམིགས་པ། the degenerated lineage of the lower vehicle which contradicts the Mahāyāna lineage 7. འབྲས་བུ་ཁྱད་པར་ཅན་ལ་དོན་གཉེར་མེད་པ་ལ་དམིགས་པ། persons not interested in the superior fruits 8. རྣམ་མཁྱེན་གྱི་རྒྱུ་ཤེར་ཕྱིན་གྱི་ཉམས་ལེན་མེད་པ་ལ་དམིགས་པ། persons lacking the practice of the perfection of wisdom that is a cause for producing omniscience 9. འགལ་རྐྱེན་བདུད་ལ་སོགས་པས་ཟིན་པ་ལ་དམིགས་ནས་བདེན་གྲུབ་ཏུ་ཞེན་པ། those being seized by demons which are obstacles to one's practice. The mode of grasping is conceiving the person imputed by these nine practices as being truly existent.

མཐོང་སྤང་ལོག་པ་གཟུང་རྟོག་དགུ

The nine conceptions of grasping at the objects of elimination to be abandoned on the path of seeing. The grasping at: 1. ཉན་རང་གི་ལམ་འབྲས་རྟོགས་པ་དམན་པ་ལ་དམིགས་པ། the lesser path; results and insights of the Hearer's vehicle 2. བདག་རྐྱེན་ཡོངས་འཛིན་དམན་པ་ལ་དམིགས་པ། the lesser spiritual master who is the fundamental cause 3. གཞན་དོན་སྒྲུབ་པའི་ཐབས་དམན་པ་ལ་དམིགས་པ། the lesser means of fulfilling other's purpose 4. རང་དོན་སྒྲུབ་པའི་ཐབས་དམན་པ་ལ་དམིགས་པ། the lesser means of fulfilling one's own purpose 5. རང་གཞན་གཉིས་ཀའི་དོན་སྒྲུབ་པའི་ཐབས་དམན་པ་ལ་དམིགས་པ། the lesser means of fulfilling the purposes of both 6. སྤང་བྱ་དམན་པ་ལ་དམིགས་པ། the lesser objects of elimination 7. རྟོགས་པ་དམན་པ་ལ་དམིགས་པ། the lesser insights or realizations 8. ལམ་ཁྱད་པར་ཅན་མ་ཐོབ་པས་ཉམས་པ་ལ་དམིགས་པ། the degeneration caused by the failure to attain superior paths 9. འབྲས་བུ་ཁྱད་པར་ཅན་མ་ཐོབ་པས་ཉམས་པ་ལ་དམིགས་ནས་བདེན་གྲུབ་ཏུ་ཞེན་པ། the degeneration caused by the failure to attain superior fruits. The mode of grasping is conceiving those as being the truly existent objects of elimination.

མཐོང་སྤང་རྫས་འཛིན་རྟོག་པ་དགུ

The nine conceptions of grasping at the substantial objects to be abandoned on the path of seeing. Grasping at: 1. བླང་དོར་ལ་ཞེན་པ། those to be cultivated and abandoned 2. དེའི་ཀུན་སློང་ལ་ཞེན་པ། their motivation 3. དེའི་ཉེས་དམིགས་ལ་ཞེན་པ། their faults 4. དེ་དག་བདེན་པར་ཞེན་པ་ལ་དམིགས་པ། their truly existent nature 5. དེ་དག་བདེན་མེད་དུ་ཞེན་པ་ལ་དམིགས་པ། their lack of truly existent nature 6. བཏགས་པ་ཙམ་དུ་ཞེན་པ་ལ་དམིགས་པ། their mere imputation 7. མི་མཐུན་ཕྱོགས་ལ་ཞེན་པ་ལ་དམིགས་པ། their opposite aspects 8. གཉེན་པོ་ལ་ཞེན་པ་ལ་དམིགས་པ། their antidotes 9. འབྲས་བུ་རྣམ་མཁྱེན་ལས་ཉམས་པ་ལ་ཞེན་པ་ལ་དམིགས་ནས་བདེན་གྲུབ་ཏུ་ཞེན་པ། the degeneration from the resultant omniscient mind. The mode of grasping is by conceiving the persons engaged in those practices as being truly existent practitioners.

མཐོང་བའི་ས།

Darśana bhūmi/ The stage of seeing. One of the seven stages of a Hearer (see nyan-thos-kyi sa bdun), the realization within the mental continuum of a person abiding on the level of fruit of the stream-winner, where the selflessness of person is cognized directly for the first time via a transworldly path.

མཐོང་ལམ།

Bhāvanā mārga/ The path of seeing. The third of the five paths to enlightenment, where a practioner cognizes reality directly for the first time.

མཐོང་ལམ་གྱི་བཟོད་པ་བརྒྱད།

Aṣṭa bhāvanā mārga dharmakṣāntayaḥ/ The eight moments of forbearance of the path of seeing. These are the eight moments of wisdom of the path of seeing known as the uninterrupted paths (bar-chad med-lam, see mthong-lam shes-bzod skad-cig bcu-drug—the eight forbearances and subsequent forbearances connected to the four noble truths).

མཐོང་ལམ་གྱི་ཤེས་པ་བརྒྱད།

The eight moments of cognition of the path of seeing. These are the eight moments of wisdom of the path of seeing known as the path of thorough liberation (rnam-grol-lam, see mothong-lam shes-bzod skad-cig-ma bcu-drug—the eight cognitions and subsequent cognitions connected to the four noble truths).

མཐོང་ལམ་རྩེ་སྦྱོར་གྱི་སྤང་བྱ་རྟོག་པ་བཞི།

The four conceptions to be abndoned on the peak training of the path of seeing. 1-2. གཟུང་རྟོག་གཉིས། two conceptual graspings at the object (see gzung-rtog gnyis) 3-4. འཛིན་རྟོག་གཉིས། two conceptual graspings at the subject (see 'dzin-rtog gnyis).

མཐོང་ལམ་ཤེས་བཟོད་སྐད་ཅིག་བཅུ་དྲུག

Ṣoḍaśa darśanamārgakṣāḥ/ The sixteen moments of cognition and forbearance of the path of seeing. 1. སྡུག་བསྔལ་ཆོས་བཟོད། duḥkhe dharmakṣānti/ forbearance with the reality of suffering 2. སྡུག་བསྔལ་ཆོས་ཤེས། duḥkhe dharmajñānam/ cognition of the reality of suffering 3. སྡུག་བསྔལ་རྗེས་བཟོད། duḥkhe 'nvayakṣānti/ subsequent forbearance with suffering 4. སྡུག་བསྔལ་རྗེས་ཤེས། duḥkhe 'nyayajñānam/ subsequent cognition of suffering 5. ཀུན་འབྱུང་ཆོས་བཟོད། samudaye dharmakṣāṇti/ forbearance with the reality of the origin of suffering 6. ཀུན་འབྱུང་ཆོས་ཤེས། samudaye dharmajñānam/ cognition of the reality of the origin of suffering 7. ཀུན་འབྱུང་རྗེས་བཟོད། samudaye 'nyayakṣānti/ subsequent forbearance with the origin of suffering 8. ཀུན་འབྱུང་རྗེས་ཤེས། samudaye 'nvayajñānam/ subsequent cognition of the origin of suffering 9. འགོག་པ་ཆོས་བཟོད། nirodhe dharmakṣānti/ forbearance with reality of the cessation of suffering 10. འགོག་པ་ཆོས་ཤེས། nirodhe dharmajñānam/ cognition of the reality of the cessation of suffering 11. འགོག་པ་རྗེས་བཟོད། nirodhe 'nyayaakṣānti/ subsequent forbearance with the cessation of suffering 12. འགོག་པ་རྗེས་ཤེས། nirodhe anvayajñānam/ subsequent cognition of the cessation suffering 13. ལམ་ཆོས་བཟོད། mārge dharmakṣānti/ forbearance with the reality of the path 14. ལམ་ཆོས་ཤེས། mārge dharmajñānam/ cognition of the reality of the path 15. ལམ་རྗེས་བཟོད། mārge 'nyayakṣāntiḥ/ subsequent forbearance with the path 16. ལམ་རྗེས་ཤེས། mārge 'nvayajñānam/ subsequent cognition of the path.

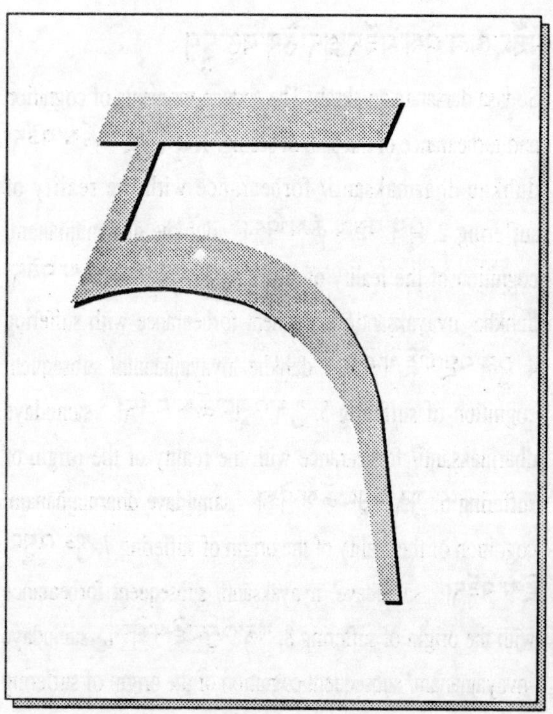

ད་ན་ཤཱི་ལ།

Dānaśīla. An Indian pandit of the eighth century born in Kashmir. He was invited to Tibet during the reign of King Trisong Deutsan and made considerable contributions in the translation of Buddhist texts into Tibetan.

དག་པ་གཉིས་ལྡན།

The state free from the two delusions, obstructions to liberation and omniscience; Buddhahood.

དག་པ་བཞི།

Catvāri pariśuddhaḥ/ The four purities; the four total purities of a Tathāgata. A. 1. ལུས་དག་པ། pure body 2. དམིགས་པ་དག་པ། pure objectives 3. སེམས་དག་པ། pure mind 4. ཡེ་ཤེས་དག་པ། pure primordial wisdom. B. 1. གནས་དག་པ། pure abode 2. ལུས་དག་པ། pure body 3. ལོངས་སྤྱོད་དག་པ། pure resources 4. ཡེ་ཤེས་དག་པ། pure wisdom.

དག་པ་ས་གསུམ།

The three pure stages of Bodhisattva; the last three grounds of a Bodhisattva—the eigth, ninth and tenth, where he or she is totally free of pride.

དག་པའི་སྒྱུ་ལུས།

Pariśuddha māyakāya/ The pure illusory body. One of the practices carried out in the completion stage practice of tantra. Meditating upon the illusory nature of the entire residence and resident maṇḍala.

དག་རྫོགས་སྨིན་གསུམ།

The three principles of purification, completion and ripening. A feature explained in the Nyingma tantra where each step of the generation stage practice is qualified by these three basic principles.

དང་པོ་ཐུགས་བསྐྱེད་ཚུལ།

The way in which Buddha first generated the Bodhimind. A According to the Hīnayāna tradition, Buddha Śākyamuni first generated the mind of enlightenment in the presence of Buddha Śakya Mahāmuni (sha-kya thub-chen). B. According to Mahāyāna tradition, he first generated the Bodhimind while yoked to a chariot in the hell realm; this follows the tradition of the sūtra called *Repaying the Kindness*.

དང་པོ་སྦྱོར་བའི་ཏིང་ངེ་འཛིན།

The concentration of first union. One of the three concentrations of the generation stage practice. It is the first because the concentration of the principal male and female deities which become the origin or source of emanating all other deities of the maṇḍala, take over the other two concentrations in series, and the unity of method and wisdom is inseparably maintained by this practice.

དད་པ་རྣམ་གསུམ།

The three types of faith. 1. ཡིད་ཆེས་པའི་དད་པ། convinced faith 2. དང་བའི་དད་པ། pure faith 3. མངོན་འདོད་ཀྱི་དད་པ། longing faith.

དད་པ་བཞི།

The four types of faith. 1-3 (see above) 4. ཕྱིར་མི་ལྡོག་པའི་དད་པ། the irreversible faith.

དད་པའི་སྟོབས།

Śraddhā bala/ The power of faith. One of the five powers of the thirty-seven auxiliaries to enlightenment (see byang-phyogs so-bdun); an overwhelming faith in the three jewels free of any obstacles that oppose faith.

དད་པའི་ནོར།

Śraddhā dhanam/ The wealth of faith. One of the seven possessions of the noble ones (see 'phags-pa'i nor-bdun); the convinced faith in the law of causality which helps turning one's mind towards the dharma; analogous to a precious wheel.

དད་པའི་དབང་པོ།

Śraddhendriya/ Faculty of faith. One of the five faculties of the thirty-seven auxiliaries to enlightenment (see byang-phyogs so-bdun); an overwhelming conviction in the four noble truths.

དད་པའི་ས།

Śraddhā bhūmi/ The ground of faith. The stage of a spiritual path where a practitioner is predominantly skillful in the practice of faith, efforts, mindfulness, concentration and wisdom.

དམ་པ་དྲུག་ལྡན།

The six-fold supreme ways. The six fundamental ways of accomplishing the six perfections (see phar-phyin drug). These are: 1. རྟེན་དམ་པ་བྱང་ཆུབ་ཀྱི་སེམས་དང་ལྡན་པ། maintaining the mind of enlightenment as the fundamental basis 2. དངོས་པོ་དམ་པ་སྦྱིན་སོགས་ཕྱོགས་རེ་བ་མ་ཡིན་པར་གཞི་ཐམས་ཅད་ལ་འཇུག་པ། engaging in all six perfections in an unbiased manner as the fundamental approach 3. ཆེད་དུ་བྱ་བ་དམ་པ་སེམས་ཅན་ཐམས་ཅད་ཀྱི་དོན་དུ་སྤྱོད་པ། working for the welfare of all sentient beings as the fundamental beneficiary of one's practices 4. ཐབས་དམ་པ་འཁོར་གསུམ་རྣམ་པར་མི་རྟོག་པའི་ཤེས་རབ་ཀྱིས་ཟིན་པ། conjoining all one's practices with the thought of purity of the three factors (see 'khor-gsum yongs-su dag-pa'i 'jug-sgrub) through skillful wisdom as the fundamental means 5. ཡོངས་སུ་བསྔོ་བ་དམ་པ་བླ་མེད་བྱང་ཆུབ་ཏུ་བསྔོ་བ། dedicating all one's virtues to the attainment of the sublime state of enlightenment as the fundamental dedication 6. རྣམ་དག་དམ་པ་སྒྲིབ་གཉིས་ཀྱི་དངོས་གཉེན་དུ་སྤྱོད་པ། applying antidotal forces against the two types of delusions (see sgrib-pa gnyis) as the fundamental purification.

དམ་པ་རིགས་བརྒྱ།

The hundred supreme divinities. The one hundred deities according to Guhyasamāja meditation, visualized as the Victorious one's རྒྱལ་བའི་ཕུང་པོ་ལྔ་བདེ་གཤེགས་ལྔ། five aggregates as the five Tathāgatas; ཁམས་བཞི་ཡུམ་བཞི། four elements as the four consorts; སྐྱེ་མཆེད་དྲུག་སེམས་དཔའ་དྲུག six sources of perception as the six Bodhisattvas; ཡུལ་ལྔ་རྡོ་རྗེ་མ་ལྔ། five objects of perception as the five Vajra Ḍākinīs. Each of these twenty is further visualized into a class of five deities each making a cycle of one hundred deities in all.

དམ་ཚིག་གི་རྫས་ཤ་ལྔ།

Pañca samaya māṁsāḥ/ The five fleshes of commitment. 1. མིའི་ཤ manuṣya māṁsa/ human flesh 2. གླང་པོ་ཆེའི་ཤ hasti māṁsa/ elephant flesh 3. བ་གླང་གི་ཤ go māṁsa/ ox flesh 4. ཁྱིའི་ཤ kukkura māṁsa/ dog flesh 5. རྟའི་ཤ aśva māṁsa/ horse flesh.

དམ་ཚིག་སེམས་དཔའ།

Samayasattva/ The commitment being. Generating oneself in the form of a deity according to the generation stage practice of tantra.

དམ་ཚིག་གསུམ་བཀོད།

The threefold commitment beings. A. A type of Buddha Śākyamuni images known as Dam-tshig sum-bkod, three samayas or pledges related to a Buddha's body, speech and mind (see dam-tshig sems dpa', ye-shes sems-dpa' and ting-nge-'dzin sems-dpa'). B. The three commitments to be observed: 1. ཁྲི་ལ་མི་ཉལ་བ། not sleeping on an elevated bed 2. ཆང་མི་འཐུང་བ། not taking intoxicants 3. ཕྱག་རྒྱ་འདྲ་བ་མི་ཟ་བ། not consuming edible things made in the shape of the various implements of deities such as lotus, vajra, etc.

དར་དཔྱངས།

Paṭṭāṅka/ Silk ribbons; tassels of silk threads that hang over the ears from a tantric ritual head-dress.

དལ་བ་བརྒྱད།

The eight leisures; the eight freedoms. A. Four freedoms from the four fetters within human existence: 1. ལོག་ལྟ་ཅན་མ་ཡིན་པ། not holding wrong views 2. ཀླ་ཀློར་སྐྱེ་བ་མིན་པ། not born in a barbaric land 3. རྒྱལ་བའི་བཀའ་མེད་པའི་ཡུལ་དུ་སྐྱེ་བ་མིན་པ། not born in a place where Buddha has not appeared 4. གླེན་ལྐུགས་ཅན་མ་ཡིན་པ། not born as a mute or fool. B. Four freedoms from the four fetters of non-human existence: 1. དམྱལ་བར་སྐྱེ་བ་མིན་པ། not being a hell being 2. ཡི་དྭགས་སུ་སྐྱེ་བ་མིན་པ། not being a hungry ghost 3. དུད་འགྲོར་སྐྱེ་བ་མིན་པ། not being an animal 4. ལྷ་ཚེ་རིང་པོར་སྐྱེ་བ་མིན་པ། not being a long living god.

དལ་འབྱོར་གྱི་རྟེན།

A fully endowed human rebirth. A human life which is characterized by the eight leisures (see dal-ba brgyad, above) and the ten endowments (see sbyor-ba bcu) thus making it suitable for practising Dharma.

དུག་གསུམ།

The three poisons; the three poisonous delusions. 1. འདོད་ཆགས། rāga/ desire-attachment 2. ཞེ་སྡང་། krodha/ hatred-anger 3. གཏི་མུག moha/ closed mindedness.

དུར་ཁྲོད་ཀྱི་ཆས་བརྒྱད།

The eight adornments of an ascetic who dwells in a cemetery; the eight costumes of a cemetery Yogi. 1. མི་མགོའི་དབུ་རྒྱན། he is crowned with human skulls 2. མི་མགོའི་དོ་ཤལ། he wears a rosary of human heads carved in crystal 3. གླང་ཆེན་གྱི་པགས་པའི་སྟོད་གཡོག he wears an elephant skin as an upper garment 4. ཞིང་ལྤགས་ཀྱི་གཡང་གཞི། he uses the skin of a human being who has committed heinous non-virtues as his skin 5. ཞག་གི་སོར་རིས། his forehead bears three greased lines horizontally and vertically 6. སྟག་ལྤགས་ཀྱི་ཤམ་ཐབས། he wears a tiger skin as his lower garment 7. ཁྲག་གི་ཐིག་ལེ། he uses blood for the tilaka between his eyes 8. ཐལ་ཆེན་གྱི་ཚོམ་བུ། his body is covered with ashes.

དུར་ཁྲོད་ཆེན་པོ་བརྒྱད།

Aṣṭa mahā śmaśāna/ The eight great cemeteries. 1. ཤར་དུ་གཏུ་དྲག The Fiery One to the east 2. བྱང་དུ་ཚང་ཚིང་འཁྲིགས་པ། The Wilderness to the north 3. ནུབ་ཏུ་རྡོ་རྗེ་འབར་བ། The Vajra Fire to the west 4. ལྷོར་ཀེང་རུས་ཅན། The Skeleton Bound to the south 5. དབང་ལྡན་དུ་དྲག་ཏུ་རྒོད་པ། The Terrific Laugh to the north-east 6. མེར་བཀྲ་ཤིས་ཚལ། The Auspicious Garden to the south-east 7. བདེན་བྲལ་དུ་མུན་པ་དྲག་པོ། The Gloomy One to the south-west 8. རླུང་དུ་ཀི་ལི་ཀི་ལིའི་སྒྲ་སྒྲོག་པ། The One Pronouncing Ki-li Ki-li to the north-west.

དུར་ཁྲོད་པ།

Smśānika/ He who dwells in a cemetery; an ascetic dwelling in a cemetery. There are three types of such practitioners: the initial practitioner dwells in the remains of the former charnel ground, the intermediate in the temporary charnel ground and the advanced in the permanent charnel ground.

དུས་ཀྱི་འཁོར་ལོ།

Kālacakra/ A tantric deity belonging to the highest class of tantra. When referred to it as a tantra, it can be understood as having three levels. 1. the outer Kālacakra comprising the universe 2. the inner Kālacakra comprising the system of energy channels, winds and drops of the inhabitants of the universe 3. the alternative Kālacakra comprising the residence and resident Kālacakra maṇḍala and meditation on the energy-channel, winds and essential drops.

དུས་ཁྲིམས་ཡན་ལག་བརྒྱད།

The eight precepts of a specific period (see bsnyen-gnas yan-lag brgyad).

དུས་ཆེན་བཞི།

The four great festivals; the four holy occasions in Buddha's life. 1. དང་པོའི་ཡར་ངོ་ལ་ཆོ་འཕྲུལ་དུས་ཆེན། the period when Buddha performed miracles from the 1st through 15th of the first Tibetan month 2. བཞི་པའི་བཅོ་ལྔར་མངོན་པར་རྫོགས་པར་སངས་རྒྱས་པའི་དུས་ཆེན། the day when Buddha attained full enlightenment on the 15th of the fourth Tibetan month. 3. དྲུག་པའི་བཞི་ལ་ཆོས་འཁོར་བསྐོར་བའི་དུས་ཆེན། the day which Buddha turned the wheel of dotrine on the 4th of the sixth Tibetan month. 4. དགུ་པའི་ཉེར་གཉིས་ལ་ལྷ་བབས་དུས་ཆེན། the day which Buddha descended from Tuṣita heaven on the 22nd of the ninth Tibetan month.

དུས་ཆེན་གསུམ་འཛོམས།

The combination of three festivals. The 15th of the 4th Tibetan month celebrated as Buddha's entering into the womb of his mother for conception; complete enlightenment; and passing away into parinirvāṇa.

དུས་མཐའི་སྐད་ཅིག་མ།

The single instant of the end of time. According to *Abhidharmkośa* this is the period of time equivalent to one fraction of the sixty parts of a normal person's finger snap.

དུས་གཞན་ལ་དགོངས་པ།

Kālāntarābhiprāya/ Determining another time. Interpretive sūtra taught with reference to another time, e.g. the sūtra in which the Buddha taught, 'If you recite Sukhāvatī prayers you will immediately be born there', where the intention of the Buddha was that through proper practice of the precepts of the Buddha of the Blissful Realm, one may be born there in the future.

དེ་ཁོ་ན་ཉིད་བཞི།

The four types of thatnesses; the four thatnesses of the Action tantra. 1. བདག་གི་དེ་ཁོ་ན་ཉིད། thatness of self 2. སྔགས་ཀྱི་དེ་ཁོ་ན་ཉིད། thatness of mantra 3. ལྷའི་དེ་ཁོ་ན་ཉིད། thatness of the deity 4. བསམ་གཏན་གྱི་དེ་ཁོ་ན་ཉིད། thatness of concentration.

དེ་ཉིད་བཅུ།

Daśatattva/ The ten suchnesses (see nang-gi de-nyid bcu and also phyi'i de-nyid-bcu).

དེ་ལྟར་བྱུང་བའི་སྡེ།

Itivṛttika/ Legendary teachings. One of the twelve scriptural categories of Buddha's teachings reaching its audience through legends.

དེ་མ་ཐག་རྐྱེན།

Samanantara pratyaya/ Immediate condition. One of the four conditions (see rkyen-bzhi) which produce a cognition; that perception just preceding the actual understanding of an object.

དེ་ཙམ་ལྔ།

Pañca tanmātrāṇi/ The five mere existents. According to the Sāṁkhya school of Hindu philosophy all phenomena are included into six categories. 1. གཟུགས། rūpa/ form 2. སྒྲ śabda/ sound 3. དྲི། gandha/ smell 4. རོ། rasa/ taste 5. རེག་བྱ། sparśa/ object of touch.

དེ་བཞིན་ཉིད་གསུམ།

The three suchnesses. According to *The Compendium of Precepts* (abhidharma-samuccaya), there is no difference in the suchness of all phenomena, however, due to the difference in their basis of existence there can be three suchnesses which are: 1. དགེ་བའི་དེ་བཞིན་ཉིད། suchness of virtues 2. མི་དགེ་བའི་དེ་བཞིན་ཉིད། suchness of non-virtues 3. ལུང་མ་བསྟན་གྱི་དེ་བཞིན་ཉིད། suchness of the unspecified phenomena.

དེ་བཞིན་གཤེགས་པ་བཞི།

The four Tathāgatas. 1. རྒྱལ་བ་རིན་ཆེན་མང་། Jinaratnabahulya 2. གཟུགས་མཛེས་དམ་པ། Jinasarūpottama 3. སྐུ་འབྱམས་ཀླས། Jinarūpaparyānta 4. འཇིགས་པ་ཐམས་ཅད་དང་བྲལ་བ། Jinasarkāyavimuktasena.

དེ་བཞིན་གཤེགས་པའི་སྟོབས་བཅུ།

Daśa tathāgata balāni/ The ten powers of a Buddha. 1. གནས་དང་གནས་མིན་མཁྱེན་པའི་སྟོབས། sthānāsthāna jñāna balam/ power of knowing right from wrong 2. ལས་ཀྱི་རྣམ་པར་སྨིན་པ་མཁྱེན་པའི་སྟོབས། karma vipāka jñāna balam/ power of knowing the consequences of actions 3. མོས་པ་སྣ་ཚོགས་མཁྱེན་པའི་སྟོབས། nānādhimukti jñāna balam/ power of knowing various mental inclinations 4. ཁམས་སྣ་ཚོགས་མཁྱེན་པའི་སྟོབས། nānā dhātu jñāna balam/ power of knowing various mental faculties 5. དབང་པོ་སྣ་ཚོགས་མཁྱེན་པའི་སྟོབས། indriya varāvara jñāna balam/ power of knowing various degrees of intelligence 6. ཐམས་ཅད་དུ་འགྲོ་བའི་ལམ་མཁྱེན་པའི་སྟོབས། sarvatra gāmanī pratipaj jñāna balam/ power of knowing the paths to all goals 7. ཀུན་ནས་ཉོན་མོངས་པ་དང་རྣམ་པར་བྱང་བ་མཁྱེན་པའི་སྟོབས། saṁkleśa vyavadāna vyutthāna jñāna balam/ power of knowing the ever-afflicted and purified phenomena 8. སྔོན་གྱི་གནས་རྗེས་སུ་དྲན་པ་མཁྱེན་པའི་སྟོབས། pūrva nivāsānusmṛti jñāna balam/ power of knowing past lives 9. འཆི་འཕོ་བ་དང་སྐྱེ་བ་མཁྱེན་པའི་སྟོབས། cyutyutpatti jñāna balam/ power of knowing death and birth 10. ཟག་པ་ཟད་པ་མཁྱེན་པའི་སྟོབས། āśrava kṣaya jñāna balam/ power of knowing the exhaustion of contaminations.

དོན་གྱི་འོད་གསལ།

The meaning clear light. The transformation of the basic clear light mind into its final form through meditation; a completion stage practice of tantra.

དོན་གྲུབ་ཀྱི་དམ་ཚིག་གཉིས།

The two pledges concerning the Buddha Amoghasiddhi. 1. སྡོམ་པ་གསུམ་གྱི་བཅས་པ་མཐའ་དག་བསྲུང་བའི་དམ་ཚིག safeguarding all precepts of the three vows 2. མཆོད་པའི་དམ་ཚིག pledges concerning the practices of offering and worship.

དོན་གཉིས།

Two purposes; two goals. 1. རང་དོན། the purpose of self 2. གཞན་དོན། the purpose of others.

དོན་དམ་གཉིས།

The two types of ultimate truths. A. 1. རྣམ་གྲངས་པའི་དོན་དམ། the nominal ultimate truth 2. རྣམ་གྲངས་མ་ཡིན་པའི་དོན་དམ། the real ultimate truth. B. 1. མཐུན་པའི་དོན་དམ། the approximate ultimate truth 2. དོན་དམ་དངོས། the actual ultimate truth.

དོན་དམ་གསུམ།

The three types of ultimate truth. 1. དོན་དོན་དམ་པ། arthaparamārtha/ ultimate meaning 2. ཐོབ་པ་དོན་དམ་པ། prāptaparamārtha/ ultimate accomplishment 3. སྒྲུབ་པ་དོན་དམ་པ། siddhaparamārtha/ ultimate practice.

དོན་དམ་བདེན་པ།

Paramārtha satya/ Ultimate truth. Generally referring to emptiness as opposed to the conventional phenomena.

དོན་དམ་པ་སྟོང་པ་ཉིད།

Paramārtha śūnyatā/ The emptiness of that which is ultimate. One of the sixteen types of emptinesses; the emptiness of nirvāṇa.

དོན་དམ་པའི་སྐྱབས།

Paramārtha śaraṇam/ The ultimate object of refuge, i.e. the Buddha Śākyamuni.

དོན་དམ་པའི་མཚན་ཉིད་ལྔ།

The five characteristics of the ultimate truth; emptiness. 1. བརྗོད་དུ་མེད་པ། inexpressible 2. གཉིས་སུ་མེད་པ། non-dual 3. རྟོག་གེའི་ཡུལ་མིན་པ། not being an object of logicians 4. རོ་གཅིག་པ། single-taste 5. མཚན་ཉིད་མེད་པ། signlessness.

དོན་དམ་པའི་སྲུང་འཁོར།

The ultimate protection wheel; meditation on the protection wheel by means of the primordial wisdom.

དོན་བདུན་ཅུ།

Arthasaptati/ The Seventy Topics. The seventy divisions of the eight realizations or topics (see dngos-po brgyad). 1-10. རྣམ་མཁྱེན་མཚོན་བྱེད་ཀྱི་ཆོས་བཅུ། the ten topics that characterize the omniscient mind (see rnam-mkhyen mtshon-byed-kyi chos-bcu) 11-21. ལམ་ཤེས་མཚོན་བྱེད་ཀྱི་ཆོས་བཅུ་གཅིག the eleven topics that characterize the knowledge of the paths (see lam-shes mtshon-byed-kyi chos-dgu) 22-30. གཞི་ཤེས་མཚོན་བྱེད་ཀྱི་ཆོས་དགུ the nine topics that characterize the knowledge of the basis (see gzhi-shes mthson-byed-kyi chos-dgu) 31-41. རྣམ་རྫོགས་སྦྱོར་བ་མཚོན་བྱེད་ཀྱི་ཆོས་བཅུ་གཅིག the eleven topics that characterize the training of the complete aspects (see rnam-rdzogs sbyor-ba mtshon-byed-kyi chos bcu-gcig) 42-49. རྩེ་མོའི་སྦྱོར་བ་མཚོན་བྱེད་ཀྱི་ཆོས་བརྒྱད། the eight topics that characterize the peak training (see rtse-mo'i sbyor-ba mtshon-byed-kyi chos-brgyad) 50-62. མཐར་གྱིས་སྦྱོར་བ་མཚོན་བྱེད་ཀྱི་ཆོས་བཅུ་གསུམ། the thirteen topics that characterize the serial training (see mthar-gyis sbyor-ba mtshon-byed-kyi chos bcu-gsum) 63-66. སྐད་ཅིག་མའི་སྦྱོར་བ་མཚོན་བྱེད་ཀྱི་ཆོས་བཞི། the four topics that characterize the momentary training (see skad-cig-ma'i sbyor-ba mtshon-byed-kyi chos-bzhi) 67-70. འབྲས་བུ་ཆོས་སྐུ་མཚོན་བྱེད་ཀྱི་ཆོས་བཞི། the four topics that characterize the resultant truth body (see 'bras-bu chos-sku mtshon-byed-kyi chos-bzhi).

དོན་སྤྱི།

Meaning generality; generic image. The image of an object in thought or idea, e.g. the vase as it would appear in the imagination.

དོན་བྱེད་ནུས་པ།

Arthakriyāśakti/ A functioning thing; effective phenomena. The class of phenomena that has the ability or power to effect changes. Synonymous to impermanence.

དོན་གཞན་ལ་དགོངས་པ།

Arthāntarābhiprāya/ Determining another meaning; intending another meaning. Interpretive sūtra indicating another meaning, e.g. the sūtra, 'all phenomena lack inherent existence', to those who accept inherent existence as their basic philosophy.

དོན་གཟུངས།

Meaning retention; retaining the meaning. Spiritual power of retaining the meaning of teachings that are received from the Buddhas and Bodhisattvas, e.g. the practice of the Bodhisattva levels and the ten perfections. This may also mean the power to retain the specific or general meaning of all that exists.

དོར་བ་མེད་པ་སྟོང་པ་ཉིད།

Anavakāra śūnyatā/ The emptiness of that which is not to be abandoned. One of the sixteen types of emptinesses (see stong-pa nyid bcu-drug); the lack of inherent existence of the reality of all phenomena which is neither to be abandoned nor discarded.

དྭགས་པོ་བཀའ་བརྒྱུད།

Dakpo Kagyud Tradition. The Kagyud tradition that comes from Marpa, Milarepa and Dagpo Lhaje (Gampopa); because this tradition flourished extensively during Dagpo Lhaje (1079-1153), the sun-like disciple of Milarepa, it is known as Dagpo Kagyud. A sub-school of Kagyud's mainstream.

དྲང་སྲོང་།

Ṛṣi/ A Sage (Rishi); Lit. 'the righteous one'. Ancient vedic masters and practitioners; Mahārṣi is used as an epithet for Buddha.

དྲན་པ་བཅུ།

Daśa smṛtiayaḥ/ The ten mindfulnesses (see rjes-su dran-pa bcu).

དྲན་པ་ཉེ་བར་བཞག་པ་བཞི།

Catvāri smrtyūpasthānāḥ/ The four close mindfulnesses; the four close contemplations. The four objects of mindfulness for mental quiescence meditation. 1. ལུས་དྲན་པ་ཉེ་བར་བཞག་པ། kāya smṛtyūpasthāna/ close contemplation of body 2. ཚོར་བ་དྲན་པ་ཉེ་བར་བཞག་པ། vedanā smṛtyūpasthāna/ close contemplation of feelings 3. སེམས་དྲན་པ་ཉེ་བར་བཞག་པ། citta smṛtyūpasthāna/ close contemplation of mind 4. ཆོས་དྲན་པ་ཉེ་བར་བཞག་པ། Dharma smṛtyūpasthāna/ close contemplation of Dharma.

དྲན་པ་ཉེ་བར་བཞག་པ་གསུམ།

The three mindfulnesses of a Buddha. 1. གུས་ཏེ་ཉན་པ་ལ་ཆགས་པ་མེད་པ། he has no attachment towards those who listen respectfully 2. གུས་པས་མི་ཉན་པ་ལ་ཁྲོང་བ་མེད་པ། he has no hatred towards those who do not listen respectfully 3. འདྲེས་མར་འདུག་པ་ལ་གཉིས་ཀ་མེད་པ། he has neither attachment nor hatred to those who listen him with mixed feeling.

དྲི་བཅས་རྣམ་བརྫུན།

The False Aspect (Cittamātrin) School. A sub-school of the Mind Only school which asserts that the Buddha's primordial awareness is conjoined with the stains of dualistic appearence.

དྲི་དྲུག

Ṣad gandhāḥ/ The six types of smells; the six odours. 1. དྲི་ཞིམ་པ། sugandha/ sweet smell 2. དྲི་ངང་། durgandha/ bad smell 3. དྲི་མཉམ་པ། samagandha/ indifferent smell 4. ལྷན་སྐྱེས་ཀྱི་དྲི། sahaja gandha/ natural smell 5. སྦྱོར་བྱུང་གི་དྲི། samyojaka gandha/ artificial smell 6. སྒྱུར་བ་ལས་བྱུང་བའི་དྲི། converted smell.

དྲི་མ་དྲུག

A. The six waste products of the body. 1. དྲི་ཆེན། excrement 2. དྲི་ཆུ། urine 3. མིག་སྐྱག eye mucus 4. རྣ་སྤབས། ear wax 5. མཆིལ་མ saliva 6. སྣབས། snot. B. The six wrong attitudes to be discarded while listening to a teaching. 1. ང་རྒྱལ། pride 2. མ་དད་པ། lack of faith 3. དོན་གཉེར་མེད་པ། lack of interest 4. རྣམ་པར་གཡེང་བ། distraction 5. རྨུགས་པ། mental sloth 6. སྐྱོ་དང་པ། despair.

དྲི་མ་མེད་པ།

Vimala bhūmi/ The Stainless Ground. The second of the ten Bodhisattva grounds (see sa-bcu) during which there is special practice of the perfection of moral discipline and self-control.

དྲི་མ་གསུམ།

The three waste products. The three waste products of our body. 1. ཁ་ཟས་སྙ་བའི་སྙིགས་མ་བཤང་བ། faeces as the waste product of gross food 2. སྣ་བའི་སྙིགས་མ་གཅིན། urine as the waste product of liquids 3. རྡོད་ཀྱི་སྙིགས་མ་རྔུལ་ནག sweat as the waste product of the body's warmth.

དྲི་མེད་རྣམ་བརྫུན།

The True Aspect (Cittamātrin) School. A sub-school of the Cittamātrins who assert that the primordial awareness of the Buddha is free from the stains of dualistic appearance.

དྲི་ཟ།

Gandharva/ The smell eaters. The intermediate beings, categorized as belonging to the class of hungry ghosts, who sustain on the smoke of burnt offerings.

དྲིན་ཅན་གྱི་ལོ་པཎ་གསུམ།

The three kind master-translators. The three great translators of the eighth century in Tibet during the reign of King Trisong Deutsan: 1. Jinamitra 2. Dhānaśīla 3. Zhang Yeshede.

དྲུག་པ་ཚེས་བཞི།

The 6th of the 4th Tibetan month. The celebration of Buddha's turning of the wheel of doctrine of the four noble truths at Vārāṇasī. One of the important Buddhist festivals.

དྲུག་སྡེ།

Ṣaḍ vargika/ The six close disciples of Buddha Śākyamuni, who were punished by Buddha Śākyamuni for their breach of disciplines. 1. དགའ་བོ། Nanda 2. ཉེ་དགའ་བོ། Upananda 3. འགྲོ་མགྱོགས། Aśvaka 4. ནབས་སོ། Punarvasu 5. འདུན་པ། Chanda 6. འཆར་ཀ། Udāyī.

དྲེགས་པ་བཅོ་ལྔ།

The fifteen types of arrogance. 1. ཚུལ་ཁྲིམས་ཀྱིས་དྲེགས་པ། arrogance of observing moral discipline 2. ཐོས་པས་དྲེགས་པ། arrogance of being learned 3. སྤོབས་པས་དྲེགས་པ། arrogance of being proud 4. རྙེད་པས་དྲེགས་པ། arrogance of finding wealth 5. བཀུར་སྟིས་དྲེགས་པ། arrogance of being respected by others 6. རིག་གནས་མཁས་པས་དྲེགས་པ། arrogance of being a scholar in the sciences of learning 7. དབེན་གནས་ཀྱིས་དྲེགས་པ། arrogance of being a hermit 8. སྦྱངས་པའི་ཡོན་ཏན་གྱིས་དྲེགས་པ། arrogance of the knowledge and trainings received 9. ཡོ་བྱད་ཉུང་བས་དྲེགས་པ། arrogance of owning only a few material possessions 10. གཟུགས་བཟང་བས་དྲེགས་པ། arrogance of possessing excellent physical features 11. ལོངས་སྤྱོད་ཀྱིས་དྲེགས་པ། arrogance of being rich 12. དབང་ཆེ་བས་དྲེགས་པ། arrogance of being powerful 13. འཁོར་གཡོག་བཟང་བས་དྲེགས་པ། arrogance of having an excellent circle of followers and servants 14. བསམ་གཏན་མངོན་ཤེས་ཀྱིས་དྲེགས་པ། arrogance of possessing meditative concentrations and extra-sensory perceptions 15. ལྷ་ཀླུ་སོགས་ཀྱིས་བསྟོད་པས་དྲེགས་པ། arrogance of being praised by gods and nagas.

གདགས་གཞི།

A basis of imputation, e.g. the five psycho-physical aggregates which are the basis for imputing 'person', 'I' or 'self'.

གདན་གསུམ་གྱི་དཀྱིལ་འཁོར།

The maṇḍala of threefold seats. The meditation of visualizing one's own physical aggregates, sensory faculties and sources of perceptions as a divine maṇḍala of threefold seats in their entirety. 1. ཕུང་ཁམས་གཤེགས་པ་གཤེགས་མའི་གདན། visualizing one's aggregates and sensory faculties as the seat for the male and female Tathāgathas 2. སྐྱེ་མཆེད་སེམས་དཔའ་སེམས་མའི་གདན། visualizing one's sources of perceptions as the seat for the male and female Bodhisattvas 3. ཡན་ལག་ཁྲོ་བོ་ཁྲོ་མོའི་གདན། visualizing one's limbs as the seat for the male and female wrathful deities.

གདམས་ངག

Upadeśa/ Instruction. The essential spiritual communication—oral, written or intuitive, given by a guru to his disciple.

དཔལ་པ་ཆོས་ཉིད་ཀྱི་ས།

The exalted ground of reality. According to the Nyingma teachings this refers to the ninth ground attained at the fifth level of yoga when a trainee transcends all apprehensions of the ãctivity and appearance of reality through his experience of the inseparability of the objective ultimate meaning clear light mind and the subjective divine body appearances.

གདུང་རྒྱུད།

Blood lineage; a hereditary hierarch. The patriarchal or matriarchal lineage holder of an exalted being, e.g. the heirs of the Śākya tradition.

གདོད་མའི་སངས་རྒྱས།

Ādibuddha/ The primordial Buddha. The primordial Buddha, Samantabhadra. However, the basic primordial Buddha is recognized as the Tathāgata essence within the mental continuum of all sentient beings.

གདོན་གསུམ།

The three evil forces. 1. སྟེང་གདོན་གཟའ་དང་རྒྱུ་སྐར། the planet of the upper world 2. བར་གདོན་བཙན་དང་རྒྱལ་པོ། the mountain-gods of the intermediate world 3. འོག་གདོན་ཀླུ་དང་ས་བདག the nāgas and earth-lords of the subterranean world.

བདག་རྐྱེན།

The fundamental condition. Something which is the main producer of a result but does not actually transform it into its substantial continuity, e.g. the eye sense power that generates eye consciousness.

བདག་བསྐྱེད།

Sādhana/ Self-generation. A tantric practice of generating oneself into a deity and carrying out incantations of mantras and then dissolving into the sphere of emptiness at the conclusion, etc., according to a ritual-text (sādhana).

བདག་གི་དེ་ཁོ་ན་ཉིད།

The suchness of self. One of the four suchnesses in action tantra meditation. In this meditation, also known as the pure reality deity of the right view, a trainee visualizes a deity within the understanding of one's mind being empty and clear and free of any elaboration and total pacification of all conventional appearances. Hence, his experience qualifies six features (see bde-gshegs snying po'i chos-drug).

བདག་གི་གཞི།

The self-basis. In performance tantra it is the practice of self-generation in the form of a deity.

བདག་གཅིག་འབྲེལ།

Relationship of identical nature, e.g. the relationship between a functional thing and an impermanent thing.

བདག་འཇུག

Self-empowerment; self-initiation. The practice of receiving initiation directly from the deity in the maṇḍala without a tantric preceptor; a lama before giving initiation to others receives self-initiation from the wisdom-beings and meditates himself being inseparable from the deity.

བདག་ཏུ་རྨོངས་པའི་མ་རིག་པ།

The ignorance of self-nescience. This refers to the ignorance that is the root of cyclic existence. The lack of knowledge of reality through which one sees one's aggregates as permanent, blissful, being the self, being solid and being the person contradicting the real nature of phenomenal status.

བདག་ལྟ་གཉིས།

The two types of view of self. The two wrong views of self to be refuted through logical reasoning. 1. ཆོས་ཀྱི་བདག་ཏུ་ལྟ་བ། dharma ātmagrāha/ the view of a self of person 2. གང་ཟག་གི་བདག་ཏུ་ལྟ་བ། puruṣātmagrāha/ the view of self of phenomena.

བདག་ལྟ་ཉི་ཤུ།

The twenty views of self; the twenty wrong views of self. 1. གཟུགས་བདག་ཏུ་ལྟ་བ། the view of form as self 2. གཟུགས་བདག་དང་ལྡན་པར་ལྟ་བ། the view of self as possessing form 3. གཟུགས་ལ་བདག་ཡོད་པར་ལྟ་བ། the view of self as abiding in form 4. བདག་ལ་གཟུགས་ཡོད་པར་ལྟ་བ། the view of form as abiding in self 5. ཚོར་བ་བདག་ཏུ་ལྟ་བ། the view of feeling as self 6. བདག་ཚོར་བ་དང་ལྡན་པར་ལྟ་བ། the view of self as possessing feeling 7. ཚོར་བ་ལ་བདག་ཡོད་པར་ལྟ་བ། the view of self as abiding in feeling 8. བདག་ལ་ཚོར་བ་ཡོད་པར་ལྟ་བ། the view of feeling as abiding in self 9. འདུ་ཤེས་བདག་ཏུ་ལྟ་བ། the view of perception as self 10. བདག་འདུ་ཤེས་དང་ལྡན་པར་ལྟ་བ། the view of self as possessing perception 11. འདུ་ཤེས་ལ་བདག་ཡོད་པར་ལྟ་བ། the view of self as abiding in perception 12. བདག་ལ་འདུ་ཤེས་ཡོད་པར་ལྟ་བ། the view of perception as abiding in self 13. འདུ་བྱེད་བདག་ཏུ་ལྟ་བ། the view of compositional factors as self 14. བདག་འདུ་བྱེད་དང་ལྡན་པར་ལྟ་བ། the view of self as possessing compositional factors 15. འདུ་བྱེད་ལ་བདག་ཡོད་པར་ལྟ་བ། the view of self as abiding in compositional factors 16. བདག་ལ་འདུ་བྱེད་ཡོད་པར་ལྟ་བ། the view of compositional factors as abiding in self 17. རྣམ་ཤེས་བདག་ཏུ་ལྟ་བ། the view of consciousness as self 18. བདག་རྣམ་ཤེས་དང་ལྡན་པར་ལྟ་བ། the view of self as possessing consciousness 19. རྣམ་ཤེས་ལ་བདག་ཡོད་པར་ལྟ་བ། the view of self as abiding in consciousness 20. བདག་ལ་རྣམ་ཤེས་ཡོད་པར་ལྟ་བ། the view of consciousness as abiding in self.

བདག་ལྟ་ཉེར་ལྔ།

The twenty-five views of self; the wrong views of self (see 1-20, bdag-lta nyi-shu, above) plus: 21. བདག་གཟུགས་ལས་གཞན་དུ་ལྟ་བ། the view of self as other than form 22. བདག་ཚོར་བ་ལས་གཞན་དུ་ལྟ་བ། the view of self as other than feeling 23. བདག་འདུ་ཤེས་ལས་གཞན་དུ་ལྟ་བ། the view of self as other than perception 24. བདག་འདུ་བྱེད་ལས་གཞན་དུ་ལྟ་བ། the view of self as other than compositional factors 25. བདག་རྣམ་ཤེས་ལས་གཞན་དུ་ལྟ་བ། the view of self as other than consciousness.

བདག་པོའི་འབྲས་བུ།

Adhipatiphala/ Environmental results. One's own experience of environment which is a result of one's previous actions in association with the community or surrounding in which one resides, e.g. the local fields which will not yield crops.

བདག་བྱིན་གྱིས་བརླབ་པའི་རིམ་པ།

The stage of blessing oneself. The ritual and rite of purifying one's impure body and faculties, thereby blessing these into three vajras—vajra body, speech and mind.

བདག་འབྲས།

Adhipatiphala/ The environmental result (see bdag-po'i 'bras-bu).

བདག་མེད།

Nairātmya/ Selflessness. The view of selflessness or the lack of an identity of independently existing phenomenon. There are two types: 1. གང་ཟག་གི་བདག་མེད། puruṣa nairātmya/ the elflessness of person 2. ཆོས་ཀྱི་བདག་མེད། dharma nairātmya/ the selflessness of phenomena.

བདག་མེད་མ།

Nairātmyā/ She the Non-ego (Anātma). The consort of Hevajra. Marpa's consort is also knwon by this name because of his spiritual association with the deity Hayagrīva.

བདག་མེད་ཕྲ་རགས།

The gross and subtle selflessnesses. The lack of an independent and self-suficient person and the lack of the inherent existence of a person.

བདག་འཛིན་གཉིས།

Two types of graspings at the self; the conceptual misapprehension of a truly existent self of either a person or a phenomenon. 1. བདག་འཛིན་ཀུན་བཏགས། intellectual grasping at the self 2. བདག་འཛིན་ལྷན་སྐྱེས། innate grasping at the self.

བདུད་ཀྱི་མདའ་ལྔ།

The five evil arrows; the five evil influences. 1. ཆགས་པར་བྱེད་པའི་མདའ། that causing desirious attachment 2. རྨོངས་བྱེད་ཀྱི་མདའ། that causing ignorance 3. ང་རྒྱལ་གྱི་མདའ། that causing pride 4. འཐབ་བྱེད་ཀྱི་མདའ། that causing conflict 5. གཡེང་བྱེད་ཀྱི་མདའ། that causing distraction.

བདུད་དགའ་རབ་དབང་ཕྱུག་གི་མེ་ཏོག་གི་མདའ་ལྔ།

The five flower-arrows of the Lord of Desire; the five evil influences of lust. 1. དྲེགས་པར་བྱེད་པའི་མདའ། that causing arrogance 2. རྨོངས་པར་བྱེད་པའི་མདའ། that causing ignorance 3. ཀུན་ཏུ་རྨོངས་པར་བྱེད་པའི་མདའ། that causing strong ignorance 4. བརྒྱལ་བར་བྱེད་པའི་མདའ། that causing one to faint 5. སེམས་མེད་པར་བྱེད་པའི་མདའ། that causing unconsciousness.

བདུད་རྩི་ལྔ།

Pañcāmṛtāni/ The five nectars; the five substances fo preparing an inner offering in tantric practices. 1. དྲི་ཆེན། excrement 2. དྲི་ཆུ། urine 3. རཀྟ། blood 4. མཾ་ས། flesh 5. རྡོ་རྗེའི་ཟིལ་པ། white and red regenerative substances.

བདུད་བཞི།

Catvāri mārāḥ/ The four devils; the four evil forces. 1. ཕུང་པོའི་བདུད། skandhamāra/ the evil of the aggregates 2. ཉོན་མོངས་པའི་བདུད། kleśamāra/ the evil of afflictions 3. འཆི་བདག་གི་བདུད mṛtyupatimāra/ the evil of death 4. ལྷའི་བུ་ཡི་བདུད devaputramāra/ the evil of the son of god (lust).

བདུད་བཞི་ཕྲ་མོ།

Catvāri sūkṣma mārāḥ/ The four subtle evils; the four subtl hinderances. 1. ཕུང་པོའི་བདུད་ཕྲ་མོ། skandha sūkṣma māra/ th subtle evil of the aggregates, i.e. the aggregates caused by th latency of ignorance and uncontaminated actions 2. ཉོན་མོངས་པའི་བདུད་ཕྲ་མོ། kleśa sūkṣma māra/ the subtle evil of affliction i.e. the latency of ignorance 3. འཆི་བདག་གི་བདུད་ཕྲ་མོ། mṛtyupa sūkṣma māra/ the subtle evil of death, i.e. inconceiveabl death 4. ལྷའི་བུ་ཡི་བདུད་ཕྲ་མོ། devaputra kleśa sūkṣma māra/ th subtle evil of lust, i.e. those evils other than the first three.

བདུད་བཞི་རགས་པ།

Catvāri sthūla mārāḥ/ The four gross evils; the four gros hinderances. 1. ཕུང་པོའི་བདུད་རགས་པ། skandha sthūla māra/ th gross evil of the aggregates, i.e. the contaminated aggregate 2. ཉོན་མོངས་པའི་བདུད་རགས་པ། kleśa sthūla māra/ the gross evil o afflictions, i.e. the six root delusions (see rtza-nyon drug) an the twenty secondary delusions (see nye-nyon nyi-shu) 3. འཆི་བདག་གི་བདུད་རགས་པ། mṛtyupati sthūla māra/ the gross evil c death, i.e. natural death through severance of the life force

ལྷའི་བུ་ཡི་བདུད་རགས་པ། devaputra sthūla māra/ the gross evil of lust, i.e. the evil of Kāmadeva.

བདུན་རྣམ་དག

The seven pure practices. 1. བཤགས་པ། confession 2. རྗེས་སུ་ཡི་རང་། rejoicing 3. དོན་དམ་པའི་བྱང་ཆུབ་ཀྱི་སེམས་བསྐྱེད་པ། generating the ultimate mind of enlightenment 4. སྐྱབས་འགྲོ taking refuge 5. སྨོན་སེམས་བསྐྱེད་པ། generating the aspiring mind of enlightenment 6. འཇུག་སེམས་བསྐྱེད་པ། generating the engaging mind of enlightenment 7. བསྔོ་བ། dedication.

བདེ་སྐྱོང་འཁོར་ལོ།

Sukhapāla cakra/ The wheel of sustaining bliss. The channel wheel located at the region of the secret organ which has thirty-two petals spreading out from the central channel like the ribs of an umbrella spreading downwards.

བདེ་འགྲོ

Sugati/ Fortunate beings; happy migrators. Beings in the fortunate realm—humans, gods and demi-gods.

བདེ་ཆེན་འཁོར་ལོ།

Mahāsukha cakra/ The wheel of great bliss. The channel wheel located at the level of the third eye which has thirty-two petals spreading out from the central energy channel like the ribs of an umbrella spreading downwards.

བདེ་ཆེན་ཕྱག་རྒྱ་ཆེན་མོ།

Mahāmudrā/ The Mahāmudrā of great bliss. The Mahāmudrā meditation according to the Kagyud tradition known as the Mahāmudrā of the path of liberation (grol-lam phyag-rgya chen-mo)—the union of emptiness and the unchanging great bliss.

བདེ་ཆེན་ཞིང་།

Sukhāvatī/ The Sukhāvatī Buddha field. The abode of Buddha Amitābha called the Buddha field of great bliss in the western direction.

བདེ་སྟོང་དབྱེར་མེད།

The inseparability of bliss and void; the unity of great bliss, the method, and emptiness, the wisdom aspect. Also the Guru Pūja rite and meditation in the Gelug tradition.

བདེ་གཤེགས་མཆེད་བརྒྱད།

The eight Medicine Buddhas (see sman-bla bde-gshegs brgyad).

བདེ་གཤེགས་སྙིང་པོའི་ཆོས་དྲུག

The six features of the Tathāgata essence. 1. གཟུང་འཛིན་ལ་སོགས་པའི་རྟོག་པ་མེད་པ། being free of grasping at subjective or objective phenomena 2. རྣམ་པར་མི་རྟོག་པའི་སྣང་བ་མེད་པ། being free of a non-conceptual appearances 3. རྡུལ་ཕྲ་རབ་ཀྱི་གཟུགས་མེད་པ། being free of body of subtle particles 4. མཚན་མའི་གཡོ་བ་མེད་པ། being free of disturbances from imaginative signs 5. དེ་རྣམས་ཀྱིས་སྟོང་པའི་མེད་དགག་ལས་འདས་པའི་རང་བཞིན་འོད་གསལ་བ། being naturally clear because their emptiness transcends non-affirming negatives 6. རང་གི་ངོ་བོ་སོ་སོ་རང་གིས་རིག་པའི་མཚན་ཉི་ཅན། experiencing the self-nature by intuitive awareness.

བདེན་པ་གཉིས།

The two truths; the two divisions of truth. 1. ཀུན་རྫོབ་བདེན་པ། saṁvṛti satya/ the conventional truth 2. དོན་དམ་བདེན་པ། paramārtha satya/ the ultimate truth.

བདེན་པ་དང་པོ་གསུམ་གྱི་རྣམ་པ་བཅུ་གཉིས།

The twelve aspects of the first three noble truths. 1. མེད་པའི་རྣམ་པ། aspect of non-existence 2. མི་སྐྱེ་བའི་རྣམ་པ། aspect of non-production 3. དབེན་པའི་རྣམ་པ། aspect of isolation 4. མི་བརྫི་བའི་རྣམ་པ། aspect that cannot be repressed 5. གནས་མེད་པའི་རྣམ་པ། aspect lacking a base 6. ནམ་མཁའི་རྣམ་པ། aspect of space 7. བརྗོད་དུ་མེད་པའི་རྣམ་པ། inexpressible aspect 8. མིང་མེད་པའི་རྣམ་པ། nameless aspect 9. འགྲོ་བ་མེད་པའི་རྣམ་པ། non-going aspect 10. མི་འཕྲོག་པའི་རྣམ་པ། non-grasping aspect 11. མི་ཟད་པའི་རྣམ་པ། inexhaustible aspect 12. སྐྱེ་བ་མེད་པའི་རྣམ་པ། aspect without genesis.

བདེན་པ་བཞི།

Catvāri satyāni/ The four noble truths. 1. སྡུག་བསྔལ་བདེན་པ། duhkha satya/ the truth of suffering 2. ཀུན་འབྱུང་བདེན་པ། samudaya satya/ the truth of the origin of suffering 3. འགོག་པའི་བདེན་པ། nirodha satya/ the truth of cessation 4. ལམ་གྱི་བདེན་པ། mārga satya/ the truth of the path.

བདེན་བཞི་ཆོས་འཁོར།

Catuḥ satya dharma cakra/ The Turning of the Wheel of the Four Noble Truths. The teachings given by Buddha Śākyamuni, after his enlightenment, on the four noble truths to the five ascetics at Vārāṇasī in which Buddha introduced the nature, function and effect of each truth thereby elucidating the twelve aspects of the four noble truths.

མདོ།

Sūtra; the Discourses. The classification of Buddha's teachings, other than his tantric teachings, dealing with the gradual way of enlightenment.

མདོ་སྒྱུ་སེམས་གསུམ།

The sūtra, māyā and citta. The three fundamental texts of generation, completion and rDzogs-chen tradition of the Nyingma school of Tibetan Buddhism. 1. མདོ་དགོངས་པ་འདུས་པ། *The Sūtra Integerating Essential Thoughts* 2. རྒྱུད་སྒྱུ་འཕྲུལ་དྲྭ་བ་སྟེ་དཔལ་གསང་བ་སྙིང་པོ། *The Tantra of Illusory Net* (Māyājāla tantra—Guhyagarbha tantra) 3. སེམས་མདོ་མ་བུ་བཅོ་བརྒྱད། *The Eighteen Father and Mother Treatises on Mind* (sems-mdo ma-bu bco-brgyad).

མདོ་སྡེ་པ།

Sautrāntika School. A school of Buddhist tenets of the lesser vehicle relying mainly on the original discourses of the Buddha and not on their commentaries. This school asserts the existence of self-awareness (rang-rig) and the existence of an external entity (phyi-don).

མདོའི་སྡེ་སྣོད།

Sūtra piṭaka/ Sets of discourses. That category of Buddha's teaching which consists chiefly of the instructions on higher training in meditative concentration.

མདོས།

Crossed-thread ritual. This signifies either offering to gods or giving ransom to the spirits. In the case of the latter it may be called the Demon-trap ritual (mas-stags).

འདུ་བྱེད་ཀྱི་ཕུང་པོའི་རིགས་ཀྱི་ཆོས་ལྔ།

The five phenomena on the level of the aggregate of compositional factors. 1. འདུ་བྱེད་ཀྱི་ཕུང་པོ། the aggregate of compositional factors 2. གཞི་དུས་ཀྱི་བྱ་སྒྲུབ་ཡེ་ཤེས། the basic wisdom of accomplishment 3. རླུང་གི་ཁམས། the element of wind 4. ལྗེའི་དབང་པོ། the tongue sense 5. རང་རྒྱུད་ཀྱི་འདུས་པའི་རོ། the taste included within one's continuum.

འདུ་བྱེད་ཀྱི་ལས་གསུམ།

The three types of compositional karmas. 1. བསོད་ནམས་ཀྱི་ལས། kuśala karma/ meritorious karma 2. བསོད་ནམས་མ་ཡིན་པའི་ལས། akuśala karma/ non-meritorious karma 3. མི་གཡོ་བའི་ལས། acala karma/ unfluctuating karma.

འདུ་ཤེས་ཀྱི་ཕུང་པོའི་རིགས་ཀྱི་ཆོས་ལྔ།

The five phenomena on the level of the aggregate of recognition. 1. འདུ་ཤེས་ཀྱི་ཕུང་པོ། the aggregate of recognition 2. གཞིའི་སོར་རྟོགས་ཡེ་ཤེས། the basic wisdom of analysis 3. མེའི་ཁམས། the element of fire 4. སྣའི་དབང་པོ། the nose sense 5. རང་རྒྱུད་ཀྱི་འདུས་པའི་དྲི། the odours within one's continuum.

འདུ་ཤེས་ལྔ།

The five attitudes. The five attitudes to be maintained while giving a discourse. 1. རང་ལ་སྨན་པའི་འདུ་ཤེས། thinking of oneself as a physician 2-5 (see chos-nyan pa'i skabs-kyi 'du-shes drug—2, 4-6).

འདུ་ཤེས་དྲུག

A. The six recognitions. 1. མཚན་བཅས་ཀྱི་འདུ་ཤེས། lakṣana saṃjñā/ recognition with signs 2. མཚན་མེད་ཀྱི་འདུ་ཤེས། anaudārika saṃjñā/ recognition without signs 3. ཆུང་ངུའི་འདུ་ཤེས anaudārika saṃjñā/ limited recognition 4. རྒྱ་ཆེ་བའི་འདུ་ཤེས། vistāra saṃjñā/ extensive recognition 5. ཚད་མེད་པའི་འདུ་ཤེས། aparimāṇa saṃjñā/ immeasurable recognition 6. ཅི་ཡང་མེད་པའི་འདུ་ཤེས། akiṁcana saṃjñā/ recognition of nothing whatsoever. B. The six attitudes (see chos-nyan-pa'i skabs kyi 'du-shes drug).

འདུན་པ་གསུམ།

The three types of wishes. 1. འཕུད་འདོད་ཀྱི་འདུན་པ། wish to accomplish one's aspirations 2. མི་བྲལ་བར་འདོད་པའི་འདུན་པ། wish not to be separated from one's aspirations 3. དོན་དུ་གཉེར་བའི་འདུན་པ། aspired wish to fulfill one's aspirations.

འདུན་པ་སེམས་པའི་རྣལ་འབྱོར།

The yoga of wishing aspiration. One of the five yogas (see rnal-'byor lnga) according to the Nyingma tradition. This refers to the wish to attain the clear light of emptiness and the deity that has been visualized only at an imagination level on the path of accumulation.

འདུལ་བ་མདོ་རྩ་བ།

The Root Sūtra of Monastic Discipline (vinayamūlasūtra). An extensive treatise on monastic discipline that summarizes the essential meanings of the four Vinaya sūtras (see, next) by Ācārya Guṇaprabha who is renowned for his authority on Vinaya teachings.

འདུལ་བ་ལུང་སྡེ་བཞི།

Catvāri vinayāgama/ The four categories of scriptures on the monastic discipline. 1. འདུལ་བ་ལུང་གཞི། *Basic Transmission on Monastic Discipline* (vinaya vastu) 2. འདུལ་བ་རྣམ་འབྱེད། *Distinguishing the Transmissions on Monastic Discipline* (vinaya vibhaṅga) 3. འདུལ་བ་ཕྲན་ཚེགས། *Minor Transmissions on Monastic Discipline* (vinaya-agama) 4. འདུལ་བ་གཞུང་དམ་པ། *The Sublime Teachings on Monastic Discipline* (vinaya-uttama).

འདུས་བྱས་སྟོང་པ་ཉིད།

Saṁskṛta śūnyatā/ The emptiness of conditioned phenomena. One of the sixteen types of emptinesses; the lack of inherent existence of the three realms produced from the collection of causes and conditions.

འདུས་མ་བྱས་བརྒྱད།

Asaṁskṛta/ The eight types of uncollected phenomena; the eight permanent phenomena. 1-3. དེ་བཞིན་ཉིད་གསུམ། the three suchnesses (see de-bzhin nyid gsum) 4-5. འདུ་ཤེས་མེད་པ་དང་། འགོག་པའི་སྙོམས་འཇུག་གི་དུས་ཀྱི་སེམས་འགག་པའི་གནས་སྐབས་གཉིས། the two moments of the cessation of the mind at the state of meditative absorption without perception and the absorption of cessation 6-8. འདུས་མ་བྱས་གསུམ། the three uncollected phenomena (see 'dus ma-byas gsum).

འདུས་མ་བྱས་སྟོང་པ་ཉིད།

Asaṁskṛta śūnyatā/ The emptiness of uncollected phenomena. One of the sixteen types of emptinesses; the emptiness of permanent phenomena which exist without depending on the collection of causes and conditions, such as the lack of truly independent existence of space.

འདུས་མ་བྱས་བཞི།

The four types of uncollected phenomena; the four permanent phenomena. 1. སོ་སོར་བརྟགས་འགོག the analytical cessation (see so-sor brtags-'gog) 2. སོ་སོར་བརྟགས་མིན་གྱི་འགོག་པ། the non-analytical cessation (see so-sor brtags-min gyi 'gog-pa) 3. ནམ་མཁའ། space 4. དེ་བཞིན་ཉིད། suchness.

འདུས་མ་བྱས་གསུམ།

The three types of uncollected phenomena; the three permanent phenomena according to *Abhidharmakośa*. 1. སོ་སོར་བརྟགས་འགོག the analytical cessation 2. སོ་སོར་བརྟགས་མིན་གྱི་འགོག་པ། the non-analytical cessation 3. ནམ་མཁའ། space (see above).

འདོད་ཁམས།

Kāma dhātu/ Desire realm. One of the three realms of existence; the realm in which consciousness is preoccupied with desire for the five sensual objects and sustains on gross food. This realm includes the states of hell beings, hungry ghosts, animals, humans, demigods and the gods of the desire realm.

འདོད་ཁམས་ཉི་ཤུ།

The twenty states of the desire realm. 1-8. ཚ་དམྱལ་བརྒྱད། the eight hot hells (see tsha-dmyal brgyad) 9-12. གླིང་དམྱལ་བརྒྱད། the four continents (see gling-bzhi) 13-18. འདོད་ལྷ་རིགས་དྲུག the six classes of gods within the desire realm (see 'dod-lha rigs-drug) 19-21. ཡི་དྭགས་དང་དུད་འགྲོའི་གནས། hungry ghosts and animals.

འདོད་ཁམས་ཀྱི་སྒོམ་སྤང་དྲུག

The six objects of abandonment within the desire realm, to be eliminated by the path of meditation. 1. མ་རིག་པ། ignorance 2. འདོད་ཆགས། desire-attachment 3. ཁོང་ཁྲོ hatred-anger 4. ང་རྒྱལ། pride 5. འཇིག་ལྟ། view of the transitory collection 6. མཐར་ལྟ། extreme view.

འདོད་ཁམས་ཀྱི་མཐོང་སྤང་སོ་གཉིས།

The thirty-two objects of abandonment within the desire realm, by the path of seeing. According to *Abhidharmakośa* text there are: འདོད་པར་སྡུག་བདེན་གྱི་སྤང་བྱ་བཅུ། ten related to the truth of suffering, ཀུན་འབྱུང་གི་སྤང་བྱ་བདུན། seven related to the truth of the origin of suffering, འགོག་བདེན་གྱི་སྤང་བྱ་བདུན། seven related to the truth of cessation, ལམ་བདེན་གྱི་སྤང་བྱ་བརྒྱད། eight related to the truth of the path.

འདོད་པའི་ཁམས་ཀྱི་སྤང་བྱ་དྲུག

The six objects of abandonment within the desire realm. The six types of delusions within the desire realm to be eliminated on the path of meditation (see 'dod-pa'i sgom-spang drug).

འདོད་ཆགས་ལྔ།

The five types of attachments. Attachment to: 1. ཕྱི་ལ་ཆགས་པ། the outer 2. ནང་ལ་ཆགས་པ། inner 3. སྡུག་བསྔལ་ལ་ཆགས་པ། suffering 4. གཟུགས་ལ་ཆགས་པ། form 5. འཇིག་ཚོགས་ལ་ཆགས་པ། the collection of the transitory phenomena, i.e. the aggregates of the body.

འདོད་ཆགས་རིགས་བཞི།

The four types of desire; the four ways of utilizing desire as the path in tantra. 1. གཉིས་གཉིས་འཁྱུད་པའི་འདོད་ཆགས། desire through looking 2. ལག་པ་བཅངས་པའི་འདོད་ཆགས། desire throughsmiling 3. རེག་པའི་འདོད་ཆགས། desire through touching 4. འཁྱུད་པའི་འདོད་ཆགས། desire through embracing.

འདོད་ཉོན།

The delusions within the desire realm. This includes the six root delusions (see rtsa-nyon drug) and the twenty near-delusions (see nye-nyon nyi-shu).

འདོད་ཉོན་སྐོར་དགུ

The nine types of delusions within the desire realm; the nine delusions within the desire realm, to be abandoned by the path of meditation. The nine levels of delusion within the desire realm, categorized into three grades of strong, moderate and weak intensity for each of the three—strong, moderate and weak.

འདོད་པ་བཅུ་གཅིག

The eleven types of beings in the desire realm. 1. ཚ་དམྱལ། hot hells 2. གྲང་དམྱལ། cold hells 3. ཀླུ nāgas 4. ལྷ་མ་ཡིན། demigods 5. མི། humans 6-11. འདོད་ལྷ་རིགས་དྲུག the six classes of gods in the desire realm (see 'dod-lha rigs-drug).

འདོད་པའི་སྒོམ་སྤང་དགུ

The nine types of delusions within the desire realm to be abandoned on the path of meditation (see 'dod-nyon skor dgu). This division is based on the principle of taking all those delusions within the desire realm to be abandoned on the path of meditation as one delusion and then are divided into nine phases according to the process of their purification.

འདོད་པའི་སྒོམ་སྤང་ང་བཅུ་རྩ་བཞི།

The fifty-four types of delusions within the desire realm to be abandoned on the path of meditation. When each of the six delusions within the desire realm to be abandoned on the path of meditation (see 'dod-pa'i sgom-spang drug) are divided into nine phases such as strong, moderate and small, each of which are further divided into three phases as such, this comes to fifty four delusions.

འདོད་པའི་སྒོམ་སྤང་དྲུག

The six types of delusions within the desire realm to be abandoned on the path of meditation. These are the six delusions within the desire realm: 1-4. འདོད་པའི་སྒོམ་སྤང་བཞི། the four types of delusions within the desire realm (see 'dod-pa'i sgom spang bzhi) 5. འདོད་པའི་ལྷན་སྐྱེས་ཀྱི་འཇིག་ལྟ། the innately born view of the transitory collection within the desire realm 6. མཐར་ལྟ། the extreme view.

འདོད་པའི་སྒོམ་སྤང་བཞི།

The four types of delusions within the desire realm to be abandoned by the path of meditation. 1. མ་རིག་པ། ignorance 2. འདོད་ཆགས། desire-attachment 3. ཁོང་ཁྲོ། hatred-anger 4. ང་རྒྱལ། pride.

འདོད་པའི་དད་པ།

Longing faith. One of the four types of faith (see dad-pa bzhi), the wish with respectful devotion to train on the paths leading to the attainment of unsurpassable enlightenment.

འདོད་པའི་རིག་འཛིན།

The wish granting boon. A result of secret mantra practice attained at the heat level of the path of preparation, whereupon one's body retains the equal-state with that of a deity, one is able to perform powerful knowledge-mantras (rig-sngags) and siddhis, and gains control of longevity.

འདོད་ཡོན་ལྔ།

A. The sensual objects: གཟུགས་སྒྲ་དྲི་རོ་རེག་བྱ། form, sound, smell, taste and touch. B. The five articles representing the five sensual objects དེ་དག་སོ་སོར་མཚོན་པར་བྱེད་པའི་མཆོད་རྫས། 1. མེ་ལོང་།

mirror 2. པི་ཝང་། guitar 3. དུང་ཆོ། conch-filled with water 4. ཤིང་འབྲས། fruits 5. གོས་དར། five silken scarves.

འདོད་ལྷ་རིགས་དྲུག

The six classes of gods of the desire realm. 1. རྒྱལ་ཆེན་རིགས་བཞི། cātur mahārājakāyikāḥ/ the four great Kings (see rgyal-chen rigs-bzhi) 2. སུམ་ཅུ་རྩ་གསུམ། trāyāstrimśaḥ/ the gods of the heaven of Thirty-three 3. འཐབ་བྲལ། yāmāḥ/ the gods of non-combat 4. དགའ་ལྡན། tusitāḥ/ the gods of Tuṣita heaven 5. འཕྲུལ་དགའ། nirmāṇaratayaḥ/ the gods enjoying emanation 6. གཞན་འཕྲུལ་དབང་བྱེད། paranirmitavaśavartinaḥ/ the gods controlling others' emanations.

འདོད་ལྷའི་འཆི་ལྟས་ལྔ།

The five signs of death for a god of the desire realm. 1. གོས་ལ་དྲི་མ་ཆགས་པ། a bad smell is formed on his clothes 2. མེ་ཏོག་གི་ཕྲེང་བ་རྙིངས་པ། his flower garlands fade away 3. མཆན་ཁུང་དུ་རྔུལ་འབྱུང་བ། sweat if formed in his armpits 4. ལུས་ལ་དྲི་ང་བ། his body smells badly 5. སྟན་ལ་མི་དགའ་བ། he feels discontent with his usual seat.

རྡུལ་རྫས་བརྒྱད་འདུས་ཀྱི་གོང་བུ།

The entity composed of eight components. The objects compounded of different entities within the desire realm, for instance, an atom particle comprises earth, water, fire and wind as well as form, sound, smell and contact.

རྡུལ་རྫས་དྲུག་འདུས།

The entity composed of six components. The atom particles within the form realm, which comprise form, touch and the four basic elements.

རྡོ་རྗེ།

Vajra/ Diamond-hard; adamantine sceptre. A symbol of strength and indestructibility; also a tantric ritual object consisting of a cylindrical axis from which two sets of curved spokes, generally five or nine in number, radiate.

རྡོ་རྗེ་འཇིགས་བྱེད།

Vajrabhairava; The Vajra Terrifier. A wrathful embodiment of Mañjuśī belonging to the highest yoga tantra.

རྡོ་རྗེ་ལྟ་བུའི་སེམས་བསྐྱེད།

Vajropama samādhi/ Diamond-hard like bodhicitta. The mind of enlightenment associated with the perfection of enthusiastic perseverance possessed by a Bodhisattva on the fourth ground.

རྡོ་རྗེ་གདན།

Bodhgayā. The holy place where Buddha Śākyamuni achieved complete enlightenment under the Bodhi tree; a major site for Buddhist pilgrims situated about five miles south of the town of Gayā in Bihar state, India.

རྡོ་རྗེ་གདན་བཞི།

The four diamond-hard seats; the four vajra seats. 1. བདག་གི་གདན། of self 2. གཞན་གྱི་གདན། of others 3. སྦྱོར་བའི་གདན། of practice 4. གསང་བའི་གདན། of secret.

རྡོ་རྗེ་སྤུན་གྲོགས།

Vajra brothers and sisters. Fellow disciples who have received initiation together from the same master.

རྡོ་རྗེ་དམྱལ་བ།

Vajra naraka/ Vajra hell. The hell of non-respite (mnar-med) destination for those who abuse the tantric path and break their tantric precepts or have committed any of the five heinous crimes (see mtshams-med lnga).

རྡོ་རྗེ་བཟླས་པ།

Vajra japa/ Vajra-recitation. A way of reciting mantras according to tantra.

རྡོ་རྗེ་བཞི་བསྐྱེད།

The four steps of vajra visualization. The meditation on the generation of a deity, in which one first meditates on emptiness and within this visualizes cushions of lotus, sun and so forth, then imagines rays of light coming out of the cushions and the seed syllable, and withdrawing these back into emptiness, one then arises in the form of a deity bearing the syllables at three points of one's body—crown, throat and heart.

རྡོ་རྗེ་གསུམ།

The three diamond-hard convictions (of the Kadampa masters). 1. ཐེབས་མེད་རྡོ་རྗེ། the conviction to reject objections to one's secluded practices by parents and relatives 2. ཁྲེལ་མེད་རྡོ་རྗེ། the conviction to face embarrassment 3. ཡེ་ཤེས་རྡོ་རྗེ་དང་འགྲོགས་པ། the conviction to abide by practices one has promised to do.

རྡོ་རྗེ་སེམས་དཔའ།

Vajrasattva. A tantric deity dedicated to purification and elimination of unwholesome deeds; appears both in peaceful and wrathful forms.

རྡོ་རྗེ་སློབ་དཔོན།

Vajrācārya. Tantric master who gives initiations and precepts.

རྡོ་འཇོག

Taxila. An ancient site situated in the kingdom of Kapila which extended from the present day Bamiyan in Afghanistan to Swat in north-west Pakistan. Taxila was a renowned centre of Buddhist learning in the 7th century.

ལྡན་མིན་འདུ་བྱེད།

Viprayukta saṁskāra/ Non-associated compositional factor. Impermanent phenomena being neither form nor consciousness, e.g. a person.

ལྡན་མིན་འདུ་བྱེད་བཅུ་བཞི།

Caturdaśa viprayuktasaṁskārāḥ/ The fourteen non-associated compositional factors. 1. ཐོབ་པ། prāpta/ attainment 2. མ་ཐོབ་པ། aprāpta/ non-attainment 3. སྐལ་མཉམ། equal state 4. འདུ་ཤེས་མེད་པ། sambhāga/ non-perception 5. འདུ་ཤེས་མེད་པའི་སྙོམས་འཇུག asaṁjñā samāpatti/ absorption without perception 6. འགོག་པའི་སྙོམས་འཇུག nirodha samāpatti/ absorption in cessation 7. སྲོག life-force 8. སྐྱེ་བ། jāti/ birth 9. རྒ་བ། jarā/ aging 10. གནས་པ། sṭhita/ endurance 11. འཇིག་པ། anitya/ impermanence 12. མིང་། nāma/ name 13. ཚིག pada/ words 14. ཡི་གེ vyañjana/ letters.

ལྡན་མིན་འདུ་བྱེད་ཉེར་བཞི།

The twenty-four non-associated compositional factors. 1-14 (see ldan-min 'du-byed bcu-bzhi, above). 15. སོ་སྐྱེ། ordinary person 16. འཇུག་པ། engagement or involvement 17. སོ་སོར་ངེས་པ། specific discernment 18. འབྱོར་འབྲེལ། combination 19. མགྱོགས་པ། speediness 20. གོ་རིམ། ranks 21. དུས། time 22. ཡུལ། object 23. གྲངས། number 24. ཚོགས་པ། collection.

ལྡན་མིན་འདུ་བྱེད་ཉེར་གསུམ།

The twenty-three non-associated compositional factors (see gang-zag ma-yin-pa'i ldan-min 'du-byed nyer-gsum).

ལྡེམ་དགོངས་བཞི།

The four interpretative sūtras (see dgongs-pa gtso-bo ston-pa'i ldem-dgongs-kyi mdo bzhi—the four interpretative sūtras primarily stressing the intention of the Buddha).

ལྡོག་ཁྱབ།

Counter pervasion. The third logical mark or pervasion in a correct logical syllogism, stating that whatever is not the predicate is not the reason. Synonymous with the correct counter pervasion (see ldog-khyab rnal-ma, below).

ལྡོག་ཁྱབ་རྣལ་མ།

Correct counter pervasion. The pervasion in a correct logical syllogism that whatsoever is not the predicate is not the reason.

ལྡོག་ཁྱབ་ཕྱིན་ཅི་ལོག

Wrong counter pervasion. The pervasion in a logical syllogism that whatsoever is not the predicate is not that which is not the reason.

ལྡོག་པ།

Nivṛtti/ Reverse identity; isolated identity of the same thing. Apparently contradictory aspects of a thing having the same nature, e.g. the two faces of a coin which is a single entity with two distinct aspects.

ལྡོག་ཆོས་གསུམ།

The three types of reverse identity. 1. རང་ཡིན་པའི་ལྡོག་ཆོས། reverse identity of being itself 2. རང་མ་ཡིན་པའི་ལྡོག་ཆོས། reverse identity of not being itself 3. ལྡོག་ཆོས་ཕུང་གསུམ་ཙམ་པོ་བ། reverse identity of being neither.

སྡིག་སྒྲིབ།

Pāpāvaraṇa/ Evils; non-virtues and obscurations. Misdeeds acquired in the past lives or this life.

སྡུག་བསྔལ་གྱི་སྡུག་བསྔལ།

Duḥkha duḥkhatā/ The suffering of pain. The literal and gross sufferings sometimes called the double suffering, e.g. the feeling of sharp pain in the kidneys.

སྡུག་བསྔལ་བརྒྱད།

Aṣṭa duḥkhatāḥ/ Eight kinds of suffering. The eight sufferings that Buddha introduced while explaining the faults of the truth of suffering. 1. སྐྱེ་བའི་སྡུག་བསྔལ། jāti duḥkham/ suffering of birth 2. རྒ་བའི་སྡུག་བསྔལ། jarā duḥkham/ suffering of aging 3. ན་བའི་སྡུག་བསྔལ། vyādhi duḥkham/ suffering of sickness 4. འཆི་བའི་སྡུག་བསྔལ། maraṇa duḥkham/ suffering of death 5. སྡུག་པ་དང་བྲལ་བའི་སྡུག་བསྔལ། priya viprayogo duḥkham/ suffering of separation from cherished objects 6. མི་སྡུག་པ་དང་འཕྲད་པའི་སྡུག་བསྔལ། apriya saṁprayogo duḥkham/ suffering of meeting with revolting objects 7. འདོད་པའི་དངོས་པོ་བཙལ་ཀྱང་མི་རྙེད་པའི་སྡུག་བསྔལ། yad apīcchaya paryeṣamāno na labhate tadapi duḥkham/ súffering of not finding desired objects 8. ཕུང་པོ་ལྔ་སྡུག་བསྔལ་བ་ཡིན་པ། saṁkṣepanam pañcoskandha duḥkham/ the suffering of the five aggregates.

སྡུག་བསྔལ་དྲུག

Ṣaḍ duḥkhatāḥ/ Six types of suffering. The six miseries within cyclic existence. 1. ངེས་པ་མེད་པའི་སྡུག་བསྔལ། suffering of uncertainty 2. ངོམས་པ་མེད་པའི་སྡུག་བསྔལ། suffering of dissatisfaction 3. ཡང་ནས་ཡང་དུ་ལུས་འདོར་བའི་སྡུག་བསྔལ། suffering of discarding one's body time and again 4. ཡང་ནས་ཡང་དུ་ཉིང་མཚམས་སྦྱོར་བའི་སྡུག་བསྔལ། suffering of frequent conception 5. ཡང་ནས་ཡང་དུ་མཐོ་དམན་དུ་འགྱུར་བའི་སྡུག་བསྔལ། suffering of frequent change of status 6. གྲོགས་མེད་པའི་སྡུག་བསྔལ། suffering of loneliness.

སྡུག་བསྔལ་བདེན་པའི་ཁྱད་ཆོས་བཞི།

The four attributes of the noble truth of suffering. 1. མི་རྟག་པ། anityam/ impermanence 2. སྡུག་བསྔལ་བ། duhkhita/ suffering/ misery 3. སྟོང་པ། śūnyam/ emptiness 4. བདག་མེད་པ། anātmakam/ selflessness.

སྡུག་བསྔལ་བཞི།

The four types of suffering. 1. སྐྱེ་བའི་སྡུག་བསྔལ། jāti duḥkham/ suffering of birth 2. རྒ་བའི་སྡུག་བསྔལ། jarā duḥkham/ suffering of old age 3. ན་བའི་སྡུག་བསྔལ། vyādhi duḥkham/ suffering of sickness 4. འཆི་བའི་སྡུག་བསྔལ། maraṇa duḥkham/ suffering of death.

སྡུག་བསྔལ་གསུམ།

The three types of suffering. 1. སྡུག་བསྔལ་གྱི་སྡུག་བསྔལ། duḥkha duḥkhatā/ suffering of pain 2. འགྱུར་བའི་སྡུག་བསྔལ། vipriṇāma duḥkhatā/ suffering of change 3. ཁྱབ་པ་འདུ་བྱེད་ཀྱི་སྡུག་བསྔལ། saṁskāra duḥkhatā/ pervasive suffering.

སྡུག་བདེན་གྱི་སྤང་བྱ་བཅུ།

The ten objects to be abandoned by the truth of suffering. The realization of the truth of suffering within this desire realm involves abandoning 1-5. ལྟ་བ་ལྔ། the five views (see lta-ba lnga) 6-10. ལྟ་མིན་ལྔ། the five non-views (see lta-min lnga).

སྡུག་པའི་རྣམ་ཐར།

Emancipation of a beautiful form. This is a kind of concentration within the form realm cultivated by a Yogi visualizing himself as having a very attractive form and taking all appearances to be of the same taste; one of the eight emancipations (see rnam-thar brgyad).

སྡེ་སྣོད་གསུམ།

Tripiṭaka/ The three baskets of teachings. The way in which Buddha's teaching is classified in general into three divisions according to their subject matter and trainings they describe. 1. འདུལ་བའི་སྡེ་སྣོད། vinaya pitaka/ the basket of teachings on moral discipline mainly emphasizes the training of ethics 2. མདོ་སྡེའི་སྡེ་སྣོད། sūtra piṭaka/ the basket of teachings in discourses mainly emphasizes the training of concentration 3. མངོན་པའི་སྡེ་སྣོད། abhidharma piṭaka/ the basket of teaching on knowledge mainly emphasizing the training of wisdom.

སྡེ་སྣོད་གསུམ་ངོས་འཛིན་གྱི་ཕྱག

The obeisance for identifying the three baskets of teachings (see above sde-snod gsum). All Vinaya texts begin with the line, 'obeisance to the all-knowing one'. All Sūtrapiṭaka texts begin with the line, 'obeisance to Buddhas and Bodhisattvas', and all Abhidharmapiṭakas begin with the line, 'obeisance to the youthful Mañjuśrī'.

སྡོམ་རྣམ་གཉིས།

The Two Compendiums. The two works of Asaṅga. 1. ཐེག་བསྡུས། *Compendium of the Greater Vehicle* (Mahāyānasaṁgraha) 2. མངོན་པ་ཀུན་བཏུས། *Compendium of Knowledge* (Abhidharmasamuccaya).

སྡོམ་པ་ཉམས་པའི་རྒྱུ་བཞི།

The four ways of losing vows (see ltung-ba'i sgo bzhi).

སྡོམ་པ་རྣམ་གསུམ།

Trisaṁvara/ A. The three classes of vows. 1. སོ་ཐར་གྱི་སྡོམ་པ། pratimokṣa saṁvara/ the individual liberation vows 2. བྱང་སེམས་ཀྱི་སྡོམ་པ། bodhicitta saṁvara/ the Bodhisattva vows 3. གསང་སྔགས་ཀྱི་སྡོམ་པ། mantra saṁvara/ the tantric vows. B. 1. འདོད་པའི་སས་བསྡུས་པ་སོ་ཐར་གྱི་སྡོམ་པ། the individual liberation vows of those within the desire realm 2. གཟུགས་ཀྱི་སས་བསྡུས་པ་བསམ་གཏན་གྱི་སྡོམ་པ། the concentration vows of those within the form realm 3. ཁམས་གསུམ་ལས་འདས་ཤིང་འཕགས་པའི་སས་བསྡུས་པ་ཟག་མེད་ཀྱི་སྡོམ་པ། the uncontaminated vows of those at the level of an Ārya's path transcending all those vows within three realms.

བརྡའི་འགོག་པ།

Symbolic negative phenomena, e.g. although emptiness is a

mere absence of a truly existent nature it is not a negative thing.

བསྡུ་བ་རྣམ་བཞི།

Catuḥsaṁgraha/ The four compendiums; the four works of Asaṅga on the Yogacāra tenet. 1. གཏན་ལ་དབབ་པའི་བསྡུ་བ། *Compendium of Ascertainment* (Nirṇayasaṁgraha) 2. གཞི་བསྡུ་བ། *Compendium of Bases* (Vastusaṁgraha) 3. རྣམ་གྲངས་བསྡུ་བ། *Compendium of Enumerations* (Paryāyasaṁgraha) 4. རྣམ་པར་བཤད་པའི་བསྡུ་བ། *Compendium of Explanations* (Vivaraṇa-saṁgraha).

བསྡུ་བའི་དངོས་པོ་བཞི།

Catvāri saṁgraha vastūni/ The four means of conversion; the four means of assembling disciples. 1. སྦྱིན་པ་སྦྱིན་པ། dānam/ giving whatever is necessary 2. སྙན་པར་སྨྲ་བ། priya vāditā/ speaking pleasantly 3. དོན་མཐུན་པ། samānārthatā helping others 4. དོན་སྤྱོད་པ། artha caryā/ consistency between words and deeds.

བསྡུས་གྲྭ

The Collected Topics. The basic texts on the Buddhist study of logic. Chapa Choekyi Senge (12th century A.D.) and others formulated this study as a key for studying Buddhist logic taught in Valid Cognition (Pramāṇa). This text is studied in all the monastic universities of the Gelug order as a part of their basic curriculum.

བསྡུས་དོན་གསུམ།

The three summarized topics; the three basic wisdoms. 1. གཞི་ཤེས། vastu jñāna/ the basic wisdom 2. ལམ་ཤེས། mārga jñāna/ the path wisdom 3. རྣམ་མཁྱེན། sarvajñāna/ the omniscient wisdom.

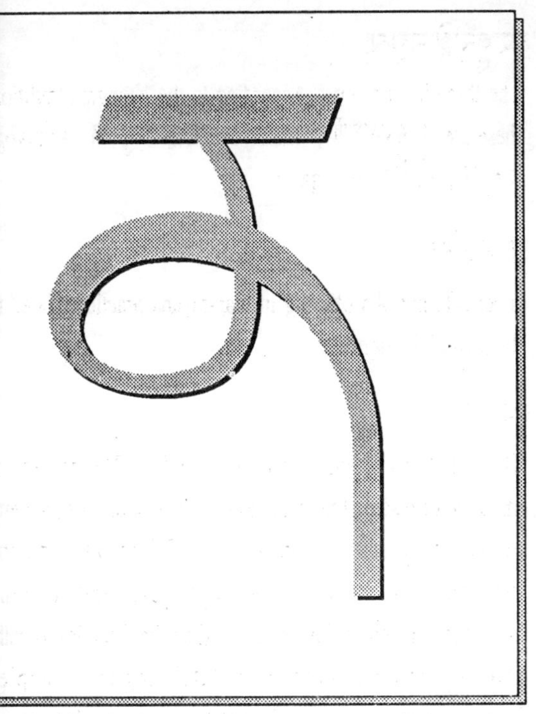

ནཱ་རོ་པ།

Naropa. A great Indian scholar and adept who, after serving as abbot of Nalanda, obtained the highest tantric teachings from Tilopa. His disciple, Marpa, took those teachings to Tibet and propagated the doctrine.

ནཱ་ལནྡཱ།

Nālanda. The great monastery of Nālanda in ancient Magadha in Bihar, India. One of the main places of pilgrimage for Buddhist devotees, also known as the birth place of Śariputra.

ནག་པོའི་ཆོས་བཞི།

The four negative conducts. The four transgressions of the Bodhisattva vows. 1. བླ་མར་དཔུ་བསྐོར་བ། misleading the teacher 2. གཞན་གྱི་དགེ་བ་ལ་འགྱོད་དུ་བཅུག་པ། leading others to regret their virtuous deeds 3. ཐེག་ཆེན་དུ་ཞུགས་པ་ལ་སྐྱོན་འདོགས་པ། disparaging those in the Mahāyāna doctrine 4. གཡོ་སྒྱུ། cheating others.

ནགས་ཁྲོད་པ།

Vānaprastha/ A forest dweller. One who forsakes his home to seek freedom from suffering and dwells as an ascetic in the forest.

་རོ་མཁའ་སྤྱོད་མ།

Sarvabuddhaḍākinī. A mantra practice of a female deity, Vajrayoginī, with its lineage coming from the great Naropa.

་རོ་ཆོས་དྲུག

The six doctrines of Naropa; the six yogas of Naropa. There are two ways of listing these six yogas. A. 1. གཏུམ་མོའི་རྣལ་འབྱོར། caṇḍālī yoga/ yoga of psychic heat 2. འོད་གསལ། prabhāsvara yoga/ yoga of clear light 3. སྒྱུ་ལུས། māyākāya yoga/ yoga of illusory body 4. བར་དོ། antarābhava yoga/ yoga of intermediate rebirth 5. འཕོ་བ། saṁkrānti yoga/ yoga of consciousness transference 6. གྲོང་འཇུག yoga of entering a corpse. B. 1. གཏུམ་མོ། yoga of psychic heat 2. འོད་གསལ། yoga of clear light 3. སྒྱུ་ལུས། yoga of illusory body 4. ཟུང་འཇུག yoga of the state of union 5. འཕོ་བ། yoga of consciousness transference 6. གྲོང་འཇུག yoga of entering a corpse.

ནང་གི་དཀྱིལ་འཁོར་གསུམ།

The three inner maṇḍalas. 1. ཀུན་རྫོབ་ཀྱི་དཀྱིལ་འཁོར། saṁvṛti maṇḍala/ conventional maṇḍala 2. བྷ་གའི་དཀྱིལ་འཁོར། bhaga maṇḍala/ the female genital maṇḍala 3. དོན་དམ་བྱང་ཆུབ་སེམས་ཀྱི་དཀྱིལ་འཁོར། paramārtha bodhicitta maṇḍala/ the maṇḍala of ultimate bodhicitta.

ནང་གི་སྐྱེ་མཆེད་དྲུག

Ṣaḍ antarāyatanāni/ The six inner sources of perception (see dbang-po drug).

ནང་གི་ཁམས་དྲུག

Ṣaḍ antara dhātavaḥ/ The six inner sense powers (see khams-bco brgyad B.)

ནང་གི་དེ་ཉིད་བཅུ།

The ten internal qualities; the ten inner qualities of a Vajrācārya. 1. བསྲུང་འཁོར་བསྒོམས་ནས་ཕྱིར་བཟློག་ལ་མཁས་པ། adept in dispelling interferences by means of meditation on the wheel of protection 2. འཁོར་ལོ་བྲིས་པ་ལུས་ལ་བཏགས་པ་སོགས་ཀྱི་སྒོ་ནས་ཕྱིར་བཟློག་ལ་མཁས་པ། adept in dispelling interferences by means of drawing mystic circles and tying them to the body 3. བུམ་དབང་དང་གསང་དབང་བསྐུར་བ་ལ་མཁས་པ། adept in bestowing the vase and secret initiation 4. ཤེས་རབ་ཡེ་ཤེས་དང་དབང་བཞི་པ་བསྐུར་བ་ལ་མཁས་པ། adept in bestowing the wisdom and fourth initiation 5. དགྲ་བོའི་བསྲུང་མ་དང་ཕྱལ་བའི་ཁ་སྤྱོར་དབྱེ་བ་ལ་མཁས་པ། adept in sending off and scattering the protectors of the enemy 6. གཏོར་མའི་ཆོ་ག་ལ་མཁས་པ། adept in the practice of ritual cake offerings 7. བཟླས་པའི་རྩལ་ལ་མཁས་པ། adept in the practice of vajra recitations 8. རྩལ་བཞིན་བསྒྲུབས་ཀྱང་མ་འགྲུབ་ན་ སྡོག་ཆོག་བྱ་བར་དྲག་ཤུལ་གྱི་ལས་ལ་མཁས་པ། adept in the means of aggressively reversed practice when unable to actualize the results through the usual order of practice 9. རབ་གནས་ཀྱི་ཆོ་ག་ལ་མཁས་པ། adept in the consecration rituals 10. དཀྱིལ་འཁོར་སྒྲུབ་མཆོད་ལ་མཁས་པ། adept in the creation and worship of maṇḍalas.

ནང་གི་བདུད།

The internal demons. The mental adversities or demonic impulses created through imbalanced and disturbed attitudes of desire, hatred and closed-mindedness.

ནང་གི་གཡེང་བ།

The inner distractions. One of the six distractions (see rnam-g-yeng drug). Mental sloth, agitation and clinging to the experience that are obstructions to generating concentration.

ནང་རྒྱུད་སྡེ་གསུམ།

The three inner tantras. According to the Nyingma traditior these are: 1. རྒྱུ་མ་ཧཱ་ཡོ་ག Mahāyoga 2. ལུང་ཨ་ནུ་ཡོ་ག Annuyog 3. མན་ངག་ཨ་ཏི་ཡོ་ག Atiyoga.

ནང་མཆོད།

Inner offering. An offering in mantrayāna practice related t the secret initiation.

ནང་འཇུག

The initiations of entering into a maṇḍala. The process o initiation of placing the disciples into the maṇḍala of the deit by opening the curtain of the mansion. This involves enterin the maṇḍala from the eastern gate and makin circumambulation of the deities, binding the disciples to oat showing wisdom beings and stabilizing the disciple inseparable from the commitment being and wisdom bein throwing flowers by reciting verses of truth, and choosing th lord of the Buddha family and the offering of flowers fc auspicious reasons and connection.

ནང་སྟོང་པ་ཉིད།

Adhyātma śūnyatā/ Internal emptiness. One of the sixtee types of emptinesses (see stong-pa nyid bcu-drug); the lack c the true and independent existence of objects conjoined wit consciousness, such as the cognitive eye power, and so forth.

ནང་དོན་ཁེམ་པོ།

Internal matter. Something which is composed of interna matter, e.g. such as the sense faculties.

ནང་ནས་པའི་དབང་ལྔ།

The five initiations of inner yoga practice. The initiations th are gateways to mahāyoga tantra practice in the Nyingm tradition. For those with potentials to fulfill one's purposes: 1. ཉན་དབང་། initiation to listen 2. སྒོམ་དབང་། initiation to meditation. For those with potentials to fulfill the goals of others: 3. འཆད་དབང་། initiation to teach 4. ཕྲིན་དབང་། initiation to perform the activities. For those with potentials to fulfill the goals of both self and others: 5. རྡོ་རྗེ་རྒྱལ་པོ་བཀའ་རབ་འབྱམས་ཀྱི་དབང་། the Vajrarāja's precious word initiation.

ང་པ་སངས་རྒྱས་པ།

A Buddhist. One who accepts the Buddha, Dharma and Saṅgha as the ultimate objects of refuge and protection.

ང་པའི་གྲུབ་མཐའ།

The Buddhist tenet. A philosophy that accepts the Three Jewels as the perfect object of refuge and the four seals of Buddhist doctrine (see lta-ba bkar-btags kyi phyag-rgya-bzhi).

ང་མཛོད།

The Nang Dzod scarf. A traditional offering scarf of a great quality depicting a design of auspicious symbols and writings.

་གུ་མ།

Niguma; Yoginī Niguma. The principal lama and meditational deity of the master Khyungpo Naljor, the founder of the Shangpa Kagyud lineage.

་གུའི་ཆོས་དྲུག

The six doctrines of Yoginī Niguma. The transmission of tantric practice that comes from Niguma. 1. གཏུམ་མོ་བདེ་དྲོད་རང་འབར། self-ignition of bliss through the yoga of psychic heat 2. སྒྱུ་ལུས་ཆགས་སྡང་རང་གྲོལ། self-liberation from attachment and hatred through the yoga of the illusory body 3. རྨི་ལམ་ཉིད་འཁྲུལ་རང་དག incineration of wrong conceptions through the yoga of dreams 4. འོད་གསལ་གཏི་མུག་རང་གསལ། self-awakening from ignorance through the yoga of clear light 5. འཕོ་བ་མ་བསྒོམས་སངས་རྒྱས། full awakening without meditation through the yoga of consciousness transference 6. བར་དོ་རྒྱལ་བ་ལོངས་སྐུ། meditation on the Sambhogakāya Buddha through the yoga of the intermediate state of rebirth.

ནུས་པ་བརྒྱད།

The eight types of inherent powers. The eight different powers of medicines rooted in their elemental composition. 1-2. ལྕི་བ་དང་སྣུམ་པ་གཉིས་ཀྱིས་རླུང་ནད་སེལ་བ། heavy and oily, powerful for wind disease. 3-4. བསིལ་བ་དང་རྟུལ་བ་གཉིས་ཀྱིས་མཁྲིས་ནད་སེལ་བ། coolness and dullness, for bile diseases. 5-8. ཡང་བ་དང་རྩུབ་པ་ཚ་བ་རྣོ་བ་བཅས་བཞི་པོས་བད་ཀན་གྱི་ནད་སེལ་བ། lightness, roughness, hot and sharpness, for phlegm.

ནོར་བུ་ཆ་བདུན།

The seven secondary jewels; the seven secondary precious objects. 1. རྒྱལ་པོའི་རྣ་ཆ། a king's ear ring 2. བཙུན་མོའི་རྣ་ཆ། a queen's ear ring 3. བློན་པོའི་རྣ་ཆ། a minister's ear ring 4. ནོར་བུ་མིག་གསུམ། the three-eyed jewel 5. བསེ་རུའི་རྭ། a rhinoceros horn 6. བྱུ་རུའི་སྡོང་པོ། a coral branch 7. གླང་ཆེན་མཆེ་བ། an elephant's tusk.

གནད་གསུམ།

A. The three principles. The principal psycho-physical discipline to be maintained in the leap-over (thod-rgal) system of rDzogs-chen meditation. 1. བཅའ་བ་ལུས་ཀྱི་གནད་སྐུ་གསུམ་གྱི་བཞུགས་སྟངས་གསུམ་ལས་མི་གཡོ་བ། stillness as the principle of the body seated in the manners of three kāyas 2. འཁྲིད་པ་དབྱིངས་ཀྱི་གནད་སྐུ་གསུམ་གྱི་གཟིགས་སྟངས་ལས་མི་འགྱུལ་བ། guidance as the principle of absorption in reality immutable from the manner of looking into three kāyas 3. སྣང་བ་ཡུལ་གྱི་གནད་དབྱིངས་རིག་མི་འབྲལ་ཞིང་རླུང་དལ་བར་སྡོད་པ། appearance as the principle of the object of meditation inseparable from primordial awareness and reality, and maintaining a gentle pace of the flow of energy wind. B. The three essential practices. 1. སྣང་བ་སེམས་སུ་སྒྲུབ་པ། taking all appearances as the (nature of) mind 2. སེམས་སྒྱུ་མར་སྒྲུབ་པ། taking mind as illusory 3. སྒྱུ་མ་རང་བཞིན་མེད་པར་སྒྲུབ་པ། taking all illusories as lacking inherent existence.

གནམ་ལྕགས།

A. Thunder and lightning B. An adamantine vajra, normally a discovered treasure-object of metal that has a soothing sound when beaten with a shadowy dark metal, unbeatable by other metals. Powerful for clearing hindrances and curing insanity.

གནས་ཀྱི་བླ་མའི་མཚན་ཉིད་བཅུ།

The ten qualities of a resident teacher or guru. 1. བརྟན་པ། he is stern/firm 2. མཁས་པ། he is wise 3. ལུས་ཐ་མལ་དུ་གནས་པ། he abides in his ordinary physical form 4. ས་རང་བཞིན་དུ་གནས་པ། he is constantly aware of his vows and commitments 5. སྙིང་རྗེ་དང་ལྡན་པ། he is compassionate 6. བཟོད་པ་དང་ལྡན་པ། he is patient 7. ནང་འཁོར་དག་པ། he has a close circle of disciples 8. ཆོས་ཀྱིས་ཕན་འདོགས་པ། he benefits others with teachings 9. ཟང་ཟིང་གིས་ཕན་འདོགས་པ། he benefits others with material gifts 10. དུས་སུ་གདམས་པ། he gives instructions in time of need.

གནས་སྐབས་བརྒྱད།

The eight stages; the eight stages of the dissolution of elements and minds at death according to tantra. 1-4. ས་ཆུ་མེ་རླུང་། the earth into water, water into fire, fire into wind, wind into consciousness 5. དཀར་ལམ། consciousness into the mind of radiant white appearance 6. དམར་ལམ། radiant white into the the mind of radiant red 7. ནག་ལམ། radiant red into mind of black near-attainment 8. སྣང་བ། འོད་གསལ། near-attainment into clear light mind.

གནས་སྐབས་ཉེར་ལྔ།

The twenty-five occasions of mental impulses; the twenty-five principles. 1. བདེ་བ། sukha/ happiness 2. སྡུག་བསྔལ། duḥkha/ suffering 3. བཏང་སྙོམས། upekṣā/ indifference 4. ཆུང་ངུ། alpa/ weak 5. འབྲིང་། madhya/ moderate 6. ཆེན་པོ། bṛhat/ strong 7. དགེ་བ། kuśala/ virtuous 8. མི་དགེ་བ། akuśala/ non-virtuous 9. ལུང་མ་བསྟན། avyākṛta/ unspecified 10. ཐོས་པ། śruta/ hearing 11. བསམ་པ། cintā/ contemplation 12. སྒོམ་པ། bhāvanā/ meditation 13. ཚུལ་ཁྲིམས་ཀྱི་བསླབ་པ། śila śikṣā/ training in morality 14. ཏིང་ངེ་འཛིན་གྱི་བསླབ་པ། samādhi śikśā/ training in concentration 15. ཤེས་རབ་ཀྱི་བསླབ་པ། prajñā śikṣā/ raining in wisdom 16. ཕྱི། bāhya/ the external 17. ནང་། ādhyātmika/ the internal 18. གཟུང་བ། grāhya/ the object of perception 19. འཛིན་པ། grahīta/ the object perceiver 20. སྤོང་བ། prahāṇa/ the abandonment 21. གཉེན་པོ། pratipakṣa/ antidotes 22. མངོན་གྱུར། pratyakṣa/ manifest 23. ལྐོག་གྱུར། parokṣa/ hidden 24. རྒྱུ་དུས། hetuḥkāla/ causal 25. འབྲས་དུས། phalam kāla/ resultant.

གནས་སྐབས་བཞི།

The four states; the four states of experiencing objects through the six-fold consciousnesses following the maturation of energy channels, energy winds and essential drops in the human body. 1. གཉིད་འཐུག་པོའི་གནས་སྐབས། deep sleep state 2. རྨི་ལམ་གྱི་གནས་སྐབས། dream state 3. སད་པའི་གནས་སྐབས། awakening state 4. སྙོམས་འཇུག་གི་གནས་སྐབས། absorption in a dormant state.

གནས་བསྐལ་གྱི་དུས་བཞི།

The four periods of endurance of this universe. 1. རྫོགས་ལྡན། the perfected aeon (see bskal-pa rdzogs-ldan). 2. བསྐལ་པ་གསུམ་ལྡན། the three-fold aeŏn (see bskal-pa gsum-ldan) 3. བསྐལ་པ་གཉིས་ལྡན། the two-fold aeon (see bskal-pa gnyis ldan). 4. རྩོད་ལྡན་གྱི་བསྐལ་པ། the quarrelsome period.

གནས་འགྱུར་མཐར་ཕྱིན་པ་གསུམ།

The three types of perfect transformation. 1. བྲལ་སེམས་ཀྱི་གནས་འགྱུར། attainment of cessation as the transformation of mind 2. ལམ་གྱི་གནས་འགྱུར། the transformation of paths 3. ཡེ་ཤེས་ཀྱི་གནས་འགྱུར། the transformation of wisdom.

ནས་ངན་ལེན།

auṣṭhulya/ The compulsive obtainment; taking unfortunate ebirth; bad rebirth. Being born in adverse circumstances.

ནས་ལྔ།

he five points; the five points of one's body for visualization f the object of meditation. 1. སྤྱི་བོ། crown 2. མགྲིན་པ། throat 3. ང་ག heart 4. ལྟེ་བ། navel 5. གསང་གནས། secret organ.

ནས་ཆེན་ལྔ།

he five holy places. The five holy places in this universe for uddhist followers. 1. ཡུལ་དབུས་རྒྱ་གར་རྡོ་རྗེ་གདན། Bodhgayā of ndia in the centre 2. ཤར་རྒྱ་རི་བོ་རྩེ་ལྔ། the Five-peaked mountain Mt. Wu-te'i) in the east 3. ལྷོའི་པོ་ཏ་ལ། Potala palace in the outh 4. ནུབ་ཀྱི་ཨོ་ཌི་ཡ་ན། Oḍḍiyāna in the west 5. བྱང་གི་ཤམྦྷ་ལ། ambhala in the north.

ནས་བརྟན།

thavira; An Elder. A senior monk who has completed at least n years of training as a fully ordained monk, and has gained astery over the theory and practice of a monk's discipline, nd thus is authorized to give the novice and full ordination ows to others.

ས་བརྟན་བཅུ་དྲུག

he sixteen Arhats; the sixteen saints to whom Buddha ākyamuni entrusted his doctrine. 1. ཡན་ལག་འབྱུང་། Aṅgaja 2. ཕམ་པ། Ajita 3. ནགས་ན་གནས། Vanavāsin 4. དུས་ལྡན། Kālika 5. རྡོ་མོའི་བུ། Vajriputra 6. བཟང་པོ། Bhadra 7. གསེར་གྱི་བེའུ། anakavatsa 8. བྷ་ར་དྭ་ཛ་གསེར་ཅན། Kanaka Bharadvāja 9. བ་ཀུ་ལ། akula 10. སྒྲ་གཅན་འཛིན། Rāhula 11. ལམ་ཕྲན་བསྟན། Cūḍapanthaka . བྷ་ར་དྭ་ཛ་བསོད་སྙོམས་ལེན། Piṇḍola Bharadvāja 13. ལམ་ཆེན་བསྟན། ahāpanthaka 14. ཀླུའི་སྡེ། Nāgasena 15. སྦེད་བྱེད། Gopaka 16. མི་ད་པ། Abheda.

གནས་བརྟན་སྡེ་པ།

Sthaviravāda. The School of Elders. One of the four main schools of the Hīnayāna order. There are three sub-schools within this school which are: 1. རྒྱལ་བྱེད་ཚལ་ན་གནས་པ། Jetavanīyāḥ 2. འཇིགས་མེད་རི་ལ་གནས་པ། Abhayagiri vāsinaḥ 3. གཙུག་ལག་ཁང་ཆེན་ན་གནས་པ། Mahāvihāravāsinaḥ.

གནས་པ་དགུ

The nine objects of reliance. 1. སྟོན་པ། teacher 2. ཆོས། Dharma 3. དགེ་འདུན། Saṅgha 4. སློབ་དཔོན། ācārya 5. མཁན་པོ། abbot 6. བླ་མ། one's master 7. གནས། residence 8. གང་ཟག person 9. ཡུལ། environment.

གནས་པའི་བསྐལ་པ།

Aeon of endurance. The period of twenty intermediate aeons since the formation of the universe until the beginning of its destruction. It begins with the rebirth of a being born in the most heinous hell realm and lasts till the end of the teaching of the last of the thousand Buddhas to appear in this universe.

གནས་མ་བུ་པ།

Vātsīputrīya school. One of the eighteen sub-schools of the Vaibhāṣika school of thought that asserts the existence of an inexpressible self, that is neither permanent nor impermanent; neither one nor separate from the five aggregates.

གནས་མི་འགྱུར་བའི་ས།

The unchanging ground. According to the Nyingma tradition this refers to the eighth ground attained at the level of the fifth yoga, where a Bodhisattva's absorption in the inseparability of primordial wisdom and reality is immutably established.

གནོད་སྦྱིན།

A. Yakṣa; harmful spirit; demons. B. A god of wealth.

མནན་བསྲེག་འཕང་གསུམ།

Capturing, destroying and dispelling. The yogic practice of exorcism which involves སྲི་མནན་པ། capturing, གདོན་བྱེགས་བསྲེག་པ། burning and གཏོར་ཟོར་འཕངས་པ། expelling an evil spirit who is harming the practice of dharma.

མནར་མེད།

Avīci hell; the hell without-respite. The hottest of the hot hells, migration to which is a result of committing any of the five heinous crimes (see mtshams-med lnga).

མནར་སེམས་པའི་དངོས་པོ་དགུ

The nine types of grudges or ill-will. The feeling that one's enemy has harmed, is harming and would harm onself; has harmed, is harming and would harm their friends; and has helped, is helping and would help another enemy.

རྣམ་མཁྱེན་གྱི་རྣམ་པ་བརྒྱ་ཙ་བཅུ།

The one hundred and ten aspects of the omniscient mind. 1-37. ཉན་རང་དང་ཐུན་མོང་བའི་རྣམ་པ་བྱང་ཕྱོགས་སོ་བདུན། the thirty-seven auxillaries to enlightenment common to Hearers and Solitary realizers (see byang-phyogs so bdun) 38-71. བྱང་སེམས་དང་ཐུན་མོང་བའི་རྣམ་པ་སོ་བཞི། thirty-four aspects common to Bodhisattvas (see byang-sems-dang thun-mongs-ba' i rnam-pa so-bzhi) 72-110. རྣམ་མཁྱེན་གྱི་ཐུན་མོང་མ་ཡིན་པའི་རྣམ་པ་སོ་དགུ thirty-nine aspects exclusive to the omniscient mind (see sangs-rgyas-kyi thun-mongs ma-yin-pa'i rnam-pa so-dgu).

རྣམ་མཁྱེན་གྱི་རྣམ་པ་སུམ་ཅུ་སོ་བཞི བྱང་སེམས་དང་ཐུན་མོང་བའི་རྣམ་པ་སོ་བཞི བྱང་ཆུབ་སེམས་དཔའ་ལ་ཡོད་པ་དང་རྗེས་སུ་མཐུན་པའི་རྣམ་མཁྱེན་གྱི་རྣམ་པ་སོ་བཞི།

The thirty-four aspects of the omniscient mind. 1-3. རྣམ་ཐར་སྒོ་གསུམ། tri vimokṣamukha/ the three doors of emancipation (see rnam-thar sgo-gsum) 4-6. སྤྲུལ་པའི་ལམ་གསུམ། tri nirmāṇa mārga/ the three paths of emanation (see sprul-pa'i lam-gsum) 7-11. མཐོ་ ཆོས་བདེར་གནས་ཀྱི་ལམ་ལྔ། pañca dṛṣṭidharma sukhathita/ the fi paths bestowing peace in this life (see mthong-chos bde-gna kyi lam-lnga) 12-20. འཇིག་རྟེན་ལས་འདས་པའི་ལམ་དགུ na lokottaramārga/ the nine transcendental paths (see thar-gy gnas-pa'i snyoms-'jug dgu) 21-24. སྦྱོང་བའི་ལམ་རིགས་འདྲ་ཕྱི་མ་ the four forbearances with the reality (chos-bzod bzhi) of t four noble truths (see mthong-lam shes-bzod skad-cig-n bcu-drug).

རྣམ་མཁྱེན་གྱི་རྣམ་པ་སོ་དགུ

Thirty-nine qualities of the omniscient mind (see sans-rgya kyi thun-mong ma-yin-pa'i rnam-pa so-dgu).

རྣམ་མཁྱེན་མཚོན་བྱེད་ཀྱི་ཆོས་བཅུ།

The ten topics that characterize the omniscient mind. 1. སེམ བསྐྱེད། the generation of the mind of enlightenment 2. གདམས་ the Mahāyāna instruction 3. ངེས་འབྱེད་ཡན་ལག་བཞི། the four lim of definite analysis of the Mahāyāna path of preparation 4. ཆོན་སྒྲུབ་པའི་རྟེན་རང་བཞིན་གནས་རིགས། the naturally abiding Budd nature that is the basis for achieving Mahāyāna path 5. ཐེག་ཆེ སྒྲུབ་པའི་དམིགས་པ། the objects of Mahāyāna paths 6. ཐེག་ཆེན་སྒྲུབ་ ཆེད་དུ་བྱ་བ། objectives of the Mahāyāna paths 7. གོ་ཆའི་སྒྲུབ achievement through armour-like practices 8. འཇུག་སྒྲུ achievement through engagement in the Bodhisattva practic 9. ཚོགས་སྒྲུབ། achievement through the collection of merit a wisdom 10. ངེས་འབྱུང་སྒྲུབ་པ། the definitely arising achievement

རྣམ་འགྱུར་ཉེར་གསུམ།

The twenty-three principles. According to the Sāṁkh school of Hindu philosophy one is born in cyclic existen because of being ignorant of these principles. 1. སྤྱི་གཙོ་བོ། fundamental principle 2. ང་རྒྱལ། I-pride 3-13. དབང་པོ་བཅུ་གཅིག eleven faculties (see bdang-po bcu-gcig) 14-18. དེ་ཙམ་ལྔ།

five mere phenomena (see de-tsam lnga) 19-23. འབྱུང་བ་ལྔ། the five elements (see 'byung-ba lnga).

རྣམ་གྲངས་པའི་ཀུན་བཏགས།

Nominally imputed phenomena. One of the two imputed phenomena (see kun-brtags gnyis), the generic image (see don-spyi) of thoughts and the clear appearances of non-existent phenomena.

རྣམ་གྲངས་པའི་དོན་དམ།

Paryāya paramārtha/ The nominal ultimate. There are two: 1. ཡུལ་གྱི་རྣམ་གྲངས་པའི་དོན་དམ། the nominal ultimate object, e.g. conglomerate matter of a vase 2. ཡུལ་ཅན་གྱི་རྣམ་གྲངས་པའི་དོན་དམ། the nominal ultimate object perceiver, e.g. the inferential understanding of emptiness.

རྣམ་གྲངས་མ་ཡིན་པའི་དོན་དམ།

The actual ultimate. There are two: 1. ཡུལ་གྱི་རྣམ་གྲངས་མ་ཡིན་པའི་དོན་དམ། the actual ultimate object, e.g. the emptiness of true existence of a vase 2. ཡུལ་ཅན་གྱི་རྣམ་གྲངས་མ་ཡིན་པའི་དོན་དམ། the actual ultimate object perceiver, e.g. the concentration of an Ārya who comprehends that emptiness.

རྣམ་གྲོལ་ལམ།

Vimuktimārga/ Path of thorough liberation. A path of single-pointed concentration in which the practitioner gains a cessation through abandoning the particular object of elimination.

རྣམ་རྟོག

Saṁkalpa/ vikalpa. A. Conceptual cognition; imagination B. Suspicion; superstition. C. Idea; thought.

རྣམ་རྟོག་བཞི།

The four conceptualizations; the four thoughts. A. གཟུང་རྟོག་གཉིས། the two conceptions of grasping at objects. 1. ཉོན་མོངས་གཟུང་རྟོག grasping at deluded phenomena 2. རྣམ་བྱང་གཟུང་རྟོག grasping at purified phenomena B. འཛིན་རྟོག་གཉིས། The two conceptions of grasping at the subject. 1. རྫས་འཛིན་རྟོག་པ། grasping at substantial phenomena 2. བཏགས་འཛིན་རྟོག་པ། grasping at imputed phenomena.

རྣམ་ཐར་སྒོ་གསུམ།

The three doors of emancipation; the three types of concentrations for liberation. 1. རྣམ་པར་ཐར་པའི་སྒོ་སྟོང་པ་ཉིད། śūnyatā vimokṣamukha/ emancipation through emptiness 2. མཚན་མ་མེད་པ། animitta vimokṣamukha/ emancipation through signlessness 3. སྨོན་པ་མེད་པ། praṇihita vimokṣamukha/ emancipation through wishlessness.

རྣམ་ཐར་བརྒྱད།

The eight emancipations. A. གཟུགས་ཀྱི་རྣམ་པར་ཐར་པ་གསུམ། The three emancipations within the form realm: 1. གཟུགས་ཅན་གཟུགས་ལ་བལྟ་བའི་རྣམ་ཐར། emancipation of one with body looking at a form 2. གཟུགས་མེད་གཟུགས་ལ་བལྟ་བའི་རྣམ་ཐར། emancipation of one without form body looking at a form 3. སྡུག་པའི་རྣམ་ཐར། emancipation through beautiful form B. གཟུགས་མེད་ཀྱི་རྣམ་པར་ཐར་པ་ལྔ། The five emancipations within the formless realm: 1. ནམ་མཁའ་མཐའ་ཡས་ཀྱི་རྣམ་ཐར། emancipation of infinite space 2. རྣམ་ཤེས་མཐའ་ཡས་ཀྱི་རྣམ་ཐར། emancipation of infinite consciousness 3. ཅི་ཡང་མེད་ཀྱི་རྣམ་ཐར། emancipation of nothingness 4. སྲིད་རྩེའི་རྣམ་ཐར། emancipation of the peak of existence 5. འགོག་པའི་རྣམ་ཐར། emancipation of cessation.

རྣམ་སྣང་གི་དམ་ཚིག་དྲུག

The six pledges concerning Vairocana. 1-3. ཚུལ་ཁྲིམས་རྣམ་གསུམ་ཉམས་སུ་ལེན་པ། practice of the three types of morality (see tshul-khrims rnam-gsum) 4-6. དཀོན་མཆོག་གསུམ་ལ་སྐྱབས་སུ་འགྲོ་བ། taking refuge in the Three Jewels.

རྣམ་སྣང་ཆོས་བདུན།

The seven-fold posture of Buddha Vairocana; the seven physical disciplines to be maintained during a formal meditation in Buddhist practice. 1. ཀང་པ་སྐྱིལ་ཀྲུང་། sitting cross-legged 2. ལག་པ་མཉམ་བཞག hand in the gesture of equipoise—the right hand lying palm upward on the upturned left hand 3. སྒལ་ཚིག་དྲང་པོ་བསྲང་བ། a straight back 4. མགྲིན་པ་ཅུང་ཟད་གུག་པ། neck bent slightly forward 5. དཔུང་པ་གཤོལ་ལྟར་བརྐྱངས་པ། མིག་སྣ་རྩེར་ཕབ་པ། shoulders straight like a yoke 6. མིག་སྣ་རྩེར་ཕབ་པ། eyes looking at the tip of the nose 7. ལྕེ་རྩེ་ཡ་ཀན་ལ་སྦྱར་བ། tongue touching the upper palate.

རྣམ་པ་ཐམས་ཅད་ཡོངས་སུ་དག་པ་བཞི།

The four absolute purities. 1. ཡུལ་དག་པ། purity of object 2. ཡུལ་ཅན་དག་པ། purity of object perceiver 3. རྟོག་པ་དག་པ། purity of thought 4. ཤེས་པ་དག་པ། purity of mind.

རྣམ་པར་རྒྱུ་བ།

The thoroughly moving energy-wind; the intensely moving wind. The energy-wind for cognitive faculties of hearing; one of the five secondary wind energies (see yan-lag-gi rlung lnga).

རྣམ་པར་དག་པའི་རྒྱུ་ལྔ།

Pañca viśuddha hetavaḥ/ The five causes of purity. 1. ལམ་དངོས་ཡོངས་སུ་དག་པ། total purity of the path 2. ཉེར་བསྡོགས་ཡོངས་སུ་དག་པ། total purity of the preparatory stage 3. རྣམ་པར་རྟོག་པས་མ་སླད་པ། lack of conceptual concoction 4. དྲན་པས་ཡོངས་སུ་ཟིན་པ། total mindfulness 5. མྱ་ངན་ལས་འདས་པར་བསྔོས་པ། dedication towards nirvāṇa.

རྣམ་པར་སྨིན་པ་མ་ཡིན་པའི་སྐད་ཅིག་སྦྱོར་བ།

Avipāka ekakṣaṇika prayoga/ Non-fruitional momentary training. The yogic practice of a Bodhisattva which is the wisdom directly opposing the obstructions to omniscience an which in actualizing the non-contaminated, non-maturin dharma, also actualizes the other concordant dharmas, all i the space of one instant (i.e. the 1/60th of a finger snap).

རྣམ་པར་སྨིན་པའི་སྐད་ཅིག་སྦྱོར་བ།

Vipāka ekakṣaṇika prayoga/ Fruitional momentary training The yogic practice of a Bodhisattva, which is the wisdon directly opposing the obstructions to omniscience, and which in actualizing the non-contaminated, maturing dharma, als actualizes the other concordant dharmas, all in the space o one instant (i.e. the 1/60th of a finger snap).

རྣམ་པར་རིག་བྱེད་ཀྱི་གཟུགས།

Vijñaptirūpa/ Revelatory form. The physical or verba expressions of a person's attitude or feeling.

རྣམ་པར་རིག་བྱེད་མ་ཡིན་པའི་གཟུགས།

Avijñaptirūpa/ Non-revelatory form. For instance, the vow possessed by a Bhikṣu while in deep sleep. There are fiv types: 1. འདུས་པ་ལས་བྱུང་བ། those arising from an aggregation c potential substance 2. མངོན་པར་སྐབས་ཡོད་པ། those appearing onl to a mental consciousness 3. ཡང་དག་པར་བླངས་པ་ལས་བྱུང་བ། thos arising from taking precepts 4. ཀུན་བརྟགས་པ། those arising fror imputation 5. དབང་འབྱོར་བ། those arising from powers.

རྣམ་དཔྱོད་རྣམ་པ་བདུན།

The seven-fold analysis of the emptiness of a chariot. T analyse whether: 1. གཅིག་གམ། the chariot is one with its parts 2 ཐ་དད། the chariot is different from its parts 3. ལྡན་པའམ། th chariot possesses its parts 4. རྟེན་དང་། the chariot is the par dependent upon the chariot 5. བརྟེན་པ། the chariot is that whic depends upon its parts 6. ཚོགས་པའམ། the chariot is a me collection of its parts 7. དབྱིབས། the chariot is merely its shape

རྣམ་བྱང་གི་དབང་པོ་བརྒྱད།

Aṣṭa vaivadānikendriyāṇi/ The eight purified mental faculties; the eight pure powers: 1. དད་པའི་དབང་པོ། śraddhendriya/ the faculty of faith 2. བརྩོན་འགྲུས་ཀྱི་དབང་པོ། viryendriya/ the faculty of virtuous efforts 3. དྲན་པའི་དབང་པོ། smṛtīndriya/ the faculty of mindfulness 4. ཏིང་ངེ་འཛིན་གྱི་དབང་པོ། samādhīndriya/ the faculty of concentration 5. ཤེས་རབ་ཀྱི་དབང་པོ། prajñendriya/ the faculty of wisdom 6. མི་ཤེས་པ་ཀུན་ཤེས་པའི་དབང་པོ། anajñātam ājñāsyām indriya/ the faculty of knowing all that is unknown 7. ཀུན་ཤེས་པའི་དབང་པོ། ajñendriya/ the faculty of knowing all 8. ཀུན་ཤེས་པ་དང་ལྡན་པའི་དབང་པོ། ajñātendriya/ the faculty of that which has the knowledge of knowing all.

རྣམ་བྱང་ཕྱོགས་ཀྱི་འགྲེལ་ཀྲང་ང་ལྔ།

The fifty-five topics of purified phenomena; the fifty-five classes of virtuous phenomena. 1-6. སྤྱོད་པའི་ལམ་ཕར་ཕྱིན་དྲུག the six perfections (see pha-rol-tu phyin-pa drug) as paths of practice 7-24. ལྟ་བའི་ལམ་སྟོང་ཉིད་བཅོ་བརྒྱད། the eighteen emptinesses (see stong-pa nyid bco-brgyad) 25-31. རྣལ་འབྱོར་གྱི་ལམ་བྱང་ཕྱོགས་སོ་བདུན། the thirty-seven limbs of enlightenment (see byang-phyogs so-bdun) 32. ཞི་གནས་ཀྱི་ལམ་འཕགས་པའི་བདེན་པ་བཞི། the four noble truths (see 'phags-pa'i bden-pa bzhi) as paths of mental quiescence meditation 33. བསམ་གཏན་བཞི། the four meditative concentrations (see bsam-gtan bzhi) 34. ཚད་མེད་བཞི། the four immeasurables (see tshad-med bzhi) 35. གཟུགས་མེད་སྙོམས་འཇུག་བཞི། the four absorptions of the formless realm (see gzugs-med snyoms-'jug bzhi) 36. རྣམ་ཐར་བརྒྱད། the eight emancipations (see rnam-thar brgyad) 37. མཐར་གྱིས་གནས་པའི་སྙོམས་པར་འཇུག་པ་དགུ the nine absorptions in series (see mthar-gyis gnas-pa'i snyoms-'jug dgu) 38. ལྷག་མཐོང་གི་ལམ་རྣམ་ཐར་སྒོ་གསུམ། the three concentrations of the three doors of emancipation (see rnam-thar sgo-gsum) as paths of penetrative insight meditation 39. ཡོན་དན་ཁྱད་པར་ཅན་གྱི་ལམ་མངོན་ཤེས་ལྔ། the five clairvoyances (see mngon-par shes-pa lnga) as paths for higher qualities 40. ཏིང་ངེ་འཛིན་བཞི། the four concentrations (see ting-nge 'dzin bzhi) 41. གཟུངས་ཀྱི་སྒོ་བཞི། the four doors of retention (see gzungs-kyi sgo bzhi) 42. འབྲས་བུའི་ལམ་སྟོབས་བཅུ། the ten powers (see de-bzhin gshegs-pa'i stobs-bcu) as the resultant paths 43. མི་འཇིགས་པ་བཞི། the four fearlessnesses (see mi-'jigs-pa bzhi) 44. སོ་སོར་ཡང་དག་པ་རིག་པ་བཞི། the four perfect specific understandings (see so-sor yang-dag rig-pa bzhi) 45. བྱམས་པ་ཆེན་པོ། great love 46. སྙིང་རྗེ་ཆེན་པོ། great compassion 47. ཆོས་མ་འདྲེས་པ་བཅོ་བརྒྱད། the eighteen unshared qualities of a Buddha (see ma-'dres-pa bco-brgyad) 48-52. གང་ཟག་ལྔ། the five aspirants to the above (see gang-zag-lnga) 53-55. མཐར་ཐུག་གི་འབྲས་བུ་གསུམ། the three ultimate fruits (see mkhyen-gsum) the basis, path and omniscient wisdom.

རྣམ་བྱང་བཞི།

The four types of purified phenomena. 1. རང་བཞིན་གྱི་རྣམ་བྱང་། the natural purified phenomena 2. དམིགས་པའི་རྣམ་བྱང་། purified phenomena of the object of meditation 3. རྣམ་དག་གི་ལམ་སྒྲུབ་པའི་རྣམ་བྱང་། purified practice 4. ཐོབ་པའི་རྣམ་བྱང་། purified attainment.

རྣམ་སྨིན་གྱི་རྒྱུ།

Vipāka hetu/ The ripening cause; maturing cause. All contaminated virtuous and non-virtuous karma.

རྣམ་སྨིན་གྱི་འབྲས་བུ།

Vipāka phala/ The ripening results; the maturing fruits. One of the five types of results (see 'bras-bu-lnga); results of the contaminated virtues and non-virtues.

རྣམ་སྨིན་གྱི་ཡོན་དན་བརྒྱད།

The eight qualities of fully ripened karma. 1. ཚེ་རིང་བ། long life 2. ཁ་དོག་ཕུན་སིམ་ཚོགས་པ། excellent features 3. རིགས་ཕུན་སུམ་ཚོགས་པ། excellent family lineage 4. དབང་ཕྱུག་ཕུན་སུམ་ཚོགས་པ། excellent wealth and power 5. ཚིག་བཙན་པ། respected speech 6. དབང་ཆེ་བར་

གྲགས་པ། renowned authority 7. སྐྱེས་པ་ཡིན་པ། being a male 8. སྤོབས་དང་ལྡན་པ། strong will-power.

རྣམ་རྫོགས་སྦྱོར་བ།

The training of the complete aspects. A Bodhisattva path or wisdom which meditates in a condensed way upon the hundred and seventy-three aspects of the three wisdoms of the basis, paths and omniscient mind. This wisdom exists from the Mahāyāna path of accumulation to the last instant of the path of meditation.

རྣམ་རྫོགས་སྦྱོར་བ་མཚོན་བྱེད་ཀྱི་ཆོས་བཅུ་གཅིག

The eleven topics that characterize the training of the complete aspects. 1. རྣམ་པ། aspects 2. སྦྱོར་བ། training 3. སྦྱོར་བའི་ཡོན་ཏན། qualities of trainings 4. སྦྱོར་བའི་སྐྱོན། faults of trainings 5. སྦྱོར་བའི་མཚན་ཉིད། characteristics of trainings 6. ཐར་པ་ཆ་མཐུན། aids to liberation 7. ངེས་འབྱེད་ཆ་མཐུན། aids to definite discrimination 8. སློབ་པ་ཕྱིར་མི་ལྡོག་པའི་ཚོགས། the irreversible trainees 9. སྲིད་ཞི་མཉམ་ཉིད་ཀྱི་སྦྱོར་བ། training in the sameness of existence and peace 10. ཞིང་དག་སྦྱོར་བ། training of the pure field 11. ཐབས་མཁས་སྦྱོར་བ། training in skillful means.

རྣམ་གཡེང་གི་རྟོག་པ་བཅུ།

The ten conceptual distractions; the ten mental wanderings: 1. དངོས་པོ་མེད་པར་རྟོག་པ། conception of the lack of things 2. དངོས་པོ་ཡོད་པར་རྟོག་པ། conception of the existence of things 3. སྒྲོ་འདོགས་པའི་རྟོག་པ། conception of exaggeration 4. སྐུར་འདེབས་ཀྱི་རྟོག་པ། conception of underestimation 5. གཅིག་ཏུ་རྟོག་པ། conception of being one 6. ཐ་དད་དུ་རྟོག་པ། conception of being different 7. ངོ་བོ་ཉིད་དུ་རྟོག་པ། conception of the identityness 8. ཁྱད་པར་དུ་རྟོག་པ། conception of being the qualities 9. མིང་ཇི་ལྟ་བ་བཞིན་དུ་རྟོག་པ། conception in accord with the name 10. དོན་ཇི་ལྟ་བ་བཞིན་དུ་རྟོག་པ། conception in accord with the meaning.

རྣམ་གཡེང་དྲུག

The six types of distractions; six distractions towards sensual objects. 1. རང་བཞིན་གྱི་རྣམ་གཡེང་ natural distraction 2. ཕྱི་རོལ་དུ་རྣམ་གཡེང་། distraction towards outer objects 3. ནང་གི་རྣམ་གཡེང་། inner distraction 4. མཚན་མའི་གཡེང་བ། distraction towards signs (mtshan-ma) 5. གནས་ངན་ལེན་གྱི་གཡེང་བ། distraction towards non-virtuous causes 6. ཡིད་ལ་བྱེད་པའི་གཡེང་བ། obsessive-mental-distraction.

རྣམ་ཤེས་ཀྱི་ཕུང་པོའི་རིགས་ཀྱི་ཆོས་ལྔ།

The five phenomena on the level of the aggregate of consciousness. 1. ཀུན་རྟོག་བརྒྱད་ཅུ། the eighty indicative thoughts 2. སྣང་བ་དཀར་ལམ་པའི་སེམས། the mind of radiant white appearance 3. མཆེད་པ་དམར་ལམ་པའི་སེམས། the mind of radiant red increase 4. ཉེར་ཐོབ་ནག་ལམ་པའི་སེམས། the mind of radiant black near attainment 5. འཆི་བ་འོད་གསལ་གྱི་སེམས། the mind of the clear light of death.

རྣམ་ཤེས་ཀྱི་ཟས།

Vijñānāhāra/ Mental nourishment; food of consciousness. The energy of consciousnesses that assists the survival of a person's life.

རྣམ་ཤེས་གཉིས།

The two types of consciousness; the two kinds of mind. 1. རྒྱུ་དུས་ཀྱི་རྣམ་ཤེས། hetuḥkāla vijñāna/ causal consciousness 2. འབྲས་དུས་ཀྱི་རྣམ་ཤེས། kāryakāla vijñāna/ resultant consciousness.

རྣམ་ཤེས་འཕོ་བའི་བུ་ག་དགུ

Nava vijñāna saṁkrānti mukhāḥ/ The nine orificies for consciousness transference. 1. ཚངས་བུག brahmarandhra/ crown of the head 2. སྨིན་མཚམས། ūrṇa/ between the eyes 3. མིག caksu/ eyes 4. རྣ་བ། karṇa/ ears 5. སྣ། ghrāṇa/ nose 6. ཁ། mukha/

nouth 7. ལྟེ་བ། nābhi/ navel 9. ཆུ་ལམ། mūtramārga/ urethra 10. ཤང་ལམ། varcomārya/ anus.

རྣམ་ཤེས་ཚོགས་བརྒྱད།

The eight groups of consciousness; the eight consciousnesses. 1. མིག་གི་རྣམ་པར་ཤེས་པ། caksụ vijñānam/ eye consciousness 2. རྣ་བའི་རྣམ་པར་ཤེས་པ། śrotra vijñānam/ ear consciousness 3. སྣའི་རྣམ་པར་ཤེས་པ། ghrāṇa vijñānam/ nose consciousness 4. ལྕེའི་རྣམ་པར་ཤེས་པ། jihvā vijñānam/ tongue consciousness 5. ལུས་ཀྱི་རྣམ་པར་ཤེས་པ། kāya vijñānam/ body consciousness 6. ཡིད་ཀྱི་རྣམ་པར་ཤེས་པ། mano vijñānam/ mental consciousness 7. ཉོན་ཡིད་རྣམ་པར་ཤེས་པ། kleśa vijñānam/ afflictive consciousness 8. ཀུན་གཞི་རྣམ་པར་ཤེས་པ། ālaya vijñānam/ foundational consciousness, the mental basis of all.

རྣམ་གསུམ་དག་པའི་ཤ།

Meat free from the three objections. Any meat or flesh of an animal that one has not seen, heard or even suspected to have been killed for oneself.

རྣལ་འབྱོར་གྱི་ས་ལྔ།

Pañca yogibhūmayaḥ/ The five yogic stages. 1. གཞིའི་ས། the basic stage 2. བསྐྱེད་པའི་ས། the generated stage 3. མེ་ལོང་ལྟ་བུའི་ས། the mirror-like stage 4. སྣང་བའི་ས། the luminous stage 5. གནས་པའི་ས། the stage of abidance.

རྣལ་འབྱོར་རྒྱུད།

Yoga tantra. The third of the four classes of tantras that stresses the importance of internal activities, i.e. meditation rather than external or physical practices.

རྣལ་འབྱོར་རྒྱུད་ཀྱི་དམ་ཚིག་བཅུ་བཞི།

The fourteen commitments related to Yoga tantra. 1-3. མཆོག་གསུམ་ལ་སྐྱབས་སུ་འགྲོ་བ་དེ་བཞིན་གཤེགས་པའི་རིགས་ཀྱི་ས། taking refuge in the Three Jewels, as the three commitments related to the Tathāgata family 4-6. རྡོ་རྗེ་དང་། དྲིལ་བུའི་ཕྱག་རྒྱ་དང་། སློབ་དཔོན་བཟུང་བ་སྟེ་རྡོ་རྗེའི་རིགས་ཀྱི་དམ་ཚིག་གསུམ། commitment of accepting vajra, bell and ācārya, as the three commitments related to the Vajra family 7-10. ཆོས་དང་། ཟང་ཟིང་དང་། མི་འཇིགས་པ་དང་། བྱམས་པའི་སྦྱིན་པ་སྟེ་རིན་ཆེན་རིགས་ཀྱི་དམ་ཚིག་བཞི། practicing the giving of dharma, material possession, protection from fear and love, as the four commitments related to the Ratna family 11-13. ཕྱི་བྱ་སྤྱོད་དང་། ནང་རྣལ་འབྱོར་རྒྱུད་དང་། ཐེག་པ་གསུམ་གྱི་ཆོས་འཛིན་པ་སྟེ་པད་མའི་རིགས་ཀྱི་དམ་ཚིག་གསུམ། accepting the outer action tantra, inner yoga tantra, and the dharma of the three vehicles, as the three commitments related to the Padma family 14. མཆོད་པའི་ལས་ལ་བརྩོན་པ་ལས་ཀྱི་རིགས་ཀྱི་དམ་ཚིག་གཅིག་སྟེ་སྒྲུབ་ཕྱོགས་ཀྱི་དམ་ཚིག striving in the activities of offering service, as the commitment related to the Karma family.

རྣལ་འབྱོར་རྒྱུད་ཀྱི་དབང་བདུན།

Sapta yoga tantra abhiṣekha/ The seven initiations of Yoga tantra. 1. མེ་ཏོག་ཕྲེང་བའི་དབང་། initiation of the flower garland 2. ཆུ་དབང་། water initiation 3. ཅོད་པཎ་གྱི་དབང་། crown initiation 4. རྡོ་རྗེའི་དབང་། vajra initiation 5. དྲིལ་བུའི་དབང་། bell initiation 6. མིང་གི་དབང་། name initiation 7. རྡོ་རྗེ་སློབ་དཔོན་གྱི་དབང་། vajrācārya initiation.

རྣལ་འབྱོར་རྒྱུད་ཀྱི་རིགས་ལྔ།

The five families of Yoga tantra. 1. སངས་རྒྱས་ཀྱི་རིགས། Buddha family 2. རྡོ་རྗེའི་རིགས། Vajra family 3. རིན་ཆེན་གྱི་རིགས། Jewel family 4. པད་མའི་རིགས། Lotus family 5. ལས་ཀྱི་རིགས། Action family.

རྣལ་འབྱོར་རྒྱུད་ལས་བྱུང་བའི་ཕྱག་རྒྱ་བཞི།

The four seals according to the Yoga tantra system. 1. ཕྱག་ཆེན། mahāmudrā/ the great seal 2. དམ་རྒྱ། samayamudrā/ the pledge seal 3. ཆོས་རྒྱ། dharmamudrā/ the dharma seal 4. ལས་རྒྱ། karmamudrā/ the action seal.

རྣལ་འབྱོར་ལྔ།

The five stages of yoga. According to the Anuyoga teaching of the Nyingma tradition there are five stages of yoga within the five paths. 1. ཚོགས་ལམ་འདུན་པ་སེམས་ཀྱི་རྣལ་འབྱོར། the yoga of an aspirational mind of enlightenment on the path of accumulation 2. སྦྱོར་ལམ་རིགས་ཆེན་འབྱེད་པའི་རྣལ་འབྱོར། the yoga of distinguishing great families on the path of preparation 3. མཐོང་ལམ་དབུགས་ཆེན་འབྱིན་པའི་རྣལ་འབྱོར། the yoga of releasing great breadth on the path of seeing 4. བསྒོམ་ལམ་ལུང་ཆེན་ཐོབ་པའི་རྣལ་འབྱོར། the yoga of obtaining great oral transmission on the path of meditation 5. མི་སློབ་ལམ་རྩལ་ཆེན་རྫོགས་པའི་རྣལ་འབྱོར། the yoga of perfecting great skills on the path of no-more learning.

རྣལ་འབྱོར་མངོན་སུམ།

Yogi pratyakṣa/ Yogic bare perception; yogic direct cognition. The non-mistaken, non-conceptual mind of an Ārya which arises in dependence upon its exclusive condition; the union of mental quiscence and penetrative insight.

རྣལ་འབྱོར་བླ་མེད་རྒྱུད།

Anuttarayoga tantra/ The highest yoga tantra. The highest of the four classes of tantra which stresses the supreme importance of inner activity, regardless of the purificatory practices of external activities.

རྣལ་འབྱོར་པ།

Yogi/ A Yogi; an adept. In its loose sense it is applied to any male practitioner, in contrast to a female practitioner who is known as a Yoginī (rnal-'byor-ma).

རྣལ་འབྱོར་བཞི།

The four yogas. The four stages of Mahāmudrā meditation according to the Kagyud tradition. 1. སེམས་ལ་དམིགས་པ་རྩེ་གཅིག་ཏུ་གཏད་པས་རྩེ་གཅིག་གི་རྣལ་འབྱོར། yoga of single-pointed concentration upon one's mind 2. སེམས་སྤྲོས་བྲལ་དུ་རྟོགས་པས་སྤྲོས་བྲལ་གྱི་རྣལ་འབྱོར yoga free of conceptual elaborations lacking an entertainment of thoughts upon one's mind 3. སྣང་སེམས་རོ་གཅིག་ཏུ་རྟོགས་པས་རོ་གཅིག་གི་རྣལ་འབྱོར། yoga of single-taste experiencin the inseparability of appearances and mind 4. མཚན་བཅས་ཀྱིས་སྒོམ་དུ་མེད་པས་སྒོམ་མེད་ཀྱི་རྣལ་འབྱོར། yoga without meditation free c any signs.

རྣལ་འབྱོར་ས་གསུམ།

The three yogic grounds. 1. གང་ཟག་གི་བདག་མེད་རྟོགས་པའི་རྣལ་འབྱོར་གྱི་ས། the yogic ground realizing the selflessness of persons 2 གཟུང་འཛིན་གཉིས་སྟོང་རྟོགས་པའི་རྣལ་འབྱོར་གྱི་ས། the yogic groun realizing the non-duality of subject and object 3. བདེན་སྟོང་རྟོགས་པའི་རྣལ་འབྱོར་གྱི་ས། the yogic ground realizing the lack of tru existence of phenomena.

རྣལ་མའི་རླུང་སེམས།

The subtle wind and mind of reality. The wind energy an mind inherent in the body of a person; the primordial win energy and intuitive awareness.

སྣ་འགའ་སྤྱོད་པའི་དགེ་བསྙེན།

A lay-person observing only some vows. One of the fou nominally ordained lay persons (see dge-bsnyen btags-pa-b bzhi) observing two or three precepts.

སྣ་གཅིག་སྤྱོད་པའི་དགེ་བསྙེན།

A lay-person observing only one vow. One of the fou nominally ordained lay persons (see dge-bsnyen btags-pa-b bzhi) observing only one of the precepts.

སྣ་ཚོགས་རྡོ་རྗེ།

Viśva vajra/ The multiple vajra. A ritual implement (vajra) with three, five or more spokes.

སྣང་སྟོང་དབྱེར་མེད།

The inseparability of appearance and emptiness. The indivisibility of appearing objects as the method and emptiness as the wisdom; thus a unity of the two from the object's side.

སྣང་བ་བདུན།

The seven conceptions (see snang-ba rnam-bdun).

སྣང་བ་བརྡའི་བླ་མ།

The symbolic guru. One's own teacher who is the symbol of reality or total enlightenment.

སྣང་བ་རྣམ་གསུམ།

The three-fold appearances; the three types of visions according to the Path and Fruit teachings of the Sakya tradition (see snang-gsum).

སྣང་བ་རྣམ་བདུན།

The seven deceptive conceptions; the seven appearances. 1. རྨི་ལམ། like a dream 2. སྒྱུ་མ། like an illusion 3. སྨིག་རྒྱུ། like a mirage 4. སྒྲ་བརྙན། like an echo 5. གཟུགས་བརྙན། like a reflection in a mirror 6. དྲི་ཟའི་གྲོང་ཁྱེར། like a city of smell-eaters (bar-do) 7. སྤྲུལ་པ། like a hallucination.

སྣང་བ་བཞི།

The four types of experiences. The experiences attained as a result of practicing rDzogs-chen meditation covering the experiences from the path of a trainee to the path of no-more learning. 1. ཆོས་ཉིད་མངོན་སུམ་གྱི་སྣང་བ། the experience of seeing reality directly 2. ཉམས་སྣང་གོང་འཕེལ་གྱི་སྣང་བ། the experience of advancing in one's spiritual development 3. རིག་པ་ཚད་ཕེབས་ཀྱི་སྣང་བ། the experience of reaching a correct realization of the intuitive awareness (rig-pa) 4. ཆོས་ཟད་བློ་འདས་ཀྱི་སྣང་བ། the experience of the total withdrawal of all phenomena into the sphere of intrinsic awareness (rig-pa) beyond imagination.

སྣང་ལ་མ་ངེས་པ།

Inattentive perception. One of the seven perceptions (see blo-rigs bdun) which an object, though it appears clearly, is not properly discerned, e.g. reception of sound to an ear consciousness while one's eye consciousness is totally absorped in observing a beautiful form.

སྣང་སྲིད་རྣམ་དག

The purity of appearance and existence. The appearance of everything in its pure nature; a yogic way of experiencing phenomena.

སྣང་སྲིད་རང་གྲོལ།

Self-liberation from the world of appearances. One who has gained liberation from this impure world.

སྣང་གསུམ།

The Three visions; the three basic paths. A Preliminary practice of the Path and Fruit teachings of the Sakya tradition. (see snang-gsum). B. Three types of visions: 1. མ་དག་པའི་སྣང་བ། the impure visions 2. རྣལ་འབྱོར་ཉམས་ཀྱི་སྣང་བ། the pure visions of yogic experience 3. དག་པའི་སྣང་བ། the pure vision.

སྣོད་ཀྱི་སྐྱོན་གསུམ།

The three faults of a receptacle; the three faults to be removed while listening to a discourse. 1. རྣ་བ་མི་གཏད་ཁ་སྦུབ་ལྟ་བུའི་སྐྱོན། fault of not paying attention to the teachings like a pot turned upside down 2. ཡིད་ལ་མི་འཛིན་ཞབས་རྡོལ་ལྟ་བུའི་སྐྱོན། fault of not retaining the teachings in one's mind like a pot which is leaking 3. ཉོན་མོངས་དང་འདྲེས་དུག་ཅན་ལྟ་བུའི་སྐྱོན། fault of having a deluded mind like a dirty or poisonous vessel.

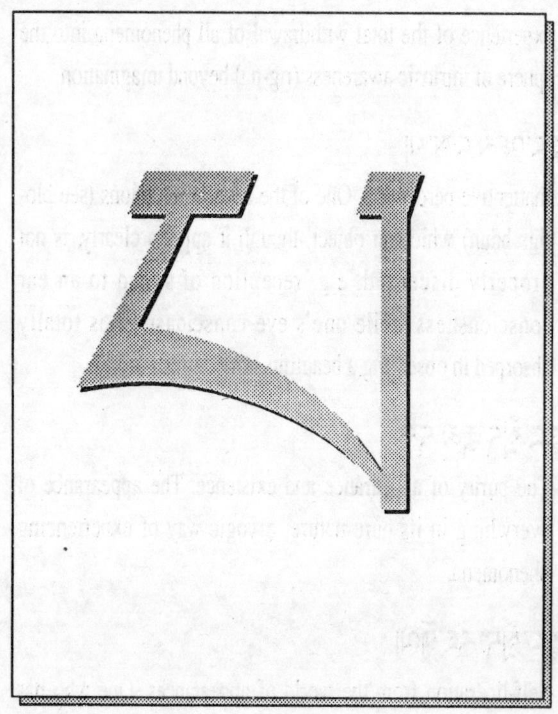

པཱ་ལ་རྣམ་གསུམ།

The three Pāla kings. The three kings of the Pāla dynasty in ancient India—Sadhupāla, Gunapāla and Prajñāpāla; the three principal followers of Indian Ācārya Pandita Dharmapāla, who was invited by Guge King Yeshe Od of the Ngari region of Tibet during the early eleventh century. His three disciples also came with him and worked for the revival of Buddhism in Tibet.

པད་མ།

Padma/ Lotus. It symbolizes the purity of a Bodhisattva's motive, just as a lotus blooms unblemished upon the mire of a swamp, a Bodhisattva remains in cyclic existence without being polluted by its negative aspects. The white lotus in particular symbolizes the pure nature of discriminative wisdom analyzing the nature of reality.

པད་མ་འབྱུང་གནས།

Padmasambhava. The great Indian Ācarya who brought the tantric teachings to Tibet in the eighth century. He founded Samye monastery and propagated the tantric form of Buddhism in Tibet.

པྲ་ཀ་ར་ཎ་སྡེ་བརྒྱད།

The eight treatises of Vasubandhu; the eight Prakaraṇas. 1. མདོ་སྡེ་རྒྱན་གྱི་བཤད་པ། Śūtrālaṁkāra bhāṣya/ Commentary on the Ornament of Discourses 2. དབུས་མཐའ་རྣམ་འབྱེད་ཀྱི་བཤད་པ། Madhyāntavibhaṅgaṭīka/ Commentary on the Distinction Between the Middle Way and the Extreme Way 3. ཆོས་ཉིད་རྣམ་འབྱེད་ཀྱི་བཤད་པ། Dharma dharmatāvibhaṅga vṛtti/ Commentary on the Distinguishing the Phenomena and its Reality 4. སུམ་ཅུ་པའི་ཚིག་ལེའུར་བྱས་པ། Triṁśika kārika/ The Thirty Verses (on Cittamātra) 5. ཉི་ཤུ་པའི་ཚིག་ལེའུར་བྱས་པ། Viṁśika kārikā/ The Twenty Verses 6. ཕུང་པོ་ལྔའི་རབ་བྱེད། Pañca skandhaprakaraṇa/ The Chapter on the Five Aggregates 7. རྣམ་བཤད་རིག་པ། Vyākhyayukti/ The Thorough Exposition 8. ལས་གྲུབ་པའི་རབ་ཏུ་བྱེད་པ། The Chapter on Establishing the Law of Karma.

དཔག་ཚད།

Yojana. A. According to the Abhidharma tradition it is a measurement of length equal to eight krosa (see gyang-grags), equal to 500 armspans. B. According to the Kālacakra measurement, four fingernails long becomes a cubit (see khru), four cubits equals an armspan, two thousand armspans equals one gyang-dak (see rgyang-grags), and four gyang-dak equals one yojana (see dpag-tsad).

དཔལ་ཀུན་ཏུ་བཟང་པོའི་གོ་འཕང་།

The state of glorious Samantabhadra. The state of Buddhahood according to Nyingma tradition, the entity of the three kāyas (see sku-gsum) and five wisdoms (se ye-shes-lnga).

དཔལ་ལྡན་རྡོ་རྗེ་འཛིན་པ།

Śrīmat vājradhāra/ The glorious Vajra master. Vajra master in the secret mantra tradition fulfilling six qualities: 1. འཁོར་བའི་ཆོས་རྒྱབ་ཏུ་དོར་བ། one who has fully renounced saṃsāric concerns 2. འདོད་པ་ཆུང་ཞིང་ཆོག་ཤེས་པ། one who is content with few desires 3. ལག་ལེན་ལ་མཁས་ཤིང་ཉམས་མྱོང་ཡོད་པ། one who is experienced in practice and ritual activities 4. རྒྱུད་ཀྱི་ཚིག་དོན་ལ་མཁས་ཤིང་སྒྲུབ་པ་ལ་མཆོན་པ། one who is knowledgeable of tantric treatises, can explain their literal and implied meaning, and is devoted to practice 5. ལྟ་བའི་དོན་ལ་མཁས་ཤིང་ནུས་པ་རྫོགས་པ། one who is learned in the meaning of the right view and fully accomplished in it 6. སྙིང་རྗེ་ཆེ་ཞིང་གཏོང་བ་ལ་དགའ་བ། one who is highly compassionate and generous.

དཔའ་ཆས་བརྒྱད།

The eight adornments of a Tantric Yogi. 1. སྤྱི་གཙུག་ཏུ་མི་འགྱུར་རྡོ་རྗེ་ཕྱེད་པའི་ཆས། a half vajra on his crown is a sign of the immutability of his goals 2. ཁམས་གསུམ་ཟིལ་གནོན་ལྷང་ལོ་རལ་པའི་ཆས། his matted hair is a sign of outshining the three realms 3. རྫུ་འཕྲུལ་ཤུགས་ལྡན་ཐབས་ཤེས་གཤོག་པའི་ཆས། the wings of method and wisdom are a sign of his miraculous powers 4. ཕ་རོལ་དཔུང་འཇོམས་ཕྱག་མཚན་ཚོགས་ཀྱི་ཆས། the different hand mudrās (gestures) are a sign of overcoming the opponent forces 5. གཞན་གྱིས་མྱ་ཐུབ་བསྲུང་བ་གོ་ཁྲབ་ཆས། his armour protects him against harms caused by others 6. ཉམ་ང་ཀུན་བྲལ་རྟག་མེད་རོ་ལྡན་ཆས། he wears the skins of different beings as a sign of his freedom from all fears 7. འཁོར་འདས་རོ་སྙོམས་ཁྲག་ཞག་རྒྱ་མཚོའི་ཆས། he uses blood and animal fat freely as a sign of his realizations of the sameness of existence and peace 8. ཉོན་མོངས་ཀུན་བསྲེགས་བསྐལ་པའི་མེ་དཔུང་ཆས། he uses fire freely as a sign of his freedom from all delusions.

དཔའ་བོ་དཔའ་མོ།

Heroes and Heroines. The male and female practitioners residing in the celestial heavens; more loosely used for male and female tantric practitioners.

དཔའ་བོའི་གད་མོ་བརྒྱད།

The eight-fold laughs of a Hero. 1. ཧ་ཧ་བཞིགས་པའི་གད་མོ། Ha-Ha the frightening laugh 2. ཧི་ཧི་དགྱེས་པའི་གད་མོ། Hi-Hi the pleasing laugh 3. ཧེ་ཧེ་རྔམ་པའི་གད་མོ། Heh-Heh the majestic laugh 4. ཧོ་ཧོ་ཟིལ་གྱིས་གནོན་པའི་གད་མོ། Ho-Ho the subduing laugh.

དཔུང་ཚོགས་ཡན་ལག་བཞི།

The four kinds of warriors. 1. གླང་པོ་ཆེའི་དམག hasti kāya/ those fighting on elephants 2. རྟའི་དམག aśva kāya/ those fighting on horses 3. ཤིང་རྟའི་དམག ratha kāya/ those fighting on chariots 4. རྐང་ཐང་གི་དམག patti kāya/ those who fight on foot.

དཔེ་དགུ

The nine examples; the nine illustrations to prove the existence of Buddha nature within the mental stream of all sentient beings. 1. པད་མའི་ནང་གི་སངས་རྒྱས། a Buddha in a lotus 2. སྦྲང་རྩིའི་ནང་གི་སྦྲང་མ། bees in the honeycomb 3. སྦུན་གྱི་ནང་གི་སྙིང་པོ། grain in the husk 4. མི་གཙང་ནང་གི་གསེར། gold in a rubbish heap 5. ས་འོག་གི་གཏེར། treasure beneath the earth 6. མྱུ་གུ་ལས་འབྲས་བུ་སྐྱེ་བའི་ནུས་པ། the potential in a seedling to produce fruit 7. གོས་རྙལ་ནང་གི་རྒྱལ་བའི་སྐུ། a statue of Buddha wrapped in dirty rags 8. བུད་མེད་ངན་པའི་ལྟོ་ནང་གི་འཁོར་ལོས་བསྒྱུར་བའི་རྒྱལ་པོའི་སྐུ། a universal king in the womb of an ugly woman 9. ས་འོག་གི་རིན་ཆེན། a precious object buried in the ground.

དཔེ་བྱད་བཟང་པོ་བརྒྱད་ཅུ།

Aśītyanuvyañjanāni/ The eighty minor marks of a Buddha. 1. སེན་མོ་ཟངས་ཀྱི་མདོག his nails are copper-coloured 2. སེན་མོ་མདོག་སྣུམ་ཅན། his nails are moderately shiny 3. སེན་མོ་མཐོ་བ། his nails are raised 4. སོར་མོ་རྣམས་ཟླུམ་པ། his nails are round 5. སོར་མོ་རྣམས་རྒྱས་པ། his nails are broad 6. སོར་མོ་རྣམས་བྱིན་གྱིས་ཕྲ་བ། his nails are tapered 7. རྩ་མི་མངོན་པ། his veins do not protrude 8. རྩ་མདུད་པ་མེད་པ། his veins are free of knots 9. ལོང་བུ་མི་མངོན་པ། his ankles do not protude 10. ཞབས་མི་མཉམ་པ་མེད་པ། his feet are not uneven 11. སེང་གེའི་སྟབས་སུ་གཤེགས་པ། he walks with a lion's gait 12. གླང་པོ་ཆེའི་སྟབས་སུ་གཤེགས་པ། he walks with an elephant's gait 13. ངང་པའི་སྟབས་སུ་གཤེགས་པ། he walks with the gait of a goose 14. ཁྱུ་མཆོག་གི་སྟབས་སུ་གཤེགས་པ། he walks with a bull's gait 15. གཡས་ཕྱོགས་སུ་ལྡོག་ཅིང་གཤེགས་པ། his gait tends to the right 16. མཛེས་པར་གཤེགས་པ། his gait is elegant 17. མི་གཡོ་བར་གཤེགས་པ། his gait is steady 18. སྐུ་འཁྲིལ་བག་ཆགས་པ། his body is well-covered 19. སྐུ་བྱི་དོར་བྱས་པ། his body looks as if it were polished 20. སྐུ་རིམ་པར་འཚམས་པ། his body is well-porportioned 21. སྐུ་གཙང་ཞིང་རྣམ་པར་དག་པ། his body is clean and pure 22. སྐུ་འཇམ་པ། his body is smooth 23. སྐུ་རྣམ་པར་དག་པ། his body is perfect 24. མཚན་རྣམ་པར་རྫོགས་པ། his sex organs are fully developed 25. སྐུ་ཁོ་ལག་ཡངས་ཤིང་བཟང་བ། his physical bearing is excellent and dignified 26. གོམ་པ་སྙོམས་པ། his steps are even 27. སྤྱན་རྣམ་པར་དག་པ། his eyes are perfect 28. སྐུ་གཞོན་ཤ་ཅན། he is youthful 29. སྐུ་ཞུམ་པ་མེད་པ། his body is not sunken 30. སྐུ་རྒྱས་པ། his body is broad 31. སྐུ་ཤིན་ཏུ་གྲིམས་པ། his body is not loose 32. ཡན་ལག་དང་ཉིང་ལག་རྣམ་པར་འབྱེས་པ། his limbs are well-proportioned 33. གཟིགས་པ་རབ་རིབ་མེད་ཅིང་རྣམ་པར་དག་པ། his vision is clear and unblurred 34. སྐུ་ཟླུམ་པ། his belly is round 35. སྐུ་སྐབས་ཕྱིན་པ། his belly is perfectly moderate 36. སྐུ་མ་རྙོངས་པ། his belly is not long 37. སྐུ་ཕྱལ་ཕྱང་ངེ་བ་མ་ཡིན་པ། his belly does not bulge 38. ལྟེ་བ་ཟབ་པ། his navel is deep 39. ལྟེ་བ་གཡས་ཕྱོགས་སུ་འཁྱིལ་བ། his navel winds to the right 40. ཀུན་ནས་མཛེས་པ། he is perfectly handsome 41. ཀུན་ཏུ་སྤྱོད་པ་གཙང་བ། his habits are clean 42. སྐུ་ལ་སྨེ་བ་སྣགས་སྦག་མེད་པ། his body is free of moles and discolouration 43. ཕྱག་ཤིང་བལ་ལྟར་འཇམ་པ། his hands are soft as cotton wool 44. ཕྱག་གི་རི་མོར་མདངས་ཡོད་པ། the lines of his palms are clear 45. ཕྱག་གི་རི་མོ་ཟབ་པ། the lines of his palms are deep 46. ཕྱག་གི་རི་མོ་རིང་བ། the lines of his palms are long 47. ཞལ་ཧ་ཅང་མི་རིང་བ། his face is not too long 48. མཆུ་བིམ་པ་ལྟར་དམར་བ། his lips are red like copper 49. ལྗགས་མཉེན་པ། his tongue is pliant 50. ལྗགས་སྲབ་པ། his tongue is thin 51. ལྗགས་དམར་བ། his tongue is red 52. གསུང་འབྲུག་གི་སྒྲ་དང་ལྡན་པ། his voice is like thunder 53. གསུང་སྙན་ཅིང་འཇམ་པ། his voice is sweet and gentle 54. མཆེ་བ་ཟླུམ་པ། his teeth are round 55. མཆེ་བ་རྣོ་བ། his teeth are sharp 56. མཆེ་བ་དཀར་བ། his teeth are white 57. མཆེ་བ་མཉམ་པ། his teeth are even 58. མཆེ་བ་བྱིན་གྱིས་ཕྲ་བ། his teeth are tapered 59. ཤངས་མཐོ་བ། his nose is prominent 60. ཤངས་གཙང་བ། his nose is clean 61. སྤྱན་ཡངས་པ། his eyes are clear and wide 62. རྫི་མ་སྟུག་པ། his eyelashes are thick 63. སྤྱན་དཀར་ནག་འབྱེད་ཅིང་པད་མའི་འདབ་མ་ལྟར་རངས་པ། the black and white parts of his eyes are well-defined and are like lotus petals 64. སྨིན་ཚུགས་རིང་བ། his eyebrows are long 65. སྨིན་མ་འཇམ་པ། his eyebrows are smooth 66. སྨིན་མ་སྣུམ་པ། his eyebrows are soft 67. སྨིན་མའི་སྤུ་མཉམ་པ། his eyebrows are evenly haired 68. ཕྱག་རིང་ཞིང་རྒྱས་པ། his hands are long and extended 69. སྙན་མཉམ་པ། his ears are of equal size 70. སྙན་གྱི་དབང་པོ་མ་ཉམས་པ། his ear sense power is perfect 71. དཔྲལ་བ་ལེགས་པར་འབྱེས་པ། his forehead is well-formed and well-defined 72. དཔྲལ་བ་འབྱེས་ཆེ་བ། his forehead is broad 73. དབུ་ཤིན་ཏུ་རྒྱས་པ། his head is very large 74. དབུ་སྐྲ་བུང་བ་ལྟར་གནག་པ། his hair is as black as a bumble bee 75. དབུ་སྐྲ་སྟུག་པ། his hair is thick 76. དབུ་སྐྲ་འཇམ་པ། his hair is soft 77. དབུ་སྐྲ་མ་འཛིངས་པ། his hair is untangled 78. དབུ་སྐྲ་མི་གཤོར་བ། his hair is not unruly 79. དབུ་སྐྲ་དྲི་ཞིམ་པ། his hair is fragrant 80. ཕྱག་ཞབས་དཔལ་བེའུ་དང་བཀྲིས་དང་གཡུང་དྲུང་འཁྱིལ་བ། his hands and feet are marked with auspicious emblems such as the Śrīvasta a.. Svastika.

དཔེའི་སྒྱུ་མ།

Upamā māyā/ The exemplary illusion. The magical creation of the conjurers such as elephants and others.

དཔེའི་འོད་གསལ།

Upamā prabhāsvara/ The examplary clear light mind. A

completion stage practice of tantra in which the energy-wind is integrated into the central energy channel at the heart-centre and the subtle mind is brought to a manifest level for the elimination of delusions.

དཔྱད་སྒོམ།

Vicāra bhāvanā/ Analytical meditation. Meditation of checking or reviewing the topic through applying analysis.

དཔྱད་པ་གསུམ།

The three-fold analysis; the three criteria for validating a phenomenon. 1. མངོན་པ་མངོན་འགྱུར་ལ་མངོན་སུམ་ཚད་མས་གནོད་པ་མེད་པ། obvious things are not contradicted by valid bare perception 2. ཅུང་ཟད་ལྐོག་གྱུར་ལ་རྗེས་དཔག་ཚད་མས་གནོད་པ་མེད་པ། slightly obscure things are not contradicted by valid inference based on the force of evidence 3. ཤིན་ཏུ་ལྐོག་གྱུར་ལ་ལུང་ཚད་མས་གནོད་པ་མེད་པ། extremely obscure things are not contradicted by valid inference based on scriptural authority.

དཔྱད་གསུམ་དག་པའི་ལུང་།

A citation pure of the three-fold analysis. A citation in Buddhist teachings and practice qualified by the three-fold analysis (see dpad-pa gsum, above).

དཔྱོད་པ་པ།

Mīmāṁsaka school of thought. A Hindu school of philosophy, which considers Vedāntic teachings as self-originated and ultimate, and asserts that the self is permanent, partless and a substantially existent consciousness. They deny the existence of the omniscient mind and true speech, and also assert that there is no liberation which is the cessation of defilement, since the defilements are an intrinsic part of the mind. However, they assert that a person can attain Brahmahood through the practice of sacrifice.

སྤང་ལྟུང་།

Pāyantika/ Abandoning downfalls. A class of monk's transgression of vows that can be confessed in the presence of the Sangha community through abandoning the causal object of the downfall.

སྤང་པ་ཟུང་འཇུག

The unity of abandonment; the union of the pure illusory body and the abandonment of deluded obscurations to liberation; the state of unity of a trainee.

སྤང་བྱ་ཅིག་ཅར་བ།

He who abandons the obstacles simultaneously.

སྤང་བྱ་ཡན་ལག་བཅུ།

The ten limbs of abandonment; the ten abandonments (see dge-tshul-gyi spang-bya yan-lag bcu).

སྤང་བྱ་རིམ་གྱིས་པ།

He who abandons the obstacles serially.

སྤངས་པ་ཁྱད་པར་གསུམ་ལྡན།

The three exalted abandonments; the three qualities of abandonment exclusive to Buddhas. 1. ལེགས་པར་སྤངས་པ། excellent abandonment 2. སླར་མི་ལྡོག་པའི་ཚུལ་གྱིས་སྤངས་པ། irreversible abandonment 3. མ་ལུས་པར་སྤངས་པ། complete abandonment.

སྤོ་མགུ་དབྱུང་གསུམ།

Demotion, pleasing and expulsion. The monastic rules for confessing a transgression of the 'remainder' category of vows by accepting the demotion of ranks, by offering services to the monk community which pleases them, or by accepting expulsion from the community.

སྤོང་བདུན་འཁོར་བཅས་ཀྱི་ཚུལ་ཁྲིམས།

The moral discipline of seven-fold abandonments and their auxiliaries. A moral discipline primarily requiring the abandonment of the three non-virtues of body (see mi-dge-ba bcu, 1-3), and the four non-virtues of speech (see mi-gde-ba bcu, 4-7) and other minor misdeeds such as abandoning taking intoxicants.

སྤོབས་པ་སོ་སོར་ཡང་དག་རིག་པ།

Pratibhāna pratisaṁvit/ Specific understanding of confidence. A skillful way of a Bodhisattva's training of redressing their doubts through listening to dharma discourses and passing the transmission to others with tireless effort.

སྤྱད་པ་རྣམ་སྦྱོང་གི་དམིགས་པ།

Object for overcoming obsession. One of the four objects of calm abiding meditation (see zhi-gnas-kyi dmigs-pa bzhi), e.g. one who is obsessed with lust must take ugliness as its object of antidote for developing calm abiding meditation.

སྤྱན་ལྔ།

Pañca cakṣu/ The five eyes; the five eyes possessed by Buddhas. 1. ལྷའི་སྤྱན། divya cakṣu/ divine eye 2. ཤའི་སྤྱན། carma cakṣu/ fleshy eye 3. ཤེས་རབ་ཀྱི་སྤྱན། prajñā cakṣu/ wisdom eye 4. ཆོས་ཀྱི་སྤྱན། dharma cakṣu/ dharma eye 5. ཡེ་ཤེས་ཀྱི་སྤྱན། jñāna cakṣu/ primordial wisdom eye.

སྤྱི་མཐུན་གྱི་ལས།

Collective karma; common karma, e.g. karma of a society or locality.

སྤྱི་གཙོ་བོ།

Prakṛti/ The Fundamental Nature; the Universal Principle. The fundamental principle as asserted by the Saṁkhyā school of Hindu philosophy, which is permanent, pervasive over all animate and inanimate objects, is the creator of all activities and is an undifferentiable unit.

སྤྱི་མཚན།

Sāmānya lakṣaṇa/ Generally characterized phenomena. Phenomena that are ultimately unable to perform a function, e.g. space.

སྤྱི་བཞི།

The four types of generality. 1. ཚོགས་སྤྱི། saṁgraha sāmānya/ collective generality 2. རིགས་སྤྱི། gotra sāmānya/ categorical generality 3. དོན་སྤྱི། artha sāmānya/ meaning generality 4. སྒྲ་སྤྱི། śabda sāmānya/ sound generality.

སྤྱོད་རྒྱུད།

Cārya Tantra; Performance Tantra. The second of the four classes of tantras, stressing the importance of a balanced approach in both the external rites and internal mental activity.

སྤྱོད་རྒྱུད་ཀྱི་དམ་ཚིག་བཅུ་བཞི།

The fourteen commitments related to performance tantra. 1-10. མི་དགེ་བ་བཅུ་སྤོང་བ། The abandonment of the ten non-virtues (see mi-ba bcu), 11. དམ་པའི་ཆོས་མི་གཏོང་བ། not to abandon the sublime Dharma 12. བྱང་ཆུབ་ཀྱི་སེམས་མི་གཏོང་བ། not giving up the mind of enlightenment 13. སེར་སྣས་མི་གཏོང་བ། not abandoning practicing giving due to miserliness 14. སེམས་ཅན་ལ་གནོད་མི་བྱེད་པ། not harming other sentient beings.

སྤྱོད་རྒྱུད་ཀྱི་དབང་དྲུག

Ṣaḍ cārya tantra abhiṣekhāḥ/ The six initiations of performance tantra. 1. མེ་ཏོག་ཕྲེང་དབང་། initiation of flower garland 2. ཆུའི་དབང་། water initiation 3. ཅོད་པཎ་གྱི་དབང་། crown initiation 4. རྡོ་རྗེའི་དབང་། vajra initiation 5. དྲིལ་བུའི་དབང་། bell initiation 6. མིང་གི་དབང་། name initiation.

སྤྱོད་རྒྱུད་རིགས་གསུམ།

Tri cārya tantra gotrāḥ/ The three families of performance tantra. A. 1. དེ་བཞིན་གཤེགས་པའི་རིགས། the Tathāgata family 2. པད་མའི་རིགས། the lotus family 3. རྡོ་རྗེའི་རིགས། the vajra family. B. That of སྐུ་གསུང་ཐུགས་ཀྱི་རིགས། Buddha's body, speech and mind.

སྤྱོད་འཇུག

A Guide to the Bodhisattva's Way of Life (bodhisattvacāryāvatāra). A fundamental text of Mahāyāna composed by Ācārya Śāntideva during the eighth century, in which a Bodhisattva's conduct is explained.

སྤྱོད་པ་རྣམ་བཞི།

The four activities. A. 1. འགྲོ་བ། going 2. འཆག་པ། walking 3. ཉལ་བ། sleeping 4. འདུག་པ། waking. B. 1. ཀུན་བཟང་སྤྱོད་པ། all-good behaviour 2. གསང་བའི་སྤྱོད་པ། secret behaviour 3. འདུ་འཛིའི་སྤྱོད་པ། behaviour in a crowd 4. ཕྱག་ཆེན་གྱི་སྤྱོད་པ། the mahāmudrā behaviour.

སྤྱོད་པའི་སྒོ་བཞི།

The doors of activity in performance tantra. 1. འཇུག་པའི་སྤྱོད་པ། activity of entering into practice 2. སྦྱོར་བའི་སྤྱོད་པ། activity of application 3. སྒྲུབ་པའི་སྤྱོད་པ། activity of the actual stage of practice 4. གྲུབ་པའི་སྤྱོད་པ། activity of accomplishment.

སྤྲིན་ལྟ་བུའི་སེམས་བསྐྱེད།

Meghopamacittotpāda/ Cloud-like Bodhicitta. The mind of enlightenment associated with skillful means within the continuum of a Nirmāṇakāya Buddha.

སྤྲུལ་སྐུ་གསུམ།

The three emanation bodies of a Buddha. 1. བཟོ་བོ་སྤྲུལ་སྐུ། śilpa nirmāṇakāya/ artisan emanation 2. སྐྱེ་བ་སྤྲུལ་སྐུ། janma nirmāṇakāya/ miscellaneous emanation 3. མཆོག་གི་སྤྲུལ་སྐུ། uttama nirmāṇakāya/ supreme emanation.

སྤྲུལ་པའི་འཁོར་ལོ།

Nirmāṇacakra/ The wheel of emanation; the channel-wheel located at the navel.

སྤྲུལ་པའི་མུ་སྟེགས་པ།

A non-Buddhist by emanation. Buddhas and Bodhisattvas who have chosen to emanate as teachers of non-Buddhist philosophy in order to lead those beings not yet ripened to progress on the higher states of realizations.

སྤྲུལ་ལམ་གསུམ།

The three paths of manifestation; the three paths of emanation (see A. of rnam-thar brgyad).

སྤྲོས་པའི་མཐའ་བརྒྱད།

The eight extremes; the eight extreme views. 1. སྐྱེ་མཐའ། production 2. འགག་མཐའ། cessation 3. རྟག་མཐའ། eternalism 4. ཆད་མཐའ། nihilism 5. འགྲོ་མཐའ། going 6. འོང་མཐའ། coming 7. གཅིག་ཡིན་པའི་མཐའ། one 8. ཐ་དད་པའི་མཐའ། different.

སྤྲོས་བྲལ་བརྒྱད།

The lack of eight extremes. The extremes to be abandoned while establishing the view of Prāsangika Mādhyamika. Lack of inherently existent birth and so on (see spros-pa'i mtha'-brgyad, above).

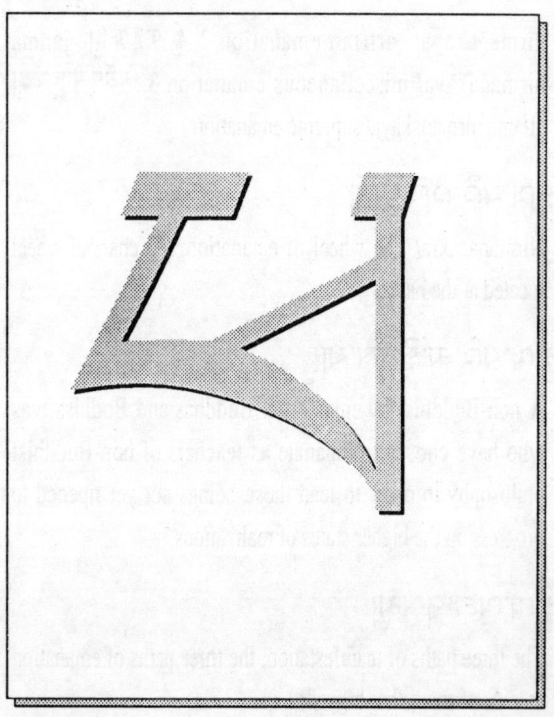

ཕ་རྒྱུད།

Pitṛ tantra/ Father Tantra. The highest class of tantra in which the primary focus is the development of an illusory body, e.g. Guhyasamāja tantra.

ཕ་ཆོས།

The father Dharma; also called the teachings of the father of the Kadam tradition, compiled by the father of the Kadampa tradition, Dromtonpa. This collection of teachings includes his questions to Atiśa and the latter's replies on many essential doctrinal points, and a short biography of Atiśa and the guru lineage of the Kadampa's sixteen drops (thig-le bcu drug) transmission.

ཕ་ཆོས་བུ་ཆོས།

The father and son dharma (see pha-chos, above and bu-chos) of the Kadampa tradition.

ཕ་རོལ་ཏུ་ཕྱིན་པ་བཅུ།

Daśa pāramitā/ The ten perfections. 1-6. The six perfections (see phar-rol-tu phyin-pa drug, below). 7. ཐབས་ཀྱི་ཕ་རོལ་ཏུ་ཕྱིན་པ། upāya pāramitā/ perfection of means 8. སྨོན་ལམ་གྱི་ཕ་རོལ་ཏུ་ཕྱིན་པ། praṇidhāna pāramitā/ perfection of aspirational prayers 9. སྟོབས་ཀྱི་ཕ་རོལ་ཏུ་ཕྱིན་པ། bala pāramitā/ perfection of power 10. ཡེ་ཤེས་ཀྱི་ཕ་རོལ་ཏུ་ཕྱིན་པ། jñāna pāramitā/ perfection of primordial wisdom.

ཕ་རོལ་ཏུ་ཕྱིན་པ་དྲུག

Ṣaḍ pāramitāḥ/ The six perfections. 1. སྦྱིན་པའི་ཕ་རོལ་ཏུ་ཕྱིན་པ། dāna pāramita/ perfection of giving 2. ཚུལ་ཁྲིམས་ཀྱི་ཕ་རོལ་ཏུ་ཕྱིན་པ། śīla pāramitā/ perfection of morality 3. བཟོད་པའི་ཕ་རོལ་ཏུ་ཕྱིན་པ། kṣānti pāramitā/ perfection of patience 4. བརྩོན་འགྲུས་ཀྱི་ཕ་རོལ་ཏུ་ཕྱིན་པ། vīrya pāramitā/ perfection of effort 5. བསམ་གཏན་གྱི་ཕ་རོལ་ཏུ་ཕྱིན་པ། dhyāna pāramitā/ perfection of concentration 6. ཤེས་རབ་ཀྱི་ཕ་རོལ་ཏུ་ཕྱིན་པ། prajñā pāramitā/ perfection of wisdom.

ཕ་རོལ་ཏུ་ཕྱིན་པའི་མི་མཐུན་ཕྱོགས་དྲུག

Ṣaḍ pāramitā pratipakṣāḥ/ The six opponents to the six perfections. 1. སེར་སྣ། matsava/ miserliness 2. ཚུལ་འཆལ། duḥśīla/ corrupt morality 3. ཞེ་སྡང་། krodha/ hatred 4. ལེ་ལོ། alasa/ laziness 5. རྣམ་གཡེང་། vikṣapana/ mental wandering 6. ཤེས་རབ་འཆལ་བ། duḥprajñā/ corrupt wisdom.

ཕ་ལས་ཐོབ་པའི་མཛོད་གསུམ།

The three treasures obtained from the father; the three constituents obtained from father. 1. ཁུ་བ། regenerative fluid 2. རྐང་། marrow 3. རུས་པ། bone.

ཕག་གྲུ་བཀའ་བརྒྱུད།

The Phagdru Kagyud Order. One of the divisions of the Kagyud order of Tibetan Buddhism founded by Phagmo Drupa (1110-1170), the chief disciple of Gampopa. He mastered the art of writing and painting without being taught. His eight disciples founded the eight sub-sects of the Kagyud.

ན་ཚུན་ཐ་དད།

Mutually exclusive things.

ན་ཚུན་སྤང་འགལ།

Mutually exclusive contradictions; mutually exclusive dichotomy, e.g. permanence and impermanence, or hot and cold.

མ་པ་བརྒྱད།

Aṣṭa parājikā dharmāḥ/ The eight moral defeats; the eight root transgressions of a fully ordained nun, Bhikṣunī. 1-4. the four moral defeats (see pham-pa bzhi) of a Bhikṣu 5. སྐྱེས་པ་ལ་ཆགས་སེམས་ཀྱིས་ལུས་འཕྲུད་ཅིང་རེག་པ། touching and embracing a man with lust 6. སྐྱེས་པ་ལ་ཆགས་སེམས་ཀྱིས་ལུས་གན་རྒྱལ་དུ་བཀན་པ། throwing a man down overwhelmed with lust 7. ལྷ་མོར་ཕམ་པ་བྱུང་བ་ཤེས་བཞིན་དུ་འཆབ་པ། knowingly concealing moral defeat of a fellow nun 8. དགེ་སློང་འགའ་ཞིག་དགེ་འདུན་གྱི་གནས་ནས་ཕྱུང་བ་ལ་སླར་ཡང་འགྲོད་པའི་སེམས་ཀྱིས་བཟོད་པར་གསོལ་བ་དེ་ཉིད་ལུས་ངག་གི་སྒོ་ནས་ཟློག་པར་བྱེད་པ། ignoring the forgiveness sought by Bhikṣus through physical and verbal gestures for their expulsion from the monastery.

མ་པ་འཆབ་བཅས།

The concealed moral defeats. Concealment of any of the four root transgressions by an ordained monk.

མ་པ་བཞི།

Catvāri parājikā dharmāḥ/ The four moral defeats; the four root transgressions of a monk, the committing of any would lead to loosing the status of a being a monk. 1. མི་བསད་པ། manuṣyabadha/ killing a human 2. མ་བྱིན་པར་ལེན་པ། adattādāna/ taking what is not given 3. མི་ཚངས་པར་སྤྱོད་པ། abrahmacārya/ indulging in sexual misconduct 4. མི་ཆོས་བླ་མའི་བརྫུན་སྨྲ་བ། uttaramanuṣya dharma pralāpa/ lying about one's attainment of suprahuman dharmas.

ཕར་ཕྱིན་ཐེག་པ།

Pāramitā yāna/ The Perfection Vehicle. The Bodhisattva vehicle as taught in the sūtras known as the causal vehicle (rgyu'i-theg-pa) in contrast to the mantrayāna vehicle known as the resultant vehicle.

ཕར་ཕྱིན་དྲུག་ལ་འཇུག་པའི་འཇུག་སྒྲུབ།

Ṣaḍ pāramitā vṛttiprasthāna pratipatti/ Achievement through engagement in the six perfections; the Bodhisattva paths encompassing the practice of the six perfections.

ཕལ་ཆེན་པའི་སྡེ་པ།

Mahāsaṁgikā school. One of the four principal schools of the Hīnayāna tradition whose direct teacher is Kāśyapa (see dge-'dun phal-po che'i sde-pa lnga).

ཕུགས་ནོར་བཅུ།

The ten innermost jewels of the Kadampa tradition (see bka'-gdams phugs-nor bcu).

ཕུང་པོ་ལྔ་།

Pañca skandhāḥ/ The five aggregates. 1. གཟུགས་ཀྱི་ཕུང་པོ། rūpa skandha/ aggregate of form 2. ཚོར་བའི་ཕུང་པོ། vedanā skandha/ aggregate of feeling 3. འདུ་ཤེས་ཀྱི་ཕུང་པོ། saṁjñā skandha/ aggregate of perception 4. འདུ་བྱེད་ཀྱི་ཕུང་པོ། saṁskāra skandha/ aggregate of compositional factors 5. རྣམ་པར་ཤེས་པའི་ཕུང་པོ། vijñāna skandha/ aggregate of consciousness.

ཕུང་པོ་དྲུག

Ṣaḍ skandhāḥ/ The six aggregates 1-5. The five aggregates (see phung-po lnga, above) 6. ཡེ་ཤེས་ཀྱི་ཕུང་པོ། jñāna skandha/ the aggregate of primordial wisdom.

ཕུང་པོ་གསུམ་པ།

The Three Heaps. A. ཕུང་པོ་གསུམ་པའི་མདོ། ལྟུང་བ་བཤགས། The sūtra of confession: 1. སྡིག་པ་བཤགས་པ། the practice of confessing non-virtues 2. རྗེས་སུ་ཡི་རང་བ། the practice of rejoicing 3. དགེ་བ་བསྔོ་བ། the practice of dedication. B. 1. སྡིག་པ་བཤགས་པ། confessing non-virtues 2. རྗེས་སུ་ཡི་རང་བ། rejoicing at the virtues 3. ཆོས་འཁོར་བསྐོར་བ། turning the wheel of doctrine.

ཕུན་ཚོགས་ལྔ།

The five excellences. A. 1. ཆོས་ཕུན་སུམ་ཚོགས་པ། dharma saṁpanna/ excellent Dharma 2. དུས་ཕུན་སུམ་ཚོགས་པ། kāla saṁpanna/ excellent period 3. སྟོན་པ་ཕུན་སུམ་ཚོགས་པ། śāstra saṁpanna/ excellent teacher 4. གནས་ཕུན་སུམ་ཚོགས་པ། sthāna saṁpanna/ excellent abode 5. འཁོར་ཕུན་སུམ་ཚོགས་པ། pariṣad saṁpanna/ excellent retinue. B. 1. སྐུ་ཕུན་སུམ་ཚོགས་པ། kāya saṁpanna/ perfect body with the major and minor marks 2. སྤངས་རྟོགས་ཕུན་སུམ་ཚོགས་པ། prahāṇa pratīta saṁpanna/ perfect abandonments and accomplishments 3. འཁོར་ཕུན་སུམ་ཚོགས་པ། pariṣada saṁpanna/ perfect retinue 4. ཞིང་ཕུན་སུམ་ཚོགས་པ། kṣetra saṁpanna/ perfect field created from the wisdom of self-awareness 5. སྤྲུལ་པ་ཕུན་སུམ་ཚོགས་པ། nirmāṇa saṁpanna/ perfect emanation of wisdom and body.

ཕུན་ཚོགས་སྡེ་བཞི།

The four excellences. A. འཇིག་རྟེན་པའི་ཕུན་ཚོགས་སྡེ་བཞི། The four worldly excellences: 1. ཆོས། Dharma 2. ནོར། wealth 3. འདོད་པ། wishes 4. ཐར་པ། liberation. B. འཇིག་རྟེན་ལས་འདས་པའི་ཕུན་ཚོགས་སྡེ་བཞི། The four transworldly excellences: 1. སངས་རྒྱས་ཀྱི་ཆོས་དར་བ། flourishing of the Buddha Dharma 2. ནོར་ལོངས་སྤྱོད་དང་ལྡན་པ། possessing riches and wealth 3. འདོད་ཡོན་ལྔ་ལ་སྤྱོད་པ། enjoying the five sensual objects (see 'dod-yon lnga) 4. ཆོས་ལ་བརྟེན་ནས་ཐར་པ་མྱང་འདས་ཀྱི་གོ་འཕང་འཐོབ་པ། attainment of the state of liberation following Dharma practices.

ཕུན་ཚོགས་གསུམ་ལྡན།

The triple excellences; the three primary requirements for a person going to receive monk vows. 1. གང་ལ་སྡོམ་པ་བླང་བའི་ཡུལ་མཁན་སློབ། the presence of an abbot and assistant abbots from whom the vows are to be received 2. གང་གིས་སྡོམ་འབོག་པར་བྱེད་པའི་ཆོ་ག the full-fledged ritual ceremony through which the vows are to be received 3. གང་བསླབ་པར་བྱ་བའི་གནས་ལ་རྩོལ་བཞིན་དུ་བསླབ་པར་འདོད་པའི་བསམ་པ། the perfect motivation to receive the vows.

ཕུན་སུམ་ཚོགས་པ་གསུམ།

A. The three excellences. 1. རྒྱུ་ཕུན་སུམ་ཚོགས་པ། excellent cause 2. འབྲས་བུ་ཕུན་སུམ་ཚོགས་པ། excellent fruit 3. ཕན་འདོགས་པ་ཕུན་སུམ་ཚོགས་པ། excellent benefit B. The three perfect accomplishments. 1. རང་དོན་ཕུན་ཚོགས། accomplishment of one's goals 2. གཞན་དོན་ཕུན་ཚོགས། accomplishment of others' goals 3 དོན་གཉིས་སྒྲུབ་པའི་ཐབས་ཕུན་ཚོགས། accomplishment of the means for achieving both goals.

ཕོ་གཅོད།

The Male Ritual of Cutting-Off. The transmission of the cutting-off ritual (gcod), of severing the ego, directly handed down from Phadampa Sangye to Yarlung Lama Ṣonam and his disciples.

ཕོ་རྩལ་སྣ་དགུ

The nine skills of a man; nine dexterities of manhood. A. ལུས་ངག་ཡིད་གསུམ་གྱི་རྩལ་གསུམ་རེ་སྟེ་དགུ The three each of body speech and mind. B. According to another tradition these are: 1. གཏམ oratorship 2. ཡི་གེ writing 3. རྩིས། calculation 4. མདའ། archery 5. རྡོ། weight lifting 6. མཆོངས། jumping 7. བང་། running 8. རྐྱལ swimming 9. ཤེ། stick-games.

ཕ་ལི་ག།

Śāta/ Evenly shaped. The perfect and refined shape of a thing.

ཕྱ་ལི་པ་མ་ཡིན་པ།

Viśāta/ Unevenly shaped. The imperfect and unrefined shape of a thing.

ཕྱག་རྒྱ།

Mudrā/ A. Hand gestures (mudrā) B. Official or non-official seal.

ཕྱག་རྒྱ་ཆེན་པོ།

Mahāmudrā; the Great Seal. The greal seal of emptiness; an exalted meditation on the nature of mind, particularly associated with the Kagyud order of Tibetan Buddhism.

ཕྱག་རྒྱ་མ།

The consort. Wife of an accomplished Lama.

ཕྱག་རྒྱ་དྲུག

A. The six symbolic ornaments. Costumes associated with tantric deities and yoginīs, made of bones representing the six perfections. 1. ནོར་བུ། jewels 2. ལག་གདུབ། bracelets 3. རྣ་ཆ། ear rings 4. སྐ་རགས belt 5. འཁོར་ལོ། wheel 6. ཐལ་བ། funerary ashes. B. The six sacred articles obtained from heaven during the reign of the Tibetan King, Lha Tho-Tho-Ri Nyan-Tsen. 1. མདོ་སྤང་སྐོང་ཕྱག་རྒྱ། the sūtra *sPang-skong phyag-rgya* 2. མདོ་ཟ་མ་ཏོག the sūtra *Za-ma-tog* 3. གསེར་གྱི་མཆོད་རྟེན། a golden stūpa 4. གཡུའི་མཆོད་རྟེན། a turquoise stūpa 5. མུ་ཏྲའི་ཕྱག་རྒྱ། a mudrā of woven pearl-net 6. ཙིནྟཱམཎིའི་སྣོད་པོར། wish-fulfilling pot.

ཕྱག་རྒྱ་བཞི།

The four seals; the four principles of meditation according to the yoga tantra tradition. 1. ལས་ཀྱི་ཕྱག་རྒྱ། karma mudrā/ seal of activity 2. དམ་ཚིག་ཕྱག་རྒྱ། samaya mudrā/ seal of pledge 3. ཆོས་ཀྱི་ཕྱག་རྒྱ། dharma mudrā/ seal of doctrine 4. སྟོང་པའི་ཕྱག་རྒྱ། śūnyatā mudrā/ seal of emptiness or great seal.

ཕྱག་རྒྱའི་ལྷ།

The Mudrā deity. One of the six kinds of deities within action tantra, involving visualizing implements such as a vajra, wheel etc., at the heart and sealing it with the commitment related to the concerned deity.

ཕྱག་ཆེན་གའུ་མ།

The Amulet Box traditon of Mahāmudrā. The Mahāmudrā transmission of the realization of the clear light mind, through meditation on the inseparability of bliss and emptiness, being likened to the two clasped sides of an amulet box.

ཕྱག་ཆེན་རྣལ་འབྱོར་བཞི།

The four mahāmudrā yogas. 1. རྩེ་གཅིག་མའི་རྣལ་འབྱོར། the yoga of single-pointed concentration on the nature of mind 2. སྤྲོས་བྲལ་གྱི་རྣལ་འབྱོར། the yoga of realizing the mind as being free from conceptual elaboration 3. རོ་གཅིག་གི་རྣལ་འབྱོར། the yoga of realizing the sameness of the appearance and mind 4. སྒོམ་མེད་ཀྱི་རྣལ་འབྱོར། the yoga of no more meditation.

ཕྱག་ཆེན་ལྷན་ཅིག་སྐྱེས་སྦྱོར།

Sahaja mahāmudrā prayoga/ The Mahāmudrā of simultaneous arisal and merging. A Mahāmudrā linage of practice taught by Gampopa for practitioners of the initial level in order that they gradually realize the beginningless, inseparable nature of the mind and finally attain the Truth Body of a Buddha.

ཕྱག་ན་རྡོ་རྗེ།

Vajrapāṇi; the Vajra Holder. A Bodhisattva who embodies the might and power of all the Buddhas.

ཕྱག་མཚན།

Mudrā/ A. Emblems, implements and hand gestures of a deity. B. Signs and marks.

ཕྱི་སྒེག་བཞི།

The four outer offering goddesses inside the maṇḍala. 1. སྒེག་མ། goddess with pleasing gesture 2. ཕྲེང་བ་མ། goddess holding garland 3. གླུ་མ། goddess of song 4. གར་མ། goddess of dance.

ཕྱི་རྒོལ།

The defender; the opponent. The respondent in a debate who defends his or her position.

ཕྱི་རྒྱུད་སྡེ་གསུམ།

The three outer tantras. According to the Nyingma tradition the Kriyā (action) tantra was taught by Buddha Śākyamuni himself and the Upayoga (performance) tantra and Yoga (union) tantra were taught by Buddha Vairocana.

ཕྱི་རྒྱུད།

The entrance from outside; the process of initiation of the disciples entering from outside the curtain of the maṇḍala. This involves having made requests to the master, placing the disciple at the eastern gate of the maṇḍala, bestowal of the common and uncommon vows and enquiring about their Buddha family and aspiration, generating the all-encompassing yogic mind and binding the disciples to the oath of secrecy.

ཕྱི་སྟོང་པ་ཉིད།

Bahirdhā śūnyatā/ The emptiness of external objects. One of the sixteen emptinesses (see stong-pa nyid bcu-drug); the lack of inherent existence of non-sentient phenomena, such as the four external elements, object of perception, etc. .

ཕྱི་དོན།

External phenomena. The assertion that form, i.e. the five objects of sensory consciousness, and the cognizing sensory consciousness are not substantially the same, but exist separately and have a special causal relationship. This is an assertion of the two lower schools of Buddhist tenets, as well as of the Prāsangika Mādhyamika school.

ཕྱི་དོན་བེམ་པོ།

External matter. For instance rocks and earth.

ཕྱི་ནང་སྟོང་པ་ཉིད།

Adhyānta bahirdhā śūnyatā/ The emptiness of external and internal objects. One of the sixteen types of emptinesses (see stong-pa nyid bcu-drug); the lack of inherent existence of objects pervaded by consciousness, such as the six faculties, six consciousnesses and the internal organs.

ཕྱི་ཕན་པའི་དབང་བཅུ།

The ten beneficial outer initiations. The initiations that are the gateway to entering the mahāyoga tantra teachings in the Nyingma tradition. 1. སྙིང་པོ་ལྔའི་དབང་། The initiations of the five essences (see snying-po lnga) 2. དབུ་རྒྱན་གྱི་དབང་། initiation of the head-dress 3. བུམ་པའི་དབང་། vase initiation 4. ཅོད་པན་གྱི་དབང་། crown initiation 5. ཕྲེང་བའི་དབང་། garland initiation 6. གོ་ཆའི་དབང་། armour initiation 7. རྒྱལ་མཚན་གྱི་དབང་། initiation of the victory banner 8. གདུགས་ཀྱི་དབང་། initiation of the umbrella 9. ཕྱག་རྒྱའི་དབང་། initiation of the mudrā 10. བཟའ་བཏུང་གི་དབང་། initiation of food and drinks.

ཕྱི་རོལ་པ།

An outsider; a non-Buddhist. Those who belong to a faith other than Buddhism.

ཕྱིན་ཅི་ལོག་བཞི།

The four misapprehensions; the four wrong thoughts. 1. གཙང་བ་ལ་གཙང་བར་འཛིན་པ། to apprehend what is impure as pure 2. བདག་མེད་པ་ལ་བདག་ཏུ་འཛིན་པ། to apprehend what is selfless a having a self 3. སྡུག་བསྔལ་བ་ལ་བདེ་བར་འཛིན་པ། to apprehend what is miserable as happiness 4. མི་རྟག་པ་ལ་རྟག་པར་འཛིན་པ། to apprehend what is impermanent as permanent.

ཕྱིན་དྲུག་གི་ཁྱད་ཆོས་བཞི།

The four qualities of the six perfections (see pha-rol-tu phyin-pa drug). 1. ཕར་ཕྱིན་རང་རང་གི་མི་མཐུན་པའི་ཕྱོགས་དང་བྲལ་བ། non-association with their respective opponents (see pha-rol-tu phyin-pa'i mi-mthun-phyogs drug) 2. གྲོགས་འཁོར་གསུམ་མི་རྟོག་པའི་ཤེས་རབ་ཀྱིས་ཟིན་པ། conjoined with the wisdom of the purity of the three circles (see 'khor-gsum) as their favourable condition 3. བྱེད་ལས་གཞན་གྱི་འདོད་དོན་རྫོགས་པར་བྱེད་པ། fulfilling others' wishes as their function 4. འབྲས་བུ་བྱང་ཆུབ་གསུམ་སྨིན་པར་བྱེད་པ། ripening of the fruits as their results.

ཕྱིའི་དཀར་པོ་གསུམ།

The three external white substances. 1. འོ་མ། kṣīra/ milk 2. ཞོ། dadhi/ curd 3. མར། ghṛta/ butter.

ཕྱིའི་དཀྱིལ་འཁོར་བཞི།

The four external maṇḍalas. 1. རྡུལ་ཚོན་གྱི་དཀྱིལ་འཁོར། coloured powder maṇḍala 2. རས་བྲིས་དཀྱིལ་འཁོར། maṇḍalas painted on cloth 3. བསམ་གཏན་གྱི་དཀྱིལ་འཁོར། concentration maṇḍala 4. ལུས་དཀྱིལ། body maṇḍala.

ཕྱིའི་སྐྱེ་མཆེད་དྲུག

The six outer sources of perception (see yul-drug).

ཕྱིའི་ཁམས་དྲུག

Ṣaḍ bahirdhā dhātavaḥ/ The six outer sensory spheres (see khams bco-brgyad, A).

ཕྱིའི་རྟེན་འབྲེལ།

The outer dependent arising; the working of the nature; the phenomena of nature.

ཕྱིའི་དེ་ཉིད་བཅུ།

The ten external qualities of a Vajrācārya. 1. དཀྱིལ་འཁོར་འབྲི་བ་ལ་མཁས་པ། skilled in the art of drawing maṇḍalas and meditating upon them 2. དང་པོ་སྦྱོར་བ་སོགས་ཀྱི་ཏིང་ངེ་འཛིན་ལ་མཁས་པ། skilled in performing the preliminary practices such as maintaining concentration 3. ཨ་ལ་རྒྱས་འདེབས་པའི་ཕྱག་རྒྱ་ལ་མཁས་པ། skilled in performing mudrās or hand gestures 4. སྟངས་སྟབས་ལ་མཁས་པ། skilled in positioning the body 5. འདུག་སྟངས་སོགས་ལ་མཁས་པ། skilled in maintaining various sitting positions 6. བཟླས་བརྗོད་ལ་མཁས་པ། skilled in mantra recitation 7. སྦྱིན་སྲེག་ལ་མཁས་པ། skilled in performing fire-rituals 8. མཆོད་པའི་ཆོ་ག་སོགས་ལ་མཁས་པ། skilled in performing offering rituals 9. ལས་ལ་སྦྱོར་བ་ལ་མཁས་པ། skilled in performing practical ritual arts 10. གཤེགས་གསོལ་དང་སླར་བསྡུ་བའི་ལས་ལ་མཁས་པ། skilled in bidding farewell to the deities and withdrawing them into the heart, etc.

ཕྱིའི་ཕྱག་རྒྱ།

Bahirdhā mudrā/ External mudrā; external seal; a tantric consort; a gesture.

ཕྱིའི་ཡོངས་འཛིན།

External tutor. The living Guru other than oneself.

ཕྱིར་བཅོས།

Pratikriyā/ Restoration of vows. Restoration of transgressed vows through a confession ceremony.

ཕྱིར་མི་འོང་བཅུ།

Ten never-returners. 1. ཕྱིར་མི་འོང་ཞུགས་པ། the enterer into never-returner 2. བར་དོར་འདའ་བ། the never-returner who attains liberation in the intermediate state 3. སྐྱེས་ནས་འདའ་བ། the never-returner who attains liberation as soon as he is born 4. འཕར་བ་གསུམ། the three never-returners of the leap-over 5. མཐོང་ཆོས་ཞི་བ། the never-returner who attains liberation in the same life-time

6. ལུས་མངོན་བྱེད། the never-returner who attains liberation with the cessation of his body.

ཕྱིར་མི་འོང་པའི་དགེ་འདུན་ལྔ།

The five irreversible aspirants to virtue. The Bodhisattvas on the peak, forbearance, and supramundane levels of the path of preparation and the path of seeing and meditation.

ཕྱིར་འོང་།

Once-returner.

ཕྱོགས་སྐྱོང་བརྒྱད།

Aṣṭa digpālāḥ/ The eight directional protectors. 1. ཤར་དུ་དབང་པོ། Indra to the east 2. ལྷོ་རུ་གཤིན་རྗེ། Yama to the south 3. ནུབ་དུ་ཆུ་བདག Varuṇa to the west 4. བྱང་དུ་གནོད་སྦྱིན། Yakṣa to the north 5. ཤར་ལྷོར་མེ་ལྷ། Agnideva to the south-east 6. ལྷོ་ནུབ་ཏུ་བདེན་བྲལ། to the south-west 7. ནུབ་བྱང་དུ་རླུང་ལྷ། Vāyudeva to the north-west 8. བྱང་ཤར་དུ་དབང་ལྡན། Indra to the north-east.

ཕྱོགས་སྐྱོང་བཅུ།

Daśa digpālāḥ/ The ten directional protectors. 1. དབང་པོ། Indra 2. གཤིན་རྗེ། Yama 3. ཆུ་བདག Varuṇa 4. གནོད་སྦྱིན། Yakṣa 5. མེ་ལྷ། Agnideva 6. སྲིན་པོ། Rakṣasa 7. རླུང་ལྷ། Vāyudeva 8. འབྱུང་པོ། Bhūta 9. ཚངས་པ། Brahma 10. སའི་ལྷ་མོ། Vanadevī.

ཕྱོགས་སྐྱོང་བཅོ་ལྔ།

Pañcadaṣa digpālāḥ/ The fifteen directional protectors. A. (see phyogs-skyong bcu, above 1-10.) 11. ཉེ་དབང་། Upendra 12. ཚོགས་བདག Gaṇapati 13. ཉི་མ། Sūrya 14. ཟླ་བ། Candra 15. ཐགས་བཟང་། Avirala. B. According to Guhyasamāja tantra, these are: 1. ཤར་དུ་རྡོ་རྗེ་མཚོན་ཆ་སེར་པོ། Yellow Vajra Weapon to the east 2. གཡས་སུ་སྒྱུ་མ་རྡོ་རྗེ་ནག་པོ། Black Vajra Illusion to his right 3. མེར་རྡོ་རྗེ་མེ་དམར་པོ། Red Vajra Fire to the south-east 4. ལྷོར་རྡོ་རྗེ་དུས་ནག་པོ། Black Vajra Time to the south 5. ལྷོ་ནུབ་དུ་རྡོ་རྗེ་གཏུན་ཤིང་། Black Vajra Club to the south-west 6. ནུབ་དུ་རྡོ་རྗེ་ཀླུ་དཀར་པོ། White Vajra Nāga to the west 7. ནུབ་བྱང་དུ་རྡོ་རྗེ་རླུང་ལྗང་ཁུ། Green Vajra Wind to the north-west 8. བྱང་དུ་རྡོ་རྗེ་འཇིགས་བྱེད་སེར་པོ། Yellow Vajra Terrifier to the north 9. གཡས་སུ་རྡོ་རྗེ་སྣ་རིང་དཀར་པོ། White Vajra Ganeś to his right side 10. བྱང་ཤར་དུ་རྡོ་རྗེ་ཁྲོ་བོ་དཀར་པོ། White Vajra Wrath to the north-east 11. དབང་ལྡན་དང་ཉི་དབང་གི་བར་དུ་རྡོ་རྗེ་འཁྱིལ་བ་དམར་པོ། Red Vajra Sun between north-east and east 12. རྡོ་རྗེ་འོད་དཀར་པོ། White Vajra Moon 13. མི་སྨྲ་རྡོ་རྗེ་སེར་པོ། Yellow Vajra Silent (Brahma) 14. ཆུ་ལྷ་དང་བདེན་བྲལ་གྱི་བར་དུ་ཐགས་བཟང་རིས་ནག་པོ། Black Tak Zangri between west and south-west 15. ས་ཡི་ལྷ་མོ་སེར་མོ། Yellow Goddess of the Earth.

ཕྱོགས་བཅུ།

The ten directions. 1-4. ཕྱོགས་བཞི། the four cardinal directions 5-8. མཚམས་བརྒྱད། the four sub-directions 9. སྟེང་། zenith 10. འོག nadir.

ཕྱོགས་ཆོས།

Pakṣa dharma/ The first logical mark. The first condition to be fulfilled in a logical syllogism, i.e. the existence or presence of a logical mark in the subject of the syllogism.

ཕྲ་རྒྱས།

Anuśaya/ Delusion; affliction. That which is subtle and multiplying. Delusions are subtle because they are difficult to see, and they are multiplying because of their auxilary mental factors or objects of grasping.

ཕྲ་རྒྱས་ཀྱི་ཐེ་ཚོམ།

The delusive doubt; the deluded doubt.

ཕྲ་རྒྱས་དགུ་བཅུ་རྩ་བརྒྱད།

The ninety-eight delusions. The ninety-eight delusions of the three realms—eighty-eight delusions to be abandoned on the path of seeing, and ten delusions to be abandoned on the path of meditation.

ཕྲ་རྒྱས་བརྒྱ་དང་ཉེར་བརྒྱད།

The hundred and twenty-eight delusions. The one hundred and twenty-eight delusions of the three realms, one hundred and twelve delusions to be abandoned on the path of seeing, and sixteen delusions to be abandoned on the path of meditation.

ཕྲ་རྒྱས་བཅུ།

The ten delusions (see mi-dge-ba bcu).

ཕྲ་རྒྱས་དྲུག

The six delusions (see rtsa-nyon drug).

ཕྲ་རྒྱས་རྟོག་པའི་རྣལ་འབྱོར།

The yoga of subtle conceptions. The subtle conceptual yoga. A generation stage practice in the highest yoga tantra in which the objects of meditation are subtle.

ཕྲེང་བ།

Mālā/ A rosary. Common religious article used for counting prayers, mantras, etc., usually strung with 108 beads. Also means a garland; a row, e.g. of votive lamps.

འཕགས་པ།

Ārya/ A Noble Being. An exalted being; a superior. One who has attained the third path, the path of seeing, on which a person becomes a real Saṅgha refuge.

འཕགས་པ་ཀླུ་སྒྲུབ།

Ārya Nāgārjuna. The pioneer of the Mādhyamika philosophy after Buddha Śākyamuni, who elucidated the subtlest profound view of emptiness.

འཕགས་པ་ཉེ་བར་འཁོར།

Ārya Upāli. A close disciple of Buddha Śākyamuni, and a barber by caste and profession, who was renowned for his mastery of the Vinaya teachings. After Buddha Śākyamuni's passing away, he was responsible for reciting the Vinaya teachings at the first Buddhist council.

འཕགས་པ་འོད་སྲུང་ཆེན་པོ།

Ārya Mahākāśyapa. A close disciple of Buddha Śākyamuni belonging to the Brahmin caste, he was the first patriach or successor of the Buddha and was responsible for reciting the *Abhidharma* teachings at the first Buddhist council.

འཕགས་པའི་བདེན་པ་བཞི།

Catvāri ārya satyāni/ The four noble truths. 1. སྡུག་བསྔལ་བདེན་པ། duḥkha satya/ the truth of suffering 2. ཀུན་འབྱུང་བདེན་པ། samudaya satya/ the truth of the origin of suffering 3. འགོག་པའི་བདེན་པ། nirodha satya/ the truth of cessation 4. ལམ་གྱི་བདེན་པ། mārga satya/ the truth of the path.

འཕགས་པའི་ནོར་བདུན།

Sapta ārya dhanāni/ The seven riches of the Noble Beings; the Seven Jewels of the Āryas. 1. དད་པ། śraddha/ faith 2. ཚུལ་ཁྲིམས། śīla/ moral discipline 3. ཐོས་པ། śruta/ hearing 4. གཏོང་བ། tyāga/ generosity 5. ངོ་ཚ་ཤེས་པ། hrī/ a sense of shame 6. ཁྲེལ་ཡོད་པ། apatrāpya/ a dread of blame 7. ཤེས་རབ། prajñā/ wisdom.

འཕགས་པའི་རིགས་བཞི།

The four types of Āryas; the four types of ascetics. 1. ཆོས་གོས་ངན་ངོན་ཙམ་གྱིས་ཆོག་ཤེས་པ། one who is content with poor clothing 2. བསོད་སྙོམས་ངན་ངོན་ཙམ་གྱིས་ཆོག་ཤེས་པ། one who is contented with meagre alms 3. གནས་མལ་ངན་ངོན་ཙམ་གྱིས་ཆོག་ཤེས་པ། one who is content with a poor dwelling 4. སྤོང་བ་སྒོམ་པ་ལ་དགའ་བ། one who takes joy in ascetic practices.

འཕགས་པའི་གསང་བ་གསུམ།

The three secret ways of the Āryas. 1. སྟོད་ཐམས་ཅད་གཞལ་ཡས་ཁང་

སྣང་བཅུད་ཐམས་ཅད་ལྷའི་རྣམ་རོལ་དུ་ལྟ་བ། viewing the environment as the divine abode and all sentient beings as divine manifestations 2. སྒྲ་ཐམས་ཅད་གཟུངས་སྔགས་དང་བདམས་ངག་ཏུ་འགྱུར་བ། taking all sounds as being mantras or teachings of the Buddha 3. ཆོས་ཐམས་ཅད་གདོད་མ་ནས་སྟོང་པར་ལྟ་བ། viewing all phenomena as being empty of true existence from beginningless time.

འཕགས་པ་ལྷ།

Āryadeva. A direct disciple of Nāgārjuna who defeated the famous Tirthika teacher Aśvaghoṣa, a highly regarded scholar, in an open debate. Author of the *Four Hundred Stanzas*.

འཕགས་ལམ་ཡན་ལག་བརྒྱད།

Āryaṣṭānga mārga/ The eight-fold Noble Path. 1. ཡང་དག་པའི་ལྟ་བ། samyakdṛṣṭi/ right view 2. ཡང་དག་པའི་རྟོག་པ། saṁyaksaṁkalpa/ right thought 3. ཡང་དག་པའི་ངག saṁyagvāk/ right speech 4. ཡང་དག་པའི་རྩོལ་བ། saṁyag vyāyāma/ right effort 5. ཡང་དག་པའི་འཚོ་བ། saṁyagājiva/ right livelihood 6. ཡང་དག་པའི་དྲན་པ། saṁyaksmṛti/ right mindfulness 7. ཡང་དག་པའི་ཏིང་ངེ་འཛིན། saṁyaksamādhi/ right concentration 8. ཡང་དག་པའི་ལས་ཀྱི་མཐའ། saṁyakkarmānta/ right action.

འཕངས་པའི་ཡན་ལག

The projected results; the four propelled fruits within the twelve links of interdependent origination—name and form, sources, contact, and feeling.

འཕེན་བྱེད་ཀྱི་ཡན་ལག

Projecting causes; the three causes within the twelve links of interdependent origination which implant the causes for ripening karmas to be reborn in cyclic existence (saṁsāra)—ignorance, karmic formation and consciousness.

འཕེལ་གདུང་།

Multiplied relics. Relics like mustard seeds, off-white in colour, found in the cremated ashes of holy lamas; they are placed inside statues, stūpas, or amulet boxes as articles of protection and devotion.

འཕོ་བ།

Saṁkrānti/ Consciousness transference. A type of exalted purification practice in which one's or other's consciousness is transfered to a pure land; one of the six yogas of Naropa (see na-ro chos-drug).

འཕོ་བ་གྲོང་འཇུག

The consciousness transference of entering a corpse (see grong-'jug).

འཕྲུལ་གྱི་འཁྲུལ་རྒྱུ།

Causes for temporary deception.

འཕྲིན་ལས།

Virtuous activity; Buddha's grace. Synonymous with the virtue, merits or positive energy received through the blessings of the Buddha and his teachings.

འཕྲིན་ལས་ལྔ།

The five types of virtuous activities. The five activities of a Buddha: 1. ཞི་བའི་ལས། activity of peace 2. རྒྱས་པའི་ལས། activity of increase 3. དབང་གི་ལས། activity of power 4. དྲག་པོའི་ལས། activity of wrath 5. ལྷུན་གྱིས་གྲུབ་པའི་ལས། the spontaneous activity.

འཕྲིན་ལས་བཞི།

The four types of virtuous activity (see phrin-las lnga 1-4 above).

པ་དན།

Patāka/ Flags; prayer flags.

པ་སྦྱང་ལྔ།

The five products of a cow; fresh substances produced from a cow, collected before they drop to the ground. 1. ཆུ། urine 2. ལྕི་བ། dung 3. འོ་མ། milk 4. མར། butter 5. ཞོ། curd.

པ་སྦྱང་རིལ་བུ།

Pills made out of cow products (see above).

བག་ཆགས།

Vāsanā/ Latencies; instincts; karmic imprints.

བག་ཆགས་ཀྱི་ལུས།

Vāsana kāya/ The instinct body; the body of a dream state mainly impelled by the instincts left upon one's mind.

བག་ཆགས་བཞི།

The four types of instincts. 1. མངོན་བརྗོད་ཀྱི་བག་ཆགས། instinct of intuition 2. བདག་ལྟའི་བག་ཆགས། instinct of the view of grasping at self 3. སྲིད་པའི་ཡན་ལག་གི་བག་ཆགས། instinct of samsaric experiences 4. རིགས་མཐུན་པའི་བག་ཆགས། instinct of similar factors.

བག་ཆགས་གསུམ།

The three types of instincts. That of body, speech and mind.

བག་མེད་པ།

Lack of conscientiousness; recklessness; negligence. An attitude of not guarding one's actions.

བག་ལ་ཉལ་བ་བདུན།

Sapta anuśayāḥ/ The seven subconscious minds. The different subconscious experiences activated in conjunction with one's own experiences. 1. འདོད་པའི་འདོད་ཆགས་ཀྱི་བག་ཉལ། subconscious attachment to the desire realm 2. ཁོང་ཁྲོའི་བག་ཉལ། subconscious anger 3. སྲིད་པའི་འདོད་ཆགས་ཀྱི་བག་ཉལ། subconscious attachment within saṁsāra 4. ང་རྒྱལ་གྱི་བག་ཉལ། subconscious pride 5. མ་རིག་པའི་བག་ཉལ། subconscious ignorance 6. ལྟ་བའི་བག་ཉལ། subconscious view 7. ཐེ་ཚོམ་གྱི་བག་ཉལ། subconscious doubt.

བང་མཛོད་ལྟ་བུའི་སེམས་བསྐྱེད།

Treasure-like Bodhicitta. The mind of enlightenment possessed by Bodhisattvas on the three pure stages—the eighth, ninth and tenth, surpassing the two accumulations of merits and insights.

བམ་པོ།

Volume. Generally a standard number of three hundred verses forming the sub-divisions of a text; a device to ensure accurate translation and classification of a manuscript; but it may vary from text to text.

བར་བསྐལ།

Antarakalpa/ The intermediate aeon. The period of time taken for each of the four intermediate aeons (see below) to begin and end in themselves.

བར་བསྐལ་བཞི།

The four intermediate aeons. 1. ཆགས་པའི་བསྐལ་བ། aeon of formation 2. གནས་པའི་བསྐལ་བ། aeon of endurance 3. འཇིག་པའི་བསྐལ་བ། aeon of destruction 4. སྟོང་པའི་བསྐལ་བ། aeon of vacuity.

བར་བསྐལ་ཉི་ཤུ།

The twenty intermediate aeons; consisting of: 1. མིའི་ཚེ་ལོ་དཔག་མེད་ནས་ཚེ་ལོ་བཅུད་ཁྲིའི་བར་བྲི་བ་ནས་ཚེ་ལོ་བཅུའི་བར་བྲི་བ་དེ་བར་བསྐལ་པ་གཅིག one aeon of decline, during which the infinite human lifespan decreases to 80,000 to 10 years. 2. དེ་ནས་ཡང་ཚེ་ལོ་བརྒྱད་ཁྲིའི་བར་དུ་ཡར་འཕེལ་ཞིང་མར་ལོ་བཅུའི་བར་དུ་བྲི་བའི་བསྐལ་པ་བཅོ་བརྒྱད། eighteen aeons of increase and decrease, during which the lifespan of human beings goes from 10 to 80,000 and back to 10. 3. ཡང་ཚེ་ལོ་བཅུ་པ་ནས་བརྒྱད་ཁྲིའི་བར་ཡར་འཕེལ་བའི་བསྐལ་པ་གཅིག one aeon of increase, during which the human life span increases from 10 to 80,000 years.

བར་ཆད་མེད་པའི་ཏིང་ངེ་འཛིན།

Ānantarya samādhi/ The uninterrupted concentration. The moment of capturing a meditative concentration that realizes emptiness directly.

བར་ཆད་མེད་པའི་རྩེ་སྦྱོར།

Ānantaryamūrdhaprayoga/ Uninterrupted peak training. The final moment of the Bodhisattva path that results in the immediate attainment of Buddhahood. Synonymous with the wisdom of the last moment within the mental continuum of a Bodhisattva.

བར་ཆད་མེད་ལམ།

Ānantarya mārga/ Uninterrupted path. A path of single-pointed concentration that overcomes its respective object of abandonment, e.g. the first instant of the path of seeing.

བར་ཆད་བཞི།

The four interruptions. The four interruptions in the course of maintaining meditative concentration: 1. རོ་མྱང་ཅན། obsession of taste 2. ང་རྒྱལ་ཤས་ཆེ་བ། strong pride 3. མ་རིག་པ་ཤས་ཆེ་བ། strong ignorance 4. ལྟ་བ་ཤས་ཆེ་བ། strong view.

བར་དོ།

Antarābhava/ Intermediate state. The state of existence between death and rebirth, during which the consciousness takes a mental body projected by the previous karmic tendencies.

བར་དོ་དྲུག

Six classes of intermediate states. 1. སྐྱེ་བའི་བར་དོ། intermediate state of birth 2. མི་ལམ་གྱི་བར་དོ། intermediate state of dreams 3. བསམ་གཏན་གྱི་བར་དོ། intermediate state of concentration 4. འཆི་ཁའི་བར་དོ། intermediate state of near-death 5. ཆོས་ཉིད་བར་དོ། intermediate state of reality 6. སྲིད་པའི་བར་དོ། intermediate state of becoming.

བར་མ་རབ་བྱུང་།

The probationary novice. One who has received layman's ordination but has not yet received novice vows.

བས་མཐའ།

Prānta/ Wilderness retreat. A retreat place completely set apart from the town life.

བུ་ག་སྒོ་དགུ

The nine orifices or gates of exit for consciousness to exit from the human body (see rnam-shes 'pho-ba'i bu-ga dgu).

བུ་དགོན།

A branch monastery. A subsidiary centre of learning founded by a later disciple of a master affiliated to the monastic centre, which is called the 'mother monastery' (ma-dgon).

བུ་ཆོས།

The son dharma. The collection of teachings of Atiśa and Drom Tonpa as received and compiled by their spiritual son, Ngog Legpe Sherab comprising many anecdotes in the life of Dromtonpa, and the entrustment of the Kadampa's doctrine to Dromtonpa during the last days of Atiśa's life. This collection is also known as the Kadampa's miraculous text (sprul-pa'i glegs-bam).

བུ་སྟོན་རིན་ཆེན་གྲུབ།

The great scholar Buton (1290-1364). Born in central Tibet, he became famous for his scholarship of all sciences of learning. He compiled all the treatises translated from Sanskrit into Tibetan in a systematic order of index, and has also left more than two dozen volumes of collected writings. Je Tsong Khapa also became his disciple and received many tantric teachings from him. His lineage is known as the Buton lineage (bu-lugs).

བུ་རམ་ཤིང་པ།

Ikṣvāku/ The sugarcane descendant. An epithet for Buddha Śākyamuni whose ancestral lineage is traced to a child born of an egg that was dropped from semen which had dripped onto a sugarcane leaf.

བུད་རྙེད་ཐོབ་གསུམ།

The expulsion, finding and attainment. The Kadampa principles of: 1. མི་གྲལ་ནས་བུད། expulsion from the ranks of worldly people 2. ཁྱི་གྲལ་བསྙེགས། finding the ranks of dogs 3. ལྷ་གྲལ་ཐོབ། attaining the rank of a god.

བུམ་པ་བསྐྱེད་པ།

The generation of the vase. A tantric practice of generating the ritual vase as a deity by connecting vajra threads (multi-coloured thread) from the vase to the heart of the master. First the vase to the heart of the master visualizes the deities, then they are offered blessed scented water from a conch, then are immersed in the nature of bliss and void and transformed as inseparable from the scented water contained in the vase etc., following a ritual text and tradition.

བུམ་པ་སྔ་གོན།

The preparatory vase ritual. A part of the preparatory rite for an initiation. The commitment beings (see dam-tshig sems-dpa') are generated in the vase and the wisdom beings (see ye-shes sems-dpa') are immersed into it, and then the initiation is bestowed following a rite and tradition of a lineage.

བུམ་དབང་།

The Vase Initiation. A tantric empowerment (see bum-dbang bcu-gcig, next) meant for ripening a disciples's mental continuum and allowing the practice of the generation stage paths aimed at gaining Buddhahood.

བུམ་དབང་བཅུ་གཅིག

The eleven vase initiations. 1. བུམ་དབང་། water initition 2. ཅོད་པན་གྱི་དབང་། crown initiation 3. རྡོ་རྗེའི་དབང་། vajra initiation 4. དྲིལ་བུའི་དབང་། bell initiation 5. མིང་གི་དབང་སྟེ་སློབ་མའི་དབང་ལྔ། name initiation 6. རྡོ་རྗེ་སློབ་དཔོན་གྱི་དབང་། vajrā-cārya initiation 7. སྔགས་ཀྱི་དབང་། mantra initiation 8. ལུང་བསྟན་དང་དབུགས་དབྱུང་གི་དབང་། prophecy and relief granting initiation 9. རྡོ་རྗེའི་བརྟུལ་ཞུགས་ཀྱི་དབང་། vajra practice initiation 10. སྤྱོད་པའི་བརྟུལ་ཞུགས་ཀྱི་དབང་། ascetic practice initiation 11. རྗེས་སྣང་གི་དབང་། permission initiation.

བུའི་འོད་གསལ།

Putraprabhāsvara/ The son clear light. The clear light mind recognized through the power of meditation while on the trainee's path arising during the dissolution of winds within the central channel through the force of meditation; the son clear light is the experience of various levels of clear light mind gained on the path towards total perfection. This has two types: 1. དབེན་པའི་འོད་གསལ། the clear light of isolation 2. མི་དབེན་པའི་འོད་གསལ། the clear light of non-isolation.

བེ་ཅོན།

Danda/ Club with an ornamental human, vajra, or human head at its top; generally depicted as an implement in the hands of Asuras.

བེམ་པོ།

Matter. Any existent thing that is neither form nor consciousness, e.g. a person. There are two types of matter. 1. ཕྱི་དོན་བེམ་པོ། external matter, e.g. a clay pot 2. ནང་དོན་བེམ་པོ། internal matter, e.g. sense organs.

བྱ་དཀའ་རྣམ་གསུམ།

Three difficult aspects of practice. 1. ཆེད་དུ་བྱ་དཀའ་བ། fulfilling the goals 2. སྤྱོད་པ་བྱ་དཀའ་བ། executing the conduct 3. ལས་བྱ་དཀའ་བ། pursuing the practice.

བྱ་ཁྱུང་།

Garuḍa; celestial eagle. A bird in Buddhist and Hindu mythology which is half man and half eagle symbolizing anger or wrath.

བྱ་ཁྲུས།

A purification ceremony conducted by a lama in which he sprinkles blessed water on one's head and gives water to sip.

བྱ་རྒོད་ཕུང་པོའི་རི།

Gṛdhrakūṭa/ Vulture Peak. The holy place near Rajgiri where Buddha Śākyamuni turned the second wheel of doctrine, e.g. the *Perfection of Wisdom Sūtras*.

བྱ་རྒྱུད།

Kriyātantra/ Action tantra. The first of the four classes of tantra, stressing the importance of purifying external activities.

བྱ་རྒྱུད་ཀྱི་དངོས་གྲུབ་གསུམ།

The three types of siddhis of action (kriyā) tantra. The power of gaining proficiency in caryatantra practices 1. རབ་རིག་འཛིན་དང་མངོན་ཤེས་དང་བསྟན་བཅོས་ཀུན་ཤེས་པ་སོགས་དང་། the siddhi of knowledge of all sciences of learning as the supreme result 2. འབྲིང་མི་སྣང་བ་དང་བཅུད་ལེན་དང་རྐང་མགྱོགས་སོགས་དང་། the siddhi of disappearance, extracting the essence/ art of elixir and swift footedness as the middling result 3. ཐ་མ་གཞན་དབང་དུ་འདུ་བ་དང་བསད་བསྒྲད་སོགས་སམ་ཛས་ལུས་ལོངས་སྤྱོད་གསུམ་སོགས་དབང་དུ་འདུ་བ། the siddhi of capturing, killing and expelling others or gaining control over matter, body and resources as the modest result.

བྱ་རྒྱུད་ཀྱི་དེ་ཁོ་ན་ཉིད་བཞི།

The four suchnesses according to action tantra. The four primary applications of the action tantra practices (see de-kho-na-nyid bzhi).

བྱ་རྒྱུད་ཀྱི་དབང་གསུམ།

The three initiations according to action tantra. 1. མེ་ཏོག་ཕྲེང་བའི་དབང་། the flower garland initiation 2. ཆུ་དབང་། water initiation 3. ཅོད་པཎ་གྱི་དབང་། crown initiation.

བྱ་རྒྱུད་ཀྱི་བསམ་གཏན་གསུམ།

The three types of concentration according to the action tantra. The three suchnesses of concentration. 1. མེར་གནས་ཀྱིདེ་ཉིད། suchness of abiding in fire 2. སྒྲར་གནས་ཀྱི་དེ་ཉིད། suchness of abiding in sound 3. སྒྲ་མཐའི་དེ་ཉིད། suchness of abiding in the finality of sound.

བྱ་རྒྱུད་ཀྱི་ལྷ་དྲུག

The six deities of the action tantra. 1. སྟོང་པའི་ལྷ། śūnyatā deva/ emptiness deity 2. ཡི་གེའི་ལྷ། akṣara deva/ letter deity 3. སྒྲའི་ལྷ། śabda deva/ sound deity 4. གཟུགས་ཀྱི་ལྷ། rūpa deva/ form deity 5. ཕྱག་རྒྱའི་ལྷ། mudrā deva/ seal deity 6. མཚན་མའི་ལྷ། lakṣaṇa deva/ symbol deity.

བྱ་རྒྱུད་སྤྱིའི་དམ་ཚིག་བཅུ་བཞི།

The fourteen commitments of action tantra in general. 1-3. དཀོན་མཆོག་གསུམ་ལ་དད་པ། maintaining faith in the Three Jewels 4. སྔགས་ལ་དད་པ། faith in mantra 5. ཐེག་ཆེན་ལ་མོས་པ། possessing aspiration in the greater vehicle teachings 6. བླ་མ་དང་ཆོས་གྲོགས་ལ་གུས་པ། being respectful to spiritual masters and friends 7. འདས་མ་འདས་ཀྱི་ལྷ་གཞན་ལ་མི་སྡང་བ། having no hatred towards other deities of the past and future 8. ཉ་སྟོང་དུས་བཞིའི་མཆོད་པ་མི་གཙོག་པ། not failing in carrying out one's commitments during the four days of a month, i.e., the eighth, fifteenth, twenty-fifth and thirtieth 9. ཀླ་ཀློ་དང་མུ་སྟེགས་པའི་གཞུང་གཞན་ལ་མི་མཆོད་པ། not worshipping other barbarian and non-buddhist doctrines or philosophies 10. གློ་བུར་ལྷགས་པའི་མགྲོན་ལ་ཟས་སྐོམ་སོགས་མཆོད་པ། offering of feast to strangers 11. སེམས་ཅན་ལ་བྱམས་པ་མི་གཏོང་བ། not giving up one's love and affection towards sentient beings 12. བསོད་ནམས་ཀྱི་ཚོགས་གོང་དུ་སྤེལ་བ། accumulating the collection of merits 13. བཟླས་བརྗོད་ལ་བརྩོན་པ། devotion to incantation of mantras 14. དམ་ཚིག་གཞན་རྣམས་ཀྱང་བསྲུང་བ། observing other commitments.

བྱ་རྒྱུད་རིགས་དྲུག

The six families of action tantra. 1. དེ་བཞིན་གཤེགས་པའི་རིགས། the Tathāgata family 2. པདྨའི་རིགས། the Padma family 3. རྡོ་རྗེའི་རིགས། the Vajra family, known as the three transworldly families 4. ནོར་བུའི་རིགས། the Ratna family 5. ལྔས་རྩེན་གྱི་རིགས། the Spirit (lngas-rtsen) family 6. འཇིག་རྟེན་ཕལ་པའི་རིགས། the common family, known as the three worldly families.

བྱ་རྒྱུད་རིགས་གསུམ།

The three families of action tantra. (see bya-rgyud rigs-drug, 1-3, above).

བྱ་རྫོགས་སྐད་ཅིག་མ།

The time between the beginning and end of an activity. The span of time which is 1/60th of a finger-snap.

བྱང་ཆུབ་ཀྱི་སེམས།

Bodhicitta/ Mind of enlightenment. Altruistic mind of enlightenment to attain Buddhahood for the sake of other sentient beings; a Bodhisattva's way of life.

བྱང་ཆུབ་ཡན་ལག་བདུན།

Sapta bodhyangāni/ The seven limbs of enlightenment; the seven auxiliaries to enlightenment which are in an equilibrim state of concentration and wisdom. 1. དྲན་པ། smṛti/ mindfulness 2. ཤེས་རབ། prajñā/ wisdom 3. བརྩོན་འགྲུས། vīrya/ effort 4. དགའ་བ། prīti/ joy 5. ཤིན་སྦྱངས། praśrabdhi/ suppleness 6. ཏིང་ངེ་འཛིན། samādhi/ concentration 7. བཏང་སྙོམས། upekṣa/ equanimity.

བྱང་ཆུབ་ཤིང་།

Bodhivṛkṣa/ Bodhi tree. The pipal tree under which Buddha Śākyamuni attained complete enlightenment at Bodhgaya.

བྱང་ཆུབ་སེམས་དཔའ།

Bodhisattva. Practitioner of the greater vehicle teachings who has resolved to attain Buddhahood for the sake of all sentient beings; also called the son of the Victorious Ones, more strictly, one who has at least attained the first path of the greater vehicle.

བྱང་ཆུབ་སེམས་དཔའི་སྟོབས་བཅུ།

Daśa bodhisattvabalāni/ The ten powers of a Bodhisattva. 1. བསམ་པའི་སྟོབས། āśaya balam/ power of intention 2. ལྷག་པའི་བསམ་པའི་སྟོབས། adhyāśaya balam/ power of resolute intention 3. སྦྱོར་བའི་སྟོབས། prayoga balam/ power of application 4. ཤེས་རབ་ཀྱི་སྟོབས། prajñā balam/ power of wisdom 5. སྨོན་ལམ་གྱི་སྟོབས། praṇidhāna balam/ power of prayer 6. ཐེག་པའི་སྟོབས། yāna balam/ power of vehicle 7. སྤྱོད་པའི་སྟོབས། caryā balam/ power of conduct 8. སྤྲུལ་པའི་སྟོབས། vikurvaṇa balam/ power of emancipation 9. བྱང་ཆུབ་ཀྱི་སྟོབས། bodhi balam/ power of enlightenment 10. ཆོས་ཀྱི་འཁོར་ལོ་བསྐོར་བའི་སྟོབས། dharmacakra pravartana balam/ power of turning the wheel of doctrine.

བྱང་ཆུབ་སེམས་དཔའ་དང་ཐུན་མོང་བའི་རྣམ་པ་སོ་བཞི།

The thirty-four qualities common to Bodhisattvas; the thirty-four aspects of the omniscient mind (see rnam-mkhyen-gyi rnam-pa sum-cu so-bzhi).

བྱང་ཆུབ་སེམས་དཔའི་དབང་བཅུ།

The ten aspects of a Bodhisattva's control. 1. ཚེ་ལ་དབང་བ། control over life 2. སེམས་ལ་དབང་བ། control over mind 3. ཡོ་བྱད་ལ་དབང་བ། control over materials 4. ལས་ལ་དབང་བ། control over action 5. སྐྱེ་བ་ལ་དབང་བ། control over birth 6. ཆོས་ལ་དབང་བ། control over doctrine 7. སྨོན་ལམ་ལ་དབང་བ། control over prayers 8. རྫུ་འཕྲུལ་ལ་དབང་བ། control over miracles 9. མོས་པ་ལ་དབང་བ། control over different faculties 10. ཡེ་ཤེས་ལ་དབང་བ། control over wisdom.

བྱང་ཆུབ་སེམས་དཔའི་ས་བཅུ།

Daśa bodhisattva bhūmayah/ The ten Bodhisattva grounds; the ten levels of Bodhisattvas (see sa-bcu).

བྱང་ཆུབ་སེམས་དཔའི་སེམས་ཅན་གྱི་དོན་བྱ་ཚུལ་བཅུ་གཉིས།

Twelve ways in which a Bodhisattva fulfils the purposes of sentient beings; the Bodhisattva's twelve means of working for the welfare of others. 1. བྱ་བ་བྱེད་པ། performance in action 2. སྡུག་བསྔལ་གྱིས་གཟིར་བའི་དོན་བྱེད་པ། helping those who are suffering 3. ཐབས་ལ་རྨོངས་པའི་དོན་བྱེད་པ། helping those ignorant of means 4. ཕན་འདོགས་པའི་དོན་བྱེད་པ། helping those in need of help 5. འཇིགས་པས་ཉེན་པའི་དོན་བྱེད་པ། helping those oppressed by fear 6. མྱ་ངན་གྱིས་གཟིར་བའི་དོན་བྱེད་པ། helping those overcome by suffering 7. ཡོ་བྱད་ཀྱིས་ཕོངས་པའི་དོན་བྱེད་པ། helping those lacking resources 8. གནས་འཆའ་བར་བྱེད་པའི་དོན་བྱེད་པ། helping the homeless 9 བློ་མཐུན་པར་འདོད་པའི་དོན་བྱེད་པ། helping those seeking to live in harmony 10. ཡང་དག་པར་ཞུགས་པའི་དོན་བྱེད་པ། helping those wishing to enter the teaching 11. ལོག་པར་ཞུགས་པའི་དོན་བྱེད་པ། helping those holding wrong views 12. རྫུ་འཕྲུལ་གྱི་སྒོ་ནས་དོན་བྱེད་པ། helping through miraculous deeds.

བྱང་ཕྱོགས་སོ་བདུན།

The thirty-seven limbs of enlightenment; the thirty-seven auxiliaries to enlightenment. 1-4. དྲན་པ་ཉེ་བར་བཞག་པ་བཞི། four close contemplations (see dran-pa nye-bar bzhag-pa bzhi) 5-8. ཡང་དག་པར་སྤོང་བ་བཞི། four perfect abandonments (see yang-dag spong-ba bzhi) 9-12. རྫུ་འཕྲུལ་གྱི་རྐང་པ་བཞི། four limbs of miracles (see rdzu-'phrul-gyi rkang-pa bzhi) 13-17. དབང་པོ་ལྔ། five powers (see dbang-po lnga) 18-22. སྟོབས་ལ five forces (see stobs-lnga) 23-29. བྱང་ཆུབ་ཕྱོགས་ཀྱི་ཆོས་བདུན། seven limbs of enlightenment (see byang-chub yan-lag bzhi) 30-37. འཕགས་ལམ་ཡན་ལག་བརྒྱད། eight noble paths (see 'phags-pa'i lam yan-lag brgyad).

བྱང་སེམས་ཀྱི་སྡོམ་པ།

Bodhisattva saṁvara/ Bodhisattva vows; Bodhisattva precepts. The vows taken with the aim of helping others to attain the state of Buddhahood.

བྱང་སེམས་འཕགས་པ།

Ārya Bodhisattva; superior Bodhisattva. A Bodhisattva who has attained the third of the five paths—the path of seeing.

བྱམས་ཆོས་སྡེ་ལྔ།

The Five Works of Maitreya. 1. མདོ་སྡེ་རྒྱན། *Ornament of Mahāyāna Discourses* (mahāyāna sūtrālaṁkāra) 2. མངོན་རྟོགས་རྒྱན། *Ornament of Clear Realization* (abhisamayālaṁkāra) 3. དབུས་མཐའ་རྣམ་འབྱེད། *Clear Distinction Between the Middle Way and Extremes* (madhyāntavibhaṅga) 4. ཆོས་ཉིད་རྣམ་འབྱེད། *Clear Distinction Between Phenomena and their Reality* (dharma dharmatāvibhaṅga) 5. རྒྱུད་བླ་མ། *The Sublime Continuum* (uttaratantra).

བྱམས་པ།

Maitreya. A. Love; the wish for all sentient beings to be happy. B. Buddha Maitreya. Also called Maitreyanath, the future Buddha who will appear after the total disappearance of Buddha Śākyamuni's teaching, presently believed to be residing in the Tuṣita God Realm. C. Bodhisattva Maitreya. The author of the Five Works of Maitreya (see above, byams-chos sde-lnga).

བྱིན་གྱིས་བརླབས་པའི་བཀའ།

Blessed words of the Buddha; the teaching given through the force of Buddha's blessings although not spoken by him. There can be the blessings of body, speech and mind, e.g. the *Heart Sūtra* is a discourse of the Buddha blessed by his mind.

བྱིན་རླབས་བཞི།

The four types of blessings. 1. བདེན་པའི་བྱིན་རླབས། blessing of the truth 2. གཏོང་བའི་བྱིན་རླབས། blessing of giving 3. ཉེ་བར་ཞི་བའི་བྱིན་རླབས། blessing of ultimate peace 4. ཤེས་རབ་ཀྱི་བྱིན་རླབས། blessing of wisdom.

བྱིས་པ་ལྟར་འཇུག་པའི་དབང་བདུན།

The seven initiations of entering (the maṇḍala) like a child. 1. ཆུའི་དབང་། water initiation 2. ཅོད་པཎ་གྱི་དབང་། crown initiation 3. དར་དཔྱངས་ཀྱི་དབང་། ribbon initiation 4. རྡོར་དྲིལ་གྱི་དབང་། vajra and bell initiation 5. རྡོ་རྗེ་བརྟུལ་ཞུགས་ཀྱི་དབང་། vajra practice initiation 6. མིང་གི་དབང་། name initiation 7. རྗེས་སྣང་གི་དབང་། permission initiation.

བྱེ་བྲག་པ།

Vaiśeṣika/ The Particularists. Proponents of non-Buddhist tenets following the sage Kanand, who asserted that all objects of knowledge are included in six categories (see below); they also assert that ablution, initiations, fasts, and offerings of fire rituals are perfect paths to liberation; accordingly, when the self is in isolation free from desire, hatred, anger or pleasure, liberation is attained.

བྱེ་བྲག་པའི་ཚིག་དོན་དྲུག

The six principles of the Paticularists. 1. རྫས། dravya/ substance 2. ཡོན་ཏན། guṇa/ quality 3. ལས། karma 4. སྤྱི། sāmānya/ enerality 5. བྱེ་བྲག viśeṣa/ particularity 6. འདུ་བ། saṁgraha/ composition.

བྱེ་བྲག་སྨྲ་བ།

Vaibhāṣika. A lower school of Buddhist philosophy that asserts the division of all phenomena into the following five categories, and assert three times as substantially existent. 1. འདུས་མ་བྱས་རྟག་པའི་གཞི། non-composite phenomena as permanent 2. སྣང་བ་སེམས་ཀྱི་གཞི། appearances as form (objects of perception) 3. གཙོ་བོ་སེམས་ཀྱི་གཞི། primary mind 4. འཁོར་སེམས་བྱུང་གི་གཞི། secondary minds 5. ལྡན་པ་མ་ཡིན་པའི་འདུ་བྱེད་ཀྱི་གཞི། non-associated compositional factors.

བྱེ་བྲག་སྨྲ་བའི་སྡེ་པ་བཅོ་བརྒྱད།

Aṣṭadaśa Vaibhāṣika nikāyaḥ/ The eighteen schools of Vaibhāṣika. The eighteen schools of Hearers (see nyan-thos sde-pa bco-brgyad).

བྱེ་བྲག་སྨྲ་བའི་རྩ་བའི་སྡེ་པ་བཞི།

The four principal schools of Vaibhāṣika. The four mains schools of Hearers (see nyan-thos rtza-ba'i sde-pa bzhi).

བྱེ་བྲག་བཤད་མཚོ་ཆེན་མོ།

Mahāvibhāsa/ *The Great Ocean of Commentary* (mahavibhāṣa). One of the principal texts of the Vaibhāṣika school of philosophy said to have been composed collectively by five hundred Arhats lead by Upāli, after the passing away of Buddha Śākyamuni. It belongs to the *Abhidharma* class of teachings.

བྱེད་རྒྱུ།

Kāraṇahetu/ Active phenomena; active cause. A phenomenon is said to be an active cause of another when it is both substantially distinct from that phenomenon and does not obstruct its arisal. There are two types of active causes: 1. བྱེད་རྒྱུ་ནུས་ལྡན། effective active cause, e.g. food for body 2. བྱེད་རྒྱུ་ནུས་མེད། ineffective active cause, e.g. permanent phenomena.

བྱེད་རྒྱུ་ཉི་ཤུ།

Twenty types of active causes. 1. གནས་པའི་བྱེད་རྒྱུ། active cause of endurance 2. བརྟན་པའི་བྱེད་རྒྱུ། active cause-of stablization 3. འབྲལ་བའི་བྱེད་རྒྱུ། active cause of separation 4. གསལ་བའི་བྱེད་རྒྱུ། active cause of clarity 5. ཡིད་ཆེས་པའི་བྱེད་རྒྱུ། active cause of conviction 6. བསྒྱུར་བའི་བྱེད་རྒྱུ། active cause of transformation 7. ཡིད་ཆེས་པར་བྱེད་པའི་བྱེད་རྒྱུ། active cause of prompting conviction 8. འཐོབ་པའི་བྱེད་རྒྱུ། active cause of achievement 9. ཐ་སྙད་པའི་བྱེད་རྒྱུ། active cause of convention 10. ལྟོས་པའི་བྱེད་རྒྱུ། active cause of reliance 11. འཕེན་པའི་བྱེད་རྒྱུ། active cause of projection 12. མངོན་པར་འགྲུབ་པའི་བྱེད་རྒྱུ། active cause of establishment 13. ཡོངས་སུ་འཛིན་པའི་བྱེད་རྒྱུ། active cause of perfection 14. ཆུང་བར་བྱེད་པའི་བྱེད་རྒྱུ། active cause of diminishment 15. སོ་སོར་ངེས་པའི་བྱེད་རྒྱུ། active cause of specific understanding 16. ལྷན་ཅིག་བྱེད་པའི་བྱེད་རྒྱུ། active cause of co-operation 17 མི་མཐུན་པའི་བྱེད་རྒྱུ། active cause of discord 18. མི་མཐུན་པ་མ་ཡིན་པའི་བྱེད་རྒྱུ། active cause of harmony 19. འབྱུང་བའི་བྱེད་རྒྱུ། active cause of elements 20. བྱེད་རྒྱུ། active cause itself.

བྲམ་ཟེ།

Brahmin. One of the four castes of Indian society who are traditionally occupied with religious duties.

བྲམ་ཟེའི་རིག་བྱེད་བཞི།

Four Vedas of Brahmins. 1. ངེས་བརྗོད། Rig Veda 2. མཆོད་སྦྱིན། Yajur Veda 3. སྙན་ཚིག Sama Veda 4. སྲིད་སྲུང་། Atharva Veda.

བྲམ་ཟེའི་ལས་དྲུག

Six tasks of a Brahmin; six trainings of a Brahmin. 1. ཀློག་པ། reading 2. ཀློག་ཏུ་འཇུག་པ། training others to read 3. མཆོད་སྦྱིན། making sacrificial offerings 4. མཆོད་སྦྱིན་བྱེད་དུ་འཇུག་པ། encouraging others to perform sacrificial offerings 5. སྦྱིན་པ། giving alms 6. ལེན་པ། accepting offerings.

བྲལ་བའི་འབྲས་བུ།

Visaṁyoga phalam/ Fruit of cessation, e.g. the noble truth of cessation of suffering.

བླ་ན་མེད་པ་དྲུག

Ṣaḍ anuttarayāṇi/ Six unsurpassables. 1. མཐོང་བ་བླ་ན་མེད་པ། darśanānuttaryam/ unsurpassable seeing 2. ཐོས་པ་བླ་ན་མེད་པ། śravaṇānuttaryam/ unsurpassable hearing 3. རྙེད་པ་བླ་ན་མེད་པ། lābhānuttaryam/ unsurpassable finding 4. བསླབ་པ་བླ་ན་མེད་པ། śikṣānuttaryam/ unsurpassable precepts 5. རིམ་གྲོ་བླ་ན་མེད་པ། paricaryānuttaryam/ unsurpassable honour 6. རྗེས་སུ་དྲན་པ་བླ་ན་མེད་པ། anusmṛty anuttaryam/ unsurpassable recollection.

བླ་བྲང་།

Lama estate. An estate owned by a high lama.

བླ་བྲེ།

Canopy. A brocade and silk hanging above a high lama's throne.

བླ་མ།

Lama. A. Spiritual master; qualified religious teacher. Lit. 'high one' (guru) or 'weighty one', meaning one who possesses great knowledge and spiritual accomplishments.

བླ་མ་དཀོན་མཆོག

A. The entire group of objects of refuge. B. A humble and sincere person. C. Not good, not bad.

བླ་མ་ཁྱད་ཆོས་གསུམ་ལྡན།

Three qualities of a Guru. 1. ཚུལ་ཁྲིམས་རྣམ་པར་དག་པས་སྒོ་གསུམ་གྱི་སྤྱོད་པ་གཙང་བ། the conduct of his body, speech and mind are pure due to his strict morality 2. ཤེས་རབ་རྣམ་པར་དག་པས་བཤད་པའི་དོན་ལ་མཁས་པ། he is wise in giving teaching due to his pure wisdom 3. བསམ་པ་རྣམ་པར་དག་པས་གཞན་ལ་ཕན་འདོགས་པ། he benefits others due to his pure altruistic thoughts.

བླ་མ་རྒྱུད་པ།

A tantric monk. A monk either from the upper or lower tantric college of the Gelug order.

བླ་མ་མ་ཎི།

A Buddhist minstrel. A professional bard who moves freely, tell stories and sings poems of Buddhist ethics, karma, life stories and epics to people.

བླ་མའི་རྣལ་འབྱོར།

Guruyoga. The practice of guru devotion; the meditation and services to please one's guru in order to increase one's power to reach one's goal of ultimate enlightenment.

བླ་མེད་ཀྱི་དབང་བཞི།

The four initiations of the highest tantra (see dbang-bzhi).

བླ་མེད་རྒྱུད་གསུམ།

The three highest yoga tantras (anuttarayoga tantra). 1. ཕ་རྒྱུད། father tantra, e. g Guhyasamāja 2. མ་རྒྱུད། mother tantra, e.g. Cakrasaṁvara 3. གཉིས་མེད་ཀྱི་རྒྱུད། non-dual tantra, e.g. Kālacakra.

བླངས་འདས་སོ་དྲུག

The thirty-six precepts of observance and abandonment of a novice monk (see dge-tshul gyi blangs-'das so-drug).

བློ།

Buddhi/ 1. Mind; perception 2. Wisdom.

བློ་གྲོས།

Wisdom; intelligence; sagacity; prudence; knowledge.

བློ་ངན་གསུམ།

The three evil wisdoms. 1. མ་རྟོགས་པ། not-knowing 2. ལོག་པར་རྟོགས་པ། knowing wrong 3. ཐེ་ཚོམ། doubt.

བློ་ལྡོག་རྣམ་བཞི།

The four principles of thought transformation; the four basic mind trainings. 1. དལ་འབྱོར་རྙེད་དཀའ་བསམ་པ། realizing the preciousness of a human rebirth 2. འཆི་བ་མི་རྟག་བསམ་པ། realizing the impermanence of this life 3. འཁོར་བའི་ཉེས་དམིགས་བསམ་པ། realizing the faults of cyclic existence (saṁsāra) 4. ལས་རྒྱུ་འབྲས་བསམ་པ། realizing that pleasure and suffering result from good and bad actions respectively.

བློ་སྦྱོང་ཐུན་བརྒྱད་མ།

Eight sessions of mind training. Kadampa's mind training precepts transmitted by Dromtonpa. 1. ཟས་ལ་བརྟེན་པའི་བློ་སྦྱོང་། mind training in reliance on eating 2. དབུགས་ལ་བརྟེན་པའི་བློ་སྦྱོང་། mind training in reliance on breath 3. ལུས་གང་གཱའི བྱེ་མ་སྙེད་དུ་སྤྲུལ་པ་ལ་བརྟེན་པའི་བློ་སྦྱོང་། mind trainin through visualizing one's body as being as numerous as th grains of sand in the river Ganges 4. ཤ་ཁྲག་ལ་བརྟེན་པའི་བློ སྦྱོང་། mind training in reliance on flesh and blood 5. གཏོར་མ ལ་བརྟེན་པའི་བློ་སྦྱོང་། mind training in reliance on ritual cak offerings 6. འབྱུང་བ་ལ་བརྟེན་པའི་བློ་སྦྱོང་། mind training i reliance on the elements 7. ལུས་ཡིད་བཞིན་ནོར་བུར་སྤྲུལ་ཏེ་བློ སྦྱོང་། mind training through transforming one's body into wish-fulfilling jewel 8. འཆི་བ་མན་ངག་བློ་སྦྱོང་། mind trainin in reliance on the instructions for death.

བློ་སྦྱོང་དོན་བདུན་མ།

The seven point mind training. The Kadampa's mind trainin precepts: སྔོན་འགྲོ་རྟེན་གྱི་ཆོས་སེམས་པ། the preliminar practice 2. དངོས་གཞི་བྱང་ཆུབ་ཀྱི་སེམས་སྦྱོང་བ། generating th mind of enlightenment 3. རྐྱེན་ངན་བྱང་ཆུབ་ཀྱི་ལམ་དུ་བསྒྱུར་ transforming misfortunes into paths to enlightenment 4. ཚ གཅིག་གི་ཉམས་ལེན་དྲིལ་ནས་བསྟན་པ། synthesizing th practices of this life 5. བློ་འབྱོངས་པའི་ཚད། the yardstick mind training 6. བློ་སྦྱོང་གི་དམ་ཚིག the commitments of mir training 7. བློ་སྦྱོང་གི་བསླབ་བྱ། the precepts of mind training.

བློ་སྦྱོང་ཞེན་པ་བཞི་བྲལ།

The mind training, 'Parting Away from the Four Clinging common to the Sakya tradition. 1. ཚེ་འདི་ལ་ཞེན་ན་ཆོས་པ མིན། if you have attachment to this life, you are not religious practitioner 2. འཁོར་བ་ལ་ཞེན་ན་ངེས་འབྱུང་མིན། you are attached to cyclic existence, you have no renunciati 3. རང་དོན་ལ་ཞེན་ན་བྱང་སེམས་མིན། if you are attached your own welfare, you do not have the mind of enlightenme 4. འཛིན་པ་བྱུང་ན་ལྟ་བ་མིན། if you have grasping, you do n have the correct view.

བློ་རིག་བདུན།

Seven awarenesses; seven ways of knowing. 1. མངོན་སུམ། pratyakṣa/ direct perception 2. རྗེས་དཔག anumāna/ inferential perception 3. བཅད་ཤེས། paricchinna jñāna/ subsequent cognition 4. ཡིད་དཔྱོད། manaḥparīkṣā/ presumption 5. སྣང་ལ་མ་ངེས། darśanāniyata/ inattentive perception 6. ཐེ་ཚོམ། vicikitsā/ indecisive mind/ doubt 7. ལོག་ཤེས། mithyājñāna/ distorted awareness.

བློ་རིག་བཞི།

The four classes of awareness. The classification of mind according to the way it cognizes its respective object of perception. 1. སྣང་ལ་མ་ངེས་པ་དང་ཡིད་དཔྱོད་གཉིས་པོ་མ་རྟོགས་པའི་བློ། non-discerning mind, e.g. the presumptions and inattentive mind 2. རྟོག་བཅས་རྟོག་མེད་ཀྱི་ལོག་ཤེས་གཉིས་པོ་ལོག་པར་རྟོག་པའི་བློ། distorted mind, e.g. the conceptual and non-conceptual misconceptions 3. བློ་ཅི་གཉིས་སུ་འདུག་པ་ཐེ་ཚོམ་གྱི་བློ། doubt, e.g. wavering minds 4. མངོན་རྗེས་ཀྱི་ཚད་མ་གཉིས་པོ་རྟོགས་པའི་བློ། discerning mind, e.g. valid direct perception and inferential minds.

བློ་ལ་གཉིས་སུ་དབྱེ་བ།

Ways of dividing mind into two. A. རྟོག་པ་དང་རྟོག་མེད་གཉིས་སུ་དབྱེ་བ། Conceptual and non-conceptual minds. B. ཚད་མ་ཚད་མིན་གཉིསསུ་དབྱེ་བ། Valid and invalid cognitions. C. འཁྲུལ་བ་དང་མ་འཁྲུལ་བའི་ཤེས་པ་གཉིས་སུ་དབྱེ་བ། Mistaken and unmistaken minds. D. རྟོགས་པ་དང་མ་རྟོགས་པ་གཉིས་སུ་དབྱེ་བ། Realized and unrealized minds.

བློའི་གཞན་སེལ།

Mental exclusion of other. An affirming negative which is a mere projection of thought, e.g. the appearance of not not a vase, i.e. the generic image of a vase.

བློས་བྱས་སྟོང་པ་ཉིད།

Intellectually formulated emptiness. Wrongly conceived emptiness.

དབང་།

Abhiṣekha/ Initiation; empowerment. A tantric ceremony in which a lama empowers his disciples to engage in higher practices of tantra through ripening their mental continuum.

དབང་གི་དངོས་གཞིའི་ཆོ་ག

The actual·initiation rite. A part of the initiation programm entailing the erection of the maṇḍala and performing the accomplishment rite (sgrub-mchod), the self-initiation and bestowing initiation to others.

དབང་གི་མཐའ་རྗེས།

The concluding rite of initiation. Offering of the thanks giving maṇḍala, agreeing to abide by the commitments, offering the three gates of activities for the master's service, and dedicating virtues.

དབང་གི་སྦྱོར་བ།

The preparatory rite of initiation. This includes the ground ritual seeking permission for its use, preparatory rites of accomplishment by constructing the maṇḍala be that a powdered sand or painted maṇḍala, and the actual accomplishment rite for a couple of days.

དབང་མངོན་ལྔ།

The five sensory direct perceptions. That of eyes, ears, nose, tongue and body senses.

དབང་བཅུ།

Daśa vaśitāḥ/ The ten powers. The ten powers of Bodhisattvas having transcended the rank of being an ordinary person, i.e.

control over the ten types of harms which a common person is likely to experience. 1. ཚེ་ལ་དབང་བ། control of life-span 2. སེམས་ལ་དབང་བ། control of mind 3. ཡོ་བྱད་ལ་དབང་བ། control of resources 4. ལས་ལ་དབང་བ། control of activities 5. སྐྱེ་བ་ལ་དབང་བ། control of rebirth 6. མོས་པ་ལ་དབང་བ། control of aspiration or wishes 7. སྨོན་ལམ་ལ་དབང་བ། control of prayers 8. རྫུ་འཕྲུལ་ལ་དབང་བ། control of miracles 9. ཆོས་ལ་དབང་བ། control of dharma 10. ཡེ་ཤེས་ལ་དབང་བ། control of wisdom.

དབང་བཅུ་གཅིག

The eleven initiations; the eleven initiations that are gateways to entering yoga tantra. 1-5. སློབ་མའི་དབང་ལྔ། the five initiations of a disciple (see rig-pa'i dbang lnga). 6-11. སློབ་དཔོན་གྱི་དབང་དྲུག the six initiations of the master (see slob-dpon gyi dbang-drug).

དབང་པོ་དགུ

Navendriyāṇi/ The nine powerful faculties. The nine faculties possessed by an Ārya. 1-5. རྣམ་བྱང་གི་དབང་པོ་ལྔ། the five pure powers or purified mental faculties (see dbang-po lnga,-below,-B). 6. ཚོར་བ་བདེ་བ། pleasant feeling 7. ཡིད་བདེ་བ། unpleasant feeling 8. བཏང་སྙོམས། equanimity 9. ཡིད་དབང་། faculty of consciousness.

དབང་པོ་ལྔ།

Pañcendriyāṇi/ The five faculties; the five powers. A. དབང་པོ་གཟུགས་ཅན་པ་ལྔ། The five physical sense faculties (see khams bco-brgyad, 7-12). B. རྣམ་བྱང་གི་དབང་པོ་ལྔ། The five purified mental faculties: 1. དད་པའི་དབང་པོ། śraddhendriyam/ power of faith 2. བརྩོན་འགྲུས་ཀྱི་དབང་པོ། vīryendriyam/ power of effort 3. དྲན་པའི་དབང་པོ། smṛtīndriyam/ power of mindfulness 4. ཏིང་ངེ་འཛིན་གྱི་དབང་པོ། samādhīndriyam/ power of concentration 5. ཤེས་རབ་ཀྱི་དབང་པོ། prajñendriyam/ power of wisdom. C. སོ་སྐྱེའི་རྒྱུད་ཀྱིས་བསྡུས་པའི་ཚོར་བ་ལྔ། The five ever-afflictive faculties; the five feelings of an ordinary person. 1-2. ལུས་ཀྱི་ཚོར་བ་བདེ་སྡུག་གཉིས། the comfortable and uncomfortable feeling of the body 3-4. ཡིད་ཀྱི་ཚོར་བ་ཡིད་བདེ་དང་ཡིད་མི་བདེ་གཉིས། the pleasant and unpleasant feeling of the mind 5. ཚོར་བ་བཏང་སྙོམས། the indifferent feeling.

དབང་པོ་བཅུ་གཅིག

Ekadaśendriyāṇi/ Eleven faculties. 1-5. དབང་པོ་ལྔ། the five sense powers (see dbang-po drug, 1-5) 6. ཁ། mouth 7. ལག་པ། hands 8. རྐང་པ། feet 9. རྐུབ། anus 10. གསང་གནས། secret organs 11. ཡིད་དབང་། faculty of mind.

དབང་པོ་ཉེར་གཉིས།

The twenty-two faculties; the twenty-two powers. 1-7. རྟེན་གྱི་དབང་པོ་བདུན། The seven faculties of reliance (see rten-gy dbang-po bdun). 8-9. རྟེན་ཅན་གྱི་དབང་པོ་གཉིས། The two faculties of basis or sex (see rten-can gyi dbang-po gnyis). 10-14. ཚོར་བའི་དབང་པོ་ལྔ། The five faculties of feeling (see tshor-ba lnga). 15-19. རྣམ་བྱང་གི་དབང་པོ་ལྔ། the five purified faculties (see dbang-po lnga,-B). 20-22. ཟག་མེད་ཀྱི་དབང་པོ་གསུམ། the three uncontaminated faculties (see zag-med kyi dbang-po gsum).

དབང་པོ་དྲུག

Ṣaḍ indriyāṇi/ Six cognitive powers; six faculties; also called the six internal sources of perception (nang-gi skyed-mched drug). 1. མིག་གི་དབང་པོ། cakṣurindriyam/ eye sense power 2. རྣ་བའི་དབང་པོ། śrotrendriyam/ ear sense faculties 3. སྣའི་དབང་པོ། ghraṇendriyam/ nose sense faculties 4. ལྕེའི་དབང་པོ། jihvendriyam/ tongue sense power 5. ལུས་ཀྱི་དབང་པོ། kāyendriyam/ body sense power 6. ཡིད་ཀྱི་དབང་པོ། man indriyam/ mental sense power.

དབང་པོ་གཟུགས་ཅན་པ་ལྔ།

The five physical faculties (see khams bco-brgyad, B. 1-5).

དབང་པོ་གསུམ།

The three faculties. A. The three pure powers gained on the paths of seeing, meditation and no-more learning, respectively (see 6-8 of rnam-byang gi dbang-po brgyad; zag-med kyi dbang-po gsum). B. The three types of persons according to their level of intelligence: 1. དབང་པོ་ཐ་མ། poor intellect 2. དབང་པོ་འབྲིང་། moderate intellect 3. དབང་པོ་རབ། sharp intellect.

དབང་ཕྱུག

Īśvara/ A. Mahadeva (śiva). B. Glory and power. C. Excellence. D. Powerful attainments (siddhi).

དབང་ཕྱུག་བརྒྱད།

A. The eight sovereign qualities (see thun-mong ma-yin-pa'i dbang-phyug-gi yon-tan brgyad). B. The eight powerful attainments; the eight worldly feats (see thun-mong-ba'i dbang-phyug-gi yon-tan brgyad).

དབང་ཕྱུག་བཅུ།

The ten sovereign qualities of a Bodhisattva; the ten powers (see bdang-bcu).

དབང་ཕྱུག་པ།

Īśvara/ The followers of Īśvara. A school of Hindu philosophy which asserts that the world and its inhabitants are created by the projected thought (blo-yi gyo-ba) of Īśvara (Śiva), who they believe to be permanent, omniscient and never changing.

དབང་བཞི།

The four-fold initiations. The four-fold initiations of the highest yoga tantra. 1. བུམ་དབང་། the vase initiation 2. གསང་དབང་། the secret initiation 3. ཤེས་རབ་ཡེ་ཤེས་ཀྱི་དབང་། the primordial-wisdom initiation 4. ཚིག་དབང་། the word initiation.

དབང་བཞི་པ།

The fourth initiation. The verbal initiation of words by which a tantric master introduces his disciple to the union of the pure body (illusory body) and mind (clear light) of a Buddha.

དབང་ལུང་ཁྲིད་གསུམ།

The threefold lineages—initiations, transmissions and explanations.

དབུ་སྡེ་གཉིས།

The two holy assemblies; the two spiritual communities. 1. གོས་དཀར་ལྕང་ལོ་ཅན་གྱི་སྡེ། tantric yogis and yoginīs who wear a white lower garment 2. རབ་བྱུང་ངུར་སྨྲིག་གི་སྡེ། monks and nuns who wear red robes.

དབུ་མ་ཐལ་འགྱུར་བ།

Prāsaṅgika mādhyamika school. The highest school of Mādhyamika philosophy which asserts that phenomena do not exist by their own nature, inherently, not even on the conventional level.

དབུ་མ་པ།

Mādhyamika school. The middle-view school, who assert emptiness as being free of two extremes—the extreme of existence and extreme of non-existence.

དབུ་མ་རང་རྒྱུད་པ།

Svātantrika mādhyamika school. A sub-school of Mādhyamika philosophy which asserts that all phenomena exist by their own nature, inherently, but do not have true existence.

དབུ་མ་རིགས་ཚོགས་ལྔ།

The five middle way treatises. The five famous treatises of Ācarya Nāgārjuna 1. དབུ་མ་རྩ་བ་ཤེས་རབ། prajñāmūla/ *The Fundamental Wisdom of the Middle Way* 2. རྩོད་ཟློག vigrahavyāvartanī/ *Refutation of Arguments* 3. སྟོང་ཉིད་བདུན་ཅུ། Śūnyatāsaptati/ *Seventy Stanzas on Emptiness* 4. རིགས་པ་དྲུག་ཅུ། yuktiṣaṣṭikā/ *Sixty Stanzas of Reasoning* 5. ཞིབ་མོ་རྣམ་འཐག vaidalyasūtra/ *Fine Investigation and Discernment*.

དབུ་མ་རིག་ཚོགས་དྲུག

The six middle way treatises (see above 1-5) 6. རིན་ཆེན་ཕྲེང་བ། ratnāvali/ *The Jewel Garland*.

དབུ་མ་གཞན་སྟོང་།

The alternative emptiness; the other emptiness (see gzhan-stong). The view asserted by Kunkhyen Dolpo-pa, a prophet of Jo-nang school of Tibetan Buddhist philosophy (see gzhan-stong).

དབེན་པ་གསུམ།

The three isolations. A. མདོ་སྔགས་ཐུན་མོང་བའི་དབང་དུ། The three isolations common to both sūtra and tantra traditions. 1. ལུས་འདུ་འཛིས་དབེན་པ། body free of association in busy life 2. སེམས་མི་དགེ་བའི་རྣམ་རྟོག་གིས་དབེན་པ། mind free of non-virtuous conceptualizations 3. སྒོ་གསུམ་ཐ་མལ་གྱི་སྣང་ཞེན་གྱིས་དབེན་པ། the three gates of activities free of ordinary vision and clinging. B. གསང་སྔགས་རྫོགས་རིམ་གྱི་རྣལ་འབྱོར་ལ། According to the Vajrayāna's completion stage yoga of triple isolation (see dben-gsum rdo-rje'i rnal-'byor).

དབེན་གསུམ་རྡོ་རྗེའི་རྣལ་འབྱོར།

Vajrayoga of triple isolation. A meditation practice similiar to the completion stage yoga in highest tantra. 1. ངག་དབེན། isolation of speech 2. ལུས་དབེན། isolation of body 3. སེམས་དབེན། isolation of mind.

དབྱངས་ཀྱི་ཡན་ལག་དྲུག་བཅུ།

The sixty features of a melodic voice; the sixty mellifulous speech. 1. མཉན་པ། flexible 2. འཇམ་པ། soft 3. ཡིད་དུ་འོང་བ། attractive 4. ཡིད་ལ་ཐད་པ། delightful 5. དག་པ། pure 6. དྲི་མ་མེད་པ། faultless 7. གསལ་བ། clear 8. སྙན་ཅིང་འཇེབས་པ། pleasantly soothing 9. མཉན་པར་འོས་པ། worthy of hearing 10. མི་རྩུགས་པ། not harmful 11. སྙན་པ། beautiful 12. དུལ་བ། subdued 13. མི་རྩུབ་པ། not coarse 14. མི་བརླང་པ། not rought 15. རབ་ཏུ་དུལ་བ། completely subdued 16. རྣར་སྙན་པ། beautiful to hear 17. ལུས་སིམ་པར་བྱེད་པ། refreshing for body 18. སེམས་སིམ་པར་བྱེད་པ། refreshing for mind 19. སྙིང་དགའ་བར་བྱེད་པ། pleasing the heart 20. དགའ་བ་དང་བདེ་བ་བསྐྱེད་པ། generating pleasure and happiness 21. ཡོངས་སུ་གདུང་བ་མེད་པ། completely without sadness 22. ཀུན་ཏུ་ཤེས་པར་བྱེད་པ། being the object of universal knowledge 23. རྣམ་པར་རིག་པར་བྱ་བ། being the object of thorough understanding 24. རྣམ་པར་གསལ་བ། completely clear 25. དགའ་བར་བྱེད་པ། producing pleasure 26. མངོན་པར་དགའ་བར་བྱེད་པ། producing manifest pleasure 27. ཀུན་ཏུ་ཤེས་པར་བྱེད་པ། producing universal knowledge 28. རྣམ་པར་རིག་པར་བྱེད་པ། producing thorough understanding 29. རིགས་པ། logical 30. འབྲེལ་བ། relevant 31. ཚིག་ཟློས་པའི་སྐྱོན་མེད་པ། free of repetition 32. སེང་གེའི་སྒྲའི་ཤུགས། possessing the strength of a lion's roar 33. གླང་པོ་ཆེའི་སྒྲ་སྐད། producing the sound of an elephant 34. འབྲུག་གི་སྒྲ་སྐད། producing the sound of a cloud (thunder) 35. ཀླུའི་སྒྲ་སྐད། producing the sound of a Nāga (serpent-spirit) 36. དྲི་ཟའི་གླུ་དབྱངས། producing the sound of Gandharva (a celestial musician) 37. ཀ་ལ་པིང་ཀའི་སྒྲ་དབྱངས། producing the melody of a sparrow 38. ཚངས་པའི་སྒྲ་དབྱངས། producing the melody of Brahma 39. ཤང་ཤང་ཏེའུ་སྒྲ་དབྱངས་བསྒྲགས་པ། producing the sound of a jīvañjīvaka bird 40. ལྷའི་དབང་པོའི་དབྱངས་ལྟར་སྙན་པ། pleasant as the melodies of the lord of gods 41. རྔ་ཡི་སྒྲ། producing the sound of a dundubhi drum 42. མ་ཁེངས་པ། free of arrogance 43. མི་དམའ་བ། not degraded 44. སྒྲ་ཐམས་ཅད་ཀྱི་རྗེས་སུ་ཞུགས་པ། harmonious to all sounds 45. ཚིག་ཟུར་ཆག་པ་མེད་པ། free of corrupted words 46. མ་ཚང་བ་མེད་པ། not incomplete 47. མ་ཞུམ་པ། not crying 48. མ་ཞན་པ། not depressed 49. རབ་ཏུ་དགའ་བ། extremely joyous 50. ཁྱབ་པ། pervasive 51. རྫུབ་པ། perfected 52. རྒྱུན་ཆགས་པ། flowing 53. འགྲེལ་བ། elegantly connected 54. སྒྲ་ཐམས་ཅད་རྫོགས་པར་བྱེད་པ། making all sounds complete 55. དབང་པོ་ཐམས་ཅད་ཚིམ་པར་བྱེད་པ། satisfying all senses 56. མ་སྨད་པ། non-abusive 57. མི་འགྱུར་བ། unchanging 58. མ་བརྟགས་པ། unwavering 59. འཁོར་ཀུན་ཏུ་གྲགས་པ། popular in all circles 60. རྣམ་པ་ཐམས་ཅད་ཀྱི་མཆོག་དང་ལྡན་པ། possessing the best of all components.

དབྱངས་ཀྱིས་བསྙད་པའི་སྡེ།

Verse-form teachings. One of the twelve scriptural categories (see gsung-rab yan-lag bcu-gnyis); verses which Buddha uttered during the beginning or conclusion of a discourse.

དབྱངས་ཅན་མ།

Sarasvatīdevī. Goddess of eloquence. A goddess of both the Hindu and Buddhist pantheons, worshipped as the perfection of eloquence and regarded as the embodiment of mellifluent clarity of sound and speech.

དབྱར་སྔ་མ།

Early summer retreat. Observance of a summer or rainy season retreat by the monastic communities from the sixteenth of the sixth month of the Tibetan calendar until the thirtieth of the eighth month. The tradition followed by the monastic community in general.

དབྱར་གནས།

Vārṣika/ Summer retreat. One of the three basic observances for monks as prescribed by Buddha Śākyamuni; rainy season retreat during which time they do not go beyond the marked bounds of the monasteries and observe rules and regulations in addition to their regular routine.

དབྱར་ཕྱི་མ།

Later summer retreat. Observance of a summer retreat by the monastic communities from the sixteenth day of the seventh month of the Tibetan calendar until thirtieth of the eighth month. This tradition is followed by both the upper and lower tantric colleges of Lhasa.

དབྱིག་གཉེན།

Vasubandhu. Regarded as a renowned Buddhist scholar of the 5th century, the younger brother of Ārya Asaṅga and the author of *Abhidharmakośaṭika* and the eight treatises of Vasubandhu (see pra-ka-ra-na sde-brgyad).

དབྱིབས་སྔགས་ཆོས་གསུམ།

The threefold practices; the three generation stage yogas or practices: 1. བསྐྱེད་པ་དབྱིབས་ཀྱི་རྣལ་འབྱོར། the yoga of generating into the shape and form of a deity 2. བཟླས་པ་སྔགས་ཀྱི་རྣལ་འབྱོར། the yoga of reciting mantras of the deity 3. འོད་གསལ་འཇུག་ལྡང་ཆོས་ཀྱི་རྣལ་འབྱོར། the yoga of dissolution and arisal within the clear light experience.

དབྱིབས་གཟུགས་བརྒྱད།

Eight types of shape and form. 1. རིང་བ། long 2. ཐུང་བ།

short 3. མཐོ་བ། high 4. དམའ་བ། low 5. གྲུ་བཞི་པ། square 6. ཟླུམ་པོ། round 7. ཕྱ་ལེ་བ། even 8. ཕྱ་ལེ་བ་མ་ཡིན་པ། uneven.

དབྱེར་མེད་ཆོས་སྐུ།

Inseparable truth body. The inseparability of the emanation body, enjoyment body and the natural truth body of a Buddha.

དབྱེར་མེད་རྡོ་རྗེའི་གསུང་།

The inseparable vajra teachings. One of the five kinds of teachings of a Buddha (see bsung-lnga) according to the Nyingma tradition. This refers to the non-duality of sound and emptiness of all speeches and teachings of a Buddha being totally free of the two extremes.

འབའ་རོམ་བཀའ་བརྒྱུད།

Bamrom Kagyu tradition. One of the eight lineages of Kagyu tradition of Tibetan Buddhism founded by Gampopa's disciple, Bamrom Darma Wangchuk who is believed to have been the incarnation of Tulzug Choepa Nagpopa.

འབུར་པོ་ལྔ།

Five protruberances. That state of foetal development in the womb of a mother when the signs of five parts of body become obvious. 1-2. དཔྱིས་མོ་གཉིས། signs of two legs 3-4. དཔུང་པ་གཉིས། signs of two arms 5. མགོ། the head.

འབྱུང་འགྱུར་གྱི་རེག་བྱ་བདུན།

Seven tangible objects arising from the elements; seven objects of touch that are transformations of the four elements. 1. འཇམ་པ། smoothness 2. རྩུབ་པ། roughness 3. ཡང་བ། lightness 4. ལྗི་བ། heaviness 5. གྲང་བ། coldness 6. བཀྲེས་པ། hunger 7. སྐོམ་པ། thirst.

འབྱུར་འགྱུར་གྱི་རེག་བྱ་ཉེར་གཉིས།

Twenty-two tangible objects arising from the elements. 1-7. (see 'byung-'gyur-gyi reg-bya-bdun, above) 8. མཉེན་པ། pliancy 9. ལྷོད་པ། loseness 10. ལྷོད་པ་མ་ཡིན་པ། tauntness 11. ཚིམ་པ། contentment 12. ཉམ་ཆེ་བ། strong 13. ཉམ་ཆུང་བ། weak 14. བརྒྱལ་བ། fainting/ swooning 15. གཡའ་བ། itching 16. བགྲོད་པ། slipperiness 17. ན་བ། illness 18. རྒ་བ། aging 19. འཆི་བ། death 20. ངལ་བ། fatigue 21. ངལ་གསོ་བ། rest 22. ལྕིངས་ཆེ་བ། weighty.

འབྱུང་བ་བཞི།

The four elements. 1. ས། earth 2. ཆུ། water 3. མེ། fire 4. རླུང་། wind. When it is five add ནམ་མཁའ། space; and when six add རྣམ་ཤེས། consciousness.

འབྱོར་བ་བཅུ།

Ten endowments; ten condusive factors for a person to practise dharma. 1. མི་ཡིན་པ། being a human 2. ཡུལ་དབུས་སུ་སྐྱེས་པ། being born in a Buddhist land 3. དབང་པོ་ཚང་བ། having sound senses 4. ལས་མཐའ་མ་ལོག་པ། being free from extreme actions 5. ཆོས་ལ་དད་པ། having faith in the Dharma 6. སངས་རྒྱས་བྱོན་པ། Buddha's having appeared 7. དམ་ཆོས་གསུངས་པ། Buddha's having taught the Dharma 8. བསྟན་པ་གནས་པ། the flourishing of his teachings 9. དེའི་རྗེས་སུ་འཇུག་པ་བཞུགས་པ། there being people following his teachings 10. གཞན་ལ་ཐུག་ཏུ་བརྩེ་བ་སྙིང་རྗེ་དང་ལྡན་པ། having compassionate feelings towards others.

འབྲས་སྐྱབས།

Phala śaraṇa/ The resultant refuge. The fully enlightened state of Buddha in one's own continuum, i.e. that fully enlightened refuge developed within oneself.

འབྲས་ཆོས་ལྔ།

The five resultant phenomena; the five qualities of Buddhahood. Those of the body, speech, mind, qualities, and enlightened activities of a Buddha.

འབྲས་ཆོས་ཉེར་ལྔ།

The twenty-five resultant phenomena; the five each with respect to the body, speech, mind, qualities and enlightened activities of a Buddha according to the explanation given in the Nyingma tantras.

འབྲས་རྟགས་ཡང་དག

Correct reason of effect. A correct reason which is the effect of the predicate in a logical syllogism.

འབྲས་རྟགས་ཡང་དག་གི་དབྱེ་བ་ལྔ།

Five divisions of correct reason of result. 1. རྒྱུ་དངོས་སྒྲུབ་ཀྱི་རྟགས། that establishing the direct cause 2. རྒྱུ་སྔོན་སོང་གི་རྟགས། that establishing the preceding cause 3. རྒྱུ་སྤྱི་སྒྲུབ་ཀྱི་རྟགས། that establishing the general cause 4. རྒྱུ་ཁྱད་པར་སྒྲུབ་ཀྱི་རྟགས། that establishing the particular cause 5. རྒྱུ་ཆོས་རྗེས་དཔོག་གི་རྟགས། that establishing the quality of a cause.

འབྲས་དུས་ཀྱི་འོད་གསལ།

The resultant clear light. The perfect realization of the final reality of the basic primordial clear light existent within oneself as introduced by a qualified meditation master, and the ability to maintain this experience day and night.

འབྲས་བུ་ལྔ།

Pañca phalāni/ Five types of results; five types of fruits. 1. རྒྱུ་མཐུན་གྱི་འབྲས་བུ། niṣyanda phalam/ results that accord with the cause 2. བདག་པོའི་འབྲས་བུ། adhipati phalam/ environmental cause 3. སྐྱེས་བུའི་བྱེད་པའི་འབྲས་བུ། puruṣa kāra phalam/ results caused by persons 4. རྣམ་པར་སྨིན་པའི་འབྲས་བུ། vipāka phalam/ ripened results 5. བྲལ་བའི་འབྲས་བུ། visaṁyoga phalam/ cessational results.

འབྲས་བུ་ཆོས་སྐུ་མཚན་བྱེད་ཀྱི་ཆོས་བཞི།

Four features characterizing the resultant Truth Body of a Buddha. 1. ངོ་བོ་ཉིད་སྐུ svabhāvakāya/ the nature truth body 2. ཡེ་ཤེས་ཆོས་སྐུ jñānadharmakāya/ the wisdom truth body 3. ལོངས་སྐུ saṁbhogakāya/ the complete enjoyment body 4. སྤྲུལ་སྐུ nirmāṇakāya/ the emanation body

འབྲས་བུ་ཐོད་རྒལ།

He who attains the fruit by leaps.

འབྲས་བུ་རིམ་གྱིས་པ།

He who attains the fruit successively.

འབྲས་བུའི་ཐེག་པ་དྲུག

The five resultant vehicles; the five tantric vehicles or paths. 1-4. The four classes of tantra (see rgyud-sde bzhi) 5. ཨ་ནུ་ཡོ་ག anuyoga vehicle 6. ཨ་ཏི་ཡོ་ག atiyoga vehicle.

འབྲས་བུའི་འོད་གསལ།

The resultant clear light. The dharmakāya itself.

འབྲས་གཟུགས་བཅུ་གཅིག

Eleven resultant forms. 1-5. དབང་པོ་གཟུགས་ཅན་པ་ལྔ། five physical sense faculties (see dbang-po drug, 1-5) 6-10. གཟུང་དོན་ལྔ། five objects of perception (see yul-drug) 11. ཆོས་ཀྱི་སྐྱེ་མཆེད་པའི་གཟུགས། abstract forms that are sources for mental consciousness.

འབྲས་ཡུམ་ལ་ཉེ་བའི་གཞི་ཤེས།

Phalabhūtamāturāsannībhūta vastujñāna/ Basic wisdom close to the resultant mother. The knowledge of the basis near to omniscient wisdom; synonymous with the knowledge of the basis (gzhi-shes) within the mental continuum of a Mahāyāna Ārya that is conjoined with exalted means and wisdom, characterized as an antidote towards grasping at true existence.

འབྲས་ཡུམ་ལ་རིང་བའི་གཞི་ཤེས།

Phalabhūtamāturadūrībhūta vastujñāna/ Basic wisdom distant from the resultant mother; knowledge of the basis distant from omniscient wisdom; synonymous with the knowledge of the basis within the mental continuum of a Hīnayāna Ārya, that lacks great compassion and is bound by grasping at true existence.

འབྲི་གུང་བཀའ་བརྒྱུད།

Drikung Kagyud. One of the prominent linaeges of the Kagyud order of Tibetan Buddhism, founded by the master Kyoba Jigten Gonpo (1143-1217).

འབྲུག་པ་བཀའ་བརྒྱུད།

Drugpa Kagyud. One of the prominent lineages of the Kagyu order of Tibetan Buddhism, founded by Yogi Lingrepa Pema Dorje and Choeje Tsangpa Gyalre.

འབྲེལ་བ་གཉིས།

Two types of relationship. Relationship between any phenomena can come under these two forms. 1. བདག་གཅིག་འབྲེལ། relationship of identical nature 2. དེ་བྱུང་འབྲེལ། cause and result relationship.

འགྲོག་དགོན་པ།

Kāntāra/ Hermitage. Monastery or seat of learning for monks situated at least 500 armspans away from a town; a hermitage is situated further away then this according to the Vinaya rules.

སྦས་དོན།

Hidden meaning; implicit meaning, e.g. the teachings of emptiness presented in the text, *Ornament of Clear Realization.*

སྦོམ་པོ་བརྒྱད།

Eight major transgressions (of tantric vows). 1. མཚན་ཉིད་མི་ལྡན་པའི་རིག་མ་བསྟེན་པ། relying on an unqualified consort 2. འདུ་ཤེས་གསུམ་དང་བྲལ་བའི་སྙོམས་འཇུག་ལ་གནས་པ། being in union without the three recognitions 3. སྣོད་མིན་པ་ལ་གསང་བ་སྟོན་པ། revealing secret substances of one's Lama and his consort to those who are not proper vessels 4. ཚོགས་ཀྱི་འཁོར་ལོའི་དུས་སུ་རྩོད་པ། quarreling or arguing during an offering assembly 5. དད་པས་ཆོས་འདྲི་བ་ལ་ལན་ལོག་པ། giving wrong answers to sincere questions 6. ཉན་ཐོས་ནང་དུ་ཞག་བདུན་ལོང་བར་བསྡད་པ། spending more than seven days in the home of a Hearer 7. རྣལ་འབྱོར་པའི་མཚན་ཉིད་དང་མི་ལྡན་པར་ཕྲུགས་པར་རློམ་པ། pretending to be a great yogi when you are not 8. དད་པ་མེད་པ་ལ་དམ་ཆོས་སྟོན་པ། giving teachings to those who do not have faith in them.

སྦྱངས་པའི་ཡོན་ཏན་བཅུ་གཉིས།

Dvādaśa dhūta guṇāḥ/ Twelve ascetic practices; twelve disciplines of a strict practitioner. 1. གོས་ཕྱག་དར་ཁྲོད་པ། pāṁśukūlika/ wearing robes made of rags 2. ཆོས་གོས་གསུམ་པ། traicīvarika/ wearing the three dharma robes 3. ཕྱིང་བ་པ། nāmatika/ wearing robes made only of wool 4. སྟན་གཅིག་པ། aikāsanika/ eating one's food in one sitting 5. བསོད་སྙོམས་པ། paiṇḍapātika/ subsisting on alms 6. ཟས་ཕྱིས་མི་ལེན་པ། khalupaścād bhaktika/ not accepting food after having risen from one's seat 7. དགོན་པ་བ། āraṇyaka/ dwelling in a hermitage 8. ཤིང་དྲུང་པ། vṛkṣamūlika/ dwelling at the foot of a tree/ forest dweller 9. བླ་གབ་མེད་པ། ābhyavakāśika/ dwelling in an open and unsheltered place 10. དུར་ཁྲོད་པ། śmāśānika/ dwelling in cemeteries 11. ཙོག་པུ་བ། naiṣadika/ remaining in the sitting posture 12. གཞི་ཇི་བཞིན་པ། yāthāsaṁstarika/ sleeping wherever one may happen to be.

སྦྱིན་པ་རྣམ་གསུམ།

Three types of giving. 1. ཟང་ཟིང་གི་སྦྱིན་པ། giving material help 2. མི་འཇིགས་པའི་སྦྱིན་པ། giving protection from fear 3. ཆོས་ཀྱི་སྦྱིན་པ། giving dharma teachings. When it is five add 5. བྱམས་པའི་སྦྱིན་པ། giving of love.

སྦྱོར་སྒྲོལ་གྱི་སྤྱོད་པ།

Corrupt practice of liberation through union. The name given to the corrupt practice spread in Tibet by the so called Red Ācārya and the Paṇḍita with blue lower robes from India, the period between Lang Darma and the coming of Atiśa. They spread the erroneous teaching that liberation is attained through mere union with consorts and killing of animals.

སྦྱོར་བ།

Prayoga/ A. Trainings; practices. B. Commitment of an action; one of the four factors determining the completion of an action. C. Preliminaries to an actual practice.

སྦྱོར་བ་ཉི་ཤུ།

Twenty trainings. The twenty trainings of a Bodhisattva's meditation on the combination of the three basic trainings. 1. བདེན་ཞེན་ལ་མི་གནས་པའི་སྦྱོར་བ། training that does not focus on grasping at true existence 2. བདེན་ཞེན་བཀག་པའི་སྦྱོར་བ། training free from grasping at true existence 3. ཟབ་པའི་སྦྱོར་བ། profound training 4. གཏིང་དཔག་དཀའ་བའི་སྦྱོར་བ། training that is hard to fathom 5. ཚད་མེད་པའི་སྦྱོར་བ། immeasurable training 6. ཚེགས་ཆེན་ཡུན་རིང་རྟོགས་པའི་སྦྱོར་བ། training that leads to enlightenment painfully after a long period 7. ལུང་བསྟན་ཐོབ་པའི་སྦྱོར་བ། training bestowed with prediction 8. ཕྱིར་མི་ལྡོག་པའི་སྦྱོར་བ། irreversible training 9. ངེས་པར་འབྱུང་བའི་སྦྱོར་བ། training of definite actualization 10. བར་ཆད་མེད་པའི་སྦྱོར་བ། training free of impediments 11. བྱང་ཆུབ་ལ་ཉེ་བའི་སྦྱོར་བ། training that is close to enlightenment 12. མྱུར་དུ་འཚང་རྒྱ་བའི་སྦྱོར་བ། training leading to quick enlightenment 13. གཞན་གྱི་དོན་གྱི་སྦྱོར་བ། training for the welfare of others 14. འཕེལ་མེད་གྲིབ་མེད་ཀྱི་སྦྱོར་བ། training without progression or regression 15. ཆོས་དང་ཆོས་མིན་སོགས་མི་མཐོང་བའི་སྦྱོར་བ། training in not seeing either dharma or non-dharma 16. བསམ་མི་ཁྱབ་པའི་སྦྱོར་བ། inconceiveable training 17. རྣམ་པར་མི་རྟོག་པའི་སྦྱོར་བ། training free from conceptual elaboration 18. འབྲས་བུ་རིན་ཆེན་སྦྱིན་པའི་སྦྱོར་བ། training bestowing the jewel of fruits 19. གནས་ངན་ལེན་ཕྲ་མོ་དག་པར་བྱེད་པའི་སྦྱོར་བ། training purifying subtle negativities 20. ས་མཚམས་ཀྱི་སྦྱོར་བ། training within prescribed limits.

སྦྱོར་བ་བཞི།

Four trainings; the four Bodhisattva trainings. 1. རྣམ་རྫོགས་སྦྱོར་བ། training of complete aspects 2. རྩེ་མོའི་སྦྱོར་བ། peak training 3. མཐར་གྱིས་སྦྱོར་བ། serial training 4. སྐད་ཅིག་མའི་སྦྱོར་བ། momentary training.

སྦྱོར་བ་ཡན་ལག་བཅུ།

The ten approaches; བྱ་རྒྱུད་ཀྱི་སྦྱོར་བའི་སྤྱོད་པའི་ཡན་ལག་སྟེ། the ways of approaching or undertaking action tantra practices. 1. སྔགས་པ་སྒྲུབ་པ་པོ། tantrika as the practitioner 2. རང་སྔགས་བསྒྲུབ་པར་བྱ་བའི་ལྷ། oneself as the deity for accomplishing the mantra 3. གཡོག་སྒྲུབ་པའི་གྲོགས་མཆོག helpers as the supreme friends for one's accomplishments 4. ལྡོང་རོས་ལ་སོགས་པའི་རྫས། possessing ldong-ros stones and others as the substances or articles 5. སྦྱོར་བའི་བརྩོན་འགྲུས། application as the enthusiastic perseverance 6. དབུས་ལ་སོགས་པའི་ཡུལ་ཕྱོགས། living in a central land or otherwise as the place of living 7. རི་རྩེ་ལ་སོགས་པའི་གཞིའི་གནས། location in the mountains etc., as the environment 8. དཔྱིད་ཟླ་དང་སྔ་དྲོ་ལ་སོགས་པའི་དུས། spring time and mornings as the period of practice 9. རི་མོ་དང་གཟུགས་སྐུ་ལ་སོགས་པའི་

ཡན་ལག་རྫོགས་པའི་ལྷ། possessing qualified images and paintings of deities 10. འཇིགས་པ་མེད་ཅིང་སྲན་ཆེ་བའི་སེམས་སྟོབས། fearlessness and forbearance as the spirit of carrying out practices.

སྦྱོར་བ་ཡན་ལག་དྲུག

The six yogas of the Kālacakra tantra. The yogas of wind meditation according to the completion stage practices in the Kālacakra tantra. 1. སོར་སྡུད། withdrawal 2. བསམ་གཏན། concentration 3. སྲོག་རྩོལ། pinpointing the life-sustaining wind 4. འཛིན་པ། retention 5. རྗེས་དྲན། recollection 6. ཏིང་འཛིན། single-pointed concentration.

སྦྱོར་བའི་ཆོས་དྲུག

Six preparatory practices. The six ways to prepare oneself for a daily session of meditation. 1. གནས་ཁང་བྱི་དོར་བྱས་པ། cleaning the room or place of practice 2. རྟེན་བཀྲམས་ཤིང་མཆོད་པ་གཡོ་མེད་པར་གཤམས་པ། arranging symbolic objects of refuge and pure offerings 3. ལུས་རྣམ་སྣང་ཆོས་བདུན་གྱི་སྒོ་ནས་སྐྱབས་འགྲོ་སེམས་བསྐྱེད་བྱ་བ། sitting on a comfortable cushion and maintaining the seven-fold posture of Vairocana (see rnam-snang chos-bdun), then taking refuge and generating the mind of enlightenment (bodhicitta) 4. ཚོགས་ཞིང་གསལ་བཏབ་པ། visualizing the merit-field 5. མཎྜལ་དང་འབྲིལ་ཡན་ལག་བདུན་པ་བྱ་བ། offering the seven branch practice and the maṇḍala of the universe 6. རྒྱུད་དང་འདྲེས་ངེས་ཀྱི་གསོལ་བ་བཏབ་པ། making powerful supplication and prayers from one's heart.

སྦྱོར་བའི་ཡོན་ཏན་བཅུ་བཞི།

Fourteen qualities of (a Bodhisattva's) training. 1. བདུད་ཀྱི་མཐུ་བཅོམ་པ། annihilation of demonic powers 2. སངས་རྒྱས་ཀྱི་དགོངས་ཤིང་མཁྱེན་པ། attention and knowledge of the Buddhas 3. སངས་རྒྱས་ཀྱི་མངོན་སུམ་དུ་མཛད་པ། being within the sight of the Buddhas 4. རྫོགས་བྱང་ལ་ཉེ་བར་འགྱུར་བ། nearing the state of enlightenment 5. རྣམ་པར་སྨིན་པ་ཆེ་བ། greatness of ripened results 6. ཤེར་ཕྱིན་ཟབ་མོ་སྨྲ་བའི་སྐྱེ་བོ་ཉིད་དུ་འགྱུར་བ། becoming a proponent of the perfection of wisdom teaching 7. རྫོགས་བྱང་ལ་མི་ཕྱེད་པ། non-deflection from complete enlightenment 8. དགེ་བའི་རྩ་བ་ཐུན་མོང་མ་ཡིན་པ་སྐྱེ་བ། cultivation of special roots of virtues 9. དམ་བཅའ་བའི་དོན་ཐམས་ཅད་སྒྲུབ་པ། accomplishment of all the pledges and vows 10. རྣམ་སྨིན་གྱི་འབྲས་བུ་རྒྱ་ཆེ་བ། achievement of extensive and great fruits of merits 11. སེམས་ཅན་གྱི་དོན་སྒྲུབ་ནུས་པ། ability to work for the welfare of other sentient beings 12. ཚེ་བརྗེས་ཀྱང་ཤེར་ཕྱིན་ཟབ་མོ་ངེས་པར་ཐོབ་པ། attainment of profound perfection of wisdom from life to life 13. ཤེས་ཕྱིན་ཟབ་མོ་གང་དུ་དར་བའི་ཡུལ་དེར་སྐྲིས་ནས་འབྲི་བ་དང་ཁ་ཏོན་དུ་བྱ་བ། copying and reciting the perfection of wisdom teachings everywhere that the teachings flourish 14. ཡོན་ཏན་ཐམས་ཅད་ཡོངས་སུ་རྫོགས་པ། accomplishment of all good qualities.

སྦྱོར་བྱུང་གི་མུ་སྟེགས་པ།

Two types of forders; two types of non-Buddhists. These non-Buddhists are said to be possessing the five extra-sensory perceptions and the ability to fly. 1. non-buddhist through meditation 2. non-Buddhist through logic.

སྦྱོར་ལམ།

Prayoga mārga/ Path of preparation. The second of the five paths, where a practitioner gains conceptual understanding of emptiness.

སྦྱོར་ལམ་དྲོད་ཀྱི་རྣམ་པ་བཅུ།

Ten aspects of the heat level of the path of preparation. 1. སེམས་ཅན་ཐམས་ཅད་ལ་སེམས་མཉམ་པ། equality of attitude towards all sentient beings 2. བྱམས་པའི་སེམས་དང་ལྡན་པ།

attitude of love towards all sentient beings 3. ཕན་པའི་སེམས་དང་ལྡན་པ། attitude of benefit towards all sentient beings 4. ཁོང་ཁྲོ་བ་མེད་པའི་སེམས་དང་ལྡན་པ། attitude free from anger towards all sentient beings 5. རྣམ་པར་འཚེ་བ་མེད་པའི་སེམས་དང་ལྡན་པ། attitude of non-violence towards all sentient beings 6. རྒན་པ་རྣམས་ལ་ཕ་མའི་སེམས་དང་ལྡན་པ། attitude of regarding elders as one's parents 7. ན་མཉམ་པ་རྣམས་ལ་སྤུན་དང་སྲིང་མོའི་སེམས་དང་ལྡན་པ། attitude of regarding one's peers as brothers and sisters 8. གཞོན་པ་རྣམས་ལ་བུ་དང་བུ་མོའི་སེམས་དང་ལྡན་པ། attitude of regarding the youngsters as sons and daughters 9. བར་མ་རྣམས་ལ་མཛའ་བཤེས་དང་གྲོགས་ཀྱི་སེམས་དང་ལྡན་པ། attitude of regarding equals as one's friends 10. སེམས་ཅན་ཐམས་ཅད་ལ་གཉེན་དང་གཉེན་མཚམས་ཀྱི་སེམས་དང་ལྡན་པ། attitude of friendliness towards all sentient beings.

སྦྱོར་ལམ་དྲོད་ཕྱིར་མི་ལྡོག་པའི་རྟགས་བཅུ་གཅིག

Eleven marks of irreversibility of a Bodhisattva on the heat level of the path of preparation. 1. གཞན་དོན་དུ་གཟུགས་སོགས་ལ་བདེན་ཞེན་ལྡོག་པ། he has turned away from grasping at true forms, etc. 2. སྐྱབས་གསུམ་ལ་ཐེ་ཚོམ་ཟད་པ། he has extinguished doubts concerning the three jewels of refuge 3. མི་ཁོམས་པ་བརྒྱད་ཟད་པ། he has extinguished the eight non-condusive states (see mi-khoms-pa brgyad) 4. རང་གཞན་གཉིས་ཀ་དགེ་བའི་ཆོས་ལ་སྦྱོར་བ། he encourages both himself and others in dharma practice 5. བདག་གཞན་བརྗེ་བའི་བསམ་པས་སྦྱིན་པ། he practices giving with the thought of exchanging self-concern for concern for others 6. ཟབ་མོའི་དོན་ལ་སོམ་ཉི་མི་བྱེད་པ། he has no doubt concerning the meaning of the profound emptiness 7. སྒོ་གསུམ་གྱི་སྤྱོད་པ་བྱམས་པའི་སེམས་ཀྱིས་སྤྱོད་པ། he performs the deeds of body, speech and mind with love 8. སྒྲིབ་པ་ལྔ་དང་མི་འགྲོགས་པ། he never associates himself with the five obstructions 9. བག་ལ་ཉལ་ཀུན་འཇོམས་པ། he has subdued all evil latencies 10. རྟག་ཏུ་དྲན་ཤེས་དང་ལྡན་པ། he is always mindful and alert 11. གོས་སོགས་ཡོངས་སུ་སྤྱོད་པ་གཙང་བ། he wears neat and clean cloth, etc.

སྦྱོར་ལམ་རྩེ་སྦྱོར།

Mūrdha prayoga mārga/ Peak training of the path of preparation. The Bodhisattva practices at the the peak level of the Mahāyāna path of preparation, on which he has gained a conceptual understanding of the emptiness conjoined with the mind of enlightenment.

སྦྱོར་ལམ་བཞི།

The four levels of the path of preparation; the second of the five paths. 1. དྲོད། heat level, whereupon the first sign of attaining the wisdom of the path of seeing is felt. 2. རྩེ་མོ། peak level, where one has gained irreversible signs of one's wholesome qualities for the first time 3. བཟོད་པ། forbearance level, whereupon one initially gains confidence to overcome fear from experiencing emptiness 4. ཆོས་མཆོག supramundane level, the final level of the path of preparation liable to ensure direct bare perception of emptiness in the next immediate instant.

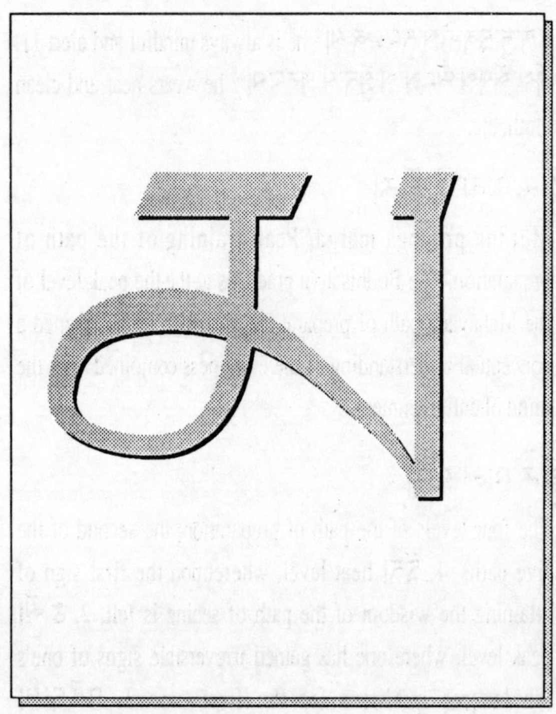

མ་སྐྱེས་དགྲ

Ajātaśatru; King Ajātaśatru of Magadha in India during the time of Buddha Śākyamuni. After Buddha's passing away into parinirvāṇa at Rājagṛha, he sponsored the first council (see bka'-bsdu gsum).

མ་འཁྲུལ་བའི་ཤེས་པ།

Abhrāntajñāna/ Unmistaken perception; non-deceptive cognition. An awareness that is unmistaken with respect to its appearing object, e.g. the first moment that eye sense perception cognizes a tree.

མ་གྲུབ་པའི་ཡིད་དཔྱོད།

Unestablished presumption; incorrect belief. Presuming what is true for an irrelevent reason.

མ་བསྒྲིབས་ལུང་མ་བསྟན།

Anivṛtāvyākṛta/ Non-obscured unspecified phenomena. Those categories of phenomena that are not deluded by nature, yet are neither virtuous nor non-virtuous with respect to their results, e.g. the universe, permanent phenomena.

མ་རྒྱུད།

Mātā tantra/ Mother tantra. The highest class of tantric teachings mainly emphasizing the development of the clear light mind, e.g. Cakrasambhava tantra.

མ་རྒྱུད་རིགས་དྲུག

Six families of the mother tantra. 1. རྡོར་སེམས་ཀྱི་རིགས། Vajrasattva tantra 2. རྣམ་སྣང་གི་རིགས། Vairocana tantra 3. ཧེ་རུ་ཀའི་རིགས། Heruka tantra 4. རྡོ་རྗེ་ཉི་མའི་རིགས། Vajrasūrya tantra 5. པད་མ་གར་དབང་གི་རིགས། Padmanarteśvara tantra 6. རྟ་མཆོག་གི་རིགས། Paramāśva tantra.

མ་ངེས་པའི་ཡིད་དཔྱོད།

Indefinite presumption. Presuming what is true to be so for an undetermined reason.

མ་ངེས་པའི་ས་མང་བརྒྱད།

Asṭāniyata bhūmikāḥ/ Eight indefinite levels of thought; eight uncertain secondary mental factors. 1. རྟོག་པ། vitarka/ rough investigation 2. དཔྱོད་པ། vicāra/ subtle investigation 3. འགྱོད་པ། kaukṛtya/ regret 4. གཉིད། nidrā/ sleep 5. ཁོང་ཁྲོ། krodha/ anger 6. ཆགས་པ། rāga/ attachment 7. ང་རྒྱལ། māna/ pride 8. ཐེ་ཚོམ། vicikitsā/ doubt.

མ་ཅིག་ལབ་སྒྲོན།

Machig Labkyi Dolma (1055-1145). A renowned female practitioner of the cutting-off ritual (gcod), a disciple of Phadampa Sangye.

མ་དག་པའི་སྒྱུ་ལུས།

Aśuddha māyakāya/ Impure illusory body. A completion stage practice of tantra in which a meditator establishes the lack of non-inherent existence of all phenomena and their illusory nature of appearances.

མ་དག་ས་བདུན།

Saptāśuddha bhūmayaḥ/ Seven impure grounds; the first seven of the ten Bodhisattva grounds (see sa-bcu, 1-7), in which a Bodhisattva possesses subtle pride still to be purified.

མ་འདྲེས་པ་བཅོ་བརྒྱད།

Aṣṭādaśāveṇika buddha dharmāḥ/ Eighteen unshared qualities of a Buddha (also see sangs-rgyas-kyi chos ma-'dres-pa bco-brgyad). A. སྤྱོད་པས་བསྡུས་པ་དྲུག Six of behaviour: 1. སྐུའི་སྤྱོད་པ་འཁྲུལ་བ་མི་མངའ་བ། nāsti tathāgatasya skhalitam/ possessing unmistaken bodily qualities 2. གསུང་ཅ་ཅོ་མི་མངའ་བ། nāsti ravitam/ not possessing unskillful (noisy) speech 3. དྲན་པ་ཉམས་པ་མི་མངའ་བ། nāsti muṣita smṛtitā/ possessing undeclined memory 4. ཐུགས་མཉམ་པར་མ་གཞག་པ་མི་མངའ་བ། nāstyasamāhita cittam/ constant abidance in meditative equipoise 5. སྤང་དོར་ངོ་བོ་ཉིད་ཀྱིས་གྲུབ་པའི་ཐ་དད་པ་ཉིད་ཀྱི་འདུ་ཤེས་མི་མངའ་བ། nāsti nānātva samjñā/ realizing that cultivation and elimination are not inherently different 6. སོ་སོར་མ་བརྟག་པའི་བཏང་སྙོམས་མི་མངའ་བ། nāstyapratisaṁkhyāyopekṣā/ possessing indiscriminate equiminity. B. རྟོགས་པས་བསྡུས་པ་དྲུག Six of insight/ wisdom: 7. འདུན་པ་ཉམས་པ་མི་མངའ་བ། nāsti cchandasya hāni/ possessing undeclining aspiration 8. བརྩོན་འགྲུས་ཉམས་པ་མི་མངའ་བ། nāsti vīryasya hāni/ possessing undeclining effort 9. སེམས་ཅན་འདུལ་བའི་ཐབས་དྲན་པ་ཉམས་པ་མི་མངའ་བ། nāsti smṛti hāni/ possessing undeclining mindfulness as a means for taming sentient beings 10. ཏིང་ངེ་འཛིན་ཉམས་པ་མི་མངའ་བ། nāsti samādhi hāni/ possessing undeclining single-pointed concentration 11. ཤེས་རབ་ཉམས་པ་མི་མངའ་བ། nāsti prajñāyā hāni/ possessing undeclining wisdom 12. རྣམ་པར་གྲོལ་བའི་ལམ་ཉམས་པ་མི་མངའ་བ། nāsti vimukti hāni/ possessing irreversibility from liberated paths. C. མཛད་པས་བསྡུས་པ་གསུམ། Three of virtuous activity: 13. སྐུའི་འཕྲིན་ལས། kāyakarma/ virtuous activity of body 14. གསུང་གི་འཕྲིན་ལས། vākkarma/ virtuous activity of speech 15. ཐུགས་ཀྱི་འཕྲིན་ལས། manaḥ karma/ virtuous activity of mind. D. དུས་ཀྱིས་བསྡུས་པ་གསུམ། Three of time: 16. འདས་པའི་དུས་མཁྱེན་པ་ལ་མ་ཐོགས་མ་ཆགས་པའི་ཡེ་ཤེས། atīte 'dhvanyasaṅgam apratihataṁ jñānadarśanaṁ parvartate/ unobstructed wisdom concerning the past 17. མ་འོངས་པའི་དུས་མཁྱེན་པ་ལ་མ་ཐོགས་མ་ཆགས་པའི་ཡེ་ཤེས། anāgate 'dhvanyasaṅgam apratihataṁ jñādarśanaṁ pravarttate/ unobstructed wisdom concerning the future 18. ད་ལྟ་བའི་དུས་མཁྱེན་པ་ལ་མ་ཐོགས་མ་ཆགས་པའི་ཡེ་ཤེས། pratyutpanne 'dhvanyasaṅgam apratihataṁ jñāna darśanaṁ pravartate/ unobstructed wisdom concerning the present.

མ་མོ།

Mātṛkā/ Mamo. A class of goddesses of which Palden Lhamo is the most prominent; most Mamos are depicted as ugly and terrifying figures; a skull full of diseases, a magic ball of thread and a black snare are their typical weapons; Mamo, as a class of deities, are quite numerous in different forms and constitute an important feminine aspect of the protectors of Buddha's doctrine.

མ་དམིགས་པའི་རྟགས་ཡང་དག

Anupalabdhi saṁyaghetu/ Correct reason of non-cognition. Correct reason arising from non-cognition in which the actual predicate that is established is a negative phenomenon, i.e. is not perceived. There are two types: 1. སྣང་རུང་མ་དམིགས་པའི་རྟགས། correct reason arising from non-cognition (of a specific thing) which is suitable to appear (to a perceiving mind). 2. མི་སྣང་བ་མ་དམིགས་པའི་རྟགས། correct reason arising from non-cognition (of a specific thing) which is unsuitable to appear (to a perceiving mind).

མ་ཟིན་པའི་སྒྲ།

Anupāttaśabda/ Unconjoined sound. Sounds that are created from elements not conjoined with consciousness, e.g. the sound of a running brook.

མ་ཡིན་དགག

Affirming negative. A negation which when expressed in words negates its specific object of negation and directly or indirectly implies the existence of another affirming (non-negative) phenomena, e.g. the statement, 'Rani does not sleep during the day,' which indirectly implies that she sleeps during the night. There are three types: 1. ཚིག་གཞན་དངོས་སུ་འཕེན་པའི་མ་ཡིན་དགག directly affirming negative 2. ཚིག་གཞན་ཤུགས་ལ་འཕེན་པའི་མ་ཡིན་དགག indirectly affirming negative 3. སྐབས་སྟོབས་ཀྱིས་འཕེན་པའི་མ་ཡིན་དགག circumstantially affirming negative.

མ་ཡིན་དགག་གི་གཞན་སེལ།

Exclusion (of others), which is an affirming negation, i.e. an affirming exclusion synonymous with negation, e.g. the statement, 'not a vase.' There are two types: 1. བློའི་གཞན་སེལ། mental exclusion of other 2. དོན་རང་མཚན་གྱི་གཞན་སེལ། ultimate self-characterized exclusion of other.

མ་རིག་པ།

Avidya/ Ignorance. One of the six root delusions (see rtsa-nyon drug); a secondary mind that is a direct antidote to the wisdom understanding the law of causality and reality of phenomena; and hence the root of misapprehension of all. There are primarily three categories, those that are induced through closed mindedness, doubt and wrong view or philosophy.

མ་ལས་ཐོབ་པའི་མཛོད་གསུམ།

Three treasures obtained from the mother. 1. ཤ། flesh 2. པགས་པ། skin 3. ཁྲག blood.

མང་བཀུར་སྡེ་པ་གསུམ།

Sammitīyāḥ/ The three schools of Sammitiya; one of the eighteen Hīnayāna schools of philosophy. 1. ས་སྒོག་རི་ལ་གནས་པའགྱི་སྡེ། Kaurukullakāḥ 2. སྲུང་བ་པའི་སྡེ། Avantakāḥ 3. གནས་མ་བུ་པའི་སྡེ། Vātsīputrīyāḥ.

མན་ངག་སྡེ།

The instruction lineage. A sub-school of the rDzogs-chen atiyoga teachings of the Nyingma order of Tibetan Buddhism.

མཎྜལ།

Maṇḍala/ A. Maṇḍala; a divine mansion. B. An offering to one's spiritual master, in which one visualizes offering the entire universe and its precious contents, etc.

མཎྜལ་བཞི།

The four types of maṇḍala offering. 1. ཕྱིའི་མཎྜལ། outer 2. ནང་གི་མཎྜལ། inner 3. གསང་བའི་མཎྜལ། secret 4. དེ་ཁོ་ན་ཉིད་ཀྱི་མཎྜལ། suchness.

མའི་འོད་གསལ།

Mother clear light. Clear light mind of the death and sleep state.

མར་གྱི་མཚམས་མེད་ཀྱི་ལས།

Boundless action leading to lower realms; action of non-respite. One of the most serious hell-states in which a person is reborn without even passing through the intermediate state of rebirth.

མར་པ།

Marpa (1012-1099). The great Tibetan yogi and translator, the disciple of Naropa and teacher of Milarepa. He was responsible for transmitting the teachings of Naropa to Tibet and for founding the Kagyud order of Tibetan Buddhism. He visited India three times and Nepal four and studied under numerous teachers.

མས་འདེད།

Removing obstacles upward. Such as in Vajrasattva meditation in which the negativities are visualized as being flushed out of your own mouth and upper orifices by an upward flow of light and nectar coming from the body of Vajrasattva at the crown of one's head.

མི་བསྐྱོད་པའི་དམ་ཚིག་བཞི།

Four pledges of Akṣobhya. 1. རྡོ་རྗེའི་དམ་ཚིག pledge concerning the vajra 2. དྲིལ་བུའི་དམ་ཚིག pledge concerning the bell 3. ཕྱག་རྒྱའི་དམ་ཚིག pledge concerning the seal 4. སློབ་དཔོན་གྱི་དམ་ཚིག pledge concerning the master.

མི་ཁོམ་པ་བརྒྱད།

Eight non-condusive factors. Eight non-free states or factors making the practice of dharma impossible. 1. དམྱལ་བར་སྐྱེ་བ། born as a hell being 2. ཡི་དྭགས་སུ་སྐྱེ་བ། born as a hungry ghost 3. དུད་འགྲོར་སྐྱེ་བ། born as an animal 4. ལྷ་ཚེ་རིང་པོར་སྐྱེ་བ། born as a long living god 5. ཀླ་ཀློར་སྐྱེ་བ། born in a barbaric land where the doctrine of the Buddha does not exist 6. དབང་པོ་མ་ཚང་བ། having incomplete sense faculties, such as being blind, deaf or insane 7. ལོག་ལྟ་ཅན། holding wrong views, such as disbelief in the law of causality 8. སངས་རྒྱས་ཀྱི་ཆོས་མེད་པའི་ཡུལ་ན་སྐྱེ་བ། born in a land where Buddha's doctrine does not flourish.

མི་དགེ་བ་བཅུ།

Daśākuśalāni/ Ten non-virtuous actions; ten unwholesome deeds. 1. སྲོག་གཅོད་པ། killing 2. མ་བྱིན་པར་ལེན་པ། stealing 3. ལོག་གཡེམ། sexual misconduct 4. བརྫུན། lying 5. ཕྲ་མ། slander 6. ཚིག་རྩུབ། harsh speech 7. ངག་འཁྱལ། idle gossip 8. བརྣབ་སེམས། covetousness 9. གནོད་སེམས། malicious intent 10. ལོག་ལྟ། wrong view.

མི་དགེ་བའི་ས་མང་གཉིས།

Two non-virtuous levels of thought. The two mental factors that accompany all non-virtuous thoughts. 1. ཁྲེལ་མེད་པ། anapatrāpya/ immodesty 2. ངོ་ཚ་མེད་པ། āhrīkya/ shamelessness.

མི་འགྱུར་རྡོ་རྗེའི་སྐུ།

The Unchanging Vajrakāya. A term common to the Nyingma tradition; one of the five types of Buddha's body or being (see sku-lnga). The inseparability of Dharmakāya and Rūpakāya.

མི་བཅུ་བཞི།

Fourteen classes of person. 1. རྐང་ཐང་པ། infantry 2. རྟ་པ། cavalry 3. གླང་ཆེན་པ། elephant cavalry 4. ཤིང་རྟ་པ་སྟེ་རྒྱལ་རིགས་བཞི། charioteer belonging to the Kṣatriya caste. 5. ནགས་ན་གནས་པ། hermit 6. ཁྱིམ་ན་གནས་པ། lay practitioner 7. དཀའ་ཐུབ་པ་སྟེ་བྲམ་ཟེའི་རིགས་བཞི། ascetic belonging to the Brahmin caste. 8. ཡིག་མཁན། scribe 9. ཚོང་པ། merchant 10. སྨན་པ་སྟེ་རྗེའི་རིགས་གསུམ། physician belonging to a noble caste. 11. ས་གཞི་རྨོ་བ། farmer 12. བ་ལང་སྐྱོང་བ། herdsman 13. འཇིམ་ལས་པ། potter 14. ཁྱིམ་ན་གནས་པ་སྟེ་དམངས་རིགས་བཞི། householder belonging to a lower caste.

མི་ཆོས་བླ་མའི་རྫུན།

Lying about the attainment of superhuman qualities; lying about spiritual realization when actually not possessing them.

མི་ཆོས་གཙང་མ་བཅུ་དྲུག

The sixteen human principles; the sixteen principles of moral conduct issued by the Tibetan King Songtsen Gampo as a decree. 1. དཀོན་མཆོག་གསུམ་ལ་གུས་པས་མཆོད་པ། respectfully worshipping the Three Jewels (Buddha, Dharma and Saṅgha) 2. དམ་པའི་ཆོས་བསྒྲུབ་པ། practising sublime Dharma 3. ཕ་མ་ལ་བཀུར་བ། honouring one's parents 4. ཡོན་ཏན་ཅན་ལ་གོང་དུ་བཀུར་བ། honouring the learned scholars 5. རིགས་མཐོ་བ་དང་རྒན་པ་རྣམས་ལ་སྲི་ཞུ་ཤུ་དུད་བྱེད་པ། honouring and respecting the elders and those belonging to higher castes 6. མཛའ་བཤེས་ལ་གཞུང་རིང་བ། being loyal and benign by avoiding a temperamental relationship with one's friends 7. ཡུལ་མི་ཁྱིམ་མཚེས་ལ་ཕན་འདོགས་པ། being benevolent as well as one is able towards people in one's locality and neighbours 8. ཡིད་དྲང་བ། being honest and incorruptible 9. མི་ཡ་རབས་ལ་ལྟ་བ། following examples of the gentle and decent 10. ཟས་ནོར་ལ་སྤྱོད་ཤེས་པ། living a moderate life free from extreme means of livelihood 11. དྲིན་ཅན་ལ་ཕན་ལན་སློག་པ། repaying kindness to the generous 12. བྲེ་སྲང་ལ་གཡོ་སྒྱུ་མེད་པ། avoiding deceptive conduct and fraud, such as in weights and measures 13. སྤྱི་སྙོམས་ཞིང་ཕྲག་དོག་མེད་པ། avoiding jealousy of others' belongings and cultivating friendship with all 14. ངན་པའི་གྲོགས་ལ་མི་ཉན་ཞིང་རང་རྒྱུགས་འཛིན་པ། avoiding the influence of evil friends and one's deceptive 15. བུད་མེད་ཀྱི་ཁ་ལ་མི་ཉན་པ། not listening to what women say 16. ཐེག་པ་ཆེ་ཞིང་བློ་ཁོག་ཡངས་པ། being patient and far-sighted and enduring hardships in carrying out one's duties.

མི་འཇིག་པའི་གནས་ལྔ།

The five holy places that cannot be destroyed (see gnas-chen lnga).

མི་འཇིགས་པ་བཞི།

Four fearlessnesses; four grounds of self-confidence of a Buddha. Fearlessness with respect to the assertion of: 1. རང་དོན་དུ་སྤངས་པ་ཐམས་ཅད་སྤངས་ཞེས་དམ་བཅས་པ་ལ་མི་འཇིགས་པ། one's complete and perfect extinguishment of all negativities for the purpose of oneself 2. རང་དོན་དུ་ཡོན་ཏན་ཐམས་ཅད་དང་ལྡན་ཞེས་དམ་བཅས་པ་ལ་མི་འཇིགས་པ། one's complete and perfect accomplishment of knowledge for the purpose of oneself 3. གཞན་དོན་དུ་གཉེན་པོའི་ལམ་འདི་དག་གོ་ཞེས་དམ་བཅས་པ་ལ་མི་འཇིགས་པ། revealing the paths of antidotes for the purpose of others 4. གཞན་དོན་དུ་འདི་དག་སྤང་བྱ་ཡིན་ཞེས་དམ་བཅས་པ་ལ་མི་འཇིགས་པ། revealing the eliminations for the purpose of others.

མི་མཉམ་པ་དང་མཉམ་པའི་ཕུང་པོ་ལྔ།

Asamasamapañcaskandhāḥ/ The five aggregates equal to the unequalled one. 1. ཚུལ་ཁྲིམས་ཀྱི་ཕུང་པོ། śila skandha/ aggregate of morality 2. བསམ་གཏན་གྱི་ཕུང་པོ། samādhi skandha/ aggregate of concentration 3. ཤེས་རབ་ཀྱི་ཕུང་པོ། prajñ[a] skandha/ aggregate of wisdom 4. རྣམ་པར་གྲོལ་བའི་ཕུང་པོ། vimukti skandha/ aggregate of thorough liberation 5. རྣམ་པར་གྲོལ་བའི་ཡེ་ཤེས་མཐོང་བའི་ཕུང་པོ། vimuktijñāna darśan[a] skandha/ aggregate of seeing the wisdom of thoroug[h] liberation.

མི་རྟག་སོགས་བཅུ་དྲུག

The sixteen attributes of the four noble truths. 1-4. སྡུག་བསྔ[ལ་] བདེན་པའི་ཁྱད་ཆོས་བཞི། four attributes of the truth o[f] suffering (see sdug-bsngal bden-pa'i khyad-chos bzhi) 5-[8] ཀུན་འབྱུང་བདེན་པའི་ཁྱད་ཆོས་བཞི། four attributes of the tru[th] of origin (see kun-'byun bden-pa'i khyad-chos bzhi) 9-12. འགོག་བདེན་གྱི་ཁྱད་ཆོས་བཞི། four attributes of the truth of cessation (see 'gog-bden-gyi khyad-chos bzhi) 13-16. ལམ་བདེན་གྱི་ཁྱད་ཆོས་བཞི། four attributes of the truth of the path (see lam-bden-gyi khyad-chos bzhi).

མི་རྟོག་པ་ཆེན་པོའི་ཐུགས།

The great non-conceptual heart. The primordial wisdom is known as the great non-conceptual heart or mind in the Nyingma tradition.

མི་ཐ་སྙད་གསུམ་ལྡན།

A person of three-fold qualities. Being able to speak, understand and having a sound mind.

མི་མཐུན་ཕྱོགས།

Pratipakṣa/ Discordant factors; dissimilar factors. That which is either contradictory to or does not share a common basis with the predicate in a logical syllogism.

མི་མཐོང་བའི་རྒྱུ་བརྒྱད།

Eight causes of invisibility. 1. ཧ་ཅང་རིང་བ། very distant 2. ཧ་ཅང་ཉེ་བ། very close 3. དབང་པོ་ཉམས་པ། weak sense faculty 4. ཡིད་དབང་ཉམས་པ། weak mental faculty 5. ཆ་ཕྲ་བ། subtle object 6. སྒྲིབ་པ་དང་བཅས་པ། obstructive factors 7. ཟིལ་གྱིས་གནོན་པ། outshining factors 8. ཡུལ་འདྲེས་པ། confusing object.

མི་ལྡན་རྣམ་གཅོད་ཀྱི་སྒྲ།

Statement rejecting other qualities; statement rejecting the existence of other features, e.g. the statement, 'sound is only an impermanent thing.'

མི་སྡུག་པའི་འདུ་ཤེས་དགུ།

Nine unlovely perceptions; nine points of meditation on ugliness. 1. རྣམ་པར་བམ་པ། perception of a swollen corpse 2. རྣམ་པར་འབུས་གཞིག་པ། perception of a worm eaten corpse 3. རྣམ་པར་རྣགས་པ། perception of a festering corpse 4. རྣམ་པར་དམར་བ། perception of a bloody corpse 5. རྣམ་པར་སྔོས་པ། perception of a bluish corpse 6. རྣམ་པར་ཟོས་པ། perception of a corpse being devoured 7. རྣམ་པར་འཐོར་བ། perception of a scattered corpse 8. རྣམ་པར་འཚིག་པ། perception of a burnt corpse 9. རྣམ་པར་དུག་ལྟ་བུ། perception of a poisonous corpse.

མི་སྡུག་པའི་མཚན་མ་བཅོ་བརྒྱད།

Eighteen signs of ugliness; eighteen unlovely signs. 1. མི་སྡུག་པ། ugliness 2. སྐྲ་ཟྲི་བ། falling hair 3. དཔྲལ་བ་ཆུང་བ། small forehead 4. མདོག་སེར་སྐྱ། pale color 5. མིག་སེར་བ། yellow color 6. མིག་ཟུམ་པ། closed eyes 7. མིག་ཆུང་བ། small eyes 8. སྨིན་མ་མཚམས་མ་སྦྱར་བ། eye-brows not joined 9. སྣ་ལེབ་པ། flat nose 10. སོ་རིང་བ། long teeth 11. ལྕེ་ལྡིག་པ། stammering 12. ཕྱི་ནང་སྒུར་བ། crooked body 13. ལྟོ་བ་ཆེ་བ། big belly 14. དཔུང་པ་རྫེ་ངར་ཐུང་བ། stooped shoulders 15. ལུས་ལ་སྤུ་མང་བ། hairy body 16. ལག་པ་དང་རྐང་པའི་མི་མ་ཉམས་པ། shrivelled hands and feet 17. ཚིག་སྦོམ་པ། thick joints 18. ཁ་དང་ལུས་ལས་དྲི་ངན་བྱུང་བ། bad smell from body and mouth.

མི་གནས་པའི་མྱང་འདས།

Aprastiṣṭhita nirvāṇa/ Non-abiding state of peace; non-abiding nirvāṇa. The full state of nirvāṇa free of the extremes of both cyclic existence and peace.

མི་དམིགས་པ་སྟོང་པ་ཉིད།

Anupalambha śūnyatā/ Emptiness of non-apprehension. One of the sixteen emptinesses (see stong-pa nyid bcu-drug); the lack of inherent existence of all phenomena within the context of any of the three times—past, present and future.

མིའམ་ཅི།

Kinnara/ Probable-human. A class of beings included within the realm of the gods of desire.

མི་ཤིགས་པའི་ཐིག་ལེ།

Indestructible drop. The indestructible drop being either the ever existent very subtle wind and mind or the white and red drop at the heart-centre during one life-time.

མི་ཤེས་པའི་རྒྱུ་བཞི།

The four causes of ignorance; the four causes of lack of knowledge. 1. ཡུལ་བསྐལ་པས་མི་ཤེས་པ། due to distant location of the object 2. དུས་བསྐལ་པས་མི་ཤེས་པ། due to distant time reference of the object 3. ངོ་བོ་བསྐལ་པས་མི་ཤེས་པ། due to the subtle nature of the object 4. ཟབ་ཅིང་མཐའ་ཡས་པས་མི་ཤེས་པ། profundity and vastness of the object.

མི་སྲིད་རྣམ་གཅོད་ཀྱི་སྒྲ།

Statement rejecting other possibilities, e.g. the statement, 'it is only possible that a calf be born from a cow.'

མི་སློབ་ལམ།

Aśaikṣa mārga/ Path of no-more learning. Last of the five paths.

མི་བསྲུན་པ་ལྔ།

The five cruelties; the five immoral activities-that deserve punishment. Those: 1. རྒྱལ་པོ་ལ་གནོད་པ། harming a king 2. ཕན་ཚུན་གཅིག་གིས་གཅིག་ལ་གནོད་པ། harming each other 3. རྒྱལ་པོའི་བཀའ་ལ་མི་ཉན་པ། disloyal to the king's advice 4. ལོག་པས་འཚོ་བའི་འཚོ་བ། practicing wrong livelihood 5. ལོག་པར་ཞུགས་པར་སྦྱོར་བ། engagement in hostile behaviours.

མིག་དར།

Blindfold. The red blindfold worn around the head during particular stages of a tantric initiation in order to prohibit the disciple from seeing the secrets of the mandala before they pass through the permission to be able to do so.

མིང་གཉིས།

Two types of name. 1. དངོས་མིང་། real name 2. བཏགས་མིང་། given name.

མིང་སྦྱོར་རྟོག་པ།

Conceptual cognition involving terms. A type of conceptual generation produced in conjuction with the name of a thing, e.g. a concept that takes for granted, 'anything that is capable of rasing a beam is a pillar.'

མིང་གཟུགས་ཀྱི་ཡན་ལག

The interdependent link of name and form. The fourth in the link of the twelve interdependent originations. Name refers to sound, smell, taste, phenomena and form as the form aggregate.

མུ་གསུམ།

Tri koti/ Three possible combinations. 1. if it is 'X' it should be 'Y' but if it is 'Y' it is not necessarily 'X' 2. that which is both 'X' and 'Y' 3. that which is neither.

མུ་བཞི།

Cātuskoti/ Four possible combinations. 1. that which is 'X' but not 'Y' 2. that which is 'Y' but not 'X' 3. that which is both 4. that which is neither.

མུ་སྟེགས་གཅེར་བུའི་དོན་དགུ

Nine topics of the Nirgrantha school. 1. སྲོག life-force 2. གང་ཟག person 3. སྡོམ་པ། precepts 4. ངེས་པར་རྒ་བ certaint of aging 5. འཆིང་བ། bindings 6. ལས། karma 7. སྡིག་པ། non-virtues 8. བསོད་ནམས། merits 9. ཐར་པ། liberation.

མུ་སྟེགས་སྟོན་པ་དྲུག

Ṣaḍ tīrthika śāstāraḥ/ The six non-buddhist teachers; These were the one's who were defeated by Buddha Śākyamuni while completing miracles, and the event is celebrated as the Great Prayer Festival. 1. འོད་སྲུང་རྫོགས་བྱེད། Pūraṇakāśyapa 2. ཀུན་དུ་རྒྱ་གནག་ལྷས་ཀྱི་བུ། Maskarīgośalīputra 3. སྣྲ་བྱེད་ཀྱི་བུ་ཡང་དག་རྒྱལ་བ་ཅན། Sañjayīvairaḍīputra 4. མི་ཕམ་སྐྲའི་ལ་བ་ཅན། Ajitakeśakambala 5. ཀ་ཏྲའི་བུ་ནོག་ཅན། Kakudakātyāyana 6. གཅེར་བུ་པ་གཉེན་གྱི་བུ། Nirgranthojñātiputra.

མུ་སྟེགས་པ་གཉིས།

Two types of non-Buddhists. 1. སྤྲུལ་པའི་མུ་སྟེགས་པ། non-Buddhist by emanation 2. ངོ་བོའི་སྒོ་ནས་མུ་སྟེགས་པ། non-Buddhist by nature or birth.

མེ་ལྟ་བུའི་སེམས་བསྐྱེད།

Fire-like bodhicitta. The mind of enlightenment associated with exertion possessed by Bodhisattvas on the path of preparation.

མེད་དགག

Non-affirming negative. A negation which when expressed in words negates its specific object of negation, but neither directly nor indirectly implies the existence of another (non-negative) phenomena, e.g. emptiness.

མེད་པ་གསལ་སྣང་ཅན་གྱི་བློ།

Awareness of the clear appearance of a non-existent object; an awareness in which something not existent seems clearly to exist, e.g. appearence of the single moon as double.

མོ་གཅོད།

Female ritual of cutting-off (gcod). A ritual of severing negative thoughts handed down from Phadampa Sangye to Yogini Machig Labkyi Dolma and her disciples.

མོས་པ་སྤྱོད་པའི་ས།

Adhimukticaryā bhūmi/ State of faith. The first two of the five paths, where a practitioner employs faith and aspiration in his practice and has only a conceptual understanding of emptiness. Hence the Bodhicitta at these stages are also known by the name—Bodhicitta preoccupied by faith.

མོས་པ་སྤྱོད་པའི་སེམས་བསྐྱེད་བཞི།

The four minds of enlightenment preoccupied by faith. The mind of enlightenment possessed by Bodhisattvas on the first two paths—the path of accumulation and preparation. 1. ས་ལྟ་བུའི་སེམས་བསྐྱེད། the earth-like mind of enlightenment (see sa lta-bu'i sems-bskyed) 2. གསེར་ལྟ་བུའི་སེམས་བསྐྱེད། the gold-like mind of enlightenment (see gser lta-bu'i sems-bskyed) 3. ཟླ་བ་ལྟ་བུའི་སེམས་བསྐྱེད། the moon-like mind of enlightenment (see zla-ba lta-bu'i sems-bskyed) 4. མེ་ལྟ་བུའི་སེམས་བསྐྱེད། the fire-like mind of enlightenment (see me lta-bu'i sems-bskyed).

མྱང་འདས།

State of peace; liberation; nirvāṇa.

དམན་པ་ས་བརྒྱད།

Eight stages of the lower vehicle (see theg-dman gyi sa-brgyad).

དམར་ཁྲིད།

Explicit teachings; bare teachings. The transmission of certain teachings in every detail, from the master's own experience in meditational practice.

དམར་ཆུང་སྐོར་གསུམ།

Three minor red protectors common to the Sakya tradition 1. ཀུ་རུ་ཀུལླེ་གསེར་གྱི་སྙིང་ཐག་ཅན། Kurukullāsuvarnaka 2. ཚོར་རྒྱུན་མ་དམར་པོ། Raktavasudhārā 3. ལྷ་མོ་ཏི་ནུ་མ། Tinudevī.

དམར་ཆེན་སྐོར་གསུམ།

Three major red protectors common to the Sakya tradition. 1. ཀུ་རུ་ཀུལླེ། Kurukullā 2. ཚོགས་བདག Gaṇapati 3. འདོད་རྒྱལ། Kāmarāja.

དམིགས་རྐྱེན།

Ālambana pratyaya/ Objective condition. One of the four conditions (see rkyen-bzhi); the objective condition held in the mind that serves as the direct cause of generating that perception, e.g. a vase, for an eye consciousness.

རྨད་དུ་བྱུང་བའི་སྡེ།

Marvelous teachings. One of the twelve scriptural categories of Buddha's teachings, describing the marvelous qualities of the Hearers, Bodhisattvas and Buddhas or their heavens.

རྨི་ལམ་གྱི་སྒྱུ་མ།

Svapana māyā/ Illusory body of the dream-state. A kind of illusory body experienced in a dream state through the force of karmic imprints; a subtle wind and mind body.

སྨད་འདུལ།

The lower Vinaya lineage. The restoration and spread of the lineage of monastic vows by the three persons known as Mar-Shakya, Yo-Gejung, and Gtang-Rabsel from Do-kham, the lower region of Tibet to central Tibet after the persecution of Buddhism in Tibet by Lang Dharma. This Vinaya lineage was received by Lachen Gongpa Rabsel, who passed the lineage to Lume Tsultrim Sherab, and subsequently to twelve persons of central Tibet.

སྨན་གྱི་རྒྱུད་བཞི།

Four medicine tantras; four basic texts of Tibetan medicine. 1. རྩ་རྒྱུད། root tantra 2. བཤད་རྒྱུད། explanatory tantra 3. མན་ངག་རྒྱུད། instruction tantra 4. རྒྱུད་ཕྱི་མ། later tantra.

སྨན་གྱི་རོ་དྲུག

Six tastes of medicine (see ro-drug).

སྨན་ལྟ་བུའི་སེམས་བསྐྱེད།

Medicine like Bodhicitta; the mind of enlightenment associated with the perfection of wisdom practice possessed by a Bodhisattva on the sixth ground; it has the potential to pacify obstructions to omniscience like a powerful medicine.

སྨན་རྣམ་བཞི།

Four types of medicine; four types of food for monks as prescribed by the Buddha. 1. དུས་རུང་གི་སྨན། food to be eaten before noon 2. ཐུན་ཚོད་དུ་རུང་བའི་སྨན། food suitable at a particular session 3. ཞག་བདུན་གྱི་སྨན། food to be taken for seven days 4. འཚོ་བཅང་གི་སྨན། food to support life.

སྨན་བླ་བདེ་གཤེགས་བརྒྱད།

Asta bhaiṣajyaguravaḥ/ Eight medicine Buddhas; eight healing Buddhas. 1. ཤཱཀྱ་ཐུབ་པ། Buddha Śakyamuni 2. སྨན་གྱི་བླ་བཻཌཱུརྱ་འོད་ཀྱི་རྒྱལ་པོ། Bhaiṣajyaguru 3. མངོན་མཁྱེན་རྒྱལ་པོ། Abhijñānarāja 4. ཆོས་བསྒྲགས་རྒྱ་མཚོ། Dharmakirtisāgara 5. མྱ་ངན་མེད་མཆོག་དཔལ། Aśokottamaśrī 6. གསེར་བཟང་དྲི་མེད། Suvarnabhadravimala 7. སྒྲ་དབྱངས་རྒྱལ་པོ། Svaraghoṣarāja 8. མཚན་ལེགས་ཡོངས་བསྒྲགས་དཔལ། Sūparikīrtita Nāmaśrī.

སྨན་བཟང་པོ་དྲུག

Six good medicines. 1. ཛ་ཏི་སྙིང་གི་བཟང་པོ། nutmeg for heart 2. ཅུ་གང་གློ་བའི་བཟང་པོ། bamboo-manna for lungs 3. གུར་གུམ་མཆིན་པའི་བཟང་པོ། saffron for liver 4. ལི་ཤི་སྲོག་གི་བཟང་པོ། clove for life force 5. སུག་མེལ་མཁལ་མའི་བཟང་པོ། lesser cardamon for kidneys 6. ཀ་ཀོ་ལ་མཆེར་པའི་བཟང་པོ། cardamon for spleen.

སྨོན་གནས་མཁྱེན་པའི་ཏིང་ངེ་འཛིན།

Praṇidhijñāna samādhi/ Concentration knowing the object of prayers; meditative concentration on prayers that one may benefit sentient beings until the end of cyclic existence.

སྨོན་པ་སེམས་བསྐྱེད།

Praṇidhāna bodhicittotpāda/ Wishing bodhicitta; aspirational thought of enlightenment.

སྨོན་ལམ་ལྔ།

The five kinds of prayers. 1. སེམས་བསྐྱེད་པའི་སྨོན་ལམ། prayers for generating bodhicitta 2. སྐྱེ་བའི་སྨོན་ལམ། prayers for good rebirth 3. སྤྱོད་ཡུལ་གྱི་སྨོན་ལམ། prayers for a better environment 4. ཡང་དག་པའི་སྨོན་ལམ། prayers for perfection 5. སྨོན་ལམ་ཆེན་པོ། the great prayer.

སྨོན་ལམ་ཆེན་མོ།

The Great Prayer Festival. This prayer festival held at Lhasa Tsuglag Khang during the first month of every year was originally instituted by Tsong Khapa in 1409.

སྨོན་སེམས་བསླབ་བྱ་བརྒྱད།

Eight precepts of the wishing bodhicitta. A. ཚེ་འདིར་སེམས་བསྐྱེད་མ་ཉམས་པར་འཕེལ་བའི་ཐབས་བཞི། Four means to prevent degeneration of Bodhicitta in this life: 1. སེམས་བསྐྱེད་ཀྱི་ཕན་ཡོན་དྲན་པ། being mindful of the benefits of Bodhicitta 2. ཉིན་མཚན་དུས་དྲུག་ཏུ་སེམས་བསྐྱེད་པ། reaffirming the Bodhicitta resolve six times a day 3. སེམས་ཅན་བློས་མི་སྤོང་བ། not neglecting sentient beings 4. ཚོགས་གཉིས་བསགས་པ། accumulating the two heaps of merits. B. སྐྱེ་བ་གཞན་དུ་སེམས་བསྐྱེད་དང་མི་འབྲལ་བའི་ཐབས་བཞི། Four means of non-separation from bodhicitta in all respects: 1. མཁན་སློབ་དབུ་མི་བསླུ་བ། not deceiving abbots, masters and lamas, etc. 2. གཞན་གྱི་དགེ་བ་ལ་འགྱོད་དུ་མི་འཇུག་པ། not inducing regret in those practising virtue 3. ཐེག་ཆེན་ལམ་ཞུགས་ལ་སྐྱོན་མི་འདོགས་པ། not disparaging those on the path of the greater vehicle 4. ལྷག་བསམ་མིན་པའི་གཡོ་སྒྱུ་སྤོང་བ། abandoning pretentious thoughts.

སྨྲ་བའི་སེང་གེ།

Vādisiṁha/ Lion of eloquence; lion amongst teachers; an epithet of Buddha Śākyamuni.

སྨྲ་བསམ་བརྗོད་མེད།

Inexpressible and inconceiveable; emptiness.

སྨྲེ་སྔགས་འདོན་པ།

To bewail; to mourn for; to grief.

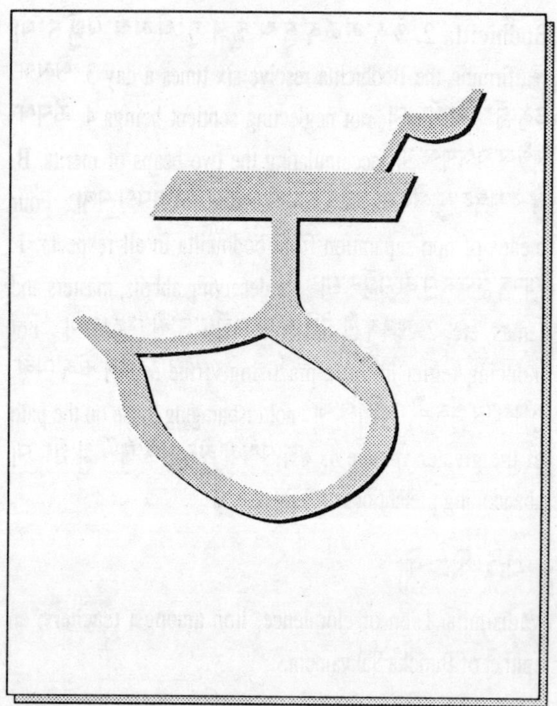

ཙ་ཀ་ལི།

A miniature painting. Small sized images and paintings of maṇḍalas, deities, implements and auspicious symbols used during the course of an initiation or other ceremonial occasions.

ཙ་རི།

The holy place, Tsari located in the southern border of Tibet. It is considered a holy place of Cakrasambhava and Vajrayoginī.

ཙནྡ་ལཱི་གསུམ།

The three types of fiery energy; the three kinds of tu-mo energy (gtum-mo) 1. ཕྱིའི་གདམས་མོ་རང་བཞིན་ཙནྡ་ལཱི། the natural fiery energy, the emptiness of all phenomena as the outer tu-mo 2. ནང་གི་གདམས་མོ་ཨ་ཐུང་ཙནྡ་ལཱི། the fiery energy of tu-mo, the short A at the navel as the inner tu-mo 3. གསང་བའི་གདམས་མོ་ཁ་སྦྱོར་ཙནྡ་ལཱི། the fiery energy of union, the union of ever-excellent emptiness and the unchanging great bliss, the secret tu-mo.

ཙོང་ཁ་པ།

Je Tsong Khapa (1357-1419). The founder of the Gelug order of Tibetan Buddhism. Renowed for his marvelous scholarship and practice. His eighteen volumes of collected writings comprises the heart of the Gelug doctrine.

གཙུག་ཏོར་སྔ་ལྔ།

Pañca uṣṇīṣabuddha/ Five Uṣṇīṣa Buddhas. 1. གཙུག་ཏོར་གདུགས་དཀར། Usṇisa Sitātapatrā 2. གཙུག་ཏོར་དྲི་མེད། Usṇisa Vimala 3. གཙུག་ཏོར་རྣམ་རྒྱལ། Usṇisa Vijayā 4. གཙུག་ཏོར་འབར་བ། Usṇisa Jvālā 5. གཙུག་ཏོར་ཕུར་པ། Usṇisa Kilaka.

གཙོ་བོ།

Jyeṣtha/ pradhāna/ Principal factor; main factor; fundamental principle; central figure; primary object; head; chief.

གཙོ་བོ་གཉིས།

Two fundamental principles according to the Sāṁkhya school of Hindu philosophy. 1. རང་བཞིན་རྒྱུའི་གཙོ་བ། causal principle of nature 2. གནས་སྐབས་འབྲས་བུའི་གཙོ་བོ། resultant principle of manifestation.

གཙོ་སེམས།

Primary mind; A consciousness or mind that is accompanied by secondary mental factors, e.g. the six consciousnesses.

བཙན།

Mountain dwelling spirits. A type of non-human spirits

believed to be living in the mountains; may enter an oracle in trance and speak through him or her.

བཙུན་པ་བཙུན་མ།

Monks and nuns.

རྩ་འཁོར་ལྔ།

The five channel wheels. 1-4. the four channel wheels (see rtsa-'khor-bzhi) 5. གསང་གནས་བདེ་སྐྱོང་གི་འཁོར་ལོ། the wheel of sustaining bliss at the secret place that has thirty two petals.

རྩ་འཁོར་དྲུག

Six channel wheels. 1-5. the five channel wheels (see rtsa-'khor-lnga) 6. ནོར་བུའི་དབུས་ཀྱི་འཁོར་ལོ། the wheel at the centre of the Jewel.

རྩ་འཁོར་བཞི།

The four channel wheels. 1. སྤྱི་བོ་བདེ་ཆེན་གྱི་འཁོར་ལོ། the wheel of great bliss at the crown that has thirty-two petals 2. མགྲིན་པར་ལོངས་སྤྱོད་ཀྱི་འཁོར་ལོ། the wheel of enjoyment at the throat that has sixteen petals 3. སྙིང་ག་ཆོས་ཀྱི་འཁོར་ལོ། the wheel of phenomena at the heart that has eight petals 4. ལྟེ་བ་སྤྲུལ་པའི་འཁོར་ལོ། the wheel of emanation at the navel that has sixty-four petals.

རྩ་འཁོར་གསུམ།

The three channel wheels (see rtsa-'khor bzhi, 1-3).

རྩ་ཉོན་དྲུག

Six root delusions; the six root defilements. 1. འདོད་ཆགས། rāga/ desire-attachment 2. ཁོང་ཁྲོ། pratigha/ hatred 3. ང་རྒྱལ། māna/ pride 4. མ་རིག་པ། avidyā/ ignorance 5. ཐེ་ཚོམ། vicikitsā/ doubt 6. ལྟ་བ། mithya drṣṭi/ wrong view.

རྩ་ལྟུང་བཞི།

Four root downfalls; four root transgressions of a monk's vows. 1. སྲོག་གཅོད་པ། taking life 2. མ་བྱིན་པར་ལེན་པ། taking what is not given 3. མི་ཚངས་པར་སྤྱོད་པ། indulging in sexual misconduct 4. བརྫུན་སྨྲ་བ། lying.

རྩ་ལྟུང་བཅུ་བཞི།

Fourteen root downfalls; fourteen root transgressions of the tantric vows/ precepts. 1. རྡོ་རྗེ་སློབ་དཔོན་ལ་བརྙས་པ། belittling the vajra master/guru 2. བདེ་གཤེགས་བཀའ་ལས་འདས་པ། despising the precepts of the Buddha 3. རྡོ་རྗེའི་སྤུན་ལ་འཁྲུ་བ། speaking badly of vajra brothers and sisters 4. བྱམས་པ་འདོར་བ། abandoning love for sentient beings 5. སྨོན་འཇུག་གི་སེམས་འདོར་བ། abandoning the wishing and committed mind of enlightenment 6. མདོ་སྔགས་ཀྱི་ཆོས་ལ་སྨོད་པ། despising the sūtra and tantra teachings 7. སྨིན་མིན་ལ་གསང་བ་སྒྲོག་པ། exposing the secret of tantra to those who are not initiated 8. ཕུང་པོ་ལ་བརྙས་པ། mistreating one's body 9. སྟོང་པ་ཉིད་སྤོང་བ། abandoning emptiness or being sceptical about it 10. གདུག་ཅན་གྱི་གྲོགས་བསྟེན་པ། associating with bad friends 11. སྟོང་པ་ཉིད་དྲན་པར་མ་བྱས་པ། not reflecting on emptiness 12. དད་ལྡན་སེམས་སུན་འབྱིན་པ། disturbing another's faith in the Dharma 13. དམ་ཚིག་ཇི་བཞིན་མི་བསྟེན་པ། not observing the pledges and commitments 14. བུད་མེད་སྨོད་པ། despising women.

རྩ་ལྟུང་བཅོ་བརྒྱད། འཇུག་སྡོམ་གྱི་བསླབ་བྱ།

Eighteen root downfalls; eighteen root transgressions of the Bodhisattva vows. 1. བདག་བསྟོད་གཞན་སྨོད། praising oneself and belittling others 2. ཆོས་ནོར་མི་སྦྱིན་པ། not giving material aid or teachings of Dharma 3. བཤགས་ཀྱང་མི་ཉན་པར་གཞན་ལ་འཚོག་པ། not listening when someone declares his or her offences 4. ཐེག་ཆེན་སྤོང་ཞིང་དམ་ཆོས་འདྲར་སྣང་སྟོན་པ། abandoning the teachings of the greater vehicle and preaching false doctrine akin to the mahāyāna teachings 5. དཀོན་མཆོག་གི་དཀོར་མ་བྱིན་པར་ལེན་པ། misusing offerings of the three jewels not given to oneself 6. དམ་པའི་ཆོས་སྤོང་བ། abandoning the sublime Dharma 7. རབ་བྱུང་ལ་འཚེ་བ། evicting monks and nuns 8. མཚམས་མེད་ཀྱི་ལས་བྱེད་པ། committing any of the five boundless actions 9. ལོག་ལྟ་འཛིན་པ། holding wrong views 10. གནས་འཇིག་པ། destroying places of worship or pilgrimage 11. སྣོད་མིན་ལ་སྟོང་ཉིད་བསྟན་པ། teaching emptiness to improper receptacles 12. རྫོགས་བྱང་ཐོབ་པའི་བློ་ལས་བཟློག་པར་བྱེད་པ། turning people away from working for enlightenment 13. སོ་ཐར་སྤོང་བ། abandoning the vows of individual liberation 14. ཉན་ཐོས་ཀྱི་ཐེག་པ་ལ་སྐུར་བ་འདེབས་པ། mistreating the lower vehicle doctrine 15. མི་ཆོས་བླ་མའི་རྫུན་སྨྲ་བ། lying exorbitantly of superhuman attainments 16. དཀོན་མཆོག་གི་དཀོར་མ་བྱིན་པར་ལེན་པ། misappropriation of the property of the three jewels 17. ཁྲིམས་ངན་འཆང་བ། holding corrupt ethical discipline 18. བྱང་ཆུབ་ཀྱི་སེམས་འདོར་བ། abandoning the mind of enlightenment.

རྩ་མདུད།

Naḍīgranthi/ Knot of the channel-wheel. In tantra, this constitutes channel-knots or coils formed from the transfiguration of the three principal energy channels of the body—central, right and left, at different locations of the standing central energy-channel.

རྩ་གནས་འཁོར་ལོ།

The wheel of energy-channels. The wheels or cakras of energy channels formed from their mode of coiling at the central energy-channel.

རྩ་བ་བཞི།

The four root precepts. The four basic vows, the transgression of which constitutes loss of monk vows (see rtsa-ltung bzhi).

རྩ་བའི་ཁ་དོག་བཞི།

Four primary colors. 1. སྔོན་པོ། blue 2. སེར་པོ། yellow 3. དཀར་པོ། white 4. དམར་པོ། red.

རྩ་བའི་ཆོས་དྲུག

Ṣaḍ mūladharmāḥ/ Six root precepts; six root vows of a probationary nun. 1. གཅིག་པུ་ལམ་དུ་མི་འགྲོ་བ། not going alone on the road 2. ཆུ་རྐྱལ་བར་མི་བྱ་བ། not swimming across to the other shore 3. སྐྱེས་པ་རེག་པར་མི་བྱ་བ། not touching a male person 4. སྐྱེས་པ་དང་ལྷན་ཅིག་འདུག་པར་མི་བྱ་བ། not living with a male person 5. ཟླ་མོའི་ཉེས་པ་འཆབ་པར་མི་བྱ་བ། not concealing a transgression of vows by a fellow nun 6. སྨྱན་དུ་འགྱུར་བ་མི་བྱ་བ། not acting as a go-between.

རྩ་བའི་ཉོན་མོངས་ཀྱི་ས་མང་ཆེན་པོ།

Mental attitudes of the root delusions (see rtsa-nyon drug).

རྩ་བའི་ཉོན་མོངས་པ་དྲུག

Ṣaḍ mūlakleśāḥ/ Six root delusions; the six root defilements (see rtsa-nyon drug).

རྩ་བའི་དམ་ཚིག་བཞི།

The four root commitments; the root samayas. The four vows of observance common to all the lower tantras. 1. འཇིག་རྟེན་པའི་ཡང་དག་པའི་ལྟ་བ། upholding right worldly view 2. དཀོན་མཆོག་གསུམ་ལ་སྐྱབས་སུ་འགྲོ་བ། taking refuge in the Three Jewels 3. བྱང་ཆུབ་ཆེན་པོར་སེམས་བསྐྱེད་པ། generating the mind of enlightenment 4. དཀྱིལ་འཁོར་དུ་དབང་བསྐུར་བ། receiving initiation into a maṇḍala.

རྩ་བའི་སྡུག་བསྔལ་གསུམ།

Tri mūla duḥkhāḥ/ The three fundamental sufferings (see sdug-bsngal gsum).

རྩ་བའི་སྡེ་པ་བཞི།

Four main Hīnayāna schools. 1. ཕལ་ཆེན་སྡེ་པ། Mahāsāṁghika, pioneered by Kāśyapa 2. གཞི་ཐམས་ཅད་ཡོད་པར་སྨྲ་བའི་སྡེ་པ། Mūlasarvāstivādin, pioneered by Rahula 3. གནས་བརྟན་པའི་སྡེ་པ། Sthavira, pioneered by Kātyāyana 4. མང་བཀུར་བའི་སྡེ་པ། Saṁmitīya, pioneered by Upāla.

རྩ་བའི་རོ་དྲུག

Six root tastes; six fundamental flavours (see sman-gyi ro-drug).

རྩ་བའི་རླུང་ལྔ།

Five principal energy winds; the energy winds retaining the nature of the five fundamental elements functioning in the human body. 1. སྲོག་འཛིན་གྱི་རླུང་། prāṇa/ life-supporting wind 2. ཐུར་སེལ་གྱི་རླུང་། apāna/ downward moving wind 3. གྱེན་རྒྱུའི་རླུང་། udāna/ upward moving wind 4. མཉམ་གནས་ཀྱི་རླུང་། samāna/ equally abiding wind 5. ཁྱབ་བྱེད་ཀྱི་རླུང་། vyāpaka/ pervasive wind.

རྩ་དབུ་མ།

Avadhūti/ Central energy channel. Located midway between the left and right channels, extending from the tip of the sex organ up to the top of the head from where it bends down in an arch and terminates between the eye-brows; the energy channel through which the essential drops passes.

རྩ་རླུང་ཐིག་ལེ་གསུམ།

Energy channels, winds and drops. The three fundamental interdependent components of our body, which can be utilized through proper yogic practice to understand the ultimate nature of all phenomena; the basis of our consciousness for sustenance and survival of our life. It is explained that the energy channels are like our home, essential drops as our property and energy wind and mind as the owner.

རྩ་གསུམ།

The three roots: A. 1. བྱིན་རླབས་ཀྱི་རྩ་བ་བླ་མ། spiritual master as the source of blessing 2. དངོས་གྲུབ་ཀྱི་རྩ་བ་ཡི་དམ། meditational deity as the source of siddhi 3. བར་གཅོད་སྲུང་བའི་རྩ་བ་མཁའ་འགྲོ་ཆོས་སྐྱོང་། Ḍākinī as the guardian for protecting oneself from hindrances. B. The energy channels: 1. རྩ་དབུ་མ། the central energy channel 2. རོ་མ། energy channel to the right 3. རྐྱང་མ། energy channel to the left.

རྩ་གསུམ་ཀུན་འདུས།

The entity of the three roots; one's personal spiritual master.

རྩལ་ཆེན་རྫོགས་པའི་རྣལ་འབྱོར།

The skillful yoga of completion. One of the five yogas according to the Nyingma tradition; the total perfection of all qualities of the state of union of a learner on the path to liberation.

རྩེ་མོའི་ཕྱིར་མི་ལྡོག་པའི་རྟགས་དྲུག

Six signs of irreversibility from the peak level of the path of preparation. 1. ལུས་ལ་སྲིན་བུའི་རིགས་མི་འབྱུང་བ། families of worms cannot arise in his body 2. སེམས་ལ་གྱ་གྱུ་མེད་པ། he has no crookedness in his mind 3. སྦྱངས་པའི་ཡོན་ཏན་བཅུ་གཉིས་བསྟེན་པ། he trains in the twelve ascetic practices (see sbyangs-pa'i yon-tan bcu-gnyis) 4. སེར་སྣ་དང་འཆལ་བའི་ཚུལ་ཁྲིམས་སོགས་མེད་པ། he has no signs of meanness or immorality 5. ཆོས་ཉིད་དང་མི་འགལ་བར་ཤེར་ཕྱིན་དང་ལྡན་པར་འགྲོ་བ། he advances in the perfection of wisdom which is not in conflict with reality 6. གཞན་དོན་དུ་དམྱལ་བར་འགྲོ་འདོད་པ། he wishes to enter hell for the welfare of others.

རྩེ་མོའི་སྦྱོར་བ།

Mūrdhaprayoga/ Peak training. Mahāyāna path of preparation at the peak of the accumulation of merits, which surpasses the meditation of the aspects of the three knowledges—that of basis, path and omniscience.

རྩེ་མོའི་སྦྱོར་བ་མཚན་ཉིད་ཀྱི་ཆོས་བརྒྱད།

Asta mūrdhaprayoga dharmāḥ/ Eight topics that characterize the peak training. 1. དྲོད་རྩེ་སྦྱོར། peak training of the heat level of the path of preparation 2. རྩེ་མོའི་རྩེ་སྦྱོར། peak training of the peak level of the path of preparation 3. བཟོད་པའི་རྩེ་སྦྱོར། peak training of the forbearance level of the path of preparation 4. ཆོས་མཆོག་རྩེ་སྦྱོར། peak training of the supramundane qualities level of the path of preparation 5. མཐོང་ལམ་རྩེ་སྦྱོར། peak training of the path of seeing 6. སྒོམ་ལམ་རྩེ་སྦྱོར། peak training of the path of meditation 7. བར་ཆད་མེད་པའི་རྩེ་སྦྱོར། peak training of the uninterrupted path 8. བསལ་བྱ་ལོག་སྒྲུབ། wrong achievements to be eliminated.

རྩོད་ལྡན་གྱི་དུས།

Kaliyuga/ Quarrelsome period; degenerated age/era. In the event of further degeneration of the second-fold aeon (see bskal-ba gnyis ldan), when people gradually begin to commit all the ten non-virtuous activities, the quarrelsome period is said to have come. This is the third phase of degenerating age.

བརྩོན་འགྲུས་ཀྱི་ཆོས་བཞི།

The four features of virtuous efforts; the four qualities of the perfection of effort, it: 1. ལེ་ལོ་སོགས་མི་མཐུན་ཕྱོགས་ཉམས་པ། quells laziness and negativities 2. ཆོས་ཀྱི་བདག་མེད་རྟོགས་པའི་རྣམ་པར་མི་རྟོག་པ། generates non-conceptual understanding of the selflessness of phenomena 3. འདོད་པ་རྫོགས་པར་བྱེད་པ། fulfills wishes 4. རིགས་ཅན་གསུམ་སྨིན་པར་བྱེད་པ། ripens the potentials for the three types of liberations—Hearer's, Solitary Realizer's and Bodhisattva's.

བརྩོན་འགྲུས་ཀྱི་སྟོབས།

Virya bala/ Power of effort. One of the five powers (see stobs-lnga) within the classification of the thirty-seven auxiliaries to enlightenment (see byang-phyogs so-bdun) that is immune to hindrances such as laziness.

བརྩོན་འགྲུས་ཀྱི་མཐར་གྱིས་སྦྱོར་བ།

Serial training in effort. A Bodhisattva training concentrated in the development of the perfection of effort.

བརྩོན་འགྲུས་ཀྱི་ཕར་ཕྱིན།

Virya pāramitā/ The perfection of effort. An effort dedicated towards virtuous goals following the Bodhisattva's way of cultivating it.

བརྩོན་འགྲུས་ཀྱི་དབང་པོ།

Vīryendriya/ Faculty of effort; power of effort. One of the five ever-purified faculties (see dbang-po lnga) within the classification of the thirty-seven auxiliaries to enlightenment; the continuous flow of virtuous hearing, contemplation and meditation.

བརྩོན་འགྲུས་ཀྱི་རྫུ་འཕྲུལ་གྱི་རྐང་པ།

Viryārddhipāda/ Limb of the miracle of effort; One of the four legs of miracles (see rdzu-'phrul-gyi rkang-pa bzhi); possessing a wish to eliminate negative conduct.

བརྩོན་འགྲུས་ལྔ།

Five types of effort; the five types of effort that generate higher qualities. 1. གོ་ཆའི་བརྩོན་འགྲུས། armour-like effort 2. སྦྱོར་བའི་བརྩོན་འགྲུས། effort of action 3. ཞུམ་པ་མེད་པའི་བརྩོན་འགྲུས། effort free of discouragement 4. མི་ཕྱོག་པའི་

བརྩོན་འགྲུས། irreversible effort 5. ཆོག་པར་མི་འཛིན་པའི་བརྩོན་འགྲུས། effort that is never contented.

བརྩོན་འགྲུས་རྣམ་གསུམ།

Three types of effort. 1. གོ་ཆའི་བརྩོན་འགྲུས། armour-like effort 2. དགེ་བ་ལ་སྦྱོར་བའི་བརྩོན་འགྲུས། joyful effort in virtuous conduct 3. སེམས་ཅན་དོན་བྱེད་ཀྱི་བརྩོན་འགྲུས། effort for the welfare of sentient beings.

ཚ་ཁང་།

Stamped clay figure house; little houses made to store clay figures (see tsa-tsa).

ཚ་དམྱལ་བརྒྱད།

Eight hot hells. 1. ཡང་སོས། sañjīvana/ reviving 2. ཐིག་ནག kālasūtra/ black-line 3. བསྡུས་འཇོམས། saṁghāta/ mass destruction 4. ངུ་འབོད། rāurava/ crying 5. ངུ་འབོད་ཆེན་པོ། mahārāurava/ great crying 6. ཚ་བ། tāpana/ hot 7. རབ་ཏུ་ཚ་བ། pratāpana/ very hot 8. མནར་མེད། avīci/ non-respite or boundless.

ཚ་ཚ། སཱཙྪ།

Sāccha/ Stamped clay figures. Clay figures stamped with the image of stūpas or deities; they are placed in a stūpa, shrine, or a place of worship and veneration.

ཚངས་པ།

Brahma. A. According to the Buddhist accounts, Brahma is the lord of the gods of the form realm. B. Hindus believe him to be the creator of the universe. C. The pure celestial domain within the form and formless realm.

ཚངས་པའི་གནས་པ་བཞི།

The four pure moral bases. The worldly paths retaining the nature of love, compassion, joy and equinimity that ensures the attainment of a state of Brahma.

ཚངས་པའི་བསོད་ནམས་བཞི།

Four immaculate merits. 1. སྔར་མཆོད་རྟེན་མེད་པའི་ས་ཕྱོགས་སུ་རིང་སྲེལ་གྱི་སྙིང་པོ་ཅན་གྱི་མཆོད་རྟེན་བརྩིགས་པ། construction of a stūpa preserving holy relics in a place where none exist 2. དགེ་འདུན་གྱི་སྡེ་ལ་ཀུན་དགའ་ར་བ་ཕུལ་བ། offering a garden or estate to the sangha community 3. དགེ་འདུན་གྱི་དབྱེན་འདུམ་པ། healing a schism in the ordained community 4. ཚད་མེད་བཞི་སྒོམ་པ། meditating on the four immeasurables.

ཚངས་སྤྱོད་དགེ་བསྙེན།

Brahmācārya upāsaka/ Celibate ordained layperson. A lay ordained practitioner who has vowed to accept the precept of not indulging in sexual conduct throughout his life, e.g. Ācārya Candragomin.

ཚངས་སྤྱོད་ཉེ་རར་གནས་ཀྱི་སྡོམ་པ།

The vows of an approximate-celibacy. An ordination ceremony accepted before taking a probationary nun's vow.

ཚད་མ་གཉིས།

Two types of valid cognition. 1. མངོན་སུམ་ཚད་མ།

pratyakṣa pramāṇa/ direct valid cognition 2. རྗེས་དཔག་ཚད་མ། anumāna pramāṇa/ inferential valid cognition.

ཚད་མ་སྡེ་བདུན།

Seven treatises on valid cognition. Seven works of Dharmakīrti on the study of valid cognition. 1. ཚད་མ་རྣམ་འགྲེལ། *Commentary on Valid Cognition* (pramāṇavartika) 2. ཚད་མ་རྣམ་ངེས། *Discernment of Valid Cognition* (pramāṇaviniścaya) 3. ཚད་མ་རིགས་ཐིག *Drop of Reasoning on Valid Cognition* (nyāyabindu) 4. གཏན་ཚིགས་ཐིག་པ། *Drop of Logical Reasoning* (hetubindu) 5. འབྲེལ་བ་བརྟག་པ། *Analysis of Relationship* (sambandhaparīkṣa) 6. རྒྱུད་གཞན་སྒྲུབ་པ། *Establishing Alternative Continuum* (saṁtānāntarasiddhi) 7. རྩོད་པའི་རིགས་པ། *Science of Debate* (vādanyāya).

ཚད་མིན་གྱི་ཤེས་པ་ལྔ།

The five types of invalid cognitions. 1. བཅད་ཤེས། subsequent cognition 2. ལོག་ཤེས། wrong perception 3. ཐེ་ཚོམ། doubt 4. ཡིད་དཔྱོད། presumption 5. སྣང་ལ་མ་ངེས་པའི་བློ། inattentive perception.

ཚད་མེད་བཞི།

Catvāryapramāṇāni/ Four immeasurables; the four immeasurable thoughts in Mahāyāna teachings. 1. བྱམས་པ་ཚད་མེད། maitrī immeasurable love 2. སྙིང་རྗེ་ཚད་མེད། karuṇā/ immeasurable compassion 3. དགའ་བ་ཚད་མེད། muditā/ immeasurable joy 4. བཏང་སྙོམས་ཚད་མེད། upekṣā/ immeasurable equanimity.

ཚལ་པ་བཀའ་བརྒྱུད།

Tsalpa Kagyud Order of Tibetan Buddhism founded by the holy master Zhand Drowe Gonpo.

ཚིག་གི་གཟུངས།

Word retention. Ability to retain names, terms and words by heart; a power gained through meditation.

ཚིག་དོན་དྲུག

Six topics; as asserted by the Vaiśeṣika school of Hindu philosophy. 1. རྫས། dravyam/ substance 2. ཡོན་ཏན། guṇa/ property 3. ལས། karma/ activity 4. སྤྱི། sāmānyam/ generality 5. བྱེ་བྲག viśeṣa/ particularity 6. འདུ་བ། samavāya/co-existence/composition.

ཚིག་དབང་།

Śabdābhiṣekha/ Word initiation; word empowerment. The last of the four-fold initiation according to the highest yoga tantra in which the master introduces the state of union (yuganada) to his disciples.

ཚུ་རོལ།

Apara/ This side, meaning cyclic existence (saṁsāra) as contrast to the state beyond suffering (nirvāṇa).

ཚུར་མཐོང་།

One who only sees the worldly view; an ordinary person.

ཚུལ་ཁྲིམས་ཀྱི་ཆོས་བཞི།

The four features of the perfection of morality. 1. ཚུལ་འཆལ་སོགས་མི་མཐུན་ཕྱོགས་ཞི་བར་བྱེད་པ། pacifies opponent forces such as corrupt morality 2. ཆོས་ཀྱི་བདག་མེད་རྟོགས་པའི་རྣམ་པར་མི་རྟོག་པ། generates non-conceptual understanding of selflessness 3. ཡོངས་སུ་སྐྱོང་བར་བྱེད་པ། gives thorough protection 4. རིགས་ཅན་གསུམ་སྨིན་པར་བྱེད་པ། ripens the fruits of the three vehicles—Hearer, Solitary Realizer and Bodhisattva.

ཚུལ་ཁྲིམས་ཀྱི་མཐར་གྱིས་སྦྱོར་བ།

Śīlānupurva prayoga/ Serial training in the perfection of morality. The Bodhisattva paths from the path of accumulation up to the moment before complete enlightenment.

ཚུལ་ཁྲིམས་རྣམ་གསུམ།

Three types of morality. A. བྱང་སེམས་ཀྱི་ཚུལ་ཁྲིམས་གསུམ། Three moralities of a Bodhisattva: 1. ཉེས་སྤྱོད་སྡོམ་པའི་ཚུལ་ཁྲིམས། duṣkṛta saṁvara śīla/ morality of abstention from misbehaviour 2. དགེ་བ་ཆོས་སྡུད་ཀྱི་ཚུལ་ཁྲིམས། kuśala dharma saṁgraha śīla/ morality of integrating virtues 3. སེམས་ཅན་དོན་བྱེད་ཀྱི་ཚུལ་ཁྲིམས། sattva kṛtya śīla/ morality for the welfare of other sentient beings. B. In general: 1. འཇིགས་སྐྱོབ་ཀྱི་ཚུལ་ཁྲིམས། morality giving protection from fear 2. ལེགས་སྨོན་གྱི་ཚུལ་ཁྲིམས། morality of admiration in virtues 3. ངེས་འབྱུང་གི་ཚུལ་ཁྲིམས། morality of seeking freedom from cyclic existence.

ཚུལ་འཆལ།

Duḥśīla/ Immorality; corrupt morality.

ཚུལ་འཆོས།

Kuhana/ A. Hypocritical. B. Cunning way of earning a living; one of the five wrong livelihoods (see log-'tsho lnga).

ཚུལ་བཞི།

Four-fold methods; four means of transmitting a tantric teaching. 1. ཚིག་གི་ཚུལ། word by word transmission 2. སྤྱིའི་ཚུལ། explicit method 3. སྦས་པའི་ཚུལ། implicit method 4. དོན་དམ་པའི་ཚུལ། ultimate method.

ཚུལ་ཤིང་།

Śalākā/ Counting sticks. Sticks measuring about one foot, that are used in monasteries during the ritual ceremony for counting the number of monks entering a rainy season retreat.

ཚུལ་གསུམ།

Three modes of reasoning; three criteria for establishing a logical reason. 1. ཕྱོགས་ཆོས། property of the subject 2. རྗེས་ཁྱབ། subsequent pervasion 3. ལྡོག་ཁྱབ། counter pervasion.

ཚེ་བུམ།

Vase of longevity; life-vase. Vase held in the hands of Buddha Amitābha or a vase in which long-life blessings has been poured.

ཚེ་དབང་རིག་འཛིན།

The immortality of life. One of the four immortalities (see rig-'dzin rnam-bzhi) according to the Nyingma tradition of attaining grounds and paths. As soon as a trainee attains the supramundane stage, i.e. the fourth level of the path of preparation, he or she has attained the pure human vajra body, and because his or her consciousness becomes fully ripened to be transformed into the path of seeing, has also attained the immortality of life.

ཚེ་རིང་མཆེད་ལྔ།

Five long living sisters; five goddesses of Tibet. 1. བཀྲ་ཤིས་ཚེ་རིང་མ། Tashi Tsering Ma, the goddess of long-life and glory 2. མཐིང་གི་ཞལ་བཟང་མ། Thingi Zahlzang Ma, the goddess of clairvoyance 3. མི་གཡོ་བློ་བཟང་མ། Miyo Lobsang Ma, the goddess of earth and environment 4. ཅོད་པན་མགྲིན་བཟང་མ། Chodpan Drinzang Ma, the goddess of precious articles 5. གཏད་དཀར་འགྲོ་བཟང་མ། Tadkar Drinzang Ma, the goddess of cattle and domestic animals.

ཚེ་རིང་དྲུག་སྐོར།

Six symbols of longevity; six objects of long life. 1. མི་ཚེ་

རིང་། long living man 2. བྱ་ཚེ་རིང་། long living bird 3. རི་དྭགས་ཚེ་རིང་། long living deer 4. ཤིང་ཚེ་རིང་། long living tree 5. ཆུ་ཚེ་རིང་། long living running water 6. བྲག་ཚེ་རིང་། long living rocky cave.

ཚེ་སྲོག་བླ་གསུམ།

The three: life-span, life-force and spirit. The first is likened to the butter-oil of a butter lamp; the wick to the life-force, and flame to the spirit. The three conditions that are basic faculties for the maintenance of our life.

ཚེ་ལྷ་རྣམ་གསུམ།

The three longevity deities. 1. ཚེ་དཔག་མེད། Amitāyus 2. སྒྲོལ་དཀར། White Tārā 3. རྣམ་རྒྱལ་མ། Vijayā.

ཚོགས།

A. The Tsok-offering; the ritual feast offering ceremony. The ceremony of offering food and drink to the host of divinities by blessing these in the form of bliss and void. B. Accumulation of merits—virtues.

ཚོགས་ཀྱི་འཁོར་ལོ།

Gaṇacakra/ The cycle of Tsok-offering. The ritual of offering tsok-feast. The feast comprises the five sensual objects (see 'dod-yon lnga) and food and drink by blessing these into uncontaminated wisdom-nectar to the host of divinities and oneself visualized in the form of a deity. A special way of accumulating merits and positive energy.

ཚོགས་སྒྲུབ།

Saṁbhāra pratipatti/ Achievement through accumulation. A Bodhisattva path of practice existing from the great level of the supramundane qualities stage of the path of preparation upto the moment before complete enlightenment.

ཚོགས་སྒྲུབ་བཅུ་བདུན།

Seventeen achievements through accumulation. That of: 1. བརྩེ་བ་སྙིང་རྗེ་ཆེན་པོའི་ཚོགས་སྒྲུབ། great compassion 2-7. ཕ་རོལ་ཏུ་ཕྱིན་པ་དྲུག་གི་ཚོགས་སྒྲུབ། six perfections (see phar-rol-tu phyin-pa drug) 8. ཞི་གནས་ཀྱི་ཚོགས་སྒྲུབ། mental quiescence 9. ལྷག་མཐོང་གི་ཚོགས་སྒྲུབ། penetrative insight 10. ཞི་ལྷག་ཟུང་འབྲེལ་གྱི་ཚོགས་སྒྲུབ། union of mental quiescence and penetrative insight 11. ཐབས་ཀྱི་ཚོགས་སྒྲུབ། skillful means 12. བསོད་ནམས་ཀྱི་ཚོགས་ཀྱི་ཚོགས་སྒྲུབ། accumulation of merits 13. ཡེ་ཤེས་ཀྱི་ཚོགས་ཀྱི་ཚོགས་སྒྲུབ། accumulation of insight 14. ལམ་གྱི་ཚོགས་སྒྲུབ། paths 15. གཟུངས་ཀྱི་ཚོགས་སྒྲུབ། retention 16. སའི་ཚོགས་སྒྲུབ grounds 17. གཉེན་པོའི་ཚོགས་སྒྲུབ། antidotes.

ཚོགས་བརྗོད་ཀྱི་སྒྲ།

Statement indicating a group, e.g. the statement, 'race.'

ཚོགས་གཉིས།

Dual accumulation; two types of meritorious collections. 1. བསོད་ནམས་ཀྱི་ཚོགས། pūnya saṁbhāra/ accumulation of merits 2. ཡེ་ཤེས་ཀྱི་ཚོགས། jñāna saṁbhāra/ accumulation of insight.

ཚོགས་སྤྱི།

Collective generality. Any group which is the combination or collection of many factors or components, e.g. a pillar.

ཚོགས་ལམ་གྱི་ཡན་ལག་ལྔ།

The five limbed practices on the path of accumulation. 1. སོ་སྐྱེའི་ཚུལ་ཁྲིམས་ལ་བརྟེན་པ། observance of the morality of ordinary persons 2. དབང་པོའི་སྒོ་སྡོམ་པ། retraining one's sensual organs 3. ཟས་ཀྱི་ཚོད་རིག་པ། maintaining a dietary balance 4. ནམ་གྱི་ཆ་སྟོད་སྨད་ལ་མི་ཉལ་བར་རྣལ་འབྱོར་ལ་བརྩོན་པ། practicing yoga at the early and latter parts of dawn without sleeping 5. དྲན་ཤེས་ལྡན་པའི་དགེ་བ་ལ་རྩེ་གཅིག་ཏུ་གནས་པར་དགའ་བ། rejoicing in the practice of remaining in single-pointed virtuous acts.

ཚོགས་ལམ་གསུམ།

The three paths of accumulation. The small, middling and great.

ཚོགས་གསུམ།

Three types of collection; three groups. 1. མིང་གི་ཚོགས། group of names 2. ཚིག་གི་ཚོགས། group of words 3. ཡི་གེའི་ཚོགས། group of letters.

ཚོགས་བསགས་ཡན་ལག་བདུན།

The seven limbed practices for the accumulation of merits (see yan-lag bdun-pa).

ཚོར་བ་ལྔ།

Pañca vedanāḥ/ Five types of feelings. 1-2. ལུས་ཀྱི་ཚོར་བ་བདེ་སྡུག་གཉིས། two of the body—pleasure and pain 3-4. ཡིད་ཀྱི་ཚོར་བ་ཡིད་བདེ་དང་ཡིད་མི་བདེ་གཉིས། two of mental—happiness and unhappiness 5. ཚོར་བ་བཏང་སྙོམས། neutral feeling.

ཚོར་བ་དྲན་པ་ཉེར་བཞག

Vedanā smṛtyūpasthāna/ Close contemplation of feelings; mindfulness of feelings. Contemplating that all feelings whatsoever have the nature of suffering and misery.

ཚོར་བ་དྲུག

Ṣaḍ vedanāḥ/ Six types of feelings. མིག་ཤེས་སུ་གྱུར་བའི་ཚོར་བ་ནས་ཡིད་ཤེས་སུ་གྱུར་བའི་ཚོར་བ་བར་དྲུག Feeling with respect to the six consciousnesses (see rnam-par shes-pa drug).

ཚོར་བའི་ཕུང་པོ་བཅུ་གཉིས།

Dvādaśa vedanā skandhāḥ/ Twelve aggregates of feeling. 1. མིག་གི་འདུས་ཏེ་རེག་པ་ལས་བྱུང་བའི་ཚོར་བ། feeling produced through visual contact 2. སྣའི་འདུས་ཏེ་རེག་པ་ལས་བྱུང་བའི་ཚོར་བ། feeling produced through olfactory contact 3. རྣ་བའི་འདུས་ཏེ་རེག་པ་ལས་བྱུང་བའི་ཚོར་བ། feeling produced through aural contact 4. ལྕེའི་འདུས་ཏེ་རེག་པ་ལས་བྱུང་བའི་ཚོར་བ། feeling produced through gustatory contact 5. ལུས་ཀྱི་འདུས་ཏེ་རེག་པ་ལས་བྱུང་བའི་ཚོར་བ། feeling produced through physical contact 6. ཡིད་ཀྱི་འདུས་ཏེ་རེག་པ་ལས་བྱུང་བའི་ཚོར་བ། feeling produced through mental contact 7. དབང་ཤེས་སུ་གྱུར་བའི་ཚོར་བ། feeling from sense powers 8. ཡིད་ཤེས་སུ་གྱུར་བའི་ཚོར་བ། feeling from mental consciousness 9. ཟང་ཟིང་དང་བཅས་པའི་ཚོར་བ། disturbed feeling 10. ཟང་ཟིང་མེད་པའི་ཚོར་བ། undisturbed feeling 11. ཞེན་པ་བསྟེན་པའི་ཚོར་བ། feelings stimulating attachment 12. མངོན་པར་འབྱུང་བ་བསྟེན་པའི་ཚོར་བ། feelings expressing experiences.

མཚན་བཅས་ཀྱི་རྣལ་འབྱོར།

Yoga with signs. A kriyā tantra practice of deity yoga lacking direct realization of emptiness, in which a practitioner meditates on the inseparability of the pledge being (see dam-tshig sems-dpa') and the wisdom being (see ye-shes sems-dpa').

མཚན་བཅས་འདུ་ཤེས་ཀྱི་ཕུང་པོ་གསུམ།

Three aggregates of perception with signs. 1. ཐ་སྙད་ལ་མཁས་པའི་འདུ་ཤེས། skillful perception of the conventions 2. འདུས་བྱས་མི་རྟག་པ་སོགས་ལ་དམིགས་པའི་འདུ་ཤེས། perception observing compositional factors, impermanence, etc. 3. དམིགས་རྣམ་གསལ་བའི་འདུ་ཤེས། perception of a clearly focused object.

མཚན་ཉིད།

Lakṣaṇa/ A. Definition; characteristics. Anything that is a definition must fulfil three qualities of a substantial existence (see rdzas-yod chos-gsum tshang-ba). B. Study of Buddhist philosophy.

མཚན་ཉིད་སྡེ་གསུམ།

The three causal vehicles; the three characteristic vehicles. A term used in the Nyingma tradition for the Hearers vehicle, Solitary realizer vehicle, and Bodhisattva vehicle.

མཚན་ཉིད་ལྡེམ་པོར་དགོངས་པ།

Lakṣaṇābhisandhi/ Interpretive sūtra concerning the characteristics (of phenomena), e.g. the sūtra included in the Third Turning of the Wheel of doctrine in which Buddha clearly explained the three categories of phenomena in terms of their true existence or lack of true existence.

མཚན་ཉིད་མེད་པའི་སྐད་ཅིག་སྦྱོར་བ།

Alakṣaṇatvaikakṣaṇābhisaṃbodha/ Signless momentary training. The last instant of the Bodhisattva paths of advancement, which is categorized as a direct antidote to the obstruction to omniscience and which has direct perception of emptiness.

མཚན་ཉིད་གསུམ།

Trīṇi lakṣaṇāni/ Three characteristics; three natures; the three types of phenomena according to the Cittamātrin school of philosophy. 1. ཀུན་བརྟགས། parikalpita lakṣaṇam/ imputed phenomena, mere objects of conceptual labelling, e.g. permanent phenomena 2. གཞན་དབང་། paratantra lakṣaṇam/ dependent phenomena, e.g. a vase 3. ཡོངས་གྲུབ། pariniṣpanna lakṣaṇam/ thoroughly established phenomena, e.g. emptiness of a vase.

མཚན་མེད་ཀྱི་རྣལ་འབྱོར།

Animitta yoga/ Yoga without signs. A kriyā tantra practice of deity yoga conjoined with the wisdom cognizing emptiness, in which a practitioner meditates on the inseparability of the pledge being (see dam-tshig sems-dpa') and the wisdom being (see ye-shes sems-dpa').

མཚན་མའི་ལྷ།

The sign-deity. One of the six types of deities according to action tantra (see bya-rgyud lha-drug) in which a trainee maintains the imagination of oneself and one's activities as that of a deity.

མཚན་གཞི་ཡིད་ཀྱི་རྣམ་ཤེས།

Exemplary mental consciousness. The mind-stream representing the conventional 'I' that acts as the basis upon which the latencies of karma abide and mature.

མཚན་བཟང་པོ་སུམ་ཅུ་རྩ་གཉིས།

Thirty-two major marks of a Buddha. 1. ཕྱག་ཞབས་འཁོར་ལོས་མཚན་པ། the palms of his hands and feet bear signs of a wheel 2. རུས་སྦལ་བཞིན་དུ་ཞབས་ཤིན་ཏུ་གནས་པ། his feet are well set upon the ground like a tortoise 3. ཕྱག་ཞབས་སོར་མོ་དྲ་བས་འབྲེལ་བ། his fingers and toes are webbed 4. ཕྱག་ཞབས་འཇམ་ཞིང་གཞོན་ཤ་ཆགས་པ། the palms of his hands and feet are smooth and tender 5. ཕྱག་དང་ཞབས་དང་ཐལ་གོང་དང་ལྟག་པའི་ཕྱོགས་མཐོ་བའི་ཕྱིར་སྐུའི་གནས་བདུན་མཐོ་བ། his body has seven prominent features: broad heels, broad hands, broad shoulder blades and broad neck 6. སོར་མོ་རིང་བ། his fingers are long 7. རྟིང་པ་ཡངས་པ། his heels are soft 8. སྐུ་ཆེ་ཞིང་དྲང་བ། he is tall and straight 9. ཞབས་ཀྱི་ལོང་བུ་མི་མངོན་པ། his ankle-bones do not protrude 10. སྐུའི་བ་སྤུ་གྱེན་དུ་ཕྱོགས་པ། the hairs on his body point upward 11. བྱིན་པ་རི་དྭགས་ཨེ་ན་ཡ་འདྲ་བ། his ankles are like an antelope's 12.

ཕྱག་རིང་ཞིང་མཛེས་པ། his hands are long and beautiful 13. མདོམས་ཀྱི་སྦ་བ་སྦུབས་སུ་ནུབ་པ། his male organ is withdrawn 14. པགས་པ་གསེར་མདོག་འདྲ་བ། his body is the colour of gold 15. པགས་པ་སྲབ་ཅིང་འཇམ་པ། his skin is thin and smooth 16. བ་སྤུ་རེ་རེ་ནས་གཡས་ཕྱོགས་སུ་འཁྱིལ་བ། each hair curls to the right 17. ཞལ་མཛོད་སྤུས་བརྒྱན་པ། his face is adorned by a coiled hair between his eyebrows 18. རོ་སྟོད་སེང་གེ་འདྲ་བ། the upper part of his body is like that of a lion 19. དཔུང་པའི་མགོ་ཤིན་ཏུ་ཟླུམ་པ། his head and shoulders are perfectly round 20. ཐལ་གོང་རྒྱས་པ། his shoulders are broad 21. རོ་མི་ཞིམ་པ་རོ་མཆོག་སྣང་བ། he has an excellent sense of taste even of the worse tastes 22. སྐུ་ཉ་གྲོ་དྷ་ར་ཆུ་ཞིང་གབ་པ། his body has the proportions of a banyan tree 23. གཙུག་ཏོར་བལྟར་མི་མངོན་པ། he has a protrusion on the crown of his head 24. ལྗགས་རིང་ཞིང་སྲབ་པ། his tongue is long and thin 25. གསུང་ཚངས་དབྱངས་ལྟ་བུ། his voice is mellifluent 26. འགྲམ་པ་སེང་གེ་འདྲ་བ། his cheeks are like those of a lion 27. ཚེམས་ཤིན་ཏུ་དཀར་བ། his teeth are white 28. ཚེམས་མཉམ་པ། there are no gaps between his teeth 29. ཚེམས་ཐགས་བཟང་བ། his teeth are evenly set 30. ཚེམས་བཞི་བཅུ་མངའ་བ། he has a total of forty teeth 31. སྤྱན་མཐོན་མཐིང་འདྲ་བ། his eyes are the colour of saphire 32. སྤྱན་གྱི་རྫི་མ་བ་མཆོག་གི་རྫི་མ་དང་འདྲ་བ། his eyelashes are like those of a magnificient heifer.

མཚམས་མེད་ལྔ།

Pañcānantarīyāṇi/ Five heinous crimes; five boundless actions. Five non-virtuous actions that propel a person immediately into the most serious hell realm. 1. ཕ་གསོད་པ། pitṛghāta/ patricide 2. མ་གསོད་པ། mātṛghāta/ matricide 3. དགྲ་བཅོམ་པ་གསོད་པ། arhadghāta/ killing an Arhat 4. དེ་བཞིན་གཤེགས་པའི་སྐུ་ལས་ངན་སེམས་ཀྱིས་ཁྲག་འབྱིན་པ། tathāgatasyāntike duṣṭacitta rudhirotpādanam/ drawing blood from the body of a Buddha with evil intent 5. དགེ་འདུན་གྱི་དབྱེན་འབྱེད་པ། saṁghabheda/ causing a schism within the Saṅgha.

མཚུངས་ལྡན་གྱི་རྒྱུ།

Samprayukta hetu/ Concomitant cause. Sharing five common factors with the result, which pertain only to a cognition; one of the six types of causes (see rgyu-drug).

མཚུངས་ལྡན་རྣམ་པ་ལྔ་མཚུངས།

Five concommitant factors. The way a secondary mind accompanies the primary mind through five-fold correlationships. 1. རྟེན་མཚུངས་པ། common sense base 2. དམིགས་པ་མཚུངས་པ། common object 3. རྣམ་པ་མཚུངས་པ། common aspect 4. དུས་མཚུངས་པ། common time 5. རྫས་མཚུངས་པ། common substantial entity.

མཚུར་ཕུ་དགོན་པ།

Tsurphu Monastic University. The principal monastic seat of the Karma Kagyud Order of Tibetan Buddhism, established in 1189 by the First Karmapa, Karmapa Dusum Khyenpa (1110-1193).

མཚོ་ལྟ་བུའི་སེམས་བསྐྱེད།

Ocean-like bodhicitta. The mind of enlightenment associated with the exalted practice of the perfection of patience possessed by a Bodhisattva on the third ground.

མཚོ་དྲུག

The six lakes. 1. སྦྲང་རྩིའི་མཚོ། lake of honey 2. མར་གྱི་མཚོ། lake of butter 3. ཞོའི་མཚོ། lake of yogurt 4. འོ་མའི་མཚོ། lake of milk 5. ཆུའི་མཚོ། lake of water 6. ཆང་གི་མཚོ། lake of liquor.

མཚོན་བྱ།

Topic to be defined. Any phenomenon that is qualified by: 1

being generally a topic to be defined 2. not being a topic to be defined other than by its definition 3. that of which there is an example.

འཚོ་བ་གསུམ།

The three types of livelihood; the three causes for our survival. 1. ཚེ། life-span 2. བསོད་ནམས། merits 3. ལས། karma.

འཚོ་བའི་ཡོ་བྱད་བཅུ་གསུམ།

Thirteen articles of livelihood for a monk. 1. སྣམ་སྦྱར། Namja: patched yellow robe worn only by a fully ordained monk 2. བླ་གོས། patched yellow robe worn by any monk 3. མཐང་གོས། undergarment 4. རྔུལ་གཟན། sweat shawl 5. རྔུལ་གཟན་གྱི་གཟན། shawl over sweat shawl 6. ཤམ་ཐབས། lower robe 7. ཤམ་ཐབས་ཀྱི་གཟན། shawl 8. སྐྲ་བཟེད། protective cloth for shaving the head 9. གདོང་ཕྱིས། towel 10. གདིང་བ། mat 11. ནག་གཟན། གཡན་དགབ། itch covering/ rash bandage 12. གཡར་གྱི་རས་ཆེན། large rain cap 13. གཏུར་བུ། cloth bag.

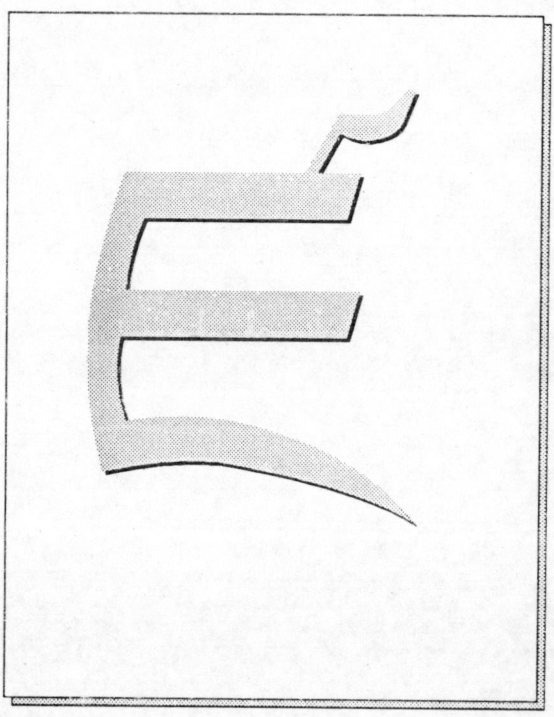

ཛ་ཡནྟུ།

Jayantu. A Sanskrit word meaning victorious or victory forever.

མཛད་པ་བཅུ་གཉིས།

Twelve deeds of Buddha Śākyamuni. 1. དགའ་ལྡན་ནས་འཕོ་བའི་མཛད་པ། descent from Tuṣita heaven 2. ལྷུམ་གྱི་ལྷུམས་སུ་ཞུགས་པའི་མཛད་པ། entering the womb of his mother 3. སྐུ་བལྟམས་པའི་མཛད་པ། taking birth 4. བཟོའི་གནས་ལ་མཁས་པར་སྟོན་པའི་མཛད་པ། displaying his skill in the worldly arts 5. བཙུན་མོའི་འཁོར་དུ་དགྱེས་པར་རོལ་པའི་མཛད་པ། life with the women of the harem 6. རབ་ཏུ་བྱུང་བའི་མཛད་པ། renunciation and ordination as a monk 7. དཀའ་བ་སྤྱད་པའི་མཛད་པ། practising arduous discipline 8. བྱང་ཆུབ་ཤིང་དྲུང་དུ་བཞུགས་པའི་མཛད་པ། meditation under the Bodhi tree 9. བདུད་བཅོམ་པའི་མཛད་པ། defeating the host of demons (māra) 10. སངས་རྒྱས་པའི་མཛད་པ། attaining full enlightenment 11. ཆོས་ཀྱི་འཁོར་ལོ་བསྐོར་བའི་མཛད་པ། turning the wheel of doctrine 12. སྐུ་མྱ་ངན་ལས་འདས་པའི་མཛད་པ། passing into the state of peace (parinirvāṇa).

མཛུབ་ཁྲིད།

A. Word by word teaching by a teacher pointing his finger at the text. B. Detailed teaching pointing out every single detail and reference.

མཛོད།

Kośa/ A. Treasure-house B. Treasure of Knowledge (Abhidharma); a major Buddhist text on metaphysics, cosmology, etc.

མཛོད་ལྟ་བུའི་སེམས་བསྐྱེད།

Treasure-house like bodhicitta. The mind of enlightenment associated with the practice of accumulations (see tshogs-gnyis), possessed by a Bodhisattva on the tenth ground.

མཛོད་སྤུ།

Ūrṇākeśa/ Coiled hair; hair-treasure. A long coiled hair between the eyebrows of a Buddha; one of the thirty-two major marks of a Buddha (see mtshan-bzang-po sum-cu rtsa-gnyis).

མཛོད་ལས་བཤད་པའི་ཤེས་པ་བཅུ།

Ten awarenesses according to the Abhidharma tradition; the ten knowledges of a Buddha. 1. ཆོས་ཤེས་པ། dharma jñānam/ knowledge of Dharma 2. རྗེས་སུ་ཤེས་པ། anvaya jñānam/ subsequent knowledge 3. སྡུག་བསྔལ་ཤེས་པ། duḥkha jñānam/ knowledge of sufferings 4. ཀུན་འབྱུང་ཤེས་པ། samudaya jñānam/ knowledge of the origin of sufferings 5. འགོག་པ་ཤེས་པ། nirodha jñānam/ knowledge of the cessation 6. ལམ་ཤེས་པ། mārga jñānam/ knowledge of the path 7. ཟད་པ་ཤེས་པ། kṣaya jñānam/ knowledge of exhaustion 8. མི་སྐྱེ་བ་ཤེས་པ།

anutpāda jñānam/ knowledge of non-production 9. ཀུན་རྫོབ་ཤེས་པ། saṁvṛti jñānam/ knowledge of conventional phenomena 10. གཞན་གྱི་སེམས་ཤེས་པ། paracitta jñānam/ knowledge of others' minds.

འཛམ་གླིང་རྒྱན་དྲུག་མཆོག་གཉིས།

The six ornaments and two excellences of this world; the great Indian pandits (see rgyan-drug mchog-gnyis).

འཛིན་རྟོག་གཉིས།

Two conceptions of grasping; two thought-apprehensions of the object-holder. 1. རྫས་འཛིན་རྟོག་པ། apprehension of the substantial entity 2. བཏགས་འཛིན་རྟོག་པ། apprehension of the imputed entity.

འཛིན་སྟངས།

Muṣṭibandha/ Mode of apprehension; apprehended object irrespective of its existence or not.

འཛིན་པ།

Grahaṇa/ A. Subjective mind; awareness; object-holder. B. Grasping; holding; apprehension; attachment.

འཛིན་པ་གཉིས།

Dvayagrāha/ Two types of apprehension; two types of grasping: A. 1. འཕྲད་ནས་འཛིན་པ། apprehension through contact 2. མ་འཕྲད་པར་འཛིན་པ། apprehension without contact B. 1. རང་མཚན་འཛིན་པ། apprehension of self-characterized phenomena 2. སྤྱི་མཚན་འཛིན་པ། apprehension of generally characterized phenomena C. 1. གང་ཟག་གི་བདག་འཛིན། grasping at the self of a person 2. ཆོས་ཀྱི་བདག་འཛིན། grasping at the self of a phenomena.

རྫས།

Dravya/ Substance. Things that are not merely labelled through concepts or ideas but are actually capable of performing a function, e.g. form.

རྫས་ཆོས།

Dravya dharma/ A. Functioning thing; things that are actually capable of performing a function, e.g. form. B. Qualities of a thing, e.g. impermanence of form.

རྫས་དགུ

Nava dravya/ Nine principles; nine phenomena as asserted by the Vaiśeṣika school of philosophy. 1. བདག ātman/ self 2. དུས། kāla/ time 3. ཕྱོགས། diśā/ direction 4. ཡིད། citta/ mind 5. ནམ་མཁའ། ākāśa/ space 6. ས། pṛthvi/ earth 7. ཆུ། apa/ water 8. མེ། agni/ fire 9. རླུང་། vāyu/ wind.

རྫས་ཡོད།

Dravyasat/ Substantial existent. A. A material entity or existent, e.g. a vase. B. A category of phenomena which can be understood without first having to understand another phenomena, e.g. the aggregate of form, or a vase.

རྫས་ཡོད་ཆོས་གསུམ།

The three features of substantial existence; the three features of those substantial entities that are themselves the definition of a phenomena. 1. རང་མཚན་ཉིད་ཡིན་པ། being a definition 2. རང་གི་མཚན་གཞིའི་སྟེང་དུ་གྲུབ་པ། that which is established upon its own basis to be defined 3. རང་གི་མཚོན་བྱ་ལས་གཞན་པའི་ཆོས་གཞན་གྱི་མཚན་ཉིད་མི་བྱེད་པ། not being a definition other than its own basis to be defined.

རྫས་ཡོད་དྲུག

Six types of substantial existents. 1-4. (see rdzas-yod bzhi, ibid) 5. རྟགས་སྒྲུབ་ཀྱི་རྫས། primordially established substantial existence 6. བདེན་གྲུབ་ཀྱི་རྫས། truly existent substantial existence.

རྫས་ཡོད་བཞི།

Four types of substantial existents. 1. རིགས་པས་གྲུབ་པའི་རྫས་ཡོད། logically established substantial existence 2. བརྟན་པས་མི་འགྱུར་བའི་རྫས་ཡོད། ever unchanging substantial existence 3. དོན་བྱེད་ནུས་པའི་རྫས་ཡོད། functional substantial existence 4. རང་རྐྱ་ཐུབ་པའི་རྫས་ཡོད། self-sufficient (independent) substantial existence.

རྫས་རིགས་གཅིག་པ།

Same substantial entities. For instance, a white and black vase made from the same lump of clay.

རྫུ་འཕྲུལ་གྱི་རྐང་པ་བཞི།

Catvāra ṛddhipādāḥ/ Four legs (causes) of miracles. A class of division within the thirty-seven auxilaries to enlightenment; qualities gained by a Bodhisattva on the great level of the path of accumulation (tshogs-lam). That of: 1. འདུན་པའི་རྫུ་འཕྲུལ་གྱི་རྐང་པ། chanda ṛddhipāda/ aspiration 2. བརྩོན་འགྲུས་ཀྱི་རྫུ་འཕྲུལ་གྱི་རྐང་པ། virya ṛddhipāda/ effort 3. བསམ་པའི་རྫུ་འཕྲུལ་གྱི་རྐང་པ། citta ṛddhipāda/ thought 4. དཔྱོད་པའི་རྫུ་འཕྲུལ་གྱི་རྐང་པ། mīmaṁsā ṛddhipāda/ analysis.

རྫུ་འཕྲུལ་ལྔ།

Five types of miracles. 1. སྒོམ་བྱུང་གི་རྫུ་འཕྲུལ། miracles acquired through meditation 2. སྐྱེས་ཐོབ་ཀྱི་རྫུ་འཕྲུལ། miracles acquired by birth 3. སྔགས་ལས་ཐོབ་པའི་རྫུ་འཕྲུལ། miracles acquired through tantric practices 4. སྨན་ལས་བྱུང་བའི་རྫུ་འཕྲུལ། miracles acquired through medicinal pills 5. ལས་ལས་བྱུང་བའི་རྫུ་འཕྲུལ། miracles acquired through karmic forces.

རྫུན་བཞི།

Four types of lying; four types of lying about monk's precepts. 1. ཕམ་པའི་ སྡེར་གཏོགས་ཀྱི་རྫུན། lying classed as a defeat 2. ལྷག་མའི་སྡེར་གཏོགས་ཀྱི་རྫུན། lying classed as a remainder 3. མ་ངེས་པའི་སྡེར་གཏོགས་ཀྱི་རྫུན། lying classed as an indefinite case 4. ཉེས་བྱས་ཀྱི་སྡེར་གཏོགས་ཀྱི་རྫུན། lying classed as a fault.

རྫོགས་ལྡན་གྱི་དུས།

The Perfected Aeon (see bskal-pa rdzogs-ldan).

རྫོགས་པ་ཆེན་པོ།

Great perfection. A term exclusive to Nyingma doctrine and meditation. The spontaneous and natural perfection of fully enlightened qualities possessed by the three kāyas within the reality of mind, i.e. the primodially empty nature dharmakāya; the naturally luminous sambhogakāya; and all-pervasive compassion nirmāṇakāya, which is otherwise the ultimate reality of all phenomena.

རྫོགས་པ་ཆེན་པོ་སྙིང་ཐིག

Heart's core great perfection. The transmission of great perfection originally received by King Trisong Deutsan from Ācarya Vimalamitra. During the later period of propagation of Buddhism (see bstan-pa phyi-dar) in Tibet. This transmission was widely disseminated by the great master Kunkhyen Longchen Rabjampa (see kun-mkhyen klong chen rab-'byams).

རྫོགས་པ་སྤྱི་ཆིབས་ཀྱི་ས།

The ground of riding the universal rDzogs-chen. According to the Nyingma tradition, this refers to the tenth Bodhisattva ground attained on the fifth stage of yoga, where a person has completely and perfectly integrated all experiences and appearances on the path to liberation into the sphere of lack of production of all projections of the Rupakaya.

རྫོགས་རིམ།

Saṁpanna krama/ Completion stage. An anuttarayoga tantra practice of meditation in which a practioner trains or is able to activate the innate primordial wisdom through experiencing the four-fold joys (see dga'-ba bzhi) and the mind of clear light through experiencing the four-fold empties (see stong-bzhi) respectively upon this vajra (deity) body.

རྫོགས་རིམ་རྣལ་འབྱོར་བཞི།

The four completion stage yogas; the four completion stage yogas of the Yamāntaka tantra. 1. སྔགས་ཀྱི་རྣལ་འབྱོར། yoga of mantra 2. དམ་ཚིག་གི་རྣལ་འབྱོར། yoga of samaya 3. དབྱིབས་ཀྱི་རྣལ་འབྱོར། yoga of shape 4. ཡེ་ཤེས་ཀྱི་རྣལ་འབྱོར། yoga of primordial wisdom.

རྫོགས་རིམ་རིམ་ལྔ།

Five levels of the completion stage. 1. ལུས་དབེན། isolation of body 2. ངག་དབེན། isolation of speech 3. སེམས་དབེན། isolation of mind 4. འོད་གསལ། clear light mind 5. སྒྱུ་ལུས། illusory body. In some cases, the first two are listed as one and the state of union (yuganaddha) is added to the list to make five. See the five profound paths (zab-lam rim-lnga).

རྫོགས་རིམ་རིམ་པ་དྲུག

Six levels of the completion stage. (see rdzog-rim rim-lnga 1-5, above) 6. ཟུང་འཇུག the state of union (yuganaddha).

རྫོགས་བྱེད་ཀྱི་ལས།

Completing karma. Karma that primarily determines the specific details of environmental and physical attributes, personality, etc., of a being irrespective of the level of rebirth, e.g. a dog enjoying comforts of living in a palace though just an animal.

རྫོགས་སྨིན་སྦྱངས་གསུམ།

Accomplishment, maturation and purification.

བརྫུས་སྐྱེས།

Upapāduka/ Miraculous birth. One of the four types of birth (see skye-gnas bzhi), e.g. the birth of Guru Padmasambhava.

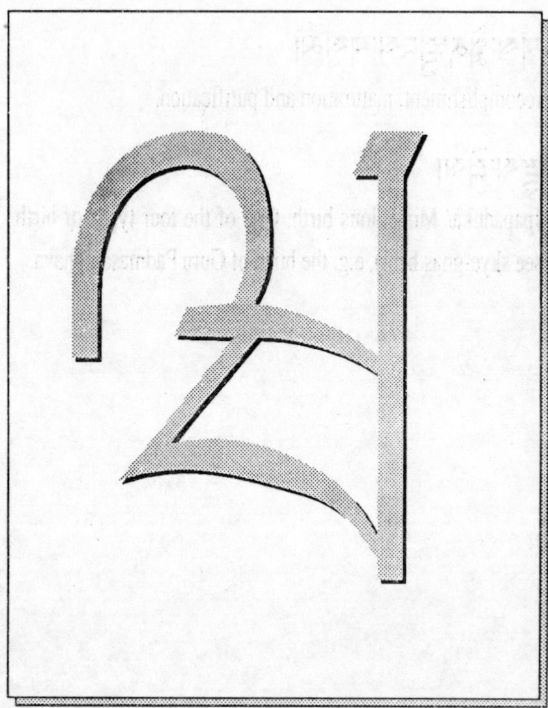

ཝ་སྐྱེས།

Fox; exemplifies cowardice and deceit in a person

ཝ་ཁ།

Gutter.

ཝ་ཁུང་།

Guttur or wolf's lair.

ཝ་པདེ།

Rhinoceros.

ཝ་ར་སྐད་ཅན།

Donkey; ass.

ཝཱ་རཱ་ཎ་སཱི།

Vārāṇasī. One of the four principal holy places of Buddhist pilgrimage, where Buddha Śākyamuni turned the first wheel of doctrine concerning the four noble truths to the the five ascetics (see 'khor lnga-sde bzang-po).

ཝ་རུ་ཎ།

Name of a nāga; a water-deity.

ཝ་ལམ་ཅན།

Cemetery.

ཝང་གང་།

Joyful state of mind; laughing expression.

ཝ་ལི་ཝ་ལི།

Clear mental comprehension of words and meanings.

ཝར་ཏུ།

Vartu. An ancient script used by Tonmi Sambhota as a model for headless Tibetan script (U-med).

ཝེར་མ།

Warrior god; god of weapon.

ཝོ་རྒྱལ། འོ་བརྒྱལ།

Tiredness; fatigue.

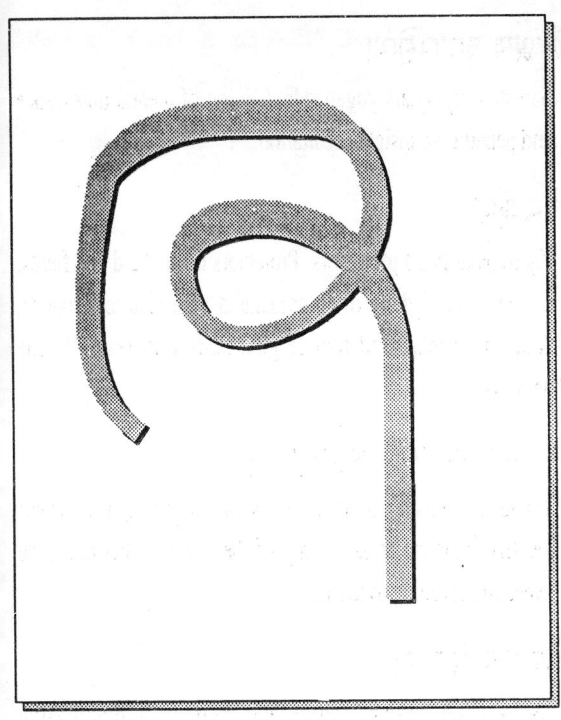

ཞ་ལུ་དགོན་པ།

Zhalu monastery. A monastery in the vicinity of Zhigatse established during the 11th century, which flourished as a principal centre of study and training of Zhalu philosophy during the time of Buton Rinchen Drup. It is believed that this monastery had many Sanskrit texts.

ཞང་ཞུང་།

Zhang-Zhung is believed to be the cradle of ancient Tibetan culture, and according to some the place of origin of the Bon religion. Some historical texts like the *Blue Annals* identify Zhang-zhung with Guge, now the Tsa-dha district in the Ngari region of western Tibet.

ཞབས་ཏོག་རྣམ་གསུམ།

The threefold services; the three ways to honour and please one's root guru. 1. རབ་སྒྲུབ་པའི་མཆོད་པ། offering of practice as the supreme 2. འབྲིང་ལུས་ངག་གི་ཞབས་ཏོག physical and vocal service as the middling 3. ཐ་མ་ཟང་ཟིང་གི་འབུལ་བ། material offering as the modest.

ཞལ་ཏ་བ།

Vārika/ Monk steward. Monk official in charge of economic affairs; especially one chosen during the three months rainy season retreat.

ཞལ་ནས་གསུངས་པའི་བཀའ།

Spoken teaching of Buddha. Teachings that Buddha actually spoke from his mouth directly; verbal teachings of Buddha.

ཞལ་གདམས།

Instruction; advice of a respected person.

ཞལ་ཟས།

Bhojya/ Food; food offerings.

ཞི་གནས།

Śamatha/ Mental quiescence meditation; calm abiding meditation. A single-pointed meditative concentration developed through the techniques of settling the mind; a practice common to both Buddhists and non-Buddhists.

ཞི་གནས་ཀྱི་སྟོབས་དྲུག།

The six powers of calm abiding meditation (see stobs-drug).

ཞི་གནས་ཀྱི་དམིགས་པ་བཞི།

Four objects of mental quiescence meditation. 1. ཁྱབ་པའི་དམིགས་པ། pervasive object 2. སྤྱད་པ་རྣམ་སྦྱོང་གི་དམིགས་པ། objects for overcoming objects of obsession 3. མཁས་པའི་དམིགས་པ། object of the wise practitioner 4. ཉོན་མོངས་རྣམ་སྦྱོང་གི་དམིགས་པ། object for purification of delusions.

ཞི་གནས་ཀྱི་ཚོགས།

The conditions for calm abiding meditation; the necessities for practicing calm abiding meditation. 1. མཐུན་པའི་ཡུལ་ན་གནས་པ། living in a harmonious place 2. འདོད་པ་ཆུང་བ། having few desires 3. ཆོག་ཤེས་པ། having contentment 4. བྱ་བ་མང་པོ་ཡོངས་སུ་སྤངས་པ། having few activities of involvement 5. ཚུལ་ཁྲིམས་རྣམ་པར་དག་པ། having pure morality 6. འདོད་པ་ལ་སོགས་པའི་རྣམ་པར་རྟོག་པ་ཡོངས་སུ་སྤངས་པ། having freedom from gross delusions such as attachment.

ཞི་གནས་ཀྱི་ཡིད་བྱེད་བཞི།

The four attentions of calm abiding meditation (see yid-byed bzhi).

ཞི་གནས་ཀྱི་གསོ་སྦྱོང་།

Restoration and purification ritual through mental quiescence meditation. A gathering of monks for purification of negativities entailing meditation on close mindfulness or contemplation.

ཞི་གནས་སྐབས་ཀྱི་ཉེས་པ་ལྔ།

The five faults of calm abiding meditation (see nyes-pa lnga).

ཞི་བ་འཚོ།

Śāntarakṣita/ Ācārya Śāntarakṣita. A highly learned master-scholar from Bengal who visited Tibet during the time of King Trisong Deutsan. He assisted Guru Padmasambhava in the building of Samye monastery and was responsible for founding the monastic community for the first time in Tibet.

ཞི་བྱེད།

The Pacifier. This is a Buddhist religious tradition founded by Phadampa Sangye at the beginning of the 12th century, and propagated the practice of gcod (cutting-off) ritual in Tibet.

ཞི་ལྷག་ཟུང་འབྲེལ།

Śamatha vipaśyanā yuganaddha/ Union of mental quiescence and penetrative insight meditation.

ཞིང་སྐྱོང་།

Kṣetrapāla/ Field protectors. Protectors of the land and fields; a kind of local deity often associated with charnel grounds. Also those male and female guardians who reside in the heavens.

ཞིང་བཅུ་ཚང་བའི་དགྲ་བོགས།

The ten heinous hindrances (see bsgral-ba'i zhing-bcu). These identify someone as an enemy of the Buddha Dharma to be expelled according to tantra.

ཞིང་དག་སྦྱོར་བ།

Kṣetraśuddhi prayoga/ Pure land training. A Bodhisattva practice by which one can transform all roots of virtue into means for establishing a Buddha field, with its inhabitants, where he will gain the state of full enlightenment; this path arises on the three pure Bodhisattva grounds, i.e. the eigth, ninth and tenth.

ཞུགས་གནས་བརྒྱད།

Eight noble persons; enterers and abiders in the four state of an ascetics—Stream-winner, Once returner, Never returner and Arhatship. 1. རྒྱུན་ཞུགས་ཞུགས་པ། enterer into the fruit of a stream-winner 2. རྒྱུན་ཞུགས་འབྲས་གནས། abider in the fruit of a stream-winner 3. ཕྱིར་འོང་ཞུགས་པ། enterer into the fruit of a once-returner 4. ཕྱིར་འོང་འབྲས་གནས། abider in the fruit of a once-returner 5. ཕྱིར་མི་འོང་ཞུགས་པ། enterer into the fruit of a never-returner 6. ཕྱིར་མི་འོང་འབྲས་གནས། abider in the fruit of a never-returner 7. དགྲ་བཅོམ་ཞུགས་པ། enterer into the fruit of a Foe-destroyer 8. དགྲ་བཅོམ་འབྲས་གནས། abider in the fruit of a Foe-destroyer.

ཞུགས་གནས་ཐིམ་གསུམ།

Entering, abiding and dissolution. The three-fold tantric practice of causing the energy winds to enter, abide and dissolve into the central channel through meditation.

ཞེན་པ་བཞི་བྲལ།

The mind training, 'Parting Away from Four Clingings' (see blo-sbyong zhen-pa bzhi-bral).

ཞེན་ཡུལ།

Object of attachment. Synonymous with the apprehended object of conception (rtog-pa'i zhen-yul).

གཞན་གྱི་དངོས་པོ་སྟོང་པ་ཉིད།

Parabhāva śūnyatā/ Emptiness of others. One of the sixteen types of emptinesses; the lack of inherent existence of transwordly phenomena as opposed to worldly existents.

གཞན་འགྱུར་བཞི།

Four changeable mental factors. 1. གཉིད། niddham/ sleep 2. འགྱོད་པ། kaukṛtyam/ regret 3. རྟོག་པ། vitarka/ grcss investigation 4. དཔྱོད་པ། vicāra/ subtle investigation.

གཞན་སྟོང་།

Other emptiness; alternative emptiness. The lack of existence of other conventional phenomena, i.e. dependent and imputed phenomena, etc., upon the thoroughly established phenomena, i.e. the non-dual wisdom understanding the inseparability of the subjective mind and objective existence. An alternative middle-view asserted by Jonangpa school of Tibetan Buddhism.

གཞན་གནོད་གཞི་དང་བཅས་པ་སྤོང་བ།

Abandonments of harms to others along with the basis. The nature of individual liberation vows; 'others', here refers to the seven non-virtuous activities of body and speech that inflicts direct harm on others, and 'bases', here refers to the causes of those non-virtues—the three non-virtues of mind. When a person holding individual liberation vows eliminates these with his or her mind conjoined with a sense of renunciation, it becomes a fully characterized individual liberation vow (pratimokṣa).

གཞན་པ་མི་མཐུན་ཕྱོགས།

Alternative dissimilar factor. That which is a dissimilar factor, yet shows a common basis with the predicate in a logical syllogism.

གཞན་དབང་གཉིས།

Two types of dependent phenomena. One of the three categories of phenomena according to the Cittamātrin school. 1. དག་པའི་གཞན་དབང་། śuddhaparatantra/ pure dependent phenomena 2. མ་དག་པའི་གཞན་དབང་། aśuddhaparatantra/ impure dependent phenomena.

གཞན་འབྱོར་ལྔ།

Five circumstantial endowments. Of the ten endowments (see 'byor-ba bcu) the five factors required to be fulfilled in the environment in which one lives: 1. སངས་རྒྱས་འཇིག་རྟེན་དུ་བྱོན་པ། Buddha's having come 2. དམ་པའི་ཆོས་གསུངས་པ། His having taught the doctrine 3. བསྟན་པ་གནས་པ། the existence of His doctrine 4. དེའི་རྗེས་འཇུག་ཡོད་པ། the existence of His followers 5. གཞན་ཕྱིར་རྟག་ཏུ་སྙིང་བརྩེ་བ། being compassionate towards others.

གཞན་ལས་ངེས་ཀྱི་ཚད་མ།

Valid cognition ascertainable from other factors, e.g. valid cognition within the continuum of a person who has no knowledge of valid cognition.

གཞན་སེལ།

Anyāpoha/ Exclusion of other; negative phenomena. An awareness that understands its own object of perception through negating the existence of its direct opposite, e.g. the generic image of a vase. Synoymous with negative phenomena. There are two types: 1. མེད་དགག་གི་གཞན་སེལ། non-affirming exclusion of other, e.g. emptiness 2. མ་ཡིན་དགག་གི་གཞན་སེལ། affirming exclusion of other, e.g. not being a vase.

གཞལ་བྱ་གཉིས།

Two types of knowable objects; two objects of knowledge. 1. སྤྱི། sāmānya/ general phenomena 2. བྱེ་བྲག viśeṣa/ particular phenomena or 1. སྤྱི་མཚན།བརྫུས་སྐྱེས། sāmānyalakṣaṇa/ generally characterized 2. རང་མཚན། svalakṣaṇa/ self-characterized phenomena or 1. རྟག་པ། nitya/ permanent 2. མི་རྟག་པ། anitya/ impermanent.

གཞལ་བྱའི་གནས་གསུམ།

Three objects of knowledge. 1. མངོན་གྱུར། pratyaksa/ manifest phenomena, e.g. pillar 2. ལྐོག་གྱུར། parokṣa/ obscure phenomena, e.g. impermanence 3. ཤིན་ཏུ་ལྐོག་གྱུར། atiparoksa/ extremely obscure phenomena, e.g. very subtle nature of the law of causality.

གཞལ་མེད་ཁང་།

Vimāna/ Inconceiveable mansion; celestial mansion; heaven.

གཞི་བཅུ་བདུན།

The seventeen basic precepts. The basic precepts of cultivation for an ordained monk. There is one precept for obtaining the vows not yet obtained; nine precepts for protecting the vows already obtained; and seven precepts for purifying the transgressed vows.

གཞི་ཇི་བཞིན་པ།

Yathāsaṁstarika/ He who sleeps wherever he happens to be. One of the twelve ascetic practice (see sbyangs-pa'i yon-tan bcu-gnyis); to sleep on a bed of grass or leaves, etc., which are laid out once without being rearranged for comfort's sake.

གཞི་ཐམས་ཅད་ཡོད་པར་སྨྲ་བའི་སྡེ་བདུན།

Sapta mūlasarvāstivādāḥ/ Seven Mūlasarvāstivādin schools. One of the eighteen schools of the Hīnayāna tradition. 1. གཞི་ཐམས་ཅད་ཡོད་པར་སྨྲ་བ། Mūlasarvāstivāda 2. འོད་སྲུང་བ། Kāśyapiyāḥ 3. ས་སྟོན་པ། Mahīśāsakāḥ 4. ཆོས་སྲུང་བ། Dharmaguptāḥ 5. མང་ཐོས་པ། Bāhuśrutīyāḥ 6. གོས་དམར་བ། Tāmraśātīyāḥ 7. རྣམ་པར་ཕྱེ་སྟེ་སྨྲ་བ། Vibhajyavādinaḥ.

གཞི་དུས་ཀྱི་འོད་གསལ།

The basic clear light mind. The Buddha nature within the mental continuum of sentient beings, i.e. the primordially pure nature of the minds of all beings.

གཞི་དུས་ཀྱི་ཡེ་ཤེས་ལྔ།

The five basic wisdoms for transforming the five delusions into wisdoms. 1. གཞི་དུས་ཀྱི་མེ་ལོང་ཡེ་ཤེས། mirror-like wisdom for self-pacification of hatred-anger 2. གཞི་དུས་ཀྱི་མཉམ་ཉིད་ཡེ་ཤེས།. wisdom of equality or sameness for self-pacification of pride 3. གཞི་དུས་ཀྱི་སོར་རྟོག་ཡེ་ཤེས། wisdom of analysis for self-pacification of desire-attachment 4. གཞི་དུས་ཀྱི་བྱ་གྲུབ་ཡེ་ཤེས། wisdom of accomplishment for self-pacification of jealousy 5. གཞི་དུས་ཀྱི་ཆོས་དབྱིངས་ཡེ་ཤེས། wisdom of reality for self-pacification of closed-mindedness.

གཞི་ཤེས་ཀྱི་རྣམ་པ་ཉེར་བདུན།

Twenty-seven aspects of the basic wisdom. 1-12. བདེན་པ་དང་པོ་གསུམ་གྱི་རྣམ་པ་བཅུ་གཉིས། twelve aspects of the first three noble truths (see bden-pa dang-po gsum-gyi rnam-pa bcu-gnyis) 13-27. ལམ་བདེན་གྱི་རྣམ་པ་བཅོ་ལྔ། fifteen aspects of the noble truth of the path (see lam-bden-gyi rnam-pa bco-lnga).

གཞི་ཤེས་མཚན་ཉིད་ཀྱི་ཆོས་དགུ

Nine topics that characterize the basic wisdom. 1. ཤེས་པས་སྲིད་ལ་མི་གནས་པའི་གཞི་ཤེས། non-abidance in the extreme of existence through knowledge 2. སྙིང་རྗེས་ཞི་ལ་མི་གནས་པའི་གཞི་ཤེས། non-abidance in the extreme of peace through compassion 3. ཐབས་མ་ཡིན་པས་འབྲས་ཡུམ་ལ་རིང་བའི་གཞི་ཤེས། distant from the mother effect due to lack of skill in means 4. ཐབས་མཁས་པས་འབྲས་ཡུམ་ལ་ཉེ་བའི་གཞི་ཤེས། close to the mother effect due to skill in means 5. མི་མཐུན་ཕྱོགས་ཀྱི་གཞི་ཤེས། basic wisdom classed as a discordant factor 6. གཉེན་པོ་ཕྱོགས་ཀྱི་གཞི་ཤེས། basic wisdom classed as an antidote 7. གཞི་ཤེས་ཀྱི་སྦྱོར་བ། training in basic wisdom 8. གཞི་ཤེས་ཀྱི་མཉམ་ཉིད་སྦྱོར་བ། training in the sameness of basic wisdom 9. གཞི་ཤེས་ཀྱི་མཐོང་ལམ། path of seeing.

གཞི་གསུམ་ཆོ་ག

The three basic rituals; the three basic ceremonies of monks. The text of rituals concerning: 1. གསོ་སྦྱོང་། bi-monthly restoration and confession ceremony 2. དབྱར་གནས། summer or rainy season retreat for three months beginning from the sixteenth of the sixth Tibetan month 3. དགག་དབྱེ། the ceremony of lifting restrictions after the completion of the three months retreat.

གཞིའི་སྐུ་གསུམ།

The three basic kāyas. 1. ཐ་མལ་པའི་སྐྱེ་བ་གཞིའི་སྤྲུལ་སྐུ the ordinary state of birth as the basic nirmāṇakāya 2. ཐ་མལ་གྱི་འཆི་བ་གཞིའི་ཆོས་སྐུ the ordinary state of death as the basic dharmakāya 3. ཐ་མལ་གྱི་བར་དོ་གཞིའི་ལོངས་སྐུ the ordinary state of intermediate rebirth as the basic sambhogakāya.

གཞུག་པ་ལྡེམ་པོར་དགོངས་པ།

Avatāraṇābhisaṁdhi/ Interpretative sūtra encouraging conversion, e.g. a sūtra explaining the existence of the self of a person in order to convert a follower into Buddhist doctrine.

གཞུང་ཆེན་མོ།

The great treatises of philosophy studied in the monastic universities or elsewhere.

གཞུང་པོ་ཏི་ལྔ།

The five treatises of Buddhist philosophy. 1. ཕར་ཕྱིན། Perfection of Wisdom 2. དབུ་མ། Middle Way 3. ཚད་མ། Valid Cognition 4. འདུལ་བ། Monastic Discipline 5. མཛོད། Treasure of Knowledge.

གཞོགས་འཕྱས།

Chiding; reprimand; upraising in an ironic manner.

གཞོལ་བ་གསུམ་གྱི་བཟླས་པ།

The three types of incantation according to action tantra; the three suchnesses of recitation in prāṇayama meditation. 1. གཞི་ལ་གཞོལ་བ། recitation while concentrating on the object deity 2. སེམས་ལ་གཞོལ་བ། recitation while concentrating on the mind deity 3. སྒྲ་ལ་གཞོལ་བ། recitation while concentrating on the sound deity.

བཞོན་པ་ལྟ་བུའི་སེམས་བསྐྱེད།

Mount-like bodhicitta. Mind of enlightenment associated with the exalted practice of compassion and resolute intention possessed by a Bodhisattva on the three pure grounds.

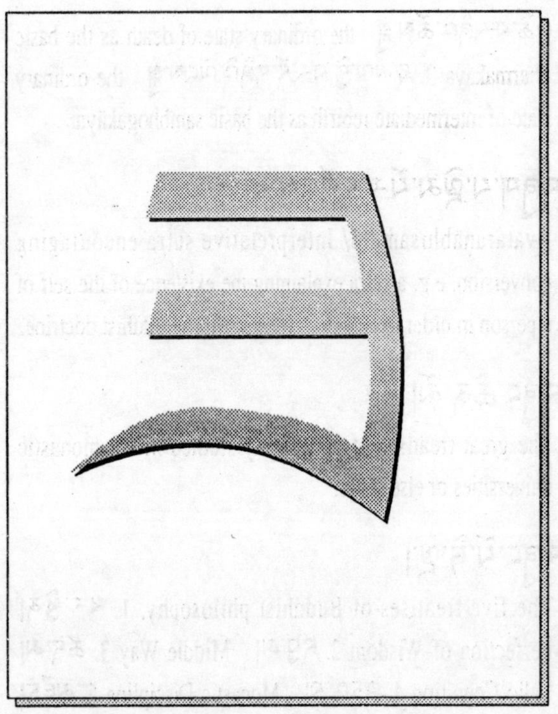

ཟ་མ་ཏོག

Karaṇḍa/ A. Food casket; carried by ascetics as their pot. B. Za-ma-tog sūtra concerning Ārya Avalokiteśvara's cycle of teachings.

ཟག་བཅས།

Sāsrava/ Contaminated phenomena. Deluded phenomena capable of increasing affliction by their presence, e.g. a human body.

ཟག་བཅས་ཀྱི་ཕུང་པོ་ལྔ།

Five contaminated aggregates (see phung-po lnga).

ཟག་པ་བཞི།

Four types of contaminations (see chu-bo bzhi).

ཟག་པའི་སྒོ་དྲུག

The six gates of contamination; the six ways in which delusions increase or become stronger. 1. ཟག་པའི་དངོས་ཉིད། being a contaminated thing, such as being any of the twenty root or near delusions (see rtsa nyon drug and nye-nyon-nyi-shu) 2. ཟག་པ་དང་འབྲེལ་བ། being connected to a contamination, such as the sense faculties that are immediate conditions for producing contaminated mental experiences 3. ཟག་པས་བཅིངས་པ། being bound by contamination, such as the contaminated virtues within the three realms of existence 4. ཟག་པའི་རྗེས་སུ་འབྲེལ་བ། being possessed by contamination, such as the inability to exploit one's body, speech and mind for positive activities 5. ཟག་པའི་རྗེས་སུ་མཐུན་པ། being similar to contamination, such as form, sound etc., that are physical sources of contamination 6. ཟག་པའི་རྒྱུ་ལས་བྱུང་བ། arisen from the contaminated, the results of contamination, such as this human body.

ཟག་མེད་ཀྱི་ཕུང་པོ་ལྔ།

Five uncontaminated aggregates; the five pure ways. 1. ཚུལ་ཁྲིམས་ཀྱི་ཕུང་པོ། śila skandha/ aggregate of moral disciple 2. ཏིང་ངེ་འཛིན་གྱི་ཕུང་པོ། samādhi skandha/ aggregate of concentration 3. ཤེས་རབ་ཀྱི་ཕུང་པོ། prajñā skandha/ aggregate of wisdom 4. རྣམ་པར་གྲོལ་བའི་ཕུང་པོ། vimukti skandha/ aggregate of thorough liberation 5. རྣམ་པར་གྲོལ་བའི་ཡེ་ཤེས་མཐོང་བའི་ཕུང་པོ། vimuktijñāna skandha/ aggregate of seeing the wisdom of thorough liberation.

ཟག་མེད་ཀྱི་དབང་པོ་གསུམ།

The three uncontaminated powers (see dbang-po gsum, B). The powers of a person who has attained the truth of the path.

ཟག་མེད་ཀྱི་ལམ་ལྔ།

The five uncontaminated paths (see zag-med kyi phung-po

lnga, above). These are known as the five uncontaminated paths when the word aggregates are replaced with the word path.

ཟག་མེད་ཡེ་ཤེས་ སྡེ་ ཚན་ ཉེར་གཅིག

Twenty-one groups of uncontaminated wisdom. 1. བྱང་ཕྱོགས་སོ་བདུན། thirty-seven auxiliaries to enlightenment (see byangs-phyog so-bdun) 2. ཚད་མེད་བཞི། four immeasurables (see tshad-med bzhi) 3. རྣམ་ཐར་བརྒྱད། asta vimokṣāḥ/ eight emancipations (see rnam-thar brgyad) 4. མཐར་གྱིས་གནས་པའི་སྙོམས་འཇུག་དགུ nine absorptions (see snyoms-'jug-dgu) 5. ཟད་པར་བཅུ། ten exhaustions/ ten totally pervasive concentrations (see zad-pa bcu) 6. ཟིལ་གྱིས་གནོན་པ་བརྒྱད། eight outshining factors/ eight surpassing concentrations (see zil-gnon brgyad) 7. ཉོན་མོངས་མེད་པའི་ཏིང་ངེ་འཛིན། concentration free of delusions 8. སྨོན་གནས་མཁྱེན་པ། praṇidhijñāsamādhi/ knowledge of one's object of prayers 9. མངོན་ཤེས་དྲུག six extra-sensory perceptions (see mngon-par shes-pa drug) 10. སོ་སོ་ཡང་དག་རིག་པ་བཞི། four specific perfect understandings (see so-sor yang-dag-pa rig-pa bzhi) 11. རྣམ་དག་བཞི། four purities: a) རྟེན་རྣམ་དག pure basis b) དམིགས་པ་རྣམ་དག pure objects c) ཐུགས་རྗེ་རྣམ་དག pure compassion d) ཡེ་ཤེས་རྣམ་དག pure primordial wisdom 12. དབང་བཅུ། ten sovereign qualities (see dbang-phug bcu) 13. སྟོབས་བཅུ། daśa balāni/ ten powers (see de-bzhin gshegs-pa'i stobs-bcu) 14. མི་འཇིགས་པ་བཞི། four fearlessnesses (see mi-'jigs-pa bzhi) 15. བསྲུང་བ་མེད་པ་གསུམ། three unguarded aspects—that of physical, verbal and mental behaviours of a Buddha 16. དྲན་པ་ཉེ་བར་གཞག་པ་གསུམ། three close contemplations (see dran-pa nye-bar gzhag-pa gsum) 17. བསྙེལ་བ་མི་མངའ་བའི་ཆོས་ཉིད། non-negligence of the purpose of sentient beings 18. བག་ཆགས་ཡང་དག་བཅོམ་པ། complete elimination of latencies of three delusions 19. ཐུགས་རྗེ་ཆེན་པོ། mahākaruṇā/ great compassion 20. སངས་རྒྱས་ཀྱི་ཆོས་མ་འདྲེས་པ་བཅོ་བརྒྱད། eighteen unshared qualities of a Buddha (see ma-'dres-pa bco-brgyad) 21. མཁྱེན་པ་གསུམ། three wisdoms (see mkhyen-gsum).

ཟག་མེད་ས་དགུ

Navānāsrava bhūmayaḥ/ Nine uncontaminated grounds; nine uncontaminated levels of concentration. 1. བསམ་གཏན་དང་པོའི་དངོས་གཞི་སྙོམས་འཇུག actual absorption of the first concentration 2. བསམ་གཏན་དང་པོའི་དངོས་གཞི་སྙོམས་འཇུག་ཙམ་པོ་བ། ordinary absorption of the first concentration 3. བསམ་གཏན་དང་པོའི་དངོས་གཞི་སྙོམས་འཇུག་ཁྱད་པར་ཅན། exalted absorption of the first concentration 4. བསམ་གཏན་གཉིས་པའི་དངོས་གཞི་སྙོམས་འཇུག actual absorption of the second concentration 5. བསམ་གཏན་གསུམ་པའི་དངོས་གཞི་སྙོམས་འཇུག actual absorption of the third concentration 6. བསམ་གཏན་བཞི་པའི་དངོས་གཞི་སྙོམས་འཇུག actual absorption of the fourth concentration 7. ནམ་མཁའ་མཐའ་ཡས་དངོས་གཞི་སྙོམས་འཇུག actual absorption of infinite space 8. རྣམ་ཤེས་མཐའ་ཡས་དངོས་གཞི་སྙོམས་འཇུག actual absorption of the infinite consciousness 9. ཅི་ཡང་མེད་ཀྱི་དངོས་གཞི་སྙོམས་འཇུག actual absorption of nothingness.

ཟང་ཐལ།

The unobstructed phenomena; The uninterrupted phenomena.

ཟངས་མདོག་དཔལ་རི།

The copper coloured glorious mountain. The legendary abode of Guru Padmasambhava.

ཟང་ཟིང་།

Āmiṣa/ A. Material goods. B. Blurred vision; confusion.

ཟད་པ་ཤེས་པ།

Kṣayajñāna/ Knowledge of exhaustion. One of the ten types of awarenesses according to the Abhidharma tradition (see mdzod-las bshad-pa'i shes-pa bcu); knowledge of one's own confidence of having abandoned all objects of elimination.

ཟད་པར་གྱི་སྐྱེ་མཆེད།

The total pervasive concentration; the concentration of exhaustion. The power of concentration gained by a person who is able to transform any phenomena into any particular element.

ཟད་པར་གྱི་སྐྱེ་མཆེད་བཅུ།

The ten exhaustions; the ten totally pervasive concentrations (see zad-par bcu, below).

ཟད་པར་བཅུ།

Ten exhaustions; ten totally pervasive concentrations the aim of which is to develop omniscience, by training in perceiving an element such as fire or a color such as blue as totally pervading all phenomena. Totally pervasive concentration with respect to 1-4. ས་ཆུ་མེ་རླུང་བཞི་དང་། five elements 5-8. སྔོ་སེར་དཀར་དམར་བཞི། four root colours—blue, yellow, white and red 9. ནམ་མཁའ་མཐའ་ཡས། infinite space 10. རྣམ་ཤེས་མཐའ་ཡས། infinite consciousness.

ཟན་གྲིལ།

The dough-ball divination. In this system the contents of divination written down on pieces of paper are rolled up in a dough-ball and thrown in front of holy images or paintings of deities of special significance through chanting invocation prayers.

ཟབ་མོ་ལྟ་བརྒྱུད།

Gaṁbhīradarśana tantra/ Lineage of the profound view; the profound view lineage. Lineage of teaching and practice coming from Mañjuśrī, Nāgārjuna and Candrakīrti which mainly emphasises the wisdom aspect of the teachings.

ཟབ་མོ་སྟོང་པ་ཉིད།

Gaṁbhīra śūnyatā/ Profound emptiness; profound voidness.

ཟབ་མོ་དག་སྣང་གི་བརྒྱུད་པ།

Lineage of profound pure perception; lineage of sacred vision. A. The transmission obtained as a result of direct vision and access of one's personal meditational deity. B. A Nyingma lineage derived from accomplished masters, who through their pure perception, have attained a vision of their root guru and meditational deity as the same, and received certain secret teachings that are transmitted only to a limited circle of disciples.

ཟབ་མོའི་ཆོས་ཉིད་རྣམ་པ་བརྒྱད།

Aṣṭa gaṁbhīra dharmatāḥ/ Eight profound realities; eight aspects of the profound reality. 1. སྐྱེ་བ་ཟབ་མོ། profound production 2. འགག་པ་ཟབ་མོ། profound stopping 3. དེ་ཉིད་ཟབ་མོ། profound thusness/reality 4. ཆོས་ཟབ་མོ། profound phenomena 5. ཤེས་པ་ཟབ་མོ། profound awareness 6. ཉམས་ལེན་ཟབ་མོ། profound practice 7. གཉིས་སྟོང་ཟབ་མོ། pro-found non-duality 8. ཐབས་མཁས་ཟབ་མོ། profound skill in means.

ཟབ་ཞི།

The profound peace; the clear light mind of a Buddha; the dharmakāya. The unfathomable omniscience and the state of nirvāṇa or cessation of sufferings within the continuum of a Buddha.

ཟབ་ཞི་སྤྲོས་བྲལ།

The profound peace free of the eight extremes (see spros-pa'i mtha'-brgyad).

ཟབ་ལམ་རིམ་ལྔ།

The five profound paths; the five stages of tantric paths

according to the highest yoga tantra. 1. ངག་དབེན། isolation of speech 2. སེམས་དབེན། isolation of mind 3. སྒྱུ་ལུས། illusory body 4. འོད་གསལ། clear light mind 5. ཟུང་འཇུག the state of unity of the illusory body and clear light mind.

ཟབ་གསལ་གཉིས་མེད་ཀྱི་རྣལ་འབྱོར།

The yoga of non-dual profundity and clarity. The yoga of union of emptiness and the primordial mind realizing it.

ཟབ་གསལ་གཉིས་མེད་ཀྱི་ཡེ་ཤེས།

The primordial wisdom of non-dual profundity and clarity. The wisdom of a yogi, who experiences a clear vision of the divine maṇḍala like the rainbow within the understanding of emptiness.

ཟས་ཀྱི་རྣལ་འབྱོར།

The yoga of foods. 1. ཁ་ཟས་སྨན་དང་འདྲ་བར་རོལ་པར་སྤྱོད་པ། the practice of relishing food like a medicine for sustenance 2. ནང་སྦྱིན་སྲེག་གི་ཚུལ་དུ་ལོངས་སྤྱོད་པ། the practice of relishing food like offering for the inner fire-ritual.

ཟས་དཀར་གསུམ།

The three white foods; yogurt, milk and butter.

ཟས་ཕུད།

The first bit of food. The tradition of offering the first portion of a meal to the objects of refuge before one eats.

ཟས་གཙང་མ།

Śuddhodana/ King Śuddhodana; the father of Buddha Śākyamuni.

ཟས་བཞི།

Catvāra-āhārāḥ/ Four types of food; four nourishments. 1. ཁམ་གྱི་ཟས། kavalikārāhāra/ coarse food, for the growth of the sense organs of this body 2. རེག་པའི་ཟས། sparśāhāra/ food of touch, for the growth of consciousness 3. སེམས་ཀྱི་ཟས། manaḥ saṁcetanāhāra/ food of mental thought, for projecting rebirth in future lives 4. རྣམ་པར་ཤེས་པའི་ཟས། vijñānāhāra/ food for consciousness, for the actualization of the next rebirth.

ཟིན་པའི་སྒྲ།

The conjoined sounds. The sound produced by a person through the force of elements such as wind, e.g. sound of clapping hands and flute.

ཟིལ་གྱིས་གནོན་པའི་སྐྱེ་མཆེད་བརྒྱད།

Aṣṭābhibhavāyatanāni/ Eight surpassing concentrations; the power of concentration through which a yogi aims to gain control of the miracles. 1. རང་གཟུགས་ཅན་དུ་འདུ་ཤེས་པས་ཕྱི་རོལ་གྱི་གཟུགས་ཆུང་ངུ་ལ་བལྟ་ཞིང་གཟུགས་དེ་དག་ཟིལ་གྱིས་གནོན་པ། imagining himself having form, he sees small external forms and overcomes them 2. རང་གཟུགས་ཅན་དུ་འདུ་ཤེས་པས་ཕྱི་རོལ་གྱི་གཟུགས་ཆེན་པོ་ལ་བལྟ་ཞིང་གཟུགས་དེ་དག་ཟིལ་གྱིས་གནོན་པ། imagining himself having form, he sees large external forms and overcomes them 3. རང་གཟུགས་མེད་པར་འདུ་ཤེས་པས་ཕྱི་རོལ་གྱི་གཟུགས་ཆུང་ངུ་ལ་བལྟ་ཞིང་གཟུགས་དེ་དག་ཟིལ་གྱིས་གནོན་པ། imagining himself as lacking form, he sees small external forms and overcomes them 4. རང་གཟུགས་མེད་པར་འདུ་ཤེས་པས་ཕྱི་རོལ་གྱི་གཟུགས་ཆེན་པོ་ལ་བལྟ་ཞིང་གཟུགས་དེ་དག་ཟིལ་གྱིས་གནོན་པ། imagining himself as lacking form, he sees large external forms and overcomes them 5. རང་གཟུགས་ཅན་མེད་པར་འདུ་ཤེས་པ་ཁོ་ནས་ཕྱི་རོལ་གྱི་གཟུགས་སྔོན་པོ་ལ་བལྟ་ཞིང་གཟུགས་དེ་དག་ཟིལ་གྱིས་གནོན་པ། merely imagining himself as lacking form, he sees external blue forms and overcomes them 6. རང་གཟུགས་མེད་པར་འདུ་ཤེས་པ་ཕྱི་ནས་ཕྱི་རོལ་གྱི་གཟུགས་སེར་པོ་ལ་བལྟ་ཞིང་གཟུགས་དེ་དག་ཟིལ་གྱིས་གནོན་པ། merely imagining himself as lacking form, he sees external yellow forms and overcomes them 7. རང་གཟུགས་མེད་པར་འདུ་ཤེས་པ་ཕྱི་ནས་ཕྱི་རོལ་གྱི་གཟུགས་དམར་པོ་ལ་བལྟ་ཞིང་གཟུགས་དེ་དག་ཟིལ་གྱིས་གནོན་པ། merely imagining himself as lacking form, he sees external red forms and overcomes them 8. རང་གཟུགས་མེད་པར་འདུ་ཤེས་པ་ཕྱི་ནས་ཕྱི་རོལ་གྱི་གཟུགས་དཀར་པོ་ལ་བལྟ་ཞིང་གཟུགས་དེ་དག་ཟིལ་གྱིས་གནོན་པ། merely imagining himself as lacking form, he sees external white forms and overcomes them.

ཟུང་འཇུག

Yuganaddha/ A. Unification; state of union, e.g. the union of calm-abiding and penetrative insight meditation or the union of bliss and void. B. One of the five levels of the completion stage practices in tantra; the union of emptiness, the wisdom aspect and great compassion, the method aspect or the union of the wisdom of spontaneous great bliss, the method aspect and the emptiness of clear light mind, the wisdom aspect or the ever-supreme emptiness, the object and the unchanging wisdom of great bliss, the object-perceiver.

ཟུང་འཇུག་ཉེར་གསུམ།

Twenty-three types of unification; twenty three states of union. 1. འཁོར་འདས་དབྱེར་མེད་ཀྱི་ཟུང་འཇུག union of the inseparability of cyclic existence and the state beyond suffering 2. ཀུན་བྱང་གི་ཟུང་འཇུག union of ever-deluded and ever-purified phenomena 3. རྣམ་བཅས་རྣམ་མེད་ཀྱི་ཟུང་འཇུག union of that with and without aspects 4. གཟུང་འཛིན་གྱི་ཟུང་འཇུག union of object and object-perceiver 5. རྟག་ཆད་བྲལ་བའི་ཟུང་འཇུག union of that which is free of the extremes of eternalism and nihilism 6. སྟོང་ཉིད་སྙིང་རྗེའི་ཟུང་འཇུག union of emptiness and compassion 7. ཐབས་ཤེས་ཟུང་འཇུག union of method and wisdom 8. ལྷག་བཅས་ལྷག་མེད་ཀྱི་ཟུང་འཇུག union of residual and non-residual cessation 9. བདག་མེད་གཉིས་ཀྱི་ཟུང་འཇུག union of two selflessnesses 10. སྒྱུ་ལུས་དང་འོད་གསལ་གྱི་ཟུང་འཇུག union of the illusory body and clear light 11. རིལ་འཛིན་གྱི་ཟུང་འཇུག union of thorough dissolution 12. རྗེས་གཞིག་གི་ཟུང་འཇུག union of gradual dissolution 13. བདེན་གཉིས་ཟུང་འཇུག union of two truths 14. མཉམ་གཞག་གི་ཟུང་འཇུག union of meditative equipoise 15. རྗེས་ཐོབ་ཀྱི་ཟུང་འཇུག union of post-meditative equipoise 16. སད་གཉིད་ཀྱི་ཟུང་འཇུག union of sleep and the awakened state 17. མཉམ་པར་འཇུག་ལྡང་གི་ཟུང་འཇུག union of engagement and arisal from meditative equipoise 18. དྲན་པ་མི་དྲན་པའི་ཟུང་འཇུག union of mindfulness and unmindfulness 19. བདེ་སྟོང་ཟུང་འཇུག union of bliss and emptiness 20. བྱ་བྱེད་ཟུང་འཇུག union of action and action-performed 21. བསྐྱེད་རྫོགས་ཟུང་འཇུག union of generation and completion stage 22. དག་མ་དག་གི་ཟུང་འཇུག union of a pure and impure state 23. གཟུགས་ཅན་གཟུགས་མེད་ཀྱི་ཟུང་འཇུག union of an embodied and unembodied entity. In the list of twenty-one, nos. 11 and 12 and nos. 14 and 15 are counted as one each the union of thorough and gradual dissolution and the union of a meditative and post-meditative state.

ཟུང་འཇུག་གཉིས།

Two types of unification; two states of union (yuganaddha). 1. སློབ་པའི་ཟུང་འཇུག state of union of a trainee or learner 2. མི་སློབ་པའི་ཟུང་འཇུག state of union of a non-trainee or a Buddha.

ཟུང་འཇུག་བཞི།

The four types of unification; the four states of union. 1. སྣང་སྟོང་ཟུང་འཇུག union of appearance and emptiness 2. རིག་སྟོང་ཟུང་འཇུག union of awareness and emptiness 3. བདེ་སྟོང་

བདེ་སྟོང་ཟུང་འཇུག union of bliss and emptiness 4. གསལ་སྟོང་ཟུང་འཇུག union of clear light and emptiness.

ཟུར་ཕུད།

Cīraka/ Top-knot; knotted hair gathered at the crown of the head.

ཟླ་གམ།

Monk's overcoat; worn during religious gatherings, especially during winter.

ཟླ་བ་འབྱུང་ངོ་ཚོག་གི་དུས་བཟང་བཞི།

Four auspicious days of every month; four special days of a month according to the Tibetan Buddhist tradition. 1. ཚེས་བརྒྱད་པར་སངས་རྒྱས་སྨན་བླའི་དུས་བཟང་། eighth is the day of the Medicine Buddha 2. ཚེས་བཅུ་པར་མཁའ་འགྲོའི་དུས་བཟང་། tenth is the day of the Ḍākinīs 3. ཚེས་བཅོ་ལྔར་སངས་རྒྱས་ཤཱཀྱ་ཐུབ་པའི་དུས་བཟང་། fifteenth is the day of Buddha Śākyamuni 4. ཚེས་སུམ་ཅུ་པར་སངས་རྒྱས་འོད་དཔག་མེད་ཀྱི་དུས་བཟང་། thirtieth is the day of Buddha Amitābha.

ཟླ་བ་ཡར་ངོ་མར་ངོ་།

Waxing and waning moon.

གཟའ་དགུ

Nava graha/ Seven planets; seven days of the week. 1. ཉི་མ། āditya/ Sun 2. ཟླ་བ། Soma/ Moon 3. མིག་དམར། aṅgāraka/ Mars 4. ལྷག་པ། budha/ Mercury 5. ཕུར་བུ། bṛhaspatiḥ/ Venus 6. པ་སངས། śukraḥ/ Jupiter 7. སྤེན་པ། śanaiścara/ Saturn. 8. སྒྲ་གཅན། rāhu/ ascending node of the moon 9. མཇུག་རིང་། ketu/ descending node of the moon.

གཟིགས་པ་ལྔ་།

Five predeterminations of Buddha Śākyamuni before conceiving to be born in this world while he was in the god realm, born as Devaputra (dam-pa tog-dkar-po). 1. དུས་ལ་གཟིགས་པ། observation of the time for his appearance 2. རུས་ལ་གཟིགས་པ། observation of the family of his birth 3. རིགས་ལ་གཟིགས་པ། observation of the caste of his lineage 4. ཡུམ་ལ་གཟིགས་པ། observation of the mother to who he would be born 5. ཡུལ་ལ་གཟིགས་པ། observation of the land in which to disseminate his doctrine.

གཟུགས་ཀྱི་སྐྱེ་མཆེད།

Rūpāyatanam/ The source of perception of form; synonymous with forms (gzugs); direct objects of sight—shape and colour.

གཟུགས་ཀྱི་ལྷ།

Rūpadeva/ The form deity. One of the six deities according to action tantra. A visualization meditation of emitting and withdrawing light from the moon maṇḍala and the circle of mantras, the transformation of which then give rise to complete features of the concerned deity of one's meditation.

གཟུགས་ཁམས།

Rūpadhātu/ Form realm. Realm in which beings are preoccupied with meditative concentration free of attachment to sensual objects within the desire realm but have attachment to forms.

གཟུགས་ཁམས་ཀྱི་སྒོམ་སྤང་བརྒྱ་དང་བརྒྱད་ཅུ།

One hundred and eighty objects of elimination within the form realm to be abandoned on the path of meditation. The four levels of concentrations—first, second, third and fourth within the form realm each have forty-five objects of elimination (see gzugs-khams-kyi sgom-spang lnga, below) when each of the five eliminations are further divided into nine levels of subtlety from within the three basic levels of great, middling and small and each of these levels are further divided into three levels, thus making one hundred and eighty in all.

གཟུགས་ཁམས་ཀྱི་སྒོམ་སྤང་ལྔ།

The five objects of elimination within the form realm to be abandoned on the path of meditation. 1. མ་རིག་པ། ignorance 2. འདོད་ཆགས། desire-attachment 3. ང་རྒྱལ། pride 4. འཇིག་ལྟ། view of transitory collection 5. མཐར་ལྟ། the extreme view.

གཟུགས་ཁམས་ཀྱི་གནས་བཞི།

The four levels of the form realm; the four states of concentration within the form realm; the four worlds of the form realm—བསམ་གཏན་དང་པོ། གཉིས་པ། གསུམ་པ། བཞི་པ། first, second, third and fourth concentration realms.

གཟུགས་ཁམས་གནས་རིས་བཅུ་བདུན།

Seventeen regions of the form realm. Three states of the first level concentration: 1. ཚངས་རིས། Brahmakāyikāḥ/ Brahma type 2. ཚངས་པ་མདུན་ན་འདོན། Brahmapurohitāḥ/ Brahma attendants 3. ཚངས་ཆེན། Mahābrahmāṇah/ great Brahma. Three states of the second level concentration: 4. འོད་ཆུང་། Parīttābhāḥ/ little light 5. ཚད་མེད་འོད། Apramāṇābhāḥ/ limitless light 6. འོད་གསལ། Ābhāsvarāḥ/ bright light. Three states of the third level concentration: 7. དགེ་ཆུང་། Parīttaśubhāḥ/ little virtue 8. ཚད་མེད་དགེ Apramāṇaśubhāḥ/ limitless virtue 9. དགེ་རྒྱས། Śubhakṛtsnāḥ/ vast virtue. Eight states of the fourth level concentration: 10. སྤྲིན་མེད། Anabharakāḥ/ cloudless 11. བསོད་ནམས་སྐྱེས། Puṇyaprasavāḥ/ born from merit 12. འབྲས་བུ་ཆེ་བ། Bṛhatphalāḥ/ great fruit 13. མི་ཆེ་བ། Avṛhāḥ/ not great 14. མི་གདུང་བ། Atapāḥ/ without pain 15. གྱ་ནོམ་སྣང་། Sudṛśāḥ/ excellent appearance 16. ཤིན་ཏུ་མཐོང་། Śudarśanāḥ/ great perception 17. འོག་མིན། Akaniṣṭāḥ/ not low.

གཟུགས་ཅན་གཟུགས་ལ་ལྟ་བའི་རྣམ་ཐར།

Emancipation of one possessing form, looking at a form. A concentration of the form realm cultivated by a yogi while considering himself as a being with physical form, in order to eliminate attachment towards external forms.

གཟུགས་ཅན་མ་ཡིན་པའི་མཚུངས་ལྡན་འདུ་བྱེད་ཀྱི་ཕུང་པོའི་སྡེ་ཚན་དྲུག

Six classes of non-physical aggregates of concomitant compositional factors. 1. སེམས་ཀྱི་ས་མང་། mental attitude 2. དགེ་བའི་ས་མང་། virtuous attitude 3. མི་དགེ་བའི་ས་མང་། non-virtuous attitude 4. ཉོན་མོངས་ཆེན་པོའི་ས་མང་། mental attitude of the major delusions 5. ཉོན་མོངས་ཆུང་ངུའི་ས་མང་། mental attitude of the minor delusions 6. མ་ངེས་པའི་ས་མང་། indefinite mental attitude.

གཟུགས་ཉེར་ལྔ།

Twenty-five types of forms. 1-4. རྩ་བའི་ཁ་དོག་བཞི། four root colors (see rtsa-ba'i kha-dog bzhi) 5-12. ཡན་ལག་གི་ཁ་དོག་བརྒྱད། eight secondary colours (see yan-lag-gi kha-dog brgyad) 13. རིང་བ། long 14. ཐུང་བ། short 15. ལྷམ་པ། squareness 16. ཟླུམ་པོ། spherical 17. རྡུལ་ཕྲ་མོ། fine particles 18. རྡུལ་རགས་པ། gross particles 19. མཐོ་བ། high 20. དམའ་བ། low 21. ཕྱ་ལེ་བ། evenness 22. ཕྱ་ལེ་བ་མ་ཡིན་པ། unevenness 23. མངོན་པར་སྐབས་ཡོད་པ། manifest form 24. རྣམ་པར་རིག་བྱེད། revelatory form 25. ནམ་མཁའ་དང་ཁ་དོག་གཅིག་པའི་གཟུགས། color identical with the sky.

གཟུགས་ཕུང་བཅོ་ལྔ།

Fifteen form aggregates. 1-4. རྒྱུ་འབྱུང་བ་ཆེན་པོ་བཞི། four causal elements (see 'byung-ba bzhi) 5-15. འབྲས་གཟུགས་བཅུ་གཅིག། eleven resultant form aggregates (see 'bras-gzugs bcu-gcig).

གཟུགས་ཕུང་རིགས་ཀྱི་ཆོས་ལྔ།

Five phenomena on the level of the form aggregate. 1. གཟུགས་ཀྱི་ཕུང་པོ། form aggregate 2. གཞི་དུས་ཀྱི་མེ་ལོང་ཡེ་ཤེས། basic mirror-like wisdom 3. སའི་ཁམས། earth element 4. མིག་གི་དབང་པོ། eye sense power 5. རང་རྒྱུད་ཀྱིས་བསྡུས་པའི་གཟུགས། form within one's mental continuum.

གཟུགས་མེད་ཁམས།

Arūpa dhātu/ Formless realm. The realm in which the beings do not have a gross body but have a pure mental body; they are free of attachment towards sensual objects, but have attachments to the formless realms.

གཟུགས་མེད་ཉེར་འགྲོའི་ཕྱིར་མི་འོང་།

Never-returner who attains liberation without effort and migrates to the formless realm.

གཟུགས་མེད་ཉེར་འགྲོའི་ཕྱིར་མི་འོང་སྐྱེས་འདའ་བ།

Never-returner who attains liberation as soon as he is born in the formless realm.

གཟུགས་མེད་ཉེར་འགྲོའི་ཕྱིར་མི་འོང་གོང་འཕོ་བ།

Never-returner who attains liberation in the highest state (either in Akaniṣṭha or the Peak of Existence) after migrating to the formless realm.

གཟུགས་མེད་ཉེར་འགྲོའི་ཕྱིར་མི་འོང་འདུ་བྱེད་དང་བཅས་པར་འདའ་བ།

Never-returner who attains liberation with great effort and migrates to the formless realm.

གཟུགས་མེད་ཉེར་འགྲོའི་ཕྱིར་མི་འོང་འདུ་བྱེད་མེད་པར་འདའ་བ།

Never-returner who atains liberation without effort and migrates to the formless realm.

གཟུགས་མེད་སྙོམས་འཇུག་བཞི།

Catasra ārūpyasamāpattayaḥ/ Four formless absorptions; four types of formless meditative absorptions. 1. ནམ་མཁའ་མཐའ་ཡས་སྙོམས་འཇུག ākāśānantyāyatanaṁ/ absorption of infinite space 2. རྣམ་ཤེས་མཐའ་ཡས་སྙོམས་འཇུག vijñānānantyāyatanaṁ/ absorption of infinite consciousness 3. ཅི་ཡང་མེད་པའི་སྙོམས་འཇུག akiñcanyāyatanaṁ/ absorption of nothingness 4. འདུ་ཤེས་མེད་འདུ་ཤེས་མེད་མིན་གྱི་སྙོམས་འཇུག naivasaṁjñānāsaṁjñāyatanaṁ/ absorption of that which is neither with discrimination nor non-discrimination.

གཟུགས་མེད་གཟུགས་ལ་ལྟ་བའི་རྣམ་ཐར།

Emancipation of one without form looking at a form. A concentration within the form realm cultivated by a yogic while considering himself as a being without form in order to eliminate his attachment to external objects.

གཟུགས་སུ་ཉེར་འགྲོའི་ཕྱིར་མི་འོང་།

Never-returner who migrates to the form realm.

གཟུགས་སུ་ཉེར་འགྲོའི་ཕྱིར་མི་འོང་གོང་འཕོ་བ།

Never-returner who attains liberation in the highest state (Akaniṣṭha) after migrating to the form realm.

གཟུགས་སུ་ཉེར་འགྲོའི་ཕྱིར་མི་འོང་སྐྱེས་འདའ་བ།

Never-returner who attains liberation as soon as he is born in the form realm.

གཟུགས་སུ་ཉེར་འགྲོའི་ཕྱིར་མི་འོང་བར་འདའ་བ།

Never-returner who attains liberation in the intermediate existence of the form realm.

གཟུགས་སུ་ཉེར་འགྲོའི་ཕྱིར་མི་འོང་འདུ་བྱེད་དང་བཅས་པར་འདའ་བ།

Never-returner who attains liberation with great effort and migrates to the form realm.

གཟུགས་སུ་ཉེར་འགྲོའི་ཕྱིར་མི་འོང་འདུ་བྱེད་མེད་པར་འདའ་བ།

Never-returner who attains liberation without effort and migrates to the form realm.

གཟུང་རྟོག་གཉིས།

Two objective graspings; two graspings at objects; two conceptual graspings at objects. 1. འཇུག་པ་གཟུང་རྟོག grasping at engagements that are to be cultivated 2. ལྡོག་པ་གཟུང་རྟོག grasping at elimination that are to be abandoned or 1. ཉོན་མོངས་གཟུང་རྟོག grasping at delusive phenomena 2. རྣམ་བྱང་གཟུང་རྟོག grasping at purified phenomena.

གཟུང་འཛིན་གཉིས་སྟོང་།

Non-duality of the object and object-perceiver. The lack of difference between the object and the object-perceiver; a view asserted by the Cittamātrin school of philosophy.

གཟུང་ཡུལ།

Grāhyaviṣaya/ Referent object. Object as seized by a perception, e.g. vase for a consciousness apprehending vase.

གཟུངས།

Dhāraṇī/ Retention power (dhāraṇī). The ability to hold words and meanings of the dharma through the force of exalted mindfulness and wisdom. Also means mantras (gzungs-sngags) through the power of which one summons blessings and the ability to eliminate interfering forces.

གཟུངས་ཀྱི་སྒོ་བཞི།

Four types of retention power; four doors of dhāraṇī. 1. བཟོད་པའི་གཟུངས། kṣāntidhāraṇī/ retention of patience, the ability to endure patiently the emptiness discerned without being terrified by it 2. སྔགས་ཀྱི་གཟུངས། mantradhāraṇī/ retention of mantra, the ability to convert any syllable or syllables into a mantra for eradicating infectious diseases and interfering forces 3. ཚིག་གི་གཟུངས། vākya dhāraṇi/ retention of word, the ability to retain names, terms or words through the power of memory 4. དོན་གྱི་གཟུངས། artha dhāraṇi/ retention of meaning, the ability to retain the specific and general meanings of all phenomena through the power of mindfulness.

བཟའ་བའི་དམ་ཚིག

The commitment related to food. The commitment according to the highest yoga tantra to accept the five fleshes (see sha-lnga) and five nectars (see bdud-rtsi lnga) without any preconceptions.

བཟོ་བོ་སྤྲུལ་སྐུ།

Śilpanirmāṇakāya/ Artisan emanation. A form of incarnate Buddha's emanation as artisans and master-craftsman in order to tame beings.

བཟོ་རིག་གི་སྒྱུ་རྩལ་སུམ་ཅུ།

The thirty skills of arts and craft. A section of the sixty-four arts. 1. ཡི་གེ literacy 2. ལག་རྩིས། calculation by hand 3. གྲངས། mathematics 4. རྩིས་ཆེན། great mathematics 5. ཁྭ་རྒོལ་ལྡགས། scare crowing 6. གོམ་སྟབས། gestures by feet 7. ལྕགས་ཀྱུས་སྐྱོར་ཐབས། art by iron rods 8. རལ་གྲིའི་ཐབས། sword slinging 9. ཞགས་པ་གདབ་པ། lasso throwing 10. མདའ་བོ་ཆེ་འཕེན་པ། archery 11. མདུན་དུ་བསྣུར་བ། offensive 12. ཕྱིར་བསྣུར་བ། defensive 13. བཅད་པ། cutting 14. དྲལ་བ། tearing 15. དབྱུག་པ། stick throwing 16. རྒྱང་ནས་འཕོག་པ། remote targeting 17. སྒྲ་གྲག་པར་འཕོག་པ། blasting 18. གནད་དུ་འཕོག་པ། blowing the target 19. མི་ཚོར་བར་འཕོག་པ། insensitive targeting 20. ཚབས་ཆེ་བར་འཕོག་པ། intense targeting 21. མཆོངས་པ། jumping 22. ཐུད་ཀྱི་འཛིན་པ། weight lifting 23. པང་། racing 24. རྐྱལ། swimming 25. བརྒལ་བ། crossing 26. གླང་པོ་ཆེའི་གཉར་ཞོན་པ། elephant riding 27. རྟ་ལ་ཞོན་པ། horse riding 28. ཤིང་རྟའི་བཟོ་

ཐབས། chariot making 29. མདའ་གཞུའི་བཟོ་ཐབས། bow and arrow making 30. གྱད་སྟོབས། wrestling.

བཟོད་པ་རྣམ་གསུམ།

The three types of patience. 1. གནོད་པ་ལ་ཇི་མི་སྙམ་པའི་བཟོད་པ། patience of not retaliating against someone who harms you 2. སྡུག་བསྔལ་དང་ལེན་གྱི་བཟོད་པ། patience of willingly enduring sufferings 3. ཆོས་ལ་ངེས་ཤེས་ཀྱི་བཟོད་པ། patience of discriminative awareness of the Dharma.

བཟོད་པ་ཕྱིར་མི་ལྡོག་པའི་རྟགས་གཉིས།

Two signs of irreversibility on the patience level of the path of preparation. 1. གཞན་གྱིས་དཀྲིར་མི་བཏུབ་པ། he cannot be led astray by others 2. ལམ་བཅོས་མ་སྟོན་པའི་བདུད་ལ་བདུད་དུ་རྟོགས་པ། he recognizes the māras preaching counterfeit paths as true māras.

བཟོད་པའི་རྩེ་སྦྱོར།

Kṣāntigata mūrdhaprayoga/ Peak training of the forbearance level of the path of preparation. A Bodhisattva path where he has gained stability in establishing his realization to progress further.

བློས་གར་གྱི་ཡན་ལག་ལྔ།

The five fundamentals of the performing arts; the five limbs of performing arts. 1. མདོ་འཛིན་པ། memorization of texts 2. རོལ་མོ། music 3. ཆས་ཀླུགས། costumes 4. བཞད་གད། comedy 5. བློས་གར། art of dance and drama.

བཟླས་བརྗོད་ཡན་ལག་བཞི།

Four branches of recitation; four types of incantation practice and meditation according to kriya tantra. 1. སྒྲའི་གཞི་ལ་གཞོལ་བ། recitation while concentrating on the sound deity 2. སེམས་ཀྱི་གཞི་ལ་གཞོལ་བ། recitation while concentrating on the mind deity 3. གཞན་གྱི་གཞི་ལ་གཞོལ་བ། recitation while concentrating on another deity 4. བདག་གི་གཞི་ལ་གཞོལ་བ། recitation while concentrating on self-deity.

བཟླས་བརྗོད་ལ་ལྟོས་པའི་བསམ་གཏན།

Japāpekṣatadhyāna/ Concentration dependent on recitation.

བཟླས་བརྗོད་ལ་མི་ལྟོས་པའི་བསམ་གཏན།

Japānāpekṣetadhyāna/ Concentration independent of recitation.

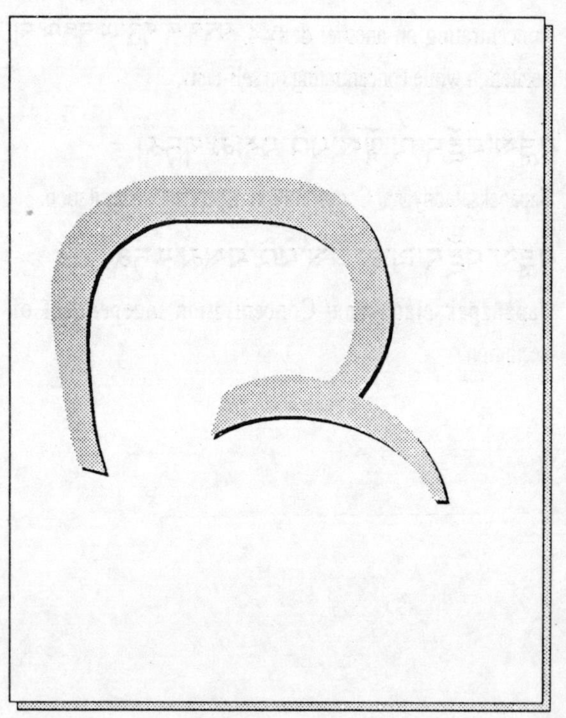

འོག་མིན།

Akaniṣṭha/ A. The Akaniṣṭa Buddha field where the sambhogakāya form of Buddhas reside, also called the 'Richly Adorned Heaven Beneath None'. B. Heaven Beneath None; the highest god realm within the form realms of the fourth concentration domain.

འོག་མའི་ཆ་མཐུན་ལྔ་།

The five delusions of the lower realms; the five delusions within the desire realm. 1. འདོད་ཆགས། desire-attachment 2. ཞེ་སྡང་། hatred-anger 3. འཇིག་ཚོགས་ལ་ལྟ་བ། view of the transitory collection 4. ཚུལ་ཁྲིམས་དང་བརྟུལ་ཞུགས་མཆོག་འཛིན། view of holding wrong moral disciplines and ascetic practices as supreme 5. ཐེ་ཚོམ། doubt.

འོད་དཔག་མེད།

Amitābha/ Buddha Amitābha. The Buddha of the western direction.

འོད་དཔག་མེད་ཀྱི་དམ་ཚིག་གསུམ།

Three pledges related to Amitābha Buddha. 1. ཕྱི་བྱ་སྤྱོད། performance and action tantra as the outer practice 2. གསང་བ་རྣལ་འབྱོར་དང་བླ་མེད། yoga and anuttarayoga tantra as the secret practice 3. ཐེག་པ་གསུམ་གྱིས་བསྡུས་པའི་དམ་ཚིག all practices encompassing the doctrine of the three vehicles.

འོད་མའི་ཚལ།

Veṇuvana/ A. Bamboo grove; a park near Rājagṛha that was offered to Buddha Śākyamuni by King Bimbisāra.

འོད་སྲུང་།

Kāśyapa/ A. Kāśyapa Buddha. The third of the thousand Buddhas and sixth of the Seven Heroid Buddhas (see sangs-rgyas dpa'-bo bdun) B. Mahākāśyapa. The first of the seven hierarchs (see ston-pa'i gtad-rabs-bdun) and one of the ten close disciples of Buddha Śākyamuni, famous for his scholarship, and was also responsible for collecting all the Abhidharma class of teachings during the First Council.

འོད་གསལ།

Prabhāsvara/ Clear Light. A. A domain of gods within the second concentration realm. B. Clear light mind; the fundamental state of consciousness which manifests at the time of death. A qualified tantric practitioner employs this subtle mind to realize emptiness. There are two types: 1. བུའི་འོད་གསལ། son clear light (see bu'i 'od-gsal) 2. མའི་འོད་གསལ། mother clear light (see ma'i-'od-gsal).

འོད་གསལ་སྒྱུ་མ།

Prabhāsvara māyā/ The clear light illusory body. One of the types of illusory bodies, the empty-body, like a reflection on a mirror, that is attained as a result of successful meditation on the completion stage of tantra.

འོད་གསལ་སྒྲིབ་མེད།

Non-obscured clear light mind. In the Sakya tradition this refers to the Buddha nature present in all sentient beings.

འོད་གསལ་མཚན་ཉིད་པ།

Actual clear light. The fully characterized clear light mind.

ཡང་དག་པའི་རྟོག་པ།

Saṁyak saṁkalpa/ Right thought. Engaging in the study of scriptures and teachings with proper motivation.

ཡང་དག་པའི་ལྟ་བ།

Saṁyag dṛṣṭi/ Right view. Discerning the meanings of the four noble truths and the two truths through proper analytical and contemplative means.

ཡང་དག་མཐའ།

Saṁyag ānta/ The perfect finality. The sphere of reality or emptiness at the cessation of the pervasive suffering, nirvāṇa.

ཡང་དག་པའི་དྲན་པ།

Saṁyak smṛti/ Right mindfulness. Retaining the object of clam abiding and penetrative insight through application of balanced approach of meditation techniques.

ཡང་དག་ཀུན་རྫོབ།

Saṁyak saṁvṛtti/ Real conventional truth; perfect conventional truth. The causes and results giving rise to the ten virtues and other wholesome activities as a result of a perfect examination of the outer and inner nature of dependent-arising principles.

ཡང་དག་པའི་ངག

Saṁyag vāk/ Right speech. To speak correct and show others means of teaching, debate and writing, aimed at generating correct views.

ཡང་དག་པའི་ཏིང་ངེ་འཛིན།

Saṁyak samādhi/ Right concentration. Establishing meditative concentrations free of the faults of laxity and excitement; an antidote to the hinderences in meditation.

ཡང་དག་པའི་རྩོལ་བ།

Saṁyag vyāyāma/ Right effort. Application of perseverance in one's practice of eliminating the obscuration to liberation and omniescence.

ཡང་དག་པའི་འཚོ་བ།

Saṁyagājīva/ Right livelihood. Right physical and vocal behaviour free of wrong means such as wheedling behavior, flattery and so forth, to earn one's livelihood.

ཡང་དག་པའི་ལས་ཀྱི་མཐའ།

Saṁyak karmānta/ Right action; right conduct. Maintenance of one's behavior free from negative techniques in contrast with the principles of teachings.

ཡང་དག་པར་བླངས་པ་ལས་གྱུར་པ།

Forms arising from pledges, e.g. a vow or an obeisance of vows revealed through physical, verbal and mental activities.

ཡང་དག་སྤོང་བ་བཞི།

Catvāri prahāṇāni/ Four perfect abandonments; four right eliminations. A section of the thirty-seven auxilaries to enlightenment. 1. མི་དགེ་བ་སྐྱེས་པ་སྤོང་བ། abandonment of non-virtues that have not been produced 2. མི་དགེ་བ་མ་སྐྱེས་པ་མི་བསྐྱེད་པ། non-generation of non-virtues that have not yet been produced 3. དགེ་བ་མ་སྐྱེས་པ་བསྐྱེད་པ། increasing virtues that have been produced 4. དགེ་བ་སྐྱེས་པ་སྤེལ་བ། making effort in generating virtues that have not yet been produced.

ཡངས་པ་ཅན།

Vaiśālī/ A. Vaiśālī. The city of Vaiśālī in the vicinity of Patna where Buddha Śākyamuni turned the Third Wheel of Doctrine; the doctrine of good distinction between the three divisions of phenomena—imputed, dependent and thoroughly established (reality). B. A chapel in Ganden monastery.

ཡན་ལག་གི་ཁ་དོག་བརྒྱད།

Eight secondary colors. 1. སྤྲིན་གྱི་ཁ་དོག cloudy 2. དུ་བའི་ཁ་དོག smoky 3. རྡུལ་གྱི་ཁ་དོག dusty 4. ཁུག་རྣའི་ཁ་དོག misty 5. གྲིབ་མའི་ཁ་དོག shadowy 6. ཉི་འོད་ཀྱི་ཁ་དོག sunny 7. སྣང་བའི་ཁ་དོག brightness 8. མུན་པའི་ཁ་དོག darkness .

ཡན་ལག་གི་རླུང་ལྔ།

Five secondary energy winds. The five energy winds in the body produced through the force of basic elements within the body. 1. རྒྱུ་བའི་རླུང་། caraṇa vāyu/ moving wind for the cognitive faculty of vision 2. རྣམ་པར་རྒྱུ་བའི་རླུང་། vicaraṇa vāyu/ thoroughly moving wind for the cognitive faculty of hearing 3. ཡང་དག་པར་རྒྱུ་བའི་རླུང་། samudācaraṇa vāyu/ perfectly moving wind for the cognitive faculty of smell 4. ངེས་པར་རྒྱུ་བའི་རླུང་། avicarata vāyu/ definitely moving wind for the cognitive faculty of touch or contact 5. རབ་ཏུ་རྒྱུ་བའི་རླུང་། upacāra vāyu/ strongly moving wind for the cognitive faculty of taste. There is another way of listing these five energy winds from the perspective of their dynamic reaction within the body. ལུས་ལ་གནས་པའི་འབྱུང་འགྱུར་གྱི་རླུང་ལྔ། 1. ཀླུའི་རླུང་ས་ཁམས། the earth element as the nāga's wind 2. རུས་སྦལ་གྱི་རླུང་རླུང་ཁམས། the wind element as the tortoise's wind 3. རྩངས་པའི་རླུང་མེ་ཁམས། the fire element as the lizard's wind 4. ལྷས་བྱིན་གྱི་རླུང་ཆུ་ཁམས། the water element as devadatta's wind 5. ནོར་རྒྱལ་གྱི་རླུང་ས་ཁམས། the earth element as vasurāja's wind.

ཡན་ལག་བརྒྱད་ལྡན་གྱི་ཆུ།

The river or water fulfilling eight qualities (see chu-yan lag brgyad-ldan).

ཡན་ལག་ལྔ།

Pañcāṅga/ The five limbs. Two arms, two legs and head.

ཡན་ལག་ལྔ་ལྡན་གྱི་སྦྱོར་བ།

The five preparatory stages. The five preliminary steps of Mahāmudrā meditation according to the Drigung Kagyud tradition. 1. བྱང་ཆུབ་ཀྱི་སེམས་བསྒོམ་པ། meditation on the mind of enlightenment 2. རང་ལུས་ལྷར་བསྒོམ་པ། meditation on oneself as a deity 3. བླ་མ་ལ་མོས་གུས་བསྒོམ་པ། meditation on faith and devotion to one's spiritual master 4. མི་རྟོག་པའི་ལྟ་བ་བསྒོམ་པ། meditation on the non-conceptual view 5. བསྔོ་སྨོན་གྱིས་རྒྱས་འདེབས་པ། concluding one's practice by dedication.

ཡན་ལག་བདུན་པ།

Saptāṅga pūja/ Seven branch practice; seven limbed practice. The seven priliminaries for carrying out a Dharma practice. 1.

ཕྱག་འཚལ་བ། vandana/ prostration 2. མཆོད་པ་ཕུལ་བ། pūjanā/ offering 3. བཤགས་པ་ཕུལ་བ། deśaya/ confession 4. རྗེས་སུ་ཡི་རང་བ། anumoda/ rejoicing 5. བསྐུལ་བ། saṁcodana/ requesting 6. གསོལ་བ་འདེབས་པ། adhyeṣaṇa/ supplication 7. བསྔོ་བ། pariṇāmana/ dedication (see sngags-phyogs-kyi yan-lag bdun-pa, and rgyun-bshags-kyi yan-lag bdun-pa).

ཡབ།

Pitṛ/ Male deity. Male deity or protector in the tantric system representing the method aspect of practice.

ཡབ་ཀྱི་ཕྱག་རྒྱ་དྲུག

Six ornaments of a male deity. 1. དབུ་རྒྱན། head-dress 2. རྣ་རྒྱན། earrings 3. མགུལ་རྒྱན། necklace 4. གདུ་བུ། bracelets 5. མཆོད་ཕྱིར་ཐོགས་པ། skull cup 6. ཐལ་ཆེན་གྱི་ཚོམ་བུ། daubing of ashes.

ཡར་གྱི་མཚམས་མེད་ཀྱི་ལས།

Higher boundless action. Positive action of higher potentiality that leads one to the higher attainments, as opposed to the boundless non-virtue which directly drives one to the hell realm.

ཡས་འདེད།

Removing obstacles downwards. Such as in the practice of Vajrasattva meditation; the elimiantion of obstacles of the body through visualizing them being flushed out of one's lower orifices with the downward flow of light and nectar from Vajrasattva at the crown of one's head.

ཡས་བབས་ཀྱི་དགའ་བཞི།

The four joys of the descending order. A skill gained through successful meditation on psychic heat by way of melting bodhicitta induced in the wheels of the energy channels, according to the completion stage meditation of the mother tantra in the highest yoga practice. Thus when the bodhicitta melts and descends it produces: 1. བྱང་སེམས་སྤྱི་བོ་ལས་བབ་པས་དགའ་བ། joy from the level of the crown 2. མགྲིན་པར་བབ་པས་མཆོག་དགའ། supreme joy at the level of the throat 3. སྙིང་གར་དགའ་བྲལ། extraordinary joy at the level of the heart 4. ལྟེ་བར་ལྷན་ཅིག་སྐྱེས་དགའ། spontaneous joy at the level of the navel.

ཡས་བབས་མས་བརྟན།

The descending and ascending order of joys from the melting of bodhicitta from crown level to the secret organ and vice-versa.

ཡི་གེའི་ལྷ།

Akṣara deva/ Letter deity. One of the six types of deities in performance (kriyā) tantra; meditation of the syllables visualized upon a moon cushion generated out of emptiness.

ཡི་དམ།

Meditational deity; personal deity; tutelary deity. Buddhas or Bodhisattvas relied upon by a practitioner having special bond or relationship in accordance with the tantric values.

ཡི་དགས་གསུམ།

Three types of hungry ghosts. 1. ཕྱི་སྒྲིབ་ཅན། those with external obstructions (food) 2. ནང་སྒྲིབ་ཅན། those with internal obstructions (drink) 3. ཟས་སྐོམ་གཉིས་ཀའི་སྒྲིབ་པ་ཅན། those with obstructions to both food and drink.

ཡིག་བརྒྱ།

Hundred Syllable mantra. Such as of Vajrasattva, Heruka, Yamāntaka and others.

ཡིག་ཆ།

A. Text book. Treatises on Buddhist philosophy studied in each of the monastic universities that form their basic curriculum of religious study. B. Documents old or new.

ཡིད་མངོན་ལྔ།

The five types of direct mental perception. Those related to: 1. གཟུགས་འཛིན་ཡིད་མངོན། form 2. སྒྲ་འཛིན་ཡིད་མངོན། sound 3. དྲི་འཛིན་ཡིད་མངོན། smell 4. རོ་འཛིན་ཡིད་མངོན། taste 5. རེག་འཛིན་ཡིད་མངོན། objects of touch.

ཡིད་ཆེས་ཀྱི་དད་པ།

Pratyayita śraddhā/ Convinced faith; trusting faith. Total faith in the working of karma and the three objects of refuge.

ཡིད་དཔྱོད།

Manaḥparīkṣa/ Presumption; correct belief. A fresh awareness that apprehends the correct object, without depending on experience or correct reasoning as its basis, e.g. the presumption that sound is impermanent merely through hearing the statement, 'sound is changeable'. There are three types of presumptions: 1. རྒྱུ་མཚན་མེད་པའི་ཡིད་དཔྱོད། presumption for no reason 2. རྒྱུ་མཚན་ལྟར་སྣང་ལ་བརྟེན་པའི་ཡིད་དཔྱོད། presumption for an incorrect reason 3. རྒྱུ་མཚན་མ་ངེས་པའི་ཡིད་དཔྱོད། presumption for an indefinite reason.

ཡིད་བྱེད་དྲུག

Six attentions. 1. མཚན་ཉིད་སོ་སོར་རིག་པ་ཡིད་བྱེད། attention to individual characteristics 2. མོས་པ་ཡིད་བྱེད། attention arisen from belief 3. རབ་ཏུ་དབེན་པ་ཡིད་བྱེད། attention of complete isolation 4. དགའ་བ་བསྡུད་པའི་ཡིད་བྱེད། attention encompassing joy 5. དཔྱོད་པ་ཡིད་བྱེད། attention to analysis 6. སྦྱོར་བ་མཐའི་ཡིད་བྱེད། attention to the conclusion of activity.

ཡིད་བྱེད་བཞི།

Four attentions; the four ways of attending to an object of meditation while practicing concentration meditation. 1. བསྒྲིམས་ཏེ་འཇུག་པ། painstaking attention 2. ཆད་པ་དང་བཅས་ཏེ་འཇུག་པ། repeated attention 3. ཆད་པ་མེད་པར་འཇུག་པ། uninterrupted attention 4. རྩོལ་བ་མེད་པར་འཇུག་པ། effortless attention.

ཡིད་བཞིན་ནོར་བུ།

Cintāmaṇi/ A. Wish-fulfilling gem. B. Dalai Lama. 3. Human body. 4. Gems obtained from the ocean.

ཡིད་བཞིན་ནོར་བུ་ལྟ་བུའི་སེམས་བསྐྱེད།

Cintāmaṇyupamacittotpāda/ Wish-fulfilling gem like bodhicitta. The mind of enlightenment associated with the perfection of prayers possessed by a Bodhisattva on the eighth ground of advancement.

ཡིད་འོང་གི་བྱམས་པ།

Manojñamaitrī/ Appealing love; heart-warming love.

ཡིད་ལས་བྱུང་བ།

Manobhava/ Mind-arisen; synonymous with the intermediate state of rebirth (bardo).

ཡུམ།

Mātṛ/ Female aspect; tantric consort; a female counterpart of a male deity or tantric practitioner symbolizing the wisdom aspect of practice.

ཡུམ་གྱི་ཕྱག་རྒྱ་ལྔ།

Five adornments of a female deity. 1. དབུ་རྒྱན། head-dress 2. སྙན་རྒྱན། earrings 3. མགུལ་རྒྱན། necklace 4. གདུ་བུ། bracelets 5. སྐུ་རགས། belt.

ཡུམ་གྱི་འགྲེལ་རྐང་བརྒྱ་དང་བརྒྱད།

One hundred and eight topics of the *Perfection of Wisdom* text. 1-53. ཀུན་ནས་ཉོན་མོངས་ཕྱོགས་ཀྱི་འགྲེལ་རྐང་ང་གསུམ། fifty-three topics of the ever afflicted phenomena (see kun-nas nyon-mongs phyogs-kyi 'grel-rkang nga-gsum) 54-108. རྣམ་བྱང་ཕྱོགས་ཀྱི་འགྲེལ་རྐང་ལྔ་བཅུ་རྩ་ལྔ། fifty-five topics of the purified phenomena (see rnam-byang phyogs-kyi 'grel-rkang nga-lnga).

ཡུམ་རྒྱས་འབྲིང་བསྡུས་གསུམ།

The large, medium and short *Wisdom Perfection* sūtras (prajñāpāramitā sūtra). 1. འབུམ། *The One Hundred Thousand Verse* (śatasāhasrikā) 2. ཉི་ཁྲི། *The Twenty Thousand Verse* (viṁśatisāhasrikā) 3. བརྒྱད་སྟོང་པ། *The Eight Thousand Verse* (Aṣṭasāhasarikā).

ཡུལ་གྱི་འོད་གསལ།

Objective clear light; the emptiness.

ཡུལ་ངེས་ལྔ།

Five determining mental factors; five determinants. 1. འདུན་པ། chanda/ aspiration 2. མོས་པ། adhimokṣa/ belief 3. དྲན་པ། smṛti/ mindfulness 4. ཏིང་འཛིན། samādhi/ concentration 5. ཤེས་རབ། prajñā/ wisdom.

ཡུལ་ཅན་གྱི་འོད་གསལ།

Subjective clear light; the wisdom cognizing emptiness in tantra.

ཡུལ་ཅན་གསུམ།

Three object-perceivers; three object possessors. A. 1. སྒྲ། śabda/ sound 2. བློ། manas/ awareness 3. སྐྱེས་བུ། purusa/ person. B. 1. གཟུགས། rūpa/ form 2. ཤེས་པ། jñāna/ consciousness 3. ལྡན་མིན་འདུ་བྱེད། viprayukta saṁskara/ those that are neither.

ཡུལ་དང་ཡུལ་ཅན།

Viṣaya viṣāyin/ Object and object-perceiver; object and subject.

ཡུལ་དྲུག

Six types of objects. 1. གཟུགས། rūpa/ form 2. སྒྲ། śabda/ sound 3. དྲི། gandha/ odors 4. རོ། rasa/ tastes 5. རེག་བྱ། sparśa/ object of touch 6. ཆོས། dharma/ phenomena.

ཡུལ་དབུས་ཀྱི་གྲོང་ཁྱེར་དྲུག

The six cities of central India; six cities in ancient India connected to Buddhist culture. 1. རྒྱལ་པོའི་ཁབ། Rājagṛha 2. ཡངས་པ་ཅན། Vaiśālī 3. མཉན་ཡོད། Śrāvastī 4. ཙམ་པ་ཀ། Campaka 5. གནས་བཅས། Sāketā 6. ཝ་རཱ་ཎ་སཱི། Vārānasī.

ཡུལ་བཞི

Four types of objects. 1. སྣང་ཡུལ། apparent object 2. གཟུང་ཡུལ། apprehended object 3. འཇུག་ཡུལ། focussed object 4. ཞེན་ཡུལ། implied object.

ཡུལ་ལ་གཉིས་སུ་དབྱེ་བའི་རྣམ་གྲངས།

Two-fold division of objects; two-fold divisions of all phenomena. A. རང་མཚན་དང་སྤྱི་མཚན། Self characterized and generally characterized phenomena B. མངོན་གྱུར་དང་ལྐོག་གྱུར། Manifest and hidden phenomena C. འདུས་བྱས་འདུས་མ་བྱས། Compositional and non-compositional phenomena D. དགག་པ་དང་སྒྲུབ་པ། Negative and affirmative phenomena E. འགལ་བ་དང་འབྲེལ་བ། Contradictory and non-contradictory phenomena F. སྣང་བ་དང་སེལ་བ། Apparent and excluding phenomena G. སྤྱི་བྱེ་བྲག General and particular phenomena H. རྫས་ཆོས་དང་ལྡོག་ཆོས། Substantial and opposite phenomena I.

མཚན་ཉིད་དང་མཚོན་བྱ། definition and defined phenomena J. ཀུན་རྫོབ་དང་དོན་དམ། conventional and ultimate phenomena.

ཡེ་ཤེས་ཀྱི་མཁའ་འགྲོ་མ།

Jñāna ḍākinī/ The wisdom ḍākinī; the primordial wisdom ḍākinī. A. The transworldly female Bodhisattvas. B. Vajra Yoginī.

ཡེ་ཤེས་ཀྱི་ཐིག་ལེ།

Jñāna bindu/ The primordial wisdom drop. The indestructible drop within the heart center in the central energy channel.

ཡེ་ཤེས་ཀྱི་རྡོར་དྲིལ།

Jñāna vajra/ The primordial wisdom vajra and bell. The inner method and wisdom, i.e. the great bliss and emptiness, symbolized by the nine-spoked vajra and bell.

ཡེ་ཤེས་ཀྱི་སྣང་བ།

The primordial wisdom appearance; the primordial wisdom vision. The vision of everything seen as totally pure.

ཡེ་ཤེས་ཀྱི་སྤྱན།

Jñāna cakṣu/ The primordial wisdom eye; the wisdom eye; the divine look. In its highest sense it is the ability to see everything that exists.

ཡེ་ཤེས་ཀྱི་ཕྱག་རྒྱ།

Jñāna mudrā/ The primordial wisdom mudrā. The wisdom of non-dual profundity and clarity.

ཡེ་ཤེས་ཀྱི་ཚོགས།

Jñāna sambhāra/ Collection of wisdom; accumulation of insight. The virtuous energy conjoined with the mind of enlightenment and wisdom understanding emptiness that is a cause for producing the resultant wisdom-body of the Buddha.

ཡེ་ཤེས་སྒྱུ་མ།

Jñāna māyā/ The illusory body of wisdom. The inconceivable activities of all Tathāgatas; the emanation of their wisdom projected in action.

ཡེ་ཤེས་ལྔ།

Pañca jñānāni/ The five wisdoms of a Buddha. 1. མེ་ལོང་ལྟ་བུའི་ཡེ་ཤེས། ādarśā jñānam/ mirror-like wisdom 2. སོར་རྟོགས་ཡེ་ཤེས། pratyavekṣaṇā jñānam/ wisdom of discrimination 3. མཉམ་ཉིད་ཡེ་ཤེས། samatā jñānam/ wisdom of equality 4. བྱ་སྒྲུབ་ཡེ་ཤེས། kṛtyānusthāna jñānam/ wisdom of accomplishment 5. dharmadhātu jñānam/ wisdom of reality.

ཡེ་ཤེས་ཆོས་སྐུ།

Jñānakāya/ Wisdom truth body; the omniscient mind of a Buddha.

ཡེ་ཤེས་སེམས་དཔའ།

Jñānasattva/ Wisdom being. The actual meditational deity that is meditated upon or visualized; a generation stage practice of meditation in tantra in which a wisdom being is meditated at the heart of one's pledge being (dam-tshig-pa) seated on a sun and moon cushion.

ཡོ་བྱད་བཅུ་གཉིས།

Twelve ritual articles of a Yogi. 1. རྡོར་དྲིལ་གཉིས། vajra and bell 2. ཅང་ཏེའུ། small hand drum 3. ཐོད་པ། skull cup 4. ཁ་ཊྭཱཾ་ག staff 5. རུས་རྒྱན། bone ornaments 6. རིན་ཆེན་བརྒྱད། eight jewel ornaments (see rin-po che'i rgyan-brgyad) 7. གཙུག་ཏོར་ཐོག་གཞུ། hair knot at crown 8. དཀར་གླུགས། ritual ladle 9. བུམ་པ། vase 10. ཕྲེང་བ། rosary 11. སྟག་ལྤགས་ཤམ་

ཐབས། a tiger-skin garment 12. སྟོད་གཡོག་སྨད་གཡོག upper and lower garment.

ཡོ་བྱད་བཅུ་གསུམ།

Thirteen articles of a monk (see 'tsho-ba'i yo-byad bcu-gsum).

ཡོ་བྱད་དྲུག

Six articles of a monk; six basic articles of a monkhood. 1-3. ཆོས་གོས་རྣམ་གསུམ། the three Dharma robes—two upper and one lower garment 4. ལྷུང་བཟེད། begging bowl 5. ཆུ་ཚགས། water strainer 6. གདིང་བ། cushion.

ཡོངས་གྲུབ་གཉིས།

Two thoroughly established phenomena. 1. ཕྱིན་ཅི་མ་ལོག་པའི་ཡོངས་གྲུབ། correct thoroughly established phenomena 2. འགྱུར་མེད་ཡོངས་གྲུབ། unchangeable thoroughly established phenomena.

ཡོངས་འཛིན་གཉིས།

Two types of tutors. 1. ཕྱིའི་ཡོངས་འཛིན། the external tutor 2. ནང་གི་ཡོངས་འཛིན། the internal tutor.

ཡོངས་སུ་དག་པ་བཞི།

Four total purities; the four features to be meditated in their pure entities for cultivating higher tantric practices connected to a deity-practice. 1. གནས། adhiṣṭhāna/ environment 2. ལུས། kāya/ body 3. ལོངས་སྤྱོད། upakarana/ riches 4. མཛད་པ། kārya/ deeds.

ཡོངས་སུ་འཚོལ་བ་དྲུག

Six thorough investigations. That of: 1. དོན། artha/ meaning 2. དངོས་པོ། bhāva/ existence/ things 3. མཚན་ཉིད། laksna/ characteristics 4. ཕྱོགས། paksa/ directions 5. དུས། kāla/ time 6. རིགས་པ། nyāya/ logic.

ཡོད་པ།

Existence; synonymous with objects of knowledge.

ཡོན་ཆབ།

Water-bowl offering; offering of waters to the objects of refuge.

ཡོན་ཏན་བརྒྱ་ཕྲག་བཅུ་གཉིས།

Twelve sets of a hundred qualities; qualities attained by a Bodhisttva on the first ground, i.e. on the path of seeing. 1. དུས་སྐད་ཅིག་མ་གཅིག་ལ་སངས་རྒྱས་བརྒྱའི་ཞལ་མཐོང་བ། seeing a hundred Buddhas in a single instant 2. སངས་རྒྱས་བརྒྱའི་བྱིན་གྱིས་བརླབ་པར་ཤེས་པ། knowing that he is being blessed and inspired by a hundred Buddhas 3. སྤྲུལ་པ་བརྒྱ་འགྱེད་པ། sending a hundred emanations 4. དུས་སྐད་ཅིག་མ་གཅིག་ལ་བསྐལ་བ་བརྒྱར་སྣོན་པ། travelling to a hundred Buddha fields in a single instant 5. སྔོན་དང་ཕྱི་མའི་མཐའ་བརྒྱ་ལ་ཡེ་ཤེས་ཀྱི་གཟིགས་པ་འཇུག་པ། seeing the past and future rebirths over a hundred aeons 6. ཏིང་ངེ་འཛིན་བརྒྱ་ལ་སྙོམས་པར་འཇུག་ཅིང་ལྡང་བ། remaining absorbed and rising in a hundred concentrations in one instant 7. སེམས་ཅན་བརྒྱ་སྨིན་པར་བྱེད་པ། maturing a hundred disciples 9. ཞིང་ཁམས་བརྒྱ་གཡོ་བར་བྱེད་པ། shaking a hundred Buddha fields 10. ཞིང་ཁམས་བརྒྱ་འོད་ཀྱིས་གསལ་བར་བྱེད་པ། illuminating a hundred Buddha fields 11. ཆོས་ཀྱི་སྒོ་མོ་བརྒྱ་འབྱེད་པ། opening a hundred entrances to dharma 12. རང་གི་ལུས་བརྒྱར་སྟོན་པ། ལུས་རེ་རེ་ཡང་འཁོར་ཕུན་སུམ་ཚོགས་པ་བརྒྱས་བསྐོར་བར་སྟོན་པ། manifesting a hundred physical forms, each of which are surrounded by a hundred Bodhisattva disciples.

ཡོན་ཏན་ལྔ།

Pañca gunāh/ Five qualities; A. As asserted by the Vaiśesika school of philosophy. 1. སྒྲ་ནམ་མཁའི་ཡོན་ཏན། sound as the quality of space 2. དྲི་སའི་ཡོན་ཏན། smell as the quality of earth 3. རོ་ཆུའི་ཡོན་ཏན། taste as the quality of water 4. རེག་བྱ་རླུང་གི་ཡོན་ཏན། sensation as the quality of wind 5. ཁ་དོག་མེའི་ཡོན་ཏན། color as the quality of wind. B. According to the Nyingma tradition—the five qualities of a Buddha are: 1. རྣམ་པར་དག་པའི་ཞིང་ཁམས། a pure Buddha field 2. རྒྱ་ཚད་བྲལ་བའི་ཞལ་ཡས་ཁང་། an inconceivable celestial mansion 3. གསལ་ཞིང་དག་པའི་འོད་ཟེར། a clear and luminous light 4. ཁྱད་པར་དུ་འཕགས་པའི་གདན་ཁྲི། a sublime throne 5. དགོས་རྒུར་སྤྱོད་པའི་ལོངས་སྤྱོད། inexhaustible resources.

ཡོན་ཏན་འོད།

Guṇaprabha/ Ācārya Gunaprabha. A disciple of Ācārya Vasubandhu famous for his scholarship in Vinaya teachings. His works include the *Root Sūtra of Vinaya* and *Treatise on the Bodhisattva Levels.*.

གཡང་འགུག་ཆོ་ག

The fortune summoning ritual. The ritual of invoking wealth deities such as Vaiśravaṇa, Zambala or Gaṇeś for affluent resources.

གཡའ་བཟང་བཀའ་བརྒྱུད།

Yazang Kagyud Order. One of the sub-sects of the Kagyud order of Tibetan Buddhism originally founded by Drogon Phagmo Drupa's disciple Kalden Yeshi Senge; the main monastery of this tradition in Tibet was built in the upper region of Yalung valley by Yazang Chokyi Monlam.

གཡོ་སྒྱུ།

Saṭha/ Deceit; cunning. Ambitious attitude similar to pretention, trying to gain advantage by hiding one's faults from others; a form of dishonesty.

རཀྟ།

Rakta/ Blood.

རགས་པ་ཉེར་ལྔ།

Twenty-five gross objects. 1-5. ཕུང་པོ་ལྔ། five aggregates (see phung-po lnga) 6-9. ཁམས་བཞི། four elements (see khmas-bzhi) 10-15. སྐྱེ་མཆེད་དྲུག six sources of perception (see dbang-po drug) 16-20. ཡུལ་ལྔ། five objects (see yul-lnga) 21-25. གཞི་དུས་ཀྱི་ཡེ་ཤེས་ལྔ། five basic wisdoms (see gzhi-dus-kyi ye-shes-lnga).

རང་རྐྱ་ཐུབ་པའི་རྫས་ཡོད་ཀྱི་བདག

Self-sufficiently existent independent self. An independent self as asserted by the lower schools of Buddhist philosophy.

རང་གི་མཚན་ཉིད་ཀྱིས་གྲུབ་པ།

Svalakṣaṇasiddha/ Existence by its own nature or characteristics. The assertion that phenomena exist not as mere objects of conceptual labelling but in their own right.

རང་གི་མཚན་ཉིད་སྟོང་པ་ཉིད།

Svalakṣana śūnyatā/ Emptiness of own characteristics; lack of true independent existence of the characteristics or marks of all conventional things, of all paths to enlightenment and of all qualities of an enlightened being; one of the sixteen emptinesses.

རང་གི་གཞི་ལ་གཞོལ་བ།

Concentration on self-basis/ deity. A tantric practice of self-generation through meditation on the emptiness deity, letter deity, form deity, seal deity and sign deity, while simultaneously reciting and counting mantras.

རང་གྲོལ།

Self-liberation. A rDzogs-chen meditation technique of naturally releasing all conceptual experiences into the sphere of self-arisen intuitive awareness without being forced through the application of antidotes, similar to a snake's self-loosening of its coiled body.

རང་རྒྱལ།

Pratyekabuddha/ Solitary Realizer. Hīnayāna practitioner who works only for his own liberation from cyclic existence, and who does not rely on a teacher during the last phase of his rebirth; some teach Dharma by means of physical gestures and some by means of miracles; a Solitary Realizer's path is very similar to that of a Hearer (nyan-thos).

རང་རྒྱལ་གྱི་ཐེག་པ།

Pratyekabuddha yāna/ The Solitary Realizer vehicle; the path of Pratekyabuddhas. The paths are similar to that of a Hearer (Śrāvaka); asserts the selflessness of a person and meditates on the twelve links of interdependent origination, and attains the state of aFoe-destroyer (Arhatship).

རང་རྒྱལ་གྱི་ལམ་ལྔ།

Pañca pratyekabuddha mārgāḥ/ The five paths of the Solitary Realizer's vehicle. The path of accumulation, preparation, seeing, meditation and no-more learning of this vehicle.

རང་རྒྱལ་གསུམ།

The three types of Solitary Realizers; the three categories of Pratekya Buddhas who have not transcended the Śrāvaka's path before. 1. བསེ་རུ་ལྟ་བུའི་རང་སངས་རྒྱས། the Rhinoceros-like solitary realizer 2. ཚོགས་སྤྱོད་ཀྱི་རང་སངས་རྒྱས། the sociable solitary realizer 3. རྒྱུན་ཞུགས་ཀྱི་རང་སངས་རྒྱས། the solitary realizer of the stream-winner.

རང་རྒྱུད་པ།

Svātantrika School. A school of Mādhyamika, who assert the lack of true existence of all phenomena and specifically that of functional phenomena, even nominally; but assert inherent existence. The name of the school is derived from their assertion that, in dependence upon a correct reason (established inherently by its inherent characteristics), the view of true existence can be severed in the mind of correct opponent.

རང་རྒྱུད་པའི་མུ་སྟེགས་པ།

Non-Buddhist by nature. Those who assert and are naturally attracted to views describing Buddha as wrong. There are two types: 1. non-Buddhist by birth 2. non-Buddhist by learning.

རང་ངོས་ནས་གྲུབ་པ།

Objective existence; existence from its own-side. True and independent existence established only in reference to the thing itself.

རང་སྟོང་།

Svaśūnyatā/ Self-emptiness. The middle view of the emptiness of self; reality that all phenomena are empty of inherent existence.

རང་དོན་རྗེས་དཔག

Svārthānumāna/ Inference for self, e.g. an inference generated for one's own understanding, e.g. impermanence through logical reasons.

རང་བྱུང་ཡེ་ཤེས།

Svayambhū vijñāna/ Self-born wisdom; spontaneously arisen wisdom in the mental continuum of all sentient beings.

རང་འབྱོར་ལྔ།

Five personal endowments. 1. མིར་སྐྱེས་པ། born as a human being 2. ཡུལ་དབུས་སུ་སྐྱེ་བ། born in a central land (a Buddhist country) 3. དབང་པོ་ཚང་བ། possessing complete sensory faculties 4. སངས་རྒྱས་བསྟན་པ་དད་པ། having faith in the teachings of Buddha 5. ལས་ཀྱི་མཐའ་མ་ལོག་པ། not being subject to extremely wrong deeds.

རང་མཚན།

Svalakṣana/ Self-characterized phenomena. A phenomenon which is established from its own side without being labelled by thought, e.g. a vase.

རང་བཞིན་བསྐལ་དོན།

The naturally obscure phenomena. Those phenomena that cannot be seen directly by sight, e.g. spirits or demons.

རང་བཞིན་གྱི་ཁ་ན་མ་ཐོ་བ།

Misdeed by nature; improbity by nature. Such as the transgression of moral values through killing, lying, etc., which are unwholesome by nature and not specifically prohibited by Buddha.

རང་བཞིན་གྱིས་གྲུབ་པ།

Svabhāvasiddha/ Inherent existence. Self existent without being dependent on causes and conditions.

རང་བཞིན་གྱི་རྟགས་ཡང་དག

Svabhāva samyaghetu/ Correct reason of (the same) nature. A correct reason which has the same nature as the predicate in a logical syllogism. There are two types: 1. ཁྱད་པར་ལྡན་པ་པོའི་རང་བཞིན་གྱི་རྟགས་ཡང་དག direct correct reason of the same nature 2. ཁྱད་པར་དགག་པ་པོའི་རང་བཞིན་གྱི་རྟགས་ཡང་དག indirect correct reason of the same nature.

རང་བཞིན་རྒྱུའི་གཙོ་བོ།

Fundamental principal by nature. The threefold principle of motility, darkness and lightness existing in a state of equilibrium; philosophical view of the Sāṁkhya school of thought.

རང་བཞིན་སྟོང་པ་ཉིད།

Prakṛtiśūnyatā/ Emptiness of nature; natural emptiness. Lack of inherent existence of the nature of all phenomena; one of the sixteen emptinesses.

རང་བཞིན་གནས་རིགས།

Naturally abiding Buddha nature; natural Buddha lineage. The reality of a stained mind that is liable to transform into the nature truth body of a Buddha.

རང་བཞིན་རྣམ་དག་གི་ཆར་གྱུར་བའི་ངོ་བོ་ཉིད་སྐུ།

Svabhāvaviśuddhabhūta svabhāvakāya/ Intrinsically pure nature body (of Buddha); i.e. the emptiness of the Buddha's mental continuum.

རང་བཞིན་ལྷུན་གྲུབ།

Svabhāvasahajasiddha/ The natural spontaneity. A. The existence of phenomena independent of effort B. According to rDzogs-chen meditation this refers to the primordial quality of mind inherently possessed within the three kāyas of a Buddha.

རང་རིག

Svasaṁvedanā/ Apperception; self-awareness. A non-conceptual awareness which only apprehends internal phenomena, i.e. a consciousness.

རང་རིག་མངོན་སུམ།

Svasaṁvedanā pratyakṣa/ Direct appreception; direct self-awareness. A direct perception that is devoid of conceptualization and only takes aspects of awareness as its object.

རང་ལས་ངེས་ཀྱི་ཚད་མ།

Self-evident direct perception. A valid cognition that cognizes itself as being a valid perception, e.g. a valid cognition of a person who has the knowledge of valid perceptions.

རང་སངས་རྒྱས།

Pratyekabuddha/ Solitary Realizer (see rang-rgyal).

རབ་གནས།

Pratiṣṭhā/ Consecration. Blessing representation of Buddha, Dharma and Saṅgha through a ceremony and transforming them into sacred religious articles.

རབ་བྱུང་།

Pravrajyā/ A. Monks and nuns; fully ordained monks or nuns; probationary nuns and novice monks and nuns. B. Sexantry; a cycle of sixty years in the Tibetan calendar commencing from the year 1027, as introduced by Gyijo Dawe Ozer after the translation of the Kālacakra tantra in Tibet.

རབ་བྱུང་གི་སྡོམ་པ་ལྔ།

Five types of ordination vows; five kinds of vows. 1-2. དགེ་ཚུལ་ཕ་མའི་སྡོམ་པ། śrāmaṇera śrāmanerikā/ novice monk and nun's vows 3. དགེ་སློབ་མའི་སྡོམ་པ། śikṣāmāṇa/ probationary nun's vows 4-5. དགེ་སློང་ཕ་མའི་སྡོམ་པ། Bhikṣu bhikṣuṇī/ fully ordained monk and nun's vows.

རབ་བྱུང་གི་ཡོ་བྱད་བཞི།

Four articles of a monk; belongings of a monk categorized into four sets: 1. འཚོ་བའི་ཡོ་བྱད། jīvitopakaraṇa/ articles of livelihood 2. མགོ་བའི་ཡོ་བྱད། basic necessities 3. ལྷག་པའི་ཡོ་བྱད། supplementary articles 4. ཡོ་བྱད་ཕྲན་ཚེགས། minor articles.

རབ་བྱེད།

Chapter; a textual division. Also a treatise written by Ācārya Vasubandhu.

རབ་རིབ་ཅན་གྱི་མིག་ཤེས།

Taimiracakṣuvijñāna/ Blurred vision; the visual consciousness of someone with a cataract.

རི་དགུ

Nine mountains; nine mountains according to the Abhidharma tradition. 1. རི་རབ་ལྷུན་པོ། sumeru/ Mt. Meru 2-8. གསེར་གྱི་རི་བདུན། the seven golden mountains 9. ཁོར་ཡུག་གི་རི། the encircling iron mountains.

རི་ལྟ་བུའི་སེམས་བསྐྱེད།

Parvatopamacittotpāda/ Mountain-like bodhicitta. The mind of enlightenment associated with the practice of the perfection of concentration possessed by a Bodhisattva on the fifth ground.

རི་བོང་རྭ།

Śaśaviṣāṇa/ Rabbit's horn. A popular example illustrating non-existence.

རི་རབ་ལྷུན་པོ།

Meru/ Mt. Meru; Sumeru; the king of mountains; central axis of Buddhist cosmology. Founded on a base of gold, the east of which is made of shiny white silver, south of blue lapiz lazuli, west of red crystal and north of yellow gold.

རིག་གྲོལ་གྱི་ཡོན་ཏན་བརྒྱད།

Aṣṭa saṁgharatna guṇāḥ/ Eight qualities of the Sangha Jewel; the Sangha's qualities of wisdom and liberation. 1. ཇི་ལྟ་བ་མཁྱེན་པའི་ཡོན་ཏན། quality of knowing what is reality 2. ཇི་སྙེད་པ་མཁྱེན་པའི་ཡོན་ཏན། quality of knowing whatever exists (conventionality) 3. རང་རིག་པའི་ཡོན་ཏན། quality of knowing inner features 4. རིག་པའི་ཡོན་ཏན། quality of knowledge itself 5. ཆགས་སྒྲིབ་ལས་གྲོལ་བའི་ཡོན་ཏན། quality of liberation from alluring delusions 6. ཐོགས་སྒྲིབ་ལས་གྲོལ་བའི་ཡོན་ཏན། quality of liberation from obstructive delusions 7. དམན་སྒྲིབ་ལས་གྲོལ་བའི་ཡོན་ཏན། quality of liberation from lower delusions 8. གྲོལ་བའི་ཡོན་ཏན། quality of liberation itself.

རིག་སྔགས།

Vidyā mantra/ The knowledge mantra. The mantras primarily meant for establishing the wisdom aspect of realizations and divine activities. In a more generalized sense this comprises the female form of deities, her mantras, mudrās, etc.

རིག་སྟོང་དབྱེར་མེད།

Inseparability of awareness and emptiness; the oneness of mind and emptiness.

རིག་གནས་བཅུ།

Ten fields of study; ten knowledges; ten sciences (see rig-gnas chung-ba lnga & rig-gnas che-ba lnga).

རིག་གནས་བཅོ་བརྒྱད།

Eighteen sciences. A. According to the Abhidharma tradition these are: 1. རོལ་མོ། music 2. འཁྲིག་འཐབ། amorous skills 3. འཚོ་ཆས། སོ་ཆས། house-keeping 4. གྲངས་ཅན། mathematics 5. སྒྲ། grammar 6. གསོ་བ། medicine 7. ཆོས་ལུགས། theology 8. བཟོ་བོ། arts and crafts 9. འཕོང་སྦྱོང་། archery 10. གཏན་ཚིག logic 11. སྨན་སྦྱོར། pharmacology 12. རང་གི་བཙས་པ། self-discipline 13. ཐོས་པ་དྲན་པ། contemplation 14. སྐར་མའི་དཔྱད། astronomy 15. རྩིས། astrology 16. མིག་འཕྲུལ། magic 17. སྔོན་རབས། history 18. སྔོན་བྱུང་བརྗོད་པ། legends. B. according to the Vinaya tradition these are: 1. སངས་སྡགས་ཀྱི་རྒྱུད།། 2. ཆོ་ག་ཞིབ་མོ། 3. གཏན་ཚིགས་རིག་པ། 4. རིག་བྱེད། 5. བརྡ་སྤྲོད། 6. སྒྲ་ངེས་པར་སྦྱོར་བ། 7. ཤེས་གསལ། 8. ངེས་པའི་ཚིག 9. སྡེབ་སྦྱོར་མཁས་པ། 10. སྐར་མའི་རིག་པ། 11. རྟགས་བྱེད་ཀྱི་རིག་པ། 12. ཆུར་ལྷུང་གི་རིག་པ། 13. ཆེར་སྤྱོད་ཀྱི་རིག་པ། 14. འཇིག་རྟེན་རྒྱང་ཕན་པའི་རིག་པ། 15. བྱེ་བྲག་པའི་རིག་པ། 16. རྒྱུད་དྲུག་ཅུ་པ། 17. ཁྱུར་མིད་ཀྱི་རིག་པ། 18. གནས་འདུག་པའི་རིག་པ།

རིག་གནས་ཆུང་བ་ལྔ་།

Five minor sciences; five minor fields of study. 1. སྙན་ངག kāvya/ poetry 2. མངོན་བརྗོད། abhidhāna/ synonyms 3. སྡེབ་སྦྱོར། chanda/ lexicography 4. སྐར་རྩིས། jyotiṣa/ astro-science 5. ཟློས་གར། nāṭaka/ dance and drama.

རིག་གནས་ཆེ་བ་ལྔ་།

Five major sciences; five major fields of study. 1. བཟོ་རིག་པ། śilpa/ arts and crafts 2. གསོ་བ་རིག་པ། cikitsā/ medicine 3. སྒྲ་རིག་པ། śabdavidyā/ grammar 4. གཏན་ཚིགས་རིག་པ། hetu/ logic 5. ནང་དོན་རིག་པ། adhyātma/ philosophy.

རིག་པ།

Vidyā/ A. Knowledge. B. Awareness. C. Wisdom. D. Intelligence. E. Science of learning.

རིག་པ་འཛིན་པའི་སྡེ་སྣོད།

The set of discourses of a knowledge-bearer; Mantrayāna vehicle. An antidote against all the three delusions (see du-gsum) in an balanced manner.

རིག་པ་གསུམ།

Three types of knowledge; three clairvoyances possessed by a person on the path of no-more learning. 1. སྔོན་གྱི་གནས་སམ་སྔོན་གྱི་མཐའ་རིག་པ། knowledge of beginninglessness 2. འཆི་འཕོ་བ་དང་སྐྱེ་བའམ་ཕྱི་མའི་མཐའ་རིག་པ། knowledge of endlessness 3. ཟག་པ་ཟད་པ་རིག་པ། knowledge of the exhaustion of contamination.

རིགས་པ་ཅན་པ།

Naiyāyika/ Logicians. Proponents of non-Buddhist tenets who follow Brahma Akṣapāda in asserting that all objects of knowledge are included in six categories (see tshig-don drug). This school is known by the name 'logician,' because they follow the logical system taught by their teacher Akṣapāda. The general presentation of their tenets are basically the same as those asserted by the Vaiśeṣika (particularist) school of Hindu philosophy.

རིག་པའི་རྒྱལ་པོ་བདུན།

Seven lords of knowledge. 1. རབ་ཏུ་གྲུབ་པ། Susiddhi 2. དབུ་རྒྱན་ཅེ་གསུམ་པ། Mauli 3. བཛྲ་ཀི་ལི་ཀ Vajrakilika 4. རིན་

ཆེན་ཀི་ལི་ཀ། Ratnakilika 5. གཟུགས་ལེགས། Surūpa 6. རྡོར་ཐིག Vajrabindu 7. རྡོ་རྗེ་རོལ་པ། Vajralalita.

རིག་པའི་དབང་ལྔ།

The five initiations of the knowledge-bearer. The five initiations that are gateways to enter performance tantra (kriyā tantra). 1. ཞེ་སྡང་མེ་གསོད་ཆུ་ཡི་དབང་། the water initiation to extinguish the fire of hatred-anger 2. ང་རྒྱལ་རི་བཤིག་དབུ་རྒྱན་དབང་། the crown initiation to demolish the mountain of pride 3. འདོད་ཆགས་དུག་འཇོམས་རྡོ་རྗེའི་དབང་། the vajra initiation to pacify the poison of desire-attachment 4. ཕྲག་དོག་ལྕགས་སྒྲོལ་དྲིལ་བུའི་དབང་། the bell initiation to release the chain of jealousy 5. གཏི་མུག་མུན་སེལ་མིང་གི་དབང་། the name initiation to quell the darkness of ignorance.

རིག་པའི་རྩལ་དབང་བཞི།

The four initiations of intuitive awareness. The four initiations that are the gateway to enter into rDzogs-chen meditation practice. 1. སྤྲོས་བཅས་བུམ་པའི་དབང་། the vase initiation with elaboration 2. སྤྲོས་མེད་གསང་བའི་དབང་། the secret initiation without elaboration 3. ཤིན་ཏུ་སྤྲོས་མེད་ཤེས་རབ་ཡེ་ཤེས་ཀྱི་དབང་། the primordial-wisdom initiation that is without extreme elaboration 4. རབ་ཏུ་སྤྲོས་མེད་ཚིག་གི་དབང་། the word initiation that is extraordinarily supreme without elaboration.

རིག་བྱེད་བཞི།

Catur vedāḥ/ Four Vedas; four ancient sciences of Hindu religion. 1. སྙན་ངག sāma veda/ science of poetry 2. སྲིད་སྐྱོང་། atharva veda/ science of administration 3. མཆོད་སྦྱིན། yajur veda/ science of sacrifice 4. ངེས་བརྗོད། ṛg veda/ science of aphorisms.

རིག་འཛིན་གྱི་སྡེ་སྣོད།

The Vidyādhāra's doctrine; set of teachings concerning tantra.

རིག་འཛིན་བརྡའ་བརྒྱུད།

The symbolic lineage of Vidyādhāras. A guru lineage within the Nyingma tradition of Tibetan Buddhism responsible for the transmission of rDzogs-chen meditation through bare introduction by a master.

རིག་འཛིན་རྣམ་བཞི།

The four types of Vidyādhāras; the four knowledge-holders. According to Nyingma tradition these are the stages of attaining the wisdom knowledge from the path of a trainee to the path of no-more learning. 1. རྣམ་སྨིན་རིག་འཛིན། the fully ripened vidyādhāra 2. ཚེ་དབང་རིག་འཛིན། the immortal-life vidyādhāra 3. ཕྱག་ཆེན་རིག་འཛིན། the mahāmudrā vidyādhāra 4. ལྷུན་གྲུབ་རིག་འཛིན། the spontaneously arisen vidyādhāra.

རིགས་ཀྱི་བུ་དང་རིགས་ཀྱི་བུ་མོ།

Blessed sons and daughters; the customary way in which Buddha addressed his disciples.

རིགས་ངེས་བྱང་སེམས།

Bodhisattva of definite lineage or family. Bodhisattvas who follow and enter the Mahāyāna path from the beginning without first entering the Hearer or Solitary realizer paths.

རིགས་ཅན་བཞི།

The four types of followers; disciples of the four families. 1. ཉན་ཐོས་ཀྱི་རིགས་ཅན། those belonging to the Hearer's family 2. རང་རྒྱལ་གྱི་རིགས་ཅན། those belonging to the Solitary realizer's family 3. ཐེག་ཆེན་གྱི་རིགས་ཅན། those belonging to the Greater Vehicle's family 4. མ་ངེས་པའི་རིགས་ཅན། those belonging to an indefinite family.

རིགས་ཅན་གསུམ།

The three types of followers; disciples of three families (see above 1-3).

རིགས་བརྗོད་ཀྱི་སྒྲ།

Sounds expressing class or category, e.g. the expression 'object of knowledge'.

རིགས་ནས་རིགས་སྐྱེས།

Kulaṁkula/ One born from family to family, e.g. a god taking rebirth again as a god.

རིགས་པའི་དགག་བྱ་གཉིས།

Two types of objects of negation by reason. 1. ཕྱིན་ཅི་ལོག་གི་ལྟ་བ། wrong view 2. དེ་ར་འཛིན་པའི་ལྟ་བ། the thought grasping at it.

རིགས་སྤྱི།

Categorical generality, e.g. a vase as compared to a golden vase.

རིགས་ཚོགས་དྲུག

Collection of six treatises; six treatises on the Middle Way by Nāgārjuna. 1. དབུ་མ་རྩ་བ་ཤེས་རབ། *The Fundamental Treatise on the Middle Way* (Mūlaprajñā) 2. རིན་ཆེན་ཕྲེང་བ། *The Precious Garland* (Ratnāvali) 3. རིགས་པ་དྲུག་ཅུ་པ། *The Sixty Verses of Reasoning* (Yuktisaṣtikā) 4. སྟོང་ཉིད་བདུན་ཅུ་པ། *The Seventy Verses on Emptiness* (Śūnytāsaptati) 5. རྩོད་བཟློག *The Refutation of Wrong Views* (Vigrahavyāvartanī) 6. ཞིབ་མོ་རྣམ་འཐག *The Thorough Investigation* (Vaidalyasūtra).

རིགས་བཞི།

Four castes of Hindu society. 1. བྲམ་ཟེའི་རིགས། priest caste 2. རྒྱལ་རིགས། warrior or royal caste 3. རྗེ་རིགས། merchant caste 4. དམངས་རིགས། laborer or working caste.

རིགས་གསུམ།

The disciples of the three families; A. According to tantra: 1. དེ་བཞིན་གཤེགས་པའི་རིགས། Tathāgata family 2. རྡོ་རྗེའི་རིགས། Vajra family 3. པད་མའི་རིགས། Padma family. B. The three types of disciples (see rigs-can gsum).

རིགས་གསུམ་མགོན་པོ།

The lords of the three families; in accordance with the Kriyā tantra tradition: 1. འཇམ་དཔལ་དབྱངས། Mañjuśrī, lord of wisdom 2. ཕྱག་ན་རྡོ་རྗེ། Vajrapāṇi, the lord of might and power 3. སྤྱན་རས་གཟིགས། Avalokiteśvara, the lord of compassion.

རིགས་གསུམ་རྡོ་རྗེ་འཛིན་པའི་ས།

The ground of the three vajra families. The entity of Buddha's body, speech and mind according to action tantra (cārya), represented by Buddha Vairocana, Amitābha and Vajra Akṣobhya respectively.

རིང་བརྒྱུད་བཀའ་མ།

Distant lineage of instruction. The texual lineage of the Nyingma tantras received by master Ma-Rinchen Chog and Nyag Janan Kumara from the great pandita Vimalamitra, who came to Tibet during the reign of King Trisong Deutsan. This transmission was wide spread in Tibet during the later period of propagation.

རིང་བསྲེལ།

Sarīra/ Relic pills. Tiny grain-like pills, sacred writings or physical remains of a saint or holy master, preserved at their cremation ground. Such relics are preserved in tombs and amulet boxes as objects of devotion and protection. There are three types: 1. གཟུངས་ཀྱི་རིང་བསྲེལ། relics of sacred writing 2. དབུ་སྐྲ་དང་ཕྱག་སེན་སོགས་ཀྱི་རིང་བསྲེལ། relics of bodily parts such as hairs, nails, etc. 3. འཕེལ་གདུང་གི་རིང་བསྲེལ། multiplied relics (see 'phel-gdung). 1. ཆོས་སྐུའི་རིང་བསྲེལ། relics of dharmakaya 2. སྐུ་བལ་གྱི་རིང་བསྲེལ། relics of physical parts 3. སྐུ་གདུང་གི་རིང་བསྲེལ། relics of the cremated body.

རིན་ཆེན་གཏེར་མཛོད།

The Treasure of Precious Collection. The collection of teachings and works of hundreds of treasure masters of the Nyingma tradition systematized into a set of collected works as compiled by the great master Kongtrul Yonten Gyatso comprising sixty-two volumes.

རིན་ཆེན་སྣ་བདུན།

A. Seven precious royal emblems. (see rgyal-srid sna-bdun) B. Seven precious stones. 1. པདྨ་རཱ་ག ruby 2. ཨིནྡྲ་ནཱི་ལ། sapphire 3. བཻཌཱུརྻ། lapiz lazuli 4. མརྒད། emerald 5. རྡོ་རྗེ་ཕ་ལམ། diamond 6. མུ་ཏིག pearl 7. བྱུ་རུ། coral. Or 1. གསེར། gold 2. དངུལ། silver 3. རྡོ་ཤེལ། crystal 4. སྤུག spug (karketana?) 5. མུ་ཏིག་དམར་པོ། red pearl 6. རྡོའི་སྙིང་པོ། emerald.

རིན་པོ་ཆེའི་རྒྱན་བརྒྱད།

Aṣṭa ratnālaṁkārāḥ/ Eight jewel ornaments; eight adornments of a deity. 1. དབུ་རྒྱན། mukuṭa/ crown 2. སྙན་རྒྱན། kaṃika/ earrings 3. མགུལ་རྒྱན། kaṇṭhābharaṇa/ necklace 4. ཕྱག་གདུབ། cūḍi/ bracelets 5. ཞབས་གདུབ། pāyala/ anklets 6. སེ་མོ་དོ། a jewel sash worn across one shoulder hanging to the level of the navel 7. དོ་ཤལ། a jewel sash worn across both shoulders hanging to the level of the thighs 8. འོག་པགས། a jewel net sash worn as a girdle.

རིན་པོ་ཆེའི་འབྱུང་གནས་ལྟ་བུའི་སེམས་བསྐྱེད།

Ratnakaropamacittotpāda/ Jewel source-like bodhicitta. The mind of enlightenment associated with the perfection of morality possessed by a Bodhisattva on the second of the ten grounds.

རིན་འབྱུང་གི་དམ་ཚིག་བཞི།

Four pledges concerning Ratnasambhava Buddha. 1. ཟང་ཟིང་གི་སྦྱིན་པ། giving material help 2. མི་འཇིགས་པའི་སྦྱིན་པ། giving protection from fear 3. ཆོས་ཀྱི་སྦྱིན་པ། giving teaching 4. བྱམས་པའི་སྦྱིན་པ། giving love.

རིམ་གྲོ

Upasthāna/ A. Offering of services and honoring spiritual persons and communities. B. Pujas or ritual ceremonies to pacify hinderances.

རིམ་པ་གཉིས།

Two stages; two stages of tantric practice. 1. བསྐྱེད་རིམ། utpannakrama/ generation stage 2. རྫོགས་རིམ། sampanna-krama/ completion stage. Or 1. སྒྱུ་ལུས། illusory body 2. འོད་གསལ། clear light.

རིལ་པ་སྤྱི་བླུགས།

Karakiṇī/ Monk's water pot; this is now sybolized by a bag tied to their sash that hangs in their lap.

རིས་ཆད་བློ་ཡི་མི་ཁོམས་པ་བརྒྱད།

The eight mental dregs of an unfortunate person. 1. ཉོན་མོངས་པའི་འཆིང་བ་དམ་པོ་ཡོད་པ། he or she is strongly bound by delusions 2. ཀུན་སྤྱོད་ཤིན་ཏུ་ངན་པ། is extremely bad mannered 3. འཁོར་བ་ལ་ཡིད་མི་སྐྱོ་བ། has no remorse about living in saṁsāra 4. དད་པ་ཅུང་ཟད་ཀྱང་མེད་པ། has total lack of faith in Dharma 5. མི་དགེའི་སྡིག་པ་སྤྱོད་པ། commits non-virtues 6. ཆོས་ལ་མི་སེམས་པ། has no interest in the Dharma 7. སྡོམ་པ་ཉམས་པ། has lost his or her vows 8. དམ་ཚིག་འཆལ་བ། has corrupted the samaya or commitment.

རུང་བ་བྱ་ཚུལ་གསུམ།

Three ways to transforming a thing into an object which a

monk may use. 1. སྦྱིན་བདག་བདག་པོ་ཉིད་དུ་མོས་པ་གཞུག་པའི་རུང་བ། by means of considering the benefactor himself as the owner 2. ཞལ་ཏ་བ་བདག་པོ་ཉིད་དུ་ཁས་ལེན་དུ་གཞུག་པའི་མོས་པའི་སྒོ་ནས་རུང་བ། by means of considering the steward himself as the owner 3. ཆོ་གའི་སྒོ་ནས་རུང་བ། by means of ceremonial rituals and rites.

རུས་པའི་རྒྱན་དྲུག

Six bone ornaments; six types of ornaments made of bone worn by a tantrika. 1. རུས་པའི་མགུལ་རྒྱན། bone necklace 2. རུས་པའི་གདུ་བུ། bone bracelet 3. རུས་པའི་རྣ་ཆ། bone earrings 4. རུས་པའི་དབུ་རྒྱན། bone crown 5. མཆོད་ཕྱིར་ཐོགས། bone wheel at the heart held by a bone bead sash across the shoulders 6. ཐལ་ཆེན། daubing crematory ashes.

རེ་ལྟ་ཐོགས་ཀྱི་སྲིད་པ་ལན་བདུན་པ།

One who takes seven rebirths at the most to attain liberation; a stream-winner who attains liberation after seven successive births as a human or god of the desire realm.

རེག་པ་དྲུག

Ṣaṭ sparśāḥ/ Six types of contact; six types of touch through association with the six faculties: མིག་གི་འདུས་ཏེ་རེག་པ་ནས་ཡིད་ཀྱི་འདུས་ཏེ་རེག་པའི་བར་དྲུག། eye, nose, ear, tongue, body and mind.

རེག་པ་གསུམ།

The three types of contact. A. 1. རིག་པའི་རེག་པ། contact through wisdom, the uncontaminated contact 2. མ་རིག་པའི་རེག་པ། contact through ignorance, the deluded contact 3. དེ་གཉིས་ཀ་མ་ཡིན་པའི་རེག་པ། contact that is neither, such as an indifferent contact. B. Three types of contact in view of the resultant feelings: 1. བདེ་བ་མྱོང་འགྱུར་གྱི་རེག་པ། contact giving rise to pleasant feelings/happiness 2. སྡུག་བསྔལ་མྱོང་འགྱུར་གྱི་རེག་པ། contact giving rise to unpleasant feelings/suffering 3. བཏང་སྙོམས་མྱོང་འགྱུར་གྱི་རེག་པ། contact giving rise to a neutral or indifferent feeling which is neither.

རེག་པའི་ཟས།

Sparśāhāra/ Food of touch; nourishment through touch. The contentment or satisfaction gained through contact with a pleasant object, e.g. forgetting to feel hungry while engrossed in watching an exciting movie.

རེག་བྱ་བཅུ་གཅིག

Ekādaśa sparśāḥ/ Eleven objects of touch; eleven tangible objects. 1-4. འབྱུང་བ་ས་ཆུ་མེ་རླུང་བཞི། the four elments—earth, water, fire and wind 5. འཇམ་པ། mṛduka/ smoothness 6. རྩུབ་པ། kakarśa/ roughness 7. ལྕི་བ། gurutva/ heaviness 8. ཡང་བ། laghutva/ lightness 9. བཀྲེས་པ། jighatsā/ hunger 10. སྐོམ་པ། tṛṣā/ thirst 11. གྲང་བ། śīta/ coldness.

རོ་གཅིག

Ekarasa/ One taste; single taste. The ultimate taste or experience of the reality of phenomena.

རོ་བཅུ་གཉིས།

Twelve types of taste. 1-6. (see ro-drug) 7. ཡིད་དུ་འོང་བ། appetizing 8. ཡིད་དུ་མི་འོང་བ། non-appetizing 9. དེ་གཉིས་ཀ་མ་ཡིན་པ། neither appetizing nor non-appetizing 10 . ལྷན་ཅིག་བྱེད་པ། natural 11. སྦྱར་བ་ལས་བྱུང་བ། artificial 12. འགྱུར་བ་ལས་བྱུང་བ། transformed taste.

རོ་སྙོམས་སྐོར་དྲུག

Sixfold transmissions of single taste; six instructions on experiencing the single taste of all phenomena. 1. རྣམ་རྟོག་ལམ་འཁྱེར། taking conceptualization as a path 2. ཉོན་མོངས་ལམ་འཁྱེར། taking delusions as a path 3. ན་ཚ་ལམ་འཁྱེར། taking illness as a path 4. ལྷ་འདྲེ་ལམ་འཁྱེར། taking gods and ghosts as a path 5. སྡུག་བསྔལ་ལམ་འཁྱེར། taking sufferings as a path 6. འཆི་བ་ལམ་འཁྱེར། taking death as a path.

རོ་དྲུག

Six types of taste. 1. མངར་བ། madhura/sweet 2. སྐྱུར་བ། amla/sour 3. ཁ་བ། tikta/bitter 4. བསྐ་བ། kaṣāya/astringent 5. ཚ་བ། kaṭuka/hot/burning 6. ལན་ཚ་བ། lavaṇa/salty.

རོ་མ།

Rasanā/ Right channel; right energy-channel. Red in color and stands adjacent to the central energy channel, it runs from the level of the eye-brows, to some what below the navel, the specific details varying according to the lineage and practice of the tantra concerned.

རོ་མྱག་འདམ།

Kuṇapa/ Corpse filled swamp; swamp of filth. One of the neighbouring hells (see nye-'khor-ba'i dmyal-ba).

རོ་ལངས།

Vetāla/ Zombie.

རོ་སོ་དྲུག

Thirty-six types of taste. Six types of tastes within each of the six tastes (see ro-drug).

རོལ་མོའི་སྒྲ་རྩལ་བཅོ་བརྒྱད།

The eighteen arts of music. 1. གར། dance (gar-dang-bro) 2. བྲོ། fairy dance 3. རྔ་བོ་ཆེ། beating big drums 4. རྫ་རྔ། clay drum 5. རྔ་ཕྲན། accessory drums 6. རྔ་ཆེན་པོ། big drums 7. འཁར་རྔ། bronze gongs 8. པི་ཝང་རྒྱུད་གཅིག་པ། single-stringed guitar 9. རྫ་རྔ་ཁ་གཅིག་པ། one sided clay drum 10. ལྕགས་ཀྱི་སིལ་སྙན། iron cymbal 11. འཁར་བའི་སིལ་སྙན། bronze staff carried by monks 12. པི་ཝང་རྒྱུད་གསུམ་པ། three-stringed guitar 13. རྔ་མུ་ཀུནྡ། mu-kunda 14. སིལ་སྙན་གླུ་དབྱངས་དང་བསྟུན་པ། music accompanied by bells and cymbals 15. ཐེག་རྡོབ། clapping 16. རོལ་མོའི་སྒྲ། musical sounds 17. པི་ཝང་། guitar 18. གླིང་བུ། flue.

རླུང་བུམ་པ་ཅན།

The vase-like wind meditation. A tantric practice or yoga of wind meditation in which, roughly speaking, air from the bottom of one's body is drawn up and air from the upper part of the body is compressed down so as to form a vase-shape at the navel level, and then retained and released at appropriate intervals according to the instruction of the master.

རླུང་འོད་གསལ་ལྔ་པ།

Energy-wind with five-fold rays. The subtle wind that serves as the mount for the clear light mind of death.

རློམ་སེམས།

Arrogance; superiority complex; self-aggrandizement.

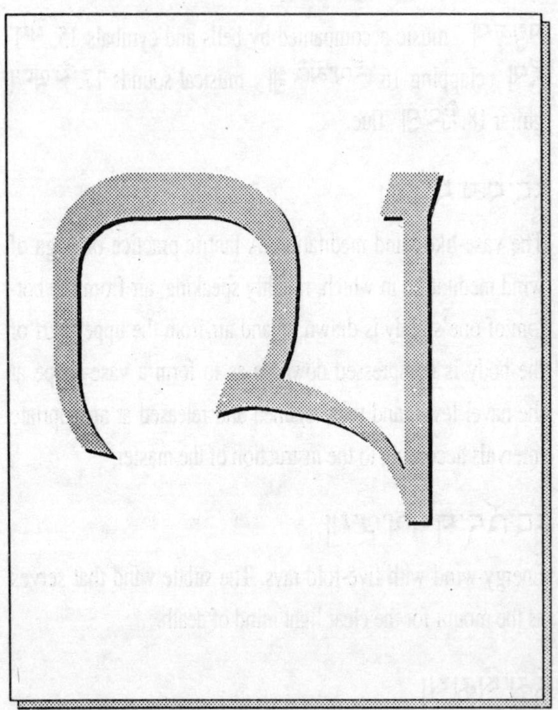

ལག་ལེན།

Practice; practical experience.

ལན་གྲངས་གཞན་དུ་མྱོང་འགྱུར་གྱི་ལས།

Aparaparyāyavedanīyam karma/ Karma whose fruits will be experienced or ripened in subsequent lives.

ལན་གཅིག་ཕྱིར་འོང་།

Sakṛdāgāmin/ Once Returner; a Hīnayāna path.

ལན་ཆགས།

Karmic debt; karmic retribution.

ལམ་གྱི་དགག་བྱ།

Mārgapratiṣedhya/ Objects to be negated by the path. There are three types: A. 1. ཉོན་སྒྲིབ། kleśāvaraṇa/ obscurations to liberation 2. ཤེས་སྒྲིབ། jñeyāvaraṇa/ obscurations to omniscience 3. སྙོམས་འཇུག་གི་སྒྲིབ་པ། samāpattyāvaraṇa/ obscurations to absorption. B. 1. ཆགས་སྒྲིབ། rāgāvaraṇa/ obstruction through attachment 2. ཐོགས་སྒྲིབ། sapratighāvaraṇa/ obstruction through obstacles 3. དམན་སྒྲིབ། hīnāvaraṇa/ obstruction of the lower.

ལམ་ལྔ་།

Five paths. 1. ཚོགས་ལམ། saṁbhāra mārga/ path of accumulation 2. སྦྱོར་ལམ། prayoga mārga/ path of preparation 3. མཐོང་ལམ། darśana mārga/ path of seeing 4. སྒོམ་ལམ། bhāvanā mārga/ path of meditation 5. མི་སློབ་ལམ། aśaikṣa mārga/ path of no-more learning.

ལམ་གཉིས།

The two types of paths. A. འཇིག་རྟེན་དང་འཇིག་རྟེན་ལས་འདས་པའི་ལམ། The worldly or transworldly path. B. ཐེག་ཆེན་དང་ཐེག་དམན་གྱི་ལམ། The path of higher and lower vehicles. C. སོ་སྐྱེ་དང་འཕགས་པའི་ལམ། The ordinary and exalted path. D. མདོ་སྔགས་གཉིས་ཀྱི་ལམ། The path of the sūtra and tantra tradition. E. ཐབས་ཤེས་གཉིས་ཀྱི་ལམ། The path of method and wisdom. F. སྨིན་བྱེད་དང་གྲོལ་བྱེད་ཀྱི་ལམ། The ripening and liberating path.

ལམ་བདེན་གྱི་ཁྱད་ཆོས་བཞི།

Four features of the noble truth of the path. 1. ལམ། mārga/ path 2. རིགས་པ། nyāya/ awareness 3. སྒྲུབ་པ། pratipatti/ achievement 4. ངེས་འབྱིན། nairyāṇika/ definite freedom.

ལམ་བདེན་གྱི་རྣམ་པ་བཅོ་ལྔ་།

Fifteen aspects of the noble truth of the path. 1. བྱེད་པ་པོ་མེད་པའི་རྣམ་པ། aspect of lacking an agent 2. ཤེས་པ་པོ་མེད་པའི་རྣམ་པ། aspect of lacking a knower 3. འཕོ་བ་མེད་པའི་རྣམ་པ། aspect of lacking transmigration 4. འདུལ་བ་མེད་པའི་རྣམ་པ། aspect of lacking discipline 5. མི་ལམ་གྱི་རྣམ་པ། aspect of a dream 6. སྒྲ་བརྙན་གྱི་རྣམ་པ། aspect of an echo 7. མིག་གཡོར་གྱི་རྣམ་པ། aspect of a hallucination 8. སྨིག་སྒྱུའི་རྣམ་པ། aspect of a mirage 9. སྒྱུ་མའི་རྣམ་པ། aspect of an illusion 10. ཉོན་མོངས་མེད་པའི་རྣམ་པ། aspect free from delusion 11. རྣམ་པར་བྱང་བ་མེད་པའི་རྣམ་པ། aspect of lacking purified phenomena 12. གོས་པ་མེད་པའི་རྣམ་པ། aspect of being free from impediments 13. སྤྲོས་པ་མེད་པའི་རྣམ་པ། aspect of being free from conceptual elaborations 14. རློམ་པ་མེད་པའི་རྣམ་པ། aspect of being free from pride 15. མི་གཡོ་བའི་རྣམ་པ། aspect of immutability.

ལམ་བདེན་གྱི་རྣམ་པ་བདུན།

Seven aspects of the noble truth of the path. 1. ཚད་མེད་པའི་རྣམ་པ། immeasurable aspect 2. མཐའ་གཉིས་དང་མ་འདྲེས་པའི་རྣམ་པ། aspect of not being mingled with the two extremes 3. ཐ་མི་དད་པའི་རྣམ་པ། undifferentiable aspect 4. མཆོག་ཏུ་འཛིན་པ་མེད་པའི་རྣམ་པ། aspect of the non-apprehension of superiority 5. རྣམ་པར་མི་རྟོག་པའི་རྣམ་པ། aspect of non-discrimination 6. གཞལ་དུ་མེད་པའི་རྣམ་པ། aspect of inconceivability 7. ཆགས་པ་མེད་པའི་རྣམ་པ། aspect of non-attachment.

ལམ་བདེན་གྱི་སྤང་བྱ་བརྒྱད།

The eight abandonments of the noble truth of the path. The abandonments to be eliminated by virtue of attaining the noble truth of the path within the desire realm. 1. མ་རིག་པ། ignorance 2. འདོད་ཆགས། desire-attachment 3. ཁོང་ཁྲོ། hatred-anger 4. ང་རྒྱལ། pride 5. ཐེ་ཚོམ། doubt 6. ལོག་ལྟ། wrong view 7. ལྟ་བ་མཆོག་འཛིན། holding wrong views as superior 8. ཚུལ་ཁྲིམས་དང་བརྟུལ་ཞུགས་མཆོག་འཛིན། holding wrong discipline and morality as superior.

ལམ་པོ་ཆེ་ལྟ་བུའི་སེམས་བསྐྱེད།

Mahāmārgopamacittotpāda/ Highway-like bodhicitta. The mind of enlightenment associated with the limbs of enlightenment possessed by a Bodhisattva on the tenth ground.

ལམ་དབུ་མ།

Madhyamamārga/ The Middle Path. A path free of the two extremes.

ལམ་འབྲས།

The Paths and Fruits. The profound and precious teachings of the Sakya tradition of Tibetan Buddhism. This lineage of teaching rooted in Hevajra tantra comes from Mahāsiddha Virūpa as transmitted to Kṛṣṇa and Dombhipa, and was brought to Tibet by Drogmi Lotsawa, who then passed the transmission to Sachen Kunga Nyingpo. Then to Sonam Tzemo and Dragpa Gyaltsen and then to Sakya Paṇḍita and then to Drogon Choegyal Phagpa. The lineage has been successfully preserved to this day by many masters of the Sakya tradition.

ལམ་འབྲས་ཚོགས་བཤད།

The open lineage of the paths and fruits. The transmission of the cycle of teachings of the paths and fruits successively passed down from the five foremost masters of the Sakya tradition to Mahāsiddha Buddhaśrī, then to Ngorchen Kunga Zangpo exclusive to Ngorpas—a sub-school of the Sakya tradition which came to be known as the open lineage of the paths and fruits of the Ngor sect.

ལམ་འབྲས་སློབ་བཤད།

The restrictive lineage of the paths and fruits. The transmission of the cycle of teachings of the paths and fruits passed down from Doring Kunpang to Tsarchen Losel Gyatso, then to Jamyang Khyentse Wangchuk and Mangthoe Ludub Gyatso; is known as the restrictive lineage of the paths and fruits exclusive to Tsarpa, a sub-sect of the Sakya tradition.

ལམ་གཙོ་རྣམ་གསུམ།

Three principal aspects of the path. 1. ངེས་འབྱུང་། niḥsaraṇa/ renunciation 2. བྱང་སེམས། bodhicitta/ mind of enlightenment 3. ཡང་དག་པའི་ལྟ་བ། saṁyagdrsti/ right view.

ལམ་རིམ་གྱི་ཆེ་བ་བཞི།

Four pre-eminent qualities of the *Graded Path to Enlightenment*. 1. བསྟན་པ་ཐམས་ཅད་འགལ་མེད་དུ་རྟོགས་པའི་ཆེ་བ། one understands that there is no contradiction in the entire teaching of the Buddha 2. གསུང་རབ་མ་ལུས་པ་གདམས་ངག་ཏུ་འཆར་བའི་ཆེ་བ། one discovers that all the teachings of the Buddha are sound instructions 3. རྒྱལ་བའི་དགོངས་པ་བདེ་བླག་ཏུ་རྟོགས་པའི་ཆེ་བ། one understands easily and unmistakenly the purpose of Buddha's teachings 4. ཉེས་སྤྱོད་ཆེན་པོ་རང་འགག་ཏུ་འགྲོ་བའི་ཆེ་བ། one will automatically stop committing great negativities.

ལམ་རིམ་པ་ལྔ།

The five stages of paths (see rdzogs-rim-pa lnga).

ལམ་ཕྱིར་ཕྱིན།

Mārga prajñāpāramitā/ Path perfection of wisdom. The Bodhisattva yoga of the union of clam-abiding and penetrative insight meditation, aimed at attaining a resultant perfection of wisdom.

ལམ་ཤེས།

Mārgajñāna/ Path wisdom; Knowledge of the paths. Mahāyāna paths within the mental continuum of a superior Bodhisattva.

ལམ་ཤེས་ཀྱི་རྣམ་པ་སོ་དྲུག

Thirty-six aspects of the path wisdom; thirty-six aspects of the knowledge of the paths. 1-8. ཀུན་འབྱུང་བདེན་པའི་རྣམ་པ་བརྒྱད། eight aspects of the noble truth of the origin of suffering (see kun-'byung bden-pa'i rnam-pa brgyad) 9-15. ལམ་བདེན་གྱི་རྣམ་པ་བདུན། seven aspects of the noble truth of the path (see lam-bden-gyi rnam-pa bdun) 16-20. སྡུག་བདེན་གྱི་རྣམ་པ་ལྔ། five aspects of the noble truth of suffering (see sdug-bden-gyi rnam-pa lnga) 21-36. འགོག་བདེན་གྱི་རྣམ་པ་བཅུ་དྲུག sixteen aspects of the noble truth of cesstion (see 'gog-bden-gyi rnam-pa bcu-drug).

ལམ་ཤེས་ཀྱི་ཡན་ལག་ལྔ།

Five limbs of the path wisdom; the five limbs of the knowledge of the paths. 1. ལམ་ཤེས་སྐྱེ་བའི་གེགས་ང་རྒྱལ་མངོན་འགྱུར་དང་བྲལ་བ། freedom from manifest pride impeding the generation of path wisdom 2. ཉེར་ལེན་ཐེག་ཆེན་གྱི་རིགས་སད་པ། ripening the Mahāyāna lineage as the principal cause 3. མཐུན་རྐྱེན་བྱང་སེམས་བསྐྱེད་པ། generating bodhicittta as the auxiliary cause 4. ལམ་ཤེས་ཀྱི་རང་བཞིན། the nature of the path wisdom 5. ལམ་ཤེས་ཀྱི་བྱེད་ལས། the function of the path wisdom.

ལམ་ཤེས་མཚོན་བྱེད་ཀྱི་ཆོས་བཅུ་གཅིག

Eleven topics that characterize the knowledge of the paths. 1. ལམ་ཤེས་ཀྱི་ཡན་ལག limbs of the path wisdom (see lam-shes-kyi yan-lag, above) 2. ཉན་ཐོས་ཀྱི་ལམ་ཤེས་པའི་ལམ་ཤེས། the path wisdom that understands the Hearer's path 3. རང་རྒྱལ་གྱི་ལམ་ཤེས་པའི་ལམ་ཤེས། the path wisdom that understands the Solitary Realizer's path 4. ཕན་ཡོན་ཅན་གྱི་མཐོང་ལམ། the beneficial Mahāyāna path of seeing 5. སྒོམ་ལམ་གྱི་བྱེད་པ། the function of the path of meditation 6. མོས་པ་སྒོམ་ལམ། the Mahāyāna path of belief 7. བསྟོད་བཀུར་བསྔགས་གསུམ་གྱི་སྒོམ་ལམ། the Mahāyāna path of praise, exhortation and eulogy 8. བསྔོ་བ་སྒོམ་ལམ། the Mahāyāna path of dedication 9. རྗེས་སུ་ཡི་རང་སྒོམ་ལམ། the Mahāyāna path of meditation of rejoicing 10. སྒྲུབ་པ་སྒོམ་ལམ། the

Mahāyāna path of meditation of achievement 11. རྣམ་དག་སྦྱོར་ལམ། the Mahāyāna path of complete purity.

ལས།

Karma; law of causality. ལས་ལ་གཉིས་སུ་དབྱེ་བ། The way karma is divided into two types: A. 1. མྱོང་བར་ངེས་པའི་ལས། karma whose fruits will definitely be experienced 2. མྱོང་བར་མ་ངེས་པའི་ལས། karma whose fruits will not definitely be experienced. B. 1. དགེ་བའི་ལས། virtuous karma 2. མི་དགེ་བའི་ལས། non-virtuous karma. C. 1. ཟག་བཅས་ཀྱི་ལས། contaminated karma 2. ཟག་མེད་ཀྱི་ལས། uncontaminated karma. D. 1. བླང་བྱའི་ལས། karma to be accumulated 2. དོར་བྱའི་ལས། karma to be abandoned. E. 1. སེམས་པའི་ལས། mental activity 2. བསམ་པའི་ལས། intended activities. ལས་ལ་གསུམ་དུ་དབྱེ་བ། The way karma is divided into three types: A. འབྲས་བུའི་སྒོ་ནས། According to their nature of fruition: 1. བདེ་བ་མྱོང་འགྱུར་གྱི་ལས། karma giving rise to happiness 2. སྡུག་བསྔལ་མྱོང་འགྱུར་གྱི་ལས། karma giving rise to suffering 3. བཏང་སྙོམས་ཀྱི་ལས། karma giving rise to indifference. B. དུས་ཀྱི་སྒོ་ནས། According to the time of their fruition: 1. མཐོང་ཆོས་མྱོང་འགྱུར་གྱི་ལས། karma whose fruits will be experienced in this life 2. སྐྱེས་ནས་མྱོང་འགྱུར་གྱི་ལས། karma whose fruits will be experienced in the next life 3. ལན་གྲངས་གཞན་དུ་མྱོང་འགྱུར་གྱི་ལས། karma whose fruits will be experienced in other subsequent live.s C. ངོ་བོའི་སྒོ་ནས། According to their nature: 1. བསོད་ནམས་ཀྱི་ལས། virtuous karma 2. བསོད་ནམས་མ་ཡིན་པའི་ལས། non-virtuous karma 3. མི་གཡོ་བའི་ལས། unfluctuating karma. D. གསོག་ཚུལ་གྱི་སྒོ་ནས། According to the way a karma is accumulated: 1. བྱས་བསགས་གཉིས་ཀ་ཚང་བའི་ལས། karma which is both caused and accumulated 2. བསགས་ལ་མ་བྱས་པའི་ལས། karma which is accumulated but not caused 3. བྱས་ལ་མ་བསགས་པའི་ལས། karma which is caused but not accumulated.

ལས་ཀྱི་སྒྲིབ་པ།

Karmāvaraṇa/ Karmic obscurations; karmic negativities; obstructions arising from the actions of henious crimes that are accumulated in the past or present life.

ལས་ཀྱི་ངོ་བོ་བཞི།

Four features of karma; four characteristics of an action. 1. ལས་ངེས་པ། karma is definite 2. ལས་འཕེལ་ཆེ་བ། karma multiplies greatly 3. ལས་མ་བྱས་པ་དང་མི་འཕྲད་པ། karma not accumulated will not be experienced 4. ལས་བྱས་པ་ཆུད་མི་ཟ་བ། karma commited will not dissipate.

ལས་ཀྱི་ཕྱག་རྒྱ།

Karma mudrā/ A. Action seal; tantric consort; the female partner of a male tantric practitioner. A completion stage practice. B. The hand mudrā symbolizing enlightened activities ('phrin-las).

ལས་ཀྱི་འབྲས་བུ་གསུམ།

Three types of karmic fruit. 1. རྣམ་སྨིན་གྱི་འབྲས་བུ། fully matured fruit/ result 2. རྒྱུ་མཐུན་གྱི་འབྲས་བུ། results corresponding to its cause 3. བདག་པོའི་འབྲས་བུ། environmental result.

ལས་ཀྱི་ཡན་ལག་བཞི།

The four branches of karma. A. གཞི། བསམ་པ། སྦྱོར་བ། མཐར་ཐུག The object, intention, actual activity and completion. B. (see las-kyi ngo-bo bzhi).

ལས་ལྔ།

Five types of karma; five activities; five functions. 1. འདེགས་པ། lifting up 2. འཇོག་པ། putting down 3. བརྐྱང་པ། extending 4. བསྐུམ་པ། withdrawing 5. འགྲོ་བ། going.

ལས་བུམ།

Action vase. The ritual vase used during various religious ceremonies such in the consecration and purification of a maṇḍala, offering articles, self-generation, abode, disciples and so on.

ལས་ཆོགས།

Liturgy; set of manuals for rituals concerning individual deities and their practice.

ལས་ལམ་གསུམ།

Three paths of activity; three mediums of activity through body, speech and mind.

ལུང་།

Āgama/ Reading transmission. A discourse in which a text is thoroughly read to the disciples in order to transmit the oral tradition to the disciples. This then authorizes a disciple to read, contemplate and meditate on that particular cycle of teachings.

ལུང་གི་བསྟན་པ།

Scriptural teachings. The transmission of Buddha's teachings extant in oral and scriptural form.

ལུང་དུ་བསྟན་པའི་སྡེ།

Prophetic teachings. One of the twelve scriptural categories that concerns prophesies given by Buddha about the past and future lives of an individual.

ལུང་འདྲེན།

Citation; quotation; scriptural support.

ལུང་མ་བསྟན།

Avyākṛta/ Unspecified phenomena. Something Buddha has not specified as being either virtuous or non-virtuous, e.g. a person.

ལུང་མ་བསྟན་གྱི་ལྟ་བ་བཅུ་བཞི།

Caturdaśāvyākṛta mūlāni/ Fourteen unspecified views; Concerning: 1. འཇིག་རྟེན་རྟག་པ། śāśvato loka/ a permanent world 2. འཇིག་རྟེན་མི་རྟག་པ། aśāśvato loka/ an impermanent world 3. འཇིག་རྟེན་རྟག་ཀྱང་རྟག་ལ་མི་རྟག་ཀྱང་མི་རྟག་པ། śāśvataś cāśvataś ca/ a world which is both permanent and impermanent 4. འཇིག་རྟེན་མཐའ་ཡོད་པ། antavān loka/ a world which has an end 5. འཇིག་རྟེན་རྟག་པ་ཡང་མ་ཡིན་མི་རྟག་པ་ཡང་མ་ཡིན། nāiva śāśvato nāśāśvataśca/ a world which is neither permanent nor impermanent 6. འཇིག་རྟེན་མཐའ་ཡོད་པ་མིན་པ། anantavān loka/ a world which has no end 7. འཇིག་རྟེན་མཐའ་ཡོད་ཀྱང་ཡོད་ལ་མཐའ་མེད་ཀྱང་མེད། antavāṁś cānantavāṁś ca/ a world which is both with and without an end 8. འཇིག་རྟེན་མཐའ་ཡོད་པ་ཡང་མ་ཡིན་མེད་པ་ཡང་མ་ཡིན། nāivāntavān nānantavān/ a world which is neither with nor without an end 9. དེ་བཞིན་གཤེགས་པ་ཤི་ནས་ཡོད། bhavati tathāgataḥ paraṁ maraṇāt/ the existence of Buddha after passing away into parinirvāṇa 10. དེ་བཞིན་གཤེགས་པ་ཤི་ནས་མེད། na bhavati tathāgataḥ paraṁ maraṇāt/ the non-existence of Buddha after passing away into parinirvāṇa 11. དེ་བཞིན་གཤེགས་པ་ཤི་ནས་ཡོད་ཀྱང་ཡོད་ལ་མེད་ཀྱང་མེད། bhavati ca na bhavati ca tathāgataḥ paraṁ maraṇāt/ a Buddha who is both existent and non-existent after passing away into parinirvāṇa 12. དེ་བཞིན་གཤེགས་པ་ཤི་ནས་ཡོད་པ་ཡང་མ་ཡིན་མེད་པ་ཡང་མ་ཡིན། nāiva bhavati na na bhavati tathāgataḥ paraṁmaraṇāt/ a Buddha who is neither existent nor non-existent after passing away into parinirvāṇa 13. སྲོག་དེ་ལུས་ཡིན། sajīvas tac charīram/ the life-force is the body 14. སྲོག་ཀྱང་གཞན་ལུས་ཀྱང་གཞན། anyo jīvo 'nyac charīram/ the life-force and body are independent of each other.

ལུས་ཀྱི་དགེ་བ་གསུམ།

Three virtues of body; three wholesome activities concerning the body. 1. སྲོག་གཅོད་སྤོང་བ། not killing 2. མ་བྱིན་པར་ལེན་པ་སྤོང་བ། not stealing 3. ལོག་གཡེམ་སྤོང་བ། not indulging in sexual misconduct.

ལུས་ཀྱི་དོན་ལྔ།

Five essential parts of the body. 1. གློ་བ། klomaka/ lungs 2. སྙིང་ག hṛdaya/ heart 3. མཁལ་མ། vṛkkā/ kidney 4. མཆེར་པ། yakṛt/ spleen 5. མཆིན་པ། plīha/ liver.

ལུས་ཀྱི་གནས་ལྔ།

Five vital points of the body. 1. སྤྱི་བོ། mūrdhan/ crown 2. མགྲིན་པ། grivā/ throat 3. སྙིང་ག hṛdaya/ heart 4. ལྟེ་བ། nābhi/ navel 5. གསང་གནས། secret organ.

ལུས་ཀྱི་སྣོད་དྲུག

Six hollow organs of the body. 1. རྒྱུ་མ། antram/ small intestine 2. ལོང་ཀ། pakvāśaya/ large intestine 3. ཕོ་བ། āmāśaya/ stomach 4. མངེ་མ། antraguṇa/ womb 5. སྒང་པ། audarīyakam/ bladder 6. མཁྲིས་སྣོད། pitta/ gall bladder.

ལུས་ཀྱི་མལ་ལྔ།

Five limbs of the body. A. 1. དཔྲལ་བ། forehead 2-3. པུས་མོ་གཉིས། two knees 4-5. ལག་མཐིལ་གཉིས། two palms of the hands. B. 1. མགོ head 2-3. ལག་པ་གཉིས། two arms 4-5. རྐང་པ་གཉིས། two legs.

ལུས་དཀྱིལ།

Kāyamaṇḍala/ Body maṇḍala. The tantric practice of visualizing and identifying the entire residence and resident features of the deities upon different parts of one's body through meditation.

ལུས་ཀྱི་རིག་འཛིན།

The extraordinary qualities of the body; the eight powerful attainments (see dbang-phyug brgyad, B.) common to both Buddhists and non-Buddhists attained as a result of the accomplishment of one's tantric practices.

ལུས་ཟུངས་བདུན།

Seven essential energies of the body; seven basic elements for the sustenance of the body. 1. ཁྲག rakta/ blood 2. ཤ། māṁsa/ flesh 3. ཚིལ། medaḥ/ fat 4. རུས་པ། asthi/ bone 5. རྐང་། majjā/ marrow 6. ཁུ་བ། rasa/ semen and blood 7. ཟ་བཏུང་གི་དྭངས་མ། nutrients of food and drink.

ལུས་ཤིན་སྦྱངས།

Physical ecstacy. The state of physical pliancy and flexibility gained as a result of the successful development of calm abiding meditation (śamatha) enabling the physical ability to bear the hardship of higher practices.

ལེགས་པའི་ཡོན་ཏན་དྲུག

The six excellent qualities; the six qualities exclusive to Buddha Śākyamuni. 1. དབང་ཕྱུག་ཕུན་སུམ་ཚོགས་པ། excellent resources 2. གཟུགས་ཕུན་སུམ་ཚོགས་པ། excellent physical features 3. དཔལ་ཕུན་སུམ་ཚོགས་པ། excellent glory 4. གྲགས་པ་ཕུན་སུམ་ཚོགས་པ། excellent fame 5. ཡེ་ཤེས་ཕུན་སུམ་ཚོགས་པ། excellent wisdom 6. བརྩོན་འགྲུས་ཕུན་སུམ་ཚོགས་པ། excellent effort.

ལེན་པ་བཞི།

The four negativities; the four compulsive acquisitions (see nyer-len bzhi). All the one hundred and eight delusions are condensed into these four negativities.

ལོ་འཁོར་བཅུ་གཉིས།

Twelve year cycle. 1. བྱི་བ། mouse 2. གླང་། ox 3. སྟག tiger 4. ཡོས། hare 5. འབྲུག dragon 6. སྦྲུལ། serpent 7. རྟ། horse 8. ལུག sheep 9. སྤྲེལ། monkey 10. བྱ། bird 11. ཁྱི། dog 12. ཕག pig.

ལོ་ཙྪ་བ།

Translator; lit. the eye of the universe; one who is fluent in two languages.

ལོ་ཙྪ་བ་རིན་ཆེན་བཟང་པོ།

Rinchen Zangpo (958-1055). The great translator during the later propagation of Buddha's teachings in Tibet. His translations are reputed for their authenticity and clarity.

ལོག་རྟོག་ལྔ་།

Five misconceptions; five wrong ideas. Misconception concerning: 1. དམིགས་པ་ལ་ལོག་པར་རྟོག་པ། object 2. དུས་ལ་ལོག་པར་རྟོག་པ། time 3. ངོ་བོ་ལ་ལོག་པར་རྟོག་པ། identity 4. རང་བཞིན་ལ་ལོག་པར་རྟོག་པ། nature 5. ཤེས་རབ་ལ་ལོག་པར་རྟོག་པ། wisdom.

ལོག་རྟོག་བཅུ་དྲུག

Sixteen misconceptions; sixteen wrong views. Misconception concerning: 1. དམིགས་པ་ལ་ལོག་པར་རྟོག་པ། object 2. རྣམ་པ་ལ་ལོག་པར་རྟོག་པ། aspect 3. འབྲས་བུ་ལ་ལོག་པར་རྟོག་པ། fruit 4. ཀུན་རྫོབ་བདེན་པ་ལ་ལོག་པར་རྟོག་པ། conventional truth 5. དོན་དམ་བདེན་པ་ལ་ལོག་པར་རྟོག་པ། ultimate truth 6. སྤྱོད་པའི་ངོ་བོ་ལ་ལོག་པར་རྟོག་པ། nature of conduct 7. སྐྱོབ་པའི་རྟེན་སངས་རྒྱས་ལ་ལོག་པར་རྟོག་པ། object of refuge 8. ཆོས་ལ་ལོག་པར་རྟོག་པ། Dharma 9. དགེ་འདུན་ལ་ལོག་པར་རྟོག་པ། Saṅgha 10. ཐབས་མཁས་པ་ལ་ལོག་པར་རྟོག་པ། skill in means 11. མངོན་རྟོགས་ལ་ལོག་པར་རྟོག་པ། realizations 12. སྤང་བྱ་ལ་ལོག་པར་རྟོག་པ། abandonments 13. ལམ་གྱི་ངོ་བོ་ལ་ལོག་པར་རྟོག་པ། nature of the path 14. སྤང་གཉེན་གྱི་རྣམ་དབྱེ་ལ་ལོག་པར་རྟོག་པ། distinction between objects to be abandoned and their antidotes 15. ཆོས་རྣམས་ཀྱི་མཚན་ཉིད་ལ་ལོག་པར་རྟོག་པ། characteristics of phenomena 16. རང་སྤྱིའི་མཚན་ཉིད་ལ་ལོག་པར་རྟོག་པ། general and specific nature of phenomena.

ལོག་ལྟ་ལྔ་།

Pañca mithyādṛṣṭayaḥ/ Five wrong views. 1. འཇིག་ཚོགས་ལ་ལྟ་བ། satkāya dṛṣṭi/ view of transitory collection 2. མཐར་འཛིན་གྱི་ལྟ་བ། antagrāha dṛṣṭi/ view of adhering to an extreme 3. ལྟ་བ་མཆོག་འཛིན། dṛṣṭi parāmarśa/ view holding oneself to be superior 4. ཚུལ་ཁྲིམས་དང་བརྟུལ་ཞུགས་མཆོག་འཛིན། śīlavrata-parāmarśa/ view holding bad ethics and discipline to be superior 5. ལོག་ལྟ། mithyā dṛṣṭi/ wrong view itself.

ལོག་པའི་ཀུན་རྫོབ།

Mithyā saṁvṛtti/ Wrong conventional truth; distorted conventional truth, e.g. a rabbit with horns.

ལོག་འཚོ་ལྔ་།

Five wrong livelihoods. Earning livelihood by means of: 1. ཁ་གསག flattery 2. གཞོགས་སློང་། hinting 3. རྙེད་པས་རྙེད་པ་འཚོལ་བ། seeking reward for favor 4. ཐོབ་ཀྱིས་འཇལ་བ། using force 5. ཚུལ་འཆོས། contrived means.

ལོག་ཞུགས་བཅུ་དྲུག

Sixteen distorted views; sixteen wrong conceptions concerning the four noble truths. Four of the noble truth of suffering: 1. ཟག་བཅས་ཀྱི་ཕུང་པོ་རྟག་པར་ལྟ་བ། seeing the contaminated aggregates as permanent 2. ཟག་བཅས་ཀྱི་ཕུང་པོ་བདེ་བར་ལྟ་བ། seeing the contaminated aggregates as joyful 3. ཟག་བཅས་ཀྱི་ཕུང་པོ་གཙང་བར་ལྟ་བ། seeing the contaminated aggregates as pure 4. ཟག་བཅས་ཀྱི་ཕུང་པོ་བདག་ཏུ་ལྟ་བ། seeing the contaminated aggregates as the self. Four of the noble truth of the origin of suffering: 1. སྡུག་བསྔལ་རྒྱུ་མེད་དུ་ལྟ་བ། seeing sufferings as causeless 2. རྒྱུ་གཅིག་ཁོ་ནས་བྱུང་བར་ལྟ་བ། seeing sufferings as produced by a single cause 3. དབང་ཕྱུག་སོགས་ཀྱི་བློའི་གཡོ་བ་སྔོན་དུ་བཏང་ནས་བྱུང་བར་འཛིན་པ། seeing them as projected by the whim of Īśvara and others 4. རང་བཞིན་རྟག་ལ་གནས་སྐབས་མི་རྟག་པར་ལྟ་བ། seeing them as inherently permanent but temporarily impermanent. Four of the noble truth of cessetion: 1. ཐར་པ་ཡེ་མེད་དུ་འཛིན་པ། seeing libertion as totally non-existent 2. ཟག་བཅས་ཀྱི་ཁྱད་པར་འགའ་ཞིག་ཐར་པར་འཛིན་པ། seeing certain contaminated features as liberation 3. ཉོན་མོངས་པའི་ཁྱད་པར་འགའ་ཞིག་ཐར་པར་འཛིན་པ། seeing certain levels of delusion as liberation 4. ཉོན་མོངས་ལན་ཅིག་སྤངས་ཀྱང་སླར་ལྡོག་པར་འཛིན་པ། apprehending the return of delusions which have already been discarded. Four of the noble truth of the path: 1. ཐར་པ་ཡེ་མེད་དུ་འཛིན་པ། seeing the path to liberation as totally non-existent 2. བདག་མེད་རྟོགས་པའི་ཤེས་རབ་ཐར་པ་མ་ཡིན་པར་འཛིན་པ། seeing that the wisdom understanding selflessness as not a path to liberation 3. བསམ་གཏན་གྱི་ཁྱད་པར་འགའ་ཞིག་ཐར་ལམ་དུ་འཛིན་པ། seeing certain levels of concentration as the path to liberation 4. སྡུག་བསྔལ་གཏན་ཟད་བྱེད་པའི་ལམ་མེད་པར་འཛིན་པ། seeing paths leading to total exhaustion of sufferings as non-existent.

ལོག་ཤེས།

Mithyājñāna/ Distorted cognition; wrong perception. An awareness that apprehends its object of cognition incorrectly, e.g. the visual perception cognizing a white snow mountain as yellow. There are two types: 1. རྟོག་པ་ལོག་ཤེས། kalpita/ conceptually distorted cognition 2. རྟོག་མེད་ལོག་ཤེས། akalpita/ non-conceptually distorted cognition.

ལོངས་སྐུ།

Saṁbhogakāya/ Complete Enjoyment Body; Utility Body; saṁbhogakāya. A form of Buddha's appreance possessing five definite qualities (see nges-pa lnga) and are directly accessible to Ārya Bodhisattvas only.

ལོངས་སྐུའི་ངེས་པ་ལྔ།

The five certainties of a Saṁbhogakāya Buddha (see nges-pa lnga).

ལོངས་སྐུའི་རྒྱན་ནམ་ཆ་བྱད་བཅུ་གསུམ།

The thirteen adorations of a Saṁbhogakāya Buddha. There are the five adorations made of silk: 1. དར་གྱི་ཅོད་པན། scarf crown 2. སྟོད་གཡོགས། upper garment 3. དར་དཔྱངས། ribbons hanging over ears 4. སྐ་རགས། belt 5. སྨད་དཀྲིས། lower garment; and the eight jewel ornaments: 6. རིན་པོ་ཆེའི་དབུ་རྒྱན། jewel head dress 7. སྙན་རྒྱན། earring 8. མགུལ་རྒྱན། necklace 9. དཔུང་རྒྱན། bracelets on the arms 10. དོ་ཤལ་དང་སེ་མོ་དོ། doshal and semodo, the jewel garland hanging down to the heart level and navel respectively 11. ཕྱག་གདུབ། bracelets 12. སོར་གདུབ། rings 13. ཞབས་གདུབ། anklets.

ལོངས་སྤྱོད་འཁོར་ལོ།

Saṁbhogacakra/ Wheel of enjoyment. Channel-wheel located at the level of the throat.

ལོངས་སྤྱོད་འབྲི་བའི་གནས་དྲུག

Ṣaḍ bhogānām apāyasthānāni/ Six causes of poverty; six causes of impoverishment. 1. ཆང་འཐུང་བ། madya pānam/ drinking alcohol 2. རྒྱན་པོ་འབྱེད་པ། dyūtam/ gambling 3. མཚན་མོ་འཕྱན་པ། vikāla caryā/ wandering at night 4. སྡིག་པའི་གྲོགས་པོ་བསྟེན་པ། pāpamitratā/ seeking bad company 5. འདུས་པ་ལ་ལྟ་བ། samāja darśanam/ watching social gatherings 6. ལེ་ལོ། ālasyam/ laziness.

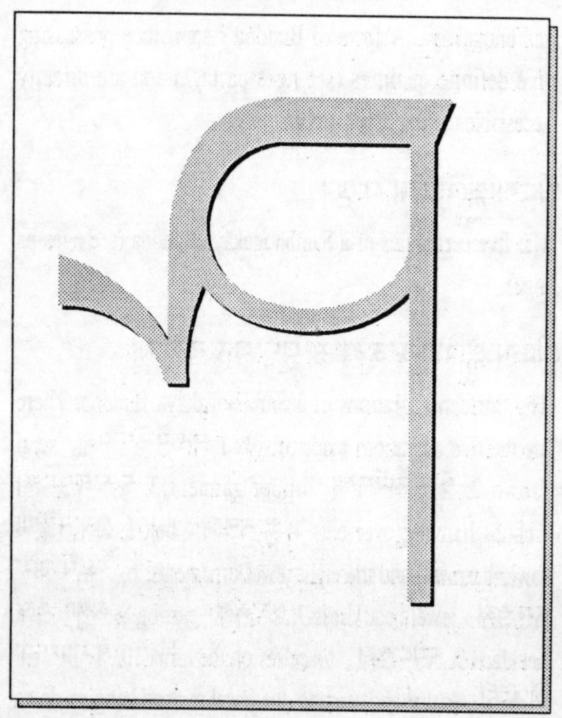

ཤ་ཁོན།

Vairin/ A. Revenge; vengeance. B. Harmful spirit who seeks to revenge a past grudge.

ཤ་ལྔ།

Five types of flesh; five meats. 1. གླང་པོ་ཆེའི་ཤ hastimāṁsa/ elephant flesh 2. མིའི་ཤ manuṣyamāṁsa/ human flesh 3. རྟའི་ཤ aśvamāṁsa/ horse flesh 4. ཁྱིའི་ཤ kukkuramāṁsa/ dog flesh 5. བ་གླང་གི་ཤ gomāṁsa/ cow flesh. Also called the five types of big-flesh (sha-chen sna-lnga).

ཤ་ཟ།

Piśāca/ Meat-eater; flesh-eater. A type of spirit living on meat, categorized as a hungry ghost.

ཤཱ་རི་པུ་ཏྲ།

Śāriputra/ One of the two principal attendents of Buddha Śākyamuni known for his wisdom and intelligence.

ཤཱཀྱ།

Śākya/ Śākya tribe. Lit: the able one; name of an ancient Indian caste in which Buddha Śākyamuni was born. Hence, he is known as the king of the Śākyas.

ཤཱཀྱ་འོད།

Śākyaprabha/. An Indian paṇḍit who was a direct disciple of Ācārya Guṇaprabha. He mastered the study of monastic discipline (vinaya) and wrote the *Treatise on Novice Vows* (śramaṇerikā-kārikā).

ཤཱཀྱ་ཤྲཱི་བྷ་དྲ།

Śākyaśrībhadra/ Śākyaśrī Bhadra (1142-1225). A Kaśmiri paṇḍit who was instrumental in establishing monastic institutions in Tibet. He became abbot of Sakya Paṇḍita Kunga Gyaltsen; stayed for twelve years at Radreng, Lodrag and others by working incessantly for the spread of Buddhism in Tibet.

ཤངས་པ་བཀའ་བརྒྱུད།

Shangpa Kagyud Order. One of the sub-sects of the Kagyud tradition of Tibetan Buddhism founded by Kherdub Khyungpo Nyaljor.

ཤམ་བྷ་ལ།

Shambala. A pure land which is the cradle of Kālacakra tantra. It was the Shambala king, Suchandra, who requested Buddha Śākyamuni to teach Kālacakra, propagated and preserved it in Shambala from where it was brought to India and later into Tibet. It is believed that in the future the twenty-five propagators of Kālacakra will emerge from Shambala and rule the universe in a righteous manner.

ཤལ་མ་ལིའི་སྡོང་པོ།

Kūṭaśālmalī vṛkṣa/ Śālmalī tree. A forest full of this tree is believed to exist in a neighbouring hell realm surrounding hot hell realms, where beings climb them and suddenly fall as the leaves transform into sharp swords and blades.

ཤིང་རྟའི་སྲོལ་གཉིས།

Two pioneering lineages of Buddha's teachings. 1. རྒྱ་ཆེན་སྤྱོད་བརྒྱུད། vaipulyacārya/ the lineage of extensive practice 2. ཟབ་མོ་ལྟ་བརྒྱུད། gaṁbhīracārya/ the lineage of the profound view.

ཤིང་རྟའི་སྲོལ་འབྱེད་གཉིས།

Two pioneers of Buddha's teachings. 1. མགོན་པོ་ཀླུ་སྒྲུབ། Nāgārjuṅa, the pioneer of the Middle Way philosophy 2. འཕགས་པ་ཐོགས་མེད། Asaṅga, the pioneer of the Mind Only philosophy.

ཤིན་ཏུ་ལྐོག་གྱུར།

Extremely obscure phenomena. Phenomena that can only be established through recourse to scriptural quotation, e.g. the subtle aspects of the law of causality.

ཤིན་ཏུ་རྒྱས་པའི་སྡེ།

Vaipulya/ Extensive teachings. One of the twelve scriptural categories; such as different levels of the perfection of wisdom teachings concerning the ten perfections of wisdom (see phar-phyin bcu).

ཤིན་སྦྱངས།

Pliancy; suppleness. The flexibility and pliancy of mind or body, or of both, gained through the power of calm-abiding meditation (śamatha). A basic necessity for firm understanding of emptiness.

ཤིས་བརྗོད།

Āśīrvāda/ Benediction; recitation or expression of verses of auspiciousness at the conclusion of a ceremony.

ཤུག་གསེབ་བཀའ་བརྒྱུད།

Shugseb Kagyud school. One of the eight sub-schools of the Phagdu Kagyud school founded by Gyergom Tsultrim Senge in the twelfth century.

ཤུགས་བསྟན།

Implied meaning; indirect reference.

ཤེར་ཕྱིན་དོན་བདུན་ཅུ།

The seventy topics of the perfection of wisdom (see don bdun-cu).

ཤེར་ཕྱིན་བཞི།

Four types of the perfection of wisdom. 1. རང་བཞིན་ཤེར་ཕྱིན། svabhāva prajñāpāramitā/ natural or real perfection of wisdom 2. གཞུང་ཤེར་ཕྱིན། textual perfection of wisdom 3. ལམ་ཤེར་ཕྱིན། mārga prajñāpāramitā/ path perfection of wisdom 4. འབྲས་བུ་ཤེར་ཕྱིན། resultant perfection of wisdom.

ཤེར་ཕྱིན་ཟབ་མོའི་སྣོད་བཞི།

Four vessels of the perfection of wisdom; four types of persons receiving the perfection of wisdom teachings. 1. ཉན་པའི་སྣོད། śrotabhjana/ vessel of hearing 2. ལེན་པའི་སྣོད། ādānabhajana/ receptive vessel 3. འཛིན་པའི་སྣོད། grāhākabhajana/ beholding vessel 4. ཚུལ་བཞིན་ཡིད་ལ་བྱེད་པའི་སྣོད། yoniśomanasi kārabhajana/ reflective vessel.

ཤེས་རྒྱུད།

Santāna/ A. Mental continuum; mind stream. B. Characteristics; personality.

ཤེས་སྒྲིབ།

Jñeyāvaraṇa/ Obscuration to omniscience. The delusions and wrong views that obstruct the attainment of omniscient mind.

ཤེས་སྒྲིབ་ཀུན་བཏགས།

Parikalpita jñeyāvaraṇa/ Intellectual obstacles to omniscience; intellectually acquired obstacles to omniscience.

ཤེས་སྒྲིབ་ཉོན་མོངས་གཟུང་རྟོག

Obstruction to omniscience that is a conception grasping at delusions.

ཤེས་སྒྲིབ་བཏགས་འཛིན་རྟོག་པ།

Obstruction to omniscience that is a conception grasping at nominal entities.

ཤེས་སྒྲིབ་རྣམ་བྱང་གཟུང་རྟོག

Obstruction to omniscience that is a conception grasping at purified phenomena.

ཤེས་སྒྲིབ་རྫས་འཛིན་རྟོག་པ།

Jñeyāvaraṇa dravyagrāhaka kalpana/ Obstruction to omniscience that is a conception grasping at substantial entities.

ཤེས་སྒྲིབ་ལྷན་སྐྱེས།

Sahaja jñeyāvaraṇa/ Innate obstruction to omniscience.

ཤེས་པ།

Jñāna/ Awareness; mind; mental; consciousness, both primary and secondary minds; clear and knowing (see blo-la gnyis-su dbye-tsul).

ཤེས་པ་བཅུ།

The ten consciousnesses; the ten awarenesses (see mdzod-las bshad-pa'i shes-pa bcu).

ཤེས་པས་སྲིད་ལ་མི་གནས་པའི་གཞི་ཤེས།

Basic wisdom not abiding in the extreme of cyclic existence through possessing the knowledge of selflessness

ཤེས་བྱ།

Jñeya/ Objects of knowledge; knowable objects. Synonymous with existents.

ཤེས་བྱ་ཉེར་ལྔ།

The twenty-five principles; the twenty-five categories of phenomena asserted by the Sāṃkhya school (see grangs-can-pa). 1. སྐྱེས་བུ། puruṣa/ person 2. རང་བཞིན། prakṛti/ fundamental principle 3. བློ། buddhi/ intellect 4. ང་རྒྱལ། ahaṃkāra/ I-principle consisting of motility (rdul), darkness (mun-pa) and lightness or courage (snying-stobs) 5. གཟུགས། rūpa/ visible forms 6. སྒྲ། śabda/ sounds 7. དྲི། gandha/ odors 8. རོ། rasa/ tastes 9. རེག་བྱ། sprastaryam/ tangible objects 10. མིག cakṣu/ eyes 11. རྣ་བ། śrota/ ears 12. སྣ། ghrāṇa/ nose 13. ལྕེ། rasana/ tongue 14. པགས་པ། sparśana/ skin 15. ཁ། vācana/ mouth 16. ལག་པ། pāṇi/ arms 17. རྐང་པ། pāda/ legs 18. རྐུབ། pāyu/ anus 19. མདོམས། upastham/ genitalia 20. ཡིད། manas/ mind 21. ས། pṛthivī/ earth 22. ཆུ། apa/ water 23. མེ། tejas/ fire 24. རླུང་། vāyu/ wind 25. ནམ་མཁའ། ākāśa/ space.

ཤེས་བྱ་མཛོད།

The Treasure of Knowledge; the encyclopedia of Buddhism.

Commonly known as *Shes-bya kun-khyab*, a very famous text by Kongtrul Yonten Gyatso (1813-1899) contain-ing ten chapters of four sections each. The book deals with every subject of Buddhist studies and meditation.

ཤེས་བཞིན།

Saṁprajanya/ Mental alertness; introspection. In calm-abiding meditation it is that mental factor which watches the activity of the mind from inclining towards mental dullness or agitation during a meditation.

ཤེས་བཟོད་སྐད་ཅིག་མ་བཅུ་དྲུག

Sixteen moments of cognition and forbearance of the path of seeing; the sixteen aspects of the path of seeing (see mthong-lam shes-bzod skad-cig-ma bcu-drug).

ཤེས་རབ།

Prajñā/ Wisdom. Discriminative awareness that understands what is to be cultivated and what is to be abandoned.

ཤེས་རབ་ཀྱི་ཆོས་བཞི།

The four qualities of wisdom. 1. ཤེས་འཆལ་སོགས་མི་མཐུན་ཕྱོགས་ཉམས་པ། pacifies discordant factors such as corrupt morality 2. ཆོས་ཀྱི་བདག་མེད་རྟོགས་པའི་རྣམ་པར་མི་རྟོག་པ། generates non-conceptual wisdom understanding the selfless-ness of phenomena 3. འདོད་པ་རྫོགས་པར་བྱེད་པ། accomp-lishes one's wishes 4. རིགས་ཅན་གསུམ་སྨིན་པར་བྱེད་པ། matures disciples of the three families (see rigs-can gsum).

ཤེས་རབ་ཀྱི་མཐར་གྱིས་སྦྱོར་བ།

Serial training in wisdom. Bodhisattva paths from the path of accumulation up to the moment preceeding the last instant of the Mahāyāna path, mainly engaged in the training in wisdom.

ཤེས་རབ་ཀྱི་ནོར།

Prajñā dhana/ Riches of wisdom; wealth of wisdom. Abundance of wit, intellect, ingenuity, understanding, etc. One of the seven riches of a Noble Person (see 'phags-nor bdun).

ཤེས་རབ་ཀྱི་ཕ་རོལ་ཏུ་ཕྱིན་པ།

Prajñāpāramitā/ Perfection of Wisdom. The Bodhisattva's training of wisdom, e.g. the understanding of emptiness and selflessness; one of the six perfections.

ཤེས་རབ་སྙིང་པོ།

Prajñāpāramitāhṛdya śūtra/ *Heart of Wisdom*; the *Heart Sūtra*. A short perfection of wisdom sūtra chiefly consisting of a dialogue between Śāriputra and Avalokiteśvara on the nature of emptiness. A teaching of Buddha through his inspiration and permission.

ཤེས་རབ་རྣམ་གསུམ།

Three types of wisdom. A. 1. ཀུན་རྫོབ་རྟོགས་པའི་ཤེས་རབ། wisdom understanding conventional phenomena 2. དོན་དམ་རྟོགས་པའི་ཤེས་རབ། wisdom understanding ultimate phenomena 3. སེམས་ཅན་དོན་བྱེད་རྟོགས་པའི་ཤེས་རབ། wisdom understanding the welfare of sentient beings. B. 1. ཐོས་པ་ལས་བྱུང་བའི་ཤེས་རབ། wisdom acquired through hearing 2. བསམ་པ་ལས་བྱུང་བའི་ཤེས་རབ། wisdom acquired through contemplation 3. བསྒོམ་པ་ལས་བྱུང་བའི་ཤེས་རབ། wisdom acquired through meditation.

ཤེས་རབ་ཡེ་ཤེས་ཀྱི་དབང་།

Prajñājñānābhiṣekha/ The primordial wisdom initiation; the wisdom-knowledge initiation. A highest yoga tantra initiation, in which the mind of disciples is initiated in reliance upon the maṇḍala of the femine consort; their mental delusions are removed; they are empowered to carry out completion stage practice meditation and the seed to obtain the dharmakāya of mind-vajra is implanted into the mental continuum of the disciples.

བཤགས་པ།

Deśanā/ Confession; declaration. Declaration of previously committed non-virtuous actions or transgressions of vows and precepts.

བཤད་གྲྭ

College. A department within the monastery where the study of philosophical texts are the primary curriculum in contrast to the training of ritual and tantric ceremonies.

བཤད་སྒྲུབ།

Study and practice; the study as well as practice of the teachings of a religious culture.

བཤད་ཐབས་ཡན་ལག་ལྔ།

Five means of teachings; five ways of presenting a text in the Buddhist tradition. 1. དགོས་དོན། purpose 2. བསྡུས་དོན། summary 3. ཚིག་དོན། literal meaning 4. མཚམས་སྦྱར། links 5. བརྒལ་ལན། debate and discussion.

བཤེས་གཉེན་ལྟ་བུའི་སེམས་བསྐྱེད།

Kalyāṇamitropamacittotpāda/ Spiritual Friend-like bodhicitta. The mind of enlightenment associated with the practice of the perfection of means, possessed by a Bodhisattva on the seventh ground.

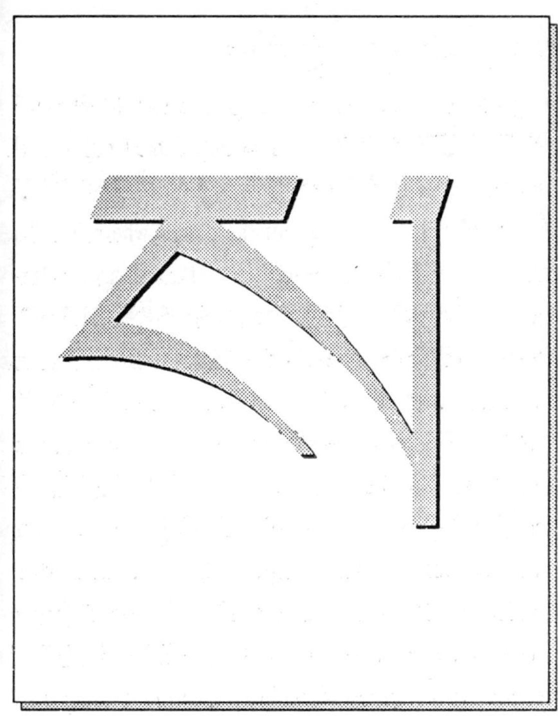

ས།

Pṛthivī/ A. Earth; solid component. B. Ground; levels of realization within the mental continuum of a practitioner who has entered the path of practice following any of the three vehicles, e.g. the Bodhisattva paths on and above the path of seeing.

ས་སྐྱ་གོང་མ་ལྔ།

Five foremost masters of Sakya; the five supreme masters of the Sakya tradition of Tibetan Buddhism. 1. ས་ཆེན་ཀུན་དགའ་སྙིང་པོ། Sachen Kunga Nyingpo (1092-1158) 2. རྗེ་བཙུན་བསོད་ནམས་རྩེ་མོ། Jetsun Sonam Tsemo (1142-1182) 3. རྗེ་བཙུན་གྲགས་པ་རྒྱལ་མཚན། Jetsun Dakpa Gyaltsen (1147-1216) 4. ས་སྐྱ་པཎྜི་ཏ་ཀུན་དགའ་རྒྱལ་མཚན། Sakya Paṇḍita Kunga Gyaltsen (1182-1251) 5. འགྲོ་མགོན་ཆོས་རྒྱལ་འཕགས་པ། Drogon Choegyal Phagpa (1232-1280).

ས་སྐྱའི་འཇམ་དབྱངས་བདུན་བརྒྱུད།

Seven Sakya masters of the Mañjuśrī lineage. 1-4. (see above, sa-skya gong-ma lnga) 5. དཔལ་ཆེན་འོད་པོ་ཆེ། Palchen Odpoche (1150-1203) 6. ཟངས་ཚ་བསོད་ནམས་རྒྱལ་མཚན། Zangtsa Sonam Gyaltsen (1184-1239) 7. འགྲོ་མགོན་འཕགས་པ་བློ་གྲོས་རྒྱལ་མཚན། Drogon Phagpa Lodoe Gyaltsen (1444-1495).

ས་སྐྱ་པ།

The Sakya Tradition; the Sakya School of Tibetan Buddhism. One of four major schools of Tibetan Buddhism established by Khon Kunchok Gyalpo and disseminated by the five foremost masters of the Sakya school (see sa-skya gong-ma lnga). The fundamental teaching of Sakya is the paths and fruits cycle of teachings. This tradition has three sub-schools: Sakya, Ngorpa and Tsarpa. The head of the tradition follows a patriarchal lineage of two houses: Phuntsok Phodrang and Dolma Phodrang. Presently, it is headed by the Drolma Phodrang patriarch His Holiness Ngawang Kunga Theckchen Palbar Trinley Samphel Wang-gi Gyalpo (b. 1945).

ས་སྐྱ་པཎྜི་ཏ།

Sakya Paṇḍita Kunga Gyaltsen (1182-1251). One of the five supreme masters and the sixth patriarch of the Sakya hierarchy of Tibetan Buddhism; famous for his mastery of the ten sciences (see rig-gnas bcu) and for creating the early Mongolian script. His works such as the *Elegant Sayings* (sa-skya legs-bshad), *Distinction Between the Three Vows* (sdom-gsum rab-dbye) and *Entering Into the Gate of the Wise One's* (mkhas-pa-la 'jug-pa'i sgo) are some of the renowned works.

ས་སྐྱ་པའི་མཁའ་སྤྱོད་སྐོར་གསུམ།

Three cycles of Ḍākinī practice in the Sakya Tradition. 1. ན་

ནཱ་རོ་མཁའ་སྤྱོད། Naro Ḍākinī 2. ཨིནྡྲ་མཁའ་སྤྱོད། Indra Ḍākinī 3. མཻ་ཏྲི་མཁའ་སྤྱོད། Maitri Ḍākinī.

ས་དགུ

Nine Grounds; the levels of attainments. 1. རིགས་ཀྱི་ས། gotrabhūmi/ level of family 2. བརྒྱད་པའི་ས། aṣṭamakabhūmi/ level of the eighth 3. མཐོང་པའི་ས། darśanabhūmi/ level of seeing 4. སྲབ་པའི་ས། tanūbhūmi/ level of discrimination 5. འདོད་ཆགས་དང་བྲལ་བའི་ས། vigatarāga bhūmi/ level free from attachment 6. བྱས་པ་རྟོགས་པའི་ས། kṛtāvibhūmi/ level understanding deeds 7. ཉན་ཐོས་ཀྱི་ས། śrāvakabhūmi/ level of the Hearer 8. རང་སངས་རྒྱས་ཀྱི་ས། pratyekabuddhabhūmi/ level of Solitary Realizer 9. བྱང་ཆུབ་སེམས་དཔའི་ས། bodhisattvabhūmi/ level of the Bodhisattva (see khams-gsum sa-dgu).

ས་དགུ་པའི་ཡོངས་སྦྱོངས་བཅུ་གཉིས།

Twelve thorough trainings on the ninth ground. 1. སྨོན་ལམ་མཐའ་ཡས་པ་འགྲུབ་པ། fulfilling infinite prayers 2. ལྷ་དང་ཀླུ་ལ་སོགས་པའི་འགྲོ་བ་སོ་སོའི་སྐད་ཇི་ལྟ་བ་བཞིན་དུ་ཤེས་པ། knowledge of the languages of nāgas, gods, and others 3. ཆོས་སྟོན་པ་ལ་སྤོབས་པ་ཆུ་བོའི་རྒྱུན་ལྟར་མི་ཟད་པར་འཇུག་པ། having inexhaustible confidence to teach Dharma like a flowing river 4. མངལ་དུ་འཇུག་པ་སྟོན་པའི་ཚེ་ཟམས་ཅད་ཀྱི་བསྔགས་པའི་ཡུམ་གྱི་ལྷུམས་སུ་འཇུག་པ། at rebirth he enters only into the womb of a respectable woman 5. རིགས་ཕུན་སུམ་ཚོགས་པ། of an excellent family 6. རུས་ཕུན་སུམ་ཚོགས་པ། of an excellent clan 7. ཆོ་འབྲང་ཕུན་སུམ་ཚོགས་པ། of an excellent caste 8. འཁོར་ཕུན་སུམ་ཚོགས་པ། with an excellent retinue 9. སྐྱེ་བ་ཕུན་སུམ་ཚོགས་པ། taking an excellent birth 10. ངེས་པར་འབྱུང་བ་ཕུན་སུམ་ཚོགས་པ། renouncing household life 11. བྱང་ཆུབ་ཀྱི་ཤིང་དྲུང་དུ་འཚང་རྒྱ་བ། gaining enlightenment under the Bodhi tree 12. ཡོན་ཏན་ཐམས་ཅད་ཡོངས་སུ་རྫོགས་པ། accomplishing all virtuous qualities.

ས་བརྒྱད་པའི་ཡོངས་སྦྱོང་བརྒྱད།

Eight thorough trainings on the eighth ground. 1. སེམས་ཅན་ཐམས་ཅད་ཀྱི་སེམས་ཤེས་པ། knowledge of the thoughts of all sentient beings 2. སངས་རྒྱས་གང་ན་བཞུགས་པའི་འཇིག་རྟེན་གྱི་ཁམས་ཤེས་པ། knowledge of the places where Buddha resides 3. སངས་རྒྱས་ཀྱི་ཞིང་སྒྲུབ་པ། establishing Buddha-fields 4. ཆོས་རྣམས་ཀྱི་རང་བཞིན་ཇི་ལྟ་བ་བཞིན་རྟོགས་པས་སངས་རྒྱས་མཉེས་པ། pleasing the Buddhas with one's correct understanding of the reality of all phenomena 5. སེམས་ཅན་རྣམས་ཀྱི་ཁམས་དང་དབང་པོ་སོགས་མཁྱེན་པ། knowledge of the different faculties of sentient beings 6. སངས་རྒྱས་ཀྱི་ཞིང་གང་དུ་འགྲུབ་པའི་སེམས་ཅན་རྣམས་ཀྱི་རྒྱུད་སྦྱོང་བ། purifying the continuum of sentient beings in those directions where Buddha-fields will be established 7. བྱང་སེམས་ཀྱི་སྤྱོད་པ་ཐམས་ཅད་སྒྱུ་མ་ལྟ་བུའི་ཏིང་ངེ་འཛིན་ལ་གནས་ནས་བྱེད་པ། performing the deeds of Bodhisattvas while abiding in an illusion like concentration 8. སེམས་ཅན་གྱི་དོན་སེམས་བཞིན་དུ་སྲིད་པ་ལེན་པ། willingly taking rebirth for the benefit of sentient biengs.

ས་ལྔ་པའི་ཡོངས་སྦྱོངས་བཅུ།

Ten thorough trainings on the fifth ground. 1. རྙེད་བཀུར་གྱི་ཆེད་དུ་ཁྱིམ་དང་འགྲོགས་འདྲིས་བྱེད་པ་སྤོང་བ། avoiding association with householders for profit and fame 2. རབ་དུ་བྱུང་བ་གཞན་ལ་སྦྱིན་བདག་དད་པ་ཅན་གྱི་ཁྱིམ་མི་སྟོན་པ་སྤོང་བ། not preventing monks from finding the homes of faithful benefectors 3. འདུ་འཛིའི་གནས་སུ་གནས་པ་སྤོང་བ། avoiding living in busy places 4. ཆགས་པས་བདག་ལ་བསྟོད་པ་སྤོང་བ། avoiding praising oneself with attachment 5. གཞན་ལ་བརྙས་པ་སྤོང་བ། avoiding deprecation of others 6. མི་དགེ་བའི་ལས་ལམ་བཅུ་སྤོང་བ། avoiding the ten unwholesome actions 7. རློམ་པས་གཞན་ལ་མི་འདུད་པ་སྤོང་བ། avoiding conceit and arrogance towards others 8. ལྷང་དོར་ཕྱིན་ཅི་ལོག་ལ་ཞེན་པ་སྤོང་བ། avoiding attachment towards wrong practices of cultivation and abandonement 9. ལོག་པར་ལྟ་བའི་སྣོ་ངན་སྤོང་བ། avoiding wrong and unwholesome views 10. སེམས་ཉོན་མོངས་ལ་ཕྱོགས་པ་སྤོང་བ། avoiding mental association with delusions.

ས་བཅུ།

Daśa bhūmayaḥ/ A. According to the Bodhisattva paths these are the grounds of: 1. རབ་ཏུ་དགའ་བ། pramuditā/ the extremely joyous 2. དྲི་མ་མེད་པ། vimalā/ the stainless 3. འོད་བྱེད་པ། prabhākarī/ the luminous 4. འོད་འཕྲོ་བ། arciṣmatī/ the radiant 5. སྦྱངས་དཀའ་བ། sudurjayā/ the difficult to overcome 6. མངོན་དུ་ཕྱོགས་པ། abhimukhī/ the approaching 7. རིང་དུ་སོང་བ། dūraṅgama/ the Gone Afar 8. མི་གཡོ་བ། acalā/ the immovable 9. ལེགས་པའི་བློ་གྲོས། sādhumatī/ the good intelligence 10. ཆོས་ཀྱི་སྤྲིན། dharmameghā/ the cloud of dharma. B. ཨ་ནུ་ཡོ་གའི་ཐུན་མོང་མ་ཡིན་པའི་བཤད་སྲོལ་ལྟར་ཚོགས་ལམ་སྐབས་ཀྱི་ས་བཅུ་ནི། According to the Anuyoga vehicle of the Nyingma tradition there are ten grounds within the path of accumulation as follows: 1. འགྱུར་བ་མ་ངེས་པའི་ས། the unchangeable ground 2. བརྟེན་པ་གཞིའི་ས། the basic ground of reliance 3. གལ་ཆེན་སྦྱོང་བའི་ས། the ground of important training 4. བསླབ་པ་རྒྱུན་གྱི་ས། the ground of continual training 5. བསོད་ནམས་རྟེན་གྱི་ས། the ground of basis for meritorious accumulation 6. བརྟན་པ་ཁྱད་པར་དུ་འགྲོ་བའི་ས། the ground of firm advancement 7. དམིགས་འབྲས་སྐྱེ་བའི་ས། the ground of achieving the fruits of one's object 8. གནས་པ་མི་འགྱུར་བའི་ས། the ground of unchangeable occupation 9. གདལ་བ་ཆོས་ཉིད་ཀྱི་ས། the ground of universal reality 10. རྫོགས་པ་སྤྱི་ཆིབས་ཀྱི་ས། the ground of unilateral completion.

ས་བཅུ་གཉིས།

Dvādaśa bhūmayaḥ/ Twelve grounds; twelve levels of the Mahāyāna paths. 1-10. (see above, sa-bchu) 11. བྱང་ཆུབ་ཏུ་སེམས་མ་བསྐྱེད་པའི་ས། ground prior to generating the mind of enlightenment 12. ཀུན་ཏུ་འོད་ཀྱི་ས། the ever-illuminating ground.

ས་བཅུ་བཞི།

The Fourteen Grounds. 1. མོས་པ་སྤྱོད་པའི་ས། The ground of faith 2-11. (see sa-bcu) 12. དཔེ་མེད་ཀྱི་ས། the incomparable ground 13. ཡེ་ཤེས་ལྡན་པའི་ས། the ground of attaining primordial wisdom 14. ཀུན་ཏུ་འོད་རྡོ་རྗེའི་ས། the ever-luminous vajra ground.

ས་ཆོགསའི་ཆོ་ག

The ground ritual. The ritual of examining, begging, purifying, owning, guarding and blessing the ground or venue intended for a tantric ceremony of constructing a maṇḍala and performing an initiation.

ས་གཉིས་པའི་ཡོངས་སྦྱོང་བརྒྱད།

Eight thorough trainings on the second ground. 1. དུས་རྟག་ཏུ་ཚུལ་ཁྲིམས་གསུམ་རྣམ་པར་དག་པ། (maintaining) purity of the three moral disciplines at all times 2. གཞན་གྱིས་ཕན་བཏགས་པ་ལ་བྱས་པ་གཟོ་བ། repaying the help rendered by others 3. གནོད་པ་ཅི་བྱུང་ཡང་བཟོད་པ། patiently accepting all harms 4. དུས་རྟག་ཏུ་དགེ་བ་སྒྲུབ་པའི་དགའ་བ། always rejoicing in wholesome deeds 5. སེམས་ཅན་རྣམས་ལ་སྙིང་རྗེ་ཆེ་བ། being compassionate towards all sentient beings 6. མཁན་སློབ་སོགས་ལ་འདུད་ཅིང་བཀུར་བསྟི་བྱེད་པ། honoring and respecting one's teachers and abbots 7. བླ་མ་རྣམས་ལ་གུས་པས་ཆོས་ཉན་པ། receiving teachings from one's teachers respectfully 8. སྦྱིན་སོགས་ཕར་ཕྱིན་རྣམས་ལ་དུས་རྟག་ཏུ་བརྩོན་པ། always practising the perfection trainings such as giving, etc.

ས་སྟེང་།

Mahītala/ Terrestial world; terrestial realm. One of the three realms of existence, which is primarily the abode of humans, animals and other earth-bound creatures.

ས་དང་པོའི་ཡོངས་སྦྱོང་བཅུ།

Ten thorough trainings on the first ground. 1. བྱ་བ་ཐམས་ཅད་ལ་གཡོ་སྒྱུ་མེད་པའི་བསམ་པ། attitude free from deceit in all activities 2. རང་གཞན་གྱི་དོན་ལ་ཕན་པ་ཐེག་ཆེན་ཉིད་འཛིན་པ། practising the Greater Vehicle for the benefit of both self and others 3. སེམས་ཅན་ཐམས་ཅད་ལ་སེམས་མཉམ་པ་ཉིད། an attitude of equanimity towards all sentient beings 4. སེར་སྣ་མེད་པས་བདོག་པ་ཐམས་ཅད་གཏོང་བ། giving away all belongings without miserliness 5. བཤེས་གཉེན་དམ་པ་རྟག་ཏུ་བསྟེན་པར་བྱེད་པ། always relying on a good spiritual friend 6. ཐེག་པ་གསུམ་གྱི་ཆོས་མ་ལུས་པའི་དམིགས་པ་འཚོལ་བ། seeking the goals of all the precepts of the three vehicles 7. དུས་རྟག་ཏུ་ངེས་པར་འབྱུང་བའི་སེམས་ཉིད་དང་ལྡན་པ། always possessing the thought of definite freedom 8. དུས་རྟག་ཏུ་སངས་རྒྱས་ཀྱི་སྐུ་མཐོང་བར་འདོད་ཅིང་དེ་ལ་དགའ་བ། always eagerly wishing to behold Buddha's presence 9. གདུལ་བྱ་རྣམས་ལ་དཔེ་མཁྱུད་མེད་པར་ཆོས་སྟོན་པ། teaching Dharma to all without restraint 10. དུས་རྟག་ཏུ་བདེན་པའི་ཚིག་སྨྲ་བར་བྱེད་པ། always speaking the truth.

ས་དྲུག་པའི་ཡོངས་སྦྱོང་བཅུ་གཉིས།

Twelve thorough trainings on the sixth ground. 1-6. ཕ་རོལ་ཏུ་ཕྱིན་པ་དྲུག་རྫོགས་པར་བྱེད་པ། accomplishing the six perfections (see phar-phyin drug) 7. ཉན་ཐོས་ཀྱི་ས་ལ་དགའ་བ་སྤོང་བ། abandoning attachment to the Hearer's level 8. རང་རྒྱལ་གྱི་ས་ལ་དགའ་བ་སྤོང་བ། abandoning attachment to the Solitary Realizer's level 9. ཟབ་མོའི་དོན་ལ་སྐྲག་པའི་སེམས་སྤོང་བ། abandoning fear of the meaning of profound emptiness 10. མགོ་ལ་སོགས་པ་བསླངས་ཀྱང་མི་ཞུམ་པ། not being discouraged even if asked for one's head 11. བདོག་པ་ཀུན་བཏང་ཡང་མི་དགའ་བ་མེད་པ། not being unhappy at renouncing all one's belongings 12. དབུལ་ཡང་སློང་བ་མི་སྤོང་བ། not abandoning beggars even in distress.

ས་བདག

Bhūpati/ A. Lord of earth; owners of the earth; non-human spirits and creatures having influence of the locality or sites.

ས་བདུན་པའི་ཡོངས་སྦྱོང་ཉི་ཤུ།

Twenty thorough trainings on the seventh ground. A. སྤང་བྱ་ཉི་ཤུ། Abandoning twenty misapprehensions: 1. བདག་ཏུ་འཛིན་པ། grasping at self 2. སེམས་ཅན་དུ་འཛིན་པ། grasping at sentient beings 3. སྲོག་ཏུ་འཛིན་པ། grasping at the life-force 4. གང་ཟག་ཏུ་འཛིན་པ། grasping at persons 5. ཆད་པའི་མཐར་འཛིན་པ། grasping at the extreme of eternalism 6. རྟག་པའི་མཐར་འཛིན་པ། grasping at the extreme of externalism 7. མཚན་མར་འཛིན་པ། grasping at signs 8. རྒྱུར་འཛིན་པ། grasping at causes 9. ཕུང་པོར་འཛིན་པ། grasping at aggregates 10. ཁམས་སུ་འཛིན་པ། grasping at elements 11. སྐྱེ་མཆེད་དུ་འཛིན་པ། grasping at sources of perception 12. ཁམས་གསུམ་པོ་ལ་གནས་པར་འཛིན་པ། grasping at the three realms as the basis 13. དེ་དག་དོར་བྱར་འཛིན་པ། grasping at the three realms to be abandoned 14. སེམས་ཀུན་ཏུ་ཞུམ་པ། mentally discouraged state 15. སངས་རྒྱས་སུ་མངོན་པར་ཞེན་པ། attachment towards Buddha 16. ཆོས་སུ་མངོན་པར་ཞེན་པ། attachment towards Dharma 17. དགེ་འདུན་དུ་མངོན་པར་ཞེན་པ། attachment towards Saṅgha 18. ཚུལ་ཁྲིམས་སུ་མངོན་པར་ཞེན་པ། attachment towards moral discipline 19. སྟོང་པ་ཉིད་ལ་རྩོད་པ། contention about emptiness 20. སྟོང་པ་དང་ཀུན་རྫོབ་འགལ་བར་འཛིན་པ། seeing the conventional and emptiness as contradictory. B. གཉེན་པོ་ཉི་ཤུ། Cultivating twenty antidotes: 1. སྟོང་པ་ཉིད་ཤེས་པ། knowledge of emptiness 2. མཚན་མ་མེད་པ་ཤེས་པ། knowledge of signlessness 3. སྨོན་པ་མེད་པ་ཤེས་པ། knowledge of wishlessness 4. འཁོར་གསུམ་རྣམ་པར་དག་པ་རྟོགས་པ། knowledge of the purity of the three factors (object, agent and action) 5. སྙིང་རྗེ་ཆེན་པོ། great compassion 6. རློམ་པ་མེད་པ། lack of pride 7. ཆོས་ཐམས་ཅད་མཉམ་པ་ཉིད་དུ་རྟོགས་པ། knowledge of the sameness of all phenomena 8. མཐར་ཐུག་ཐེག་པ་གཅིག་ཏུ་ཤེས་པ། knowledge of one final vehicle 9. དོན་དམ་པར་མི་སྐྱེ་བ་ཤེས་པ། knowledge of ultimate non-production 10. ཟབ་མོ་མི་སྐྲག་པའི་བཟོད་པ་ཤེས་པ། knowledge of patient acceptance and fearlessness of emptiness 11. ཆོས་ཐམས་ཅད་བདེན་མེད་དུ་སྟོན་པ། teaching that all phenomena lack a truly existent nature 12. བདེན་འཛིན་གྱི་རྟོག་པ་ཀུན་དུ་འཇོམས་པ། subduing all conceptions of true existence 13. མཚན་མར་འཛིན་པའི་འདུ་ཤེས་དང་འཛིག་ལྟ་སོགས་སྤོང་བ། abandoning all perception of signs, wrong views, etc. 14. རྣམ་མཁྱེན་ལ་རྩེ་གཅིག་པའི་ཞི་གནས་ངེས་པར་སེམས་པ། training in single-pointed mental quiescence meditation on omniscient mind 15. ལྷག་མཐོང་ཐབས་ཤེས་གཉིས་ལ་མཁས་པ། possessing penetrative insight skillful in both method and wisdom 16. གནས་ལུགས་བསྒོམས་པས་སེམས་དུལ་བ། taming the mind through having meditated on the mode of abidance/\reality 17. ཆོས་ཐམས་ཅད་ལ་ཐོགས་པ་མེད་པའི་ཡེ་ཤེས་དང་ལྡན་པ། having unobstructed wisdom knowing all phenomena 18. ཆོས་གང་ལའང་བདེན་པར་ཆགས་པའི་གནས་མེད་པར་རྟོགས་པ། knowledge of any phenomenon's being without a basis for true existence 19. རང་གར་ཉིད་ལྟར་འདོད་པའི་སངས་རྒྱས་ཀྱི་ཞིང་གཞན་དུ་མཉམ་དུ་འགྲོ་བ། freedom of movement to and from Buddha-fields as one wishes 20. རང་གི་ལུས་ལ་དབང་བསྒྱུར་ཐོབ་པས་ལུས་ཅི་འདོད་པར་སྟོན་པ། exhibiting all forms of bodies having gained control of one's own body.

ས་སྡེ་ལྔ།

Five Treatises of Asaṅga; five works of Asaṅga on levels of attainments. 1. རྣལ་འབྱོར་སྤྱོད་པའི་ས། *Grounds of Yogic Practices* (Yogacaryabhūmi) 2. གཏན་ལ་དབབ་པ་བསྡུ་བ། *Compendium of Ascertainment* (Nirṇayasaṁgraha) 3. གཞི་བསྡུ་བ། *Compendium of Bases* (Vastusaṁgraha) 4. རྣམ་གྲངས་བསྡུ་བ། *Compendium of Enumerators* (Paryāyasaṁgraha) 5. རྣམ་བཤད་བསྡུ་བ། *Compendium of Explanation* (Vivaraṇasaṁgraha).

ས་རྣམ་པ་དྲུག་ཏུ་གཡོ་བ།

Six ways of shaking the earth. The way nature pays its respect when a Buddha is born, enlightened or passes away into parinirvāṇa, etc. Also when a person becomes a Bodhisattva generating the mind of enlightenment. A. 1. འགུལ་བ། moving 2. གཡོ་བ། shaking 3. ལྡིག་པ། lifting 3. འཁྲུག་པ། errupting 4. ཁུར་ཁུར། humming 5. ཙེམ་ཙེམ། shimmering. B. ཤར་ཕྱོགས་མཐོ་ན་ནུབ་ཕྱོགས་དམའ་བ། if the east is higher the west is lower 2. ནུབ་ཕྱོགས་མཐོ་ན་ཤར་ཕྱོགས་དམའ་བ། if the west is higher the east is lower 3. ལྷོ་ཕྱོགས་མཐོ་ན་བྱང་ཕྱོགས་དམའ་བ། if the south is higher the north is lower 4. བྱང་ཕྱོགས་མཐོ་ན་ལྷོ་ཕྱོགས་དམའ་བ། if the north is higher the south is lower 5. མཐའ་མཐོ་ན་དབུས་དམའ་བ། if the corners are higher the central part is lower 6. དབུས་མཐོ་ན་མཐའ་དམའ་པ། if the central part is higher the corners are lower.

ས་སྟེང་།

Antarīkṣa/ Celestial world; celestial realm. One of the three realms of existence, primarily the abode of gods.

ས་གཞི་མ་དག་པ།

Aśuddhabhūmi/ Unsuitable land. Area where poisonous snakes, etc., live. Or a disputed land where according to Vinaya, building of a monastery is prohibited.

ས་བཞི་པའི་ཡོངས་སྦྱོང་བཅུ།

Ten thorough trainings on the fourth ground. 1. དགོན་པའི་ནགས་ན་གནས་པ། solitary dwelling in a forest 2. འདོད་པ་ཆུང་བ། having few desires 3. ཆོག་ཤེས་པ། being contented 4. སྦྱངས་པའི་ཡོན་ཏན་ལ་ཡིད་དམ་པ། strictly following the twelve ascetic trainings (see sbyangs-pa'i yon-tan bcu-gnyis) 5. བསླབ་ཁྲིམས་ཡོངས་སུ་མི་གཏོང་བ། not forshaking discipline 6. འདོད་པའི་ཡོན་ཏན་ལ་སྨོད་པ། loathing sensual objects 7. གདུལ་བྱ་སོ་སོའི་སྐལ་བ་དང་འཚམས་པའི་ཆོས་སྟོན་ཅིང་

ཀུན་འདྲེན་ལ་གཞོལ་བ། leading beings to the state of peace by giving teachings according to their capabilities 8. བཏོག་པ་ཀུན་གཏོང་བ། renouncing and giving away all possessions 9. དགེ་བ་སྒྲུབ་པ་ལ་སེམས་མི་ཞུམ་པ། never turning away from doing wholesome practices 10. མཐོང་ཞེན་གྱི་ལྟ་བ་མེད་པ། never holding wrong views.

ས་འོག

Bhūtala/ Subterrestial world. One of the three realms of existence, which is primarily the abode of nāgas, or serpent spirits.

ས་ལམ།

Paths and grounds. Grounds and paths of advancement to the state of liberation and omniscience.

ས་གསུམ་པའི་ཡོངས་སྦྱོང་ལྔ།

Five thorough trainings on the third ground. 1. ཆོས་ཐོས་པས་མི་ངོམས་པ། never satiated with listening to teachings 2. ཟང་ཟིང་གི་བསམ་པ་མེད་པར་གཞན་ལ་ཆོས་སྟོན་པ། teaching others without a thought for reward 3. རང་ཉིད་གང་དུ་འཚང་རྒྱ་བའི་ཞིང་ཀུན་སྦྱོང་བ། purification of the Buddha field where one is to attain enlightenment 4. འཁོར་བའི་སྐྱོན་མཐོང་བའི་གཞན་དོན་ལ་ཡོངས་སུ་མི་སྐྱོ་བ། never discouraged by seeing the faults of cyclic existence, from seeking others welfare 5. ངོ་ཚ་ཤེས་ཤིང་ཁྲེལ་ཡོད་དང་ལྡན་པ། having a sense of shame and embarrassment.

སངས་རྒྱས།

Buddha/ Fully enlightened being; Buddha. One who has completely purified himself of all faults and delusions and perfected all knowledge and wisdom; a fully enlightened being knowing all phenomena as they are.

སངས་རྒྱས་ཀྱི་ཆོས་མ་འདྲེས་པ་བཅོ་བརྒྱད།

Aṣṭādaśāveṇikabuddhadharmāḥ/ Eighteen unshared qualities of a Buddha, according to the Abhidharma tradition, (see ma-'dres-pa bco-brgyad). 1-10. སྟོབས་བཅུ། daśabalāni/ ten powers (see de-bzhin gshegs-pa'i stobs-bcu) 11-14. མི་འཇིགས་པ་བཞི། catvāri vaiśāradyāni/ four fearlessnesses (see mi-'jigs-pa bzhi) 15-17. དྲན་པ་ཉེ་བར་བཞག་པ་གསུམ། trīṇi smṛtyūpasthānāni/ three close mindfulnesses (see dran-pa nye-bar bzhag-pa gsum) 18. སྙིང་རྗེ་ཆེན་པོ། mahākaruṇa/ great compassion.

སངས་རྒྱས་ཀྱི་ཐུན་མོང་མ་ཡིན་པའི་རྣམ་པ་སོ་དགུ

Thirty-nine qualities exclusive to a Buddha. 1-10. སྟོབས་བཅུ། ten powers (see de-bzhin gshegs-pa'i stobs-bcu) 11-14. མི་འཇིགས་པ་བཞི། four fearlessnesses (see mi-'jigs-pa bzhi) 15-18. སོ་སོ་ཡང་དག་རིག་པ་བཞི། four specific perfect understandings (see so-sor yang-dag-pa rig-pa bzhi) 19-36. མ་འདྲེས་པ་བཅོ་བརྒྱད། eighteen unshared qualities of a Buddha (see ma-'dres-pa bco-brgyad) 37. དེ་བཞིན་ཉིད་ཀྱི་རྣམ་པ། aspect of thusness 38. རང་བྱུང་གི་རྣམ་པ། aspect of self-arisal 39. སངས་རྒྱས་ཉིད་ཀྱི་རྣམ་པ། aspects of the Buddha himself.

སངས་རྒྱས་ཀྱི་མཛད་པ་བཅུ་གཉིས།

The twelve deeds of Buddha Śākyamuni (see mdzad-pa bcu-bnyis).

སངས་རྒྱས་ཀྱི་རིགས།

Buddhagotra/ Buddha Nature; Buddha Lineage. The intrinsically pure mind and Buddhahood acquired through practice.

སངས་རྒྱས་དཔའ་བོ་བདུན།

Seven Heroic Budhas; the seven Buddhas of this aeon who have already appeared in this world according to the Hīnayāna tradition. 1. རྣམ་གཟིགས། Vipaśyin 2. གཙུག་ཏོར་ཅན། Śikhin

3. ཐམས་ཅད་སྐྱོབ། Viśvabhū 4. འཁོར་བ་འཇིག Krakuccanda 5. གསེར་ཐུབ། Kanakamuni 6. འོད་སྲུང་། Kaśyapa 7. ཤཱཀྱ་ཐུབ་པ། Śākyamuni.

སད་མི་མི་བདུན།

Seven Probationers; the first seven monks of Tibet ordained by Ācārya Śāntarakṣita during the reign of King Tri Ralpa Chan. 1. སྦ་གསལ་སྣང་། Ba Salnang 2. མཆིམས་ཤཱཀྱ་པྲ་བྷ། Chim Shakya Prabha 3. པ་གོར་བེ་རོ་ཙ་ན། Pagor Bero Tzana 4. ངན་ལམ་རྒྱལ་བ་མཆོག་དབྱངས། Ngan-lam Gyalwa Choryang 5. རྨ་རིན་ཆེན་མཆོག Ma Rinchen Chog 6. འཁོན་ཀླུའི་དབང་པོ། Khon Lui Wangpo 7. གཙང་ལེགས་གྲུབ། Tzang Legdrub.

སའི་ལྷ་སྔ་གོན།

Ground-ritual; preparatory-rite of the site. A part of preparatory rite in an initiation in which the goddess of the site is generated in the centre of the maṇḍala and wisdom-beings are immersed into her; she is then offered ritual-cakes (gtor-ma) and her permission is sought to allow the site to be used for an empowerment ceremony.

སའི་ཡོངས་སྦྱོང་།

Thorough trainings on the grounds; qualities of the trainings on the various levels of a Bodhisattvas' career (see sa-dang-po'i yongs-sbyong bcu, etc.).

སུན་འབྱིན།

Dūṣaṇa/ Refutation; refutation of others' position or philosophical stand. There are two types: 1. correct refutation 2. incorrect refutation.

སུམ་ཅུ་རྩ་གསུམ།

Trayastriṁśa devāḥ/ The Heaven of Thirty-Three. Celestial abode of gods of the desire realm believed to be located on top of Mt. Meru, which is inhabited by the so called 'eight wealth-gods' (nor-lha brgyad) the 'eleven wrathful' (drag-po bcu-gcig), the 'twelve suns' (nyi-ma bcu-gnyis), the 'two sons of thal-kar' (thal-skar-gyi bu-gnyis) and Indra (lha-bdang brgya-byin).

སུམ་ལྡན།

The three-fold aeon (see bskal-pa sum-ldan).

སེང་གེ་བཟང་པོ།

Haribhadra/ Ācārya Haribhadra. A student of Ācārya Śāntarakṣita known for his authority in the study of Perfection of Wisdom; the author of the *Clear Meaning* ('grel-pa don gsal) and the *Extensive Commentary on Eight Thousand Verses* (brgyad-stong 'grel-chen).

སེམས།

Citta/ Mind; primary consciousness, e.g. eye consciousness.

སེམས་ཀྱི་ཁམས་བདུན།

Seven mental constituents; seven domains of the mind. 1. མིག་གི་རྣམ་པར་ཤེས་པའི་ཁམས། cakṣu vijñānadhātu/ domain of eye consciousness 2. རྣ་བའི་རྣམ་པར་ཤེས་པའི་ཁམས། śrota vijñānadhātu/ domain of ear consciousness 3. སྣའི་རྣམ་པར་ཤེས་པའི་ཁམས། grāṇa vijñānadhātu/ domain of nose consciousness 4. ལྕེའི་རྣམ་པར་ཤེས་པའི་ཁམས། jihvā vijñānadhātu/ domain of tongue consciousness 5. ལུས་ཀྱི་རྣམ་པར་ཤེས་པའི་ཁམས། kāya vijñānadhātu/ domain of body consciousness 6. ཡིད་ཀྱི་རྣམ་པར་ཤེས་པའི་ཁམས། mano vijñānadhātu/ domain of mental consciousness 7. ཡིད་ཀྱི་དབང་པོ། mana indriyam/ domain of mental faculty.

སེམས་ཀྱི་གཞི་ལ་གཞོལ་བ།

Concentration on mind base; absorption into the object of mind. One of the four types of recitations/ incantation in lower tantra (see bzlas-brjod yan-lag bzhi); a practice of visualizing the ultimate mind of enlightenment as empty of inherent existence and the moon disk at the heart as the conventional mind of enlightenment.

སེམས་ཀྱི་ས་མང་བཅུ།

Ten mental levels; ten mental attitudes. 1-5. ཀུན་འགྲོ་ལྔ། five ever-functioning mental factors (see kun-'gro-lnga) 6-10. ཡུལ་ངེས་ལྔ། five determining mental factors (see yul-nges-lnga).

སེམས་བསྐྱེད།

Cittoptāda/ Mind generation; generation of the mind of enlightenment; an altruistic mind caused by a wish to benefit others and accompanied by a wish to attain Buddhahood for the sake of others.

སེམས་བསྐྱེད་ཉེར་གཉིས།

The twenty-two types of bodhicitta. The division of bodhicitta according to one's level of attainment and illustration. There are: 1-4. མོས་པ་སྤྱོད་པའི་སེམས་བསྐྱེད་བཞི། four preoccupied by faith (see mos-pa spyod pa'i sems bskyed bzhi) 5-11. ལྷག་བསམ་དག་པའི་སེམས་བསྐྱེད་བདུན། seven preoccupied with resolute intention (see lhag bsam dag pa'i sems bskyed bdun) 12-20. རྣམ་པར་སྨིན་པའི་སེམས་བསྐྱེད་དགུ nine fully matured ones (see) 21-22. སྒྲིབ་པ་སྤངས་པའི་སེམས་བསྐྱེད་གཉིས། two completely free of obscurations on the level of Buddhahood.

སེམས་བསྐྱེད་གཉིས།

Two types of mind of enlightenment; two kinds of bodhicitta. A. ངོ་བོའི་སྒོ་ནས། By nature: 1. ཀུན་རྫོབ་སེམས་བསྐྱེད། saṁvṛti cittotpāda/ conventional mind of enlightenment 2. དོན་དམ་སེམས་བསྐྱེད། paramārtha cittotpāda/ ultimate mind of enlightenment B. སྦྱོར་བའི་སྒོ་ནས། By means of their activity: 1. སྨོན་པ་སེམས་བསྐྱེད། praṇidhāna bodhicittotpāda/ aspiring mind of enlightenment 2. འཇུག་པ་སེམས་བསྐྱེད། prasthānacittotpāda/ engaging mind of enlightenment.

སེམས་བསྐྱེད་བཞི།

Four types of mind of enlightenment. The mind of enlightenment categorized in view of their degree of attainment. ས་མཚམས་ཀྱི་སྒོ་ནས། 1. མོས་པ་སྤྱོད་པའི་སེམས་བསྐྱེད། adhimukti-caryā cittotpāda/ mind of enlightenment preoccupied with faith—extant on the path of accumulation and the path of preparation only. 2. ལྷག་བསམ་དག་པའི་སེམས་བསྐྱེད། adhyāśayacittotpāda/ mind of enlightenment preoccupied with resolute intention—extant on the first seven Bodhisattva grounds. 3. རྣམ་པར་སྨིན་པའི་སེམས་བསྐྱེད། viśuddhicittotpāda/ fully matured mind of enlightenment—extant on the last three Bodhisattva grounds. 4. སྒྲིབ་པ་སྤངས་པའི་སེམས་བསྐྱེད། āvaraṇaprahāṇa cittotpāda/ mind of enlightenment free of obscurations—possessed by a Buddha.

སེམས་བསྐྱེད་གསུམ།

Three types of mind of the enlightenment. The mind of enlightenment categorized from the perspective of how it is initially generated. ཐོག་མར་སེམས་བསྐྱེད་ཚུལ་གྱི་སྒོ་ནས། 1. རྫི་བོ་ལྟ་བུའི་སེམས་བསྐྱེད། a shepherd-like mind of enlightenment 2. མཉན་པ་ལྟ་བུའི་སེམས་བསྐྱེད། a boatman-like mind of enlightenment 3. རྒྱལ་པོ་ལྟ་བུའི་སེམས་བསྐྱེད། a king-like mind of enlightenment.

སེམས་རྒྱུད།

Santāna/ A. Mind-stream; mental continuum. B. Mental attitude; philosophy.

སེམས་ཅན།

Sattva/ Sentient being. Lit: 'possessing a mind'; all living beings who posseses a mind, as distinct from a Buddha who possesses an enlightened mind.

སེམས་ཅན་དུ་སྟོན་པའི་སྒྲ།

Sattvākhyaśabda/ Articulate sound. Sound which intentionally indicates meaning to sentient beings, e.g. the speech of a Buddha, as opposed to the sound of a brook that does not intentionally indicate any meaning to sentient beings.

སེམས་རྟེན།

A. Souvenir. B. Brain and heart, the location of mind. C. object of meditation.

སེམས་རྟེན་གཉིས།

Two types of objects of meditation. Objects within and without one's own mind stream.

སེམས་དྲུག

Six types of mind; six attitudes. A. 1. རྩ་བའི་སེམས། mūlacitta/ root mind 2. རྗེས་སུ་དཔྱོད་པའི་སེམས། anucāritacitta/ post-analytical mind 3. རྣམ་པར་དཔྱོད་པའི་སེམས། vicāraṇacitta/ analytical mind 4. ངེས་པར་འཛིན་པའི་སེམས། avadhāraṇacitta/ discerning mind 5. སྡོམ་པའི་སེམས། saṁvaracitta/ restraining mind 6. སྨོན་པའི་སེམས། praṇidhicitta/ wishing mind. B. six consciousnesses (see rnam-shes tsogs-brgyad, 1-6).

སེམས་མདོ་བཅོ་བརྒྱད།

The eighteen tantras of the mind-system; the eighteen tantras of rDzogs-chen meditation. 1. རྒྱ་མཚོ་ལྟ་བུའི་རྒྱུད་རིག་པ་རང་ཤར། The Ocean-like Tantra called *Self Appearance of the Intuitive Awareness*. 2. ཉི་མ་ལྟ་བུའི་རྒྱུད་རྡོ་རྗེ་སེམས་དཔའ་སྙིང་གི་མེ་ལོང་། The Sun-like Tantra called *Mirror of Vajrasattva's Heart* 3. སེང་གེ་ལྟ་བུའི་རྒྱུད་སེང་གེ་རྩལ་རྫོགས། The Lion-like Tantra called *Perfection of a Lion's Skill* 4. རི་རྒྱལ་ལྟ་བུའི་རྒྱུད་ཡི་གེ་མེད་པ། The Meru-like Tantra called *The Letterless* 5. འཁོར་ལོ་ལྟ་བུའི་རྒྱུད་བཀྲ་ཤིས་མཛེས་པ། The Wheel-like Tantra called *Auspicious Adoration* 6. ལྡེ་མིག་ལྟ་བུའི་རྒྱུད་སྒྲ་ཐལ་འགྱུར། The Key-like Tantra called *Sound Consequentialist* 7. རལ་གྲི་ལྟ་བུའི་རྒྱུད་ཀུན་ཏུ་བཟང་པོ་ཐུགས་ཀྱི་མེ་ལོང་། The Sword-like Tantra called *Mirror of Samantabhadra's Heart* 8. གསལ་ཤིང་ལྟ་བུའི་རྒྱུད་སྒྲོན་མ་འབར་བ། The Multi Pronged Spear-like Tantra called *Blazing Lamp* 9. གསེར་ཞུན་ལྟ་བུའི་རྒྱུད་ནོར་བུ་ཕྲ་བཀོད། The Refined Gold-like Tantra called *Jewel Studded* 10. མ་བུ་འཕྲེལ་བ་ལྟ་བུའི་རྒྱུད་ཉི་མ་ཁ་སྦྱོར། The Tantra Like the Meeting of Mother and Child called *Union of Suns* 11. མེ་ལོང་ལྟ་བུའི་རྒྱུད་ངོ་སྤྲོད་སྤྲས་པ། The Mirror-like Tantra called *Adoration of Introduction* 12. མུ་ཏིག་སྟར་ལ་བརྒྱུས་པ་ལྟ་བུའི་རྒྱུད་མུ་ཏིག་ཕྲེང་བ། The Pearl String-like Tantra called *Pearl Garland* 13. སྦྲུལ་མདུད་ལྟ་བུའི་རྒྱུད་རིག་པ་རང་གྲོལ། The Snake's Coil-like Tantra called *Self-liberation of Intutive Awareness* 14. ཁྱུང་ཆེན་ལྟ་བུའི་རྒྱུད་ཀློང་དྲུག་པ། The Guru-like Tantra called *Six-fold Centrism* 15. ཆུ་བོ་ལྟ་བུའི་རྒྱུད་རྫོགས་པ་རང་བྱུང་། The River-like Tantra called *Spontaneous Completion* 16. སྤུ་གྲི་ལྟ་བུའི་རྒྱུད་ནག་མོ་ཁྲོས་མ། The Razor Blade-like Tantra called *Wrathful Black Goddess* 17. རྒྱལ་པོ་ལྟ་བུའི་རྒྱུད་སྐུ་གདུང་འབར་བ། The King-like Tantra called *Blazing Tomb* 18. བང་མཛོད་ལྟ་བུའི་རྒྱུད་རིན་པོ་ཆེ་སྤུངས་པ། The Treasure-like Tantra called *Jewel Heap*.

སེམས་སྡེ།

The Mind system; the mind tradition. A lineage of rDzogs-chen meditation coming from Ācarya Śrisiṁha, the great translator; primarily establishing the recognition of intrinsic awareness being free of its own plays.

སེམས་གནས་དགུ

Nine stages of setting the mind; the nine stages of establishing one's mind into a state of single-pointed concentration in calm-abiding meditation. 1. ནང་འཛོག་པ། mental setting 2. རྒྱུན་དུ་འཇོག་པ། continual setting 3. བླན་ཏེ་འཇོག་པ། patch-like setting 4. ཉེ་བར་འཇོག་པ། close setting 5. འདུལ་བར་བྱེད་པ། controlled setting 6. ཞི་བར་བྱེད་པ། pacification 7. རྣམ་པར་ཞི་བར་བྱེད་པ། complete pacification 8. རྩེ་གཅིག་ཏུ་བྱེད་པ། single-pointed setting 9. མཉམ་པར་འཇོག་པ། equal setting.

སེམས་པ།

Cintanā/ Thought; intention. A secondary mind that draws the attention of a primary mind to its object and establishes its recognition.

སེམས་པའི་ལས།

Mental activity. Activities of body, speech and mind brought to a manifest level or revealed due to mental projections.

སེམས་དཔའ་གསུམ་བརྩེགས།

Incorporation of the triple-beings. A method of generating deities one within another: 1. དམ་ཚིག་སེམས་དཔའ། samayasattva/ the pledged-being (see dam-tsig sems-dpa') 2. ཡེ་ཤེས་སེམས་དཔའ། jñānasattva/ the wisdom-being (see ye-shes sems-dpa') 3. ཏིང་ངེ་འཛིན་སེམས་དཔའ། samādhisattva/ the concentration-being (see ting-nge-'dzin sems-dpa').

སེམས་བྱུང་ལྔ་བཅུ་རྩ་གཅིག

Fifty-one secondary mental factors; fifty-one secondary minds accompanying a primary mind, 1-5. ཀུན་འགྲོ་ལྔ། the five omnipresent mental factors (see kun-'gro-lnga) 6-10. ཡུལ་ངེས་ལྔ། the five determinants (see yul-nges lnga) 11-16. རྩ་ཉོན་དྲུག the six root delusions (see rtsa-nyon drug) 17-36. ཉེ་ཉོན་ཉི་ཤུ། the twenty near-delusions (see nye-nyon nyi-shu) 37-47. དགེ་བ་བཅུ་གཅིག the eleven virtuous mental factors (see dge-ba bcu-gcig) 48-51. གཞན་འགྱུར་བཞི། the four changeable mental factors (see gzhan-'gyur bzhi).

སེམས་མེད་པའི་སྐབས་ལྔ།

The five occasions without mind; the five occasions when mind temporarily ceases to function. 1. འགོག་སྙོམས་ཀྱི་གནས་སྐབས། meditative absorption in cessation 2. འདུ་ཤེས་མེད་པའི་གནས་སྐབས། lack of discrimination 3. འདུ་ཤེས་མེད་པའི་སྙོམས་འཇུག་གི་གནས་སྐབས meditative absorption lacking discrimination 4. གཉིད་མཐུག་པོའི་གནས་སྐབས། deep sleep state 5. བརྒྱལ་བའི་གནས་སྐབས། fainting.

སེམས་ཙམ་པ།

Cittamātra/ The Mind only school; Cittamātra. A Mahāyāna school of tenets called the Yogacāra or Vijñānavāda, developed by Asaṅga and his brother Vasubandhu. This school asserts lack of duality between the object and object-perceiver and propounds eight types of consciousnesses (see rnam-shes tshogs-brgyad). There are two sub-schools.

སེམས་ཙམ་པ་རྣམ་བདེན།

True aspect mind only school. Cittamātrins who assert that the appearance of a gross form to the sensory consciousness perceiving form in the mind of a non-Ārya being (one who has not perceived emptiness directly) is not contaminated by latencies of ignorance.

སེམས་ཙམ་པ་རྣམ་རྫུན།

False aspect mind only school. Cittamātrins who assert that the appearance of a gross form to the sensory consciousness perceiving form in the mind of a non-Ārya being is contaminated by latencies of ignorance.

སེར་སྐྱ་པ།

Followers of the sage Kapila. A proponent of non-Buddhist philosophy (Hindu) called the Sāṁkhyas who assert the enumeration of all phenomena into twenty-five categories (see shes-bya nyer-lnga) and gains liberation through complete understanding of these phenomena.

སེལ་འཇུག

Eliminative engager. A subjective consciousness which engages in its object of identification by differentiating it from various aspects that are possessed by it, e.g. the idea or statement that expresses Tashi. There are two types: 1. བློའི་སེལ་འཇུག mental eliminative engager, e.g. the concept of a vase 2. སྒྲའི་སེལ་འཇུག verbal eliminative engager, e.g. the statement, 'sound is impermanent'.

སེལ་བ།

Apoha/ Elimination; eliminative phenomena; a negative phenomena. There are three: 1. དོན་གྱི་སེལ་བ། meaning eliminative phenomena, e.g. a thing that is not not a vase 2. བློའི་སེལ་བ། mental eliminative phenomena, e.g. the appearance of a thing that is not not a vase to a thought cognizing a vase 3. མེད་དགག་གི་སེལ་བ། affirming negative type eliminative phenomena, e.g. the mere absence of something that is not a vase.

སོ་ཐར་གྱི་སྡོམ་པ།

Pratimokṣa saṁvara/ Vows of individual liberation. Precepts of ordination meant for self-liberation from bad rebirth and saṁsāra. There are generally two: 1. ཁྱིམ་པའི་སྡོམ་པ། a householder's vows 2. རབ་བྱུང་གི་སྡོམ་པ། a monk's or nun's vows.

སོ་ཐར་རིགས་བརྒྱད།

Eight classes of individual liberation vows (see so-thar rigs-bdun 1-7) 8. བསྙེན་གནས་ཀྱི་སྡོམ་པ། one day ordination vows.

སོ་ཐར་རིགས་ རིས་ བདུན།

Seven classes of individual liberation vows. 1. དགེ་སློང་པའི་སྡོམ་པ། bhikṣu saṁvara/ fully ordained monk vows 2. དགེ་སློང་མའི་སྡོམ་པ། bhikṣuni saṁvara/ fully ordained nun vows 3. དགེ་ཚུལ་པའི་སྡོམ་པ། śrāmaṇera saṁvara/ novice monk vows 4. དགེ་ཚུལ་མའི་སྡོམ་པ། śrāmaṇerikā saṁvara/ novice nun vows 5. དགེ་བསྙེན་པའི་སྡོམ་པ། upāsaka saṁvara/ layman vows 6. དགེ་བསྙེན་མའི་སྡོམ་པ། upāsikā saṁvara/ laywoman vows 7. དགེ་སློབ་མའི་སྡོམ་པ། śikṣamānā saṁvara/ probationary nun vows.

སོ་ཐར་རིགས་རིས་བཞི།

The four classes of individual liberation vows. 1. དགེ་སློང་ཕ་མའི་སྡོམ་པ། fully ordained monk and nun vows 2. དགེ་ཚུལ་ཕ་མའི་སྡོམ་པ། novice vows 3. དགེ་བསྙེན་གྱི་སྡོམ་པ། layperson's vows 4. བསྙེན་གནས་ཀྱི་སྡོམ་པ། one day ordination vows.

སོ་སོ་སྐྱེ་བོ།

Pṛthagjana/ Ordinary person; beginner. Persons who have no knowledge of the reality of phenomena.

སོ་སོར་བརྟགས་འགོག

Pratisaṁkhyānirodha/ Analytical cessation. Cessation gained through the wisdom of meditation and anylysis on the four noble truths, e.g. the truth of cessation within the mental continuum of an Ārya on the path of meditation.

སོ་སོར་བརྟགས་མིན་འགོག་པ།

Apratisaṁkhyānirodha/ Non-analytical cessation. Cessation that is impermanent by nature and is not acquired through the wisdom of meditation and analysis on the four noble truths, e.g. cessation of rebirth into bad migration within the continuum of a Bodhisattva on the path of preparation.

སོ་སོར་ཐར་པ།

Pratimokṣa/ Individual liberation (see so-thar-gyi sdom-pa).

སོ་སོ་ཡང་དག་རིག་པ་བཞི།

Four specific perfect understandings. The four ways in which a Bodhisattva knows the distinct features, characteristics and states of phenomena. 1. ཆོས་སོ་སོ་ཡང་དག་རིག་པ། dharma pratisaṁvid/ specific perfect understanding of dharma 2. དོན་སོ་སོ་ཡང་དག་རིག་པ། artha pratisaṁvid/ specific perfect understanding of meaning 3. ངེས་ཚིག་སོ་སོ་ཡང་དག་རིག་པ། nirukti pratisaṁvid/ specific perfect understanding of definitive words 4. སྤོབས་པ་སོ་སོ་ཡང་དག་རིག་པ། pratibhāna pratisaṁvid/ specific perfect understanding of confidence.

སོར་མོ་ལྔ།

Pañcāṅguli/ Five fingers. 1. མཐེ་བོང་། aṅguṣṭha/ thumb 2. མཛུབ་མོ། aṅguli/ index finger 3. གུང་མོ། madhāṅguli/ middle finger 4. སྲིན་ལག anāmā/ ring finger 5. མཐེའུ་ཆུང་། anāmikā/ little finger.

སྲི།

Peśī/ A. Evil spirit; a malignant spirit or devil born of a dead person resurrected in their previous locality who create truble in the vicinity. B. Miserliness. C. A disastrous event or period believed to be a common karma, e.g. evil accidents happening one after another in the same locality.

སྲི་གནོན།

Exorcism. A type of tantric ritual to capture, bury and burn a malignant spirit (see sri, above).

སྲིད་པ།

Bhava/ A. Saṁsāra; cyclic existence. B. Existence.

སྲིད་པ་ཆགས་པའི་ལྷ་དགུ

Nine Gods of Tibet. O-de Gung-gyal, the ninth King of Tibet, son of Drigum Tzen-po and his eight sons believed to be residing and guarding Tibet throughout its three regions. 1. ཡར་ལྷ་ཤམ་པོ། Yala Shampo 2. གཉན་ཆེན་ཐང་ལྷ། Nyan-chen Thang-la 3. རྨ་ཆེན་སྤོམ་ར། Ma-chen Pom-ra 4. སྒྱོགས་ཆེན་གདོང་ར། Gyog-chen Dong-ra 5. སྒམ་པོ་ལྷ་རྗེ། Gampo-Lha-Je 6. ཞོགས་ལྷ་ཕྱུགས་པོ། Zhog-La Gyug-Po 7. ཇོ་བོ་གཡུལ་རྒྱལ། Jobo Yu-Gyal 8. ཤེའུ་ཁ་རག Sheu Kha-Rag 9. འོད་དེ་གུང་རྒྱལ། O-De Gung-Gyal.

སྲིད་པ་ཐ་མ་པ།

Caramabhavika/ One on the last existence. One who is free from being reborn again in cyclic existence through the force of his contaminated karma.

སྲིད་པ་འཚོལ་བ།

Seeker of existence. Epithet for the being in an intermediate state of rebirth (bar-do).

སྲིད་པ་བཞི།

Four states of existence; the four domains of existence. 1. སྐྱེ་སྲིད། utpatti bhava/ birth state 2. སྔོན་དུས་ཀྱི་སྲིད་པ། sakṣin bhava/ live state 3. འཆི་སྲིད། maraṇa bhava/ death state 4. བར་སྲིད། antara bhava/ intermediate state.

སྲིད་པ་གསུམ།

The three worlds: A. 1. ལྷའི་སྲིད་པ། devabhava/ world of gods 2. ཀླུའི་སྲིད་པ། nāgabhava/ world of nāgas 3. མིའི་སྲིད་པ། manuṣyabhava/ world of humans. B. 1. ས་འོག bhūtala/ sub-terrestrial world 2. ས་སྟེང་། mahitala/ terrestrial 3. ས་བླ། antarika/ heaven. C. The three states of existence: 1. སྐྱེ་སྲིད། utpattibhava/ birth-state 2. འཆི་སྲིད། maraṇabhava/ death-state 3. བར་སྲིད། antarabhava/ intermediate-state. D. According to the Nyingma tradition the three states of existence are as follows: 1. ལུས་སྣང་བ་འདོད་པའི་སྲིད་པ། the desire realm in which physical form is seen 2. ངག་ཕྱེད་སྣང་གཟུགས་ཀྱི་སྲིད་པ། the form realm in which half of speech is felt 3. ཡིད་མི་སྣང་གཟུགས་མེད་པའི་སྲིད་པ། the formless realm in which mind cannot be sensed.

སྲིད་པའི་རྩ་བ་ཕྲ་རྒྱས་དྲུག

Six root delusions of cyclic existence (see rtsa-nyon-drug).

སྲིད་པའི་ཡན་ལག

The limb of existence. The link of grasping, ninth in the twelve links of interdependent origination which has the force of activating strong karmas through negativities accumulated by body, speech and mind.

སྲིད་རྩེ།

Bhavāgra/ Peak of Existence. The highest state of the three realms within cyclic existence.

སྲིད་ཞི་མཉམ་ཉིད་ཀྱི་སྦྱོར་བ།

Bhavaśāntisamatā prayoga/ Training in the sameness of cyclic existence and peace; the Bodhisattva's meditative training in the sameness of saṁsāra and nirvāṇa as lacking inherent existence.

སྲུང་འཁོར།

Wheel of Protection. Meditation on a vajra fence, fire fence and vajra tent, etc., as a protection for the residence and resident maṇḍala of a deity. The meditation of a vajra fence throughout the ten directions before creation of a maṇḍala and bestowal of an initiation.

སྲུང་ཐབས་ཡན་ལག་ལྔ།

Five means of guarding a moral discipline; five ways of protecting one's vows from degeneration. 1. དགེ་བའི་བཤེས་གཉེན་ལ་བསྟེན་པ། relying on a spiritual teacher 2. བསམ་པ་ཕུན་སུམ་ཚོགས་པ། relying on an excellent motivation 3. འགལ་རྐྱེན་མི་མཐུན་ཕྱོགས་ངོ་ཤེས་པ། recognizing the opposing factors 4. བསླབ་པ་ཡོངས་སུ་སྦྱོང་བ། perfectly training in the precepts 5. བདེ་བར་གནས་པའི་རྐྱེན་བསྟེན་པ། relying on conditions for a peaceful life.

སྲུང་མདུད།

Protection cord. Strings that are knotted in a special way, blessed and given by Lamas as their symbol of protection and blessings.

སྲེད་པ།

Tṛṣṇā/ A. Craving; the urge to meet with pleasant feelings and to be separated from ill sensations. B. Attachment; clinging.

སྲེད་པ་གསུམ།

Three kinds of craving; cravings experienced at death. 1. འདོད་སྲེད། rāga tṛṣṇā/ craving for desired objects 2. འཇིགས་སྲེད། satkāya tṛṣṇā/ craving for fear of losing this body 3. སྲིད་སྲེད། bhava tṛṣṇā/ craving for existence.

སྲེད་པའི་ཡན་ལག

The link of craving. The link of feeling, seventh in the twelve links of interdependent origination which causes the growth of the faculty to taste various objects and develops attachment and clinging to these, thereby enhancing the state of existence.

སྲོག

Prāṇa/ Life-force. A. According to Vinaya and the Abhidharma tradition it is the vital energy that acts as the basis for consciousness and the warmth of a being; whereas in other traditions it is generally the life as opposed to death. B. In astrology, it is the life-pattern of a person.

སྲོག་སྒོམ་གཟེར་བཞི།

The four vital points. The four vital points in the practice of the generation stage of mahāyoga tantra according to the Nyingma tradition, meant for integrating the life-like essence of all phenomena into the sphere of non-dual primordial wisdom. 1. ཏིང་ངེ་འཛིན་ལྷའི་གཟེར། the vital point of a deity used for developing meditative concentration 2. སྙིང་པོ་སྔགས་ཀྱི་གནད། the vital point of the essential mantra 3. དགོངས་པ་མི་འགྱུར་བའི་གནད། the unchangeable vital point of the instruction or thought 4. འཕྲོ་འདུ་འཕྲིན་ལས་ཀྱི་གནད། the vital point of virtuous activity or energy for dissolving distractions.

སློག་འཛིན་གྱི་རླུང་།

Prānavāyu/ Life-supporting wind. One of the five principal energy winds located at the crown within the brain, responsible for wit and intelligence and the power of memory.

སློབ་དཔོན།

Ācārya/ A. Ācārya; a spiritual master who takes care of his diciples' material needs. B. Teacher; lecturer. C. An instrument of a carpenter.

སློབ་དཔོན་གྱི་དབང་དྲུག

The six initiations of a master. 1. ཕྱིར་མི་ལྡོག་པའི་དབང་། the irreversible initiation 2. གསང་བའི་དབང་། the secret initiation 3. རྗེས་གནང་གི་དབང་། permission initiation 4. ལུང་བསྟན་གྱི་དབང་། prophesy 5. དབུགས་དབྱུང་གི་དབང་། giving relief 6. གཟེངས་བསྟོད་ཀྱི་དབང་། praise and encouragement.

སློབ་དཔོན་ལྔ།

The five masters (see slob-dpon bdun, 3-7).

སློབ་དཔོན་དྲུག

Six masters; six types of teachers. 1. དམ་ཚིག་དང་སྡོམ་པ་སྦྱིན་པའི་སློབ་དཔོན། a teacher who bestows pledges and vows 2. བཟླས་ལུང་སྦྱིན་པའི་སློབ་དཔོན། a teacher who bestows oral and reading transmissions 3. རྒྱུད་བཤད་པའི་སློབ་དཔོན། a teacher who bestows tantric teachings 4. མན་ངག་སྟོན་པའི་སློབ་དཔོན། a teacher who gives quintessential instructions 5. དབང་བསྐུར་བའི་སློབ་དཔོན། a teacher who bestows initiations 6. ལས་བྱེད་པའི་སློབ་དཔོན། a teacher who gives ritual guidance.

སློབ་དཔོན་བདུན།

Seven masters; seven types of teachers according to the Vinaya tradition. 1. བསྙེན་གནས་ཀྱི་སློབ་དཔོན། master who bestows one day vows 2. དགེ་བསྙེན་གྱི་སློབ་དཔོན། master who bestows lay persons' vows 3. དགེ་ཚུལ་གྱི་སློབ་དཔོན། master who bestows novice vows 4. གསང་སྟེ་སྟོན་པའི་སློབ་དཔོན། master who is one's confidant 5. ལས་བྱེད་པའི་སློབ་དཔོན། master who gives ritual guidance 6. ཀློག་པའི་སློབ་དཔོན། master who teaches basics 7. གནས་ཀྱི་སློབ་དཔོན། resident master.

སློབ་དཔོན་དཔའ་བོ།

Ācāryavīra/ Ācārya Āryaśūra. Perhaps the greatest of all scholarly Buddhist poets, a non-Buddhist of great learning who was defeated in debate by Āryadeva, a disciple of Nāgārjuna and converted to Buddhism; he composed the *Fifty Verses of Guru Devotion.*

སློབ་དཔོན་ས་ར་ཧ།

Ācārya Saraha. Also called Brahma Rahula; the root Guru of Ācārya Nāgārjuna born in a Brahmin family at Odibida, Orissa of modern India, renowned for his tantric practice.

སློབ་མ་ཁྱད་ཆོས་གསུམ་ལྡན།

Disciple with qualities; three basic qualities of a Dharma disciple. 1. ཤེས་རབ་རྣོ་བ། he has clear wisdom 2. སྨྲ་བ་ཉུང་བ། he speaks little 3. བླ་མ་ལ་གུས་པ། he is respectful of his masters.

སློབ་མ་སྟ་གོན།

The preparatory rites of disciples. The first phase of initiations meant to prepare the disciple for the actual initiation. This involves: 1. ཀུན་སློང་བཅོས་ཤིང་ནང་དབང་བསྐུར་བ། setting motivation and granting inner initiation 2. གསོལ་བ་གདབ་ཅིང་འཛིན་དུ་གཞུག་པ། making requests and upholding the practice 3. སྡོམ་པ་གཟུང་ཞིང་བྱིན་གྱིས་བརླབ་པ། receiving vows and blessings 4. དངོས་གྲུབ་བརྟག་ཕྱིར་སོ་ཤིང་དོར་བ། examining the siddhi and throwing of the tooth stick 5. ངག་ཉེས་སྦྱང་ཕྱིར་ཁྱོར་ཆུ་སྦྱིན་པ། distributing blessed water (khyor-chu) for purifying negativities of speech 6. རྨི་ལམ་བཟློག་ཕྱིར་ཀུ་ཤ་གདང་པ། distributing kuśa grass to avoid bad dreams 7. བར་ཆད་ཞི་ཕྱིར་དཔུང་སྐུད་གདགས་པ། distributing protection thread to guard the disciples from interferences 8. སྤྲོ་བ་བསྐྱེད་ཕྱིར་ཆོས་བཤད་པ། giving a summary teaching to generate inspiration 9. མཚན་ལྟས་བརྟག་ཕྱིར་རྨི་ལམ་བརྟག་པ། examining dreams through analyzing the omens.

སློབ་མའི་ཆོས་བཞི།

The four qualities of a disciple; four basic qualities to judge the acceptance of a disciple. 1. མི་ཕྱེད་པའི་དད་པ། unfluctuating faith 2. མི་ལྡོག་པའི་བརྩོན་འགྲུས། irreversible efforts 3. གཞན་དྲིང་མི་འཇོག་པའི་གསུང་རབ། incomparable teachings/ texts to be taught 4. བཤེས་གཉེན་ལ་དད་གུས། faith and devotion in the spiritual master.

སློབ་མའི་བྱ་བ་ལྔ།

The five duties of a disciple. 1. བཤེས་གཉེན་འཚོལ་བ་ལ་སྐྱོ་བ་མེད་པ། having no regret in searching for spiritual masters 2. སྐུ་ལྟ་བས་ཆོག་མི་ཤེས་པར་བྱ་བ། being insatiable in meeting and seeing one's teachers 3. དེས་བསྟན་པ་དང་རྗེས་སུ་མཐུན་པར་འཇིན་པ། following his or her teacher's teachings and instructions 4. དེའི་ཐབས་མཁས་སྤྱོད་པ་ལ་མི་ཁྲོ་བ། having no hatred against his or her teacher's skillful behaviors 5. དེ་ལས་རྟོགས་པ་ཐེབས་པར་བགྱི་བ། working towards generating realizations.

སློབ་མའི་དབང་ལྔ།

The five initiations of a disciple (see rig-pa'i dbang lnga).

སློབ་མའི་མཚན་ཉིད་ལྔ།

The five qualities of a disciple. 1. བློ་གཟུ་བོར་གནས་པ། having an unbiased way of thinking 2. བློ་གྲོས་དང་ལྡན་པ། having good wisdom 3. དོན་གཉེར་ཆེ་བ། having interest in one's training 4. གུས་པ། being respectful 5. ཡིད་གདུང་པ། being devoted.

སློབ་མའི་མཚན་ཉིད་གསུམ།

The three qualities of a disciple. 1. བློ་གསལ་བ། having clear wisdom 2. ཤེས་འདོད་ཡོད་པ། having interest in gaining knowledge 3. བླ་མར་གུས་པ། being respectful of one's teachers.

སློབ་ལམ་བཞི།

The four paths of a trainee. 1. ཐར་པ་ཆ་མཐུན། aid to liberation 2. ངེས་འབྱེད་ཆ་མཐུན། aid to definitive separation 3. དོན་མངོན་རྟོགས། realization of the meaning 4. རྗེས་ལ་མངོན་རྟོགས། the subsequent realization. These are synonymous with the path of accumulation, preparation, seeing and meditation, respectively.

གསང་སྔགས།

Secret mantra; tantric teachings. Those cycles of teachings involving techniques to protect one's mind from misconceptions and illusions by means of cultivating the path of union of the wisdom understanding emptiness and great compassion aimed ultimately at the actualization of the great wisdom; these are to be practised secretly and cannot be declared to those who are not properly ripe to receive these (see below).

གསང་སྔགས་ཀྱི་ཁྱད་ཆོས་བཞི།

The four special qualities of secret mantra; the four features that make tantra superior compared to other practices. 1. ཐབས་ཀྱི་ཆ་ལ་མ་རྨོངས་པའི་ཁྱད་པར། rich in the methods of approach 2. ཐབས་མང་བའི་ཁྱད་པར། has many-fold methods or techniques 3. དཀའ་བ་མེད་པའི་ཁྱད་པར། easy to adopt its methods and techniques 4. དབང་པོ་རྣོ་བའི་ཁྱད་པར། suitable for persons of sharp intellect to carry the practice.

གསང་སྔགས་ཀྱི་སྡོམ་པ།

Secret mantra vows; tantric vows (see rtsa-ltung bcu-bzhi and sbom-po brgyad).

གསང་སྔགས་ཀྱི་སྣོད།

The receptacles of secret mantra; the proper disciples qualified to receive secret mantra teachings. 1. དབང་པོ་རྣོ་བ། sharp intelligence 2. དབང་གིས་རྒྱུད་སྨིན་པར་བྱས་པ། having matured or ripened one's mental continuum through initiation 3. རྩ་བ་དང་ཡན་ལག་གི་དམ་ཚིག་བསྲུང་བ། having observed the root and secondary vows properly.

གསང་སྔགས་རྙིང་མ།

Ancient secret mantra tradition; Ancient Tantra. Tantra was initially introduced into Tibet in the seventh century during the reign of King Songtsen Gampo and in the middle of the eighth century. During the reign of King Trisong Deutsan, Guru Padmasambhava visited Tibet and spread the tantric teach-ings widely through translating many tantric texts into Tibetan. In the tenth century Paṇḍita Smṛti Jñāna and others came to Tibet and further carried out translation works of the doctrine and spread it extensively. The spreading of tantric doctrines in the history of Tibet is known as the Ancient Tantra.

གསང་སྔགས་རྡོ་རྗེ་ཐེག་པ།

Secret Mantra Vajrayāna. Simply called the Vajrayāna or Diamond Vehicle concerning the tantric doctrine of the kriyā, cārya, yoga and anuttarayoga tantras; also called the resultant vehicle.

གསང་སྔགས་གསར་མ།

New secret mantra tradition; New tantra. Following the eclipse of Buddhist teachings during the reign of King Lang Darma, in the middle of the 9th century, the great translator of Ngari, Rinchen Zangpo (958-1055) translated and revised many tantric texts into Tibetan and revitalized the doctrine once again in Tibet; this period, beginning from Rinchen Zangpo is known in the religious history of Tibet as the new system of tantra.

གསང་སྤྱོད་ལྡོག་སྒོམ།

Reversed method of meditation on secret practice. One of the eight means of transmitting the Mahāmudrā doctrine, primarily a method of passing on the bare techniques of psychic heat meditation based on one's own experience.

གསང་བ་འདུས་པ།

Guhyasamāja. A tantric deity belonging to the father tantra of the highest class of tantric practices.

གསང་བ་ཟབ་མོའི་དབང་གསུམ།

The three profound secret initiations. The initiations that are gateways to enter into the mahāyoga cycle of tantric practice according to the Nyingma tradition. 1. སྤྱོད་པའི་བརྟུལ་ཞུགས་ཅན་ལ་གསང་དབང་། the secret initiation for adopting ascetic behavior 2. རིག་པའི་བརྟུལ་ཞུགས་ཅན་ལ་ཤེས་རབ་ཡེ་ཤེས་ཀྱི་དབང་། the primordial wisdom initiation for adopting ascetic practices of intuitive awareness 3. མཉམ་པའི་བརྟུལ་ཞུགས་ཅན་ལ་དབྱེར་མེད་བདེ་བ་ཆེན་པོའི་དབང་། the inseparable great bliss initiation for those adopting balanced ascetic practices.

གསང་བའི་དཀྱིལ་འཁོར།

Guhyamaṇḍala/ The secret maṇḍala. The vagina of a tantric consort.

གསང་བའི་བདག་པོ།

Guhyapati/ A. Master of secret teachings; Buddha Vajradhāra. B. Vajrapāṇi. C. Vaiśravaṇa; the god of wealth.

གསང་དབང་།

Guhyābhiṣekha/ Secret initiation; secret empowerment. One of the highest levels of initiation whereby the disciples are initiated into the conventional maṇḍala of bodhicitta of the deities in union; their stains of speech are purified; they are authorized to carry out meditation on the yogas of the energy channels and winds; and thereby the seed of attaining Sambhogakāya Buddha is implanted in their mental continuum.

གསང་མཛོད་གསུམ།

Three secret treasuries; three secret texts of the Nyingma tradition. 1. བླ་མ་གསང་མཛོད། secret treasury of the Guru 2. ཡི་དམ་གསང་མཛོད། secret treasury of the meditational deity 3. མཁའ་འགྲོ་གསང་མཛོད། secret treasury of the ḍākas and ḍākinis.

གསང་ཡུམ།

The secret mother. The consort of a master, tantrika or a tulku.

གསན་ཡིག

List of teachings, initiations, oral transmissions and discourses received by a great Lama during his lifetime; record of teachings received.

གསལ་སྟོང་དབྱེར་མེད།

Inseparability of clarity and emptiness; the intutive awareness of reality and primordial wisdom as fused into one another.

གསལ་སྟོང་འཛིན་མེད།

The view of non-apprehension regarding clarity and emptiness. A view of reality as explained in the doctrine of the Sakya tradition; the fact that our mind is primordially clear by nature and this clarity cannot be found upon any object no matter where we may search for it; and hence such an emptiness is the nature of our mind. When its clarity is found to be its emptiness and vice-versa one has found the natural and inexpressible view of the unity of clarity and emptiness of our mind.

གསལ་སྣང་།

Prasena/ A. Clarity. B. Luminosity.

གསལ་བ།

Predicate. The predicate in a logicial syllogism (see sgrub-bya'i chos).

གསུང་ཀུན་དུ་བརྗོད་པའི་ཆོ་འཕྲུལ།

Ādeśanāprātihārya/ Miracles through teachings. Buddha's way of teaching his disciples according to their need; one of the three types of miracles of a Buddha (see cho-'phrul rnam-gsum).

གསུང་ལྔ།

The five kinds of speeches; Buddha's five ways of teaching disciples as explained in the Nyingma tradition. 1. སྐྱེ་མེད་དོན་གྱི་གསུང་། the ultimate teachings lacking birth 2. དགོངས་པ་བརྡའི་གསུང་། the intended teachings through gestures 3. བརྗོད་པ་ཚིག་གི་གསུང་། the literal teachings through expression 4. དབྱེར་མེད་རྡོ་རྗེའི་གསུང་། the vajra teachings of inseparability 5. མངོན་བྱང་གི་གསུང་། the teachings through enlightened energy or blessings.

གསུང་ཆོས་ཀྱི་ཕྱག་རྒྱའི་རྣལ་འབྱོར།

The yoga of dharma mudrā of the teachings. One of the four yogas of yoga tantra (see phyag rgya-bzhi) identified with the actualization of the wisdom of discrimination by means of eliminating adventitious defilements upon the mind.

གསུང་དབྱངས་ཡན་ལག་ལྔ།

The features of melodic voice; the five limbs of enlightened speech of a Buddha. 1. འབྲུག་སྒྲ་ལྟར་ཟབ་པ། deep like that of thunder 2. སྙན་ཞིང་འཇེབས་ལ་རྣ་བར་སྙན་པ། soothing and comfortable to the ear 3. ཡིད་དུ་འོང་ཞིང་དགའ་བར་བྱེད་པ། pleasant and delightful 4. རྣམ་པར་གསལ་ཞིང་རྣམ་པར་རིག་པར་བྱེད་པ། lucid and articulate 5. མཉན་འོས་ཤིང་མི་མཐུན་པ་མེད་པ། suitable and consistent throughout.

གསུམ་ལྡན།

The three-fold period (see bskal-pa gsum ldan).

གསུང་རབ་ཡན་ལག་དགུ

Nine scriptural categories. These are No. 1-6 and 10-12 derived from the twelve sciptural categories (see gsung-rab yan-lag bcu-gnyis).

གསུང་རབ་ཡན་ལག་བཅུ་གཉིས།

Dvādaśa dharmapravacana/ Twelve scriptural categories. 1. མདོའི་སྡེ། sūtram/ sets of discourses 2. དབྱངས་ཀྱིས་བསྙད་པའི་སྡེ། geyam/ intermediate verses 3. ལུང་དུ་བསྟན་པའི་སྡེ། vyākaraṇam/ prophetic teachings 4. ཚིགས་སུ་བཅད་པའི་སྡེ། gāthā/ versified teachings 5. ཆེད་དུ་བརྗོད་པའི་སྡེ། udānam/ specific teachings 6. གླེང་གཞིའི་སྡེ། nidānam/ introductory teachings 7. རྟོགས་པ་བརྗོད་པའི་སྡེ། avadānam/ parables 8. དེ་ལྟ་བུ་བྱུང་བའི་སྡེ། itivṛttakam/ legends 9. སྐྱེས་པའི་རབས་ཀྱི་སྡེ། jātakam/ life stories 10. ཤིན་ཏུ་རྒྱས་པའི་སྡེ། vaipulyam/ grand teachings 11. རྨད་དུ་བྱུང་བའི་སྡེ། adbhūta dharma/ marvellous teachings 12. གཏན་ལ་ཕབ་པའི་སྡེ། upadeśa/ finalized teachings.

གསེར་གྱི་རི་བདུན།

Seven golden mountains. The seven mountains surrounding Mt. Meru as explained in the Abhidharma text. 1. མུ་ཁྱུད་འཛིན། Nimindhāra/ rim holder 2. རྣམ་པར་འདུད། Vinataka/ perfect bow 3. རྟ་རྣ། Aśvakarṇa/ horse-ear 4. ལྟ་ན་སྡུག Sudarśana/ lovely to behold 5. སེང་ལྡེང་ཅན། Khadiraka/ Acacia 6. གཤོལ་མདའ་འཛིན། Īsādhāra/ ploughshaft holder 7. གཉའ་ཤིང་འཛིན། Yugadhāra/ yoke holder.

གསེར་ཆོས་བཅུ་གསུམ།

The thirteen golden texts. The thirteen cycles of restrictive esoteric teachings known to the Tsarpa school of the Sakya tradition. These are: 1-3. མཁའ་སྤྱོད་སྐོར་གསུམ། the three concerning Vajrayoginī (see mkha'-spyod skor-gsum) 4-6. དམར་ཆེན་སྐོར་གསུམ། the three concerning the major red protectors (see dmar-chen skor gsum) 7-9. དམར་ཆུང་སྐོར་གསུམ། the three concerning minor red protectors (see dmar-chung skor gsum) 10. འཆི་མེད་རྡོ་རྗེ་ལྷ་མོ། the cycle of teachings of Amṛtavajra Devi 11. ཛམ་དམར། the cycle of teachings of Red Dzambala 12. སེང་གདོང་། the cycle of teachings concerning Siṁhanada 13. འཇམ་དཔལ་ནག་པོ། the cycle of teachings concerning Black Mañjuśrī.

གསེར་ལྟ་བུའི་སེམས་བསྐྱེད།

Suvarṇopamacittotpāda/ Gold-like bodhicitta. The mind of enlightenment associated with the practice of superior intention possessed by a Bodhisattva on the middling path of accumulation.

གསེར་གདུང་།

The golden-tomb. Usually stūpas of various sizes containing relics and precious articles of a deceased master.

གསོ་དཔྱད་ཡན་ལག་བརྒྱད།

Eight branches of healing; eight types of therapy in the Tibetan medical system. 1. ལུས་ནད་གསོ་བའི་དཔྱད། treatment of physical ailments 2. བྱིས་པའི་ནད་གསོ་བའི་དཔྱད། treatment of children's ailment 3. མོ་ནད་གསོ་བའི་དཔྱད། treatment of women's ailments 4. གདོན་གྱིས་འཆི་བའི་དཔྱད། treatment of disorders caused by spirits 5. མཚོན་གྱིས་འཆི་བའི་དཔྱད།

treatment of wounds caused by weapons 6. དུག་གིས་འཚེ་བའི་དཔྱད། treatment of poisoning 7. རྒས་ཁ་གསོ་བའི་དཔྱད། treatment to combat old age 8. རོ་ཙ་གསོ་བའི་དཔྱད། treatment concerning fertility.

གསོ་སྦྱོང་།

Poṣadha/ The bi-monthly confession and restortion ceremony of monks and nuns as proscribed by Buddha.

གསོ་སྦྱོང་བཅུ་བཞི་པ།

The bi-monthly confession and restoration ceremony of monks and nuns during the months of waning moon in which the ceremony cannot be held on the fourteenth day of the 12th, 2nd, 4th, 6th, 2nd phase of 8th and the 10th month of Tibetan calendar.

གསོ་སྦྱོང་བཅོ་ལྔ་པ།

The bi-monthly confession and restoration ceremony of the monks and nuns held during the months of waxing moon and the waning moons of the 11th, 1st, 3rd, 5th, 7th and during Aśvinī (tha-skar) constellation.

བསམ་གྱི་མི་ཁྱབ་པ་ལྔ་།

Five inconceiveable topics. 1. ལས་ཀྱི་རྣམ་པར་སྨིན་པ་བསམ་མི་ཁྱབ། inconceiveable ripening of karma 2. ནོར་བུ་སྔགས་སྨན་སོགས་ཀྱི་ནུས་པ་བསམ་མི་ཁྱབ། inconceiveable power of jewels, mantras and medicine 3. རྣལ་འབྱོར་གྱི་ནུ་མཐུ་བསམ་མི་ཁྱབ། inconceiveable power of yogis 4. བྱང་སེམས་ཀྱི་དབང་བཅུ་བསམ་མི་ཁྱབ། inconceiveable ten powers of a bodhisattva 5. སངས་རྒྱས་ཀྱི་འཕྲིན་ལས་བསམ་མི་ཁྱབ། inconceiveable virtuous deeds of a Buddha.

བསམ་གཏན།

Samādhi. Concentration; meditative concentration. A state of mind in which one is able to focus one's attention single-pointedly on any suitable virtuous object without wandering outside of it. Such a state of mind becomes the source of all spiritual qualities.

བསམ་གཏན་གྱི་དཀྱིལ་འཁོར།

Samādhi maṇḍala/ Concentration maṇḍala. Creation and visualization of the residence and resident maṇḍala of a deity or dieties through the power of meditation.

བསམ་གཏན་གྱི་སྐྱོན་བརྒྱད།

Eight faults of concentration. The eight faults of the desire realm and concentrations realms of the lower level. 1-2. འདོད་པ་ན་ཡོད་པའི་སྡུག་བསྔལ་དང་ཡིད་མི་བདེ་བ། suffering and mental discomfort within the desire realm 3-4. བསམ་གཏན་དང་པོ་ལ་ཡོད་པའི་རྟོག་པ་དང་དཔྱོད་པ། investigation and analysis within the first concentration level 5. བསམ་གཏན་གཉིས་པ་མན་ཆད་དུ་ཡོད་པའི་ཡིད་བདེ་བའམ་དགའ་བ། mental ecstacy or joy below the level of the second concentration 6-8. བསམ་གཏན་གསུམ་པ་མན་ཆད་ན་ཡོད་པའི་དབུགས་འབྱུང་བ་དང་། རྔུབ་པ་དང་། གསུམ་པའི་བདེ་བ། exhalation, inhalation and bliss of the third concentration level and the levels below it.

བསམ་གཏན་གྱི་དངོས་གཞིའི་སྙོམས་འཇུག

Actual meditative absorption. A virtuous state of concentration free of desire-attachment to the lower level of concentration. There are four types belonging to the four concentration levels (see bsam-gtan-bzhi, A).

བསམ་གཏན་གྱི་ཆོས་བཞི།

The four qualities of concentration. 1. རྣམ་གཡེང་སོགས་མི་མཐུན་ཕྱོགས་ཉམས་པ། quells distractions and other unfavorable factors 2. ཆོས་ཀྱི་བདག་མེད་རྟོགས་པའི་རྣམ་པར་མི་རྟོགས་པ། generates non-conceptual cognition of the selflessness of phenomena 3. འདོད་པ་རྫོགས་པར་བྱེད་པ།

fulfills one's wishes 4. རིགས་ཅན་གསུམ་སྨིན་པར་བྱེད་པ། ripens the three classes of disciples of the three vehicles.

བསམ་གཏན་གྱི་གནས།

States of concentration (see gzugs-khams gnas-ris bcu-bdun).

བསམ་གཏན་གཉིས།

Two types of concentration. 1. རྒྱུ་སྙོམས་འཇུག་གི་བསམ་གཏན། karaṇasamāpattidhyāna/ concentration in causal absorption 2. འབྲས་བུ་སྐྱེ་བའི་བསམ་གཏན། kāryasamāpattidhyāna/ concentration giving rise to result concentration.

བསམ་གཏན་གཉིས་པའི་ཡན་ལག་བཞི།

Four branches of the second level concentration. 1. ནང་རབ་ཏུ་དང་བ། adhyātmasamprasāda/ internal clarity 2. དགའ་བ། mudita/ joy 3. བདེ་བ། sukha/ bliss 4. སེམས་རྩེ་གཅིག་པ། ekāgracitta/ single-pointed mind.

བསམ་གཏན་དང་པོའི་དངོས་གཞི་གསུམ།

Three actual absorptions of the first level concentration. 1. ཉོན་མོངས་ཅན་གྱི་དངོས་གཞི། deluded concentration 2. དག་པའི་དངོས་གཞི། purified concentration 3. ཟག་མེད་ཀྱི་དངོས་གཞི། uncontaminated concentration.

བསམ་གཏན་དང་པོའི་ཡན་ལག་ལྔ།

Five branches of the first level concentration. 1. རྟོག་པ། vitarka/ investigation 2. དཔྱོད་པ། vicāra/ analysis 3. དགའ་བ། mudita/ joy 4. བདེ་བ། sukha/ bliss 5. སེམས་རྩེ་གཅིག་པ། ekāgracitta/ single-pointed mind.

བསམ་གཏན་དག་པ་བ་བཞི།

Four pure concentrations. 1. ཉམས་པ་ཆ་མཐུན། aid to degeneration 2. གནས་པ་ཆ་མཐུན། aid to endurance 3. ཁྱད་པར་ཆ་མཐུན། aid to promotion 4. ངེས་འབྱེད་ཆ་མཐུན། aid to definite separation.

བསམ་གཏན་བཞི།

Four types of concentration. A. གཟུགས་ཁམས་ཀྱི་བསམ་གཏན་བཞི། Four levels of concentration within the form realm. 1. བསམ་གཏན་དང་པོ། prathamaṁdhyāna/ first level concentration 2. བསམ་གཏན་གཉིས་པ། dvitīyadhyāna/ second level concentration 3. བསམ་གཏན་གསུམ་པ། tritīyadhyāna/ third level concentration 4. བསམ་གཏན་བཞི་པ། cathurthadhyāna/ fourth level concentration. B. རྒྱུད་སྡེ་འོག་མ་ནས་བཤད་པའི་བསམ་གཏན་བཞི། Four concentrations according to the lower tantras. 1. བཟླས་བརྗོད་ཡན་ལག་བཞིའི་བསམ་གཏན། concentration of the four limbs of recitation/ incantation (see bzlas-brjod yan-lag bzhi) 2. མེ་གནས་ཀྱི་བསམ་གཏན། concentration on abiding in fire 3. སྒྲ་གནས་ཀྱི་བསམ་གཏན། concentration on abiding in sound 4. སྒྲ་མཐར་ཐར་པ་སྟེར་བའི་བསམ་གཏན། concentration resulting in liberation at the conclusion of sound.

བསམ་གཏན་བཞི་པའི་ཡན་ལག་བཞི།

Four branches of the fourth level concentration. 1. དྲན་པ། mindfulness 2. བཏང་སྙོམས་ཡོངས་དག pure equanimity 3. ཚོར་བ་བཏང་སྙོམས། neutral feeling 4. སེམས་རྩེ་གཅིག་པ། single-pointed mind.

བསམ་གཏན་ས་དགུ

Nine states of concentration. 1. བསམ་གཏན་དང་པོའི་ཉེར་བསྡོགས་མི་ལྕོགས་མེད། preparatory stage of the first level concentration 2. བསམ་གཏན་དང་པོའི་དངོས་གཞི་ཙམ་པོ་བ། ordinary stage of the first level concentration 3. བསམ་གཏན་དང་པོའི་དངོས་གཞི་ཁྱད་པར་ཅན། exalted stage of the first level concentration 4. བསམ་གཏན་གཉིས་པའི་དངོས་གཞི་ཙམ་པོ་བ། ordinary stage of the second level concentration 5. བསམ་གཏན་གཉིས་པའི་དངོས་གཞི་ཁྱད་པར་ཅན། exalted stage of the second level concentration 6. བསམ་གཏན་གསུམ་པའི་དངོས་གཞི་ཙམ་པོ་བ། ordinary stage of the third level concentration 7. བསམ་གཏན་གསུམ་པའི་དངོས་གཞི་ཁྱད་པར་ཅན། exalted stage of the third level concentration 8. བསམ་གཏན་བཞི་པའི་དངོས་གཞི་ཙམ་པོ་བ། ordinary stage of the fourth level concentration 8. བསམ་གཏན་བཞི་པའི་དངོས་གཞི་ཁྱད་པར་ཅན། exalted stage of the fourth level concentration.

བསམ་གཏན་ས་དྲུག

Six states of concentration. 1. བསམ་གཏན་དང་པོའི་ཉེར་བསྡོགས་མི་ལྕོགས་མེད། preparatory stage of the first level concentration 2. བསམ་གཏན་དང་པོའི་དངོས་གཞི་ཙམ་པོ་བ། ordinary stage of the first level concentration 3. བསམ་གཏན་དང་པོའི་དངོས་གཞི་ཁྱད་པར་ཅན། exalted stage of the first level concentration 4. བསམ་གཏན་གཉིས་པའི་དངོས་གཞི། actual stage of the second level concentration 5. བསམ་གཏན་གསུམ་པའི་དངོས་གཞི། actual stage of the third level concentration 6. བསམ་གཏན་བཞི་པའི་དངོས་གཞི། actual stage of the fourth level concentration.

བསམ་གཏན་གསུམ་པའི་ཡན་ལག་ལྔ།

Five branches of the third level concentration. 1. དྲན་པ། smṛti/ mindfulness 2. ཤེས་བཞིན། samprajanya/ introspection 3. བཏང་སྙོམས། upekṣa/ equinimity 4. བདེ་བ། sukha/ bliss 5. སེམས་རྩེ་གཅིག་པ། ekāgracitta/ single-pointed mind.

བསམ་པའི་ལས།

Intended activity. Karma or activities of body and speech as motivated by the mind.

བསམ་ཡས།

Samye Monastery. the first monastery in Tibet built in 763 A.D. by King Trisong Deutsan under the guidance of the Great Abbot Śāntarakṣita and Ācārya Padmasambhava on the bank of the Tsang-po, south-east of Lhasa.

བསོད་ནམས།

Puṇya/ Merits. Synonymous with virtuous activity (dge-ba'i-las); positive energy.

བསོད་ནམས་ཀྱི་ཕུང་པོ་ལྔ།

Five aggregates of merit; five virtuous aggregates. Collection of merits of: 1. ཚུལ་ཁྲིམས་ཀྱི་ཕུང་པོ། śilaskandha/ morality 2. ཏིང་ངེ་འཛིན་གྱི་ཕུང་པོ། samādhiskandha/ concentration 3. ཤེས་རབ་ཀྱི་ཕུང་པོ། prajñāskandha/ wisdom 4. རྣམ་པར་གྲོལ་བའི་ཕུང་པོ། vimuktaskandha/ thorough liberation 5. རྣམ་པར་གྲོལ་བའི་ཡེ་ཤེས་མཐོང་བའི་ཕུང་པོ། vimuktajñānadṛṣṭiskandha/ understanding the wisdom of thorough liberation.

བསོད་ནམས་ཀྱི་ཚོགས།

Puṇyasaṁbhāra/ Collection of merits; accumulation of merits that is the primary cause of producing the resultant form body of a Buddha.

བསོད་ནམས་ཀྱི་ལས།

Punyakarma/ Meritorious karma. Karma that results in rebirth as a human being, demi-god or a god of the desire realm.

བསོད་ནམས་མ་ཡིན་པའི་ལས།

Apuṇyakarma/ Non-meritorious karma. Karma that results in rebirth as an animal, a hungry ghost or a hell being.

བསོད་ནམས་རྟེན་གྱི་ས།

The ground of basis for merits. According to the Nyingma tradition this refers to the fifth ground attained during the second stage of yoga which leads to actualizing the uncontaminated primordial wisdom.

བསོད་ནམས་སུ་བྱ་བའི་དངོས་པོ་བཞི།

Three kinds of meritorious deeds; three ways of collecting

merits. 1. སྦྱིན་པ་ལས་བྱུང་བའི་དངོས་པོ། merits collected through the practice of giving 2. ཚུལ་ཁྲིམས་ལས་བྱུང་བའི་དངོས་པོ། merits collected through the practice of morality 3. བསྒོམ་པ་ལས་བྱུང་བའི་དངོས་པོ། merits collected through the practice of concentration. 4. རྫས་ལསབྱུང་བའི་དངོས་པོ། merits collected through the power of substances.

བསྲུང་བ་མེད་པ་གསུམ།

Three unguarded actions; the three bases of self-confidence of a Buddha. 1. སྐུ་བག་མེད་པ་ལས་བསྲུང་བ་མེད་པ། he need not protect himself from physical faults 2. གསུང་བག་མེད་པ་ལས་བསྲུང་བ་མེད་པ། he need not protect himself from vocal faults 3. ཐུགས་བག་མེད་པ་ལས་བསྲུང་བ་མེད་པ། he need not protect himself from mental faults.

བསྲེ་འཕོ་དགུ་སྐོར།

The yoga of ninefold mixing; the nine rounds of mixing. According to the glorious Rechungpa's version these are: 1. འདོད་ཆགས་བདེ་ཆེན་དང་བསྲེ་བ་གཏུམ་མོ། the psychic heat mixing lust with great bliss 2. ཞེ་སྡང་བདེན་མེད་དང་བསྲེ་བ་སྒྱུ་ལུས། the illusory body through mixing hatred with lack of true existence 3. གཏི་མུག་མི་རྟོག་པ་དང་བསྲེ་བ་འོད་གསལ། the clear light mind mixing ignorance with non-conceptuality 4. གཏུམ་མོ་དང་སྒྱུ་ལུས་བསྲེས་ལ་ཉིན་མོ་བསྒོམ། the broad day light meditation mixing psychic heat with the illusory body 5. རྨི་ལམ་དང་འོད་གསལ་བསྲེས་ལ་མཚན་མོ་བསྒོམ། the midnight meditation mixing dreams with the illusory body 6. བར་དོ་དང་འཕོ་བ་བསྲེས་ལ་འཆི་ཁར་བསྒོམ། the meditation at death mixing the intermediate state of rebirth and consciousness transference 7. གང་ཟག་བརྩོན་འགྲུས་ཅན་ལ་གཏུམ་མོ། psychic heat for persons of great diligence 8. ལེ་ལོ་ཅན་ལ་རྨི་ལམ། dreams for lazy persons 9. ཚེ་ཐུང་འཕོ་བ་དང་བསྲེ་བ། the consciousness transference for persons of short life-span.

བསླབ་ཁྲིམས། བསླབ་སྡོམ།

Śikṣā śila/ The precepts and trainings; the vows of individual liberation, Bodhisattva and tantra.

བསླབ་པ་ཀུན་ལས་བཏུས་པ།

Śikṣāsammuccaya/ *Compendium of Precepts.* An important work by Ācarya Śantideva compiled from Mahāyāna teachings dealing with moralities, vows and precepts. This complements his *A Guide to the Bodhisattva's Way of Life* (spyod-'jug).

བསླབ་པ་རྒྱུན་གྱི་ས།

The ground of continual training. According to the Nyingma tradition this refers to the fourth ground attained at the second level of yoga where a yogi enhances his training on the continual experience of the state of union of seeing all existents as being empty like illusions and clear light appearance.

བསླབ་པ་གསུམ།

Three trainings. 1. ཚུལ་ཁྲིམས་ཀྱི་བསླབ་པ། śilaśikṣā/ training in moral discipline 2. ཏིང་ངེ་འཛིན་གྱི་བསླབ་པ། samādhi śikṣās/ training in concentration 3. ཤེས་རབ་ཀྱི་བསླབ་པ། prajñāśikṣā/ training in wisdom.

བསླབ་པའི་གཞི་བརྒྱད།

Eight fundamental precepts of a one day vow holder (see bsnyen-gnas yan-lag brgyad).

བསླབ་པ་ཡི་གཞི་ལྔ།

The five fundamental precepts of a layperson (see bsnyen-gnas yan-lag brgyad, 1-5).

བསླབ་པའི་གཞི་ཉིས་བརྒྱ་ལྔ་བཅུ་རྩ་གསུམ།

The two hundred and fifty three vows of a fully ordained

monk (Bikṣu). 1-4. ཕམ་པ་བཞི། The four downfalls 5-17. ལྷག་མ་བཅུ་གསུམ། · the thirteen remainders 18-47. སྤང་ལྟུང་སུམ་ཅུ། the thirty abandoning downfalls 48-137. ལྟུང་བྱེད་འབའ་ཞིག་པ་དགུ་བཅུ། ninety solid propelling downfalls 138-141. སོར་བཤགས་བཞི། the four individual confessions 142-253. ཉེས་བྱས་བརྒྱ་དང་བཅུ་གཉིས། the one hundred and twelve faults.

བསླབ་བྱ་གསུམ།

The three types of precepts. 1. དགག་པའི་བསླབ་བྱ། precepts of negation 2. སྒྲུབ་པའི་བསླབ་བྱ། precepts of cultivation 3. ཆ་མཐུན་གྱི་བསླབ་བྱ། auxiliary precepts.

བསླུ་བའི་ཆོས་ཅན།

Moṣadharmiṇa/ Deceptive nature; deceptive phenomena.

ཧམ་པ།

Mānya/ Avarice; conceit. An attitude of expecting and demanding; an expectation or possession of more than one's share.

ཧེ་རུ་ཀ

Heruka. A tantric deity belonging to the mother tantra of the highest class of tantra; also identified as Cakrasambhara.

ཧྭ་ཤང་།

Hashang. Equivelant to Upadhya—abbot; the master learned in Buddhist trainings. It came to be identified with the Chinese master, Hashang who spread the view of simultaneous enlightenment (cig-car-ba'i lugs) and asserted that both virtuous and non-virtuous ideas and thoughts are equally negative because both bind one within saṁsāra, hence, meditation on nothingness could only lead one to liberation. He contested a debate with Ācārya Kamalaśila during the reign of the Tibetan King Trisong Deutsan and being defeated is said to have returned to China.

ཧྲིལ་པོ།

A. Entire; whole; all. B. Spherical shaped.

ལྷ།

Deva/ A. A meditational deity in tantric practice. B. Gods; one of the six living beings of saṁsāra.

ལྷ་ཆེན་བརྒྱད།

Eight great gods; eight lords. 1. དབང་ཕྱུག Īśvara 2. བརྒྱ་བྱིན། Indra 3. ཚངས་པ། Brahma 4. ཁྱབ་འཇུག Viṣṇu 5. འདོད་པའི་དབང་ཕྱུག Kāmadeva 6. ཚོགས་བདག Gaṇeśa 7. སྣིང་གི་རི་ཏི། Bhṛṁgiriṭi 8. གཞོན་ནུ་གདོང་དྲུག Ṣaḍmukhakumāra.

ལྷ་ཆོས་དགེ་བ་བཅུ།

The ten divine principles; the ten moral principles. The moral code of law proscribed by King Songtsen Gampo (see dge-ba bcu) along with the sixteen moral conducts (see mi-chos gtzang-ma bcu-drug).

ལྷ་ཆོས་བདུན་ལྡན།

The seven-fold deity and texts (see bka'-gdams lha-chos-bdun).

ལྷ་རྗེས་སུ་དྲན་པ།

Recollection of the deity. One of the six recollections (see rjes-su dran-pa drug); reflecting upon the qualities of gods within the desire realm, form realm and the noble one's (aryas).

ལྷ་མཐོ།

Votive cairn or heaps of stones in honor of a local deity, or in memory of a holy person, erected at the top of a pass or mountain.

ལྷ་དྲུག་རྣལ་འབྱོར།

The yoga of six deities. The deity yoga of kriyā tantra can be classified into the practice of six deities (see bya-rgyud-kyi lha-drug).

ལྷ་བབས་དུས་ཆེན།

The day of Buddha Śākyamuni's descent from heaven. The 15th of the ninth Tibetan month when Buddha Śākyamuni descended from the heaven of the 'Thirty-Three' god realm to this world.

ལྷ་བླ་མ་ཡེ་ཤེས་འོད།

Lha Lama Yeshe Od. A tenth century Tibetan King of Ngari region, western Tibet, who was the younger son of the King of Guge; in the latter part of his life he offered the kingdom to his brother in order to become a monk, and was later instrumental in inviting Atiśa to Tibet.

ལྷ་མ་ཡིན།

Asura/ Demi-gods. One of the six types of beings believed to be anti-gods by birth and are in constant conflict with gods due to jealousy.

ལྷ་མ་ཡིན་གྱི་གྲོང་ཁྱེར་བཞི།

Four cities of the demi-gods. 1. འོད་ལྡན། With Light 2. སྐར་ཕྲེང་། Star-garland 3. ཟབ་པ། Profound 4. གསེར་ལྡན། Golden.

ལྷ་མོ་ཚེ་རིང་མཆེད་ལྔ།

The five female guardians of Tibet (see tse-ring mched-lnga).

ལྷ་མོ་དབྱངས་ཅན་མ།

Sarasvatīdevī. The feminine aspect of wisdom found both in Hindu and Buddhist pantheons; also called the goddess of melody.

ལྷ་མོའི་བཞོན་པའི་ཁྱད་ཆོས་གསུམ།

Three features of Palden Lhamo's (highest goddess in Tibetan Buddhism) mount. 1. རྫུ་འཕྲུལ་གྱི་རྐང་པ། miraculous legs 2. རླུང་གི་གཤོག་པ། wings of wind 3. མྱུར་མགྱོགས་ཀྱི་རྩལ། swift.

ལྷ་བཙུན་བྱང་ཆུབ་འོད།

Jangchub Od. Song of King Lhade of Ngari region of Tibet. After much hardship he invited Atiśa to Tibet on the instruction of his uncle Lha Lama Yeshe Od. At his request Atiśa wrote the famous text—*A Lamp on the Path to Enlightenment* (bodhipathapradīpa).

ལྷ་སྲིན་སྡེ་བརྒྱད།

Eight gods and spirits. 1. གཤིན་རྗེ། Yama/ Lord of Death (yama) 2. མ་མོ། Mātṛka/ Female-protector (see ma-mo) 3. བདུད། Māra/ Devil; demons 4. བཙན། Haṭa/ Mountain-dwelling spirits 5. རྒྱལ་པོ། Rāja/ Principal local gods 6. ཀླུ། Nāga/ Serpent's 7. གནོད་སྦྱིན། Yakṣa/ Harmful spirits 8. གཟའ། Graha/ Malignant stars or planets.

ལྷ་གསོལ། ལྷ་བསང་།

The incense burning ceremony. The ceremony of tying prayer flags and offering incense as a feast to appease gods, nāgas and protectors.

ལྷག་བཅས་མྱང་འདས།

Nirvāṇa with remainder; residual state of liberation. A state of liberation within the mental continuum of an Arhat who continues to live in the body derived from his previous contaminated mental and physical actions even after attaining nirvāṇa.

ལྷག་མཐོང་།

Vipaśyanā/ Penetrative Insight. Penetrative insight meditation. A single pointed concentration able to apply analysis of its object; an apex form of all concentrations able to see the indepth reality of phenomena.

ལྷག་པའི་ང་རྒྱལ།

Adhimāna/ Exalted pride. A feeling that you are better than everyone else.

ལྷག་པའི་ཡོ་བྱད།

Additional articles of a monk. The articles that a monk is allowed to possess not out of necessity but to use these in times of need for oneself or for others, e.g. an extra robe.

ལྷག་པའི་བསླབ་པ་གསུམ།

Three higher trainings. The trainings that are superior to a training undertaken by a common or a non-Buddhist practitioner. 1. ལྷག་པ་ཚུལ་ཁྲིམས་ཀྱི་བསླབ་པ། adhiśilaśikṣā/ higher training in moral discipline 2. ལྷག་པ་ཏིང་ངེ་འཛིན་གྱི་བསླབ་པ། i adhisamādhiśikṣā/ higher training in concentration 3. ལྷག་པ་ཤེས་རབ་ཀྱི་བསླབ་པ། i adhiprajñāśikṣā/ higher training in wisdom.

ལྷག་མེད་མྱང་འདས།

Nirvāṇa without remainder; non-residual state of liberation. A state of libertion within the mental continuum of an Arhat who is freed from the physical aggregates derived from contaminated action as soon as he attains nirvāna.

ལྷག་བསམ།

Adhyāśaya/ Resolute intention. A pure wish to accept responsibilities upon oneself to liberate all sentient beings from the bonds of cyclic existence; one of the fundamental causes to produce the mind of enlightenment (bodhicitta) within oneself.

ལྷག་བསམ་དག་པའི་སེམས་བསྐྱེད་བདུན།

The seven minds of enlightenment with pure resolute intention; the mind of enlightenment possessed by Bodhisattvas on the seven impure grounds—first to seven of the ten grounds. 1. གཏེར་ལྟ་བུའི་སེམས་བསྐྱེད། the treasure-like bodhicitta 2. རིན་ཆེན་འབྱུང་གནས་ལྟ་བུའི་སེམས་བསྐྱེད། the jewel-source-like bodhicitta 3. རྒྱ་མཚོ་ལྟ་བུའི་སེམས་བསྐྱེད། the ocean-like bodhicitta 4. རྡོ་རྗེ་ལྟ་བུའི་སེམས་བསྐྱེད། the vajra-like bodhicitta 5. རི་རྒྱལ་ལྟ་བུའི་སེམས་བསྐྱེད། the Meru-like bodhicitta 6. སྨན་ལྟ་བུའི་སེམས་བསྐྱེད། the medicine-like bodhicitta 7. བཤེས་གཉེན་ལྟ་བུའི་སེམས་བསྐྱེད། the spiritual teacher-like bodhicitta.

ལྷང་ངེ་བ།

Clear and lucid understanding; articulated meaning or sound; solid and vivid appearance of the object of meditation.

ལྷན་སྐྱེས།

Sahaja/ Innately born; innately produced; acquired by birth or from beginningless time, e.g. the view of holding one's transitory aggregates as oneself or as I or self (lhan-skyes-kyi 'jig-lta).

ལྷན་སྐྱེས་ཀྱི་ཉོན་མོངས་པ།

Sahajakleśa/ Innately produced delusions. The negative emotions in those whose minds or perspective of looking at things are not stained by philosophical views but are natural tendencies, e.g. the innately born ignorance (lhan-skyes-kyi ma-rig-pa).

ལྷན་སྐྱེས་ཀྱི་ལྷ་ལྔ།

The five natural gods of human beings. The gods or spirits

supposed to be born along with oneself from birth. 1. འཚོ་བའི་ལྷ། god of livelihood 2. སྲུང་བའི་ལྷ། god that protects oneself from enemies 3. སྐྱོབས་པའི་ལྷ། god that guards oneself from fears 4. འགྲོགས་པའི་ལྷ། god that associates with oneself 5. འགོ་བའི་ལྷ། personal god.

ལྷན་སྐྱེས་ཀྱི་ལྷ་འདྲེ།

Natural devils or spirits. The spirits or gods and their influence that are incorporated into one's own life from birth, perhaps caused by one's previous karma, and are separated from oneself when one is dead.

ལྷན་ཅིག་སྐྱེས་སྦྱོར།

Sahajayoga/ Simultaneous production and union; innate union. A Mahāmudrā meditation tradition of the Dvagpo Kagyud Order of Tibetan Buddhism.

ལྷན་ཅིག་སྐྱེས་པའི་ཡེ་ཤེས།

Sahajajñāna/ Wisdom of innate production; innately born wisdom. The immense joy and bliss experienced by a Yogi through the practice of making the energy wind enter, abide and dissolve within the central energy channel at the initial level of the completion stage practice of tantra.

ལྷན་ཅིག་འབྱུང་བའི་རྒྱུ།

Sahabhūhetu/ Simultaneously arisen cause. Anything that exists simultaneously not only with it cause but also integerates it as an inseparable part of the result and does not impede its production, such as the four elements co-existing and supporting each other.

ལྷན་ཅིག་བྱེད་རྐྱེན།

Sahakārikāraṇa/ Auxiliary condition; co-operative condition or factor. For instance the hammer used by a carpenter in making a table.

ལྷན་ཅིག་མི་གནས་འགལ།

Non-simultaneously abiding mutual exclusion. Things that nullify each other for co-existence, e.g. the antidotes and their direct elimination.

ལྷམ་མེ་ལྷན་ནེ་ལྷན་ནེ།

Bhāsate tapati virocate/ Outshining, majestic and illustrious. An imposing outlook.

ལྷའི་རྟེན་ཅན་གྱི་རྒྱུན་ཞུགས་སྲིད་པ་ལན་བདུན་པ་པ།

Stream-winner who attains liberation after seven successive rebirths as a god.

ལྷའི་དེ་ཁོ་ན་ཉིད།

The suchness of a deity. One of the four yogas of suchness according to action tantra (kriyā). This concerns generating oneself in the form of a deity by means of the six deity yogas within action tantra practice and inviting wisdom-beings in front, and focussing one's attention on them just as a servant would attend to his master, and requesting their virtuous energy or siddhi.

ལྷའི་རྣལ་འབྱོར།

Devayoga/ Deity yoga. Meditation on a deity or dieties; visualizing deities infront or generating onself as the deity.

ལྷའི་རྣ་བའི་མངོན་ཤེས།

Divyaṃśrotamābhijñāna/ Clairvoyance of the divine ear; extra-sensory aural perception. The divine power to hear and listen to sounds or voice of a distance covering hundreds of yojanas (see dpag-tshad).

ལྷའི་མིག་གི་མངོན་ཤེས།

Dirvyacakṣurvijñāna/ Claivoyance of the divine eyes; extra-sensory visual perception. One of six types of extra-sensory perception (see mngon-par shes-pa drug) enabling one to see where and when a person would die or be born without being impeded by any factors of time, location and nature.

ལྷའི་གཙོ་བོ་གསུམ།

Three principal gods. 1. ཚངས་པ། Brahma 2. དབང་ཕྱུག Īśvara 3. ཁྱབ་འཇུག Viṣṇu.

ལྷའི་ཡང་ལྷ།

Devātideva/ God of gods; divine among divinities. An epithet for Buddha.

ལྷའི་ང་རྒྱལ།

The divine pride. Imagination of oneself as being the deity in the generation stage meditation of tantric practices in order to remove a sense of ordinariness of oneself.

ལྷའི་གསལ་སྣང་།

The divine vision; the clear perception of a deity. The imagination and appearance of seeing each and every feature of the deity lucidly without oblivion during the course of the generation stage meditation of tantra aimed at removing attachment to the oridinariness of oneself.

ལྷས་བྱིན།

Devadatta. Cousin of Buddha Sākyamuni who was his persistent antagonist, not only after Buddha's enlightenment but even when he engaged in the Bodhisattva trainings.

ལྷས་བྱིན།

Devadatta. Cousin of Buddha Śākyamuni who was his persistent antagonist, not only after Buddha's enlightenment but even when he engaged in the Bodhisattva trainings.

ལྷས་བྱིན་གྱི་བརྟུལ་ཞུགས་ བསླབ་ཆིག ལྔ་།

Five ascetic practices of Devadatta; five precepts of Devadatta. 1. ཤ་མི་ཟ་བ། not eating meat 2. འོ་མ་མི་འཐུང་བ། not drinking milk 3. ལན་ཚྭ་མི་ཟ་བ། not taking salt 4. གོས་དྲས་དྲུབ་ཅན་མི་གྱོན་པ། not wearing ragged cloths 5. དགོན་པར་མི་གནས་པ། not living in a hermitage.

ལྷུང་བཟེད།

Piṇḍapātra/ Monk's or nun's begging bowl. Traditionally it is required to be made of stones or metal.

ལྷུན་གྲུབ་ཐོད་རྒལ།

The spontaneous leap-over path. A rDzogs-chen meditation technique especially for highly advanced followers; a speedy method of realizing rDzogs-chen.

ལྷུན་གྲུབ་རིག་འཛིན།

The state of spontaneous Vajradhāra. The Nyingmapas name for the state of Buddha Vajradhāra.

ལྷུན་ཀྱིས་གྲུབ་པ།

Spontaneous existence; natural; existence by nature; unintended incident.

ཨ།

A. The last of the thirty letters of the Tibetan alphabet; a universal vowel present in all letters. B. The shortest form of the *Perfection of Wisdom*. It is explained to contain the meaning of the entire teachings of Buddha; heavily blessed syllable.

ཨ་ཏི་ཡོ་ག

The atiyoga tantra. The peak of the nine vehicles according to the Nyingma tradition called the Great Completion stage, Dzog-pa chen-po.

ཨ་ནུ་ཡོ་ག

The anuyoga tantra. The eighth of the nine vehicles according to the Nyingma tradition dealing primarily with the completion stage practices of tantra.

ཨ་ཏི་ཤ།

Atiśa (982-1054). A renowned Indian master and scholar who visited Tibet in the early 11th century and taught extensively, thereby restoring the purity of Buddhist practice in Tibet. He wrote the famous text *A Lamp on the Path to Enlightenment* (bodhipathapradhīpa), and founded the Kadampa tradition.

ཨ་ལི།

Vowel letters of the Sanskrit alphabet.

ཨ་ལི་བཅུ་དྲུག

The sixteen vowel letters. ཨ། a, ཨཱ། ā, ཨི། i, ཨཱི། ī, ཨུ། u, ཨཱུ། ū, རྀ། ṛ, རཱྀ། ṝ, ལྀ། ḷ, ལཱྀ། ḹ, ཨེ། e, ཨཻ། ae, ཨོ། o, ཨཽ། au, ཨཾ། aṁ, ཨཿ aḥ. These represents the sixteen emptinesses (see stong-nyis bcu-drug) and are the sources of the thrity-two major marks of a Buddha (see mtshan-bzang-po sum-bcu rtsa-gnyis).

ཨིནྡྲ་ནཱི་ལ།

Indraṇīla; sapphire.

ཨུ་རྒྱན།

Oḍḍiyāna. The birth-place of Guru Padmasambhava, the kingdom of King Indrabodhi. Some identity this place with Swat in Pakistan. This is also regarded as a sacred place of Ḍākinīs.

ཨེ་ཝཾ།

E-Wam syllable. E represents emptiness as the wisdom side and Wam great bliss, the method side.

ཨེ་ཝཾ་ཟུང་འཇུག

The union of E and Wam. Represents the ever supreme reality emptiness and the supreme unchangeable great bliss.

ཨེར་ཀ་ཧྲན་གྱི་ཆོས་ལུགས།

Shaminism of Mongolia. A pre-Buddhist religious tradition in Mongolia similar to the Bon religion of pre-Buddhist Tibet, in which practice of animal sacrifice and offering of their blood to the gods and spirits was common. The Third Dalai Lama, Sonam Gyatso, (1543-1588) banned this practice and taught the virtues of Buddhism.

ཨོ་ལོ།

The monks on duty serving tea or gruel during the Great Prayer festival in Tibet.

ཨོཾ།

The head of mantras. Has many meanings such as symbolizing the Vajra body of a Buddha.

ཨོཾ་སྭསྟི།

Om svāsti/ May all be auspicious. May all enjoy peace and prosperity.

BIBLIOGRAPHY

Tibetan Sources:

dKon mchog 'jigs med dbang po. *mdo rgyud bstan bcos du ma nas 'byuung ba'i chos kyi rnam grangs shes ldan yid kyi dg'a ston.* Vol. 7, 465-531. New Delhi: Ngawang Gelek Demo, 1972.

kLong rdol bla ma. *gsang sngags rig pa 'dzin pa'i sde las byung ba'i ming gi grangs.* Vols. 1,2. New Delhi: Lokesh Changra, 1973.

—. *phar phyin las byung ba'i ming gi grangs.*

—. *theg chen gyi mngon pa'i sde sogs las byung ba'i don bsdus ming drug, bzhi brgya pa sogs kyi ming gi rnam grangs.*

—. *rgyas 'bring bsdus gsum, byams chos ssde lnga, bk'a gdams gzhung drug, bzhi brgya pa sogs kyi ming gi rnam grangs.*

—. *nang rig pa mngon pa'i sde snod las byung ba'i don bsdus ming gi rnam grangs.*

—. *'bum gyi 'grel rkang brgya rtza brgyad ngos 'dzin.*

—. *nang rig pa 'dul ba'i sde snod las byung ba'i don bsduus ming gi rnam grangs.*

—. *tsad ma rnam 'grel sogs gtan tsig rig pa las byung ba'i ming gi rnam grangs.*

lCang skya rol pa'i rdo rje. *dag yig mkhas pa'i 'byung gnas.* Delhi: Chatring Jangsar Tenzing, 1972.

Chahar Geshe, Lobsang Tsultrim. *mngon par rtogs pa'i rgyan gyi 'grel pa dngos grub kun 'byung zhes bya ba.* Vol. 3. New Delhi: Chatring Jangsar Tenzing, 1972.

rTa nag mkhan chen chos rnam rgyal. *bstan pa dang bstan 'dzin gyi lo rgyus 'du'i me tog gsar pa'i do shal zhes bya ba bzhugs so* (to be reprinted and published by LTWA, Dharamsala).

Panchen Sonam Dakpa. *shes rab kyi pha rol tu phyin pa'i man ngag gi bstan bcos mngon par rtogs pa'i rgyan gyi 'grel pa dang rtza ba'i rnam bshad snying po'i rgyan gyi don legs par bshad pa yum don gsal ba'i sgron me zhes bya ba bzhugs so.* Gangtok: Thupten Palden Ozer and others, 1970.

—. *rgyud sde spyi'i rnam par bzhag pa bskal bzang yid 'phog ces bya ba bzhugs so.* Dharamsala: LTWA, 1975.

Various Early Tibetan Translators:

Mahavyutpatti. (Tib. *bye brag tu rtogs par byed pa chen mo.*) Parts 1,2. Tokyo-Kyoto: Tibetan Tripitaka Research Institute, 19??.

—. *sgra sbyor bam po gnyis pa.* Ed. Sonam Wangdu, Leh, 1973.

Lokesh Chandra, Dr. *Tibetan-Sanskrit Dictionary.* Vol. 1, 2. New Delhi: International Academy of Indian Culture, 1976.

Sarat Chandra Das. *A Tibetan English Dictionary.* Delhi: Motilal Banarsidass, 1970.

Yeshi Gyaltsen, Kachen. *sher phyin gsal sgron.* Vol 8, 1-165. New Delhi: Tibet House, 1976.

English Sources:

A-kya yongs 'dzin dbyang can dg'a ba'i blo gros. *A Compendium of Ways of Knowing (blo rig gi sdom tshig blang dor gsal ba'i me long).* Tr. Geshe Dhargye, Sharpa Tulku and Alex Berzin, Dharamsala: LTWA, 1982.

Amipa, Sherab Gyaltsen. *A Water Drop from the Glorious Ocean.* Rikon: Tibetan Institute, 1976.

Apte, V. S. *The Student's Sanskrit-English Dictionary.* Delhi: Motilal Banarsidass, 1963.

Baresford, Brian C. *Mahayana Purification.* Dharamsala: LTWA, 1980.

Battacharya, Kamaleswar. *The Dialectical Method of Nagarjuna.* Delhi: Motilal Banarsidas, 1978.

Conze, Edward. *Astasahasarika Prajnaparamita.* Calcutta: Asiatic Society, 1970.

—. *The Prajnaparamita Literature*. Tokyo: Reiyakai, 1978.

—. *The Short Prajnaparamita Texts*. London: Luzac, 1973.

—. *Buddhism: Its Essence & Development*. London: Faber & Faber, 1951.

—. *Buddhist Scriptures*. Middlesex: Penguin Books, 1964.

—. *Materials for a Dictionary of the Prajnaparamita Literature*. Tokyo: Suzuki Research Foundation, 1973.

—. *The Perfection of the Wisdom in Eight Thousand Lines & Its Verse Summary*. Bolinas: Four Seasons Foundation, 1973.

—. *Selected Sayings from the Perfection of Wisdom*. London: The Buddhist Society, 1968.

—. *The Large Sutra of Perfection of Wisdom with the Divisions of the Abhisamayalankara*. Berkeley: University of California Press, 1975.

Adgerton, Franklin. *Buddhist Hybrid Sanskrit Reader*. Delhi: Motilal Banarsidass, 1973.

sGampo-pa. *Jewel Ornament of Liberation (sgam po thar rgyan)*. Tr. & annot. Herbert Guuenther, Berkeley: Shambala, 1971.

Guenther, Herbert V. *Philosophy and Psychology in Abhidharma*. Lucknow: Buddha Vihara, 1975.

—. *The Royal Song of Saraha: A Study in the History of Buddhist Thought*. Berkeley: Shambala, 1977.

—. *The Tantric View of Life*. Berkeley: Shambala, 1972.

—. *Tibetan Buddhism in a Western Perspective: Collected Articles*. California: Dharma, 1977.

—. *The Life & Teachings of Naropa*. London: Oxford University Press, 1971.

—. *The Dawn of Tantra*. Berkeley: Shambala, 1975.

Hopkins, Jeffrey. *Meditation on Emptiness*. London: Wisdom, 1983.

—. *Tantra of Tibet*. London: George Allen & Unwin, 1975.

—. *The Yoga of Tibet*. London: George Allen & Unwin, 1981.

—. *Tantric Practice in Nyingma*. London: Rider, 1982.

—. *Compassion in Tibetan Buddhism*. London: Rider, 1980.

—. *Practice and Theory of Tibetan Buddhism*. New Delhi: B.I. 1977.

—. *Precious Garland & the Song of Four Mindfulnesses*. London: George Allen & Unwin. 1975.

Humphreys, Christmas. *A Popular Dictionary of Buddhism*. London: Curzon Press, 1976.

Joshi, Lal Mani. *Studies in the Buddhist Culture of India*. Delhi: Motilal Banarsidass, 1977.

Karmapa, the IXth, Wanchuuk Dorjee. *The Mahamudra: Eliminating the Darkness of Ignorance*. Tr. & ed. Alexander Berzin, Dharamsala: LTWA, 1978.

Lati Rinpoche & Hopkins. *Death, Intermediate State & Rebirth*. London: Rider, 1979.

—. *Mind in Tibetan Buddhism*. Tr. & ed. Elizabeth Napper, London: Rider, 1980.

—. *Meditative States in Tibetan Buddhism*. Tr. & ed. Leah Zahler, London: Wisdom, 1981.

Lessing, Ferdinand D. & Wayman, Alex. *mKasss-Grub Je's Fundamentals of the Buddhist Tantras*. Paris: Mouton, 1968.

Lamrim, Geshe. *Necklace of Good Fortune*. Trs. lJampa Gendun, Damdul Namgyal and Tsepak Rigzin, Dharamsala: LTWA, 1982.

Longchen Rabjampa Drime Wozer. *The Four- Themed Precious Garland*. Tr. & ed. Alexander Berzin, Dharamsala: LTWA, 1979.

Lobsang Tharchin, Geshe & Engles, A.R. *The Logic and Debate Tradition of India, Tibet and Mongolia*. Howell, New Jersey: Rashi Gempilling, 1979.

—. *Nagarjuna's Letter to a Friend with Commentary by Ven. Rendawa Zon-nu Lodro*. Dharamsala: LTWA, 1979.

—. *An Explanation of Abhidharmakosa*. Unpublished translation of Gyalwa Gendun Drub's Commentary.

Mullin, Glenn H. *Essence of Refined Gold*. Dharamsala: Tushita Books, 1978.

—. *Bridging the Sutras and Tantras*. Dharamsala: Tushita Books, 1981

—. *Stanzas for a Novice Monk & Tsong Khapa's Essence of the Ocean of Vinaya*. Dharamsala: LTWA, 1978.

—. *Songs of Spiritual Change*. New York: Gabriel/Snow Lion, 1983.

—. *Meditations on the Lower Tantras*. Dharamsala: LTWA, 1983.

—. *Meditations upon Arya Tara*. Dharamsala: Dharmakaya, 1978.

Murti, T.R.V. *The Central Philosophy of Buddhism: A Study of the Madhyamika System*. London: George Allen & Unwin, 1955.

Nagarjuna. *The Precious Garland*. Tr. & ed. Jeffrey Hopkins & Lati Rinpoche with Anne Klein. London: George Allen & Unwin, 1975.

Ngawang Dhargye, Geshe. *Tibetan Tradition of Mental Development*. Dharamsala: LTWA, 1978.

Namgyal Institute of Tibetology. *Prajna: Lexicon/Dictionary of Sanskrit-Tibetan*. Gangtok: Namgyal Institute of Tibetology, 1961.

Samdhong Rinpoche. *Madyamika Dialectic and the Philosophy of Nagarjuna*. Sarnath: Tibetan Institute, 1977.

Shantideva, Acharya. *Skiksha Samuccya: A Compendium of Buddhist Doctrine*. Delhi: Motilal Banarsidass, 1971.

—. *Bodhicaryavatara: A Guide to the Bodhisattva's Way of Life*. Dharamsala: LTWA, 1979.

Sopa, Lhundup & Hopkins, Jeffrey. *Practice and Theory of Tibetan Buddhism*. New Delhi: B.I. 1977,

Stcherbatsky. F. Th. *Buddhist Logic*. Vol. 1, 2. New York: Dover, 1962.

—. *Madhanta-Vibhanga*. New Delhi: Oriental Reprints, 1978.

Taranatha. *History of Buddhism in India*. Trs. Lana Chimpa & Alaka Chattopadhyaya, Simla: Indian Institute of Advanced Study, 1970.

Trungpa, Chogyam. *Glimpses of Abhidharma*. Boulder: Prajna Press, 1978.

—. *Empowerment*. Boulder: Vajradhatu, 1976.

—. *Meditation in Action*. Berkeley: Shambala, 1976.

—. *Journey Withjout Goal*. Berkeley: Shambala, 1985.

Tenzin Gyatso, H.H. the XIVth Dalai Lama. *Opening the Mind and Generating a Good Heart*. Tr. & ed. Tsepak Rigzin & Jeremy Russel, Dharamsala: LTWA, 1985.

—. *Advice from Buddha Shakyamuni*. Tr. & ed. Tsepak Rigzin & Glenn H. Mullin, Dharamsala: LTWA, 1982.

Wangyal, Geshe. *The Door of Liberation*. New York: Maurice Girodias, 1973.

Wijikowitz, Nebesky. *Oracles & Demons of Tibet*. Austria: Akademische, Druk-u Verlagsantalt, 1975.

Wayman, Alex. *Calming the Mind and Discerning the Real*. New York: Columbia University Press, 1978.

—. *Yoga of Guhyasamaja Tantra: The Arcane Lore of Fifty Verses*. Delhi: Motilal Barnarsidass, 1984.

—. *Buddhist Insight*. Ed. & introduced by George R. Elder, Delhi: Motil Banarsidass, 1984.

Yeshe Tsondru. *The Essence of Nectar*. Tr. Geshe Lobsang Tharchin & Benjamin Alterman. Dharamsala: LTWA, 1979.

Yeshe Dhonden. *The Ambrosia Heart Tantra: The Secret Oral Teaching on the Eight Branches of the Science* of Healing. Dharamsala: LTWA, 1977.

Yu, Lu Kuan. *Practical Buddhism*. London: Rider, 1971.